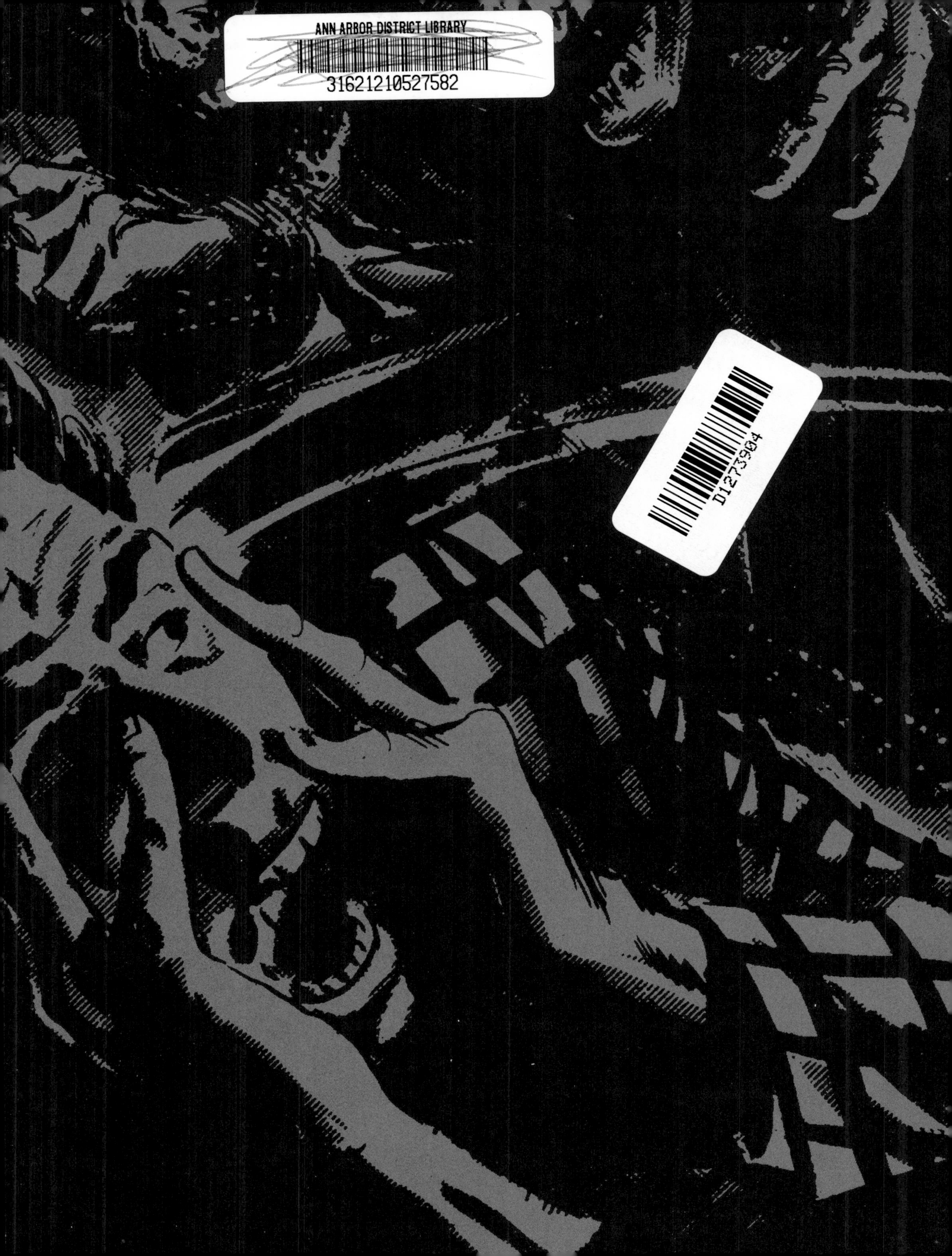

CREEPY™

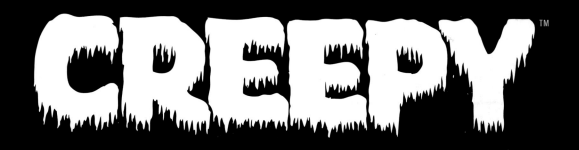

ARTISTS

Tom Sutton	Don Vaughn
William Barry	Syd Shores
Pat Boyette	Kenneth Smith
Reed Crandall	Roger Brand
Tony Williamsune	Ernie Colón
Juan Lopez Ramon	Bill Stillwell
Jack Sparling	The Brothers Ciochetti
Dan Adkins	Alan Weiss
Ken Barr	Carlos Garzón
Ken Kelly	Jerry Grandenetti
John G. Fantucchio	Rich Buckler
Richard Corben	

WRITERS

Tom Sutton	Bill Parente
Buddy Saunders	Howard Waldrop
Pat Boyette	Bill Stillwell
Robert Michael Rosen	Alan Weiss
Bill Warren	James Haggenmiller
Al Hewetson	T. Casey Brennan
Nicola Cuti	Greg Theakston
Richard Corben	

EDITORS

Bill Parente

James Warren

Archie Goodwin

Nicola Cuti

CREEPY

ARCHIVES - VOLUME SEVEN

EDITORS: Shawna Gore & Philip R. Simon   **CONSULTING EDITORS:** Dan Braun & Craig Haffner
ASSISTANT: Rachel Edidin   **DESIGNER:** Amy Arendts   **PUBLISHER:** Mike Richardson

Page 20

Page 74

Page 131

CONTENTS

NEW COMIC COMPANY: Josh Braun,
Dan Braun, Rick Brookwell, Craig Haffner

PUBLISHED BY DARK HORSE BOOKS, A DIVISION OF DARK HORSE
COMICS, INC., 10956 SE MAIN STREET, MILWAUKIE, OREGON 97222
TO FIND A COMICS SHOP IN YOUR AREA, CALL THE COMIC SHOP
LOCATOR SERVICE: (888) 266-4226

DARKHORSE.COM
FIRST EDITION: SEPTEMBER 2010 — ISBN 978-1-59582-516-2
1 3 5 7 9 10 8 6 4 2
PRINTED AT 1010 PRINTING INTERNATIONAL, LTD.,
GUANGDONG PROVINCE, CHINA

Page 43

Page 110

Page 222

FRANK FRAZETTA

LEGEND

Interview by Steve Ringgenberg

Editor's note: Steve Ringgenberg is a longtime comics journalist and Heavy Metal *magazine contributor, and has interviewed many classic* Creepy *contributors over the years—including the legendary Frank Frazetta. Interviewing Mr. Frazetta at several different times in his life, Steve Ringgenberg was able to ask the painter and icon about several key figures who pushed him to create work and who had at least a little something to do with spurring the painter in new directions as new creative periods in his life opened up. We will run two interviews with Mr. Frazetta in this volume, which help to size up the contributions illustrator Roy Krenkel and musician and publisher Glenn Danzig had on his life and work.*

February 1983 interview

Steve Ringgenberg: What was your impression of Roy Krenkel, the man?

Frank Frazetta: Roy Krenkel, the man? Oh, actually, I never knew quite what to make of Roy for all that time. I just knew that he was goddamned personable and fun to be around. I thought he was a little unstable at times, you know, because of his attitude, and I never thought he was a particularly courageous guy until the end. And I tell you I personally am very, very shocked for his courage. I always thought of myself as the macho guy. Roy [was], well, you know, just great, a lot of fun, but a big sissy and all of that. Well, he really showed me something at the end. I mean, knowing what he had, just facing up to it. I picture myself just crumbling under those conditions, tough as I thought I was. He showed me something. So, apparently, Roy's sense of humor and all that was not something to cover a cowardly personality. The guy was awfully, awfully brave. I thought of Roy as just a wonderful inspiration, a

lot of fun, a lot of laughs. Certainly he made me go. There are few people that made me go, in my career, but he was certainly a major factor. Roy really introduced me to books and showed me art and showed me just how far you could really go. I was awfully casual about it. I just did my thing my way and really didn't make any pretensions of going to high places or anything quite like that. And Roy said, "You gotta do this, Frank, look at these guys, look at these guys!" And he'd show me this wonderful art that really got me fired up. Not that I wanted to be like them, but it just amazed me as to the kind of talent that really was out there that I wasn't aware of, whether they be alive or dead, you know? And it really got me fired up just like it seems that I inspire younger artists. These guys inspired the hell out of me. But, thanks to Roy, who just dragged this stuff around, forced it on me, forced me to look! You know, it was great. It was great conversation about, oh, Jesus, the many, many nuances of art. What makes it work, what doesn't make it work, and it was quite an education.

Ringgenberg: Was it Roy who got you to start painting?

Frazetta: Well, no, no. I painted when I was eleven, but not very seriously. I painted in art school, I did occasional paintings for myself long before I met Roy, but I never, for some reason never considered doing it professionally, or at least in the field of illustration. I don't know what it was at that time, but nobody, including Roy, seemed very aware of paperbacks, you know? We collected books, but we were primarily cartoonists, I mean we worked for comics, and that's all we knew. I don't really know where my head was at, but it wasn't until they called Roy in, quite out of the blue, to do some of the Burroughs things up at Ace, that we even knew there was such a field. So Roy was kind of flabbergasted. He'd never painted at all. And at least I had dabbed around here and there. I would occasionally do a painting, just for my wall, you know, or just to fill space in the living room, that kind of thing. And suddenly, here was Roy doing these paperbacks, which they commissioned him to do a bunch, far more than he wanted to handle, and he introduced them to me. He figured, "Hell, Frank can paint, for Christ's sake. I'll get him on this." So, I said, "Well, hell, I'll try." This was very exciting for me. I didn't realize you could actually paint for a living and get paid for it, that kind of thing. I just did it for fun. But you did comics to make a buck, see? Well, that was it. And Roy, of course, collaborated, worked together, on a couple of them and off we went. But we were always together whenever we could [be] and we talked for hours and hours and he just gave me belly laughs and it was just so much fun to be with him.

Ringgenberg: I've heard from other people that Roy was a really funny guy.

Frazetta: He was extraordinarily funny and extraordinarily witty. I didn't necessarily agree with everything he had to say. He was, in my opinion, out in left field, and off the wall very often, but I don't think he really meant it half the time, it was just his way of, well, you know his great campaign against the telephone company and all that? I used to find that amusing and very strange. He had so many nasty things to say about the world, politics and all that, yet I never heard him say a negative thing about an acquaintance, or a friend, or somebody we mutually know, which is really a first, because you know, I'm not that bad a guy, but I'm pretty outspoken. And if I say a guy's a rat, he's a rat, and if I love him, I love him. I have pros and cons, but not Roy. Everybody was great. Everybody he ever met or knew personally was great . . . which I learned to appreciate later on, and that was wonderful of him, or very naive, I never knew quite which. So, this is the kind of guy [he was]: he lifted your spirits, he was always a lot of laughs. There was never a quarrel or a bad mood. To have Roy around was to have fun, to have a party, and coffee klatches, and good food, you know? Oh, God, he was just something else again. And we'd go over the art. Certainly I'm an artist. Why not talk about art, why not listen to good music, and of course, girls, and of course, heroes aside

from art? His ideas on the subjects were really something to turn your head, and it was very funny. Like I say, we would talk all night, because I would probably disagree with 80 percent of what he had to say, but it was a hell of a lot of fun trying to convince him . . . And his argument about girls having to be a certain proportion, and then I . . . [would] try to convince him that it was quality and not quantity that counted, and oddly enough, after maybe twenty-five years, or thirty years of knowing the guy, I noticed a slight change in his approach, but also in mine. We were kind of beginning to meet halfway. Without really admitting to it, his girls, as he drew them, were getting slimmer, and mine were getting [bigger] . . . and we noticed it. "Hey, Roy—look at your girls, you're cutting them down, eh, kid? Beginning to get some quality instead of those blimps." He said, "Frazetta, yours are looking a little fat," so, this is the kind of thing it was. We began to see the good in each other, and appreciate each other's opinions more and more through the years. We had really heavy arguments, but always with a chuckle. I don't know what else I can say. I know certainly Ellie loved him, and I never heard anybody, never met anybody, that didn't like him. The worst anybody said about him [was], "He's a strange duck, isn't he?" That's the worst, but God rest his soul, I did love him. I think he was a hell of a lot of fun. That's sincere, you know? I wouldn't even offer to contribute any information on someone who's died if he wasn't totally lovable anyway. You know, I'd rather say nothing. You've heard it from everyone. He was very, very special.

Ringgenberg: You don't mind if I quote from you directly, do you?

Frazetta: Pick the best part. I don't know of anybody in the world, and this is the gospel truth, that I loved as much as him.

August 1994 interview

Ringgenberg: Frank, my first question is: Why are you doing a comics project at this time?

Frazetta: Well, I'm not doing anything but supervising, really. As you know [Simon] Bisley is the guy [who's] going to do the artwork. And of course I'll just check in on it and make sure he doesn't go crazy. [*laughs*] And I guess I'll let them use my covers and stuff. As to why I'm doing it, I guess I was talked into it by [Glenn] Danzig. And it sounds like a good, profitable idea, but I'm not actually doing comics. I mean, I guess you read somewhere that Frazetta's back in comics, almost.

Ringgenberg: Well, I knew you were just doing covers, which is sort of what I figured.

Frazetta: Well, I have a few covers [that] haven't even been used, so I would guess at this point it would be more like a test run to see what happens. And I'm not about to really get involved. I want to just check out his work and make sure that he doesn't go crazy, and he keeps it in the tradition that I want.

Ringgenberg: Are you going to be doing any new Death Dealer covers or just using the ones that you've already done?

Frazetta: Well, I don't know. I'm not sure. I've got at least one that has never been used for starters, and then of course, we *could* use the others. Nobody seems to get too tired of it. And if the interior is all new, what's the difference?

Ringgenberg: What's the frequency of the comic going to be? Is it going to be a monthly, or a bimonthly?

Frazetta: I'm not sure about that. Like I say, they may just make, I don't know what they call it, a test run, just to see whether it takes off, you know? If it takes off, who knows?

Ringgenberg: So you had said that Glenn talked you into taking a stab at doing the comics stuff based on your characters. How did he approach you?

Frazetta: Glenn's been a friend for a couple of years, and a fan, and he's been to my house any number of times, and he's the guy who got me to do the pencil book. Are you familiar with that?

Ringgenberg: Oh, the *Illustrations Arcanum*? Yeah. That was beautiful.

Frazetta: Oh, you did see it, then.

Ringgenberg: Yes. I saw it at the San Diego con. It was great stuff!

Frazetta: Yeah, well, that was Glenn. Somehow he got me excited, and got me to work. Mostly because I love doing pencils, and they're relatively easy. And I just wanted to exploit that medium. Nobody's ever really gotten to see pencil drawings done up quite like that. And I just thought it might be a wonderful new idea. Plus, the subject matter is what I like to do, and if the reaction was as positive as everybody's saying, why not? I may even go on and do another one. I mean, the next one might be based on Frazetta girls, period. Done in probably as classy a manner as I can, a kind of different look. Not fantasy, you know? More real women. Do you have the book around? Have you looked at it closely?

Ringgenberg: Yes.

Frazetta: You know the drawing of the girl standing in the water, for example, and the other girl standing next to an ape? More that style. A little more photographic, a little more real. Less crazy. A whole book devoted to that. And mostly to show off my skills and stuff, I guess.

Ringgenberg: How long did it take you to do the illustrations that were in the book?

Frazetta: Those? Well, there's thirty of them, and I don't think I took longer than a day for each one.

Ringgenberg: When did you do them?

Frazetta: When? I started them last year, and I think I finished them last year. Then we finally got around to printing it.

Ringgenberg: Was this something you were just initially doing for yourself, or did you intend to publish them?

Frazetta: No--I found, I'm sure you're familiar with the *remarques* that I've been doing with *The Egyptian Queen*? A little drawing under each print?

Ringgenberg: Right.

Frazetta: And I had such fun doing them in pencil that I said, "Gee, I forgot how good I was with that medium." And I just got excited about pencil, period. And the reactions from people everywhere was *really* very exciting. And Glenn came out. We talked about doing this, that, and the other thing. I said, "How do you feel about pencils?" Glenn immediately commissioned me to do him, personally, three or four or five or more pencils. And he flipped out. He said, "Why don't we do a book on this stuff?" I said, "Yeah, man! That sounds great." And so it went from there. I drew rather easily, quickly. You know, I don't feel inhibited. And unlike when you say *pencils*, most people think in terms of sketches, you know? Like pencils are generally a preliminary to a painting or something, or at least for inking. And I said, "Why can't the pencils just speak for themselves?" And so you see what I got.

Ringgenberg: The reproduction was wonderful.

Frazetta: Oh, it was. Well, I supervised it at this end. I wasn't going to ship the pencils all over the place, so I had my guy do it down here, and made perfect reproductions.

Ringgenberg: I know a lot of people were talking about that book in San Diego.

Frazetta: Yeah. I know the question is: "Did Frazetta do this many years ago? Were they sitting around the house?" No. They're brand new.

Ringgenberg: I was talking to Glenn about the book, and I asked him how new the stuff was, and he told me. It's nice to see you working in a different medium, because everybody is so used to seeing you do the oil paintings.

Frazetta: Yeah, well even that gets boring. I've got nothing

against oils but it's so nice. An artist should change around and do different stuff. But the fact is I haven't been awfully productive in many years, and it's amazing how many skeptical people feel that, "Wow, Frazetta couldn't have just done this stuff. He must have done this stuff in his prime, back in the sixties or whatever." Didn't you get that impression?

Ringgenberg: Well, people *were* wondering how old the drawings were.

Frazetta: Well, that's the reason. Because they're looking at stuff I've done in the last ten years or so, and they feel it wasn't up to the old Frazetta, right? Pretty much?

Ringgenberg: Yeah, some of the oil paintings. I think that's some of what I heard.

Frazetta: Yeah, well I got the scam all over the place that they felt I'd seen my best days and that sort of crap, and they couldn't believe the quality of the drawings. They can't believe I just did them. They're sure these are drawings that were just laying around forever.

Ringgenberg: One thing that really struck me in looking over those drawings is just the freshness and the vitality. Those things just leaped off the page. I was talking with Bernie [Wrightson], Bill Stout, [Michael] Kaluta, various people. They were all excited about the book.

Frazetta: Yeah. Pretty good for an old guy, huh?

Ringgenberg: Very good. I also liked that painting. Glenn had a poster of a new painting of yours. I think it was a repaint of one of the Jongor paintings, showing a kind of Tarzan-like superhero fighting a bunch of monkey-men.

Frazetta: Oh, yeah, yeah. A leopard-type outfit?

Ringgenberg: Yes.

Frazetta: Yeah, well Glenn wants to do a whole bunch of

comics and wants me to do the covers and wants me to create characters, and so I redid that because I thought it was a pretty hopeless piece of work in the first place and so I redid it, very quickly. And you saw it, you saw it unfinished. He wanted me to shoot it up, just to show it around.

Ringgenberg: That wasn't finished?

Frazetta: Nope.

Ringgenberg: It looked great.

Frazetta: Oh, it looks great now.

Ringgenberg: Do you have a name for that character, or are you still playing with it?

Frazetta: I think Glenn's kicking around names and stuff, you know.

Ringgenberg: And if you did a book with that character, would you do a couple of new paintings?

Frazetta: Probably, sure.

Ringgenberg: One thing I also saw at the con was some little casts, a series of head busts, like a primitive man, a woman, and a guy who looked like your Darkwolf character from *Fire and Ice.*

Frazetta: Oh, right. Okay. You mean the heads? Yeah. They were done for the movie I made. It would appear that the artists had a lot of problems with being consistent, and so I found myself making these clay heads so they'd each have a copy and, you know, pretty much understand what the characters looked like. Because they varied all over the place with these people. You know what I mean? You've got forty or fifty people, and some are talented and some are not, and we're getting these drawings, one after another and some of them were terrible. They were just all going out into left field. So I got the brainstorm to do these heads. And they'd each get one, and they'd have it, you know, at their drawing board and they'd be far more consistent that way. That's all that was.

Ringgenberg: Oh, I thought it was something that was done for the collector's market, like a limited edition.

Frazetta: No, not at all. Not at all.

Ringgenberg: Interesting. Well, you know, Frank, for years I've heard rumors that you were doing little bronzes, but I've only ever seen a couple of things.

Frazetta: No, I'm not doing any bronzes. I did something for Dark Horse. Randy Bowen is doing a Death Dealer figure, and of course it went back and forth and I kept changing it and improving it and repairing it and changing it and improving it and so on, and I think we've got a good thing now. And we sent it out to be done in the usual manner, and these people couldn't handle it. So we decided a bronze would be safer. When I say they couldn't handle it, I hand painted some stuff like the horns on Death Dealer's head, and this and that. And they sent them off to these factories and they came back sloppy and inconsistent as hell and Randy Bowen, in disgust, said, "They can't do it, Frank. They simply can't do it." So if you go for bronze, they'll all look the same.

Ringgenberg: Well, are you happy with what Glenn's done so far?

Frazetta: Oh, you mean like the book? Sure. It's great. It's great. Well, Glenn's a great guy. Glenn will do *nothing* to screw me up, and he doesn't just come off blowing his horn.

Ringgenberg: I assume you have final approval over everything?

Frazetta: Oh, yeah. Absolutely. Well, I say I had it printed here. And the negatives were shot here and everything, and then Glenn went from there. We discussed it for many, many months.

Ringgenberg: I'm curious, Frank. How big were the original pencil drawings? Were they large?

Frazetta: Not bigger than their reproductions.

Ringgenberg: Oh, really?

Frazetta: Oh, yeah. And as good as the book appears, the originals blow them away. I don't know why. I mean they're perfectly good reproductions, but I don't know if it's size or what, but I mean the originals are looser and crazier and the reproduction, you know when you reduced it, it sort of got, it looked a little tight, just a little on the tight side. And they're not tight. They're very loose and crazy. And, yeah, it's a perfect reproduction, but the originals are so much more fun to look at you can't believe it.

Ringgenberg: You said you might want to do your next book just on women?

Frazetta: Yeah. Why not? Not that I didn't enjoy doing that subject, you know, but as I went along, and I drew those two with the women . . . Those were the last two that I [did], and I got really excited about this. Jeez, I think if I do another book, I'd like to just focus on that. And because I love drawing women, unlike what I usually do, where it's all fantasy, I wanted to do some serious but very sexy, wonderful women, just exploit the female form and do it in a way like it's never been done possibly, or you know, the way I draw women. They're not going to be just posing statically or anything. Just try to make them as beautiful and sexy as I can make them, but always in good taste. No way I'll go trashy, you know?

Ringgenberg: Aside from what you're doing with Glenn, do you have any projects in the works?

Frazetta: Well, there's going to be a big showing in New York, on Madison Avenue of my work and stuff. It's the Alexander Gallery. You can find out about that.

Ringgenberg: When is it going to be held?

Frazetta: In October.

Ringgenberg: Is that going to be all oil paintings, or also drawings?

Frazetta: Probably a little bit of everything. But I want them

to focus on my ability as an artist and not a cartoonist. But, you know, this guy has a problem with that. I don't want to be set back thirty, forty years and when he starts bringing up my comic-book days, which were minimal as far as I'm concerned . . .

Ringgenberg: Does he want to feature some of your comic-book work?

Frazetta: Well, I guess he's trying to show the "versatilities" aspect of it, and that's all very nice, but you know as well as I do somehow when people feel, "Well, he did comics," they don't think of you as a fine artist. They don't feel you can possibly work in comics and be a fine artist all at the same time. And they judge your work by the subject matter and that sort of crap. I'm trying to get rid of that label once and for all and let them appreciate my work for what it is.

Ringgenberg: You transcended comics thirty years ago.

Frazetta: Well, that's what I thought, but, you know, people are very slow to react. "Yeah, yeah. Well, he's a phenomenon, and we don't quite understand it, but we shouldn't maybe take him too seriously." But all that shit's gone down the tubes a long time ago. I mean they're teaching my work in colleges now and stuff like that. Now, come on.

Ringgenberg: Frank, on the subject of teaching your work, do you ever think that you'd want to do a "how to" book on painting or something?

Frazetta: No. It's silly. Because I have no formula. You know, with this business of teaching, I can't ever, ever teach anyone how to think like me. That's what makes my work . . . my imagination, the fact that I'm inventive. The fact that I draw well. There's no formula. I've had guys come in here, and they just fall over when they look at my palette. They just fall over, saying, "How the hell can you do such beautiful work with that horrible-looking palette?" I mean, it's an absolute mess. I just paint and draw by instinct. What I do is create images, *period*. I can't *ever* teach anybody. I can teach somebody how to apply paint. I can teach them how to swipe from me, that's about it. I'm me. That's it. It's not like the usual school of art where they have these set formulas where you go from step one to step two. Forget it. I'm a sort of a method artist. I just—it's time to work, I start reaching down into my head, see these images, and just whirl away at it. And things happen. How do you teach someone that? All I'll do is develop a hundred clones of myself. And I say "clones," but all they will have done is copy. They'll never be able to do what I do, in that I just—I'm always different, I'm always creative—and they can't do that. If they don't have that kind of ability, what'll I do from there?

Ringgenberg: There's no substitute for imagination.

Frazetta: Well, exactly . . . If you just teach them the fundamentals they wind up thinking like you, but more thinking like what you've done rather than what you might do. It simply doesn't work. There are schools of thought where they do have these absolutely cut-and-dried approaches to art, and you can learn to become a professional artist. But how good you'll get and how creative you'll get is open to conjecture. But a teacher I couldn't be. It would teach them nothing. I might get them excited. I might get them fired up. I would just stress being your own man. If you have something to say, say it. Use life as a guide. Get down what you think you see. Get down what you would like to see. Don't think in terms of how Frank might have done it or somebody else might do it. I don't sit here approaching the drawing board thinking, "Let's see now. How would so-and-so have painted this?" But that's what they do. I just sit there and imagine that I'm there, that I'm on the scene. How do you teach somebody that?

Ringgenberg: I guess you can't.

Frazetta: No, you really can't.

Ringgenberg: The last time I interviewed you, you said something that's been stuck in my head ever since. You said, if you're out there in the creative arena and you really don't have anything to say, then get the hell out.

Frazetta: Yeah. That's the way I feel about it. I don't want to condemn anybody, but, you know, if it's too hot in the kitchen, get out of there.

Ringgenberg: Do you have any projects that you'd really like to do but you just haven't lined up yet?

Frazetta: Oh, yeah, as a matter of fact. This is no big secret, but Glenn is very, very high on perhaps getting this Death Dealer comic book off the ground and getting a movie made.

Ringgenberg: A live-action Death Dealer film?

Frazetta: Yeah.

Ringgenberg: I was going to ask if you had any film projects that you were thinking about.

Frazetta: Oh, yeah, well that's it, brother. And I mean no bullshit, none of those Hollywood assholes screwing it up.

Ringgenberg: And would you direct it?

Frazetta: Pretty much. I'd be right there. Plus, getting everything *the best*, and I mean directors, writers, the whole thing. But with my input, because if we're doing Death Dealer, I think I know him a little better than anybody else. And, yeah, pretty much like I did with *Fire and Ice*. Unfortunately, I had my input, but it clashed with [Ralph] Bakshi's.

Ringgenberg: Well, even with Bakshi's input, the film still looks pretty good.

Frazetta: Oh, I think it looks great! But don't forget, I was giving art lessons every day to the background guys, and you know the backgrounds are great.

Ringgenberg: That's a movie my wife and I have gone back to again and again, and we still find it entertaining. It holds up.

Frazetta: But you know as well as I do that a lot of people are very critical of it, and many liked the action scenes, which is primarily what I did. Of course, I created characters and told them how to move and how to perform those actions and stuff like that. And Bakshi did, well, the other half of it, you know, the weird stuff, which he's prone to do. And everything spectacular, moving glaciers and stuff, that's out of my league. I don't think like that. I just wanted a simple adventure and a chase scene in the jungle, in the swamps, you know, like I do. And I'm the guy that made the lizard work, and those hero characters do their thing. That was me. But then they had other guys writing the story, and I fought like hell about that. And other guys doing this and other guys doing that, so it's not pure Frazetta. There are a lot of Frazetta moments, period. But still, it still worked pretty well. I still think it might have made money.

Ringgenberg: The action in it was solid. Those were very realistic fights.

Frazetta: Well, that's exactly what I did. I did every action scene.

Ringgenberg: You were like a second-unit director on that, right?

Frazetta: Second unit, right. I even did some of the action, *personally*.

Ringgenberg: Really?

Frazetta: Yep. Oh, yeah . . . and I jumped around, did all that silly nonsense.

Ringgenberg: Did you have a sound stage with ramps and ropes to swing on and so forth?

Frazetta: Everything. Whatever it took. But I think, right off the bat, that we could have done it live in the first place. Bakshi agreed to that after, oh, maybe two weeks of shooting. He said, "Goddamnit, Frazetta, we could have done it live!" You know he had the attitude that there was no way we could do it live and make people look like the paintings that I do, and I said, we sure can. Sure you can do it live if you know

what you're doing, if you know what you want, if you know how to cast, and you know how to costume the people, and you know, you spend some money.

Ringgenberg: Where would you find locations that look like your paintings?

Frazetta: My locations are very normal. Mountainous backgrounds, swamps, forests. What have I got that's so unusual?

Ringgenberg: It would be kind of hard right now to find the kind of lush jungles that you paint. So much of it has disappeared.

Frazetta: Oh, not really. Not at all. Hell, you can find 'em right in Mexico. You can find lush jungle anywhere if you want to.

Ringgenberg: I guess if they could make *Predator*, they could make a film from your stuff.

Frazetta: It's how you shoot it. It's the lighting you use and so on. That's no problem. It's how I would stage it and have the guy move from here to there, and his attitude and so on, like that. If you want to catch the drama, the same kind of drama, and the power. I mean I paint it, so I know what I'm doing. And a lot of those stuntmen thought I was crazy when I asked them to do certain things, and I had to show them. It was really funny. "Aw, a person can't do that." So I would do it. It's like the cameras are going and you get a little adrenaline going for you. How dare they say it's impossible, you know? But I had to prove that if I did it in a painting, it's possible.

FAMOUS MONSTERS 1970 FEAR BOOK

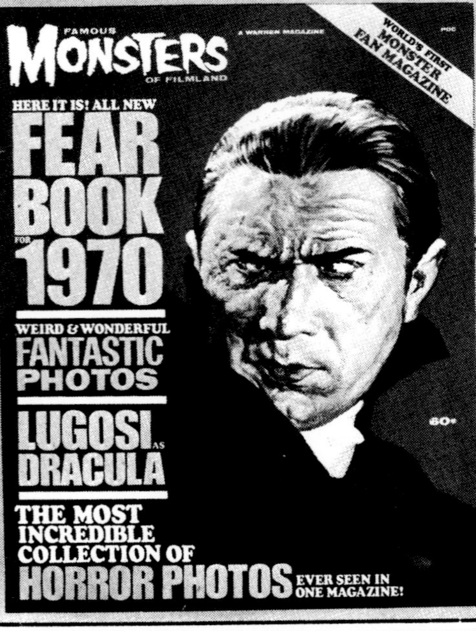
FAMOUS
MONSTERS
OF FILMLAND
A WARNER MAGAZINE
WORLD'S FIRST MONSTER FAN MAGAZINE
HERE IT IS! ALL NEW
FEAR BOOK FOR 1970
WEIRD & WONDERFUL
FANTASTIC PHOTOS
LUGOSI AS DRACULA
THE MOST INCREDIBLE COLLECTION OF
HORROR PHOTOS EVER SEEN IN ONE MAGAZINE!
60¢

Get ready, get set . . . GO GET THE FABULOUS 1970 YEARBOOK of FAMOUS MONSTERS! Bigger, better, gruesomore . . . ghastlier than ever. Just coming off the giant monster presses. 84 PAGES, and horror-packed with page after page of KARLOFF, LUGOSI, CHANEY, LEE, AND ALL your old favorites from the Monster Screen! HERE, in a huge, scare-packed 84 pages, are hundreds of exclusive FAMOUS MONSTERS photos, stories, articles and background items. A RARE COLLECTOR'S YEARBOOK, sure to increase in value and interest year after year.

ORDER BY MAIL! A LIMITED NUMBER of reserved copies will be mailed to the first readers who fill out the coupon below. Act now! Let us know that you want one of the 1st copies of the 1970 FAMOUS MONSTERS YEARBOOK. It will be rushed to you. And you can thrill to this TRULY AMAZING, 84-PAGE MONSTER ANNUAL.

Get one of the Reserved COPIES Delivered by Your Mailman!

ONLY 60¢ USE THIS COUPON!

FAMOUS MONSTERS 1970 YEARBOOK,

All Copies Mailed in a Sturdy Envelope for Protection.

Please send me an advance copy of FAMOUS MONSTERS 1970 YEARBOOK. I enclose 60c (the cost of the Yearbook) plus 15c to cover mailing & handling charges. (Total 75c) Offer good in U.S.A. only.

NAME ....

ADDRESS ....

CITY .... STATE .... ZIPCODE ....

YOU ASKED FOR IT— HERE IT IS!

For years now we've ignored the thousands of requests for FM T-SHIRTS, but we can't fight the world forever. Now at last you can own your own fine quality white cotton washable T-shirt featuring the FAMOUS MONSTERS insignia. Be the first in your neighborhood to create riots this summer with your FAMOUS MONSTERS T-SHIRT. Only **$1.50**

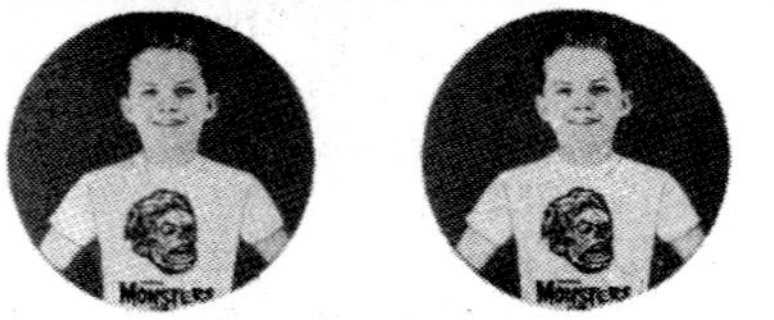

FAMOUS MONSTER T-SHIRTS

FAMOUS MONSTERS T-SHIRTS

I CAN'T WAIT! HERE'S MY $1.50 FOR EACH SHIRT AND I'VE INDICATED MY SIZE ON THE COUPON. RUSH ME MY FAMOUS MONSTERS T-SHIRT IMMEDIATELY! WE PAY ALL POSTAGE!

SMALL (size 6 to 8)	MEDIUM (size 10 to 12)	LARGE size 14 to 16

NAME ....

ADDRESS ....

CITY ....

STATE .... ZONE ....

NO. OF SHIRTS .... SIZE(S) ....

AMOUNT ENCLOSED AT $1.50 EACH ....

MAKE YOUR OWN MONSTER PHOTO CARDS

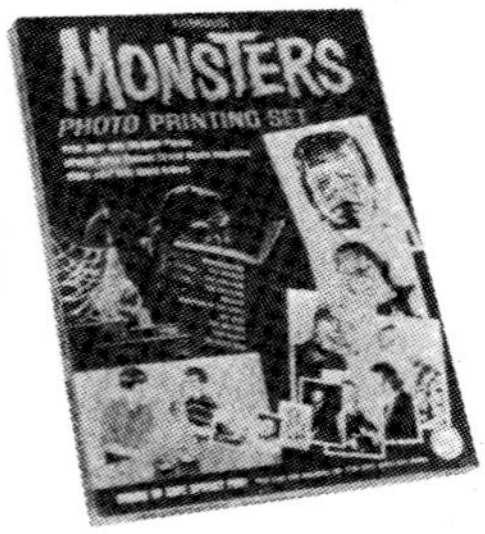
FAMOUS
MONSTERS
PHOTO PRINTING SET

SET INCLUDES ORIGINAL NEGATIVES FROM FAMOUS MONSTERS MAGAZINE

Only $3.98 plus 75¢ postage and handling.

COMPLETE MONSTER PHOTO PRINT SET INCLUDES ALL THESE 46 ITEMS . . .

10 NEGATIVES of the officially selected most popular monsters from FAMOUS MONSTERS MAGAZINE, each 2½ in. x 3⅜ in., 25 SHEETS OF FINE PHOTO PRINT PAPER, 2 PACKS OF DEVELOPER (premeasured), 2 PACKS OF FIXERS (premeasured), AMBER SAFELIGHT FOR PERFECT PRINTING, DURABLE PROFESSIONAL PRINTING FRAME, COMPLETE INSTRUCTIONS IN COMIC BOOK, 2 SWIZZLE STICKS FOR BETTER MIXING.

THE 10 MOST GRUESOME PICTURES from Famous Monsters Magazine are included in your set. Think how proud you will be as you show your finished "professional" prints to your family and friends. They just won't believe that you, yourself, made the prints. Then pull out the 10 exclusive Monster Negatives and prove that it was you, not a photo shop, that made your wonderful prints.

FIRST MAGAZINE OF ILLUSTRATED HORROR

CREEPY

CREEPY #33 JUNE

A WARREN MAGAZINE   PDC

50¢

"...CRAWLING, EVIL, SCREAMING CREATURES SLITHERED FROM THE GOLD MASK." See Page 12

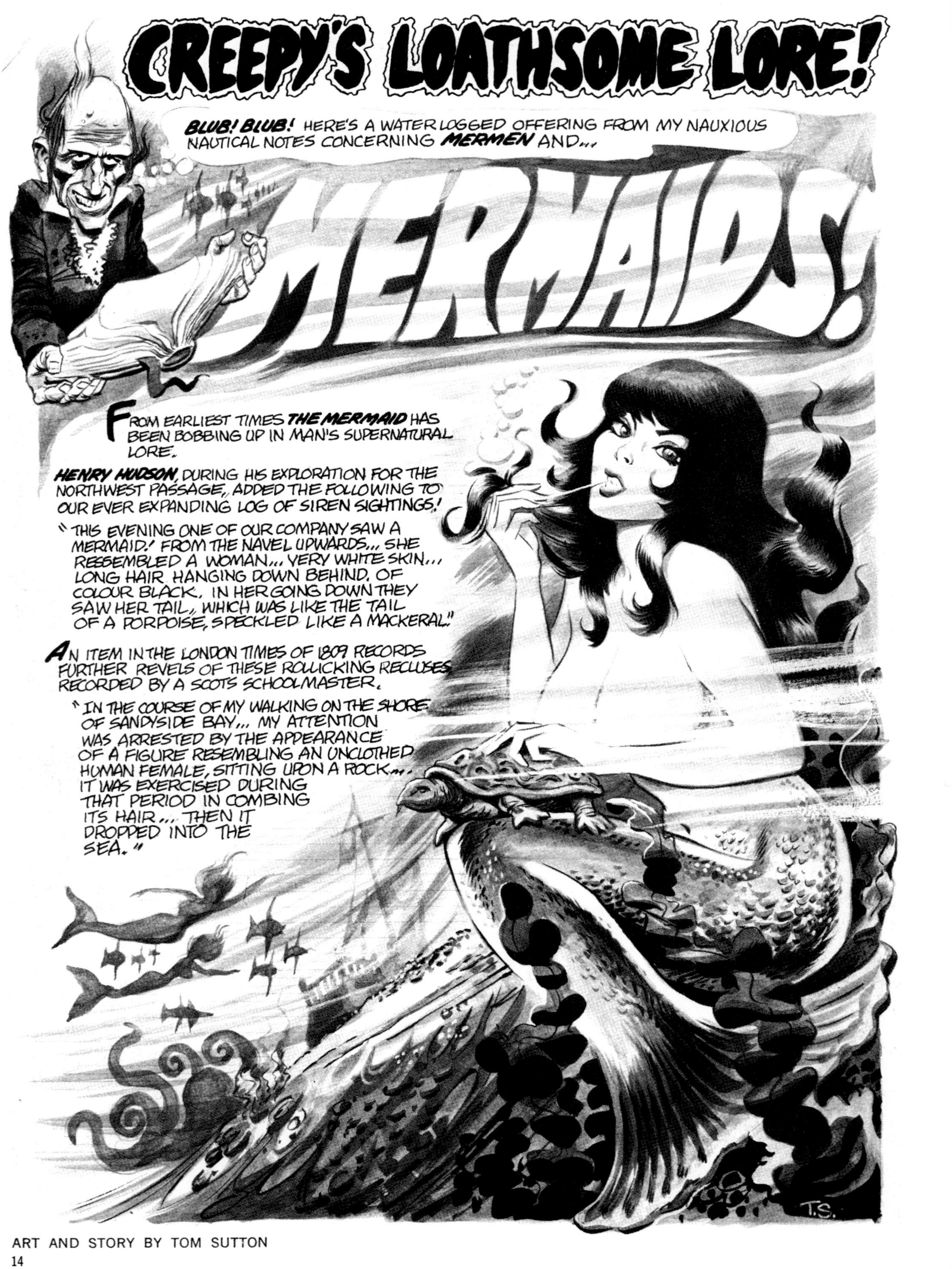
CREEPY'S LOATHSOME LORE!
BLUB! BLUB! HERE'S A WATERLOGGED OFFERING FROM MY NAUXIOUS NAUTICAL NOTES CONCERNING MERMEN AND...
MERMAIDS!
FROM EARLIEST TIMES THE MERMAID HAS BEEN BOBBING UP IN MAN'S SUPERNATURAL LORE.
HENRY HUDSON, DURING HIS EXPLORATION FOR THE NORTHWEST PASSAGE, ADDED THE FOLLOWING TO OUR EVER EXPANDING LOG OF SIREN SIGHTINGS!
"THIS EVENING ONE OF OUR COMPANY SAW A MERMAID! FROM THE NAVEL UPWARDS... SHE RESSEMBLED A WOMAN... VERY WHITE SKIN... LONG HAIR HANGING DOWN BEHIND, OF COLOUR BLACK. IN HER GOING DOWN THEY SAW HER TAIL, WHICH WAS LIKE THE TAIL OF A PORPOISE, SPECKLED LIKE A MACKERAL."
AN ITEM IN THE LONDON TIMES OF 1809 RECORDS FURTHER REVELS OF THESE ROLLICKING RECLUSES, RECORDED BY A SCOTS SCHOOLMASTER.
"IN THE COURSE OF MY WALKING ON THE SHORE OF SANDYSIDE BAY... MY ATTENTION WAS ARRESTED BY THE APPEARANCE OF A FIGURE RESEMBLING AN UNCLOTHED HUMAN FEMALE, SITTING UPON A ROCK... IT WAS EXERCISED DURING THAT PERIOD IN COMBING ITS HAIR... THEN IT DROPPED INTO THE SEA."
T.S.

ART AND STORY BY TOM SUTTON

CREEPY

NO. 33

PUBLISHER: JAMES WARREN **EDITOR:** BILL PARENTE **COVER:** PAT BOYETTE
ARTISTS THIS ISSUE: WILLIAM BARRY, PAT BOYETTE, REED CRANDALL, JUAN LOPEZ RAMON, JOHN FANTUCCHIO, TOM SUTTON, TONY WILLIAMSUNE **WRITERS THIS ISSUE:** AL HEWETSON, R. MICHAEL ROSEN, BUDDY SAUNDERS, TOM SUTTON, BILL WARREN

CONTENTS

POLICE
RRRRRRRRRRRRRR

HYDE!

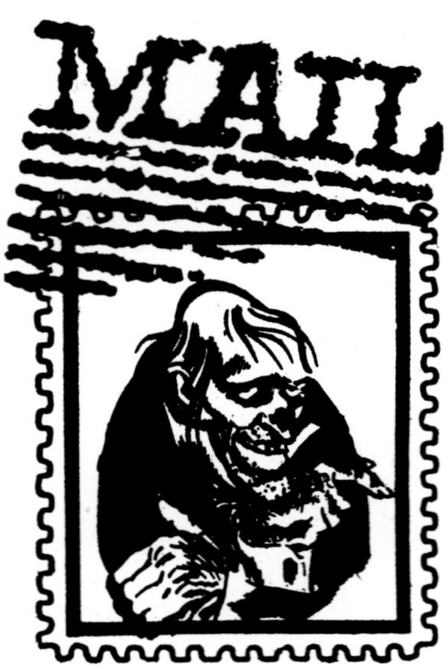
MAIL

❝$27.00 worth of CREEPYS and EERIES! Too many science-fiction stories!❞

NUTTY PICTURES?
I liked issue #31 a lot, but I didn't like the artists much. Too many of them made very nutty pictures. But I like all your magazines anyway.

LARRY QUINN
Arlington, Va.

SOMETHING YOU ATE
I buy all my magazines in a cafe. When I got issue #31, I sat down at a table with a couple of cheeseburgers. When I saw your picture of a chicken climbing out of a robot, it almost made me sick.

JOHN SIMMONS
Cincinnati, Ohio

Good thing you weren't eating fried chicken! Or roasted robots.

EAGLE EYE
You may already have fired your proofreader (if you ever had one at all!), but in case you didn't, I think you should take another look at issue #31. The whole mess starts on page 7, fourth frame, where borough is spelled "burrough." Then, if you'll get our trusty dictionary, you'll discover that you made another boo-boo on page 8—it's assassin, not "assasin." And shouldn't the story title on page 19 be "A Night's Lodging"? The other blunders were not so bad. I think even Uncle Creepy could have caught them himself: Page 29—"sinse," page 44—"beatiful," page 54—"tommorw," page 57—"woudn't" and "icey," page 58—"sanaity" and "againest." And, to end it all, "immercing" on page 60.

But don't worry, Unc. even with mistakes, your stories are still great and always have been. Maybe if you're lucky, Noah Webster will drop in to give you a few spelling lessons. We all know that nobody's purfekt.

ERIC SCHILLING
Oakland, N.J.

Strange you should mention that name Noah. That's our proofreader's name, too. —Noah Moresky. Our Noah was once umpire in the Transylvanian baseball league. He retired after 150 years' of faithful service and now works with us. You'll have to forgive his occasional mistakes. He still has difficulty with the English language. And his eyesight isn't what it used to be. Though in the tradition of all great baseball umpires, he steadfastly refuses to wear glasses. But we're sentimental about old Noah. He does his best.

GOOD CUSTOMER
I am a horror magazine collector and I have never seen any that can compare to the three great Warren magazines. I read all your letter pages and it makes me mad to see how readers put you down saying your art stinks. I'd like to see them do better! They couldn't if their **life** depended on it.

The other magazines on the market consist of stories rewritten from last year. And last year's stories were rewrites of stories that appeared in the 1930's and 1940's.

When my mother and my uncle were kids, they collected horror magazines, too. My father just bought me $27.00 worth of **CREEPYS** and **EERIES** and my mother took time to read all of them. She enjoyed them as much as I do.

I just bought the latest issues of **EERIE** and **VAMPIRELLA,** and a few weeks ago I got issue #31 of **CREEPY.** I thought all of them were just great. I thought your cover for #31 was especially good. Todd and Bode are great artists. I also like their cover for **VAMPIRELLA** #3.

It would be great if you could have your stories acted out on television.

ROSS FRANKEL
Scarsdale, N.Y.

A WHAT?
I think your magazine is pretty good. Issue #31 was the best of all, I think. I have been collecting **CREEPY** since issue #5. The art has been improving lately. I think you should give all your artists a raise.

DANNY JENKS
Wild Rose, Wisc.

A MASTERPIECE
I must say, old man, the story "Snowmen" in issue #31 was a masterpiece. Although the cover wasn't so hot, I especially liked all the stories inside. Tell me, Uncle, why don't you have more stories about werewolves in your magazine? No offense, but you've been having too many science fiction stories lately. I, myself, hate science fiction. I suggest you put in more melodrama. And more blood. You were getting out of that reprint, rut, then you slipped back last time. How come?

SAM RICCARDO
West Chester, Pa.

We've established a no-reprint rule around here. So has my miserable little cousin. But every once in a while, a story arrives too late to make our printing deadline and we're faced with three choices: Either delay the magazine (which you wouldn't like much), run it with blank pages (which wouldn't add much to your fun either), or reprint another story. We hope it never happens, and it won't very often. But when you do see a reprint, don't get the idea we don't care.

VERY BEST FAN
Though I've only been a fan of yours since issue #20, I consider myself one of your very best fans. Some people write to say that they like **CREEPY** better than **EERIE** or **EERIE** better than **CREEPY.** How can anyone say one is better than the other when both magazines are written by the same writers, drawn by the same artists, edited by the same editor, published by the same publisher and both have the same kind of stories?

CHUCK HECK
Fontana, Cal.

It's a long story. Call it loyalty. CREEPY came out a year ahead of EERIE, and all those artists, writers, and other people are more loyal to "the first one."

FROM THE ARCHIVES
I wish to inform you that you have a misprint on the cover of your screaming mag. The cover bears the wonderful message: "All New Stories."

Yet, somewhere in the back of my mind—way back among the cobwebs of horrors—I seem to recall the tale, "A Night's Lodging." So I summon my faithful Igor and we advance down into the crypts to the dead files. Then, when the dust settles, I gaze down upon issue #17, the first **CREEPY** I ever saw. Then, on page 43 of that good old '67 issue, I find "A Night's Lodging!" Was this an uintentional mistake? But, nonetheless, the rest of this issue came through for you. Issue #31 was as loaded with horror and terror as any magazine can ever hope to be.

BILL MOONEY
Camdentown, Mo.

ANOTHER LONG MEMORY
If you have to run reruns, why "A Night's Lodging"? Didn't your fans jump on you enough for that when it ran in issue #17? Even then it was modelled after "An Invitation" in issue #8.

I'm confused by one thing: In one of the Dracula movies, he was killed by running water, or at least laid to rest. But in "Dracula 2000," he committed the unspeakable crime of drinking water. In "Dracula Has Risen From the Grave," he was frozen in it, then thawed out. I must admit Maurice is a good artist, but somehow the spelling is amiss. "Snowmen" was one of Tom Sutton's best ever. I think leaving the end of "Telephoto Troll" to the reader's imagination did nothing more than stagger the reader's imagination. One more thing: if you're keeping count of the stories in the old vault, we haven't heard from "Adam Link" in a long while. I hope he hasn't rusted.

BOB KNODERER
Joliet, Ill.

Killing vampires is a little out of my line. Some of my best friends are vampires. But there is one certain little girl vampire I'd like to put out of her misery. If you hear any more about this water theory, let me know.

W.O.M.C.C.
I call you my uncle because I, too, am a creepy person. I literally feed on horror and your magazine is the best thing to come along in years for a person like me. I have seen other horror magazines, but none of them holds a candle to yours. Keep up the good work and we might even let you become a member of the W.O.M.C.C. (Western Organization of Maladjusted Creepy Characters.)

RICHIE PERLOFF
Culver City, Cal.

BURNING THOUGHTS
For the benefit of Agatha

Hulk and Hazel Gruntt who are so curious about witches, I refer them to the letter that appeared in issue #31 just above theirs (from Pete Brady) and to "The Encyclopedia of Witchcraft and Demonology." The book says that a bunch of witches is called a "coven." Some day I'm going to explore the Transylvanian Alps of Rumania. I read in a book by Sir Arthur Conan Doyle that a part of the Midwestern United States was once known as Transylvania.

To change the subject, I think the two most frightening movies of all time were: "The House on Haunted Hill," and "Terror in The Tomb." I'd like to know if your readers agree with me. I think the corniest movie of all time was "Death Takes a Holiday."

Good bye. Give my regards to Cousin Eerie and the Ackermonster and the beautiful Vampi. Are you and Vampi blood relatives? I hope you'll excuse my handwriting, but this letter is being written as I'm being burned at the stake.

MICHAEL O'BRIEN
North Haven, Conn.

COLON, ADAMS & CO.
I liked the cover on issue #31. Very colorful! I also like the bigger letters page and the possibility of subscribing for two years instead of just one (and at a saving at that!).

This is my third letter. Each time I have begged you to bring back Neal Adams. So as not to ruin my record, once again I beseech you: Bring back N.A.

In issue #31, the only story that seemed to rise above your usual fine quality was "Death of a Stranger." Ernie Colon's work was better than usual. And that makes it pretty darn good! I like his imaginative arrangement of the story panels. Such background as the last panel on page 45 and the second on page 48 make his art wonderfully realistic. Which, when talking about horror magazines is a bit of high flattery.

Lastly, E. Colon's rendering of our beloved Uncle is the best I've ever seen. Many of your artists make an attempt at U.C.'s portrait, but Colon **really** captures him. Especially on page 43.

It usually seems that you regard the last item in any letter the most important. So I'll end my letter with this: Bring back Neal Adams!

I'm losing sleep these days. I hardly ever drink blood. I repeatedly rise on the wrong side of my coffin. I'm totally upset over Adam's absence. Bring back Adams! AUGGH-H-H!

JOE BANSBACH
Media, Pa.

VOICE OF THE PEOPLE
CREEPY is becoming an increasing disappointment. Although your stories are still good, your art runs them into the ground. Since issue #17, the names of the great artists like Gray Morrow, Angelo Torres, Frank Frazetta and Reed Crandall have been replaced by comparative amateurs.

In issue #30, you had a request from a reader to bring back the old artists and you said you would. But you haven't. If you guys are trying to start a new style with **CREEPY**, forget it. Only the old version with the great artists can survive. Keep on the way you're going now and . . . well, you know the old saying: "give him enough rope and he'll hang himself."

Please. You seem to keep ignoring readers' requests for the old artists. What's wrong? Don't you pay any attention to your fans at all? Take a look at the list of artists in issue #7 and start bringing some of those people back again. Then you'll get real fan support.

Let's see the voice of the people in action.

Yes, you do have some good artists. Not great, but good. They are Carlos Prunes, Ernie Colon (probably your best!), and Billy Graham. Keep these and get back the good old ones and I'd gladly pay a buck for your magazine.

AARON ALBRECHT
Hyattsville, Md.

GREAT CRACKLING CUTICLES
Now that you've expanded your letters page to two, I thought it was time I told you what I thought about your raggy mag. That cover on issue #31 was terrific. Bode's got a real talent for interior work. Get him. His work is "cartoony," but great. As far as effect and presentation of the cover goes, it ranks up there with the best of the **CREEPY** covers. But I do wish there had been a good story to go with it.

Please, Frank, come back! We still love you. And Uncle Creepy: May your crackling creme colored cuticles curl coilingly over your cravenly coffin.

MIKE BYRD
Cocoa, Fla.

"In my opinion . . ."
What is your opinion?
Let us hear it. Address
your mail to:
DEAR UNCLE CREEPY

17

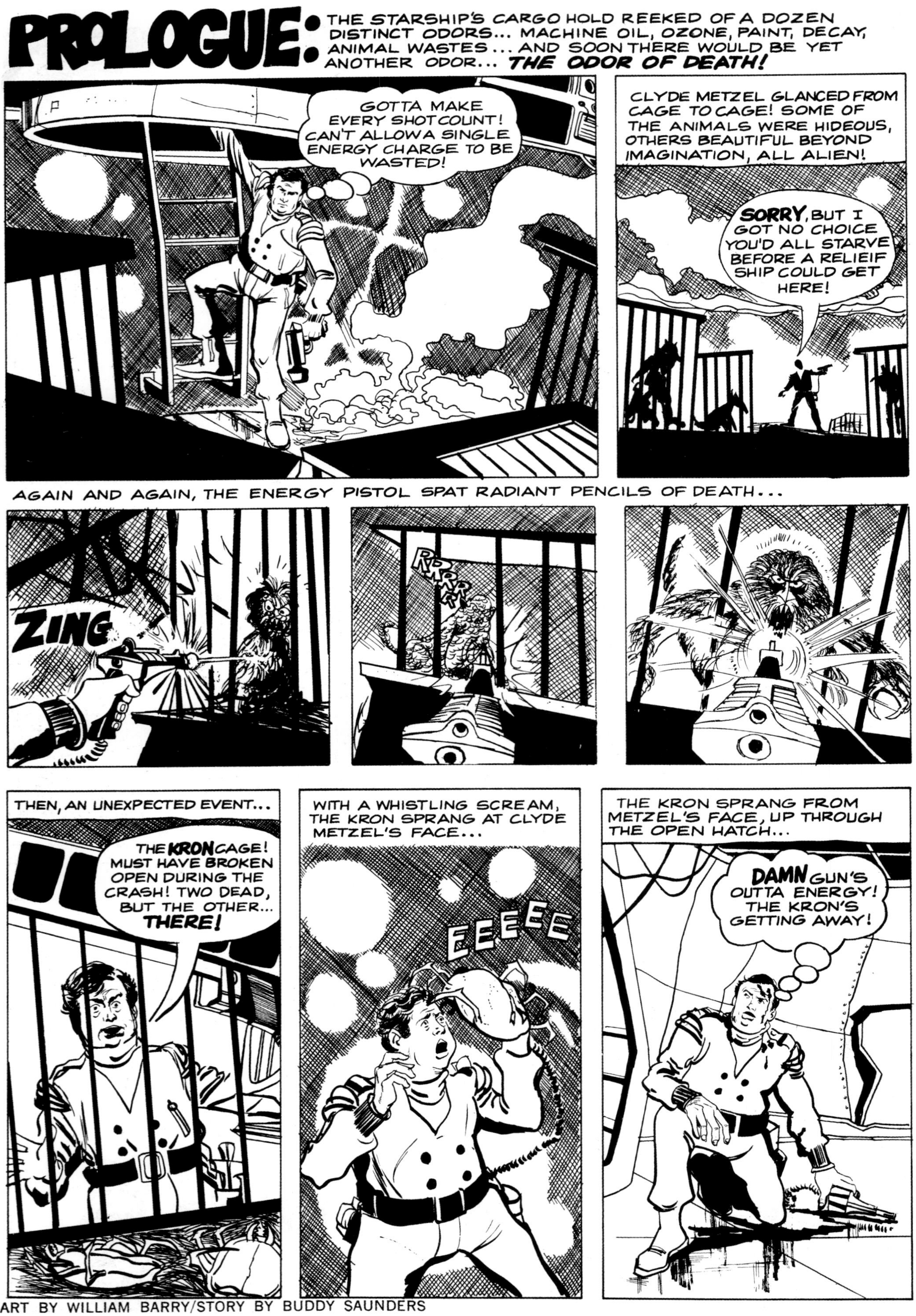
PROLOGUE: THE STARSHIP'S CARGO HOLD REEKED OF A DOZEN DISTINCT ODORS... MACHINE OIL, OZONE, PAINT, DECAY, ANIMAL WASTES... AND SOON THERE WOULD BE YET ANOTHER ODOR... THE ODOR OF DEATH!
GOTTA MAKE EVERY SHOT COUNT! CAN'T ALLOW A SINGLE ENERGY CHARGE TO BE WASTED!
CLYDE METZEL GLANCED FROM CAGE TO CAGE! SOME OF THE ANIMALS WERE HIDEOUS, OTHERS BEAUTIFUL BEYOND IMAGINATION, ALL ALIEN!
SORRY, BUT I GOT NO CHOICE YOU'D ALL STARVE BEFORE A RELIEIF SHIP COULD GET HERE!
AGAIN AND AGAIN, THE ENERGY PISTOL SPAT RADIANT PENCILS OF DEATH...
ZING
THEN, AN UNEXPECTED EVENT...
THE KRON CAGE! MUST HAVE BROKEN OPEN DURING THE CRASH! TWO DEAD, BUT THE OTHER... THERE!
WITH A WHISTLING SCREAM, THE KRON SPRANG AT CLYDE METZEL'S FACE...
EEEEE
THE KRON SPRANG FROM METZEL'S FACE, UP THROUGH THE OPEN HATCH...
DAMN GUN'S OUTTA ENERGY! THE KRON'S GETTING AWAY!

ART BY WILLIAM BARRY/STORY BY BUDDY SAUNDERS

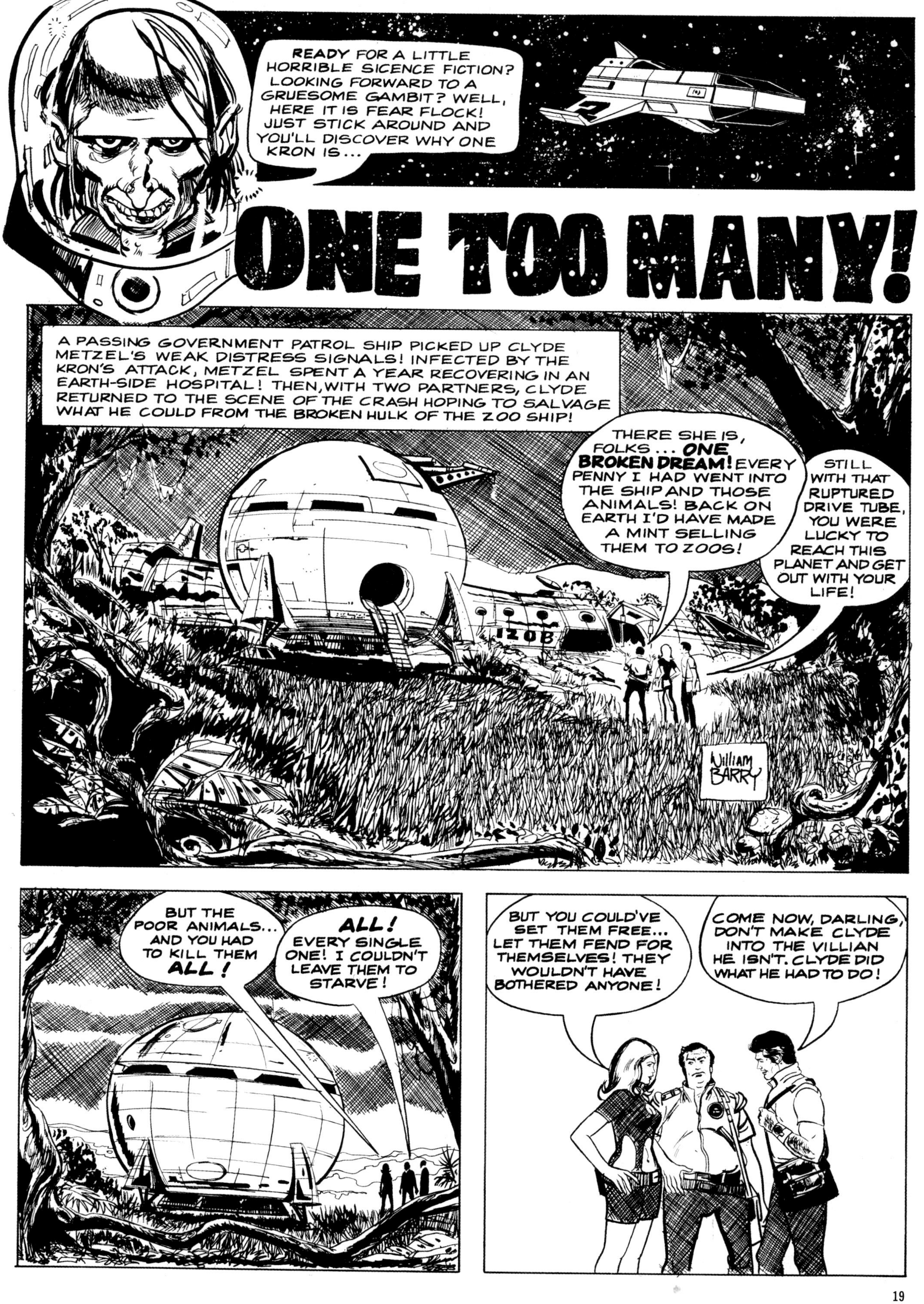
READY FOR A LITTLE HORRIBLE SICENCE FICTION? LOOKING FORWARD TO A GRUESOME GAMBIT? WELL, HERE IT IS FEAR FLOCK! JUST STICK AROUND AND YOU'LL DISCOVER WHY ONE KRON IS...
ONE TOO MANY!
A PASSING GOVERNMENT PATROL SHIP PICKED UP CLYDE METZEL'S WEAK DISTRESS SIGNALS! INFECTED BY THE KRON'S ATTACK, METZEL SPENT A YEAR RECOVERING IN AN EARTH-SIDE HOSPITAL! THEN, WITH TWO PARTNERS, CLYDE RETURNED TO THE SCENE OF THE CRASH HOPING TO SALVAGE WHAT HE COULD FROM THE BROKEN HULK OF THE ZOO SHIP!
THERE SHE IS, FOLKS... ONE BROKEN DREAM! EVERY PENNY I HAD WENT INTO THE SHIP AND THOSE ANIMALS! BACK ON EARTH I'D HAVE MADE A MINT SELLING THEM TO ZOOS!
STILL WITH THAT RUPTURED DRIVE TUBE, YOU WERE LUCKY TO REACH THIS PLANET AND GET OUT WITH YOUR LIFE!
IZOB
WILLIAM BARRY
BUT THE POOR ANIMALS... AND YOU HAD TO KILL THEM ALL!
ALL! EVERY SINGLE ONE! I COULDN'T LEAVE THEM TO STARVE!
BUT YOU COULD'VE SET THEM FREE... LET THEM FEND FOR THEMSELVES! THEY WOULDN'T HAVE BOTHERED ANYONE!
COME NOW, DARLING, DON'T MAKE CLYDE INTO THE VILLIAN HE ISN'T. CLYDE DID WHAT HE HAD TO DO!

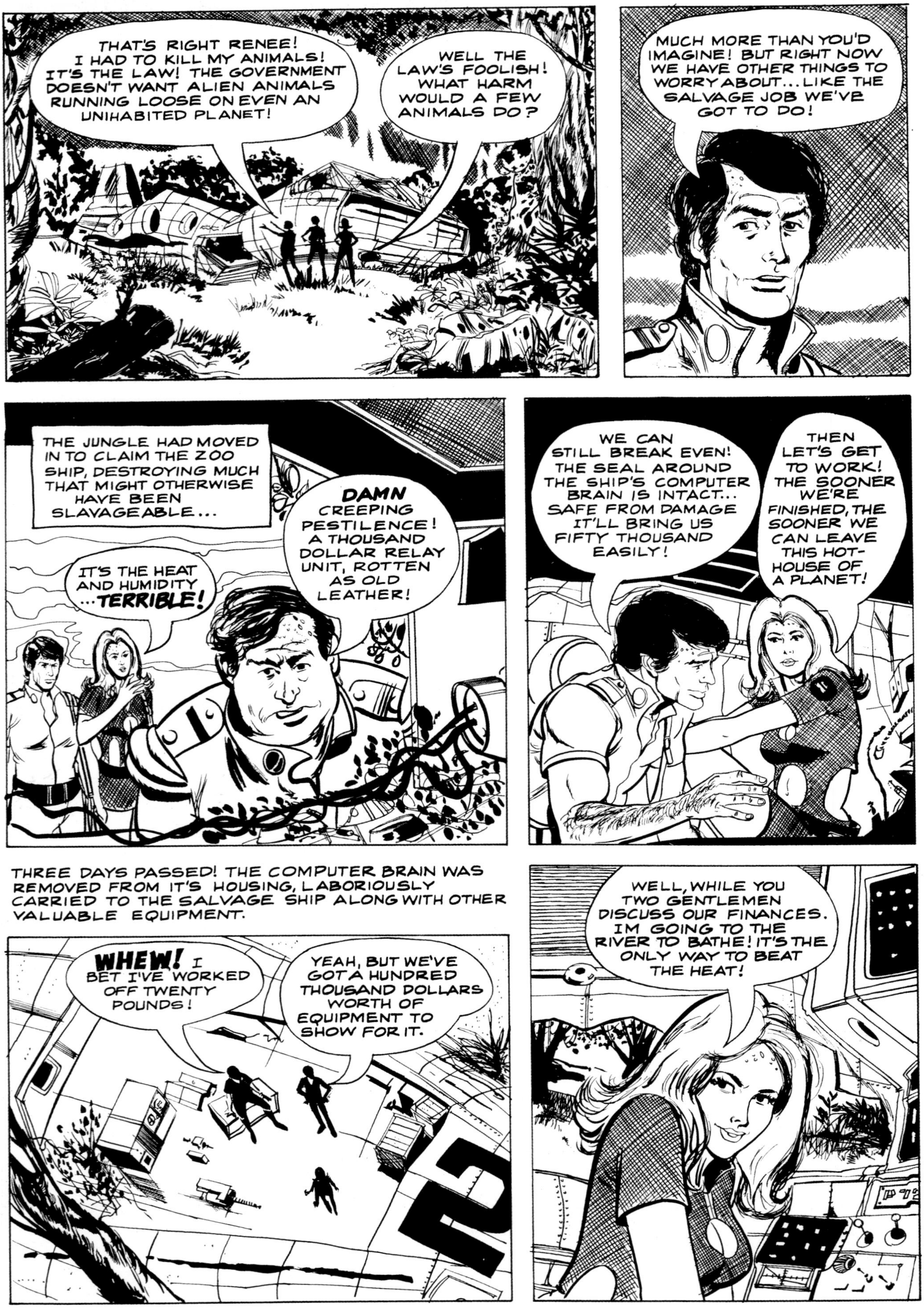
THAT'S RIGHT RENEE! I HAD TO KILL MY ANIMALS! IT'S THE LAW! THE GOVERNMENT DOESN'T WANT ALIEN ANIMALS RUNNING LOOSE ON EVEN AN UNIHABITED PLANET!
WELL THE LAW'S FOOLISH! WHAT HARM WOULD A FEW ANIMALS DO?
MUCH MORE THAN YOU'D IMAGINE! BUT RIGHT NOW WE HAVE OTHER THINGS TO WORRY ABOUT... LIKE THE SALVAGE JOB WE'VE GOT TO DO!
THE JUNGLE HAD MOVED IN TO CLAIM THE ZOO SHIP, DESTROYING MUCH THAT MIGHT OTHERWISE HAVE BEEN SLAVAGEABLE...
DAMN CREEPING PESTILENCE! A THOUSAND DOLLAR RELAY UNIT, ROTTEN AS OLD LEATHER!
IT'S THE HEAT AND HUMIDITY ...TERRIBLE!
WE CAN STILL BREAK EVEN! THE SEAL AROUND THE SHIP'S COMPUTER BRAIN IS INTACT... SAFE FROM DAMAGE IT'LL BRING US FIFTY THOUSAND EASILY!
THEN LET'S GET TO WORK! THE SOONER WE'RE FINISHED, THE SOONER WE CAN LEAVE THIS HOT-HOUSE OF A PLANET!
THREE DAYS PASSED! THE COMPUTER BRAIN WAS REMOVED FROM IT'S HOUSING, LABORIOUSLY CARRIED TO THE SALVAGE SHIP ALONG WITH OTHER VALUABLE EQUIPMENT.
WHEW! I BET I'VE WORKED OFF TWENTY POUNDS!
YEAH, BUT WE'VE GOT A HUNDRED THOUSAND DOLLARS WORTH OF EQUIPMENT TO SHOW FOR IT.
WELL, WHILE YOU TWO GENTLEMEN DISCUSS OUR FINANCES. IM GOING TO THE RIVER TO BATHE! IT'S THE ONLY WAY TO BEAT THE HEAT!

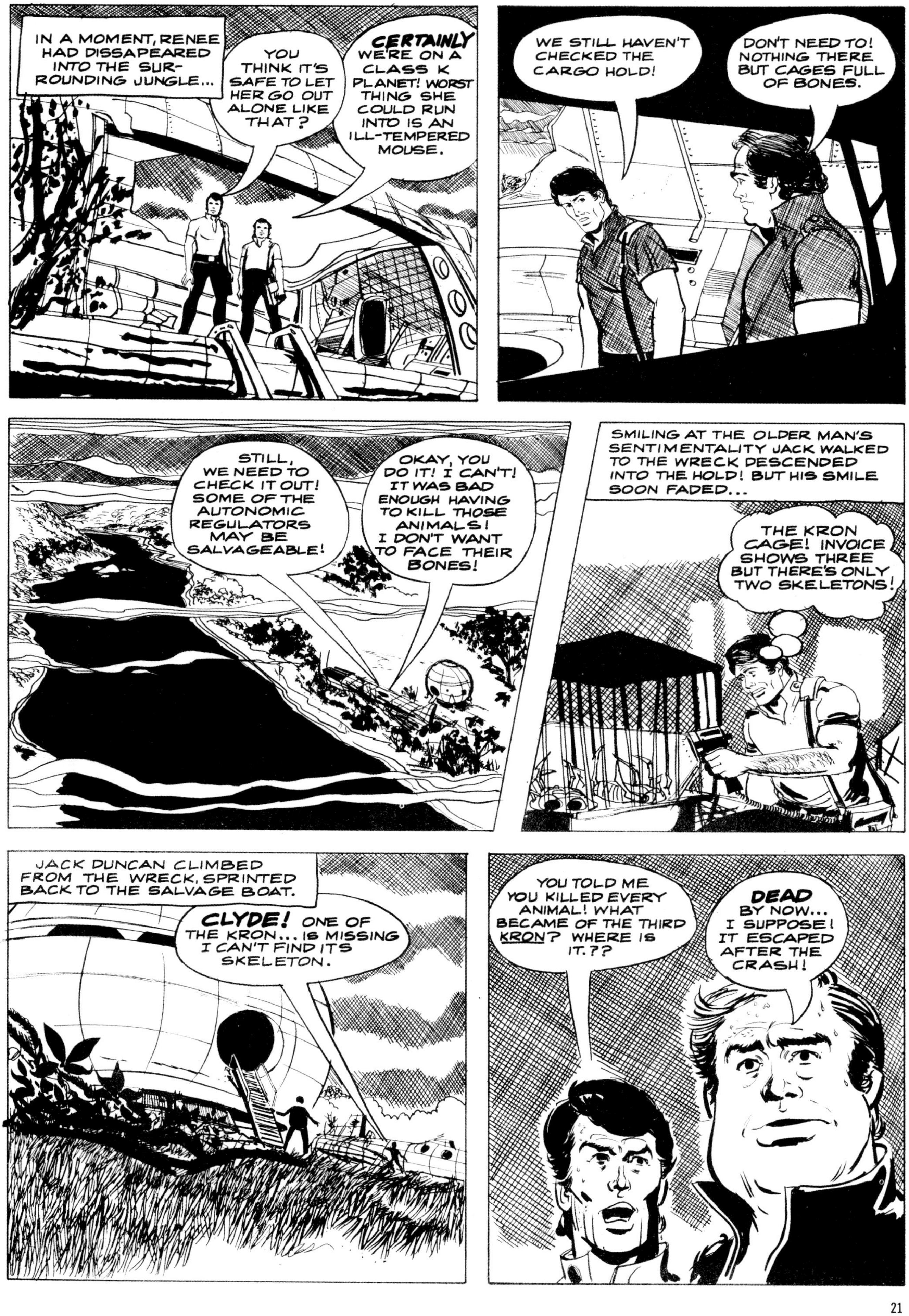
IN A MOMENT, RENEE HAD DISSAPEARED INTO THE SURROUNDING JUNGLE...
YOU THINK IT'S SAFE TO LET HER GO OUT ALONE LIKE THAT?
CERTAINLY WE'RE ON A CLASS K PLANET! WORST THING SHE COULD RUN INTO IS AN ILL-TEMPERED MOUSE.
WE STILL HAVEN'T CHECKED THE CARGO HOLD!
DON'T NEED TO! NOTHING THERE BUT CAGES FULL OF BONES.
STILL, WE NEED TO CHECK IT OUT! SOME OF THE AUTONOMIC REGULATORS MAY BE SALVAGEABLE!
OKAY, YOU DO IT! I CAN'T! IT WAS BAD ENOUGH HAVING TO KILL THOSE ANIMALS! I DON'T WANT TO FACE THEIR BONES!
SMILING AT THE OLDER MAN'S SENTIMENTALITY JACK WALKED TO THE WRECK DESCENDED INTO THE HOLD! BUT HIS SMILE SOON FADED...
THE KRON CAGE! INVOICE SHOWS THREE BUT THERE'S ONLY TWO SKELETONS!
JACK DUNCAN CLIMBED FROM THE WRECK, SPRINTED BACK TO THE SALVAGE BOAT.
CLYDE! ONE OF THE KRON... IS MISSING I CAN'T FIND ITS SKELETON.
YOU TOLD ME YOU KILLED EVERY ANIMAL! WHAT BECAME OF THE THIRD KRON? WHERE IS IT.??
DEAD BY NOW... I SUPPOSE! IT ESCAPED AFTER THE CRASH!

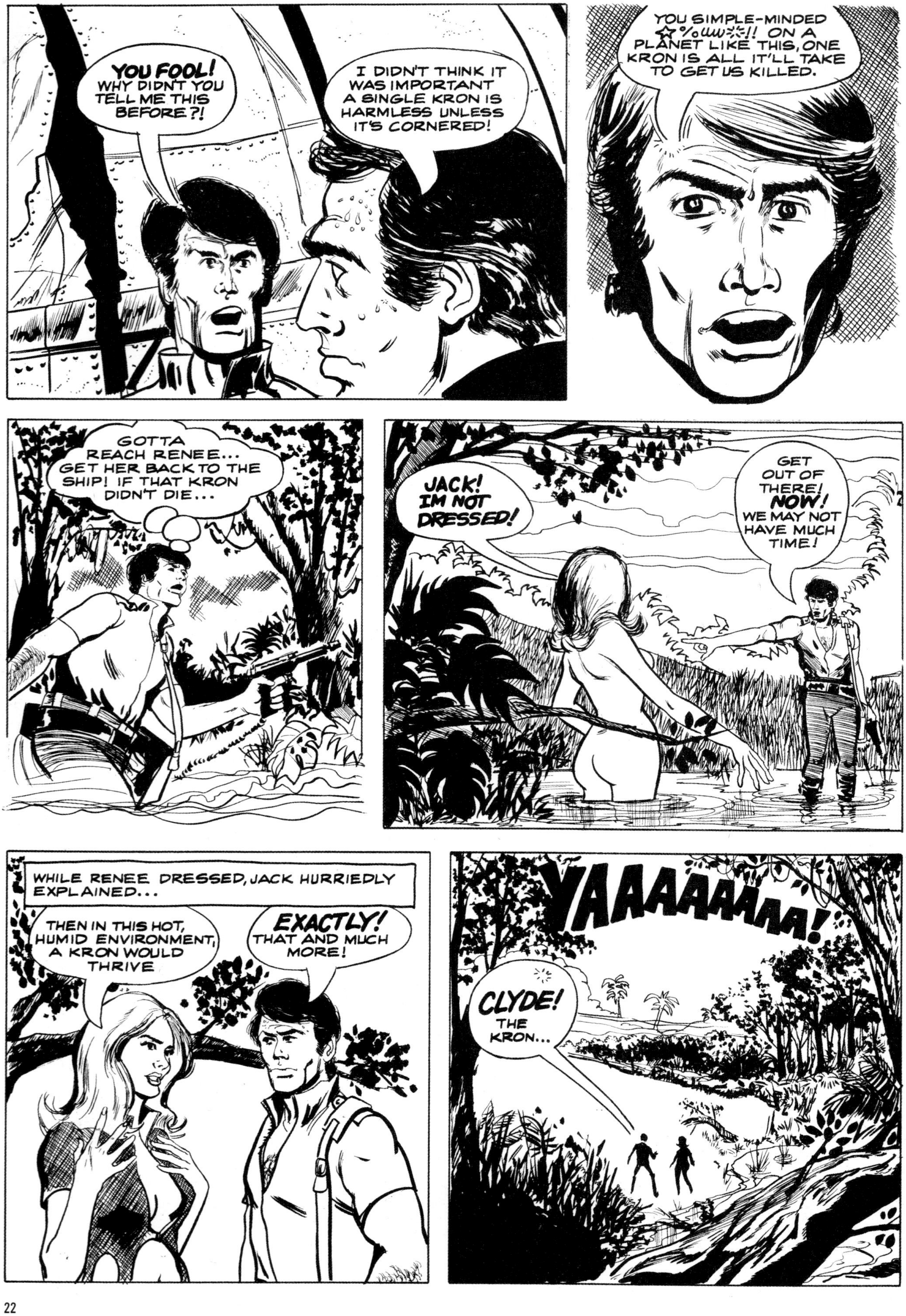
YOU FOOL! WHY DIDN'T YOU TELL ME THIS BEFORE?!
I DIDN'T THINK IT WAS IMPORTANT A SINGLE KRON IS HARMLESS UNLESS IT'S CORNERED!
YOU SIMPLE-MINDED ☆%ωω☆!! ON A PLANET LIKE THIS, ONE KRON IS ALL IT'LL TAKE TO GET US KILLED.
GOTTA REACH RENEE... GET HER BACK TO THE SHIP! IF THAT KRON DIDN'T DIE...
JACK! IM NOT DRESSED!
GET OUT OF THERE! NOW! WE MAY NOT HAVE MUCH TIME!
WHILE RENEE DRESSED, JACK HURRIEDLY EXPLAINED...
THEN IN THIS HOT, HUMID ENVIRONMENT, A KRON WOULD THRIVE
EXACTLY! THAT AND MUCH MORE!
YAAAAAAAA!
CLYDE! THE KRON...

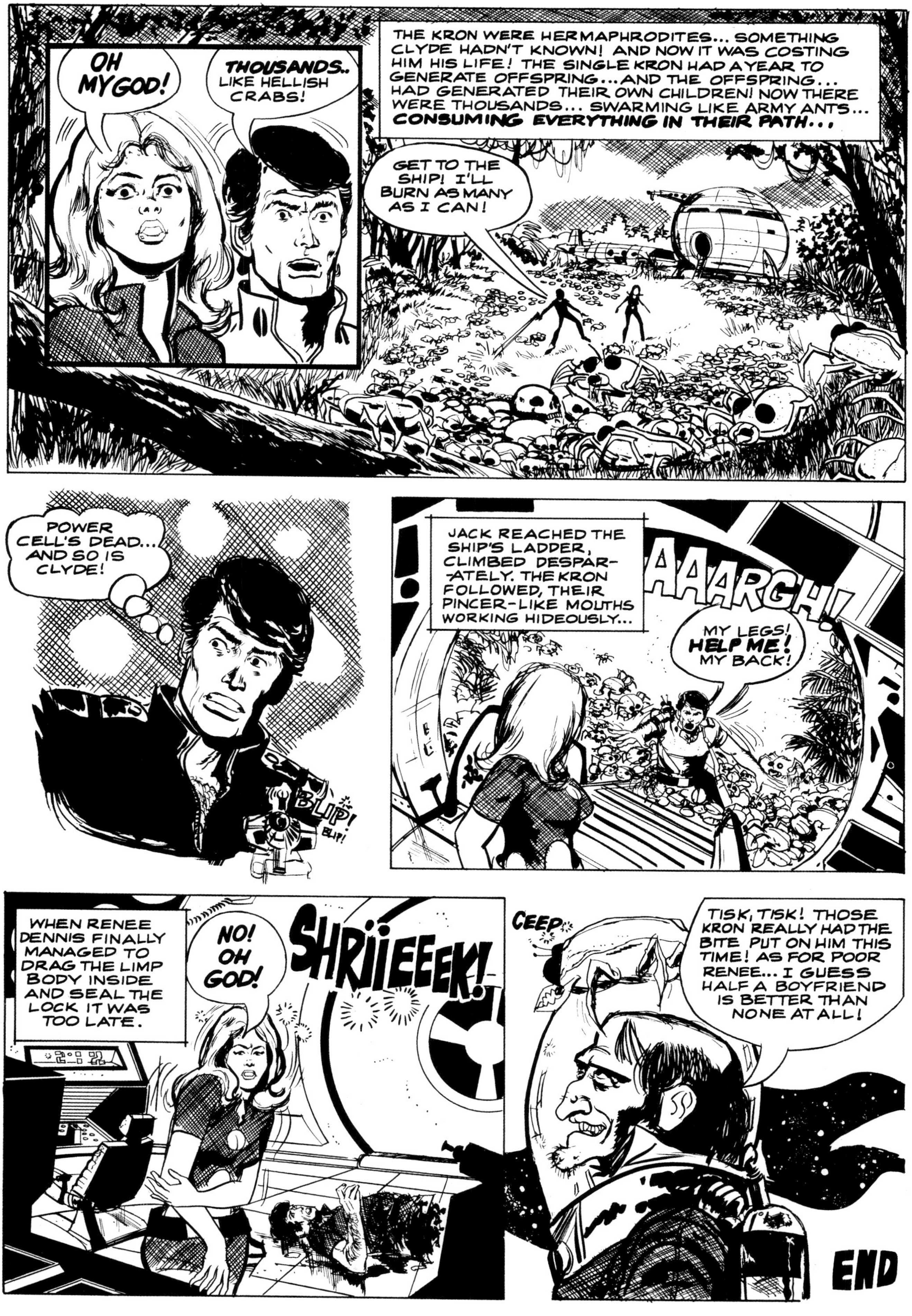

THE KRON WERE HERMAPHRODITES... SOMETHING CLYDE HADN'T KNOWN! AND NOW IT WAS COSTING HIM HIS LIFE! THE SINGLE KRON HAD A YEAR TO GENERATE OFFSPRING... AND THE OFFSPRING... HAD GENERATED THEIR OWN CHILDREN! NOW THERE WERE THOUSANDS... SWARMING LIKE ARMY ANTS... CONSUMING EVERYTHING IN THEIR PATH...
OH MY GOD!
THOUSANDS.. LIKE HELLISH CRABS!
GET TO THE SHIP! I'LL BURN AS MANY AS I CAN!
POWER CELL'S DEAD... AND SO IS CLYDE!
BLIP! BLIP!
JACK REACHED THE SHIP'S LADDER, CLIMBED DESPAR-ATELY. THE KRON FOLLOWED, THEIR PINCER-LIKE MOUTHS WORKING HIDEOUSLY...
AAARGH!
MY LEGS! HELP ME! MY BACK!
WHEN RENEE DENNIS FINALLY MANAGED TO DRAG THE LIMP BODY INSIDE AND SEAL THE LOCK IT WAS TOO LATE.
NO! OH GOD!
SHRIIEEEK!
CEEP
TISK, TISK! THOSE KRON REALLY HAD THE BITE PUT ON HIM THIS TIME! AS FOR POOR RENEE... I GUESS HALF A BOYFRIEND IS BETTER THAN NONE AT ALL!
END

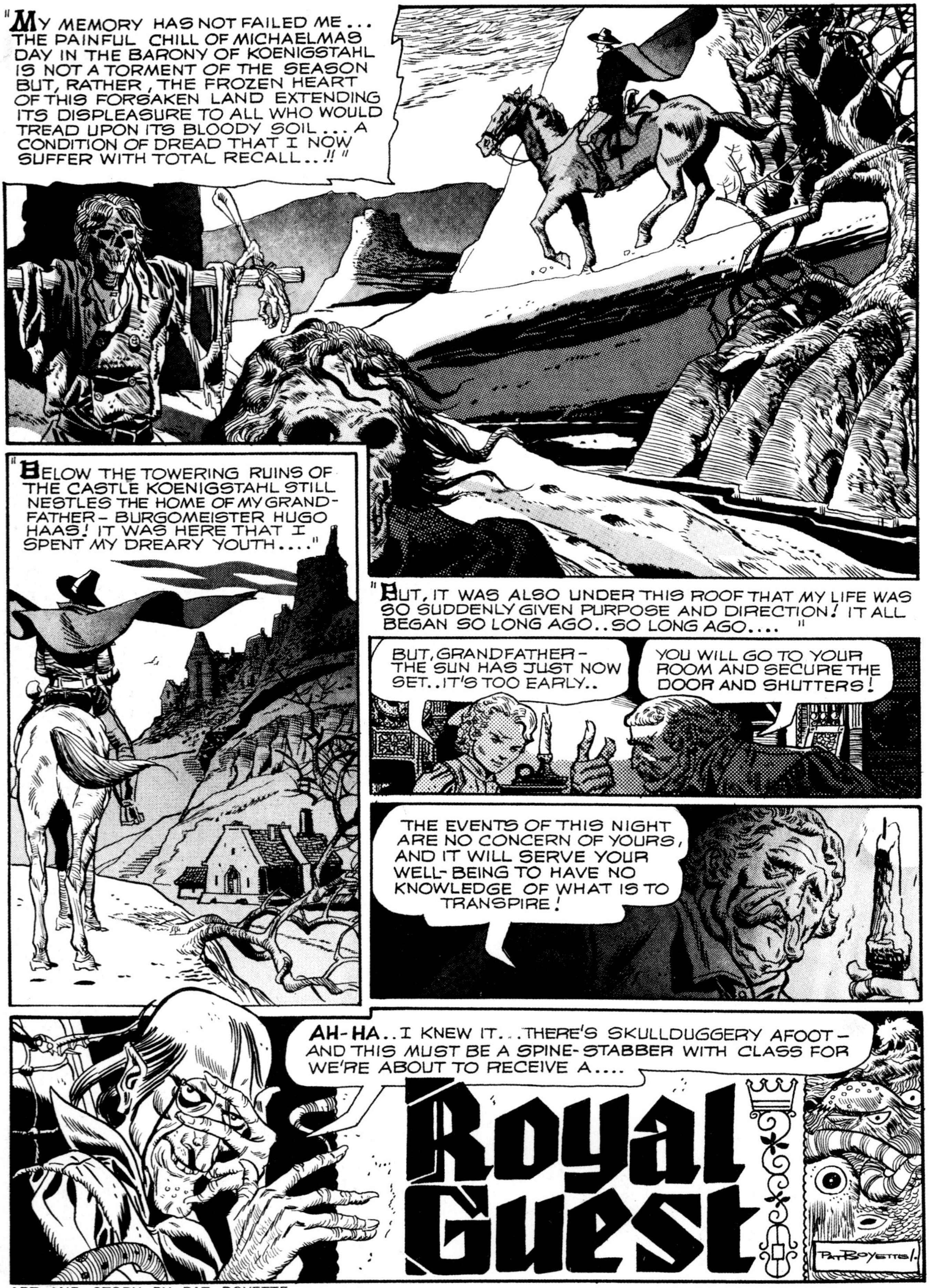
"MY MEMORY HAS NOT FAILED ME... THE PAINFUL CHILL OF MICHAELMAS DAY IN THE BARONY OF KOENIGSTAHL IS NOT A TORMENT OF THE SEASON BUT, RATHER, THE FROZEN HEART OF THIS FORSAKEN LAND EXTENDING ITS DISPLEASURE TO ALL WHO WOULD TREAD UPON ITS BLOODY SOIL... A CONDITION OF DREAD THAT I NOW SUFFER WITH TOTAL RECALL..!!"
"BELOW THE TOWERING RUINS OF THE CASTLE KOENIGSTAHL STILL NESTLES THE HOME OF MY GRAND-FATHER - BURGOMEISTER HUGO HAAS! IT WAS HERE THAT I SPENT MY DREARY YOUTH...."
"BUT, IT WAS ALSO UNDER THIS ROOF THAT MY LIFE WAS SO SUDDENLY GIVEN PURPOSE AND DIRECTION! IT ALL BEGAN SO LONG AGO..SO LONG AGO.... "
BUT, GRANDFATHER - THE SUN HAS JUST NOW SET..IT'S TOO EARLY..
YOU WILL GO TO YOUR ROOM AND SECURE THE DOOR AND SHUTTERS!
THE EVENTS OF THIS NIGHT ARE NO CONCERN OF YOURS, AND IT WILL SERVE YOUR WELL-BEING TO HAVE NO KNOWLEDGE OF WHAT IS TO TRANSPIRE!
AH-HA..I KNEW IT...THERE'S SKULLDUGGERY AFOOT - AND THIS MUST BE A SPINE-STABBER WITH CLASS FOR WE'RE ABOUT TO RECEIVE A....
Royal Guest

ART AND STORY BY PAT BOYETTE

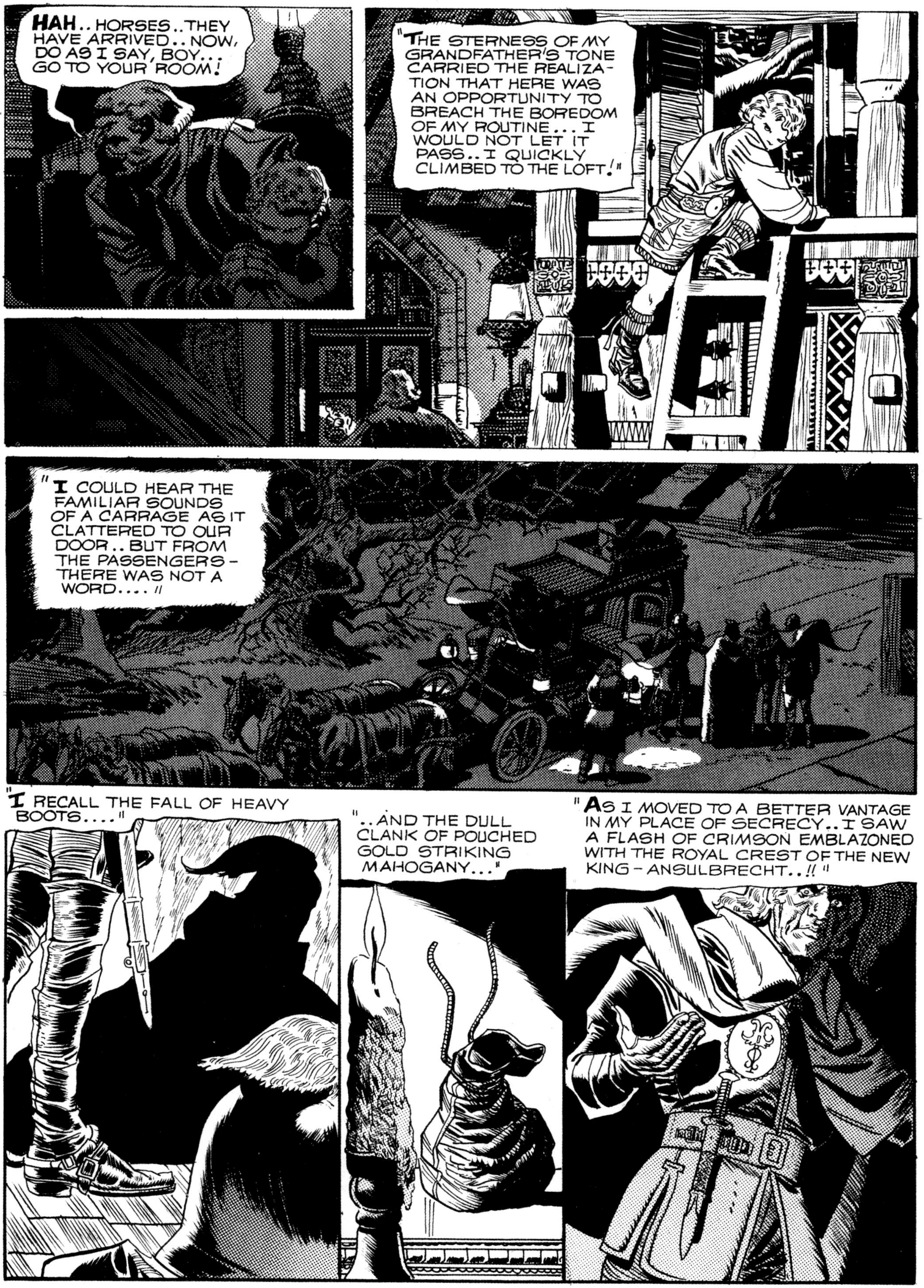
HAH.. HORSES.. THEY HAVE ARRIVED.. NOW, DO AS I SAY, BOY... GO TO YOUR ROOM!
"THE STERNESS OF MY GRANDFATHER'S TONE CARRIED THE REALIZATION THAT HERE WAS AN OPPORTUNITY TO BREACH THE BOREDOM OF MY ROUTINE... I WOULD NOT LET IT PASS.. I QUICKLY CLIMBED TO THE LOFT!"
"I COULD HEAR THE FAMILIAR SOUNDS OF A CARRAGE AS IT CLATTERED TO OUR DOOR.. BUT FROM THE PASSENGERS - THERE WAS NOT A WORD.... "
"I RECALL THE FALL OF HEAVY BOOTS...."
"..AND THE DULL CLANK OF POUCHED GOLD STRIKING MAHOGANY..."
"AS I MOVED TO A BETTER VANTAGE IN MY PLACE OF SECRECY.. I SAW A FLASH OF CRIMSON EMBLAZONED WITH THE ROYAL CREST OF THE NEW KING - ANSULBRECHT..!!"

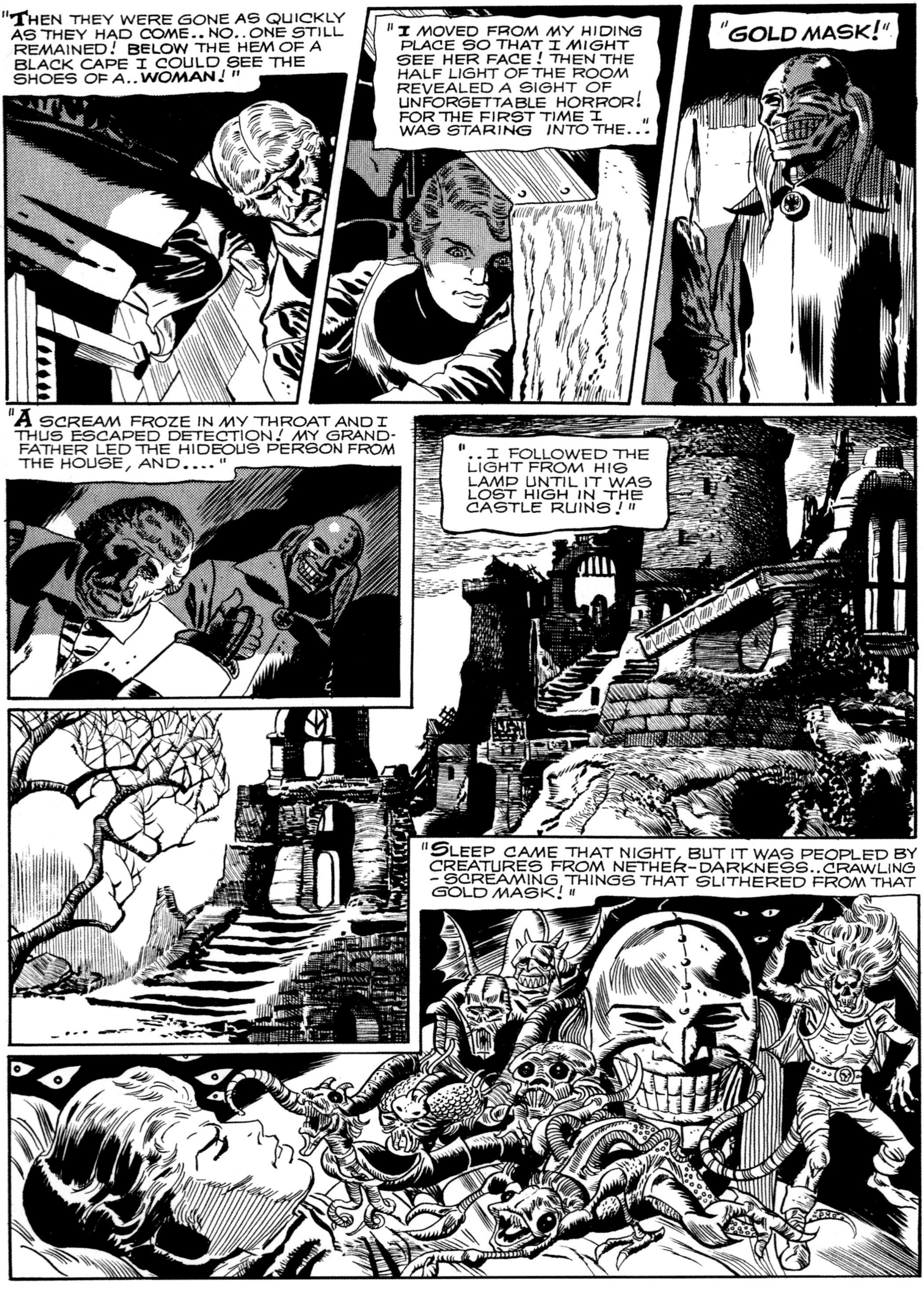
"THEN THEY WERE GONE AS QUICKLY AS THEY HAD COME.. NO.. ONE STILL REMAINED! BELOW THE HEM OF A BLACK CAPE I COULD SEE THE SHOES OF A.. WOMAN!"
"I MOVED FROM MY HIDING PLACE SO THAT I MIGHT SEE HER FACE! THEN THE HALF LIGHT OF THE ROOM REVEALED A SIGHT OF UNFORGETTABLE HORROR! FOR THE FIRST TIME I WAS STARING INTO THE..."
"GOLD MASK!"
"A SCREAM FROZE IN MY THROAT AND I THUS ESCAPED DETECTION! MY GRAND-FATHER LED THE HIDEOUS PERSON FROM THE HOUSE, AND...."
"..I FOLLOWED THE LIGHT FROM HIS LAMP UNTIL IT WAS LOST HIGH IN THE CASTLE RUINS!"
"SLEEP CAME THAT NIGHT, BUT IT WAS PEOPLED BY CREATURES FROM NETHER-DARKNESS..CRAWLING -SCREAMING THINGS THAT SLITHERED FROM THAT GOLD MASK!"

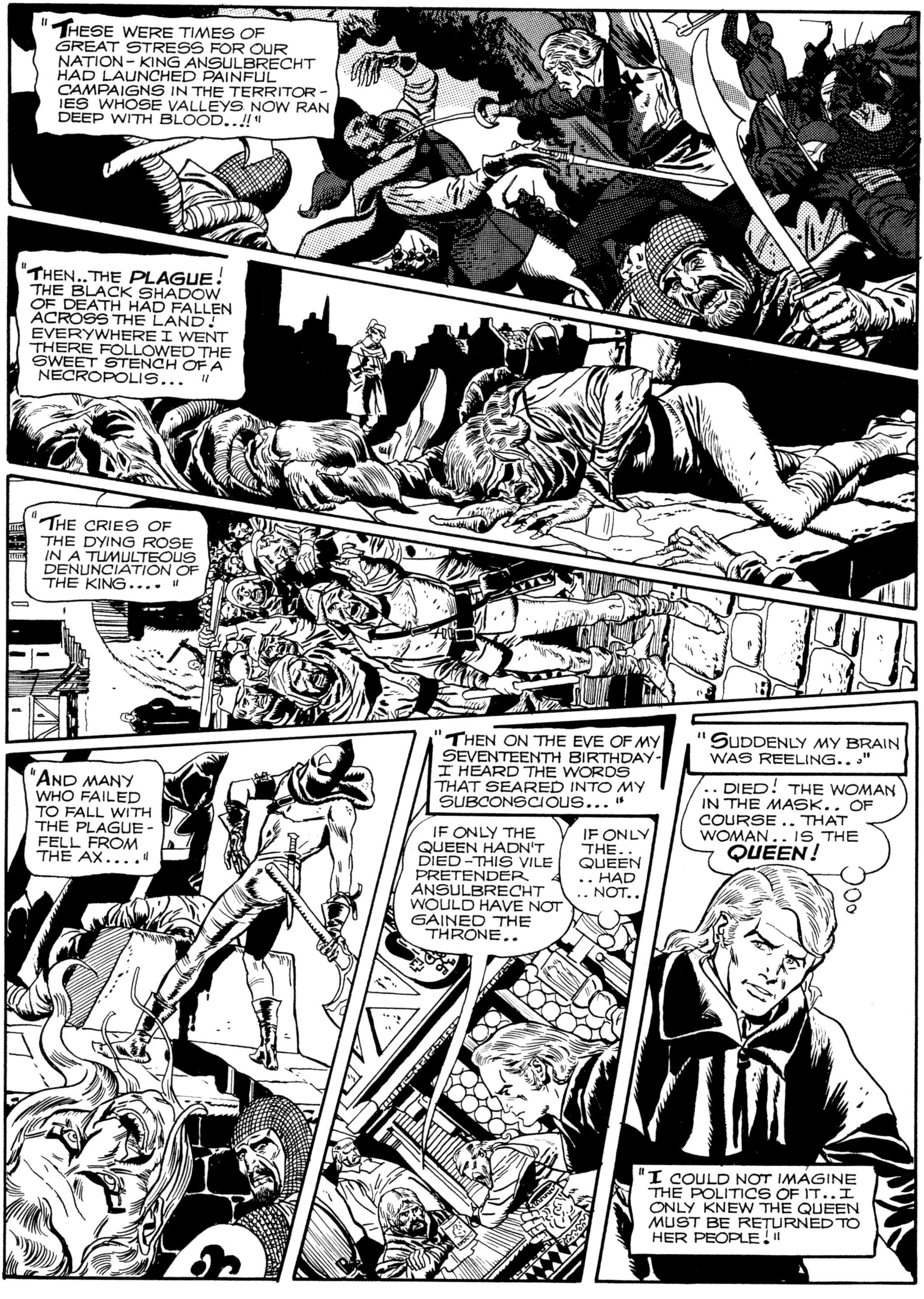
"THESE WERE TIMES OF GREAT STRESS FOR OUR NATION - KING ANSULBRECHT HAD LAUNCHED PAINFUL CAMPAIGNS IN THE TERRITORIES WHOSE VALLEYS NOW RAN DEEP WITH BLOOD..!!"
"THEN..THE PLAGUE! THE BLACK SHADOW OF DEATH HAD FALLEN ACROSS THE LAND! EVERYWHERE I WENT THERE FOLLOWED THE SWEET STENCH OF A NECROPOLIS..."
"THE CRIES OF THE DYING ROSE IN A TUMULTEOUS DENUNCIATION OF THE KING...."
"AND MANY WHO FAILED TO FALL WITH THE PLAGUE - FELL FROM THE AX...."
"THEN ON THE EVE OF MY SEVENTEENTH BIRTHDAY - I HEARD THE WORDS THAT SEARED INTO MY SUBCONSCIOUS..."
IF ONLY THE QUEEN HADN'T DIED - THIS VILE PRETENDER ANSULBRECHT WOULD HAVE NOT GAINED THE THRONE..
IF ONLY THE.. QUEEN .. HAD .. NOT..
"SUDDENLY MY BRAIN WAS REELING..."
.. DIED! THE WOMAN IN THE MASK.. OF COURSE.. THAT WOMAN.. IS THE QUEEN!
"I COULD NOT IMAGINE THE POLITICS OF IT.. I ONLY KNEW THE QUEEN MUST BE RETURNED TO HER PEOPLE!"

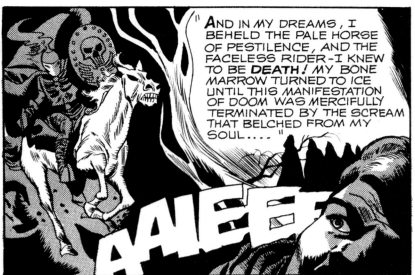

"AND IN MY DREAMS, I BEHELD THE PALE HORSE OF PESTILENCE, AND THE FACELESS RIDER–I KNEW TO BE *DEATH!* MY BONE MARROW TURNED TO ICE UNTIL THIS MANIFESTATION OF DOOM WAS MERCIFULLY TERMINATED BY THE SCREAM THAT BELCHED FROM MY SOUL.... "

AAIEE!

"As FOR OUR GUEST–SHE WENT UNMENTIONED UNTIL THE NIGHT, SOME WEEKS LATER, WHEN MY GRANDFATHER FELL DESPERATELY ILL!"

HE'S TOO WEAK ..I'LL TAKE HER FOOD!

"I CLIMBED THE RUINS, AND AFTER SOME DIFFI-CULTY–FOUND HER PLACE OF CONCEALMENT..."

"I THOUGHT I WAS PREPARED FOR THE ORDEAL.. BUT MY LEGS TURNED TO JELLY, I DROPPED THE BOWL AND RE-TREATED IN TERROR!"

"My GRANDFATHER WAS ANGERED TO EXHAUSTION, AND ONLY HIS GROWING WEAKNESS SAVED ME FROM A SE-VERE THRASHING! BY MORNING, MY GRANDFATHER WAS DEAD!"

GRANDFATHER ..PLEASE.. DON'T DIE..... GRANDFATHER!

WITH TYPICAL TEUTONIC THOROUGHNESS, HE HAD LEFT COMPLETE ARRANGE-MENTS! HULKING, DULL, LOTHAR HABEN WOULD SEE TO INTERRMENT, AND REMAIN TO SERVICE OUR GUEST! I WOULD GO TO INSDORFF FOR SCHOOL-ING! IT WAS GRAND-FATHER'S DESIRE THAT I BECOME A SOLICITOR!

HURRY, BOY- OR THE ROAD WILL BE CLOSED

JA!

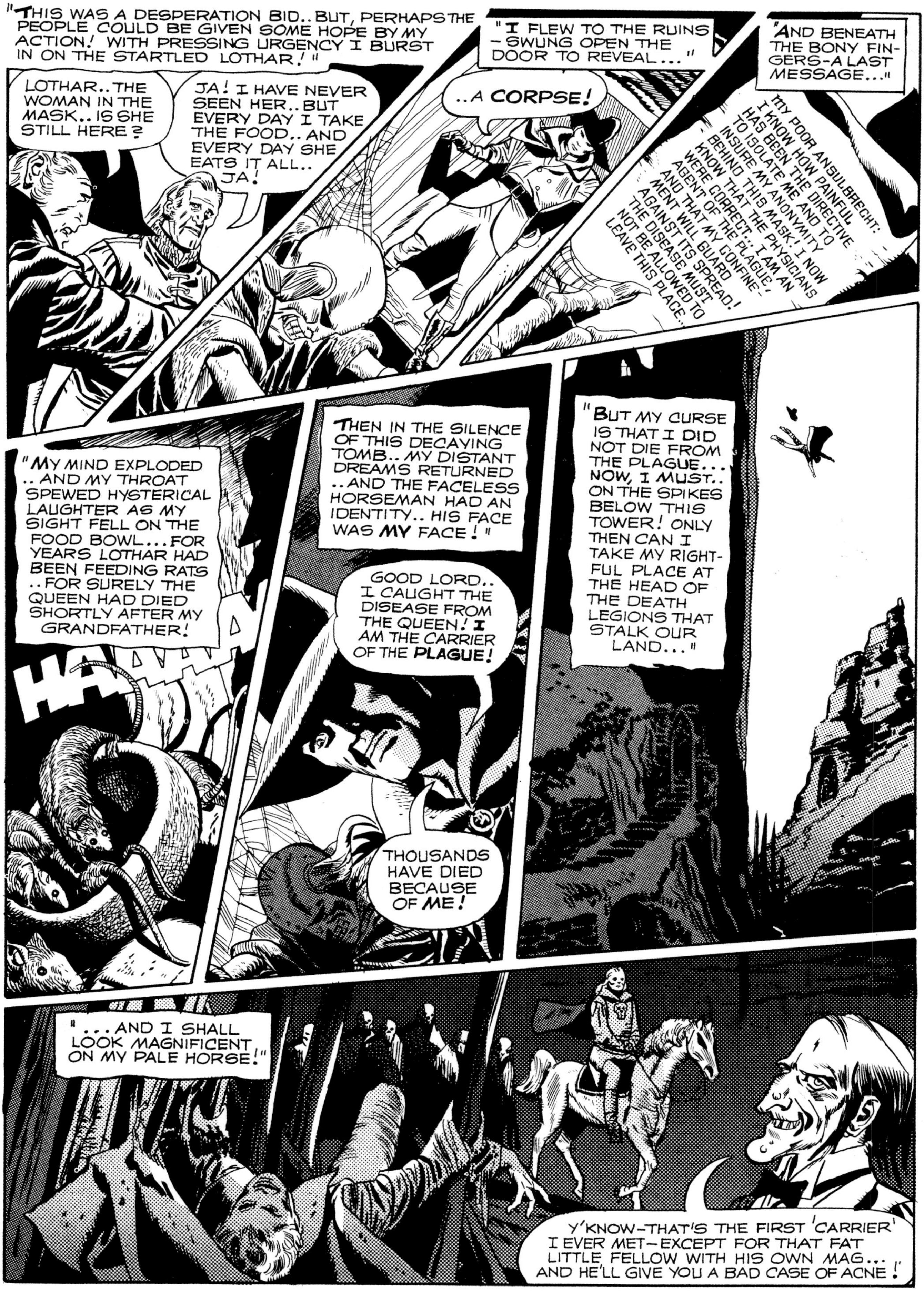
"THIS WAS A DESPERATION BID.. BUT, PERHAPS THE PEOPLE COULD BE GIVEN SOME HOPE BY MY ACTION! WITH PRESSING URGENCY I BURST IN ON THE STARTLED LOTHAR!"
LOTHAR.. THE WOMAN IN THE MASK.. IS SHE STILL HERE?
JA! I HAVE NEVER SEEN HER.. BUT EVERY DAY I TAKE THE FOOD.. AND EVERY DAY SHE EATS IT ALL.. JA!
"I FLEW TO THE RUINS - SWUNG OPEN THE DOOR TO REVEAL..."
..A CORPSE!
"AND BENEATH THE BONY FINGERS-A LAST MESSAGE..."
MY POOR ANSULBRECHT: I KNOW HOW PAINFUL HAS BEEN THE DIRECTIVE TO ISOLATE ME AND TO INSURE MY ANONYMITY BEHIND THIS MASK! I NOW KNOW THAT THE PHYSICIANS WERE CORRECT.. I AM AN AGENT OF THE PLAGUE, AND THAT MY CONFINEMENT WILL GUARD AGAINST ITS SPREAD! THE DISEASE MUST NOT BE ALLOWED TO LEAVE THIS PLACE...
"MY MIND EXPLODED.. AND MY THROAT SPEWED HYSTERICAL LAUGHTER AS MY SIGHT FELL ON THE FOOD BOWL... FOR YEARS LOTHAR HAD BEEN FEEDING RATS.. FOR SURELY THE QUEEN HAD DIED SHORTLY AFTER MY GRANDFATHER!
HA
THEN IN THE SILENCE OF THIS DECAYING TOMB.. MY DISTANT DREAMS RETURNED.. AND THE FACELESS HORSEMAN HAD AN IDENTITY.. HIS FACE WAS MY FACE!"
GOOD LORD.. I CAUGHT THE DISEASE FROM THE QUEEN! I AM THE CARRIER OF THE PLAGUE!
THOUSANDS HAVE DIED BECAUSE OF ME!
"BUT MY CURSE IS THAT I DID NOT DIE FROM THE PLAGUE... NOW, I MUST.. ON THE SPIKES BELOW THIS TOWER! ONLY THEN CAN I TAKE MY RIGHTFUL PLACE AT THE HEAD OF THE DEATH LEGIONS THAT STALK OUR LAND..."
"...AND I SHALL LOOK MAGNIFICENT ON MY PALE HORSE!"
Y'KNOW-THAT'S THE FIRST 'CARRIER' I EVER MET-EXCEPT FOR THAT FAT LITTLE FELLOW WITH HIS OWN MAG... AND HE'LL GIVE YOU A BAD CASE OF ACNE!

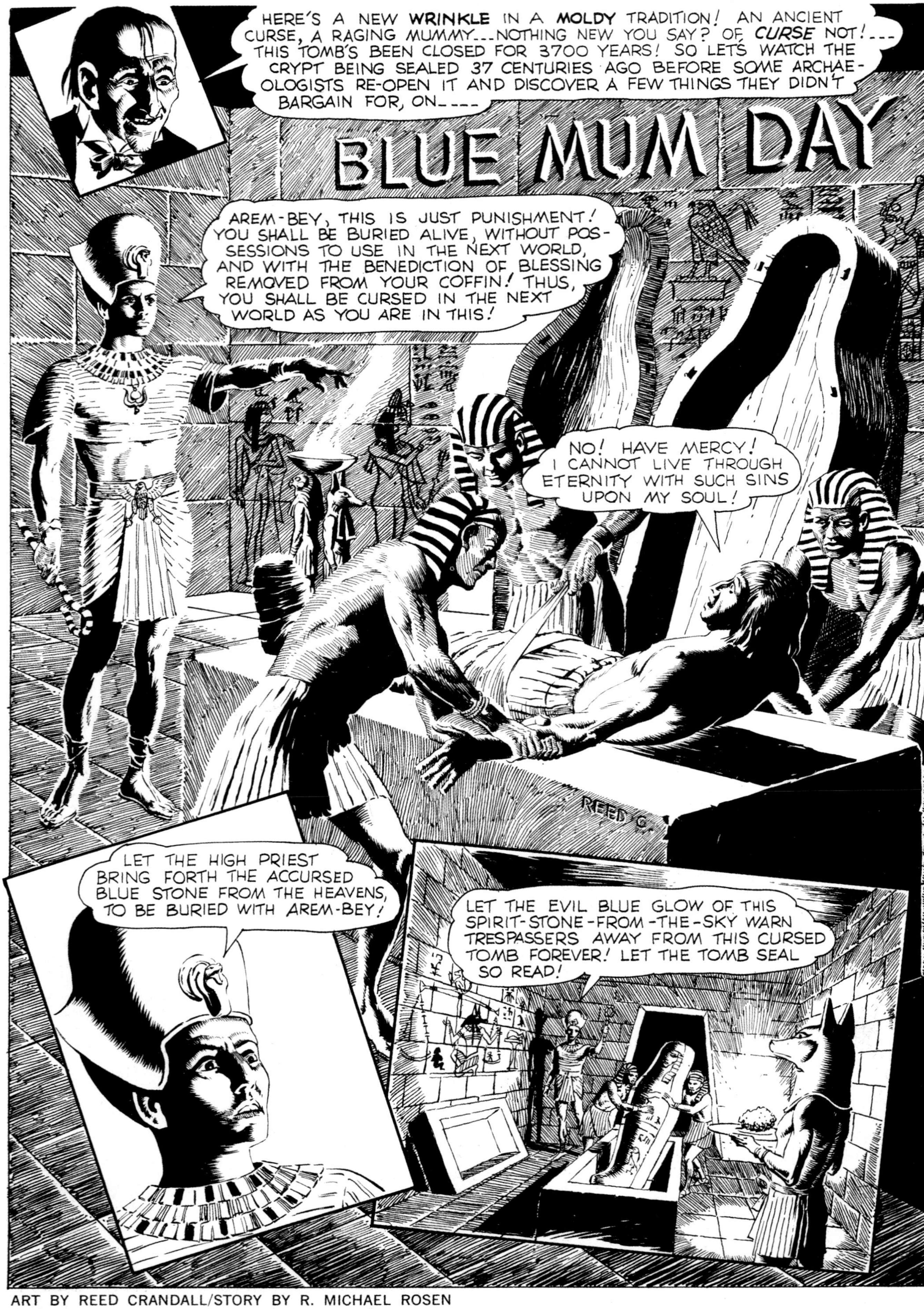
HERE'S A NEW WRINKLE IN A MOLDY TRADITION! AN ANCIENT CURSE, A RAGING MUMMY---NOTHING NEW YOU SAY? OF CURSE NOT!--- THIS TOMB'S BEEN CLOSED FOR 3700 YEARS! SO LETS WATCH THE CRYPT BEING SEALED 37 CENTURIES AGO BEFORE SOME ARCHAEOLOGISTS RE-OPEN IT AND DISCOVER A FEW THINGS THEY DIDN'T BARGAIN FOR, ON----
BLUE MUM DAY
AREM-BEY, THIS IS JUST PUNISHMENT! YOU SHALL BE BURIED ALIVE, WITHOUT POSSESSIONS TO USE IN THE NEXT WORLD, AND WITH THE BENEDICTION OF BLESSING REMOVED FROM YOUR COFFIN! THUS, YOU SHALL BE CURSED IN THE NEXT WORLD AS YOU ARE IN THIS!
NO! HAVE MERCY! I CANNOT LIVE THROUGH ETERNITY WITH SUCH SINS UPON MY SOUL!
REED C.
LET THE HIGH PRIEST BRING FORTH THE ACCURSED BLUE STONE FROM THE HEAVENS, TO BE BURIED WITH AREM-BEY!
LET THE EVIL BLUE GLOW OF THIS SPIRIT-STONE-FROM-THE-SKY WARN TRESPASSERS AWAY FROM THIS CURSED TOMB FOREVER! LET THE TOMB SEAL SO READ!

ART BY REED CRANDALL/STORY BY R. MICHAEL ROSEN

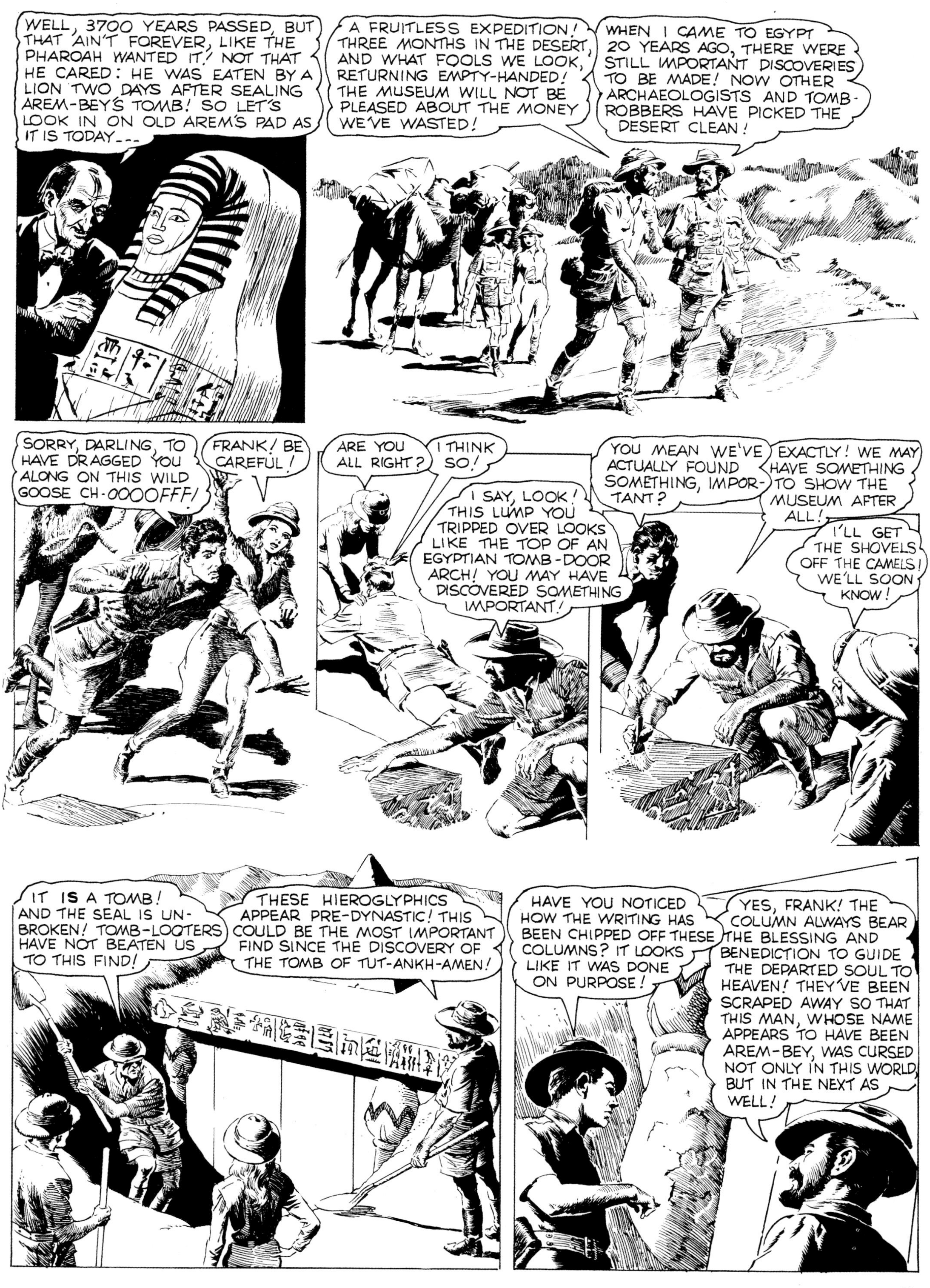

WELL, 3700 YEARS PASSED, BUT THAT AIN'T FOREVER, LIKE THE PHAROAH WANTED IT! NOT THAT HE CARED: HE WAS EATEN BY A LION TWO DAYS AFTER SEALING AREM-BEY'S TOMB! SO LET'S LOOK IN ON OLD AREM'S PAD AS IT IS TODAY---
A FRUITLESS EXPEDITION! THREE MONTHS IN THE DESERT, AND WHAT FOOLS WE LOOK, RETURNING EMPTY-HANDED! THE MUSEUM WILL NOT BE PLEASED ABOUT THE MONEY WE'VE WASTED!
WHEN I CAME TO EGYPT 20 YEARS AGO, THERE WERE STILL IMPORTANT DISCOVERIES TO BE MADE! NOW OTHER ARCHAEOLOGISTS AND TOMB-ROBBERS HAVE PICKED THE DESERT CLEAN!
SORRY, DARLING, TO HAVE DRAGGED YOU ALONG ON THIS WILD GOOSE CH-OOOOFFF!
FRANK! BE CAREFUL!
ARE YOU ALL RIGHT?
I THINK SO!
I SAY, LOOK! THIS LUMP YOU TRIPPED OVER LOOKS LIKE THE TOP OF AN EGYPTIAN TOMB-DOOR ARCH! YOU MAY HAVE DISCOVERED SOMETHING IMPORTANT!
YOU MEAN WE'VE ACTUALLY FOUND SOMETHING, IMPOR-TANT?
EXACTLY! WE MAY HAVE SOMETHING TO SHOW THE MUSEUM AFTER ALL!
I'LL GET THE SHOVELS OFF THE CAMELS! WE'LL SOON KNOW!
IT IS A TOMB! AND THE SEAL IS UN-BROKEN! TOMB-LOOTERS HAVE NOT BEATEN US TO THIS FIND!
THESE HIEROGLYPHICS APPEAR PRE-DYNASTIC! THIS COULD BE THE MOST IMPORTANT FIND SINCE THE DISCOVERY OF THE TOMB OF TUT-ANKH-AMEN!
HAVE YOU NOTICED HOW THE WRITING HAS BEEN CHIPPED OFF THESE COLUMNS? IT LOOKS LIKE IT WAS DONE ON PURPOSE!
YES, FRANK! THE COLUMN ALWAYS BEAR THE BLESSING AND BENEDICTION TO GUIDE THE DEPARTED SOUL TO HEAVEN! THEY'VE BEEN SCRAPED AWAY SO THAT THIS MAN, WHOSE NAME APPEARS TO HAVE BEEN AREM-BEY, WAS CURSED NOT ONLY IN THIS WORLD BUT IN THE NEXT AS WELL!

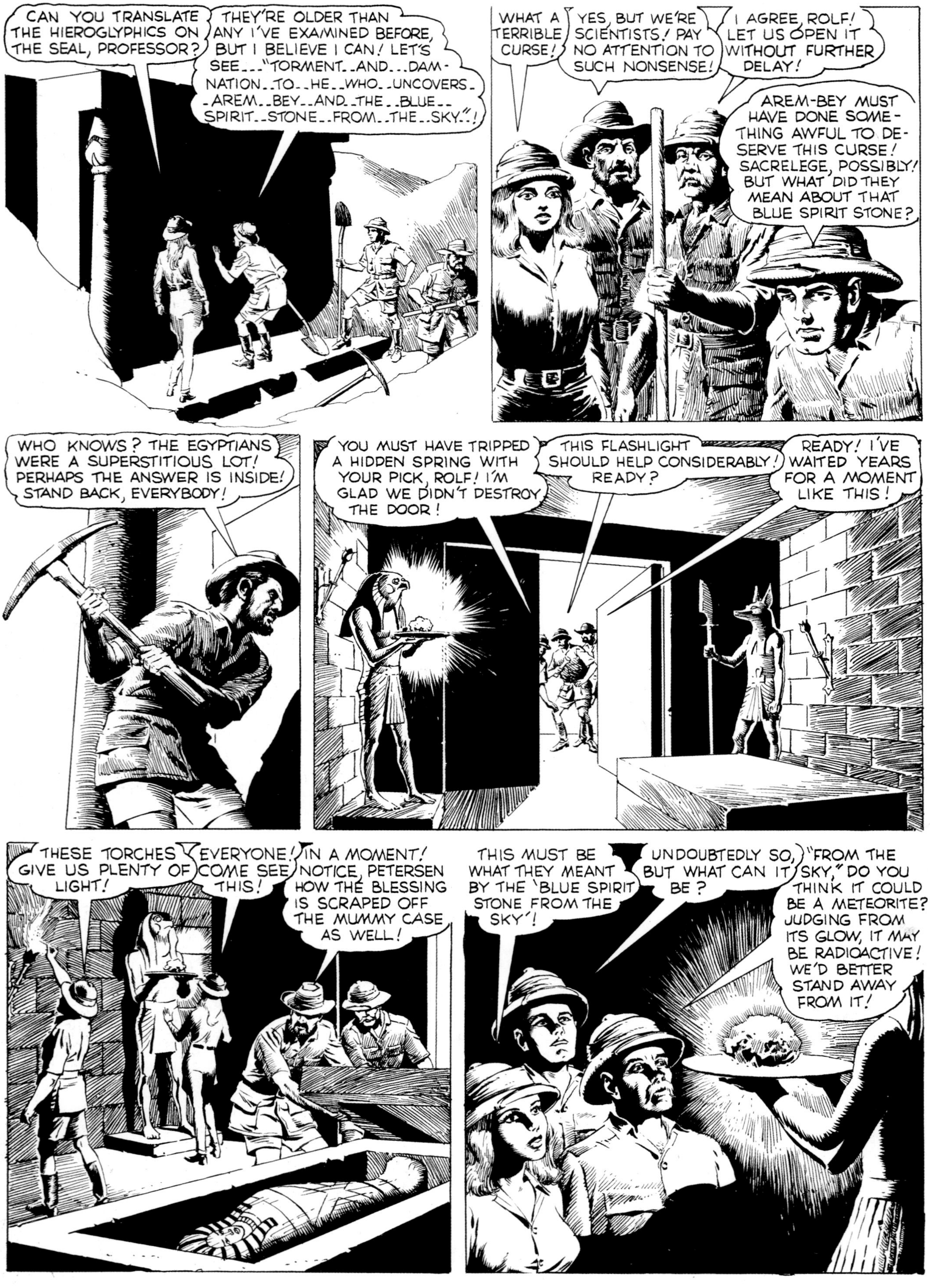
CAN YOU TRANSLATE THE HIEROGLYPHICS ON THE SEAL, PROFESSOR?
THEY'RE OLDER THAN ANY I'VE EXAMINED BEFORE, BUT I BELIEVE I CAN! LET'S SEE..."TORMENT..AND...DAMNATION..TO..HE..WHO..UNCOVERS..AREM..BEY..AND..THE..BLUE..SPIRIT..STONE..FROM..THE..SKY."!
WHAT A TERRIBLE CURSE!
YES, BUT WE'RE SCIENTISTS! PAY NO ATTENTION TO SUCH NONSENSE!
I AGREE, ROLF! LET US OPEN IT WITHOUT FURTHER DELAY!
AREM-BEY MUST HAVE DONE SOMETHING AWFUL TO DESERVE THIS CURSE! SACRELEGE, POSSIBLY! BUT WHAT DID THEY MEAN ABOUT THAT BLUE SPIRIT STONE?
WHO KNOWS? THE EGYPTIANS WERE A SUPERSTITIOUS LOT! PERHAPS THE ANSWER IS INSIDE! STAND BACK, EVERYBODY!
YOU MUST HAVE TRIPPED A HIDDEN SPRING WITH YOUR PICK, ROLF! I'M GLAD WE DIDN'T DESTROY THE DOOR!
THIS FLASHLIGHT SHOULD HELP CONSIDERABLY! READY?
READY! I'VE WAITED YEARS FOR A MOMENT LIKE THIS!
THESE TORCHES GIVE US PLENTY OF LIGHT!
EVERYONE! COME SEE THIS!
IN A MOMENT! NOTICE, PETERSEN HOW THE BLESSING IS SCRAPED OFF THE MUMMY CASE AS WELL!
THIS MUST BE WHAT THEY MEANT BY THE 'BLUE SPIRIT STONE FROM THE SKY'!
UNDOUBTEDLY SO, BUT WHAT CAN IT BE?
"FROM THE SKY," DO YOU THINK IT COULD BE A METEORITE? JUDGING FROM ITS GLOW, IT MAY BE RADIOACTIVE! WE'D BETTER STAND AWAY FROM IT!

ODD---THE CASE WASN'T EVEN SEALED! NEVER SAW A MUMMY LIKE THAT BEFORE! ALMOST NO BONE STRUCTURE! AS IF IT WAS A WAX FIGURE!

NOTICE THE MOLD? IT'S BLUE...THE SAME BLUE AS THE GLOWING STONE! ALL OVER IT! EVEN ON THE BANDAGES!

IT'S GHASTLY!

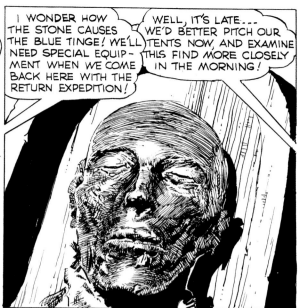

I WONDER HOW THE STONE CAUSES THE BLUE TINGE! WE'LL NEED SPECIAL EQUIPMENT WHEN WE COME BACK HERE WITH THE RETURN EXPEDITION!

WELL, IT'S LATE... WE'D BETTER PITCH OUR TENTS NOW, AND EXAMINE THIS FIND MORE CLOSELY IN THE MORNING!

I CAN'T SLEEP... I'M TOO EXCITED! WE'LL BE FAMOUS FOR THIS DISCOVERY.

I CAN'T GET THAT MUMMY OUT OF MY MIND! THAT BLUE....

EEEEEAAAAAHHHH!

THAT SOUNDED LIKE PETERSEN!

FRANK, BE CAREFUL!

WHAT'S GOING ON!

IT'S PETERSEN... I THINK HE'S DEAD!

HE IS DEAD! APPEARS TO BE STRANGULATION! AND LOOK...THAT SAME BLUISH MOLD ON HIS THROAT! IT GIVES OFF A GLOW, TOO! I WONDER HOW---

THE MUMMY! IT'S ALIVE! IT MUST BE! HOW ELSE----

NONSENSE! I REFUSE TO BELIEVE IN FOOLISHNESS LIKE A LIVING MUMMY! THE HEART AND LUNGS WOULD DISINTEGRATE IN 3700 YEARS.

WE'D BE WISE TO POST A SENTRY---

WELL, I THINK IT'S FOOLISH TO LOSE SLEEP GUARDING AN ANCIENT MUMMY! BUT IF YOU INSIST, I HAVE AN IDEA THAT MIGHT PROVE A LOT EASIER! I'LL SHOW YOU---

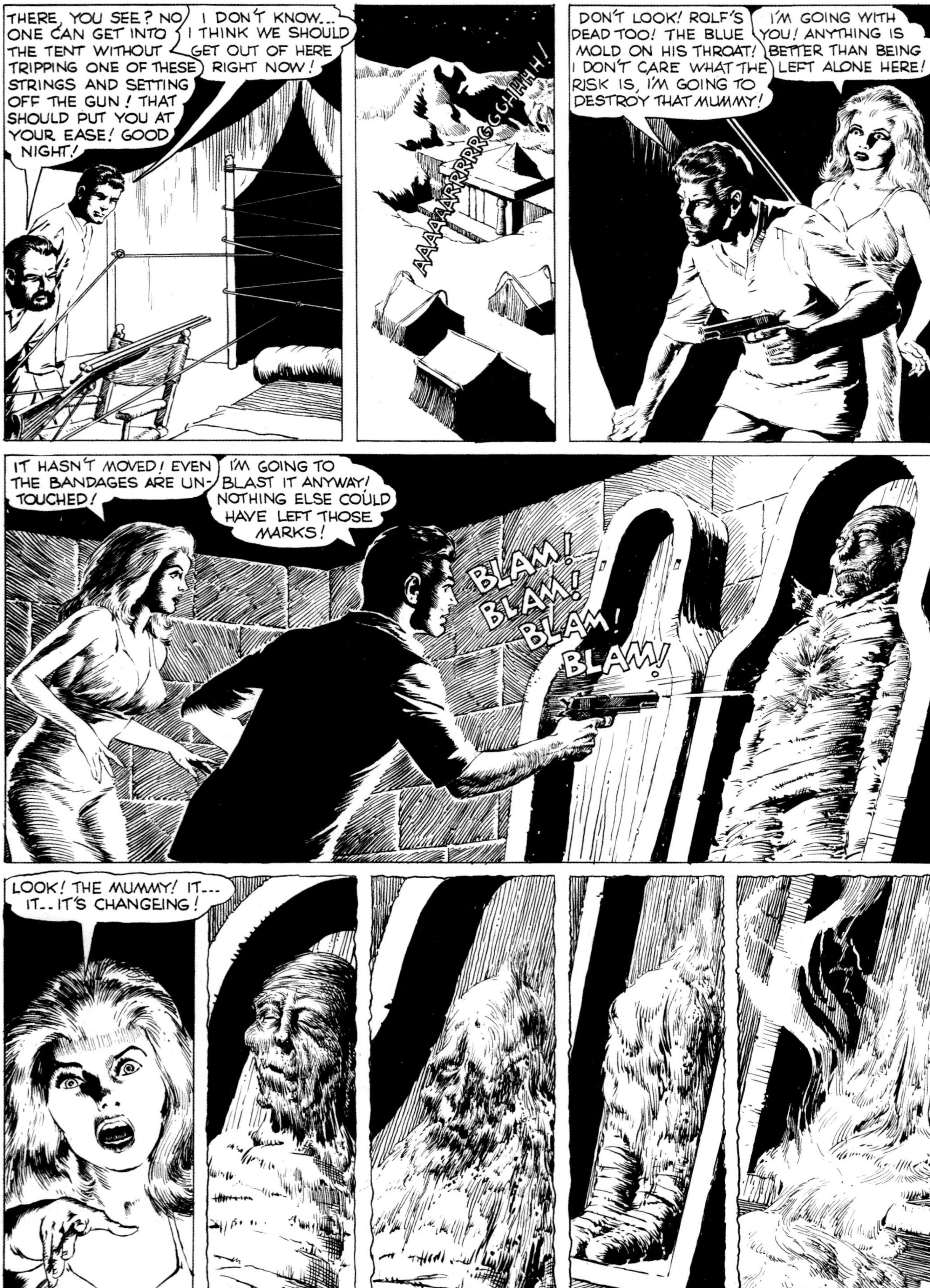
THERE, YOU SEE? NO ONE CAN GET INTO THE TENT WITHOUT TRIPPING ONE OF THESE STRINGS AND SETTING OFF THE GUN! THAT SHOULD PUT YOU AT YOUR EASE! GOOD NIGHT!
I DON'T KNOW... I THINK WE SHOULD GET OUT OF HERE RIGHT NOW!
AAAAAARRRRRGGGHHHH!
DON'T LOOK! ROLF'S DEAD TOO! THE BLUE MOLD ON HIS THROAT! I DON'T CARE WHAT THE RISK IS, I'M GOING TO DESTROY THAT MUMMY!
I'M GOING WITH YOU! ANYTHING IS BETTER THAN BEING LEFT ALONE HERE!
IT HASN'T MOVED! EVEN THE BANDAGES ARE UN-TOUCHED!
I'M GOING TO BLAST IT ANYWAY! NOTHING ELSE COULD HAVE LEFT THOSE MARKS!
BLAM! BLAM! BLAM! BLAM!
LOOK! THE MUMMY! IT--- IT-- IT'S CHANGEING!

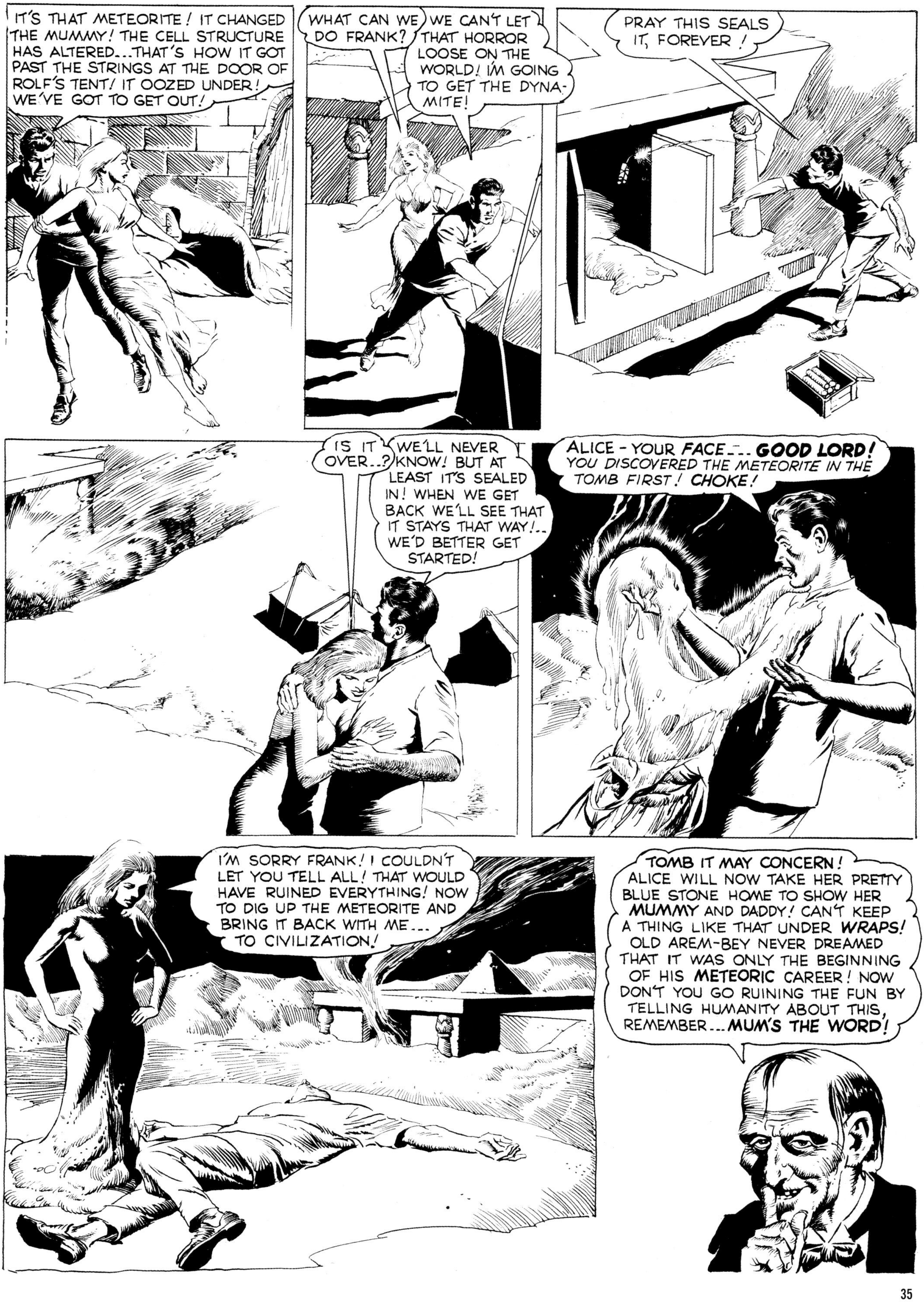

IT'S THAT METEORITE! IT CHANGED THE MUMMY! THE CELL STRUCTURE HAS ALTERED...THAT'S HOW IT GOT PAST THE STRINGS AT THE DOOR OF ROLF'S TENT! IT OOZED UNDER! WE'VE GOT TO GET OUT!
WHAT CAN WE DO FRANK?
WE CAN'T LET THAT HORROR LOOSE ON THE WORLD! I'M GOING TO GET THE DYNAMITE!
PRAY THIS SEALS IT, FOREVER!
IS IT OVER..?
WE'LL NEVER KNOW! BUT AT LEAST IT'S SEALED IN! WHEN WE GET BACK WE'LL SEE THAT IT STAYS THAT WAY!.. WE'D BETTER GET STARTED!
ALICE - YOUR FACE... GOOD LORD! YOU DISCOVERED THE METEORITE IN THE TOMB FIRST! CHOKE!
I'M SORRY FRANK! I COULDN'T LET YOU TELL ALL! THAT WOULD HAVE RUINED EVERYTHING! NOW TO DIG UP THE METEORITE AND BRING IT BACK WITH ME... TO CIVILIZATION!
TOMB IT MAY CONCERN! ALICE WILL NOW TAKE HER PRETTY BLUE STONE HOME TO SHOW HER MUMMY AND DADDY! CAN'T KEEP A THING LIKE THAT UNDER WRAPS! OLD AREM-BEY NEVER DREAMED THAT IT WAS ONLY THE BEGINNING OF HIS METEORIC CAREER! NOW DON'T YOU GO RUINING THE FUN BY TELLING HUMANITY ABOUT THIS, REMEMBER... MUM'S THE WORD!

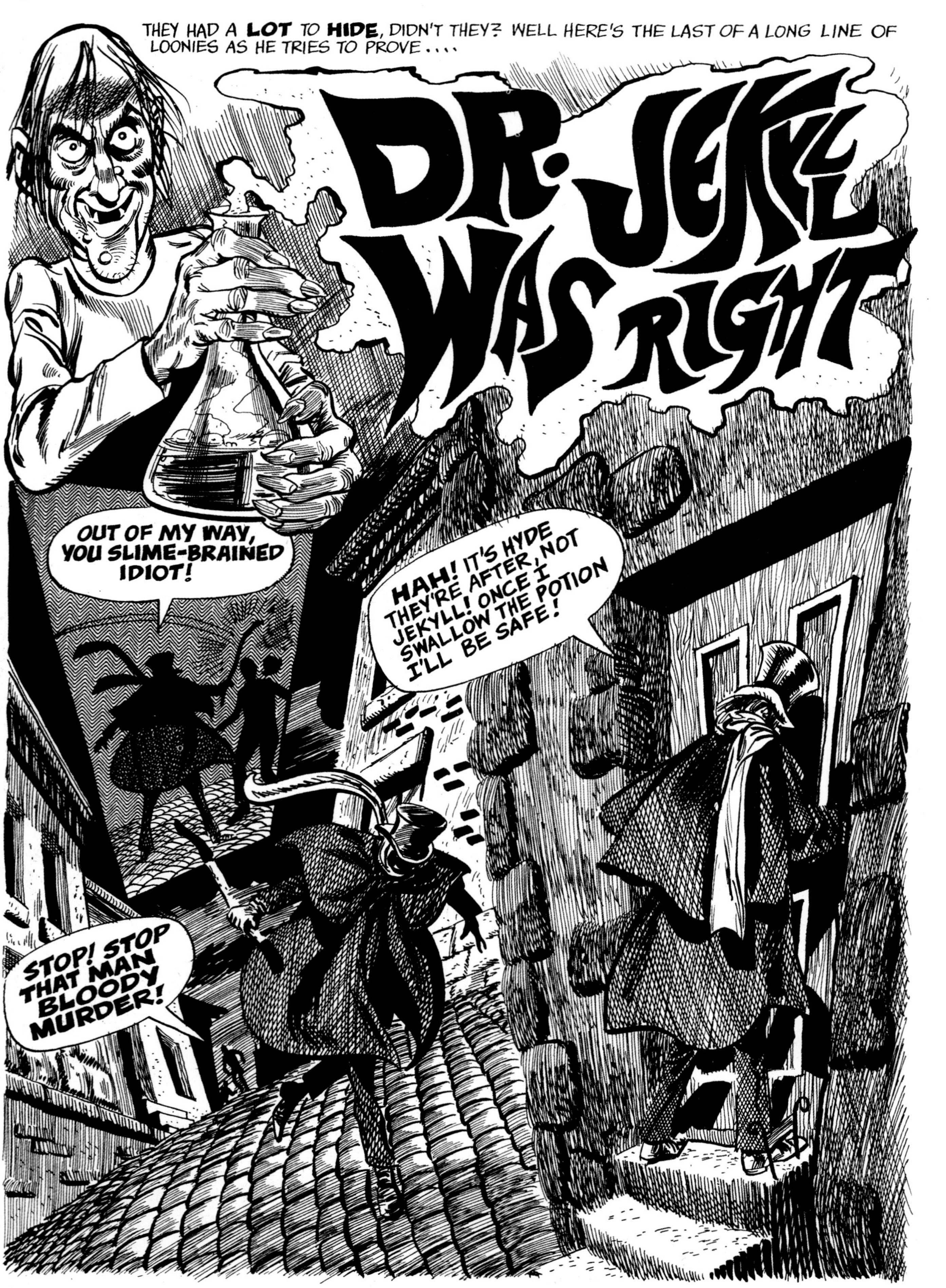
THEY HAD A LOT TO HIDE, DIDN'T THEY? WELL HERE'S THE LAST OF A LONG LINE OF LOONIES AS HE TRIES TO PROVE....
DR. JEKYL WAS RIGHT
OUT OF MY WAY, YOU SLIME-BRAINED IDIOT!
HAH! IT'S HYDE THEY'RE AFTER, NOT JEKYLL! ONCE I SWALLOW THE POTION I'LL BE SAFE!
STOP! STOP THAT MAN BLOODY MURDER!

ART BY TONY WILLIAMSUNE/STORY BY BILL WARREN

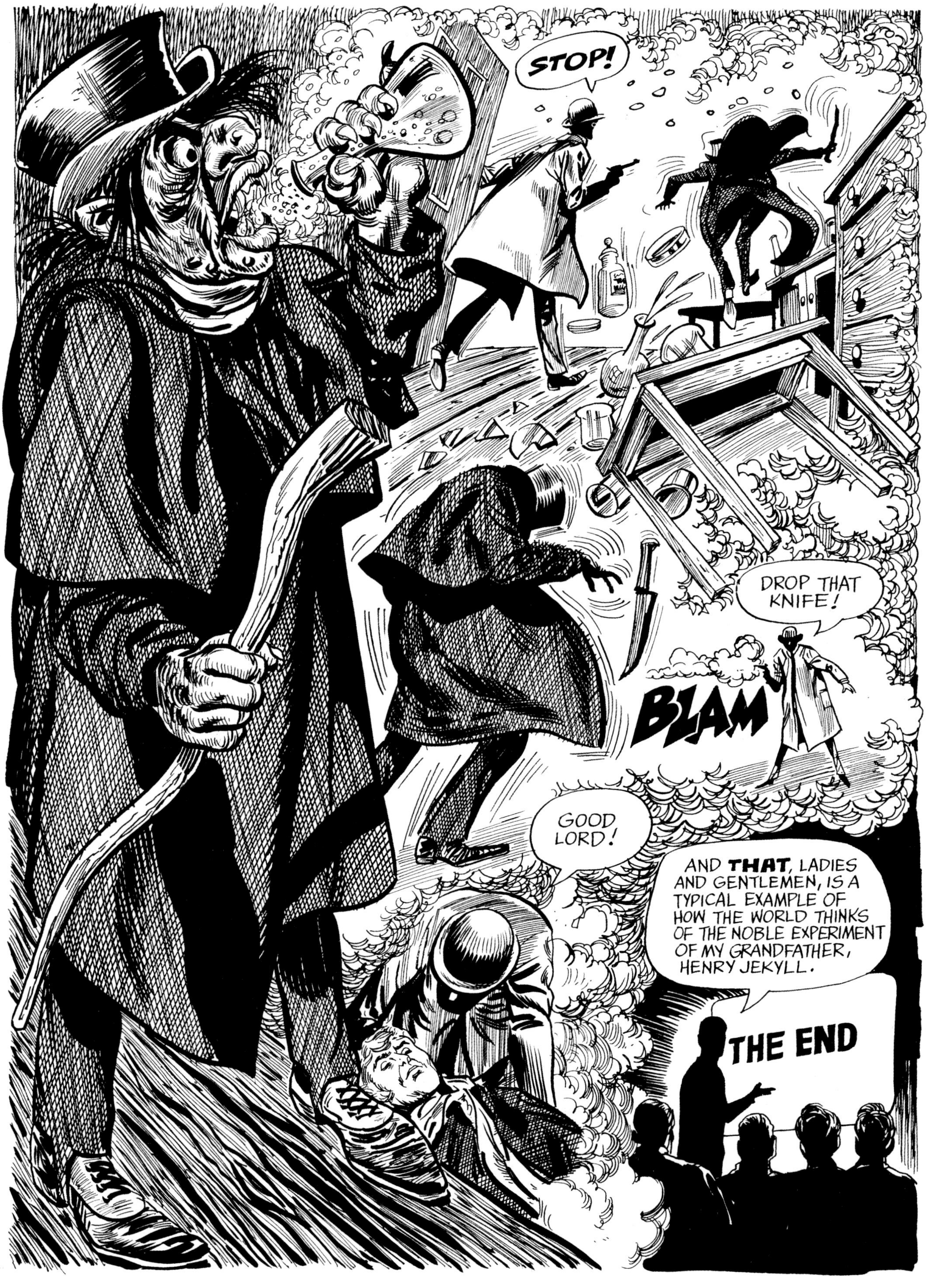
STOP!
DROP THAT KNIFE!
BLAM
GOOD LORD!
AND THAT, LADIES AND GENTLEMEN, IS A TYPICAL EXAMPLE OF HOW THE WORLD THINKS OF THE NOBLE EXPERIMENT OF MY GRANDFATHER, HENRY JEKYLL.
THE END

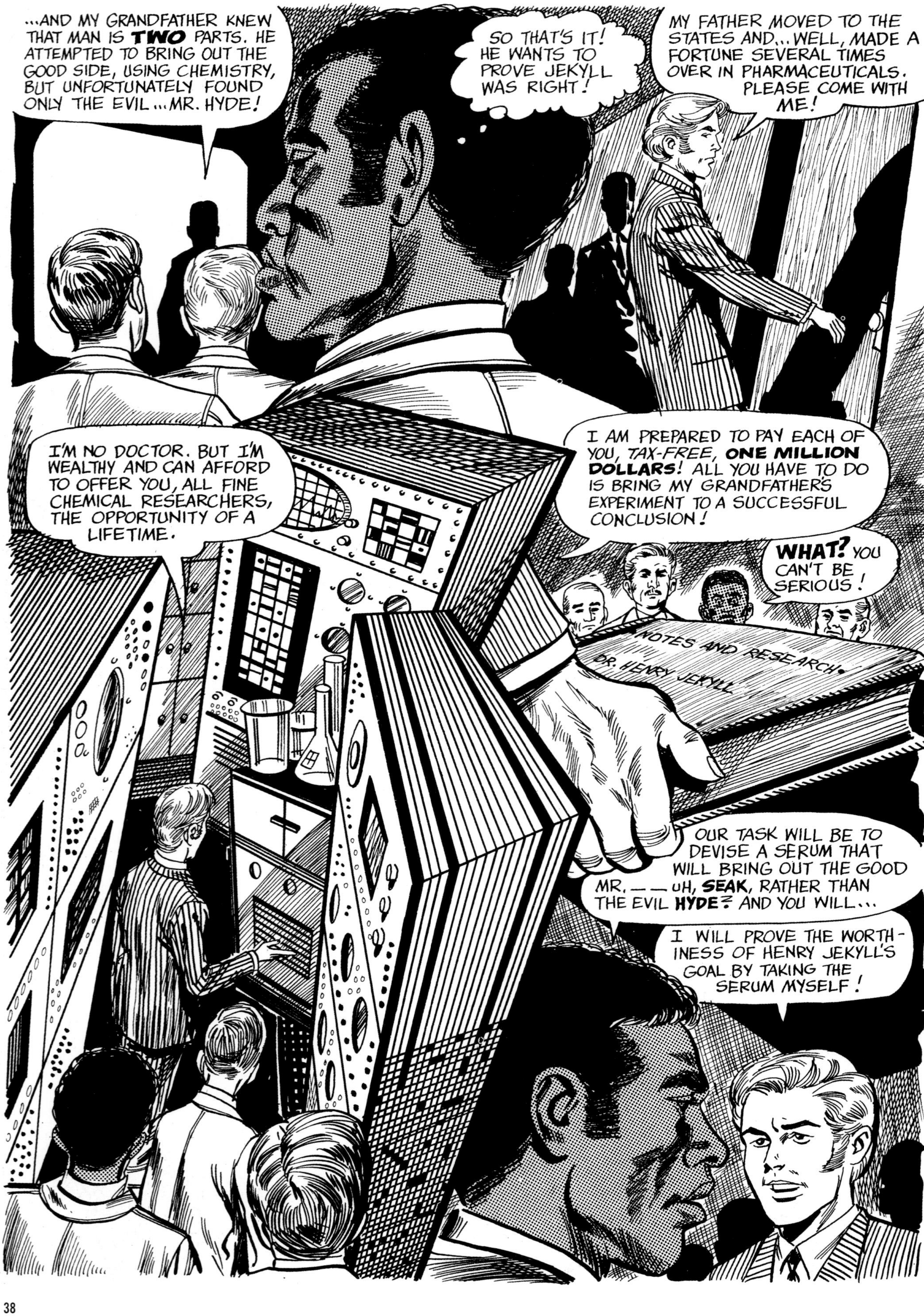
...AND MY GRANDFATHER KNEW THAT MAN IS **TWO** PARTS. HE ATTEMPTED TO BRING OUT THE GOOD SIDE, USING CHEMISTRY, BUT UNFORTUNATELY FOUND ONLY THE EVIL...MR. HYDE!
SO THAT'S IT! HE WANTS TO PROVE JEKYLL WAS RIGHT!
MY FATHER MOVED TO THE STATES AND...WELL, MADE A FORTUNE SEVERAL TIMES OVER IN PHARMACEUTICALS. PLEASE COME WITH ME!
I'M NO DOCTOR. BUT I'M WEALTHY AND CAN AFFORD TO OFFER YOU, ALL FINE CHEMICAL RESEARCHERS, THE OPPORTUNITY OF A LIFETIME.
I AM PREPARED TO PAY EACH OF YOU, *TAX-FREE*, **ONE MILLION DOLLARS**! ALL YOU HAVE TO DO IS BRING MY GRANDFATHER'S EXPERIMENT TO A SUCCESSFUL CONCLUSION!
WHAT? YOU CAN'T BE SERIOUS!
NOTES AND RESEARCH
DR. HENRY JEKYLL
OUR TASK WILL BE TO DEVISE A SERUM THAT WILL BRING OUT THE GOOD MR.--UH, **SEAK**, RATHER THAN THE EVIL **HYDE**? AND YOU WILL...
I WILL PROVE THE WORTHINESS OF HENRY JEKYLL'S GOAL BY TAKING THE SERUM MYSELF!

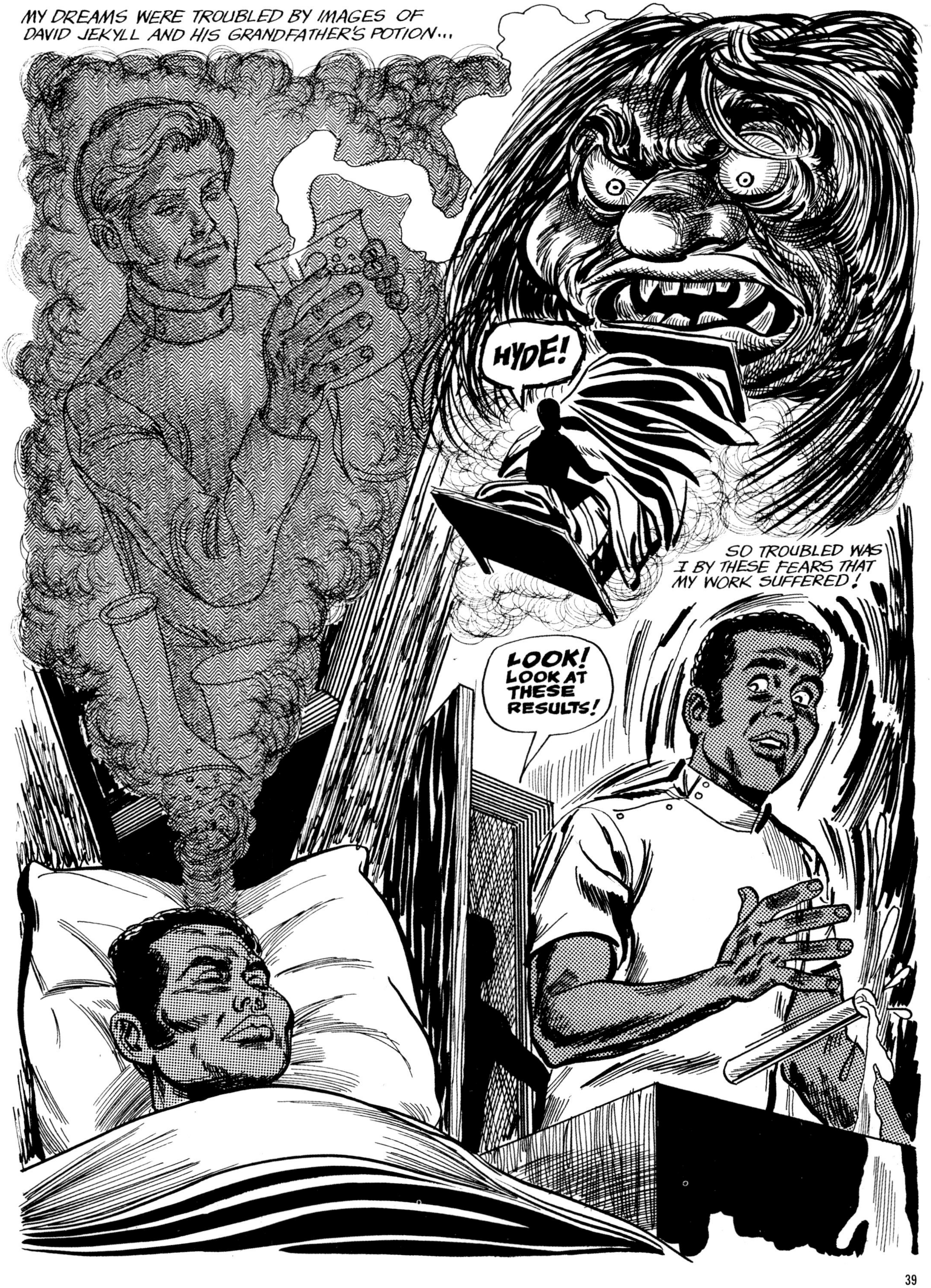
MY DREAMS WERE TROUBLED BY IMAGES OF DAVID JEKYLL AND HIS GRANDFATHER'S POTION...
HYDE!
SO TROUBLED WAS I BY THESE FEARS THAT MY WORK SUFFERED!
LOOK! LOOK AT THESE RESULTS!

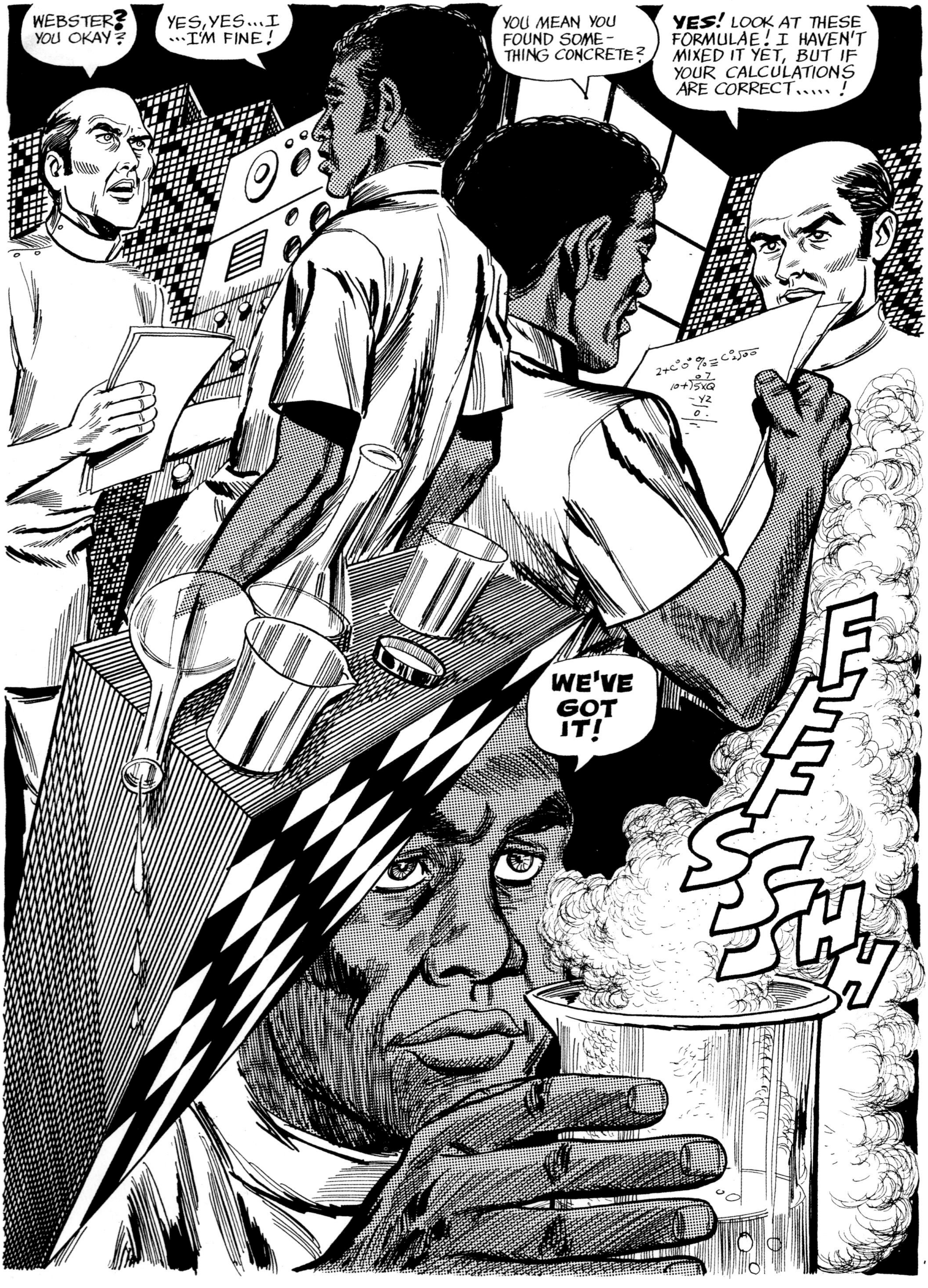
WEBSTER? YOU OKAY?
YES, YES... I ...I'M FINE!
YOU MEAN YOU FOUND SOME-THING CONCRETE?
YES! LOOK AT THESE FORMULAE! I HAVEN'T MIXED IT YET, BUT IF YOUR CALCULATIONS ARE CORRECT.....!
WE'VE GOT IT!
FFFFSSSHH

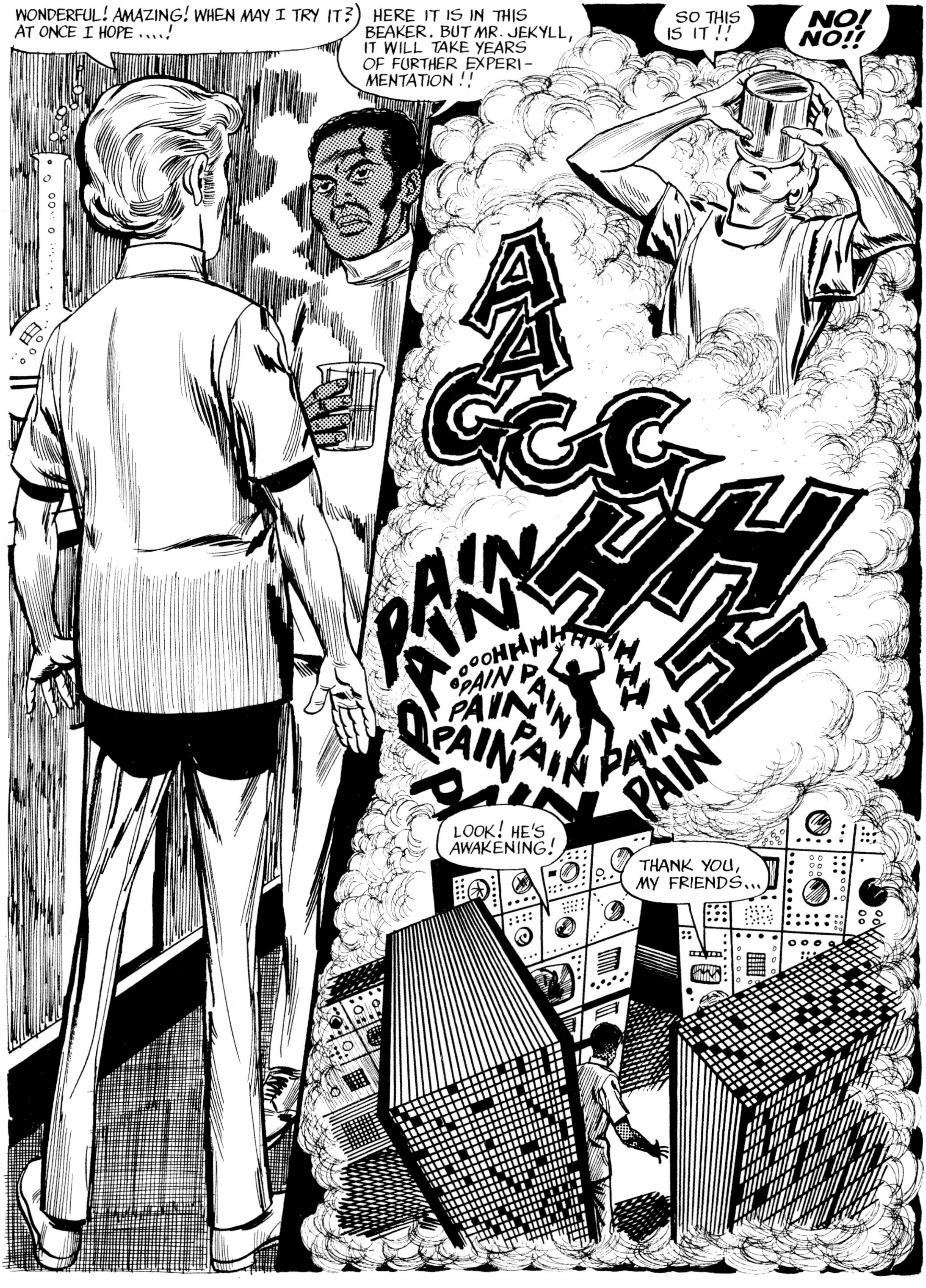
WONDERFUL! AMAZING! WHEN MAY I TRY IT? AT ONCE I HOPE.....!
HERE IT IS IN THIS BEAKER. BUT MR. JEKYLL, IT WILL TAKE YEARS OF FURTHER EXPERI-MENTATION!!
SO THIS IS IT!!
NO! NO!!
AAAGGGHHHH
PAIN PAIN
OOOHHHHHHHHHH
PAIN PAIN PAIN PAIN PAIN PAIN PAIN PAIN PAIN PAIN
LOOK! HE'S AWAKENING!
THANK YOU, MY FRIENDS...

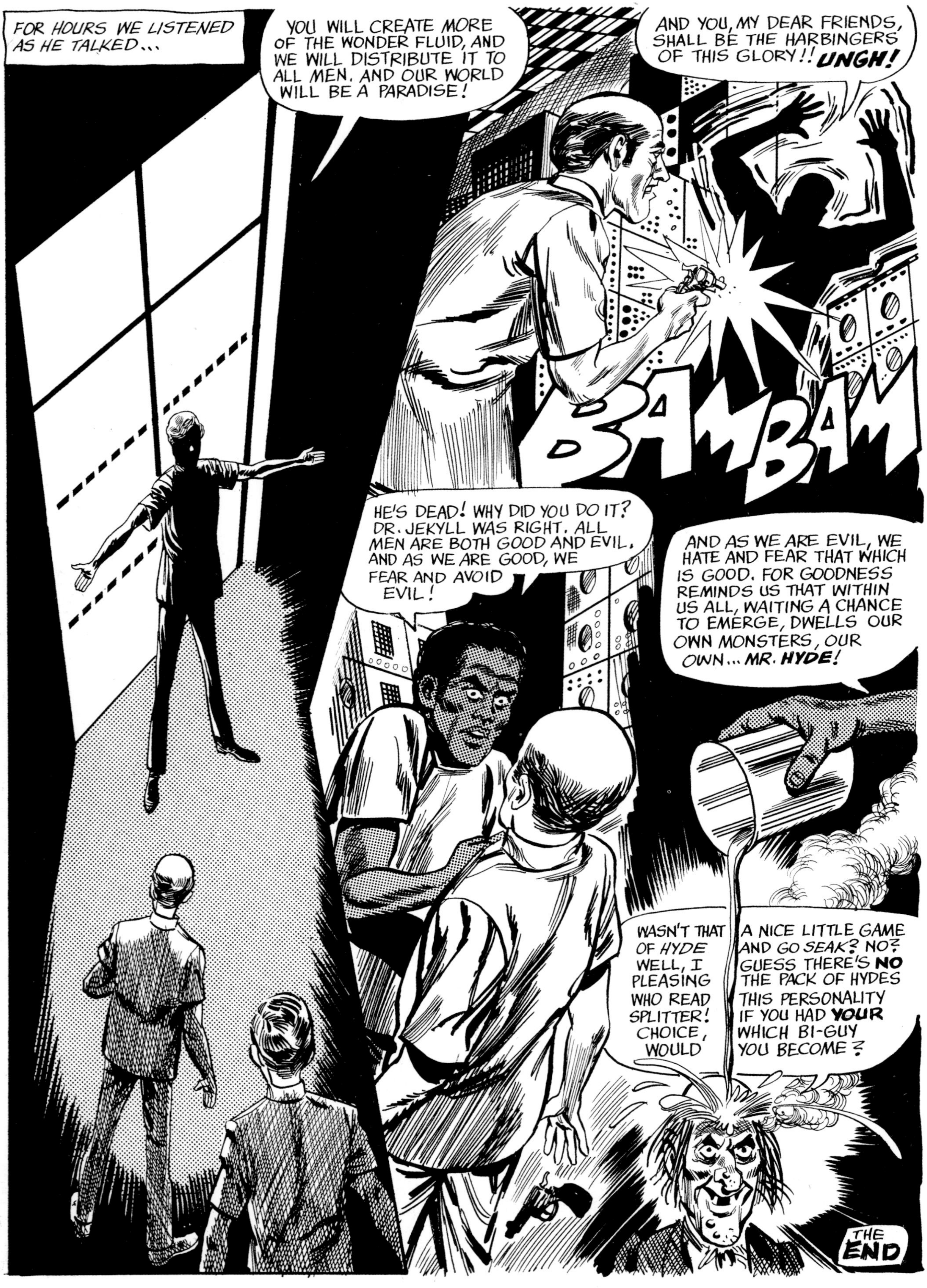
FOR HOURS WE LISTENED AS HE TALKED...
YOU WILL CREATE MORE OF THE WONDER FLUID, AND WE WILL DISTRIBUTE IT TO ALL MEN. AND OUR WORLD WILL BE A PARADISE!
AND YOU, MY DEAR FRIENDS, SHALL BE THE HARBINGERS OF THIS GLORY!! UNGH!
BAMBAM
HE'S DEAD! WHY DID YOU DO IT? DR. JEKYLL WAS RIGHT. ALL MEN ARE BOTH GOOD AND EVIL, AND AS WE ARE GOOD, WE FEAR AND AVOID EVIL!
AND AS WE ARE EVIL, WE HATE AND FEAR THAT WHICH IS GOOD. FOR GOODNESS REMINDS US THAT WITHIN US ALL, WAITING A CHANCE TO EMERGE, DWELLS OUR OWN MONSTERS, OUR OWN... MR. HYDE!
WASN'T THAT A NICE LITTLE GAME OF HYDE AND GO SEAK? NO? WELL, I GUESS THERE'S NO PLEASING THE PACK OF HYDES WHO READ THIS PERSONALITY SPLITTER! IF YOU HAD YOUR CHOICE, WHICH BI-GUY WOULD YOU BECOME?
THE END

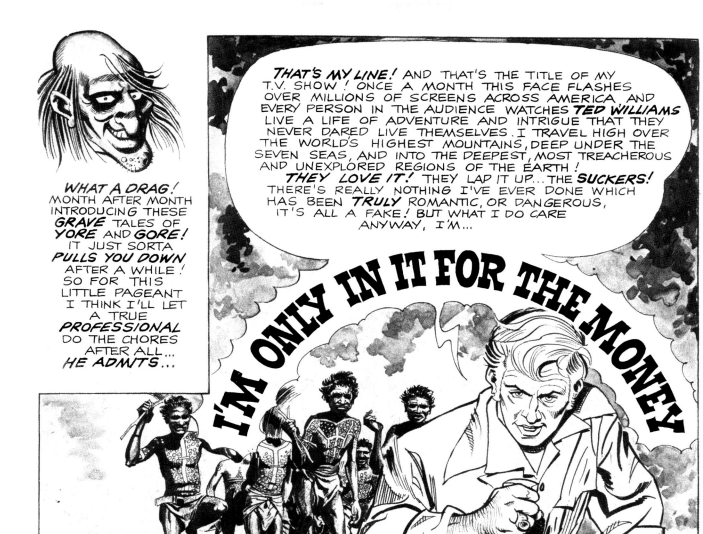

WHAT A DRAG! MONTH AFTER MONTH INTRODUCING THESE *GRAVE* TALES OF *YORE* AND *GORE!* IT JUST SORTA *PULLS YOU DOWN* AFTER A WHILE! SO FOR THIS LITTLE PAGEANT I THINK I'LL LET A TRUE *PROFESSIONAL* DO THE CHORES AFTER ALL... *HE ADMITS...*

THAT'S *MY LINE!* AND THAT'S THE TITLE OF MY T.V. SHOW! ONCE A MONTH THIS FACE FLASHES OVER MILLIONS OF SCREENS ACROSS AMERICA, AND EVERY PERSON IN THE AUDIENCE WATCHES *TED WILLIAMS* LIVE A LIFE OF ADVENTURE AND INTRIGUE THAT THEY NEVER DARED LIVE THEMSELVES. I TRAVEL HIGH OVER THE WORLD'S HIGHEST MOUNTAINS, DEEP UNDER THE SEVEN SEAS, AND INTO THE DEEPEST, MOST TREACHEROUS AND UNEXPLORED REGIONS OF THE EARTH! *THEY LOVE IT!* THEY LAP IT UP...THE *SUCKERS!* THERE'S REALLY NOTHING I'VE EVER DONE WHICH HAS BEEN *TRULY* ROMANTIC, OR DANGEROUS, IT'S ALL A FAKE! BUT WHAT I DO CARE ANYWAY, I'M...

I'M ONLY IN IT FOR THE MONEY

ART BY JUAN LOPEZ RAMON/STORY BY AL HEWETSON

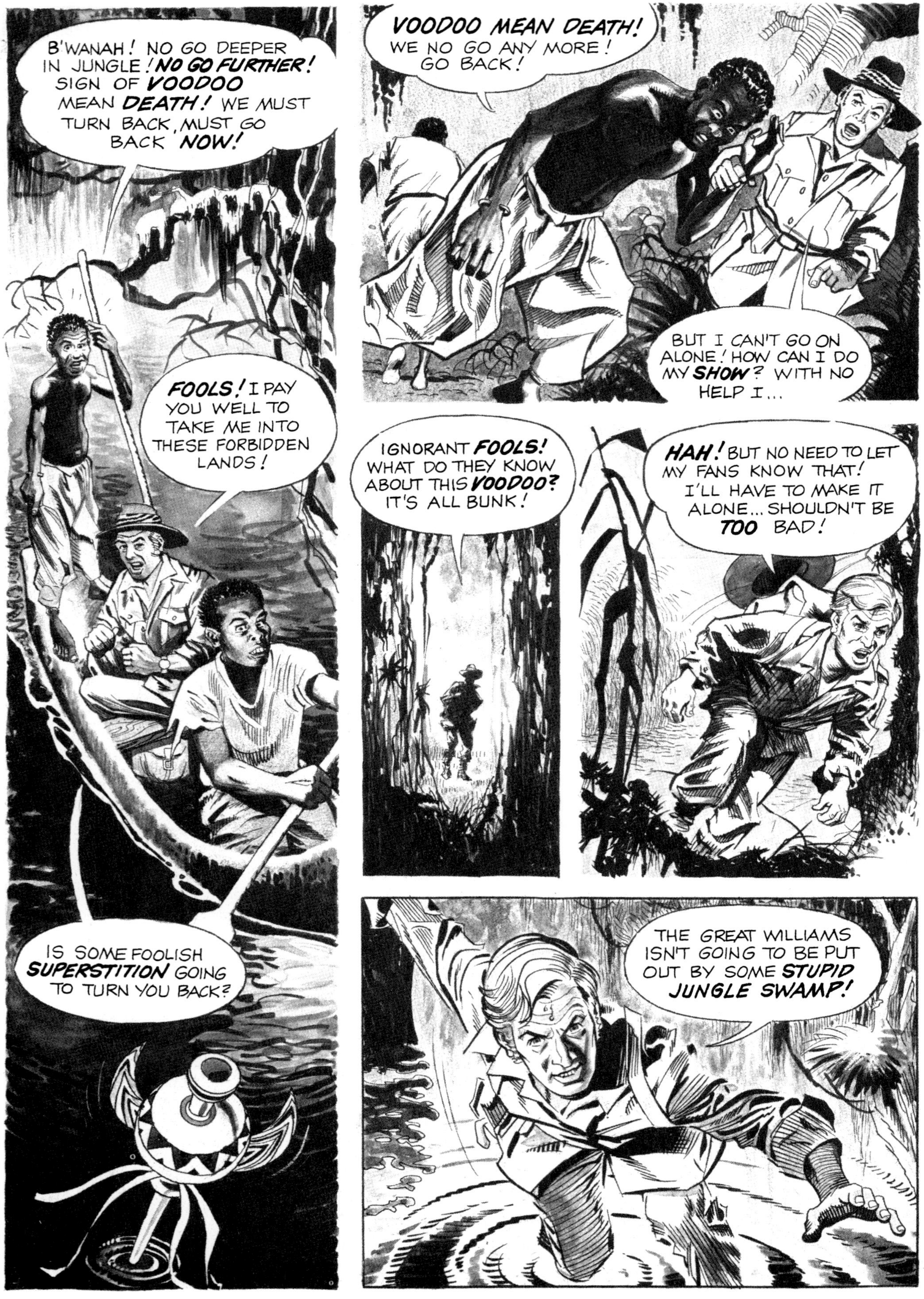
B'WANAH! NO GO DEEPER IN JUNGLE! NO GO FURTHER! SIGN OF VOODOO MEAN DEATH! WE MUST TURN BACK, MUST GO BACK NOW!
FOOLS! I PAY YOU WELL TO TAKE ME INTO THESE FORBIDDEN LANDS!
IS SOME FOOLISH SUPERSTITION GOING TO TURN YOU BACK?
VOODOO MEAN DEATH! WE NO GO ANY MORE! GO BACK!
BUT I CAN'T GO ON ALONE! HOW CAN I DO MY SHOW? WITH NO HELP I...
IGNORANT FOOLS! WHAT DO THEY KNOW ABOUT THIS VOODOO? IT'S ALL BUNK!
HAH! BUT NO NEED TO LET MY FANS KNOW THAT! I'LL HAVE TO MAKE IT ALONE... SHOULDN'T BE TOO BAD!
THE GREAT WILLIAMS ISN'T GOING TO BE PUT OUT BY SOME STUPID JUNGLE SWAMP!

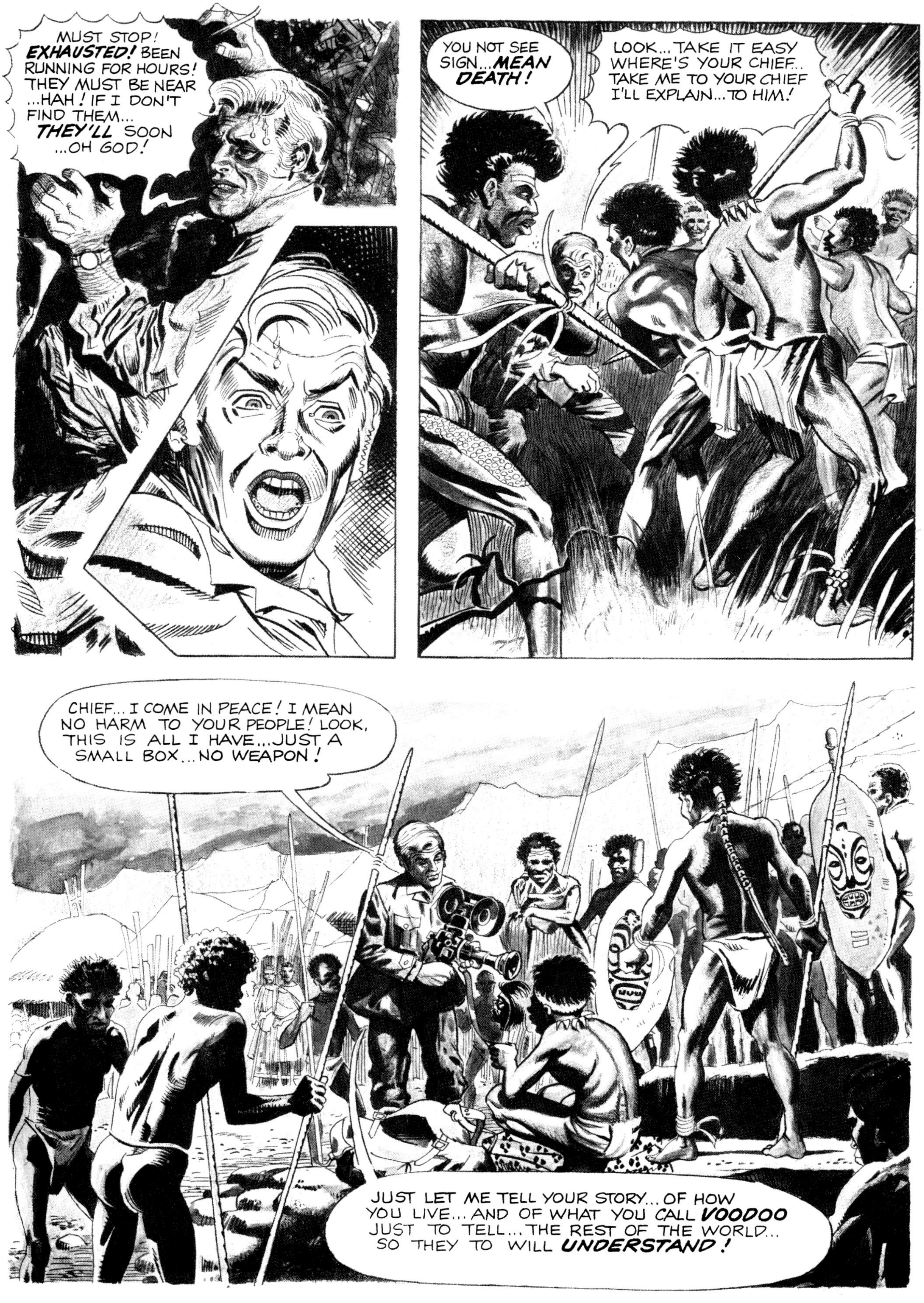
MUST STOP! EXHAUSTED! BEEN RUNNING FOR HOURS! THEY MUST BE NEAR ...HAH! IF I DON'T FIND THEM... THEY'LL SOON ...OH GOD!
YOU NOT SEE SIGN... MEAN DEATH!
LOOK... TAKE IT EASY WHERE'S YOUR CHIEF.. TAKE ME TO YOUR CHIEF I'LL EXPLAIN... TO HIM!
CHIEF... I COME IN PEACE! I MEAN NO HARM TO YOUR PEOPLE! LOOK, THIS IS ALL I HAVE... JUST A SMALL BOX... NO WEAPON!
JUST LET ME TELL YOUR STORY... OF HOW YOU LIVE... AND OF WHAT YOU CALL VOODOO JUST TO TELL... THE REST OF THE WORLD... SO THEY TO WILL UNDERSTAND!

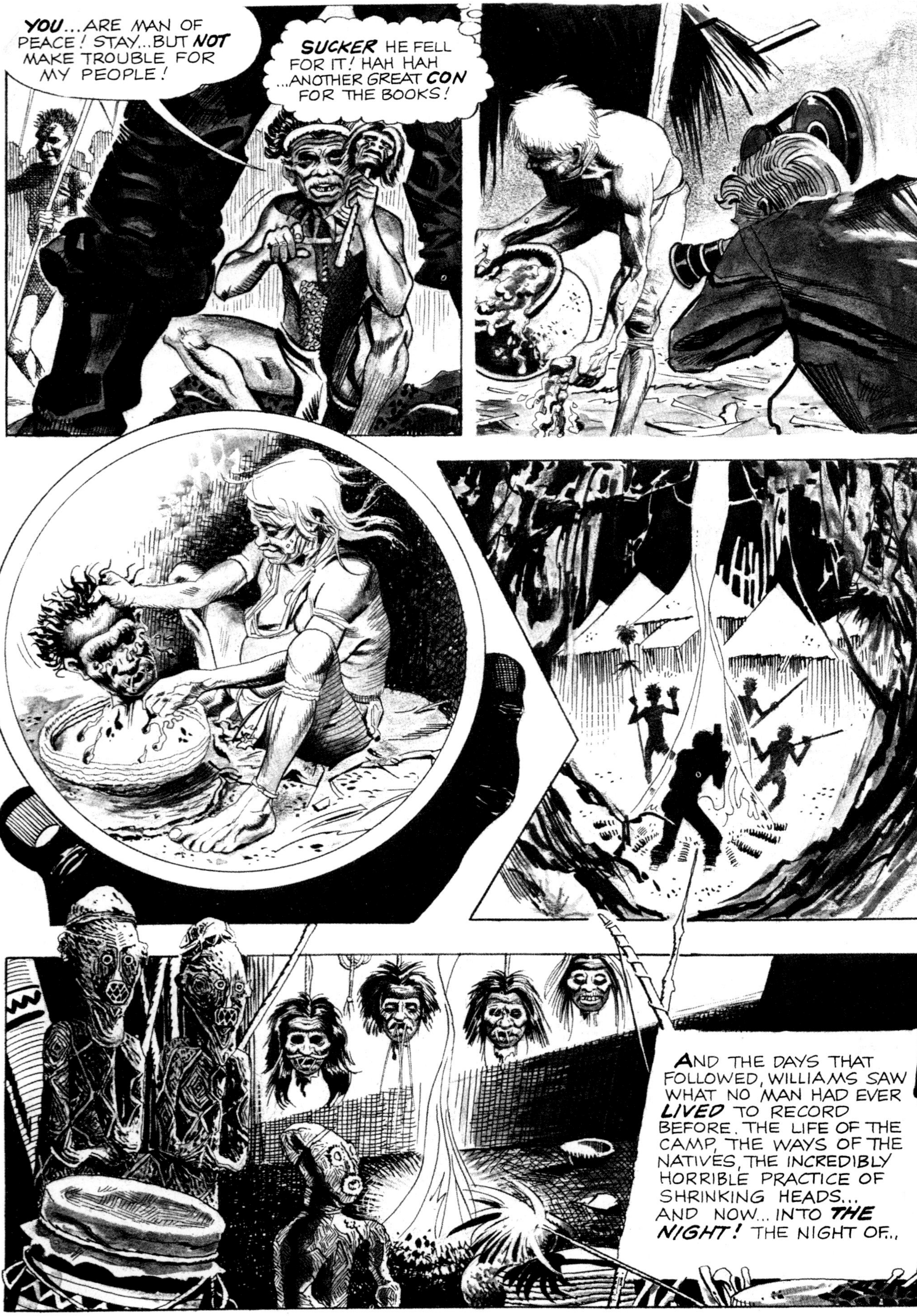
YOU... ARE MAN OF PEACE! STAY... BUT NOT MAKE TROUBLE FOR MY PEOPLE!
SUCKER HE FELL FOR IT! HAH HAH ...ANOTHER GREAT CON FOR THE BOOKS!
AND THE DAYS THAT FOLLOWED, WILLIAMS SAW WHAT NO MAN HAD EVER LIVED TO RECORD BEFORE. THE LIFE OF THE CAMP, THE WAYS OF THE NATIVES, THE INCREDIBLY HORRIBLE PRACTICE OF SHRINKING HEADS... AND NOW... INTO THE NIGHT! THE NIGHT OF...

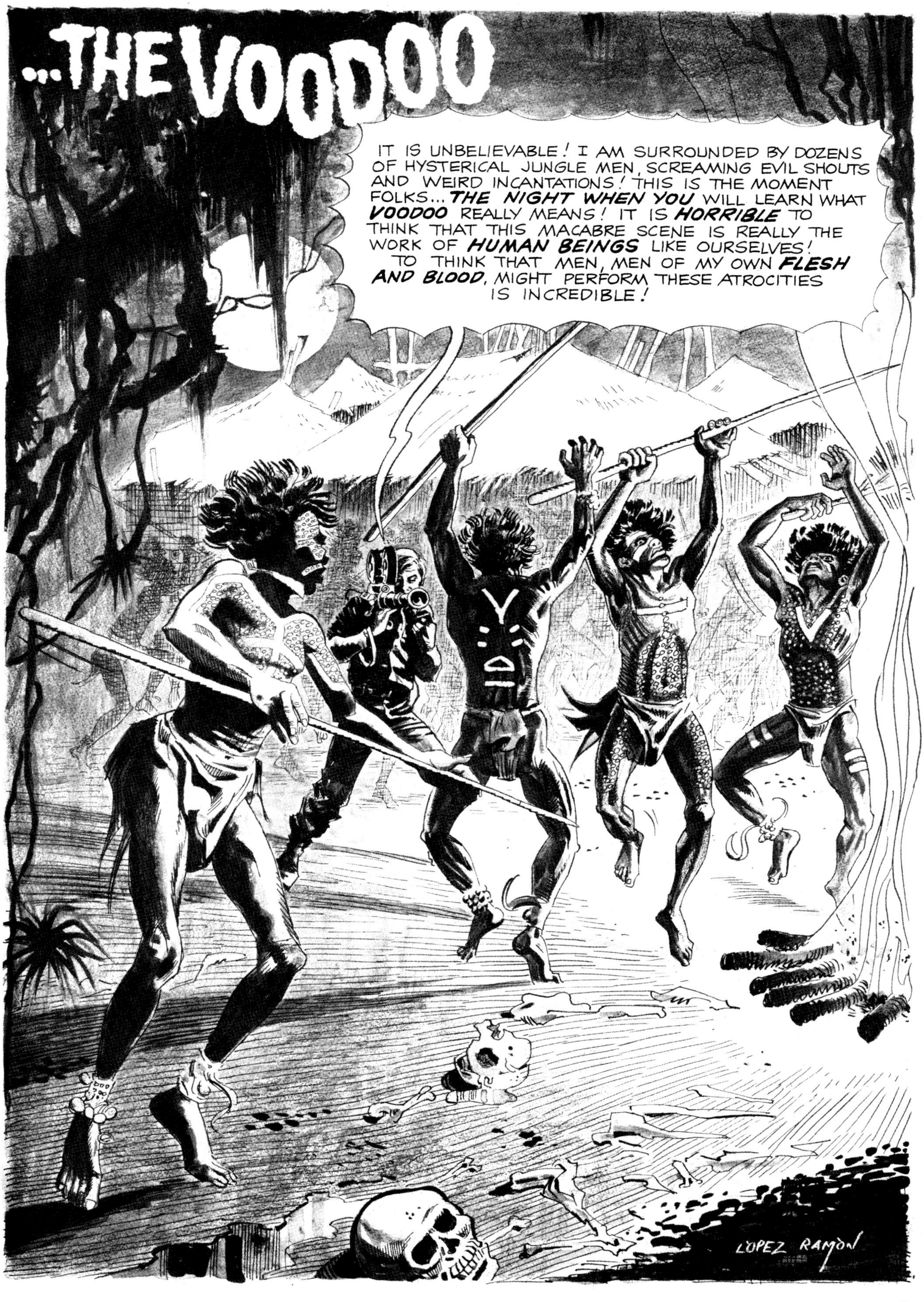
...THE VOODOO
IT IS UNBELIEVABLE! I AM SURROUNDED BY DOZENS OF HYSTERICAL JUNGLE MEN, SCREAMING EVIL SHOUTS AND WEIRD INCANTATIONS! THIS IS THE MOMENT FOLKS... THE NIGHT WHEN YOU WILL LEARN WHAT VOODOO REALLY MEANS! IT IS HORRIBLE TO THINK THAT THIS MACABRE SCENE IS REALLY THE WORK OF HUMAN BEINGS LIKE OURSELVES! TO THINK THAT MEN, MEN OF MY OWN FLESH AND BLOOD, MIGHT PERFORM THESE ATROCITIES IS INCREDIBLE!
LOPEZ RAMON

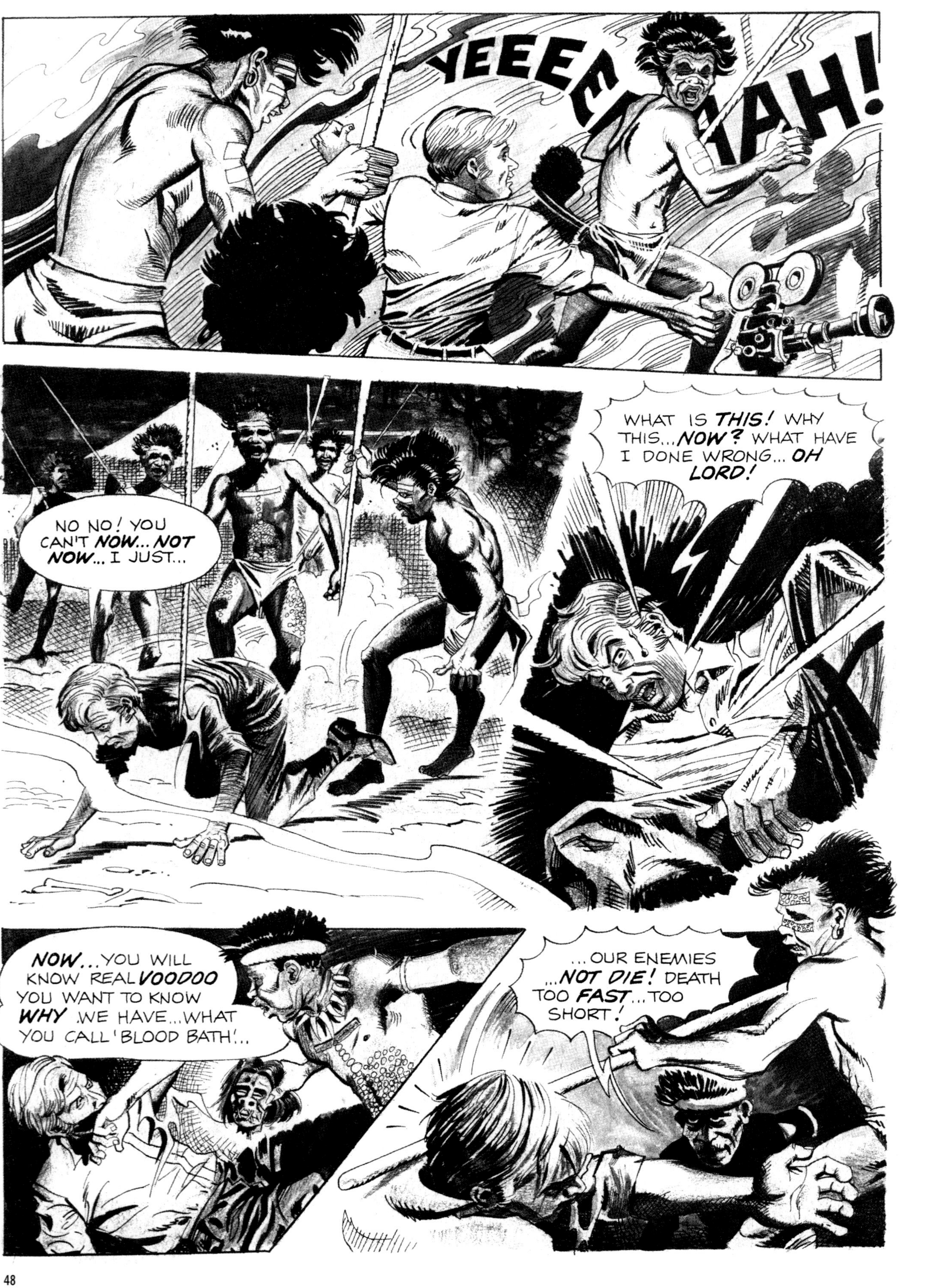
YEEEEAAH!
NO NO! YOU CAN'T NOW... NOT NOW... I JUST...
WHAT IS THIS! WHY THIS... NOW? WHAT HAVE I DONE WRONG... OH LORD!
NOW... YOU WILL KNOW REAL VOODOO YOU WANT TO KNOW WHY WE HAVE... WHAT YOU CALL 'BLOOD BATH'...
...OUR ENEMIES ...NOT DIE! DEATH TOO FAST... TOO SHORT!

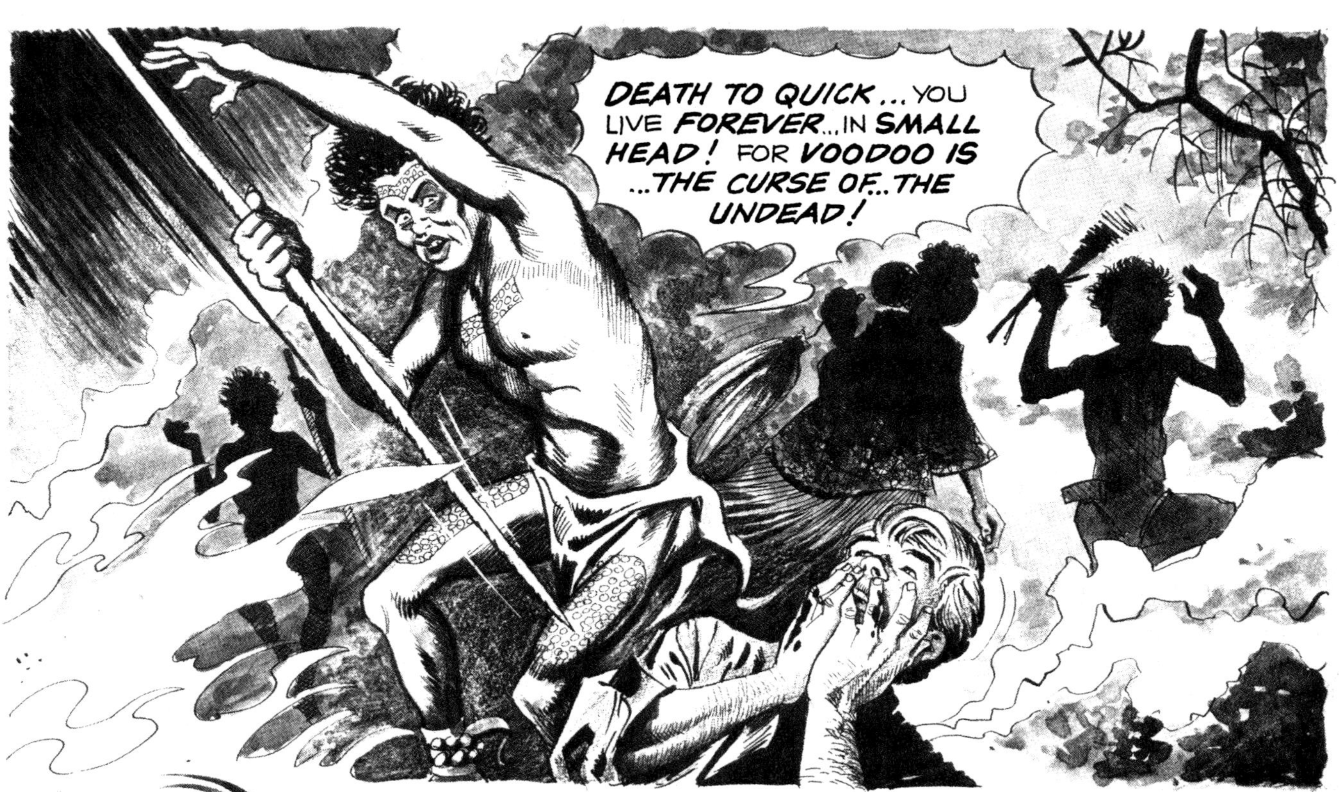
DEATH TO QUICK... YOU LIVE FOREVER... IN SMALL HEAD! FOR VOODOO IS ...THE CURSE OF... THE UNDEAD!

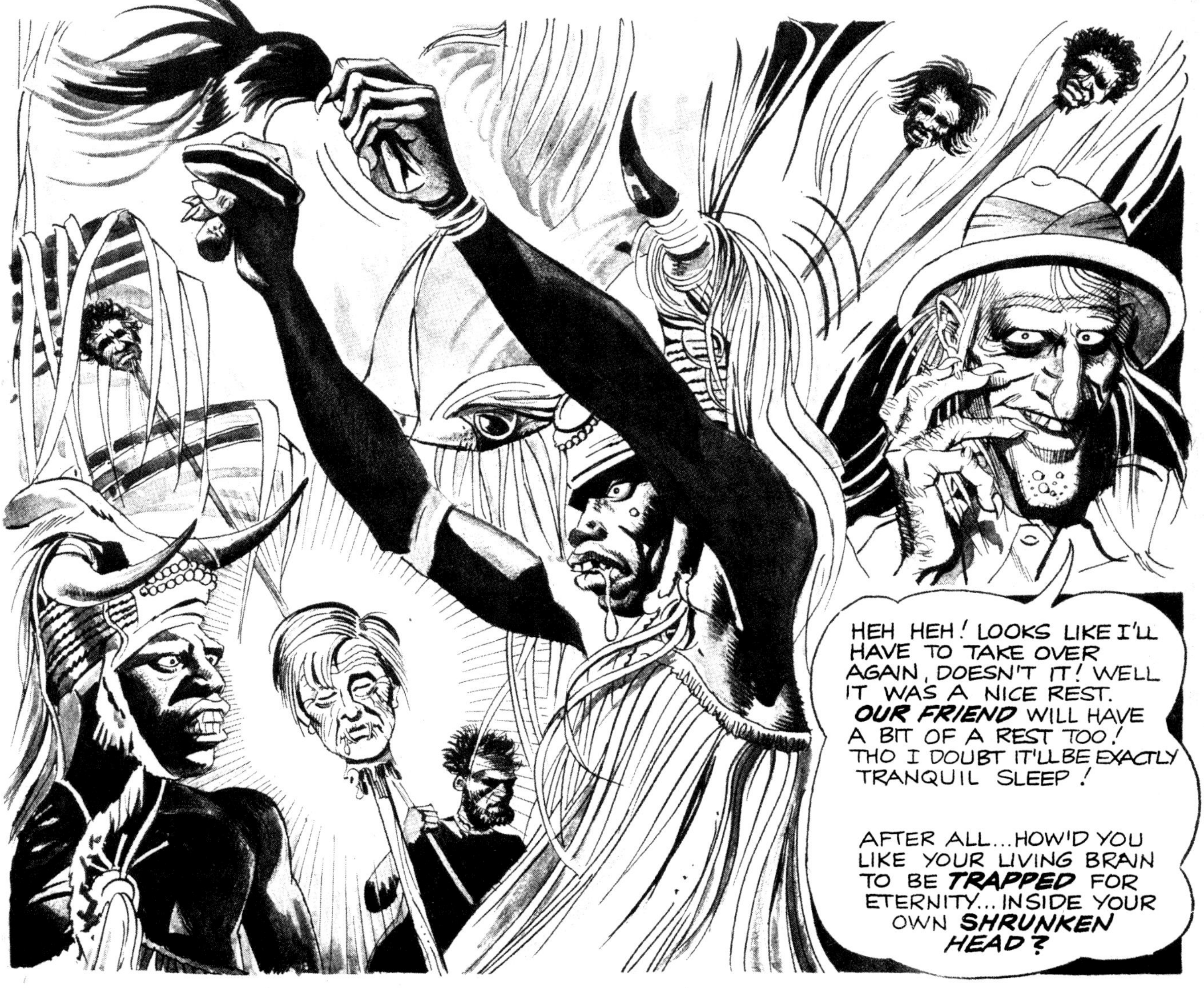
HEH HEH! LOOKS LIKE I'LL HAVE TO TAKE OVER AGAIN, DOESN'T IT! WELL IT WAS A NICE REST. OUR FRIEND WILL HAVE A BIT OF A REST TOO! THO I DOUBT IT'LL BE EXACTLY TRANQUIL SLEEP!
AFTER ALL... HOW'D YOU LIKE YOUR LIVING BRAIN TO BE TRAPPED FOR ETERNITY... INSIDE YOUR OWN SHRUNKEN HEAD?

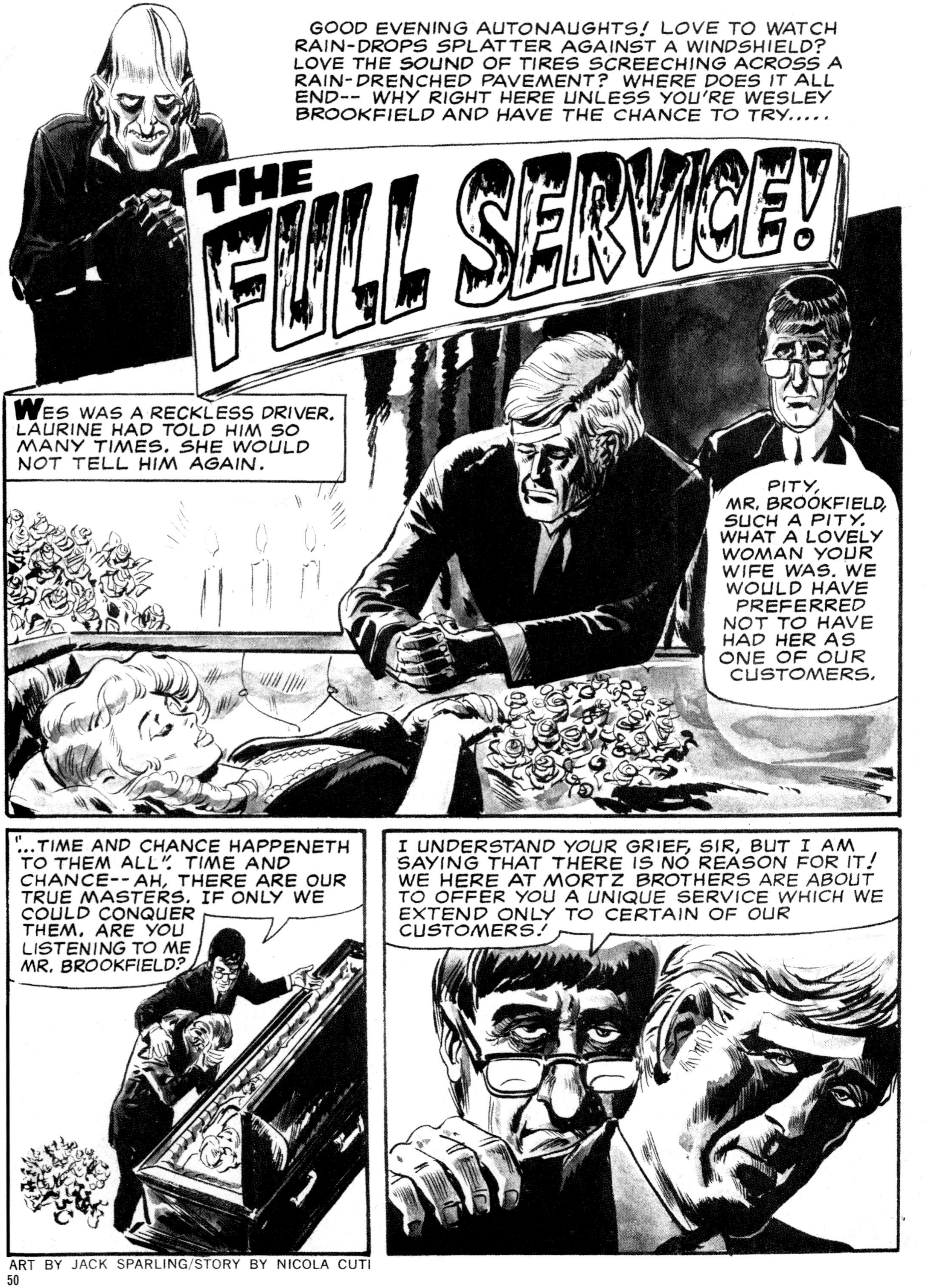
GOOD EVENING AUTONAUGHTS! LOVE TO WATCH RAIN-DROPS SPLATTER AGAINST A WINDSHIELD? LOVE THE SOUND OF TIRES SCREECHING ACROSS A RAIN-DRENCHED PAVEMENT? WHERE DOES IT ALL END-- WHY RIGHT HERE UNLESS YOU'RE WESLEY BROOKFIELD AND HAVE THE CHANCE TO TRY.....
THE FULL SERVICE!
WES WAS A RECKLESS DRIVER. LAURINE HAD TOLD HIM SO MANY TIMES. SHE WOULD NOT TELL HIM AGAIN.
PITY, MR. BROOKFIELD, SUCH A PITY. WHAT A LOVELY WOMAN YOUR WIFE WAS. WE WOULD HAVE PREFERRED NOT TO HAVE HAD HER AS ONE OF OUR CUSTOMERS.
"...TIME AND CHANCE HAPPENETH TO THEM ALL". TIME AND CHANCE--AH, THERE ARE OUR TRUE MASTERS. IF ONLY WE COULD CONQUER THEM. ARE YOU LISTENING TO ME MR. BROOKFIELD?
I UNDERSTAND YOUR GRIEF, SIR, BUT I AM SAYING THAT THERE IS NO REASON FOR IT! WE HERE AT MORTZ BROTHERS ARE ABOUT TO OFFER YOU A UNIQUE SERVICE WHICH WE EXTEND ONLY TO CERTAIN OF OUR CUSTOMERS!

ART BY JACK SPARLING/STORY BY NICOLA CUTI

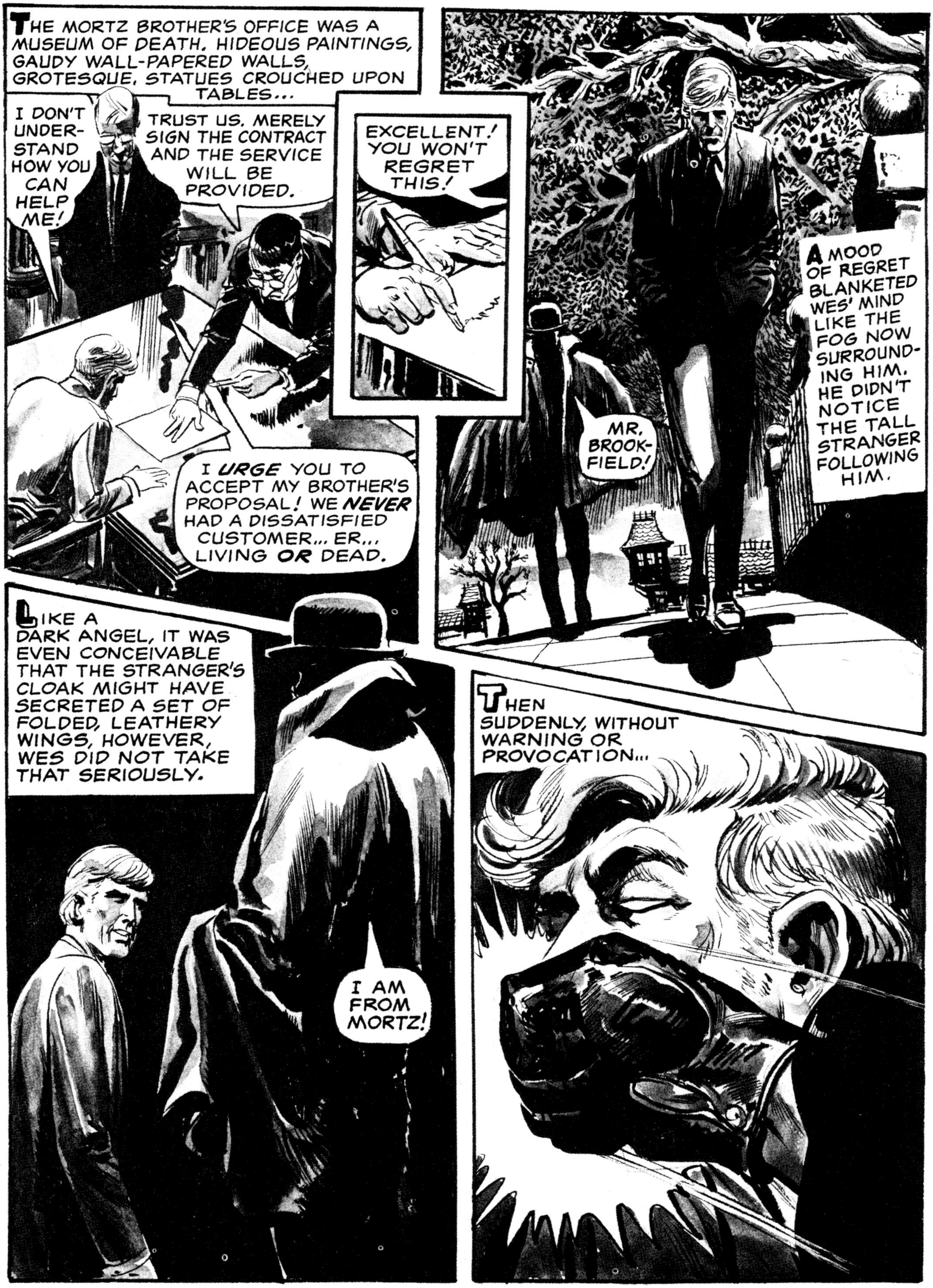
THE MORTZ BROTHER'S OFFICE WAS A MUSEUM OF DEATH. HIDEOUS PAINTINGS, GAUDY WALL-PAPERED WALLS, GROTESQUE, STATUES CROUCHED UPON TABLES...
I DON'T UNDERSTAND HOW YOU CAN HELP ME!
TRUST US. MERELY SIGN THE CONTRACT AND THE SERVICE WILL BE PROVIDED.
I URGE YOU TO ACCEPT MY BROTHER'S PROPOSAL! WE NEVER HAD A DISSATISFIED CUSTOMER... ER... LIVING OR DEAD.
EXCELLENT! YOU WON'T REGRET THIS!
A MOOD OF REGRET BLANKETED WES' MIND LIKE THE FOG NOW SURROUNDING HIM. HE DIDN'T NOTICE THE TALL STRANGER FOLLOWING HIM.
MR. BROOKFIELD!
LIKE A DARK ANGEL, IT WAS EVEN CONCEIVABLE THAT THE STRANGER'S CLOAK MIGHT HAVE SECRETED A SET OF FOLDED, LEATHERY WINGS, HOWEVER, WES DID NOT TAKE THAT SERIOUSLY.
I AM FROM MORTZ!
THEN SUDDENLY, WITHOUT WARNING OR PROVOCATION...

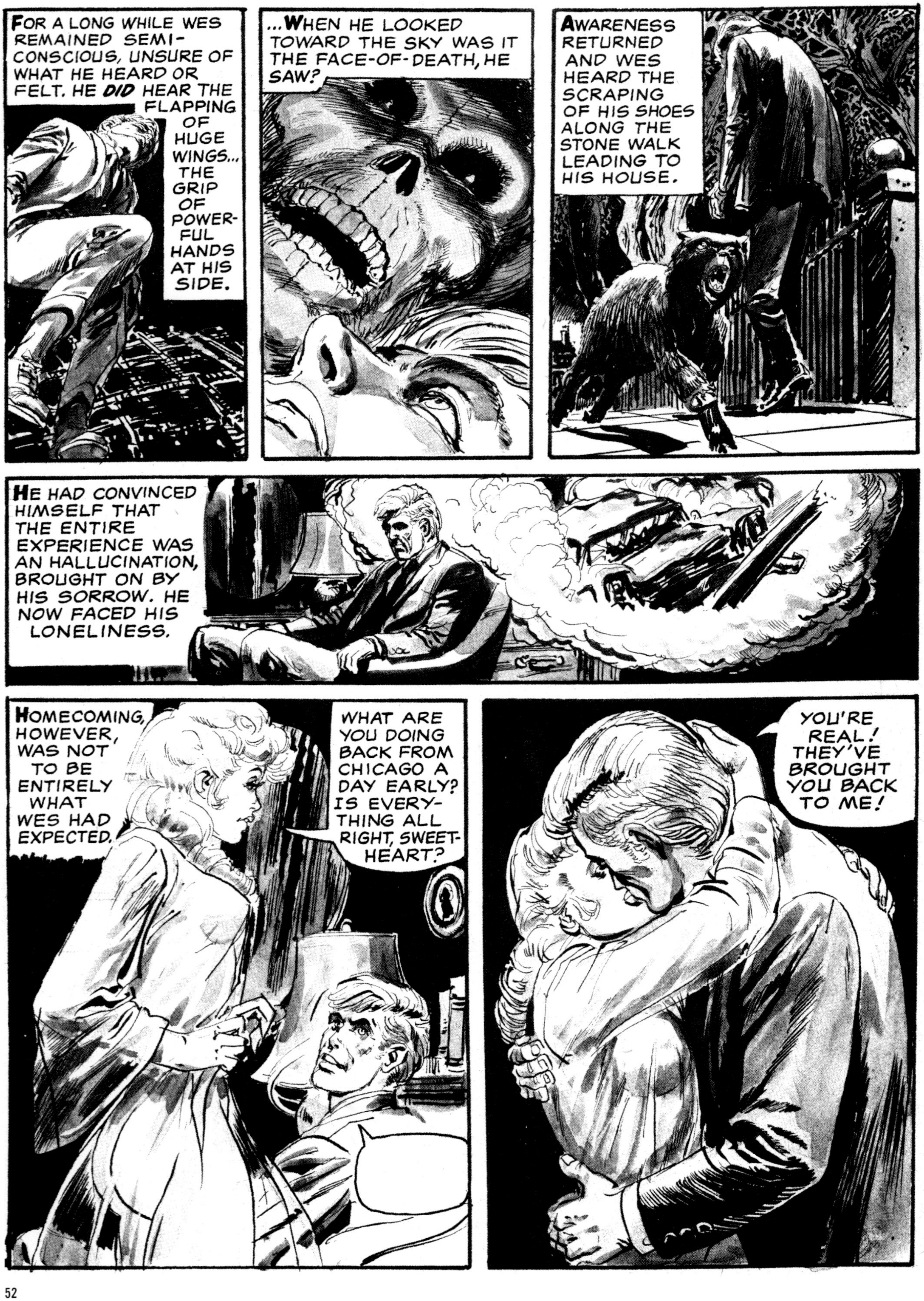
FOR A LONG WHILE WES REMAINED SEMI-CONSCIOUS, UNSURE OF WHAT HE HEARD OR FELT. HE DID HEAR THE FLAPPING OF HUGE WINGS... THE GRIP OF POWERFUL HANDS AT HIS SIDE.
...WHEN HE LOOKED TOWARD THE SKY WAS IT THE FACE-OF-DEATH, HE SAW?
AWARENESS RETURNED AND WES HEARD THE SCRAPING OF HIS SHOES ALONG THE STONE WALK LEADING TO HIS HOUSE.
HE HAD CONVINCED HIMSELF THAT THE ENTIRE EXPERIENCE WAS AN HALLUCINATION, BROUGHT ON BY HIS SORROW. HE NOW FACED HIS LONELINESS.
HOMECOMING, HOWEVER, WAS NOT TO BE ENTIRELY WHAT WES HAD EXPECTED.
WHAT ARE YOU DOING BACK FROM CHICAGO A DAY EARLY? IS EVERYTHING ALL RIGHT, SWEETHEART?
YOU'RE REAL! THEY'VE BROUGHT YOU BACK TO ME!

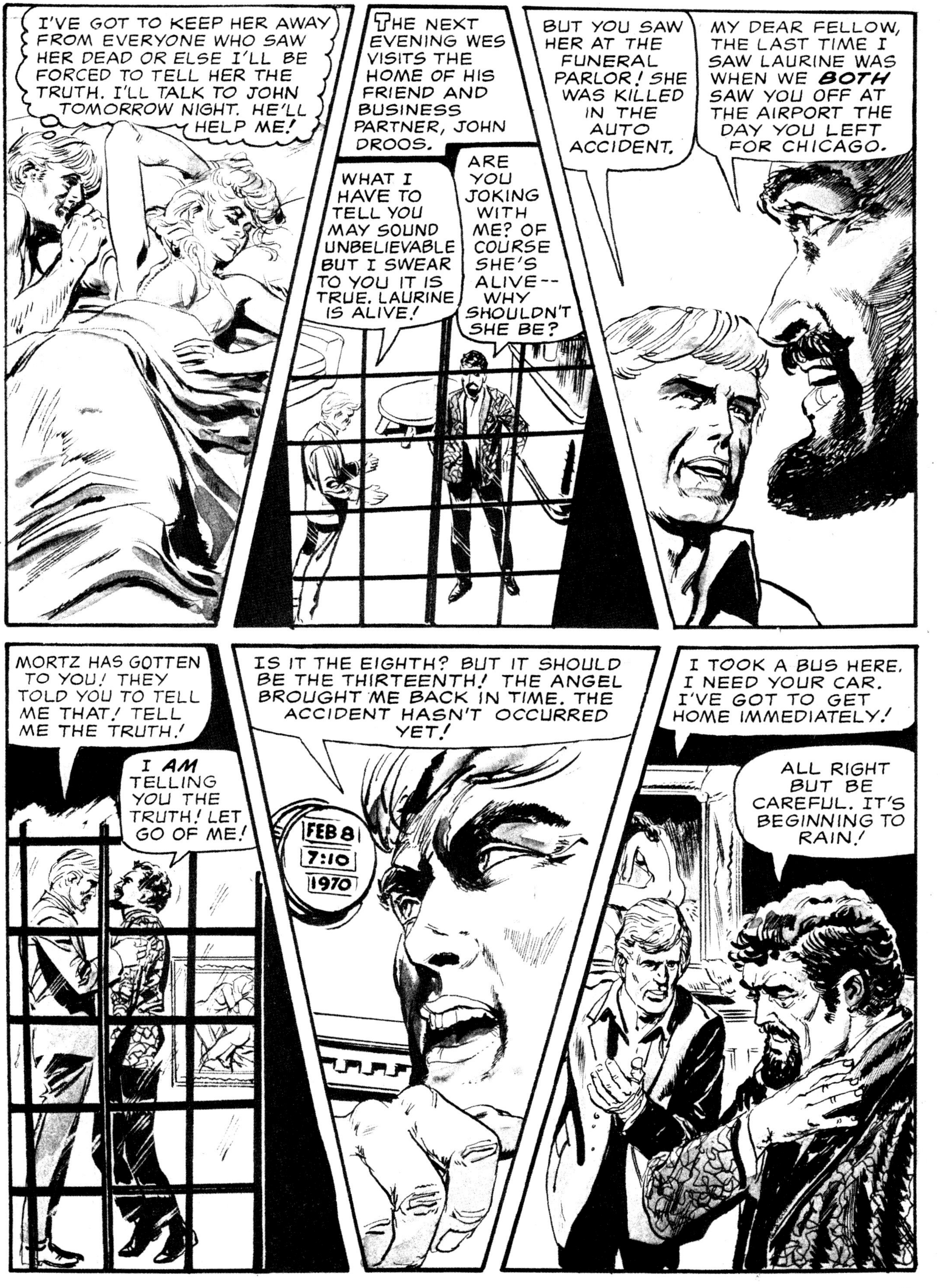
I'VE GOT TO KEEP HER AWAY FROM EVERYONE WHO SAW HER DEAD OR ELSE I'LL BE FORCED TO TELL HER THE TRUTH. I'LL TALK TO JOHN TOMORROW NIGHT. HE'LL HELP ME!
THE NEXT EVENING WES VISITS THE HOME OF HIS FRIEND AND BUSINESS PARTNER, JOHN DROOS.
WHAT I HAVE TO TELL YOU MAY SOUND UNBELIEVABLE BUT I SWEAR TO YOU IT IS TRUE. LAURINE IS ALIVE!
ARE YOU JOKING WITH ME? OF COURSE SHE'S ALIVE-- WHY SHOULDN'T SHE BE?
BUT YOU SAW HER AT THE FUNERAL PARLOR! SHE WAS KILLED IN THE AUTO ACCIDENT.
MY DEAR FELLOW, THE LAST TIME I SAW LAURINE WAS WHEN WE BOTH SAW YOU OFF AT THE AIRPORT THE DAY YOU LEFT FOR CHICAGO.
MORTZ HAS GOTTEN TO YOU! THEY TOLD YOU TO TELL ME THAT! TELL ME THE TRUTH!
I AM TELLING YOU THE TRUTH! LET GO OF ME!
IS IT THE EIGHTH? BUT IT SHOULD BE THE THIRTEENTH! THE ANGEL BROUGHT ME BACK IN TIME. THE ACCIDENT HASN'T OCCURRED YET!
FEB 8
7:10
1970
I TOOK A BUS HERE. I NEED YOUR CAR. I'VE GOT TO GET HOME IMMEDIATELY!
ALL RIGHT BUT BE CAREFUL. IT'S BEGINNING TO RAIN!

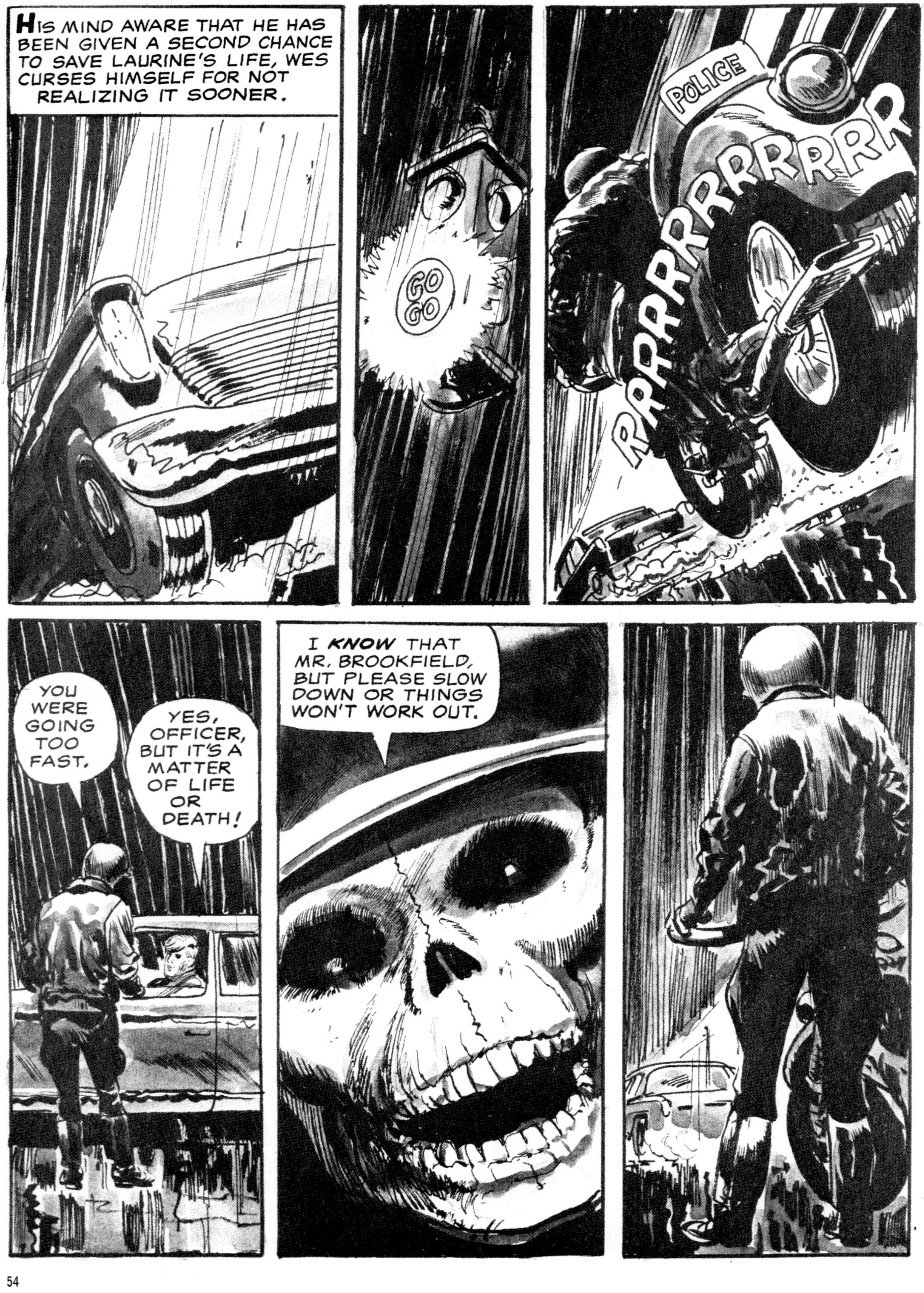
HIS MIND AWARE THAT HE HAS BEEN GIVEN A SECOND CHANCE TO SAVE LAURINE'S LIFE, WES CURSES HIMSELF FOR NOT REALIZING IT SOONER.
GO GO
POLICE
RRRRRRRRRRRRRRR
YOU WERE GOING TOO FAST.
YES, OFFICER, BUT IT'S A MATTER OF LIFE OR DEATH!
I KNOW THAT MR. BROOKFIELD, BUT PLEASE SLOW DOWN OR THINGS WON'T WORK OUT.

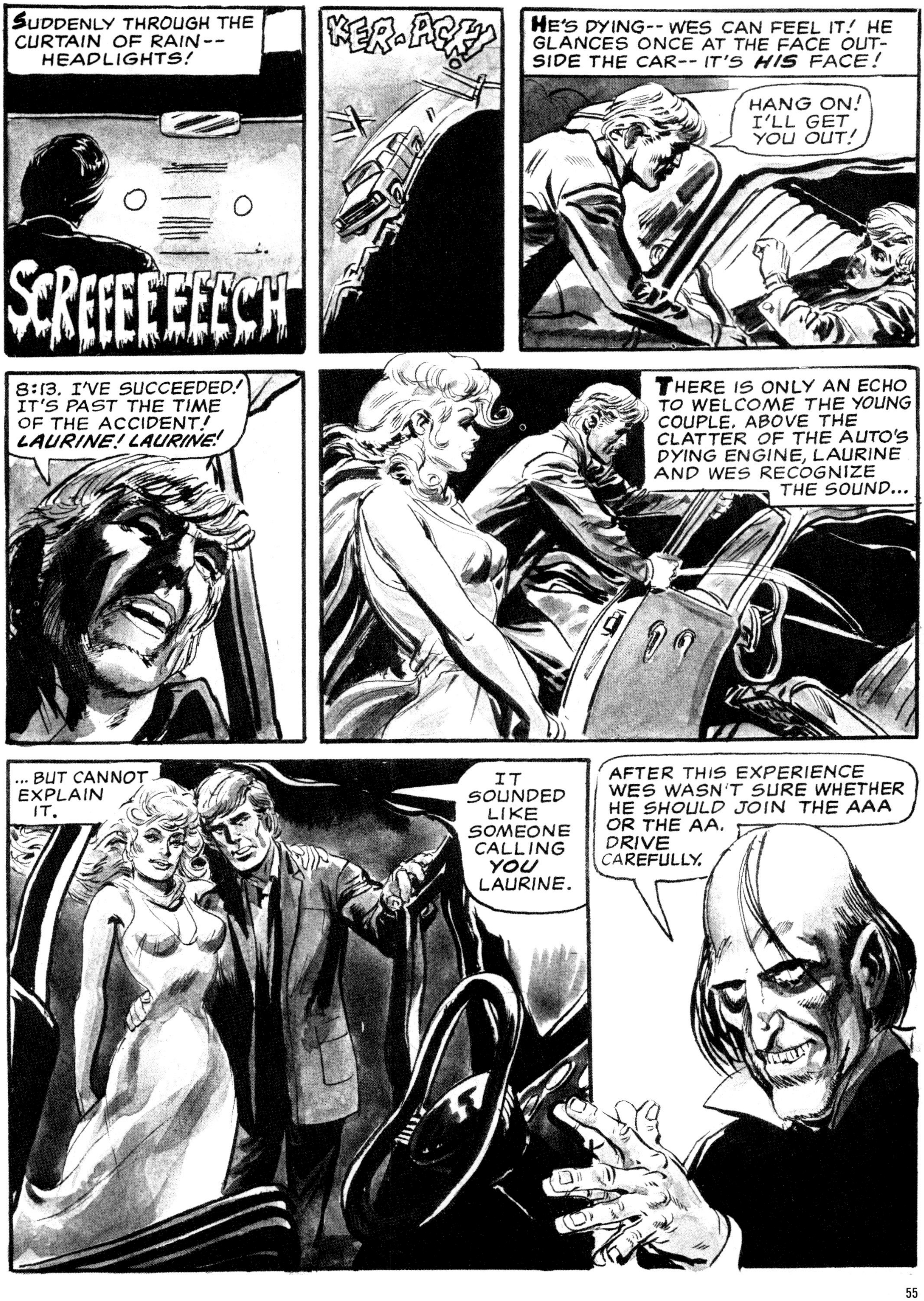
SUDDENLY THROUGH THE CURTAIN OF RAIN-- HEADLIGHTS!
SCREEEEEEECH
KER-ACK!
HE'S DYING-- WES CAN FEEL IT! HE GLANCES ONCE AT THE FACE OUTSIDE THE CAR-- IT'S HIS FACE!
HANG ON! I'LL GET YOU OUT!
8:13. I'VE SUCCEEDED! IT'S PAST THE TIME OF THE ACCIDENT! LAURINE! LAURINE!
THERE IS ONLY AN ECHO TO WELCOME THE YOUNG COUPLE. ABOVE THE CLATTER OF THE AUTO'S DYING ENGINE, LAURINE AND WES RECOGNIZE THE SOUND...
...BUT CANNOT EXPLAIN IT.
IT SOUNDED LIKE SOMEONE CALLING YOU LAURINE.
AFTER THIS EXPERIENCE WES WASN'T SURE WHETHER HE SHOULD JOIN THE AAA OR THE AA. DRIVE CAREFULLY.

THE CREEPY FAN CLUB!

Hardly a week goes by that we don't get a letter from someone who says he plans to become an illustrator. Many of them send us samples of their work, which then appear on this page. (Though, as you can see, none did this time around!)

Though many of them will surely make it, some will probably drift into other professions. That's what happened to Pat Boyette. For a while. Aren't you glad he finally drifted back in the right direction?

PAT BOYETTE— HILLBILLY MAKES GOOD

Pat Boyette sold his first one-panel cartoon at the age of ten. How could this brilliant young man, after such a successful beginning, possibly have failed to become one of America's leading humorists? It was simple, says Pat, he never sold another one.

Numbed by the realization that he was a "one-joke child," Pat turned to broadcasting and for twenty-six weeks played the son of a fictional radio family whose only topic of conversation for all those weeks was the merits of "hot spurs chili." It was a dull, but very compatable family. Until the problem of "with beans or without beans" became a big issue.

About the time a Crayola was able to fill in the gaps in Pat's first moustache, he became a hillbilly disc jockey. With great enthusiasm he entered the world of geetars, cards and letters and cowboy boots.

Then came his big opportunity. He was given a chance to work with Charlie Plumb —who was already famous for his comic strip "Ella Cinders"—on a new western comic strip. It didn't take Pat long to get shed of his geetars and cowboy boots. The cards and letters, he says, are still coming in.

The western strip went very well. Until the day Charlie decided it would be fun to have the hero, Captain

PAT BOYETTE got his first moustache from a box of Crayolas. But he swears this one's real.

Flame, attacked by five thousand screaming redskins. Now, Pat calculated that allowing only three feathers per Indian would give him fifteen thousand feathers to draw. He decided it was time he got back into show business.

Sufficiently out of focus now, Pat turned to television and news broadcasting. Somehow he was able to pull himself from the turmoil of makeup (with Crayolas?), lights, and the signing of three or four autographs to write and direct three theatrical motion pictures. These were horror movies, carefully designed to send chills up the spines of distributors and backers and to bring agonizing spasms of laughter from the audiences at all the dramatic climaxes. It was all very stimulating, if not financially rewarding, though. And it filled Pat with the warm awareness that perhaps he was more than just a one-joke child after all.

Today Pat lives in Texas on the road to the LBJ Ranch. He says that, while the excitement of a dashing to and fro news corps is gone (he doesn't miss them, they never bought any souvenirs from him anyway), the aroma of barbeque is still an important highlight of the local odor.

Comics? Oh, well—when Pat suddenly realized he was too immature to attent the

current movies, and too mature to be intellectually profound, he advanced into the wonderful world of pictures. And here he intends to stay. Because it's only here that all problems can be easily solved and all endings can be even gruesomely happy.

He never leaves Texas and doesn't expect he ever will. Some Texans are funny that way. Pat thinks all of **us** should go on down and join him.

MORE POETRY

Rod McKuen move over! In the last several months, our fan club mail has been bubbling over with budding poets. Joseph Westbrook of New Orleans is the latest. His says this is his first venture into poetry and he thinks it's fun. And after all, Shakespeare started that way!

CASTLE OF THE COUNT
by Joseph Westbrook

Here on the moors
  his castle stands,
Casting its eye on the
  surrounding lands.
Encircled by darkness,
  encased in gloom,
In an atmosphere of
  certain doom.
Its threshold rises
  from murky fog,
A footbridge crosses
  the forbidden bog.
A medieval door from
  days of old,
Hides horrible tales,
  as yet untold.
The door creaks open,
  with a will of its own,
Perhaps the wind,
  yet it has not blown.
The once great hallway,
  now covered with dust,
Drapes and hangings
  thick with must,
From bygone days,
  a great velvet chair,
And, but for it,
  the hall is bare.
A great marble staircase,
  the color of rose,
Up, up, unaware the front
  door will close.
You now see tracks in the
  deep, gray dust,
Heading upward, not down,

as you know they must.
Now a great barren hall.
  Just a red carpet on the
  floor.
Reminding you of blood
  stretching to the door.
Continue you do, you must,
  and when you draw near,
For the very first time,
  your heart knows fear.
The room is vast,
  you are here at last,
The room is shrouded,
  completely in black.
Against the smooth wall,
  your courage now does
  lack.
A magnificent chandelier
  hangs from the ceiling,
The room is bright, but you
can't shake that feeling.
Now you see a coffin
  at the end of the room.
The lid slowly rises,
  hits the floor with a boom.
He stands there before you
  with great majesty,
You suddenly know struggle
  will fruitless be.
He slowly approaches,
  his lips start to part,
He's an undead creature,
  and you are his sport.
And now you scream,
  again you scream,
This can't be real,
  it must be a dream.
But then you stop.
  You reconcile.
As he kisses your neck,
  you begin to smile.
You now realize your
  one purpose in life.
For now you are
  Count Dracula's wife.

STILL MORE!

L. Alain Portnoff, of Portland, Ore., is another poet among us. In his letter, he also said that horror poems are fun to write. Fun to read, too!

FOR THE SOULS: THEY THAT WALK THE NIGHT
by L. Alain Portnoff

I passed along
  the dusk-waved shore,
With glowing eyes,
  burned with lore,
To rest beneath
  the flaring moon,
And to drink of secrets

that should ne'er h'been
Born . . .
Mine heart reposed
with a lonely flame,
That smouldered forever
with a neophyte's blame;
That I had fled from mine
burning lair,
To set on a shore,
the waves to stare . . .
But 'twas my anguish
that cloaked my mind,
That mine blazing eyes
met a form reclined:
Reposed atop a cyclopean
tor,
Like those spectres
that haunt Tir-Na-Norg . . .
"Speak to my mind
of legend, old one,"
Thus I did him bade;
But he spoke not of
mortal worlds,
But of those beyond
the grave . . .
"They walk the night,"
he spake agape,
"In sinister, sombre
radiance;
"And not all that man
has done or will do,
"Can force them return
to their graves."
"Who be they who walk
by night"? demanded
the tongue
Of mine.
"They who've lost their
earthly souls:
lost with the devil
Of time.
And he said no more
to my pale shade;
no more to my
Ghostly visage;
For he came to walk and do
naght else; walk to Death's
Road on . . .
And now I sleep in death's
black soul
That the devils of time
have trod; and cold
Be my spirit, a'twixt
the Dark and the Light,
For now it, too, walks alone;
stalking along the night.

SCIENCE FICTION DEPT.

This story, from David Martin, of Wichita Falls, Texas, begins with these ominous words . . .

"For months the old man had tortured him . . . goaded him into taking the job. 'But you have go to take it! You are the only man for the job!' "

And with those words of prologue, we begin . . .

ROCKETS TO TERROR
by David Martin

Haily Garren, an astronaut at Garren Space Center, had been involved in a fantastic accident a month ago. An accident that had changed his life!

He was in the chemical lab when it happened. A chemical explosion in a test tube rocked the whole building. When the two M.P.'s recovered him from the wreckage, though, it was found that he was in perfect condition. Not a scratch. Scientists across the country were puzzled. Further investigation revealed that his body was unaffected by heat. The hottest flame didn't seem to bother him in the least. This was discovered one day when Haily lit a cigarette and flames spread all over his body. But when the flames were put out, he wasn't burned. And he couldn't remember feeling any pain as his body was enveloped in flames.

He became top man at Garren Space Center, and it was not long after the Center itself was named in his honor. Through all of this, one man hated and despised him—Edward Warren. Warren had been top man at the Center until he was forced into retirement because of his age. He had always been jealous of the strong young astronaut's fame and glory, but had been careful not to show it. In fact, he encouraged Haily to become involved in missions that the younger man might not otherwise have taken. Secretly, Edward was hoping to put the astronaut's life in danger.

And now, as Haily stands before him, he agrees to take on this last dangerous assignment. This is to be Warren's last project before retirement, and he has vowed that it will also be young Hailey's last mission, too.

A week later, the mission is about to begin. Officially, Hailey has been chosen for this one because he is the only man able to withstand the intense heat of deep space. It will be a dramatic mission, and newsmen by the hundreds are on hand to watch as Hailey waves his final goodbye and enters the huge ship.

Soon the monstrous roar of twinpowered neutro-sonic engines fills the air and within minutes Hailey is orbiting the earth on his way toward Mars—the red planet.

Edward Warren enters the control room and takes over control of the rocket. He hesitates. Should he do it? What if he were to be caught? He could always put the blame on the complex machinery. That's it! There can always be a malfunction! He would do it.

He pushed the red button market "Destruct."

There is a blinding flash on the view screen. "Sir! We've lost contact with Hailey!" one of the engineers screams. Warren strides out of the building and gets into his car, a satisfied smile on his face. He drives straight to his cabin in the mountains.

That night, as he sits in the quiet, savoring his victory, he hears a noise outside. He picks up a flashlight and goes out to investigate. In the sky above, he sees what seems to be a flaming meteor streaking earthward. He goes to the spot where it appears to land. There he finds a huge piece of metal glowing white-hot. Can it be?

Yes! It is! A fragment of the destroyed space ship. He walks slowly back into the house. Suddenly, he stops in his tracks. There in front of him are footprints that aren't his own. They seem burned into the carpet.

Then he hears a noise in the next room. He walks toward it.

Several screams and a choking sound follow.

An hour later, two policemen stand over the body of Edward Warren. "Think this has anything to do with that hunk of meteorite we saw a while back"? says one. "I doubt it," replies the other. "But look at those marks on his neck. They're not strangulation marks. They look more to me like radiation burns!"

LOVE STORY

If you're the sort who likes sentimental stories, you'll really dig this one written by Allan Feldman of Bayside, New York. I'll have to admit I was a bit choked up after I read it.

I LOVE HER
by Allan Feldman

Digging deep into the soggy soil, my shovel finally hit something solid. Loosing the coffin from the clutches of the grave, that feeling of coldness once more swept through my entire body. I began to sweat as I opened the dead man's box. Thoroughly drenched now, my vision was reduced to a blur. Though sweating like a mad man, my hands and feet were just as cold as those belonging to the dead man I was now staring at.

This cemetery was a horrible place to be on a night like this. It had rained earlier and the ground was still wet. The slightest sound, magnified in the eerie stillness, could send a cold chill up any man's spine and scare the living daylights out of anyone. The tombstones were lined up like so many marching soldiers.

I wouldn't dare bring my wife to a place like this. At this very moment, she's undoubtedly lying comfortably at home in front of the TV set. Just as I had left her.

Suddenly a siren sounded. Quickly I fell to the ground alongside my silent newfound friend. In a minute they passed. My foot fell asleep. How can any person rest comfortably in such a crampbed box? How can people be so inhuman as to bury their loved ones in the cold earth that is crawling with worms and insects?

The police would never understand what I was doing. That is why I was forced to work shrouded in darkness. No one would understand.

Creeping out of the grave, it was difficult to carry the body with me. Somehow I managed to drag him behind me. He made quite a burdensome bundle in my arms. But it was worth it.

After about 20 minutes of walking through alleys and down deserted streets, I finally reached my house. The light on the porch was on. It gave me my first chance to get a good look at our new house guest. He was a handsome man, no more than 30 or 40 years old. I have always been careful in choosing my wife's friends.

Life is a hard road and death is a cold and lonely state of being. I could not allow my wife to suffer through either of them.

It took me a while before I could reach my key to open the door. I heard the sound of the TV set. This would be a perfect time to introduce the new arrival to my wife, and let him get acquainted with the others. Tomorrow I would be at work all day and everyone will keep each other company.

"Honey, I'm home!"

CLOSING MESSAGE

To end this month's round, here is a word or two from "out there" sent to us by Mark Aubry of Los Angeles.

MESSAGE FROM THE DEAD
by Mark Aubry

Do you believe in ghosts? Well, I'm here to say these things exist. Your best friend may be a ghoul, vampire or ghost. Have you noticed any of them acting strangely lately? Cousin Eerie is a ghoul. Vampirella is a vampire. No one knows just what Uncle Creepy is, though.

If you ever meet up with these people, or any others like them, I can help. Just call on me. By the way, my name is Death. I think you know where you can find me.

THIS IS YOUR BIG CHANCE!
If you've always wanted to see your art, your writing, your picture in print, let us have it. Then look for it here. Send it to: CREEPY FAN CLUB

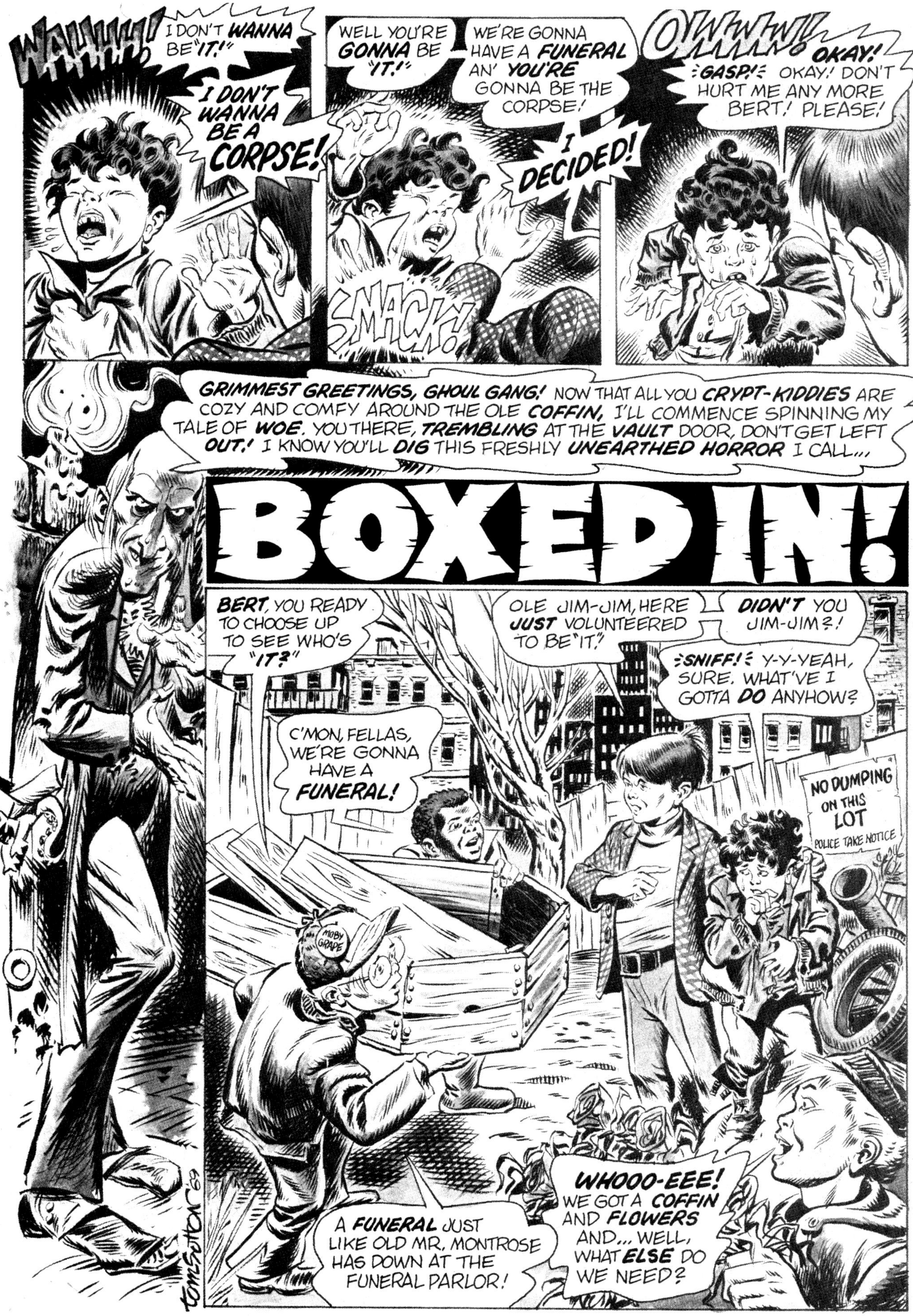
WAHHH!
I DON'T WANNA BE "IT!"
I DON'T WANNA BE A CORPSE!
WELL YOU'RE GONNA BE "IT!"
WE'RE GONNA HAVE A FUNERAL AN' YOU'RE GONNA BE THE CORPSE!
I DECIDED!
SMACK!
OWWW!
OKAY!
GASP! OKAY! DON'T HURT ME ANY MORE BERT! PLEASE!
GRIMMEST GREETINGS, GHOUL GANG! NOW THAT ALL YOU CRYPT-KIDDIES ARE COZY AND COMFY AROUND THE OLE COFFIN, I'LL COMMENCE SPINNING MY TALE OF WOE. YOU THERE, TREMBLING AT THE VAULT DOOR, DON'T GET LEFT OUT! I KNOW YOU'LL DIG THIS FRESHLY UNEARTHED HORROR I CALL...
BOXED IN!
BERT, YOU READY TO CHOOSE UP TO SEE WHO'S "IT?"
OLE JIM-JIM, HERE JUST VOLUNTEERED TO BE "IT."
DIDN'T YOU JIM-JIM?!
SNIFF! Y-Y-YEAH, SURE. WHAT'VE I GOTTA DO ANYHOW?
C'MON, FELLAS, WE'RE GONNA HAVE A FUNERAL!
NO DUMPING ON THIS LOT
POLICE TAKE NOTICE
MOBY GRAPE
WHOOO-EEE! WE GOT A COFFIN AND FLOWERS AND... WELL, WHAT ELSE DO WE NEED?
A FUNERAL JUST LIKE OLD MR. MONTROSE HAS DOWN AT THE FUNERAL PARLOR!
TOM SUTTON '69

ART AND STORY BY TOM SUTTON

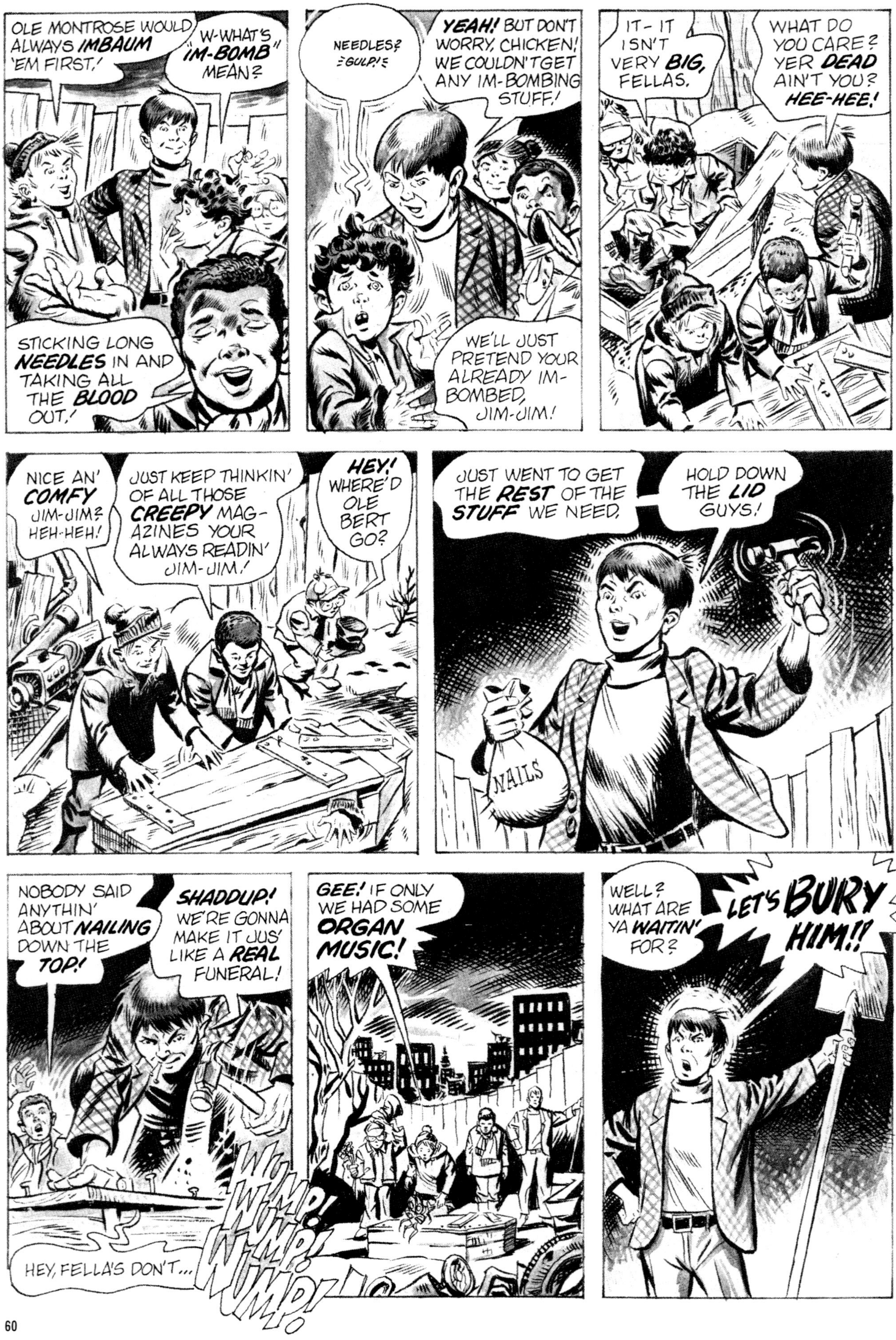
OLE MONTROSE WOULD ALWAYS IMBAUM 'EM FIRST.'
W-WHAT'S "IM-BOMB" MEAN?
STICKING LONG NEEDLES IN AND TAKING ALL THE BLOOD OUT.'
NEEDLES? GULP!
YEAH! BUT DON'T WORRY, CHICKEN! WE COULDN'T GET ANY IM-BOMBING STUFF!
WE'LL JUST PRETEND YOUR ALREADY IM-BOMBED, JIM-JIM!
IT- IT ISN'T VERY BIG, FELLAS.
WHAT DO YOU CARE? YER DEAD AIN'T YOU? HEE-HEE!
NICE AN' COMFY JIM-JIM? HEH-HEH!
JUST KEEP THINKIN' OF ALL THOSE CREEPY MAG-AZINES YOUR ALWAYS READIN' JIM-JIM!
HEY! WHERE'D OLE BERT GO?
JUST WENT TO GET THE REST OF THE STUFF WE NEED.
HOLD DOWN THE LID GUYS!
NAILS
NOBODY SAID ANYTHIN' ABOUT NAILING DOWN THE TOP!
SHADDUP! WE'RE GONNA MAKE IT JUS' LIKE A REAL FUNERAL!
HEY, FELLA'S DON'T...
WUMP! WUMP! WUMP!
GEE! IF ONLY WE HAD SOME ORGAN MUSIC!
WELL? WHAT ARE YA WAITIN' FOR?
LET'S BURY HIM!!

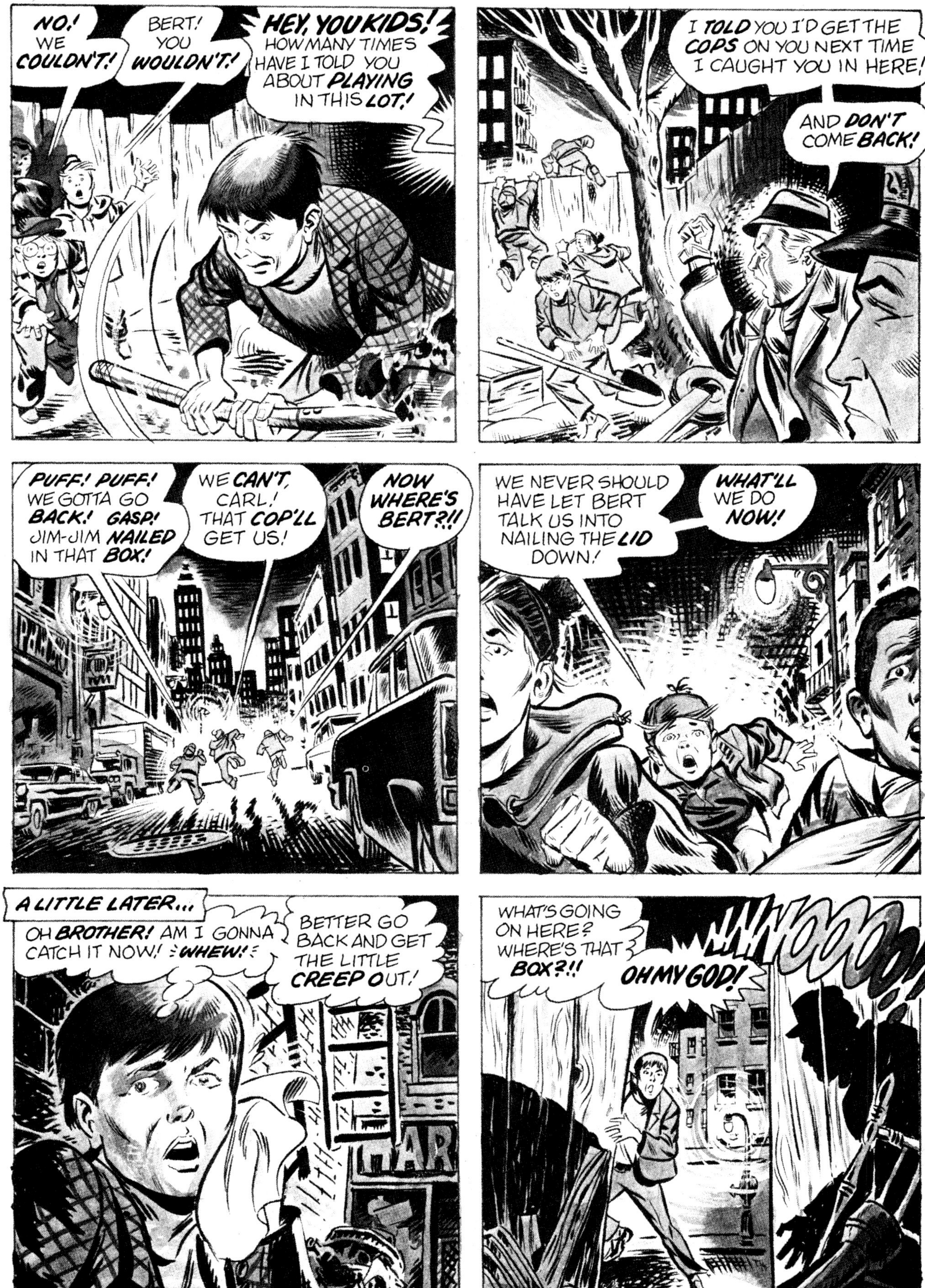

NO! WE COULDN'T!
BERT! YOU WOULDN'T!
HEY, YOU KIDS! HOW MANY TIMES HAVE I TOLD YOU ABOUT PLAYING IN THIS LOT!
I TOLD YOU I'D GET THE COPS ON YOU NEXT TIME I CAUGHT YOU IN HERE!
AND DON'T COME BACK!
PUFF! PUFF! WE GOTTA GO BACK! GASP! JIM-JIM NAILED IN THAT BOX!
WE CAN'T, CARL! THAT COP'LL GET US!
NOW WHERE'S BERT?!!
WE NEVER SHOULD HAVE LET BERT TALK US INTO NAILING THE LID DOWN!
WHAT'LL WE DO NOW!
A LITTLE LATER...
OH BROTHER! AM I GONNA CATCH IT NOW! WHEW!
BETTER GO BACK AND GET THE LITTLE CREEP OUT!
WHAT'S GOING ON HERE? WHERE'S THAT BOX?!!
OH MY GOD!
NNOOOO!!

"THEY'RE GRINDING...

...ALL THE JUNK FROM THE LOT...

...INTO THAT *TRUCK!*

GAG!

ULP!!

CITY TRASH DISPOSAL UNIT 7

GRRRUNNGG-GRRRINNNG-GRUMGLL-GRUNNGG-GRRUNNG

THANK HEAVENS NOBODY'S HOME! GOTTA THINK OF SOME WAY OUTTA THIS!

GASP!

PANT!

PANT!

GUESS THEY COULDN'T HEAR THE LITTLE CREEP'S YELLS OVER THE CHOKE! GRINDING!

UGH!

B-BERT! LET ME *OUT!* BERT! PLEASSSE!

JIM-JIM!!

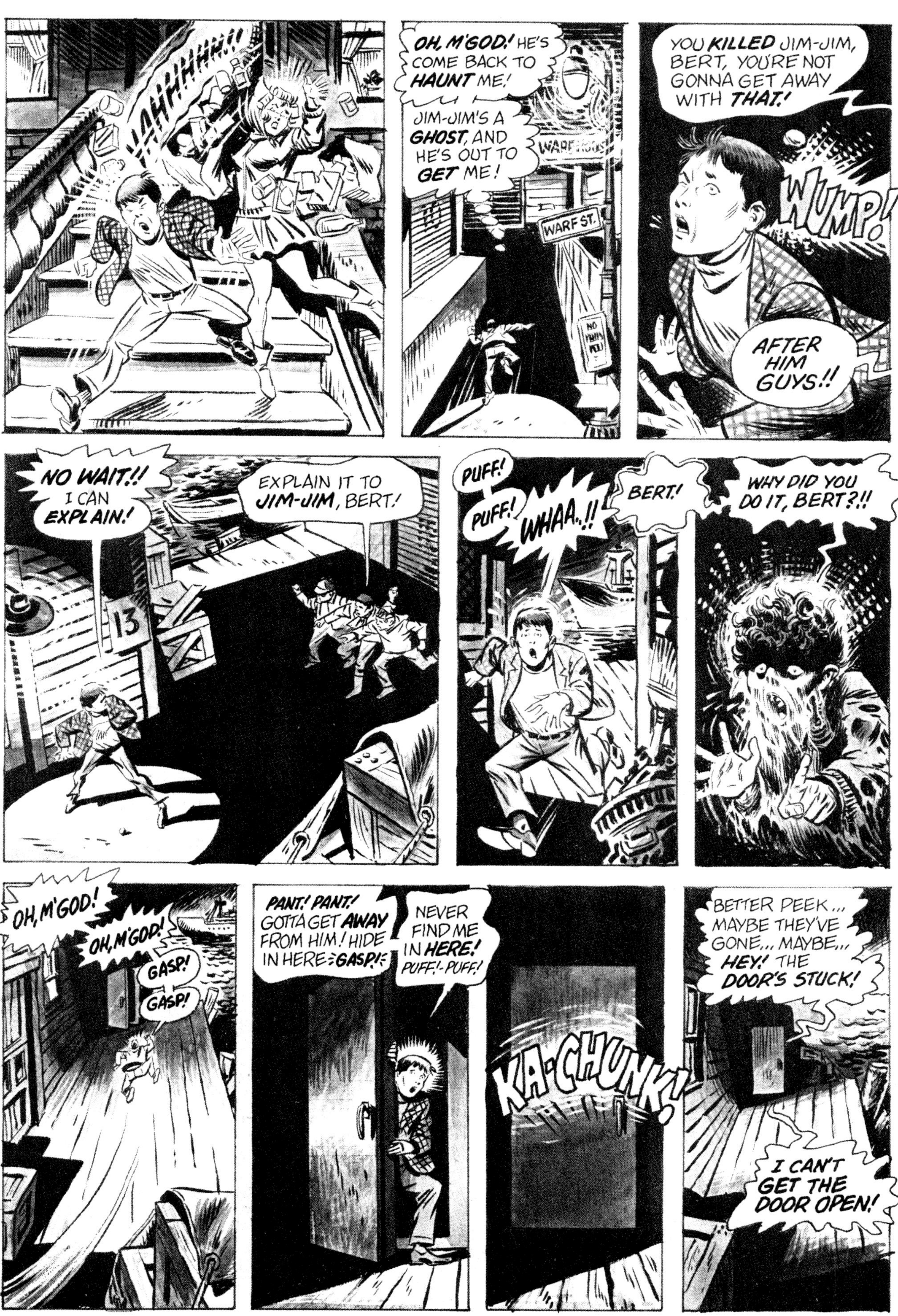
YAHHHHHH!!!
OH, M'GOD! HE'S COME BACK TO HAUNT ME!
JIM-JIM'S A GHOST, AND HE'S OUT TO GET ME!
WARF ST.
YOU KILLED JIM-JIM, BERT, YOU'RE NOT GONNA GET AWAY WITH THAT!
WUMP!
AFTER HIM GUYS!!
NO WAIT!! I CAN EXPLAIN!
EXPLAIN IT TO JIM-JIM, BERT!
13
PUFF!
PUFF!
WHAA..!!
BERT!
WHY DID YOU DO IT, BERT?!!
OH, M'GOD!
OH, M'GOD!
GASP!
GASP!
PANT! PANT! GOTTA GET AWAY FROM HIM! HIDE IN HERE -GASP!-
NEVER FIND ME IN HERE! PUFF!-PUFF!
KA-CHUNK!
BETTER PEEK... MAYBE THEY'VE GONE... MAYBE... HEY! THE DOOR'S STUCK!
I CAN'T GET THE DOOR OPEN!

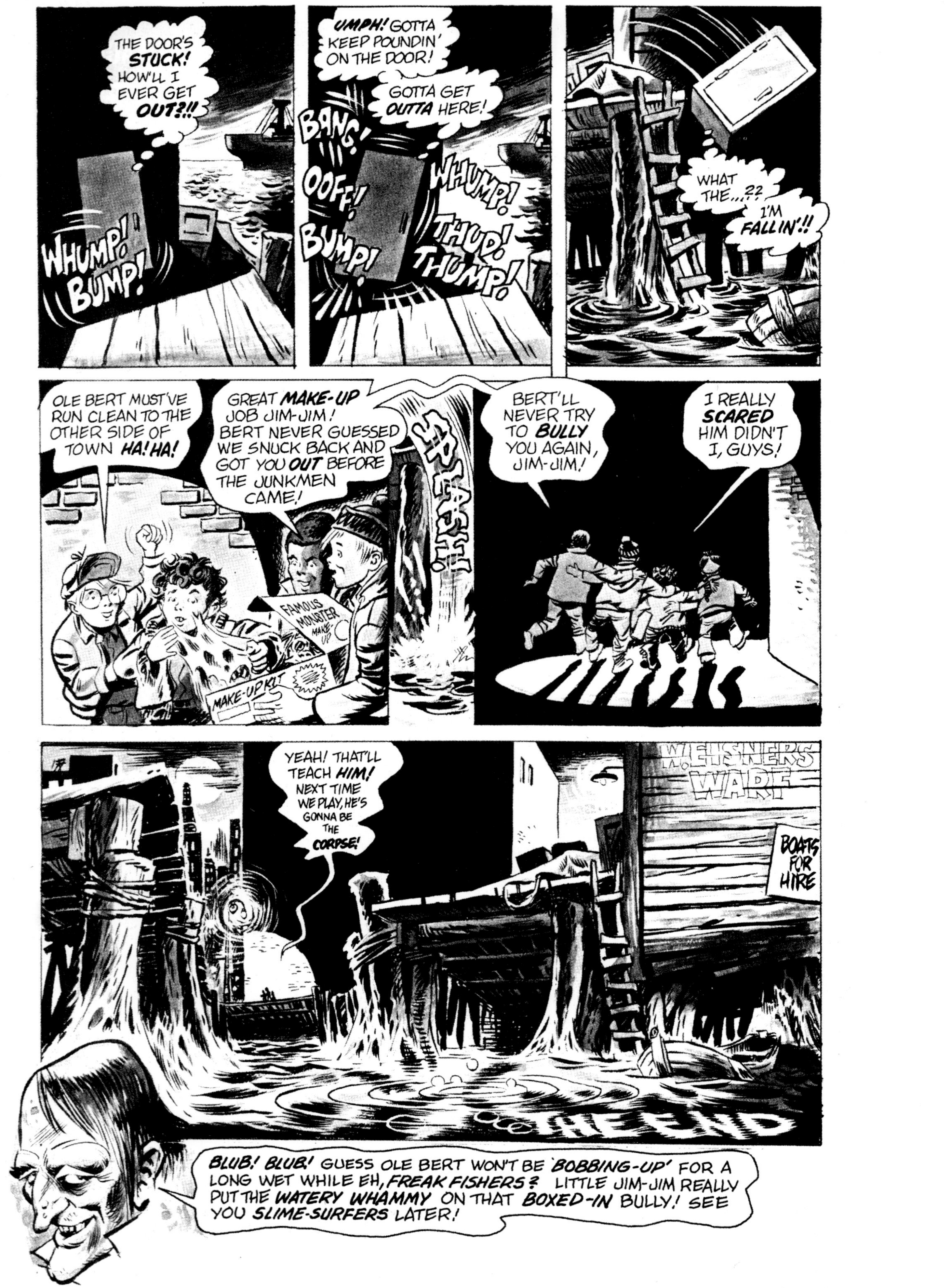

THE DOOR'S STUCK! HOW'LL I EVER GET OUT?!!
WHUMP! BUMP!
UMPH! GOTTA KEEP POUNDIN' ON THE DOOR!
GOTTA GET OUTTA HERE!
BANG! OOFF! BUMP!
WHUMP! THUD! THUMP!
WHAT THE...??
I'M FALLIN'!!
OLE BERT MUST'VE RUN CLEAN TO THE OTHER SIDE OF TOWN HA! HA!
GREAT MAKE-UP JOB JIM-JIM! BERT NEVER GUESSED WE SNUCK BACK AND GOT YOU OUT BEFORE THE JUNKMEN CAME!
FAMOUS MONSTER MAKE-UP
MAKE-UP KIT
SPLASH!
BERT'LL NEVER TRY TO BULLY YOU AGAIN, JIM-JIM!
I REALLY SCARED HIM DIDN'T I, GUYS!
YEAH! THAT'LL TEACH HIM! NEXT TIME WE PLAY, HE'S GONNA BE THE CORPSE!
W. EISNER'S WARF
BOATS FOR HIRE
THE END
BLUB! BLUB! GUESS OLE BERT WON'T BE 'BOBBING-UP' FOR A LONG WET WHILE EH, FREAK FISHERS? LITTLE JIM-JIM REALLY PUT THE WATERY WHAMMY ON THAT BOXED-IN BULLY! SEE YOU SLIME-SURFERS LATER!

500 HORROR PHOTOS IN EACH EXCITING MAGAZINE — ONLY 70¢ EACH!

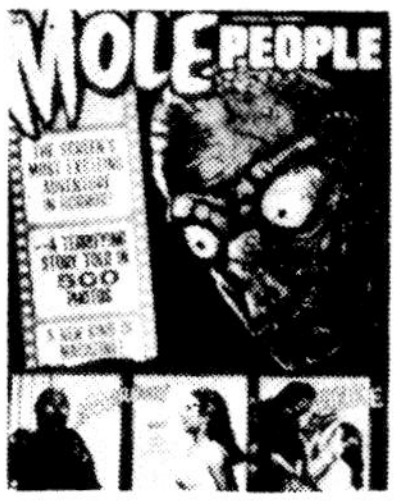
MOLE PEOPLE

EXCITING, COMPLETE FILM STORY! FAMOUS, eerie film, as made by Universal Pictures. Savage civilization of a million years ago, full of blood-lust and eerie agony. FOR THE BIG STORY, with 500 pictures, mail 70¢ plus 15¢ for postage and handling.

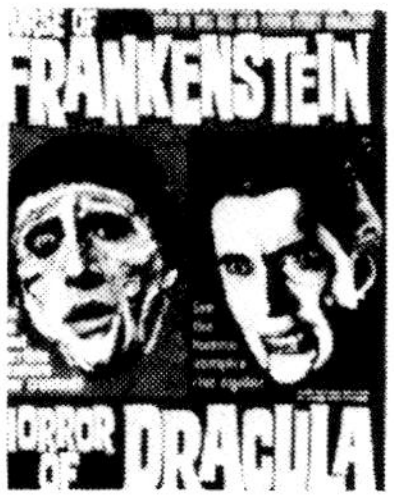
FRANKENSTEIN
HORROR OF DRACULA

DOUBLE - TROUBLE in a two-for-the money combination of Frankenstein and the Vampire. Complete individual Monster and Horror stories plus 500 exciting gruesome photos. Now at last, in one combination to thrill you. Only 70¢ plus 15¢ for postage and handling.

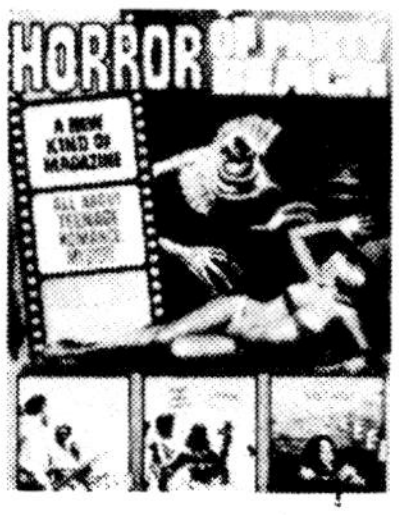
HORROR OF PARTY BEACH

HORROR OF PARTY BEACH! Just teenagers twisting at the beach . . . and then all terror breaks loose. Horrible sea-monsters crawl from the water. What happens at Party Beach will make your hair stand on end. 500 photos, only 70¢ plus 15¢ for postage and handling.

ANTS—

REAL ONES, too...

In Their Own ANT FARM!

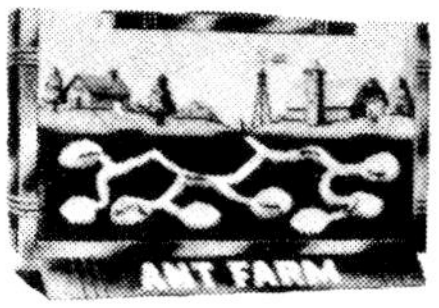
ANT FARM

YOU WON'T BELIEVE your eyes when you see this fascinating ANT FARM! An army of WORKER ANTS dig tunnels, build rooms, carry loads uphill. FEEDER ANTS see that everyone eats well. NURSEMAID ANTS take care of the baby ants. Show your ANT FARM to your science teacher, friends, classmates. Mother, father and visitors will share in this amazing nature study. Shows exactly how ant hills get that way, and what happens. Strongly built of clear plastic. Convenient 6" x 9" size. Ant Farm includes farm decorations. stand, soil and sandbar. Only $2.98 complete. We pay postage. LIVE DELIVERY GUARANTEED.

$2.98

WHO ELSE WANTS A LIVE MONKEY

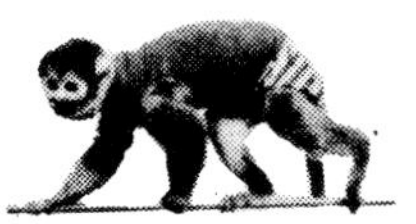

YOU can be the happiest boy on your block with your own LIVE BABY SQUIRREL MONKEY! Have loads of fun and enjoyment. Train your monkey to do tricks, come to you for food, petting and playing. These delightful monkeys grow to almost 12 inches tall and are golden in color. Slender, short-haired. Each monkey has a heart-shaped face, appealing eyes and grows a tail almost 14 inches long.

No problem caring for or feeding your monkey. It eats lettuce, carrots, fruits, almost anything you eat. Affectionate and loveable, almost a "member of the family" soon after you get your pet. Dress it in cute costumes put on shows; you and your monkey can be real pals. LIVE DELIVERY GUARANTEED! Send $19.95 in check or money order. Pay delivery man small express charges for safe delivery to you.

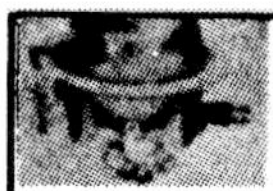

Watch the MIRACLE of BIRTH Before Your Very Eyes

NURSE embryos from egg to chick! You can do it with amazing DOME MIRACLE hatcher. A poultry farm in miniature. Set includes bulb, egg holder, thermometer & full instructions. 6" tall, 7¼" wide. Holds proper heat, humidity to hatch chicks, ducks, pheasants, quail, etc. Fascinating and educational. Only $3.98, plus 25c postage, handling.

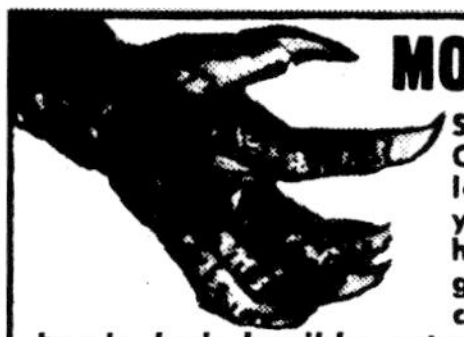

MONSTER HAND!

SANTA NEVER SAW CLAWS like these! Fierce-looking monster hands you wear over your hands, like grotesque gloves. Tucked inside a coat or shirtsleeve, the hands look horribly natural. Have fun with your own Monster Hands. $1.50 for 1 hand; $3.00 for the pair. Add 25c per hand for postage, handling.

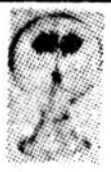

PERPETUAL MOTION SOLAR ENGINE—Energy from Light Makes it Work!

HERE IS a mysterious instrument, with flags inside that can turn forever. All by themselves. No electricity, no motor, no batteries. Works the same way sun's energy causes ocean tides. All you need is light from any source to make flags turn. Brighter the light, faster the action. A fascinating, scientific device. Only $1.75, plus 25c postage, handling.

MONSTER FLY!

- OVER 8 INCHES LONG!
- STICKS TO ANYTHING!
- CUTE AND HORRIBLE!
- SCARES EVERYONE!

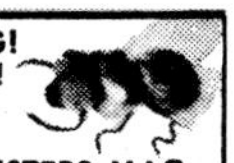

Developed especially for FAMOUS MONSTERS MAGAZINE readers. Realistic, 8" size; with transparent wings, blazing red eyes, flexible black legs, green body, black veins. Suction cup in nose lets MONSTER FLY stick to anything, any time, anywhere. Want to create a Monster Sensation. Get your MONSTER FLY right away. Only $1.75 plus 25c for shipping & handling.

HUMAN SKELETON!

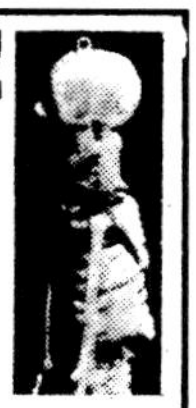

IS THAT WHAT WE LOOK LIKE INSIDE???

YOU CAN'T walk around in your bones. Next best thing is this HUMAN SKELETON. A foot-high model, scaled from a 6' man; made of BONE WHITE flexible Superlon. No gluing, no painting: parts snap together. Free Anatomy Chart included. Only $1.25 plus 25c shipping & handling.

SILENT DOG WHISTLE

MYSTERIOUS . . . Only DOGS Can Hear It!

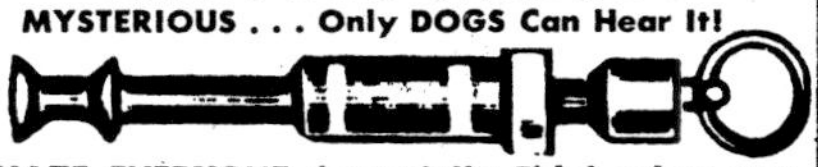

AMAZE EVERYONE (especially Fido) when you blow THE SILENT DOG WHISTLE. Supersonic features makes it silent to human ears, but your dog will respond instantly. Only $1.00 plus 25¢ for postage & handling.

MAD DOCTOR HYPODERMIC NEEDLE!

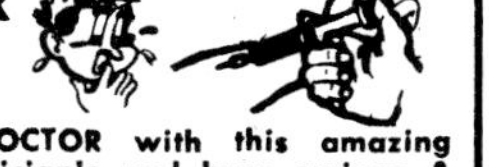

YOU'RE THE MAD DOCTOR with this amazing duplicate of your physician's real hypo syringe & needle. Take "blood" tests. Give "shots." Fool everyone. Blunt, harmless needle seems to enter vein but actually rides back into syringe. Tube seems to fill with victim's blood. Red liquid is built in to this safe, funny gadget. Only $1.50 plus 25c for postage & handling.

MONSTER FOOT!

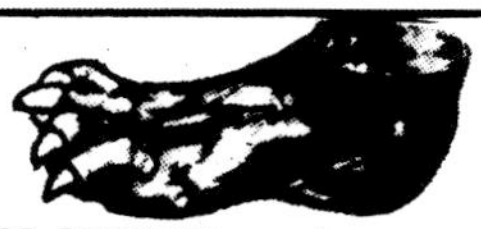

PUT YOUR BEST FOOT FORWARD wearing a grotesque MONSTER FOOT! Create a riot shuffling along, monster-style. Giant size; made of long-lasting latex rubber; riotously painted. Goes on over shoe. Full price only $1.50 each foot; $3.00 for complete pair, plus 25c per foot for postage.

GRUESOME SKULL CUP!

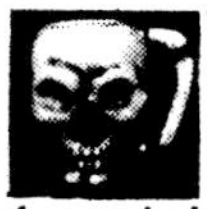

THIS MAY KILL your thirst, but think of the fun as you die laughing, drinking from your SKULL CUP. Perfect copy of a real skull. Made of fine ceramic, with bone-like handle. Order several and have a good time with your pals. Makes milk and anything else taste better. 1 SKULL MUG . . . $1.75, plus 35c postage & handling. Set of 3, only $3.50, plus 50c for postage.

A COMPLETE SET OF 5 DIFFERENT MONSTER RINGS

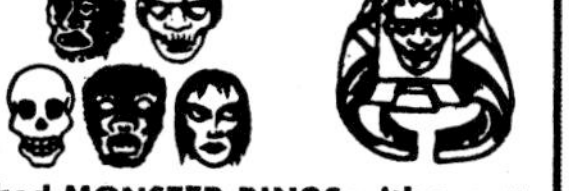

Bright silver-finished MONSTER RINGS with secret flicker designs that jump and change position with each movement of the hand! You get ALL 5 MONSTER RINGS (WEREWOLF, FRANKENSTEIN, VAMPIRE SKULL & MUMMY) for only 50¢ plus 25¢ postage & handling.

HORRIBLE HERMAN — DARES YOU TO LOOK IN THE BOX!

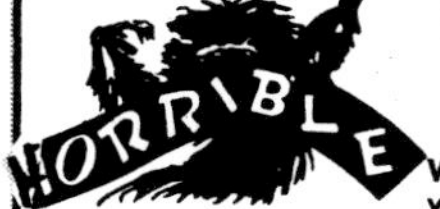
HORRIBLE

WHAT'S IN THE BOX? Only you know and you can dare anyone to look. It's HORRIBLE HERMAN, the hideous ASIATIC INSECT. Has a fur body, scaly head, red eyes, twin tendrils. You can also make him lift his head and move around. Only 50¢ plus 10¢ for postage.

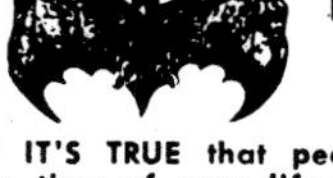

DRACULA'S OWN "RUBBER BAT"

IF IT'S TRUE that people fear bats, you'll have the time of your life when they walk in on this one. DRACULA's OWN RUBBER BAT, so real it may even scare you. Suction cup lets you put him on wall, closets, fences, beds, etc. Then have fun driving folks crazy with fear. Only 75c, plus 25c for postage and handling.

NEW! "IRON-ON" MONSTERS

The newest way to "Monsterize" your shirts, T-shirts, sweat shirts, jeans, jackets, notebooks—anything! Each "Iron-On Monster" is in FULL COLOR, 11" high and 7½" long, and completely washable. Can be pressed onto cotton, linen or woolen materials. Just place heated iron on top of the monster design—and it automatically transfers onto your shirt, jacket, etc. Any two "monsters"—only $1.00.

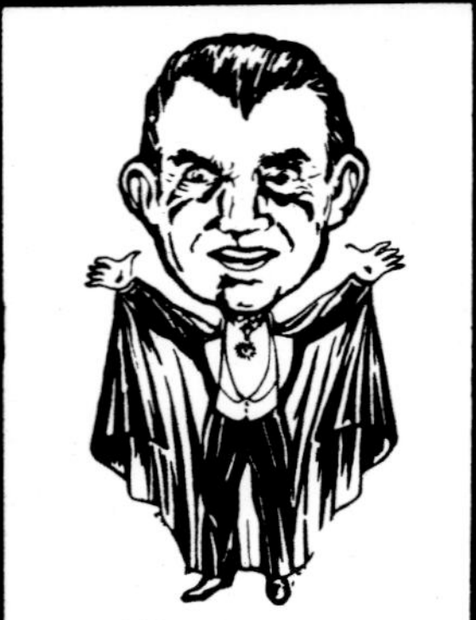
DRACULA

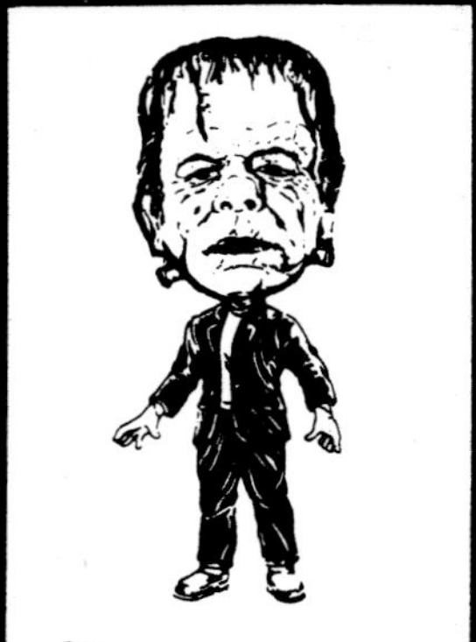
FRANKENSTEIN

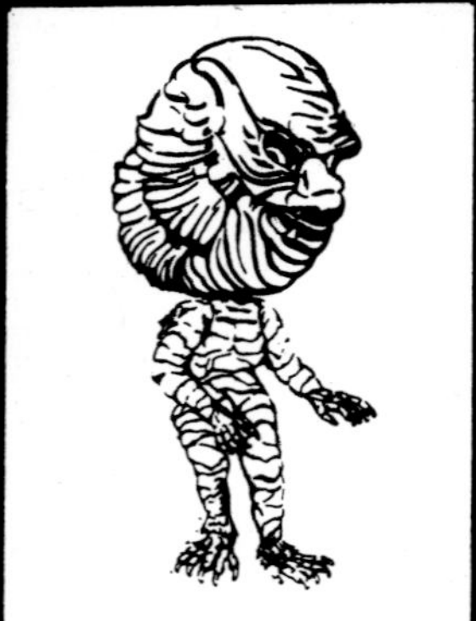
CREATURE

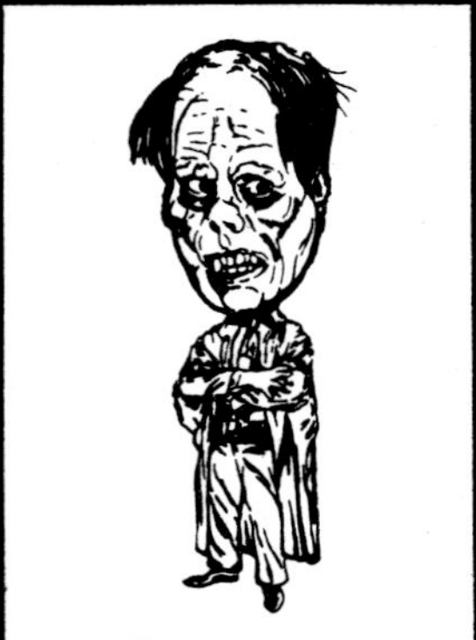
PHANTOM

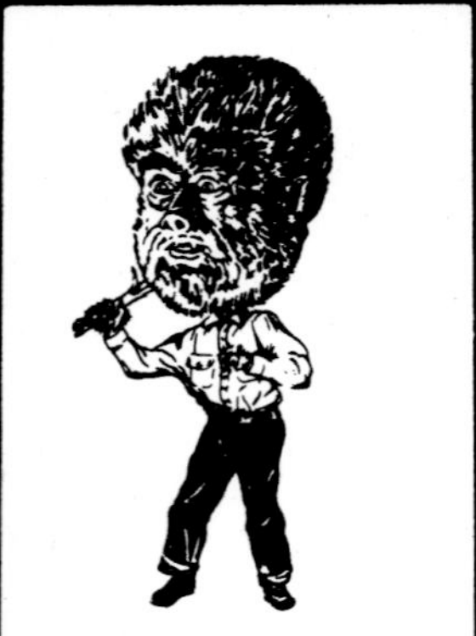
WOLF MAN

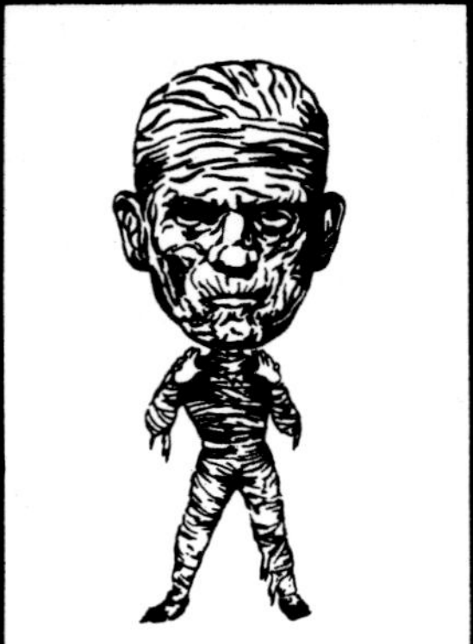
MUMMY

YOUR CHOICE OF ANY 2 "IRON-ON MONSTERS" ONLY $1.00 PLUS 25c POSTAGE & HANDLING.

TREMENDOUS 10 FOOT BALLOONS

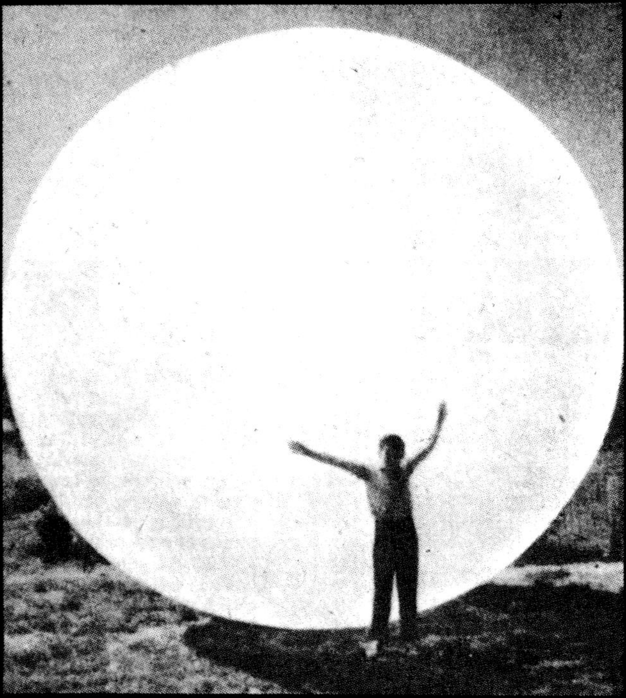

MONSTER-SIZE balloons! Special Air Force surplus balloon made of genuine Neoprene Rubber for extra durability. Never used. Out of this world (it even looks like a flying saucer when inflated!). Think of the fun you'll have: Draw a picture of a monster on the balloon with luminous paint and inflate it at night. Wow! The neighbors will run screaming! Special limited offer sold at fraction of cost. $2.95 plus 50c postage and handling

MANY USES . . . absolutely terrific for attracting attention and crowds at Sports Events, Openings, Fairs, Roadside Stands, Gas Stations, etc. ● Great fun at School Games, to promote and advertise Special Events.

Name...

Address..

City.......................................Zone...................

State..

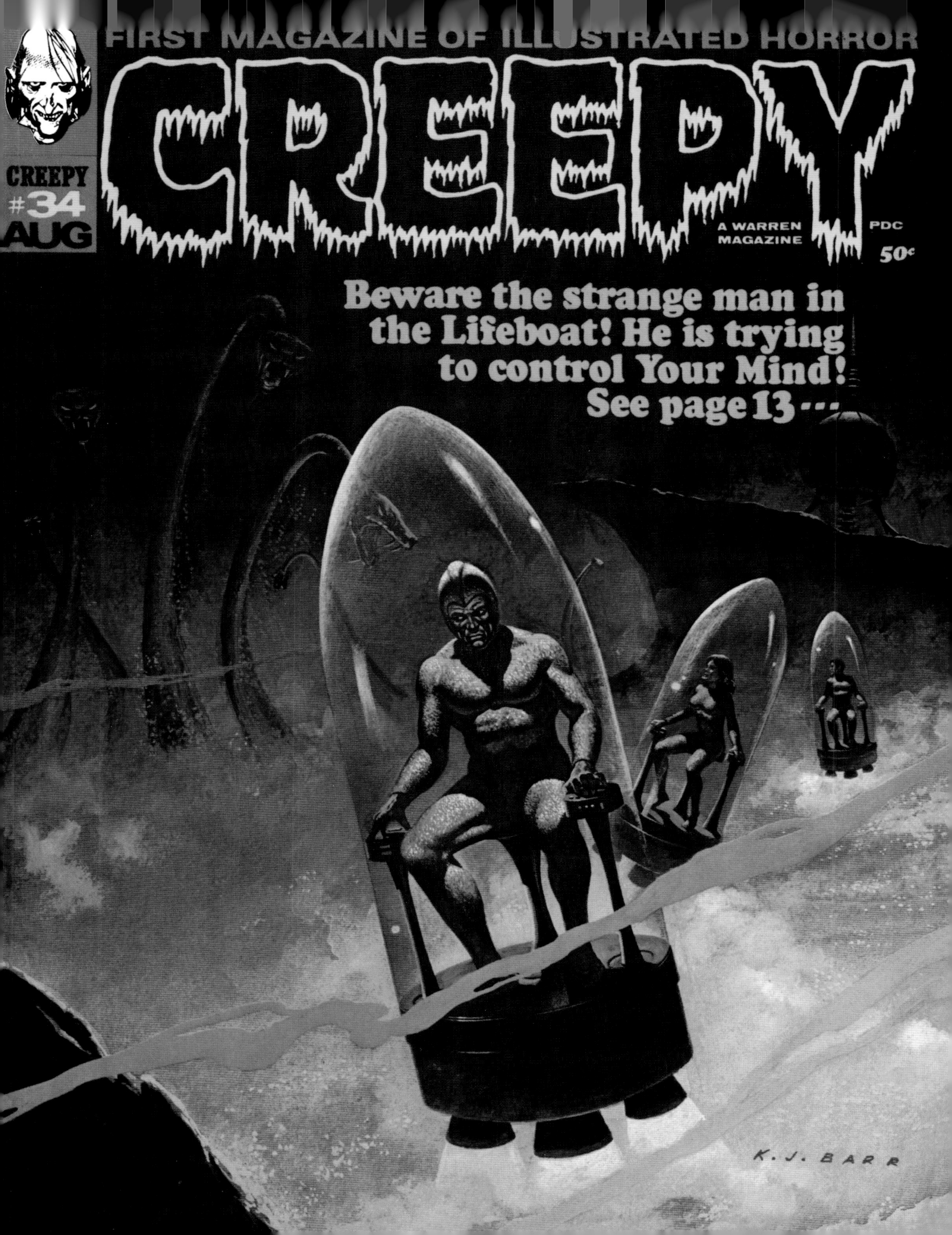
FIRST MAGAZINE OF ILLUSTRATED HORROR
CREEPY
CREEPY
#34
AUG
A WARREN MAGAZINE
PDC
50¢
Beware the strange man in the Lifeboat! He is trying to control Your Mind!
See page 13 ---
K.J. BARR

CREEPY'S LOATHSOME LORE

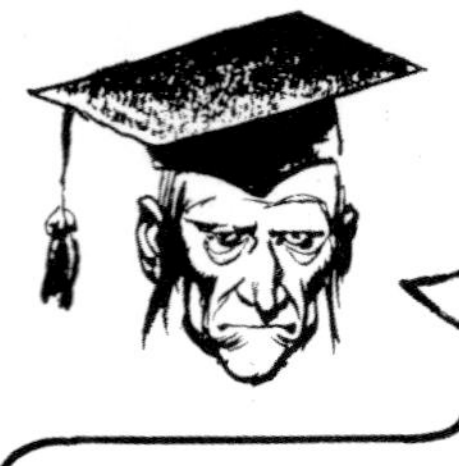

SWIMMING HAZILY THROUGH THE MURKILY MYSTICAL DEPTHS OF INDIA'S OCEAN FOLKLORE IS ***THE MAKARA*** --- SOMETIMES APPEARING TO MORTALS AS PART CROCODILE, DOLPHIN, SHARK AND ELEPHANT, THIS HINDOO MYTHOLOGICAL GOD IS SAID TO KEEP THE INDIAN OCEAN WARM. OTHER AUTHORITIES SAY THE ***MAKARA*** ITSELF DOESN'T KEEP INDIAN OCEAN WARM. THEY CLAIM SEETHING VOLCANIC MOLTEN LAVA **FISSURES** ON THE OCEAN FLOOR WHERE THE **MAKARA** MAKES ITS HOME PROVIDE THE WEIRD WATERS' WARMTH. IF YOU MEET THE ***HOT-BLOODED MAKARA***, SWIM FAR AWAY BEFORE THIS ***FABULOUS FISH FRYS YOU!***

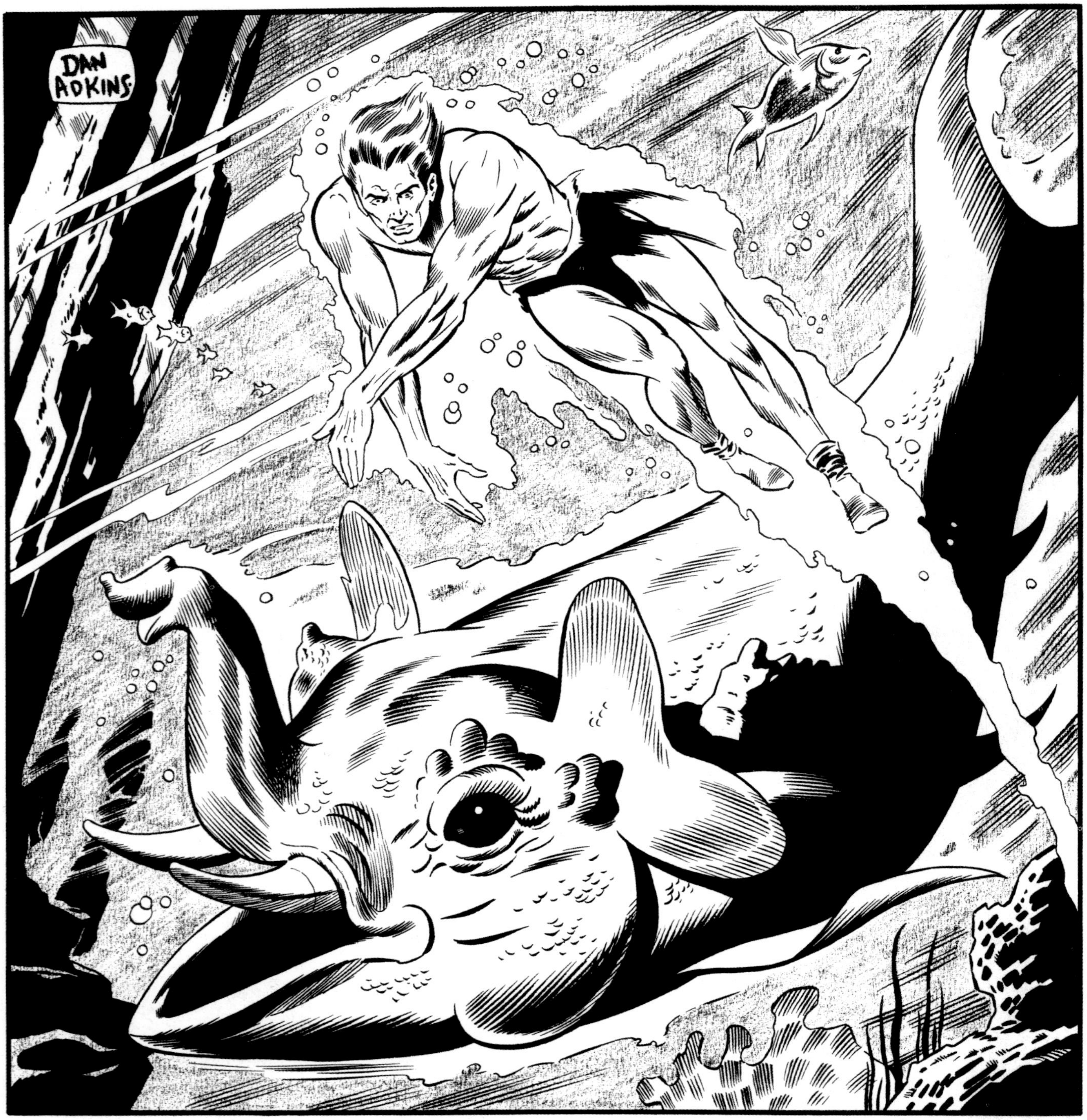
DAN ADKINS

CREEPY

NO. 34

EDITOR AND PUBLISHER: JAMES WARREN **COVER:** KEN BARR

ARTISTS THIS ISSUE: KEN BARR, JOHN G. FANTUCCIO, KEN KELLEY, SYD SHORES, JACK SPARLING, DON VAUGHN, TONY WILLIAMSUNE

WRITERS THIS ISSUE: AL HEWETSON, BILL PARENTE, ROBERT ROSEN, BUDDY SAUNDERS

NO, NO

THE SWORD WORKS THEM NO GREAT ILL! AND I SMOTHER, FOR THEY BURN THE VERY AIR!

CONTENTS

COME NOW MR. PAUL! AREN'T YOU GIVING UP THE CHANCE OF A LIFETIME!

WILDEST DREAMS!
EEEEEEEEEEEAHH!

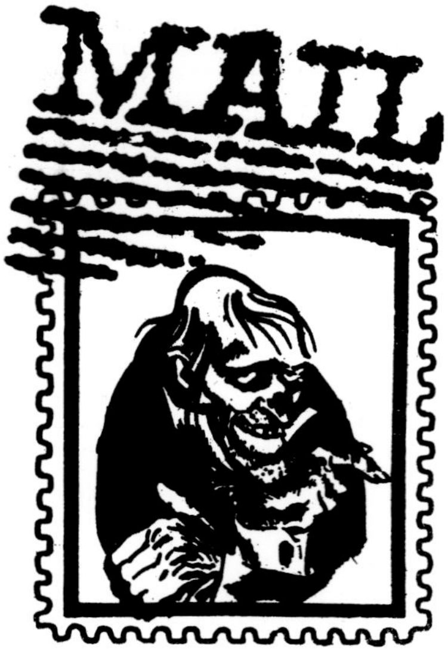
MAIL

"The pinnacle for all that is or ever has been . . ."

Issue #32 was pretty good. Frank Frazetta's cover was excellent, and Neal Adams' art on "The Rock God" was just great. But "V.A.M.P.I.R.E." was awful. "Death is a Lonely Place" was my favorite story. I never imagined a vampire could be so human.

BILL WHITAKER
Wheeling, W. Va.

It's one of the first rules of Vampirism, my boy. If you don't seem human, you'll get hungry.

I've seen and read **CREEPY** since the very beginning and I know very well what you are capable of. I thought that once the old staff left, **CREEPY** would die. But you pulled yourself up with talents like Tom Sutton and Neal Adams. And the return of Mr. Frazetta proved you could reach your top standards again. Issue #32 was just beautiful. Professional all the way. Frazetta and Adams were both up to their highest standards. Why don't you have more of the classic stories by Edgar Allen Poe and H. P. Lovecraft? I think, too, that the great Ray Bradbury would look good between your covers.

ERIC PEDERSON
Kensington, Md.

Thought we couldn't do it, eh? Old soliders never die, Ric. I've been around death for so long, I know how to avoid it.

Issue #32 was pretty good. Frank Frazetta's cover was excellent, and Neal Adams' art on "The Rock God" was just great. But "V.A.M.P.I.R.E." was awful. "Death is a Lonely Place" was my favorite story. I never imagined a vampire could be so human.

BILL WHITAKER
Wheeling, W. Va.

It's one of the first rules of Vampirism, my boy. If you don't seem human, you'll get hungry.

I've seen and read **CREEPY** since the very beginning and I know very well what you are capable of. I thought that once the old staff left, **CREEPY** would die. But you pulled yourself up with talents like Tom Sutton and Neal Adams. And the return of Mr. Frazetta proved you could reach your top standards again. Issue #32 was just beautiful. Professional all the way. Frazetta and Adams were both up to their highest standards. Why don't you have more of the classic stories by Edgar Allen Poe and H. P. Lovecraft? I think, too, that the great Ray Bradbury would look good between your covers.

ERIC PEDERSON
Kensington, Md.

Thought we couldn't do it, eh? Old soliders never die, Ric. I've been around death for so long, I know how to avoid it.

Not too long ago, a friend of mine, who also reads **CREEPY,** saw the latest edition of your mag. "Have you seen number 32? They sure have come a long way," he said. I have to agree. It took a lot of reprint issues, but you're finally back on top of the heap. The cover on issue #32 was the best I've seen in ages. It's one of Frank Frazetta's all-time best. It was only fitting that the story that went with it was just as great. I know you have your own staff of regulars, but when an old favorite like Neal Adams draws the best and longest story, he towers over the best of them. I read "Rock God" in a horror magazine not too long ago, and loved it then, also. "Death is a Lonely Place" showed that even a vampire has feelings—which was just the opposite of "V.A.M.P.I.R.E." That story finally shows that Tony Williamsune can put tones and added dimensions to his art.

I can't figure out why you call Ernie Colon "David StClair," when he signs the first panel as Ernie. Also, Tony Williamsune has more pen names than I can remember. Colon did an outstanding job on "A Wall of Privacy," and Mike Royer did a great job on "I, Executioner," which is why he's fast becoming one of my personal favorites. I liked all the stories in this issue, mainly because they were all new. And most had endings I couldn't guess. Keep up the good work. I'll bet old Cousin Eerie is turning in his grave over being stuck in third place after you and the second-place **VAMPIRELLA.**

WILLIAM SWEENEY
Weirton, W. Va.

I approve your choice of friends, Bill. You're obviously a pair of discriminating young men. Smart, too.

I don't want my first letter to your fine magazine to be a complaint, but it is. Not that I don't like your magazine—I think even **EERIE** is great. But I want to know why you're sticking Ernie Colon's name all over the place. First of all, in **EERIE** #26, on the Fan Fare page, you have a drawing supposedly from a fan who forgot to include his name. So how come at the bottom is the well-known Colon signature? Then in **CREEPY** #32, the story, "A Wall of Privacy," which is supposed to have been drawn by "David StClair," also contains Ernie Colon's signature. What goes on?

CHARLES KERNODLE
Memphis, Tenn.

What goes on, obviously, is Ernie Colon's signature. I've noticed it myself. I think Ernie has a press agent.

I used to like **EERIE** better, but lately, you've been getting better. But since becoming a fan of yours about a year ago, I'm finding it harder and harder to find your books. The best issue I've seen so far was #28. I think "The Doorway" was fantastic. I wish I had seen issue #30, though. Everyone was saying it was the coolest and the scariest. But I couldn't find a copy around here.

DENNIS O'KEEFE
Chicago, Ill.

Everything they said about #30 was the honest truth. You can order a copy from our back issue dept. And you can keep up with future issues by ordering a subscription.

"Rock God" was the best story ever published in any Warren Magazine. Harlan Ellison's script was certainly the best ever to grace the pages of **CREEPY.** Neal Adams' art was the best he's ever done, too. Even the lettering, by Ben Oda, was the best ever seen in a horror magazine. All this, coupled with a fantastically mysterious cover painted by Frank Frazetta supports my claim that "Rock God" will never be bettered by anything past, present or future. It's a shame, though. After all these years, **CREEPY** has been getting better with every issue. But now it's impossible to improve, for "Rock God" is the pinnacle for all that is or has ever been.

DAN WILDER
Jupiter, Fla.

When you're number one, Dan you try harder. Watch us! I think this may be the first time anyone has mentioned the lettering by Ben Oda. And it's about time! Ben has been with us since the beginning, and nobody deserves more praise. He's worked closely with more pros than anybody in the business and he's a favorite with all of them. We've been trying to get him to write a biography for the Fan Club page, but he's too busy to get all the facts together for us. But he will. And when he does, you're in for an exciting story. He works regularly with all the best people in the business from Milton Caniff to Neal Adams.

CREEPY #32 was without a doubt the best ever to hit the stands. "Rock God," by Harlan Ellison, was great along with the magnificent art by Neal Adams. The Frazetta cover was beyond mortal words of praise. Wasn't the same story also published in a new pulp magazine that specializes in tales of witchcraft and the supernatural? I hope "Rock God" marks the beginning of a new custom of giving short biographies with some of your stories. I liked the biography as much as the story. In your issue #9, you gave us a story by Eando Binder continuing the life story of Adam Link. This was great, and something I'd like to see much more of. Following up on novels by original writers, that is. The day after I bought that issue, a rock radio station, WMEX, in Boston had a weekend special on witches. I called the disc jockey on the phone and read him the article you had reprinted on the Fan Club page from The New York Times. (It was titled, "Late News

Item," and appeared on page 41.) He told the listening audience about the information I gave him, but he forgot to mention you, Unc. Looking over your competition, and I see you have nothing at all to worry about. Most of them are really gross. They're really downgrading the whole horror comics field. And their covers! Even your very poorest artists can outrank the best of them.

JOE VIGLIONE
Arlington, Mass.

I'm not too worried about the competition, Joe. It's The New York Times that bothers me!

Issue #32 was absolutely beautiful! Everything a ghoul could ask for. A Frazetta cover with no cover quips to quibble about. Less advertisements. Longer and better stories. Good artists. Great writers. And a really **loathsome** "loathsome Lore." Speaking of art, I really dig Billy Graham's art. I'll never forget the fantastic job he did on "Rhapsody in Red" in the second issue of **VAMPIRELLA.** I like the way he draws vampires. He really puts fury into his work. By the way, that was a perfectly pounding poem written by Michael Paumgardhen and Christopher Laube in the last ish.

JACK AGUGLIARO
Niagara Falls, N.Y.

As a long-time horror fan, I enjoy reading your magazine a lot. But let's face it, you're not up to par! First, the artists: Try to get Frazetta for covers, and maybe some inside work, too. Let's see more of Jeff Jones, Neal Adams, Berni Wrightson, Ralph Reese, Morrow, Crandall, Orlando, Ditko, Mastroserio; and less of Colon, Williamsune, Grandanetti, Stewart and others. Stories: Check them very carefully before you print them. And let us have more of the classics like "Dracula" and "Frankenstein." Covers: Cut out the margins. And words that blot out the picture. And don't put Creepy's picture in the upper left-hand corner. It just looks stupid. Inside: Make your stories gorier. Expand the Fan Club to two pages. Make the letters page longer. Instead of ads, give us another story in their place. These are only some of my ideas.

GERARD GREIS
North Olmstead, Ohio

I have an idea you haven't seen some of our recent issues. If you had, you'd know we've already taken a lot of your advice.

Your magazine has jumped into the lead again. And I must say, I'm really amazed at the quality of it. Frazetta's cover and Ellison's script and Neal's art started issue #32 with real blood. It was a real treat for one who had seen just tidbits for the past eleven issues. I've collected all your magazines since the second one. And in all that time have missed only five issues. But you have raised **CREEPY's** standard to a new high in bloody, gory, completely fantastic standards. The last issue was worth a lot more than the 50c cover price!

JOE SCOTT
Sauk Centre, Minn.

I don't know why you are so surprised, Joe. You had enough faith to stick with us all that time. Watch what we're going to do in issues coming up!

Good lord! When I saw your issue #32, I had to rub my eyes and tell myself I wasn't dreaming! If it weren't enough to have a cover by Frank Frazetta, you had to go and have Harlan Ellison write a story about it! And, on top of that, you had Neal Adams illustrate it! Wow! How much can you ask for? I am overwhelmed at this very serious attempt to restore **CREEPY** to its original level of quality. I've been watching your magazine since the first issue, and I realize you've seen some bad times. However, in the last several issues, there has been an obvious return to the original level of creativity. Don't stop now! We need you more than ever now that the rest of the industry seems to slowing down. You may not be able to have a Frazetta cover every time, nor all of your old artists back. But don't let that stop you from exploring new fields and reaching new heights. You're our only hope!

JOHN POUND
San Diego, Cal.

Issue #32 was, like every other issue of **CREEPY,** worth more than the price I paid. You should have Frank Frazetta do more covers, since your readers agree he's the best there is. Another great artist is Ernie Colon. He never fails to make chills run up my spine. I've noticed that many of your letters say you are slipping. I don't know if this is true. It's hard to imagine how you ever could have been better than you are now.

JEFF KADISH
South Windsor, Conn.

You wouldn't happen to be Ernie Colon's press agent, would you, Jeff?

Address your mail to DEAR UNCLE CREEPY

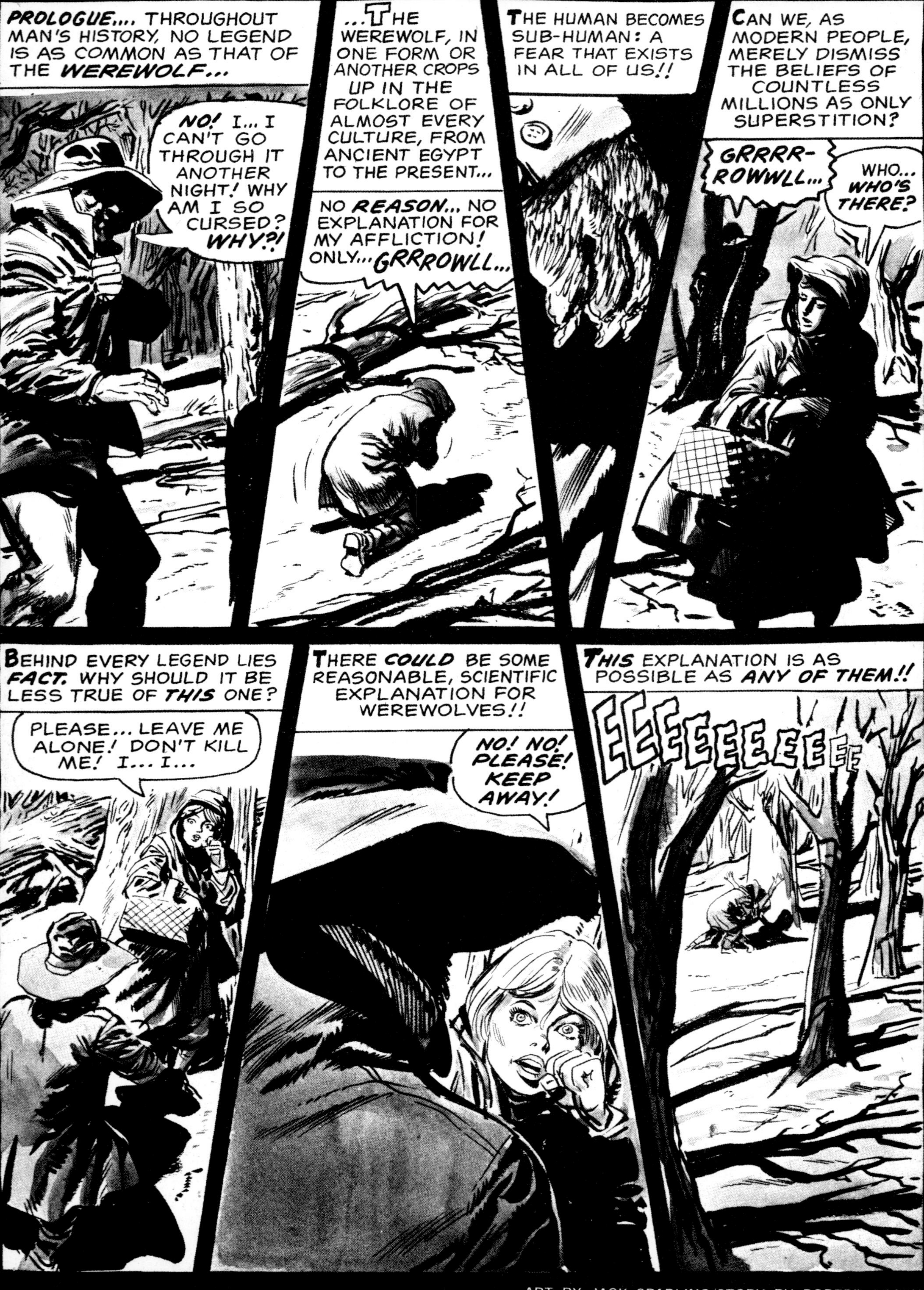
PROLOGUE.... THROUGHOUT MAN'S HISTORY, NO LEGEND IS AS COMMON AS THAT OF THE WEREWOLF...
NO! I... I CAN'T GO THROUGH IT ANOTHER NIGHT! WHY AM I SO CURSED? WHY?!
...THE WEREWOLF, IN ONE FORM OR ANOTHER CROPS UP IN THE FOLKLORE OF ALMOST EVERY CULTURE, FROM ANCIENT EGYPT TO THE PRESENT...
NO REASON... NO EXPLANATION FOR MY AFFLICTION! ONLY... GRRROWLL...
THE HUMAN BECOMES SUB-HUMAN: A FEAR THAT EXISTS IN ALL OF US!!
CAN WE, AS MODERN PEOPLE, MERELY DISMISS THE BELIEFS OF COUNTLESS MILLIONS AS ONLY SUPERSTITION?
GRRRR-ROWLL...
WHO... WHO'S THERE?
BEHIND EVERY LEGEND LIES FACT. WHY SHOULD IT BE LESS TRUE OF THIS ONE?
PLEASE... LEAVE ME ALONE! DON'T KILL ME! I... I...
THERE COULD BE SOME REASONABLE, SCIENTIFIC EXPLANATION FOR WEREWOLVES!!
NO! NO! PLEASE! KEEP AWAY!
THIS EXPLANATION IS AS POSSIBLE AS ANY OF THEM!!
EEEEEEEEEEE

ART BY JACK SPARLING/STORY BY ROBERT ROSEN

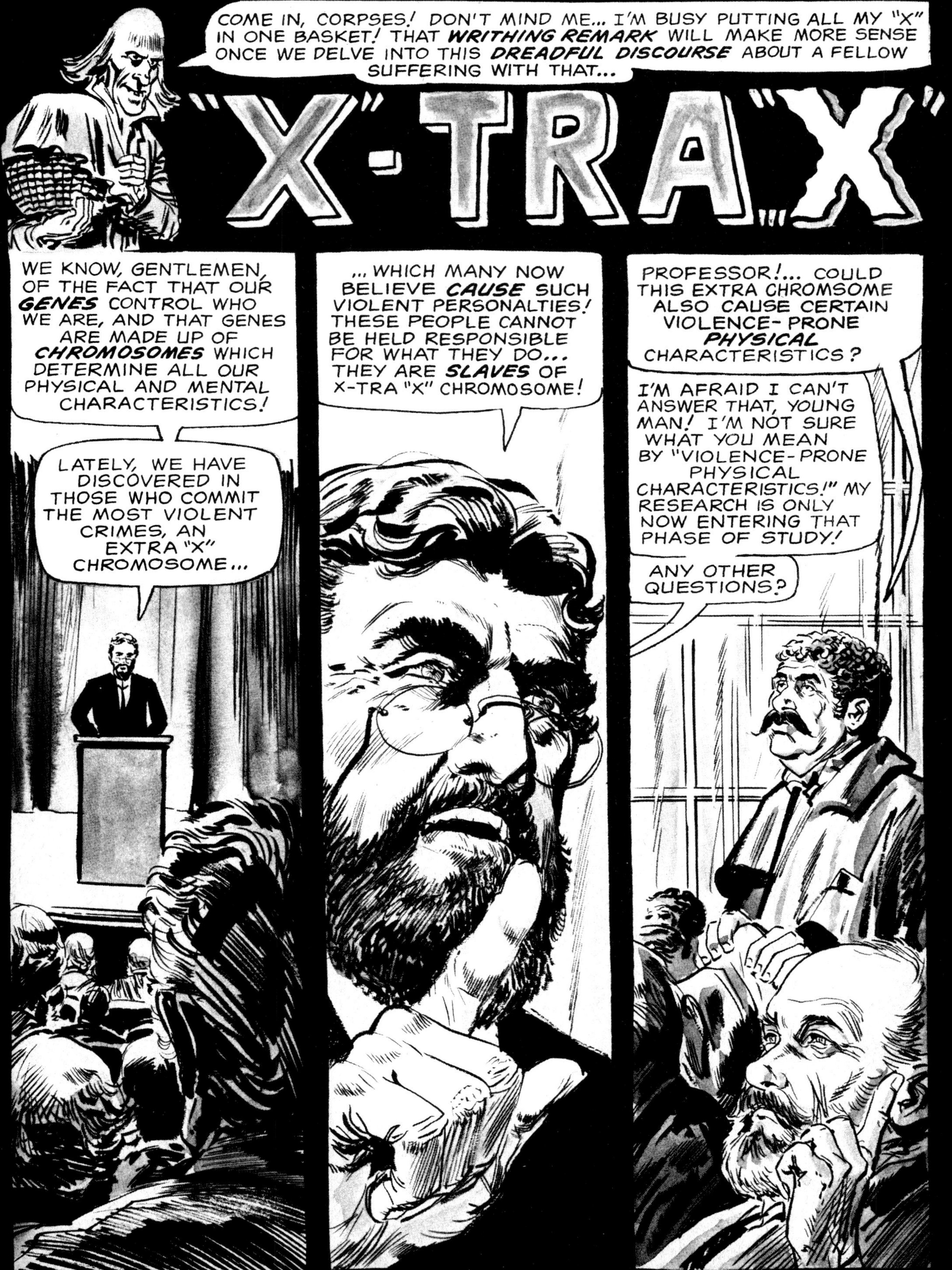

COME IN, CORPSES! DON'T MIND ME... I'M BUSY PUTTING ALL MY "X" IN ONE BASKET! THAT WRITHING REMARK WILL MAKE MORE SENSE ONCE WE DELVE INTO THIS DREADFUL DISCOURSE ABOUT A FELLOW SUFFERING WITH THAT...
"X"-TRA "X"
WE KNOW, GENTLEMEN, OF THE FACT THAT OUR GENES CONTROL WHO WE ARE, AND THAT GENES ARE MADE UP OF CHROMOSOMES WHICH DETERMINE ALL OUR PHYSICAL AND MENTAL CHARACTERISTICS!
LATELY, WE HAVE DISCOVERED IN THOSE WHO COMMIT THE MOST VIOLENT CRIMES, AN EXTRA "X" CHROMOSOME...
...WHICH MANY NOW BELIEVE CAUSE SUCH VIOLENT PERSONALTIES! THESE PEOPLE CANNOT BE HELD RESPONSIBLE FOR WHAT THEY DO... THEY ARE SLAVES OF X-TRA "X" CHROMOSOME!
PROFESSOR!... COULD THIS EXTRA CHROMSOME ALSO CAUSE CERTAIN VIOLENCE-PRONE PHYSICAL CHARACTERISTICS?
I'M AFRAID I CAN'T ANSWER THAT, YOUNG MAN! I'M NOT SURE WHAT YOU MEAN BY "VIOLENCE-PRONE PHYSICAL CHARACTERISTICS!" MY RESEARCH IS ONLY NOW ENTERING THAT PHASE OF STUDY!
ANY OTHER QUESTIONS?

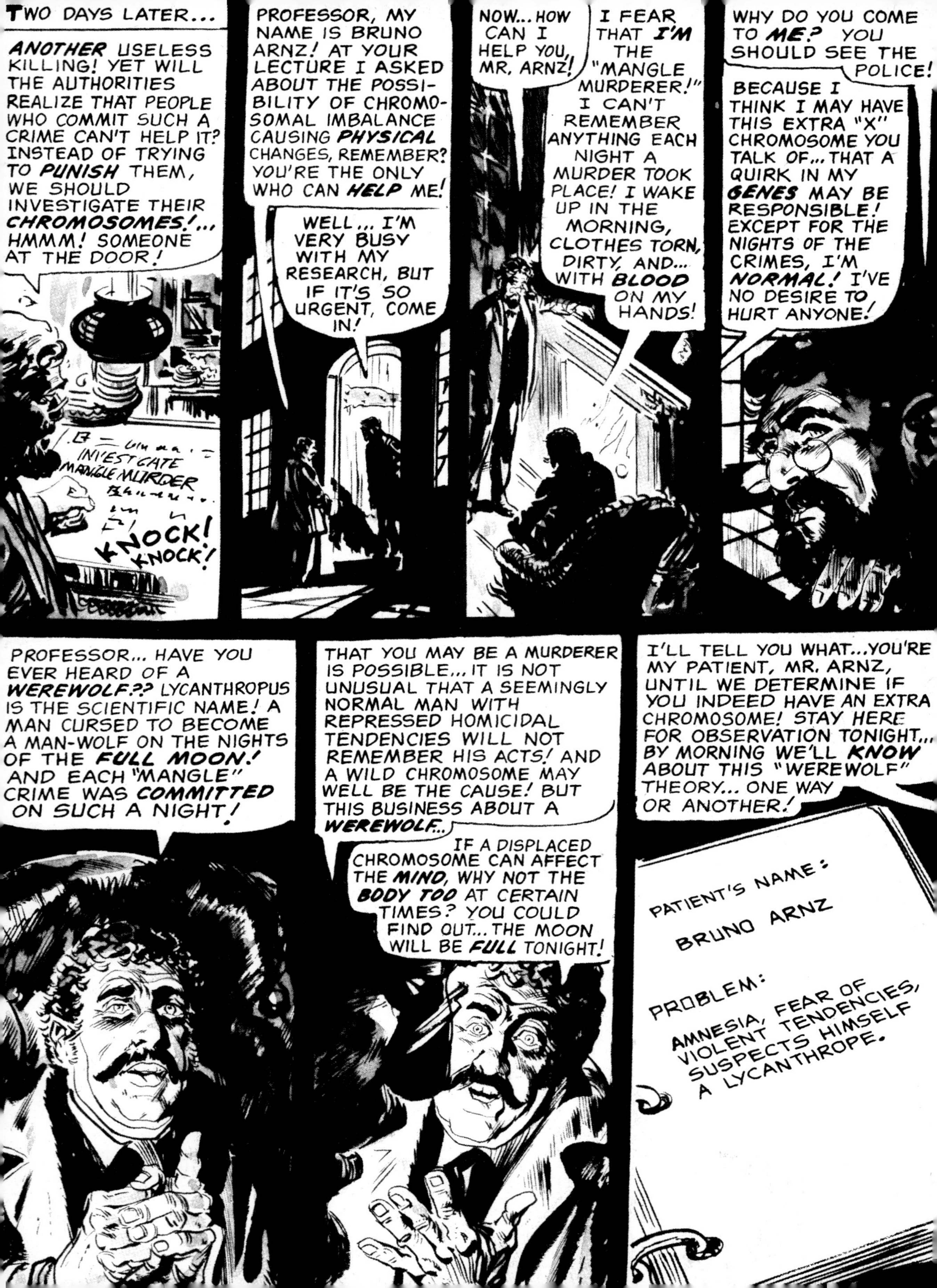
TWO DAYS LATER...
ANOTHER USELESS KILLING! YET WILL THE AUTHORITIES REALIZE THAT PEOPLE WHO COMMIT SUCH A CRIME CAN'T HELP IT? INSTEAD OF TRYING TO PUNISH THEM, WE SHOULD INVESTIGATE THEIR CHROMOSOMES!... HMMM! SOMEONE AT THE DOOR!
INVESTIGATE MANGLE MURDER
KNOCK! KNOCK!
PROFESSOR, MY NAME IS BRUNO ARNZ! AT YOUR LECTURE I ASKED ABOUT THE POSSIBILITY OF CHROMOSOMAL IMBALANCE CAUSING PHYSICAL CHANGES, REMEMBER? YOU'RE THE ONLY WHO CAN HELP ME!
WELL... I'M VERY BUSY WITH MY RESEARCH, BUT IF IT'S SO URGENT, COME IN!
NOW... HOW CAN I HELP YOU, MR. ARNZ!
I FEAR THAT I'M THE "MANGLE MURDERER!" I CAN'T REMEMBER ANYTHING EACH NIGHT A MURDER TOOK PLACE! I WAKE UP IN THE MORNING, CLOTHES TORN, DIRTY, AND... WITH BLOOD ON MY HANDS!
WHY DO YOU COME TO ME? YOU SHOULD SEE THE POLICE!
BECAUSE I THINK I MAY HAVE THIS EXTRA "X" CHROMOSOME YOU TALK OF... THAT A QUIRK IN MY GENES MAY BE RESPONSIBLE! EXCEPT FOR THE NIGHTS OF THE CRIMES, I'M NORMAL! I'VE NO DESIRE TO HURT ANYONE!
PROFESSOR... HAVE YOU EVER HEARD OF A WEREWOLF?? LYCANTHROPUS IS THE SCIENTIFIC NAME! A MAN CURSED TO BECOME A MAN-WOLF ON THE NIGHTS OF THE FULL MOON! AND EACH "MANGLE" CRIME WAS COMMITTED ON SUCH A NIGHT!
THAT YOU MAY BE A MURDERER IS POSSIBLE... IT IS NOT UNUSUAL THAT A SEEMINGLY NORMAL MAN WITH REPRESSED HOMICIDAL TENDENCIES WILL NOT REMEMBER HIS ACTS! AND A WILD CHROMOSOME MAY WELL BE THE CAUSE! BUT THIS BUSINESS ABOUT A WEREWOLF...
IF A DISPLACED CHROMOSOME CAN AFFECT THE MIND, WHY NOT THE BODY TOO AT CERTAIN TIMES? YOU COULD FIND OUT... THE MOON WILL BE FULL TONIGHT!
I'LL TELL YOU WHAT... YOU'RE MY PATIENT, MR. ARNZ, UNTIL WE DETERMINE IF YOU INDEED HAVE AN EXTRA CHROMOSOME! STAY HERE FOR OBSERVATION TONIGHT... BY MORNING WE'LL KNOW ABOUT THIS "WEREWOLF" THEORY... ONE WAY OR ANOTHER!
PATIENT'S NAME:
BRUNO ARNZ
PROBLEM:
AMNESIA, FEAR OF VIOLENT TENDENCIES, SUSPECTS HIMSELF A LYCANTHROPE.

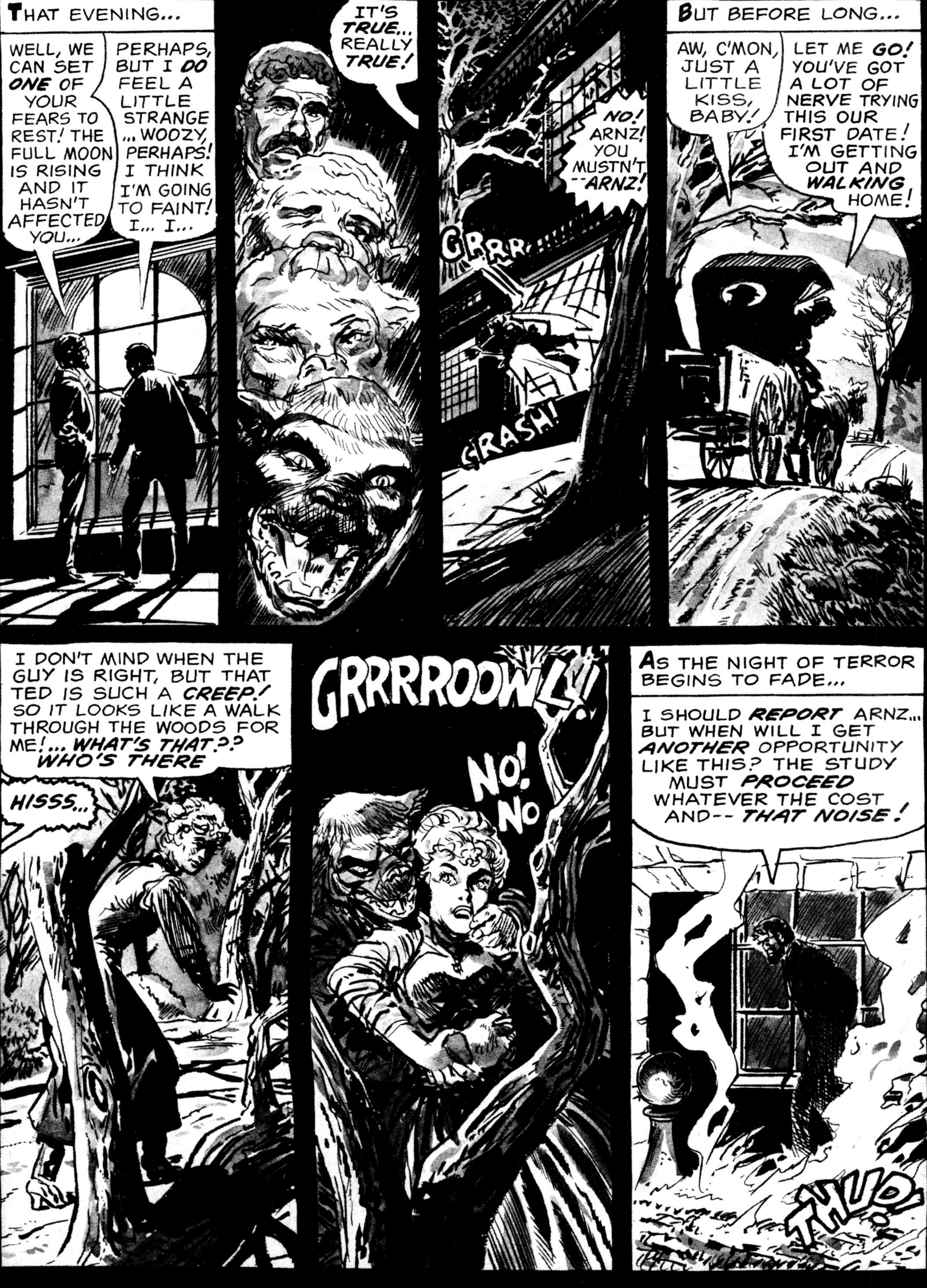

THAT EVENING...
WELL, WE CAN SET ONE OF YOUR FEARS TO REST! THE FULL MOON IS RISING AND IT HASN'T AFFECTED YOU...
PERHAPS, BUT I DO FEEL A LITTLE STRANGE ...WOOZY, PERHAPS! I THINK I'M GOING TO FAINT! I... I...
IT'S TRUE... REALLY TRUE!
NO! ARNZ! YOU MUSTN'T --ARNZ!
GRRR
CRASH!
BUT BEFORE LONG...
AW, C'MON, JUST A LITTLE KISS, BABY!
LET ME GO! YOU'VE GOT A LOT OF NERVE TRYING THIS OUR FIRST DATE! I'M GETTING OUT AND WALKING HOME!
I DON'T MIND WHEN THE GUY IS RIGHT, BUT THAT TED IS SUCH A CREEP! SO IT LOOKS LIKE A WALK THROUGH THE WOODS FOR ME! ... WHAT'S THAT?? WHO'S THERE
HISSS...
GRRRROOWL!
NO! NO
AS THE NIGHT OF TERROR BEGINS TO FADE...
I SHOULD REPORT ARNZ... BUT WHEN WILL I GET ANOTHER OPPORTUNITY LIKE THIS? THE STUDY MUST PROCEED WHATEVER THE COST AND-- THAT NOISE!
THUD!

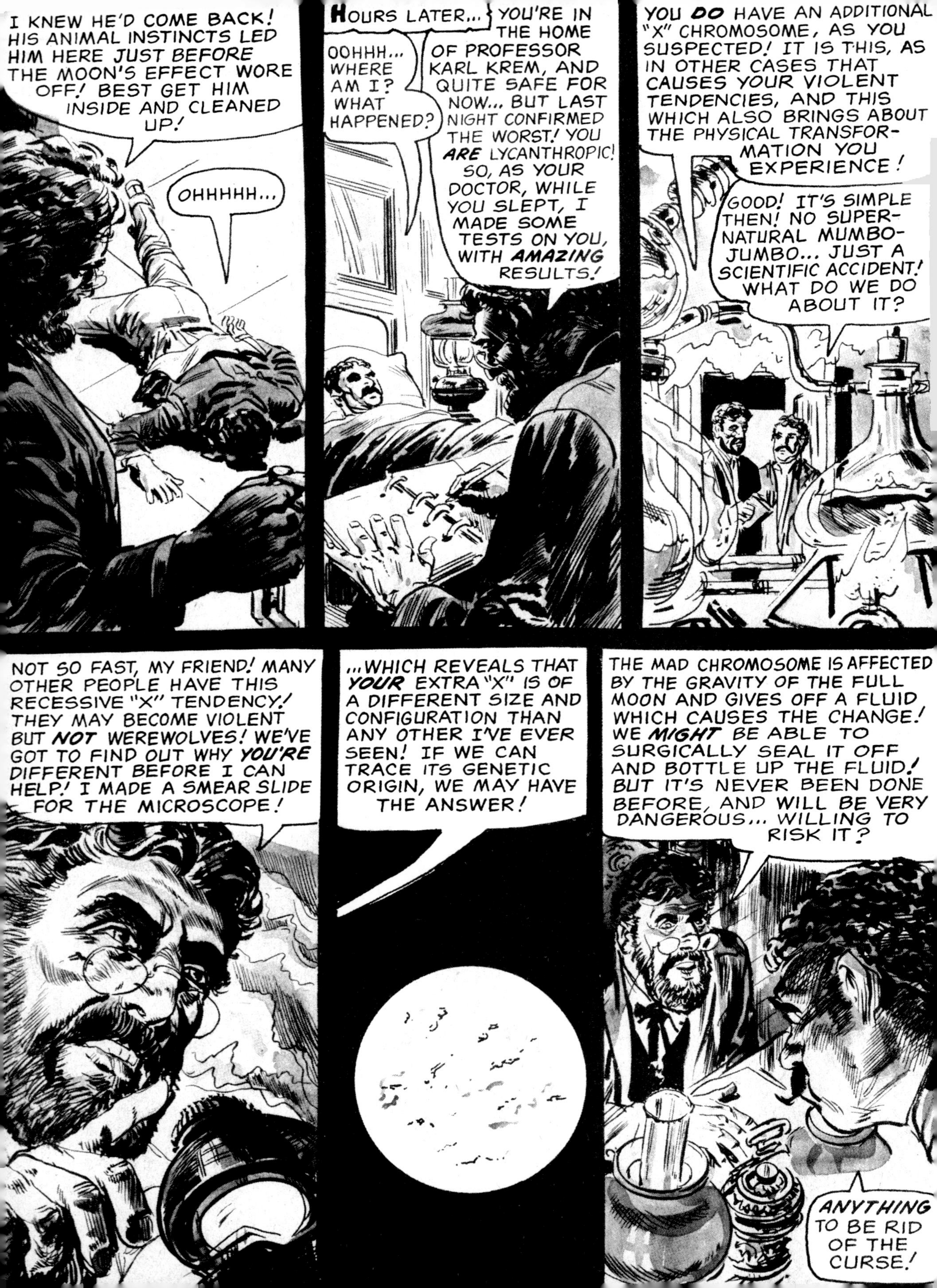
I KNEW HE'D COME BACK! HIS ANIMAL INSTINCTS LED HIM HERE JUST BEFORE THE MOON'S EFFECT WORE OFF! BEST GET HIM INSIDE AND CLEANED UP!
OHHHHH...
HOURS LATER...
OOHHH... WHERE AM I? WHAT HAPPENED?
YOU'RE IN THE HOME OF PROFESSOR KARL KREM, AND QUITE SAFE FOR NOW... BUT LAST NIGHT CONFIRMED THE WORST! YOU ARE LYCANTHROPIC! SO, AS YOUR DOCTOR, WHILE YOU SLEPT, I MADE SOME TESTS ON YOU, WITH AMAZING RESULTS!
YOU DO HAVE AN ADDITIONAL "X" CHROMOSOME, AS YOU SUSPECTED! IT IS THIS, AS IN OTHER CASES THAT CAUSES YOUR VIOLENT TENDENCIES, AND THIS WHICH ALSO BRINGS ABOUT THE PHYSICAL TRANSFORMATION YOU EXPERIENCE!
GOOD! IT'S SIMPLE THEN! NO SUPER-NATURAL MUMBO-JUMBO... JUST A SCIENTIFIC ACCIDENT! WHAT DO WE DO ABOUT IT?
NOT SO FAST, MY FRIEND! MANY OTHER PEOPLE HAVE THIS RECESSIVE "X" TENDENCY! THEY MAY BECOME VIOLENT BUT NOT WEREWOLVES! WE'VE GOT TO FIND OUT WHY YOU'RE DIFFERENT BEFORE I CAN HELP! I MADE A SMEAR SLIDE FOR THE MICROSCOPE!
...WHICH REVEALS THAT YOUR EXTRA "X" IS OF A DIFFERENT SIZE AND CONFIGURATION THAN ANY OTHER I'VE EVER SEEN! IF WE CAN TRACE ITS GENETIC ORIGIN, WE MAY HAVE THE ANSWER!
THE MAD CHROMOSOME IS AFFECTED BY THE GRAVITY OF THE FULL MOON AND GIVES OFF A FLUID WHICH CAUSES THE CHANGE! WE MIGHT BE ABLE TO SURGICALLY SEAL IT OFF AND BOTTLE UP THE FLUID! BUT IT'S NEVER BEEN DONE BEFORE, AND WILL BE VERY DANGEROUS... WILLING TO RISK IT?
ANYTHING TO BE RID OF THE CURSE!

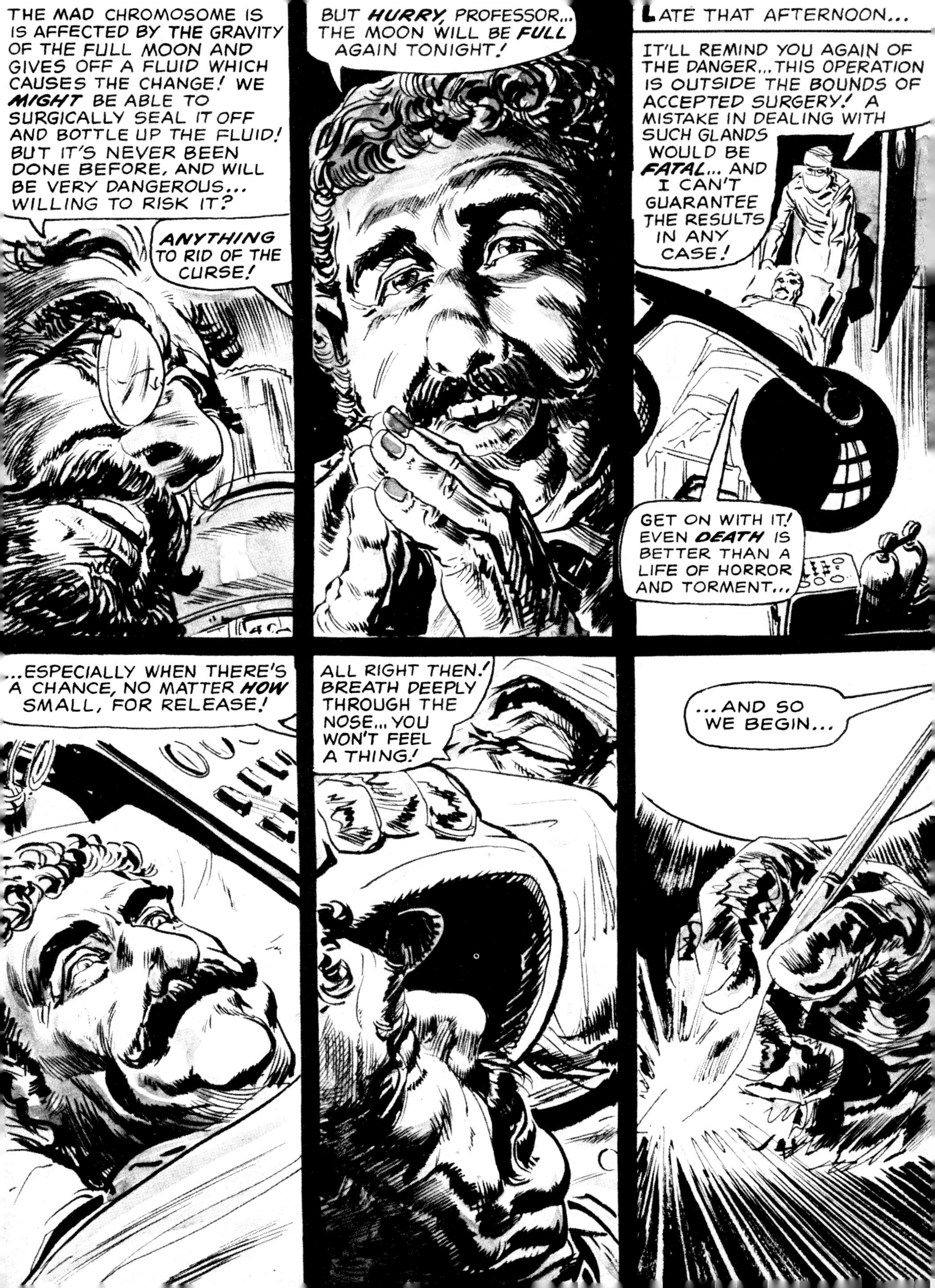
THE MAD CHROMOSOME IS IS AFFECTED BY THE GRAVITY OF THE FULL MOON AND GIVES OFF A FLUID WHICH CAUSES THE CHANGE! WE MIGHT BE ABLE TO SURGICALLY SEAL IT OFF AND BOTTLE UP THE FLUID! BUT IT'S NEVER BEEN DONE BEFORE, AND WILL BE VERY DANGEROUS... WILLING TO RISK IT?
ANYTHING TO RID OF THE CURSE!
BUT HURRY, PROFESSOR... THE MOON WILL BE FULL AGAIN TONIGHT!
LATE THAT AFTERNOON...
IT'LL REMIND YOU AGAIN OF THE DANGER... THIS OPERATION IS OUTSIDE THE BOUNDS OF ACCEPTED SURGERY! A MISTAKE IN DEALING WITH SUCH GLANDS WOULD BE FATAL... AND I CAN'T GUARANTEE THE RESULTS IN ANY CASE!
GET ON WITH IT! EVEN DEATH IS BETTER THAN A LIFE OF HORROR AND TORMENT...
...ESPECIALLY WHEN THERE'S A CHANCE, NO MATTER HOW SMALL, FOR RELEASE!
ALL RIGHT THEN! BREATH DEEPLY THROUGH THE NOSE... YOU WON'T FEEL A THING!
...AND SO WE BEGIN...

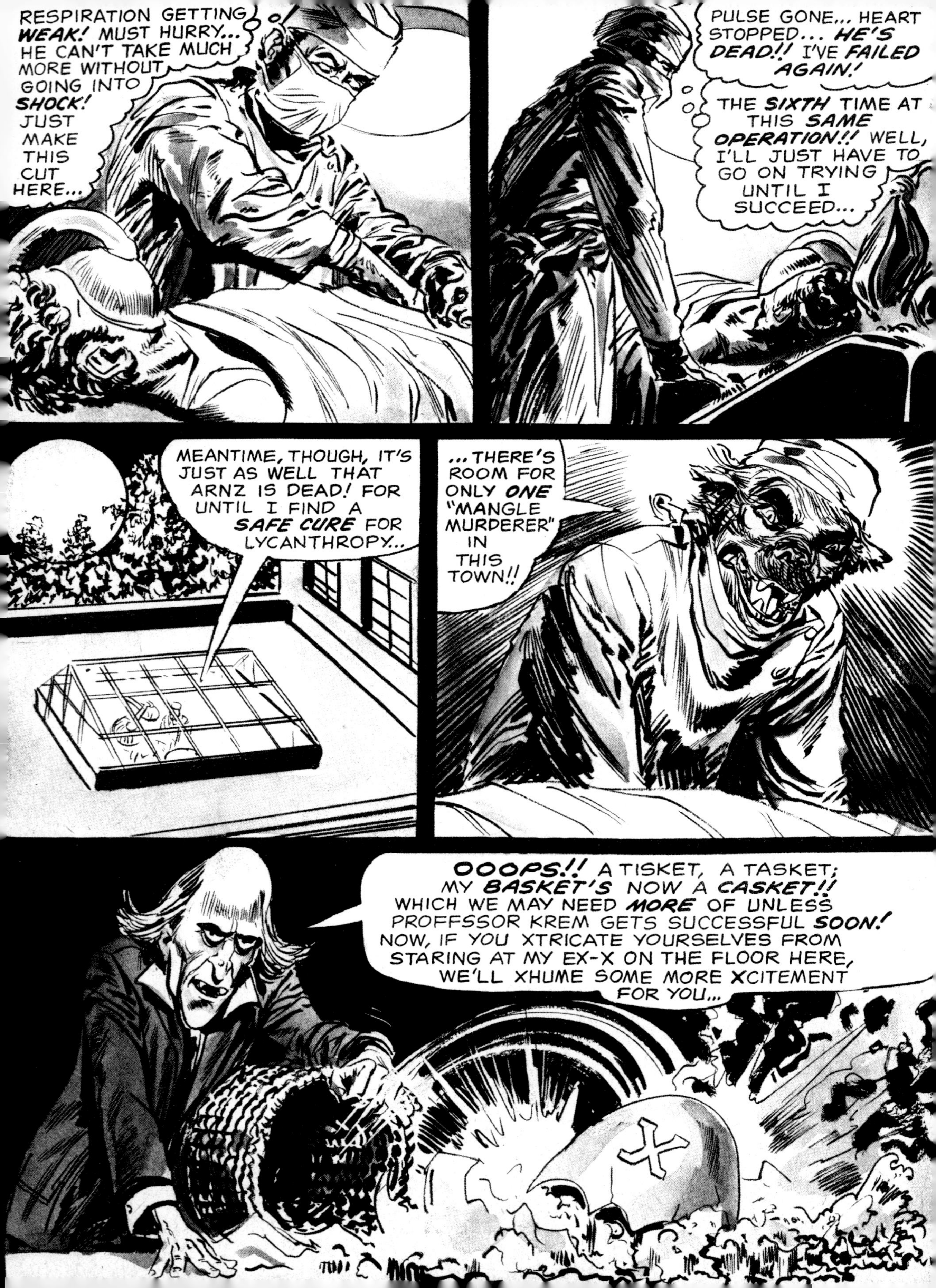

RESPIRATION GETTING WEAK! MUST HURRY... HE CAN'T TAKE MUCH MORE WITHOUT GOING INTO SHOCK! JUST MAKE THIS CUT HERE...
PULSE GONE... HEART STOPPED... HE'S DEAD!! I'VE FAILED AGAIN!
THE SIXTH TIME AT THIS SAME OPERATION!! WELL, I'LL JUST HAVE TO GO ON TRYING UNTIL I SUCCEED...
MEANTIME, THOUGH, IT'S JUST AS WELL THAT ARNZ IS DEAD! FOR UNTIL I FIND A SAFE CURE FOR LYCANTHROPY...
...THERE'S ROOM FOR ONLY ONE "MANGLE MURDERER" IN THIS TOWN!!
OOOPS!! A TISKET, A TASKET; MY BASKET'S NOW A CASKET!! WHICH WE MAY NEED MORE OF UNLESS PROFFSSOR KREM GETS SUCCESSFUL SOON! NOW, IF YOU XTRICATE YOURSELVES FROM STARING AT MY EX-X ON THE FLOOR HERE, WE'LL XHUME SOME MORE XCITEMENT FOR YOU...

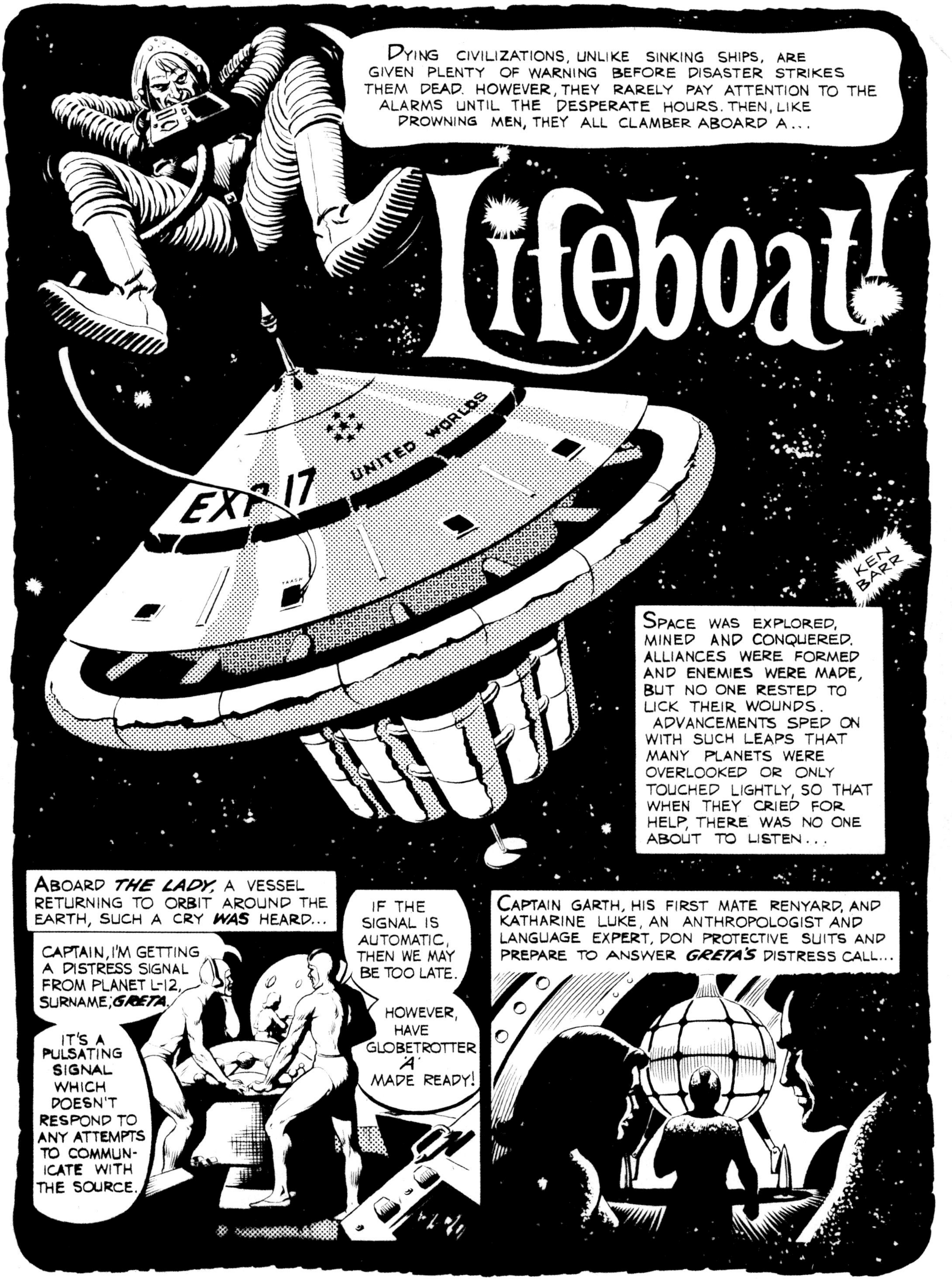
DYING CIVILIZATIONS, UNLIKE SINKING SHIPS, ARE GIVEN PLENTY OF WARNING BEFORE DISASTER STRIKES THEM DEAD. HOWEVER, THEY RARELY PAY ATTENTION TO THE ALARMS UNTIL THE DESPERATE HOURS. THEN, LIKE DROWNING MEN, THEY ALL CLAMBER ABOARD A...
Lifeboat!
UNITED WORLDS
EXP 17
TRASH
KEN BARR
SPACE WAS EXPLORED, MINED AND CONQUERED. ALLIANCES WERE FORMED AND ENEMIES WERE MADE, BUT NO ONE RESTED TO LICK THEIR WOUNDS. ADVANCEMENTS SPED ON WITH SUCH LEAPS THAT MANY PLANETS WERE OVERLOOKED OR ONLY TOUCHED LIGHTLY, SO THAT WHEN THEY CRIED FOR HELP, THERE WAS NO ONE ABOUT TO LISTEN...
ABOARD THE LADY, A VESSEL RETURNING TO ORBIT AROUND THE EARTH, SUCH A CRY WAS HEARD...
CAPTAIN, I'M GETTING A DISTRESS SIGNAL FROM PLANET L-12, SURNAME; GRETA.
IT'S A PULSATING SIGNAL WHICH DOESN'T RESPOND TO ANY ATTEMPTS TO COMMUNICATE WITH THE SOURCE.
IF THE SIGNAL IS AUTOMATIC, THEN WE MAY BE TOO LATE.
HOWEVER, HAVE GLOBETROTTER 'A' MADE READY!
CAPTAIN GARTH, HIS FIRST MATE RENYARD, AND KATHARINE LUKE, AN ANTHROPOLOGIST AND LANGUAGE EXPERT, DON PROTECTIVE SUITS AND PREPARE TO ANSWER GRETA'S DISTRESS CALL...

ART BY KEN BARR/STORY BY BILL PARENTE

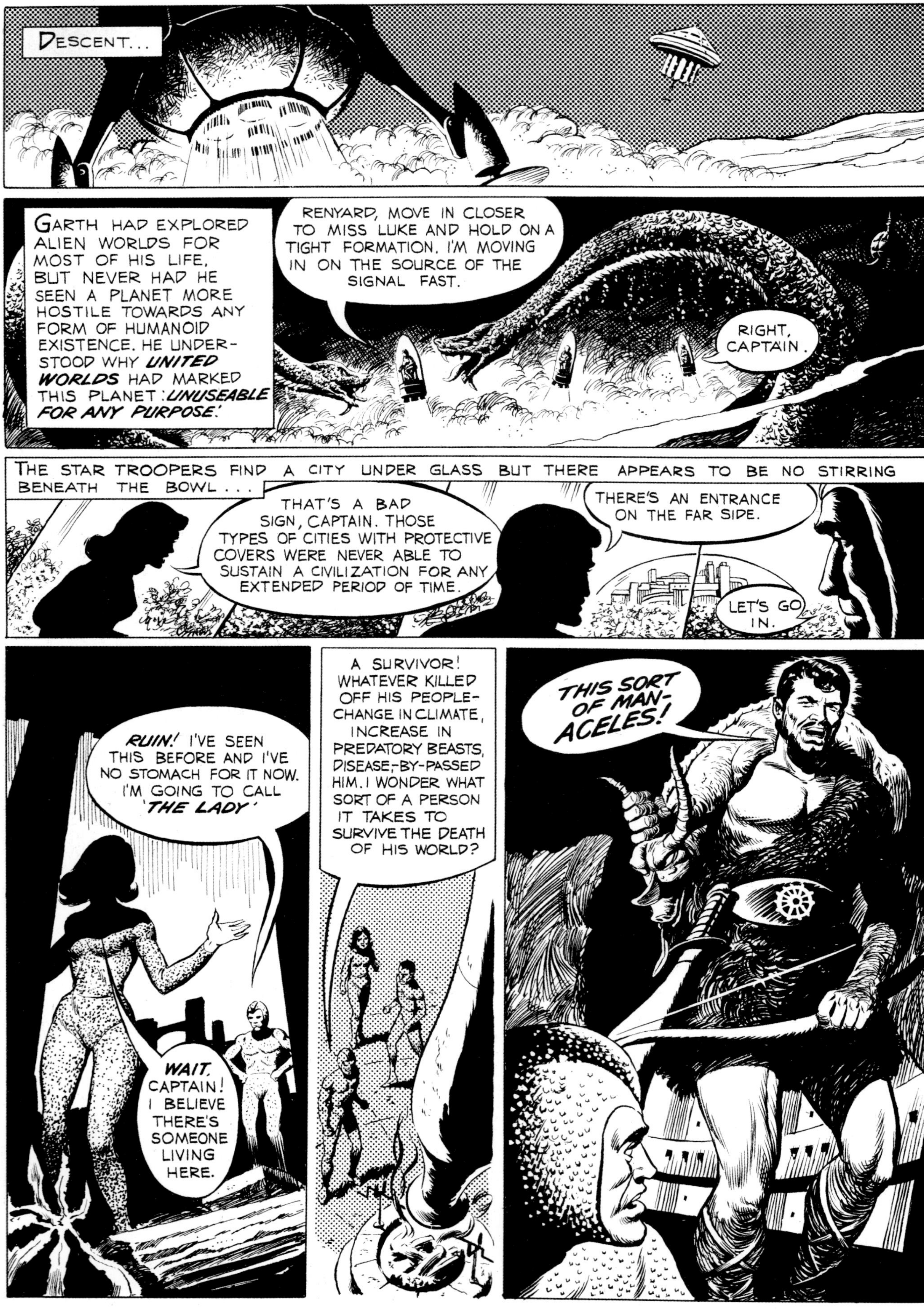
DESCENT...
GARTH HAD EXPLORED ALIEN WORLDS FOR MOST OF HIS LIFE, BUT NEVER HAD HE SEEN A PLANET MORE HOSTILE TOWARDS ANY FORM OF HUMANOID EXISTENCE. HE UNDERSTOOD WHY *UNITED WORLDS* HAD MARKED THIS PLANET: *'UNUSEABLE FOR ANY PURPOSE.'*
RENYARD, MOVE IN CLOSER TO MISS LUKE AND HOLD ON A TIGHT FORMATION. I'M MOVING IN ON THE SOURCE OF THE SIGNAL FAST.
RIGHT, CAPTAIN.
THE STAR TROOPERS FIND A CITY UNDER GLASS BUT THERE APPEARS TO BE NO STIRRING BENEATH THE BOWL...
THAT'S A BAD SIGN, CAPTAIN. THOSE TYPES OF CITIES WITH PROTECTIVE COVERS WERE NEVER ABLE TO SUSTAIN A CIVILIZATION FOR ANY EXTENDED PERIOD OF TIME.
THERE'S AN ENTRANCE ON THE FAR SIDE.
LET'S GO IN.
RUIN! I'VE SEEN THIS BEFORE AND I'VE NO STOMACH FOR IT NOW. I'M GOING TO CALL *'THE LADY'*
WAIT, CAPTAIN! I BELIEVE THERE'S SOMEONE LIVING HERE.
A SURVIVOR! WHATEVER KILLED OFF HIS PEOPLE–CHANGE IN CLIMATE, INCREASE IN PREDATORY BEASTS, DISEASE–BY-PASSED HIM. I WONDER WHAT SORT OF A PERSON IT TAKES TO SURVIVE THE DEATH OF HIS WORLD?
THIS SORT OF MAN–ACELES!

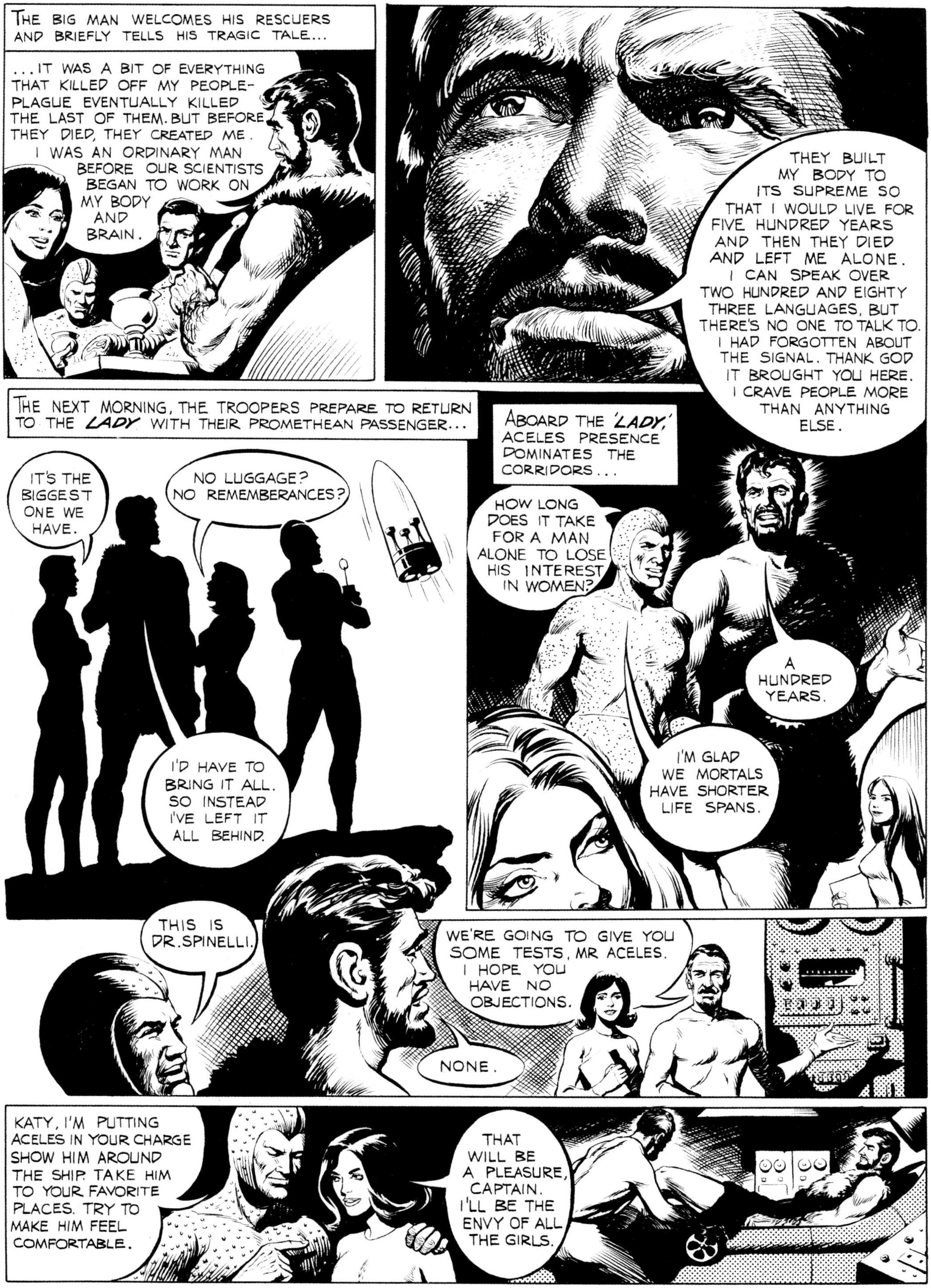

THE BIG MAN WELCOMES HIS RESCUERS AND BRIEFLY TELLS HIS TRAGIC TALE...
...IT WAS A BIT OF EVERYTHING THAT KILLED OFF MY PEOPLE- PLAGUE EVENTUALLY KILLED THE LAST OF THEM. BUT BEFORE THEY DIED, THEY CREATED ME. I WAS AN ORDINARY MAN BEFORE OUR SCIENTISTS BEGAN TO WORK ON MY BODY AND BRAIN.
THEY BUILT MY BODY TO ITS SUPREME SO THAT I WOULD LIVE FOR FIVE HUNDRED YEARS AND THEN THEY DIED AND LEFT ME ALONE. I CAN SPEAK OVER TWO HUNDRED AND EIGHTY THREE LANGUAGES, BUT THERE'S NO ONE TO TALK TO. I HAD FORGOTTEN ABOUT THE SIGNAL. THANK GOD IT BROUGHT YOU HERE. I CRAVE PEOPLE MORE THAN ANYTHING ELSE.
THE NEXT MORNING, THE TROOPERS PREPARE TO RETURN TO THE LADY WITH THEIR PROMETHEAN PASSENGER...
IT'S THE BIGGEST ONE WE HAVE.
NO LUGGAGE? NO REMEMBERANCES?
I'D HAVE TO BRING IT ALL. SO INSTEAD I'VE LEFT IT ALL BEHIND.
ABOARD THE 'LADY,' ACELES PRESENCE DOMINATES THE CORRIDORS...
HOW LONG DOES IT TAKE FOR A MAN ALONE TO LOSE HIS INTEREST IN WOMEN?
A HUNDRED YEARS.
I'M GLAD WE MORTALS HAVE SHORTER LIFE SPANS.
THIS IS DR. SPINELLI.
WE'RE GOING TO GIVE YOU SOME TESTS, MR ACELES. I HOPE YOU HAVE NO OBJECTIONS.
NONE.
KATY, I'M PUTTING ACELES IN YOUR CHARGE SHOW HIM AROUND THE SHIP. TAKE HIM TO YOUR FAVORITE PLACES. TRY TO MAKE HIM FEEL COMFORTABLE.
THAT WILL BE A PLEASURE, CAPTAIN. I'LL BE THE ENVY OF ALL THE GIRLS.

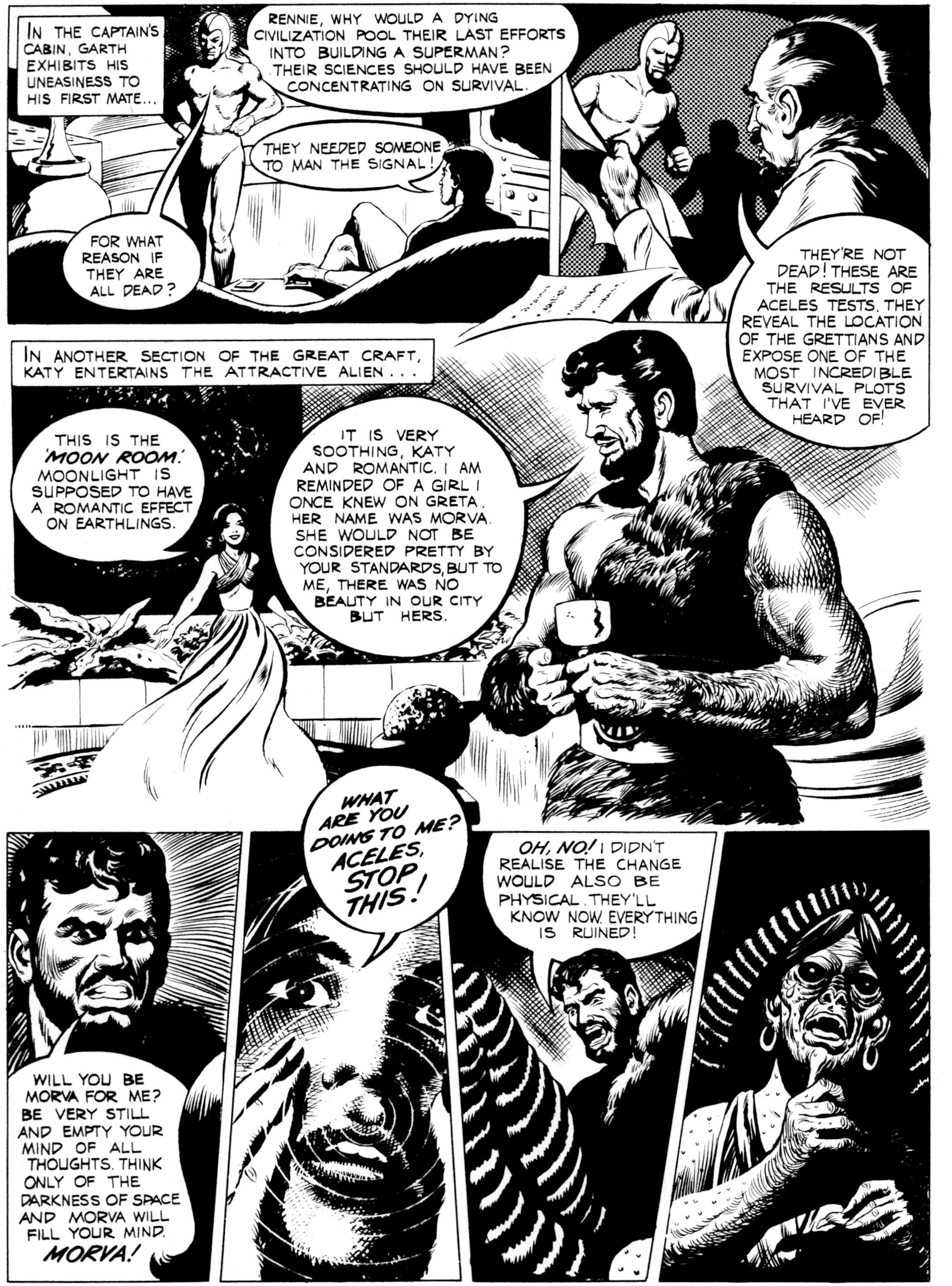

IN THE CAPTAIN'S CABIN, GARTH EXHIBITS HIS UNEASINESS TO HIS FIRST MATE...
RENNIE, WHY WOULD A DYING CIVILIZATION POOL THEIR LAST EFFORTS INTO BUILDING A SUPERMAN? THEIR SCIENCES SHOULD HAVE BEEN CONCENTRATING ON SURVIVAL.
THEY NEEDED SOMEONE TO MAN THE SIGNAL!
FOR WHAT REASON IF THEY ARE ALL DEAD?
THEY'RE NOT DEAD! THESE ARE THE RESULTS OF ACELES TESTS. THEY REVEAL THE LOCATION OF THE GRETTIANS AND EXPOSE ONE OF THE MOST INCREDIBLE SURVIVAL PLOTS THAT I'VE EVER HEARD OF!
IN ANOTHER SECTION OF THE GREAT CRAFT, KATY ENTERTAINS THE ATTRACTIVE ALIEN...
THIS IS THE 'MOON ROOM.' MOONLIGHT IS SUPPOSED TO HAVE A ROMANTIC EFFECT ON EARTHLINGS.
IT IS VERY SOOTHING, KATY AND ROMANTIC. I AM REMINDED OF A GIRL I ONCE KNEW ON GRETA. HER NAME WAS MORVA. SHE WOULD NOT BE CONSIDERED PRETTY BY YOUR STANDARDS, BUT TO ME, THERE WAS NO BEAUTY IN OUR CITY BUT HERS.
WILL YOU BE MORVA FOR ME? BE VERY STILL AND EMPTY YOUR MIND OF ALL THOUGHTS. THINK ONLY OF THE DARKNESS OF SPACE AND MORVA WILL FILL YOUR MIND. MORVA!
WHAT ARE YOU DOING TO ME? ACELES, STOP THIS!
OH, NO! I DIDN'T REALISE THE CHANGE WOULD ALSO BE PHYSICAL. THEY'LL KNOW NOW. EVERYTHING IS RUINED!

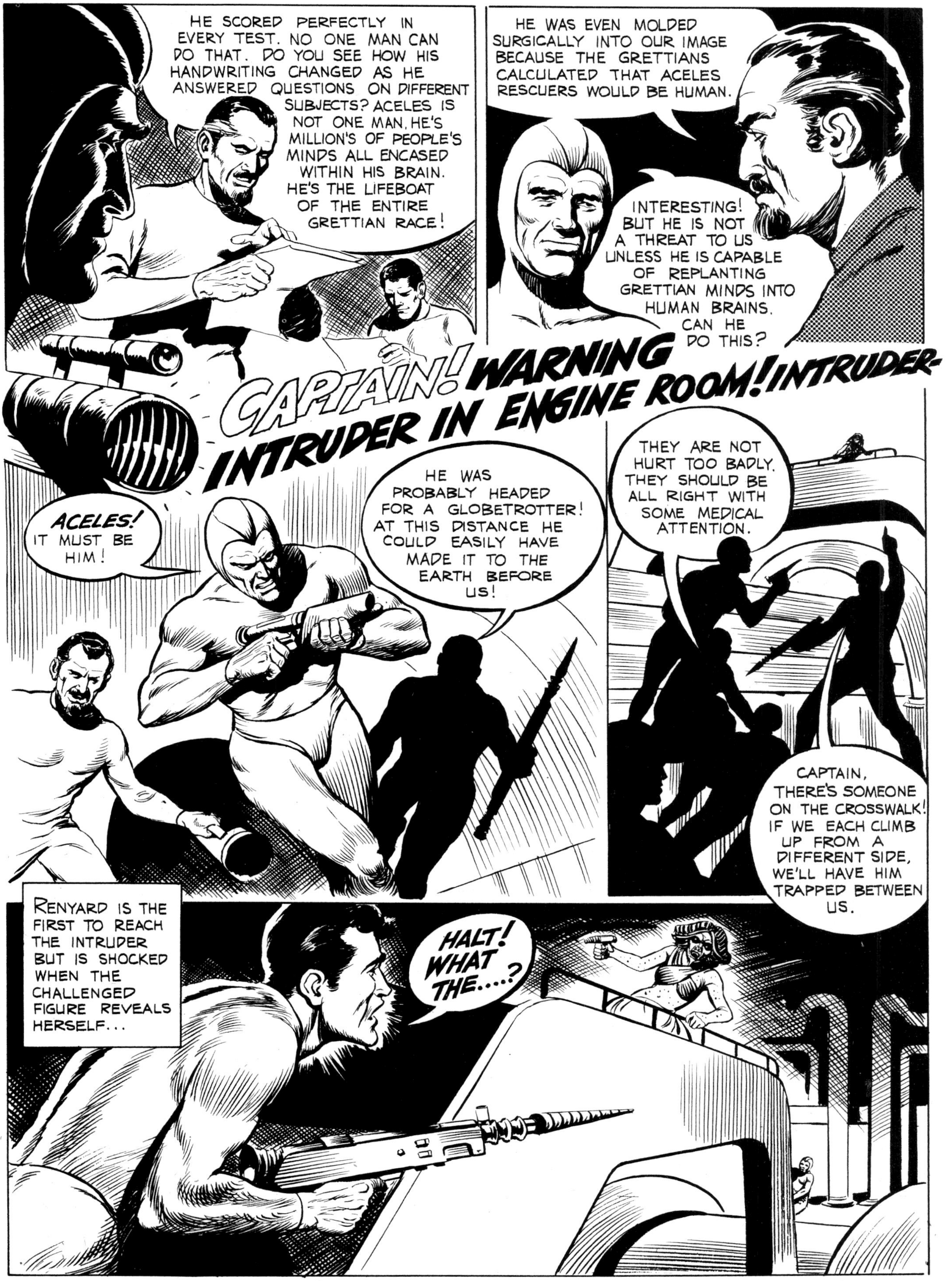
HE SCORED PERFECTLY IN EVERY TEST. NO ONE MAN CAN DO THAT. DO YOU SEE HOW HIS HANDWRITING CHANGED AS HE ANSWERED QUESTIONS ON DIFFERENT SUBJECTS? ACELES IS NOT ONE MAN, HE'S MILLION'S OF PEOPLE'S MINDS ALL ENCASED WITHIN HIS BRAIN. HE'S THE LIFEBOAT OF THE ENTIRE GRETTIAN RACE!
HE WAS EVEN MOLDED SURGICALLY INTO OUR IMAGE BECAUSE THE GRETTIANS CALCULATED THAT ACELES RESCUERS WOULD BE HUMAN.
INTERESTING! BUT HE IS NOT A THREAT TO US UNLESS HE IS CAPABLE OF REPLANTING GRETTIAN MINDS INTO HUMAN BRAINS. CAN HE DO THIS?
CAPTAIN! WARNING INTRUDER IN ENGINE ROOM! INTRUDER-
ACELES! IT MUST BE HIM!
HE WAS PROBABLY HEADED FOR A GLOBETROTTER! AT THIS DISTANCE HE COULD EASILY HAVE MADE IT TO THE EARTH BEFORE US!
THEY ARE NOT HURT TOO BADLY. THEY SHOULD BE ALL RIGHT WITH SOME MEDICAL ATTENTION.
CAPTAIN, THERE'S SOMEONE ON THE CROSSWALK! IF WE EACH CLIMB UP FROM A DIFFERENT SIDE, WE'LL HAVE HIM TRAPPED BETWEEN US.
RENYARD IS THE FIRST TO REACH THE INTRUDER BUT IS SHOCKED WHEN THE CHALLENGED FIGURE REVEALS HERSELF...
HALT! WHAT THE....?

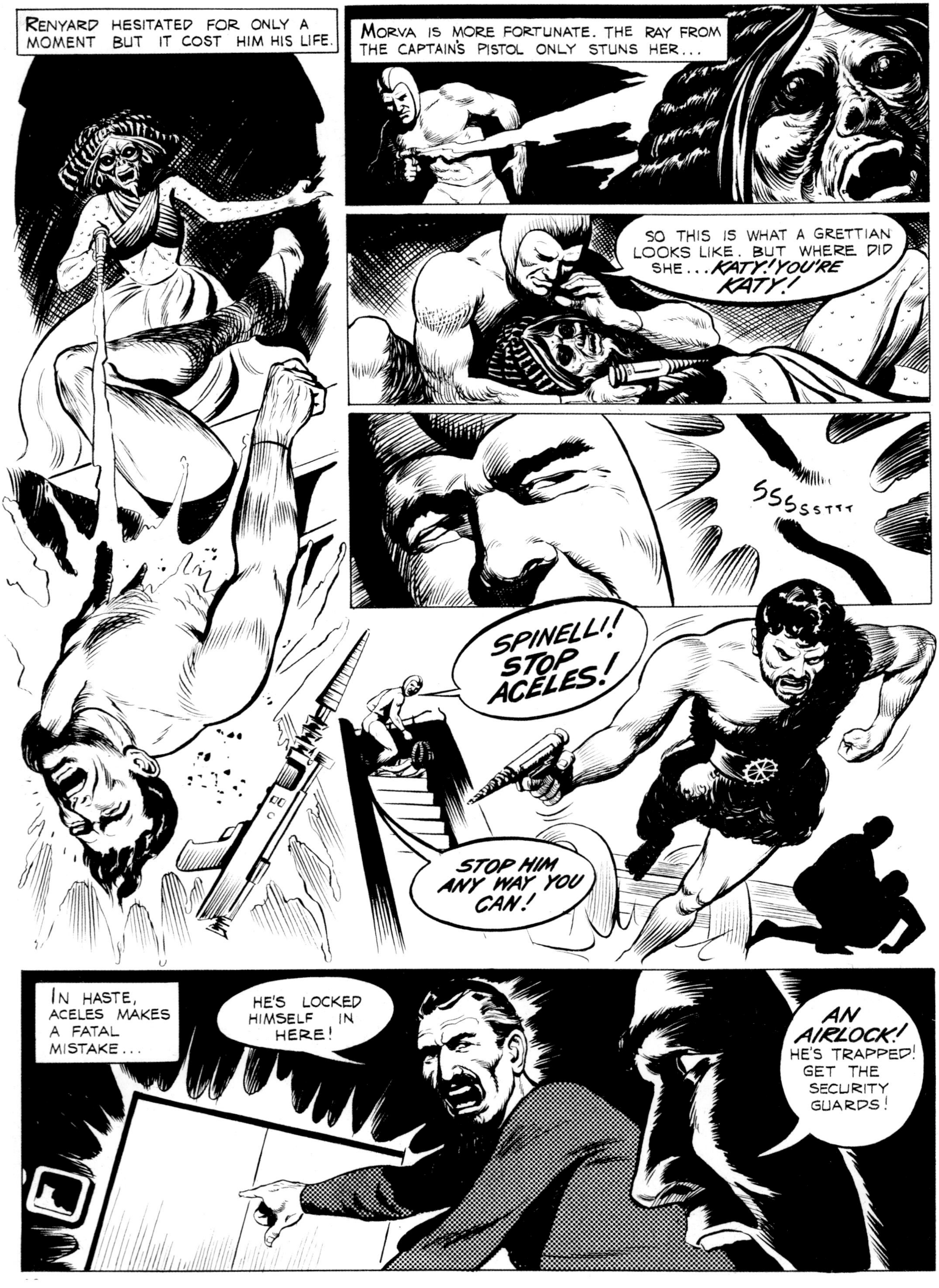
RENYARD HESITATED FOR ONLY A MOMENT BUT IT COST HIM HIS LIFE.
MORVA IS MORE FORTUNATE. THE RAY FROM THE CAPTAIN'S PISTOL ONLY STUNS HER...
SO THIS IS WHAT A GRETTIAN LOOKS LIKE. BUT WHERE DID SHE... KATY! YOU'RE KATY!
SSSSSTTT
SPINELLI! STOP ACELES!
STOP HIM ANY WAY YOU CAN!
IN HASTE, ACELES MAKES A FATAL MISTAKE...
HE'S LOCKED HIMSELF IN HERE!
AN AIRLOCK! HE'S TRAPPED! GET THE SECURITY GUARDS!

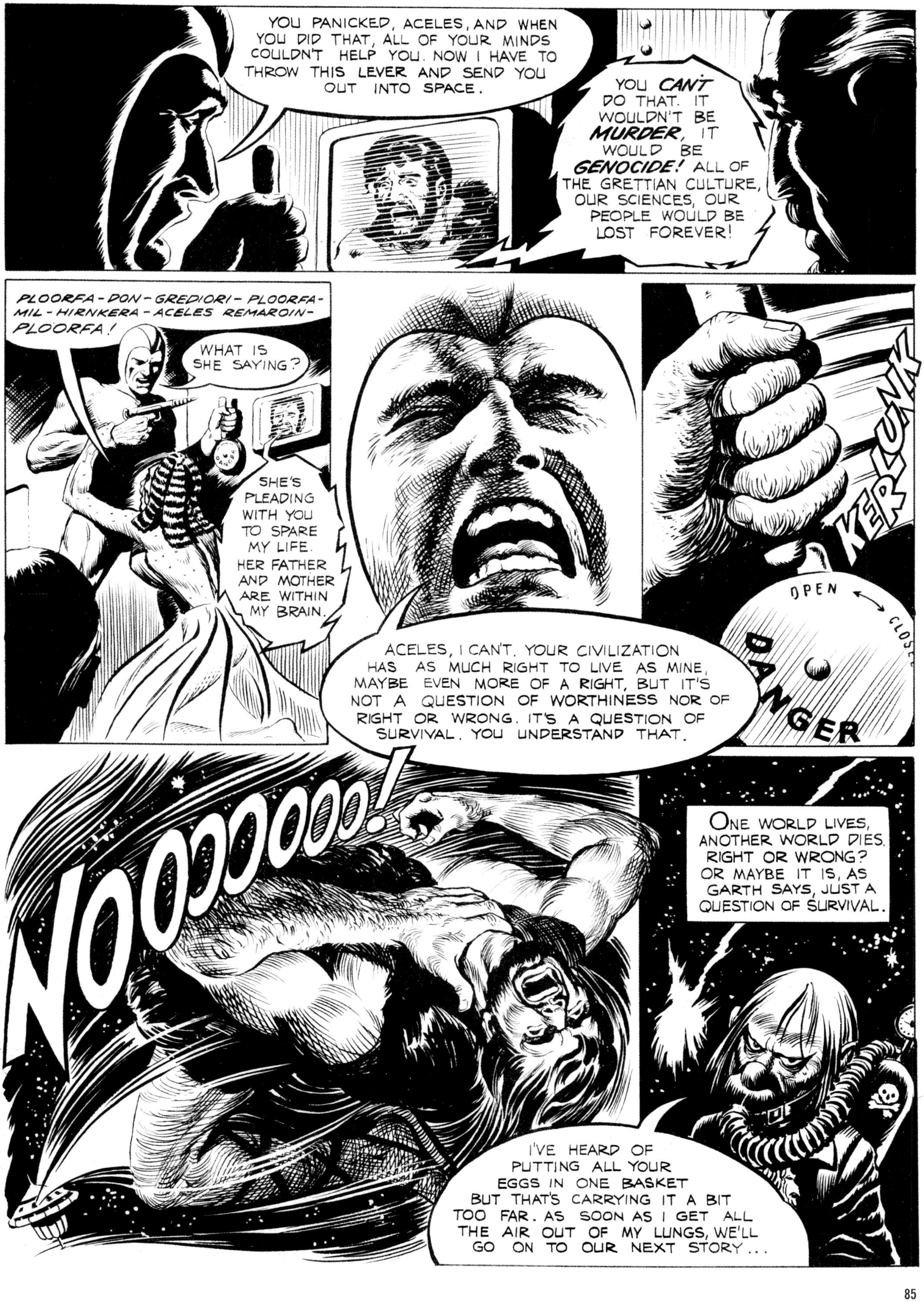
YOU PANICKED, ACELES, AND WHEN YOU DID THAT, ALL OF YOUR MINDS COULDN'T HELP YOU. NOW I HAVE TO THROW THIS LEVER AND SEND YOU OUT INTO SPACE.
YOU CAN'T DO THAT. IT WOULDN'T BE MURDER, IT WOULD BE GENOCIDE! ALL OF THE GRETTIAN CULTURE, OUR SCIENCES, OUR PEOPLE WOULD BE LOST FOREVER!
PLOORFA-DON-GREDIORI-PLOORFA-MIL-HIRNKERA-ACELES REMAROIN-PLOORFA!
WHAT IS SHE SAYING?
SHE'S PLEADING WITH YOU TO SPARE MY LIFE. HER FATHER AND MOTHER ARE WITHIN MY BRAIN.
KERLUNK
OPEN
CLOSE
DANGER
ACELES, I CAN'T. YOUR CIVILIZATION HAS AS MUCH RIGHT TO LIVE AS MINE, MAYBE EVEN MORE OF A RIGHT, BUT IT'S NOT A QUESTION OF WORTHINESS NOR OF RIGHT OR WRONG. IT'S A QUESTION OF SURVIVAL. YOU UNDERSTAND THAT.
NOOOOOOOO!
ONE WORLD LIVES, ANOTHER WORLD DIES. RIGHT OR WRONG? OR MAYBE IT IS, AS GARTH SAYS, JUST A QUESTION OF SURVIVAL.
I'VE HEARD OF PUTTING ALL YOUR EGGS IN ONE BASKET BUT THAT'S CARRYING IT A BIT TOO FAR. AS SOON AS I GET ALL THE AIR OUT OF MY LUNGS, WE'LL GO ON TO OUR NEXT STORY...

THE CREEPY FAN CLUB!

The Fan Club goes international with this picture of a vampire drawn by MONDINI GIANLUIGI of Bologna, Italy . . .

The return address on the envelope this story came in said: Thomas Isenberg, Passaic, N.J. But the story itself was signed, "The Doomed." It's also, as it turns out, the title of the story . . .

THE DOOMED
by Thomas Isenberg

My profession? I'm a scientist. I've worked in seclusion and complete privacy for a number of years. Now I feel it's time to publicize my secret findings.

I have devised a time machine. My experiments with it have been very interesting indeed. My machine is capable of transporting another being from another point in time into my laboratory. The only drawback is that I do not know from which period in time my machine is drawing until the being materializes in my lab. Risky, isn't it? Well, no matter. Here is what has happened:

The first time I operated my machine, my hopes were high. But they were soon to vanish. The lights were flashing, the gears grinding. Then, out of nowhere, a loathsome creature materialized on the floor of my lab. It didn't move at all. But in spite of the ugly result of my first experience, I felt elated. My machine worked.

But what about that thing on the floor? I examined it closely. It appeared to be a headless human body. I assumed it came from a time

in history when decapitation was more in vogue than it is today. I looked down at my feet and discovered I was standing in a pool of blood. I quickly disposed of the horrible thing and went on about my business. I was anxious to give my new machine another try.

A week later, I was ready. The machine worked even more rapidly this time and delivered to my lab floor a second corpse.

This one was riddled by hundreds of bloody holes. No doubt the unfortunate victim of a Foreign Legion firing squad.

I began to have doubts. I can bring back flesh and blood from other times. But why not a live one? I decided to try once again.

The machine went through the electronic motions of reaching back through time. Soon it delivered another body. Another dead man. The skin of this one had eaten away. This was surely the most terrifying result I had gotten yet.

I went forward to drag it away. Suddenly it moved. I gasped. I was speechless and screamless. It got up and began to stumble toward me.

I felt weak and very faint, but somehow I managed to back away from it. I ran wildly toward the door in a sudden burst of strength. Out of curiosity, I turned as I reached the door.

The thing was at the control panel of the machine. It

was using my device to bring more creatures like itself from some forgotten corner of time.

I slammed the door behind me and raced to the top of the tower above my lab. It wasn't until I had reached the top and securely bolted the door behind me that I stopped to catch my breath.

I lost no time in writing this letter. But by now I can hear them down there. There must be hundreds of them! I can hear them on the stair. They're coming for me. Send help! Now! Please . . . help . . . me . . .

This hungry guy was last seen in Long Beach, Cal., where he sat for this portrait by GERALD COLUCCI

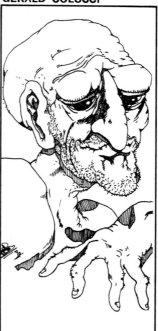

THE MOVIE CRITIC
by Steven Hart

"No, No! Keep away. EEEEYAAA!" "Hold still, Linda, or I might hit you."
"AAAAAAUGGGGHHHH!"
KAAAAAAABOOOOOO
MMM!
Then the words, "The End" appeared on the screen.
"Dad! Did you see that movie?"

"Yes, it was awful."
"Dad, every time you review a monster movie, you don't like it."
"That's because every one I've seen is badly done, John." "You always say that, Dad." "John, it's time to go home." Back home, Fred began to write his review for the local newspaper. When he turned it in, his editor gave him a new assignment: He was to review another new movie, "The War of The Monsters." At the theater, he settled down in his seat and hoped it would be better than he expected. At last, when it ended, he stayed in his seat until the others were gone. After they had left, and he was alone, he heard a voice behind him.

"Well, how did you like it?"
"I think it was terrible. One of the worst I've seen. It wasn't realistic enough." Suddenly, he was dragged from his seat and thrown to the floor. Then he realized the theater was filled with monsters that he had just seen on the screen. "If it's realism you want, you're going to get it right now."

He didn't even have time to scream.

LOST: A LIFE
by Anothony Kowalik

I'm dying! Scared, shuddering uncontrollably. Old. So old, so lonely. My children, who might have been comforting, have all departed in the starships. Starships. To find a life no longer here. Yet I remained behind. As if there were a choice. I loved them as only a mother could. But no tears! Then why do I tremble? The wind is fierce. But I cannot breathe. The air is suffocating. Tainted with ashes, dust. The sky is gray and I cannot see the sun. Choking and shivering. It's getting colder, quickly and inevitably colder. Even if there were any water left. But no, that's gone, too. It's just me. And death. A very lonely me. A very handsome death. Come soon. I have waited. Long. A lifetime. Ended! And with a final, silent cry, the Earth gave up her spirit.

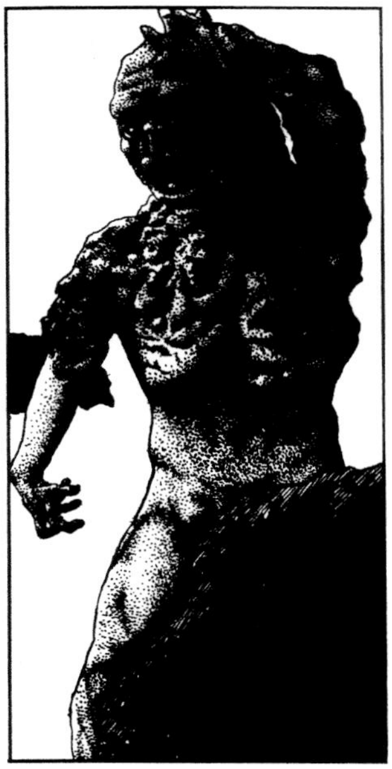

BRANT WITHERS, of Camarillo, Cal., saw this creature in a tar pit where he went for a picnic one day last spring.

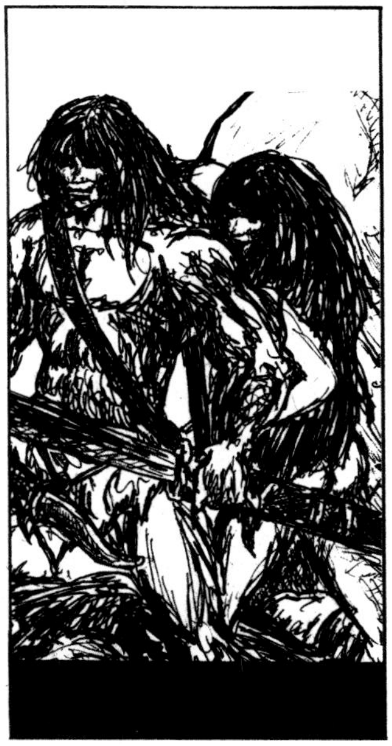

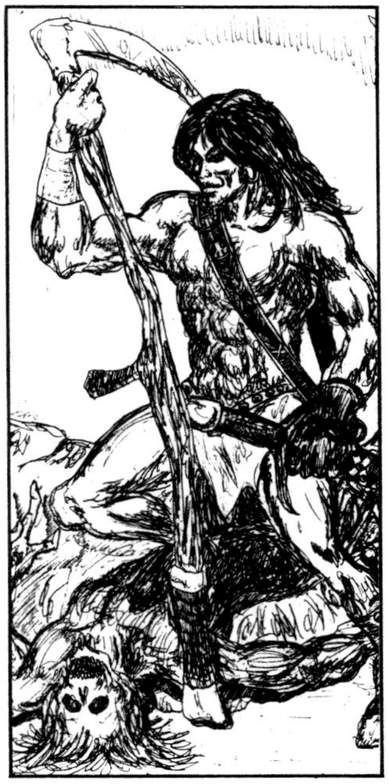

The fellow on top is Konar of Cysergia, Slayer of the Dark Fury. SCOT CASSMAN, who drew both pictures, didn't say who the girl is. The man with the scythe is Abraxis of Mescal, Slayer of Death.

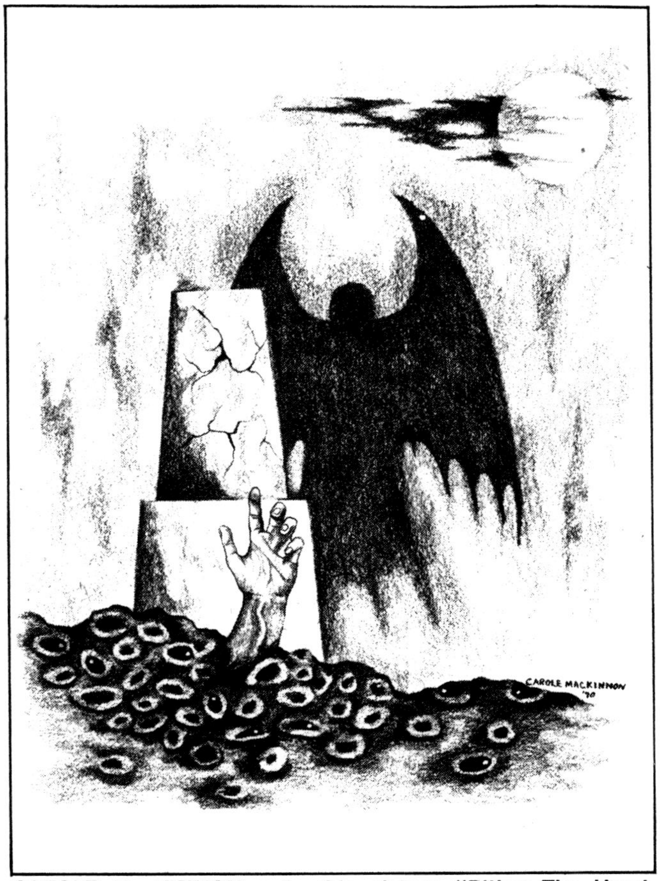
CAROLE MACKINNON '70

CAROLE MacKINNON calls this picture "Biting The Hand That Feeds You."

THE SEARCH FOR THE PHASIMARA PLANT
by John Scrofani

Jack Boltob and Joseph Philke, had traveled all over the world searching for new and different plant species. They had collected every kind of plant known to man. And a few not previously known. Except for two species: one is a plant supposed to be extinct for 1000 years. The other is also supposedly extinct, the strange Phasimara Plant.

Then, in 1968, they discovered a specimen in the frozen Arctic wastes.

The discoverey made, Joe, along with his wife, Cora, and Jack, with his new girl friend, Janet Cameron, headed for home.

It was at the same time that Jack began to experience odd stomach pains. His own doctor wasn't able to find the cause and sent him to a specialist who concluded that he had contracted the disease from exposure to the plant he had discovered in the Artic. The only possible cure, he said, was the rare Pharisma Plant, the only known cure for this strange disease. If the plant could not be found, Jack would be dead within five years.

All this had taken place three years ago. And now, with only two years of life left, there was only place left to search: the jungles of India.

In a little clearing in the Indian jungle stands a little cabin. Inside, Jack and Janet are playing a game of cards, while Joe and Cora silently read.

Suddenly, breaking the somber mood, a horrible blood-curdling sound fills the air. Then, just as suddenly, a deathly silence.

Then, a huge, reptile-like creature slithers into view.

Rearing more than nine feet in the air, it is covered with a green, horny material. Sprouting from its side are two long powerful arms like those of a man, except for the hands, which are more like claws. The head of the creature is mounted on a thick, powerful neck. Its cavern-like mouth is armed with huge curved fangs. And its dully-glowing eyes bulge beneath huge, hairy brows. The nose is flat and broad, with flaring nostrils. And running from the top of its head, down to the tip of its thrashing tail, a row of curving bony plates protruding from its scaly skin.

Reaching the cabin, the monster begins to beat at the walls .with its claws. In no time, the walls give way and the creature is inside.

Spying Janet, who by now is unconscious on the floor, it charges toward her. Jack, who has been paralized with horror, leaps forward to protect her. But just as he steps forward, his stomach tightens in pain. Everything blurs in front of his eyes. Joe picks up a chair and rushes toward the monster. He breaks it over the creature's head. The demon lashes out, sending him sprawling into a corner.

Now, undisturbed, the creature picks Janet up and retreats through the broken wall.

Minutes later, the others recover enough to go after the girl. Arming themselves with rifles, they head into the jungle.

As the trio enters a clearing, the monster rushes them from behind a huge boulder.

Jack raises his rifle. But the creature is on him before he can fire. The monster grabs Jack by the neck, hurling him into the thick underbrush. As it turns to face Joe, the gun goes off, hitting the creature in the eye. Angered by pain, the monster clamps its powerful jaws onto Joe's shoulder. Rearing up to full height, the demon hurls Joe into a tree, killing him instantly.

Cora, frightened out of her wits, empties her pistol at the creature. Two of her bullets rip into its shoulder, a third hits its stomach.

Grimacing in pain, the monster charges. But before it reaches her, Jack leaps onto its back with a long Bowie knife.

Screaming in pain and anger, the creature lashes out. It pulls Jack up toward its head, and the man pumps six bullets into its head.

The wounded creature drops to the ground. Dead. But Jack is dying, too. As Cora reaches him, he breathes his last. Looking under his outstretched arm, she sees growing there the rare Phasimara Plant.

Have you got something rare you'd like to see planted on these pages? Drop them in the mail.

Address to:
CREEPY FAN CLUB

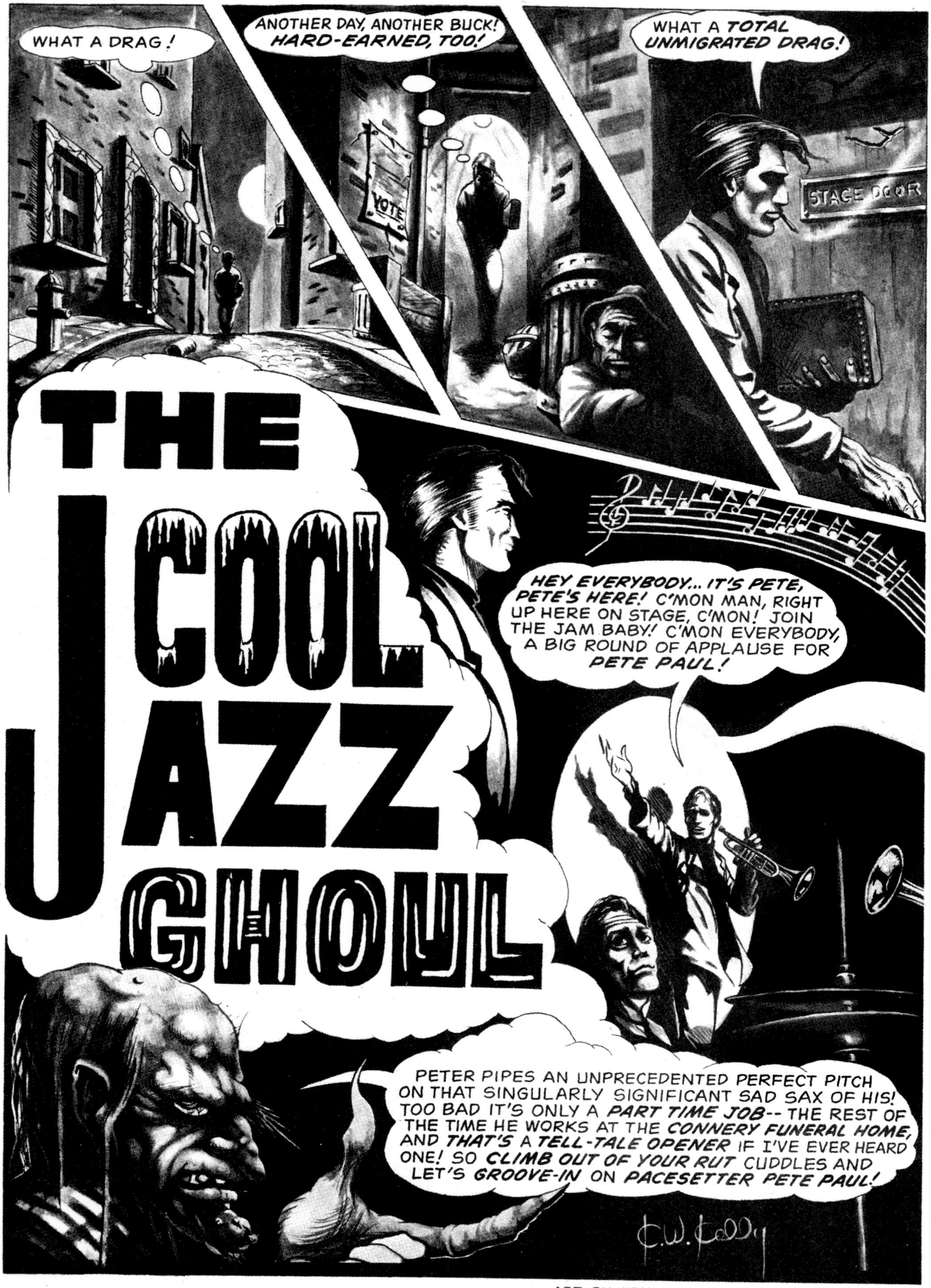
WHAT A DRAG!
ANOTHER DAY, ANOTHER BUCK! HARD-EARNED, TOO!
VOTE
WHAT A TOTAL UNMIGRATED DRAG!
STAGE DOOR
THE COOL JAZZ GHOUL
HEY EVERYBODY... IT'S PETE, PETE'S HERE! C'MON MAN, RIGHT UP HERE ON STAGE, C'MON! JOIN THE JAM BABY! C'MON EVERYBODY, A BIG ROUND OF APPLAUSE FOR PETE PAUL!
PETER PIPES AN UNPRECEDENTED PERFECT PITCH ON THAT SINGULARLY SIGNIFICANT SAD SAX OF HIS! TOO BAD IT'S ONLY A PART TIME JOB-- THE REST OF THE TIME HE WORKS AT THE CONNERY FUNERAL HOME, AND THAT'S A TELL-TALE OPENER IF I'VE EVER HEARD ONE! SO CLIMB OUT OF YOUR RUT CUDDLES AND LET'S GROOVE-IN ON PACESETTER PETE PAUL!

ART BY KEN KELLEY/STORY BY AL HEWETSON

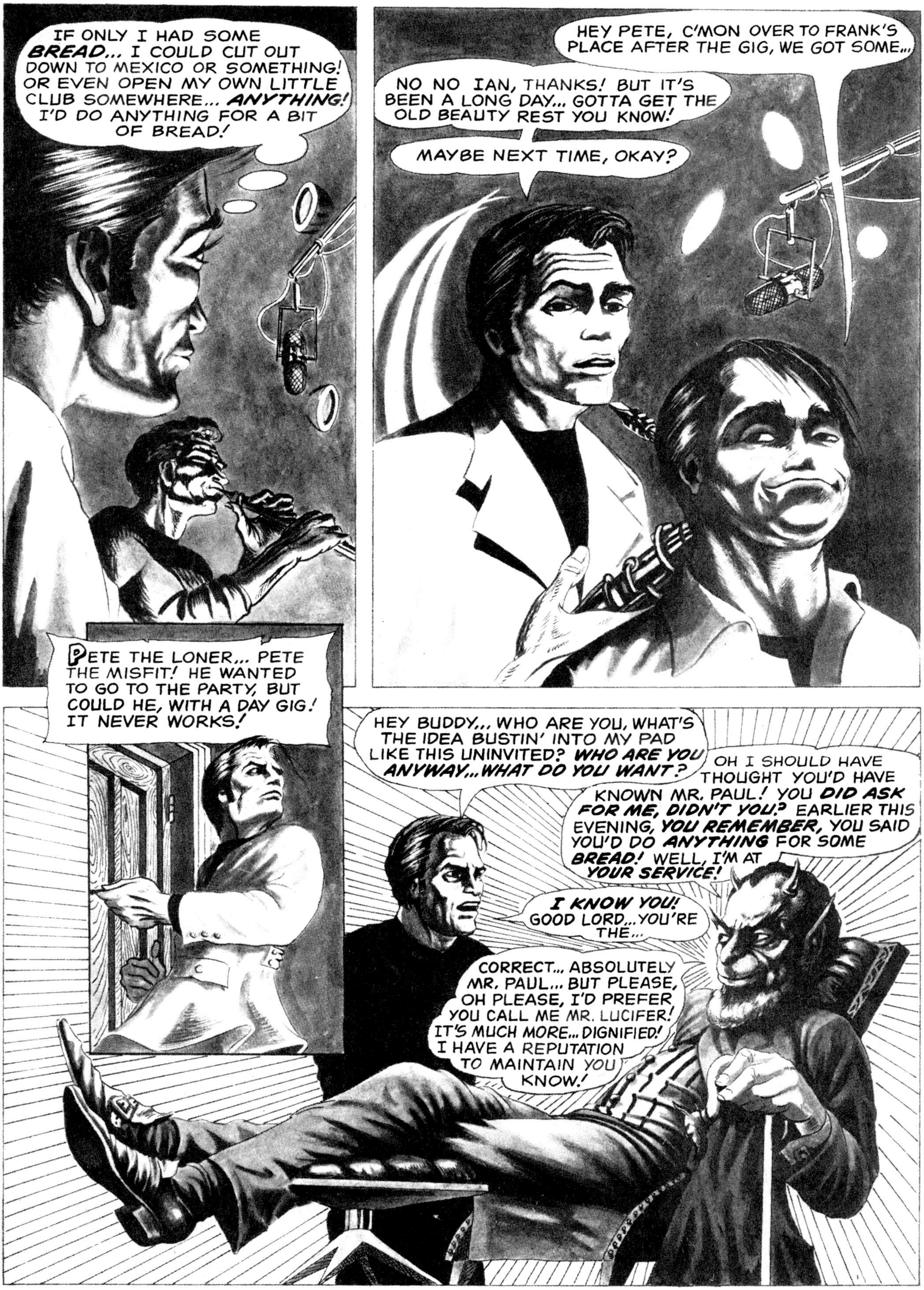

IF ONLY I HAD SOME BREAD... I COULD CUT OUT DOWN TO MEXICO OR SOMETHING! OR EVEN OPEN MY OWN LITTLE CLUB SOMEWHERE... ANYTHING! I'D DO ANYTHING FOR A BIT OF BREAD!
HEY PETE, C'MON OVER TO FRANK'S PLACE AFTER THE GIG, WE GOT SOME...
NO NO IAN, THANKS! BUT IT'S BEEN A LONG DAY... GOTTA GET THE OLD BEAUTY REST YOU KNOW!
MAYBE NEXT TIME, OKAY?
PETE THE LONER... PETE THE MISFIT! HE WANTED TO GO TO THE PARTY, BUT COULD HE, WITH A DAY GIG! IT NEVER WORKS!
HEY BUDDY... WHO ARE YOU, WHAT'S THE IDEA BUSTIN' INTO MY PAD LIKE THIS UNINVITED? WHO ARE YOU ANYWAY... WHAT DO YOU WANT?
OH I SHOULD HAVE THOUGHT YOU'D HAVE KNOWN MR. PAUL! YOU DID ASK FOR ME, DIDN'T YOU? EARLIER THIS EVENING, YOU REMEMBER, YOU SAID YOU'D DO ANYTHING FOR SOME BREAD! WELL, I'M AT YOUR SERVICE!
I KNOW YOU! GOOD LORD... YOU'RE THE...
CORRECT... ABSOLUTELY MR. PAUL... BUT PLEASE, OH PLEASE, I'D PREFER YOU CALL ME MR. LUCIFER! IT'S MUCH MORE... DIGNIFIED! I HAVE A REPUTATION TO MAINTAIN YOU KNOW!

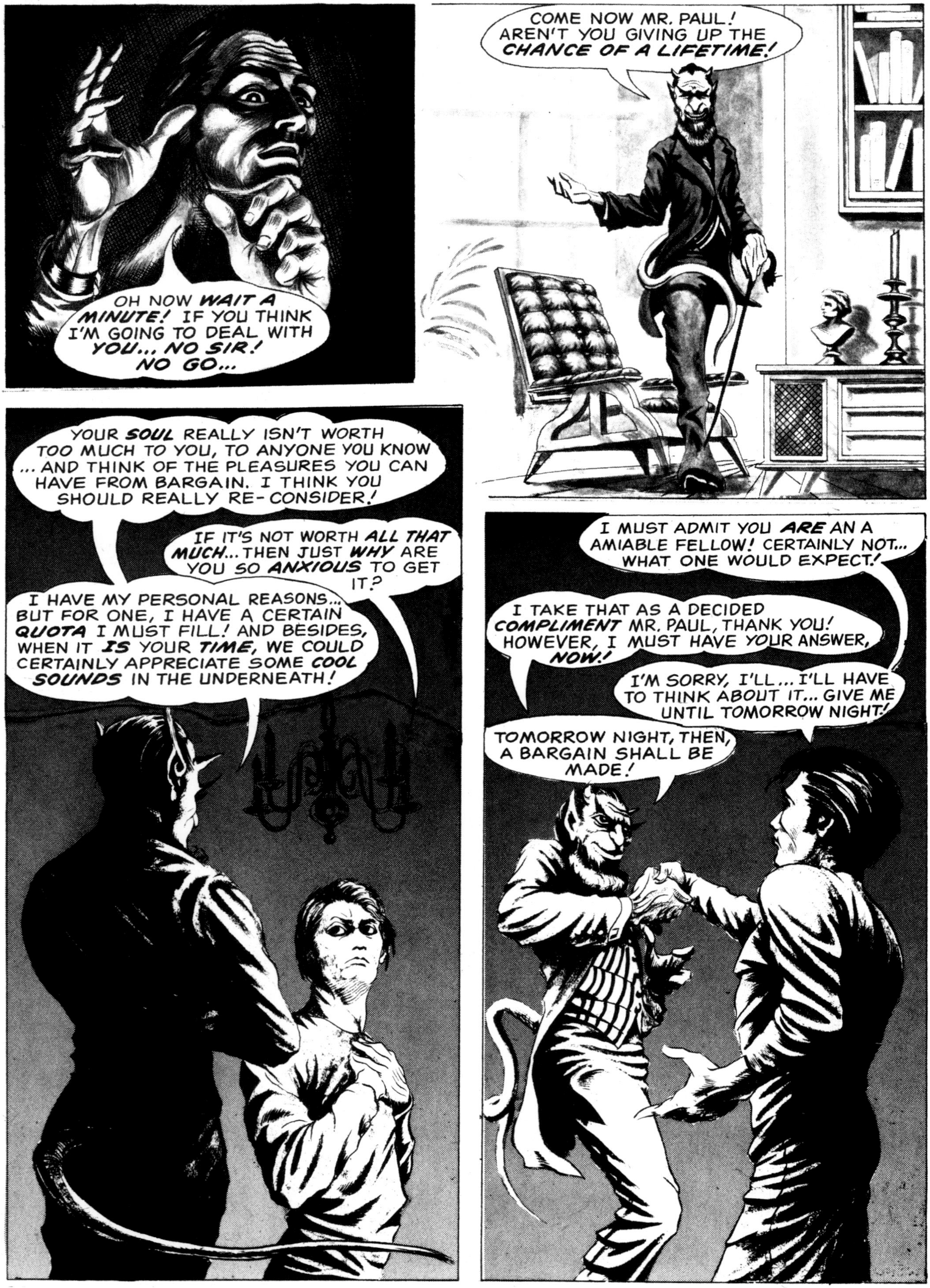

OH NOW WAIT A MINUTE! IF YOU THINK I'M GOING TO DEAL WITH YOU..., NO SIR! NO GO...
COME NOW MR. PAUL! AREN'T YOU GIVING UP THE CHANCE OF A LIFETIME!
YOUR SOUL REALLY ISN'T WORTH TOO MUCH TO YOU, TO ANYONE YOU KNOW ... AND THINK OF THE PLEASURES YOU CAN HAVE FROM BARGAIN. I THINK YOU SHOULD REALLY RE-CONSIDER!
IF IT'S NOT WORTH ALL THAT MUCH... THEN JUST WHY ARE YOU SO ANXIOUS TO GET IT?
I HAVE MY PERSONAL REASONS... BUT FOR ONE, I HAVE A CERTAIN QUOTA I MUST FILL! AND BESIDES, WHEN IT IS YOUR TIME, WE COULD CERTAINLY APPRECIATE SOME COOL SOUNDS IN THE UNDERNEATH!
I MUST ADMIT YOU ARE AN A AMIABLE FELLOW! CERTAINLY NOT... WHAT ONE WOULD EXPECT!
I TAKE THAT AS A DECIDED COMPLIMENT MR. PAUL, THANK YOU! HOWEVER, I MUST HAVE YOUR ANSWER, NOW!
I'M SORRY, I'LL... I'LL HAVE TO THINK ABOUT IT... GIVE ME UNTIL TOMORROW NIGHT!
TOMORROW NIGHT, THEN, A BARGAIN SHALL BE MADE!

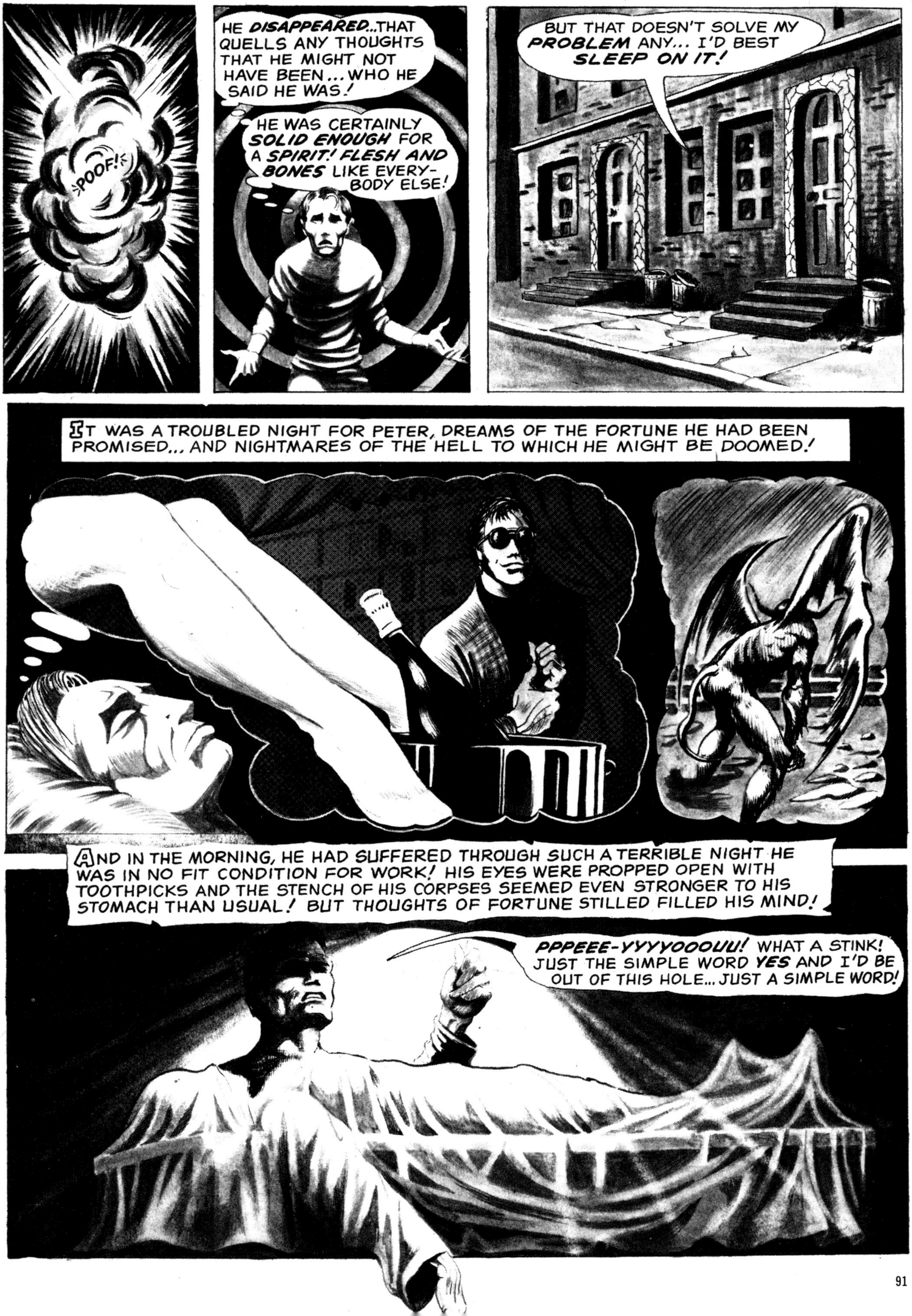
POOF!
HE DISAPPEARED...THAT QUELLS ANY THOUGHTS THAT HE MIGHT NOT HAVE BEEN... WHO HE SAID HE WAS!
HE WAS CERTAINLY SOLID ENOUGH FOR A SPIRIT! FLESH AND BONES LIKE EVERY-BODY ELSE!
BUT THAT DOESN'T SOLVE MY PROBLEM ANY... I'D BEST SLEEP ON IT!
IT WAS A TROUBLED NIGHT FOR PETER, DREAMS OF THE FORTUNE HE HAD BEEN PROMISED... AND NIGHTMARES OF THE HELL TO WHICH HE MIGHT BE DOOMED!
AND IN THE MORNING, HE HAD SUFFERED THROUGH SUCH A TERRIBLE NIGHT HE WAS IN NO FIT CONDITION FOR WORK! HIS EYES WERE PROPPED OPEN WITH TOOTHPICKS AND THE STENCH OF HIS CORPSES SEEMED EVEN STRONGER TO HIS STOMACH THAN USUAL! BUT THOUGHTS OF FORTUNE STILLED FILLED HIS MIND!
PPPEEE-YYYYOOOUU! WHAT A STINK! JUST THE SIMPLE WORD YES AND I'D BE OUT OF THIS HOLE... JUST A SIMPLE WORD!

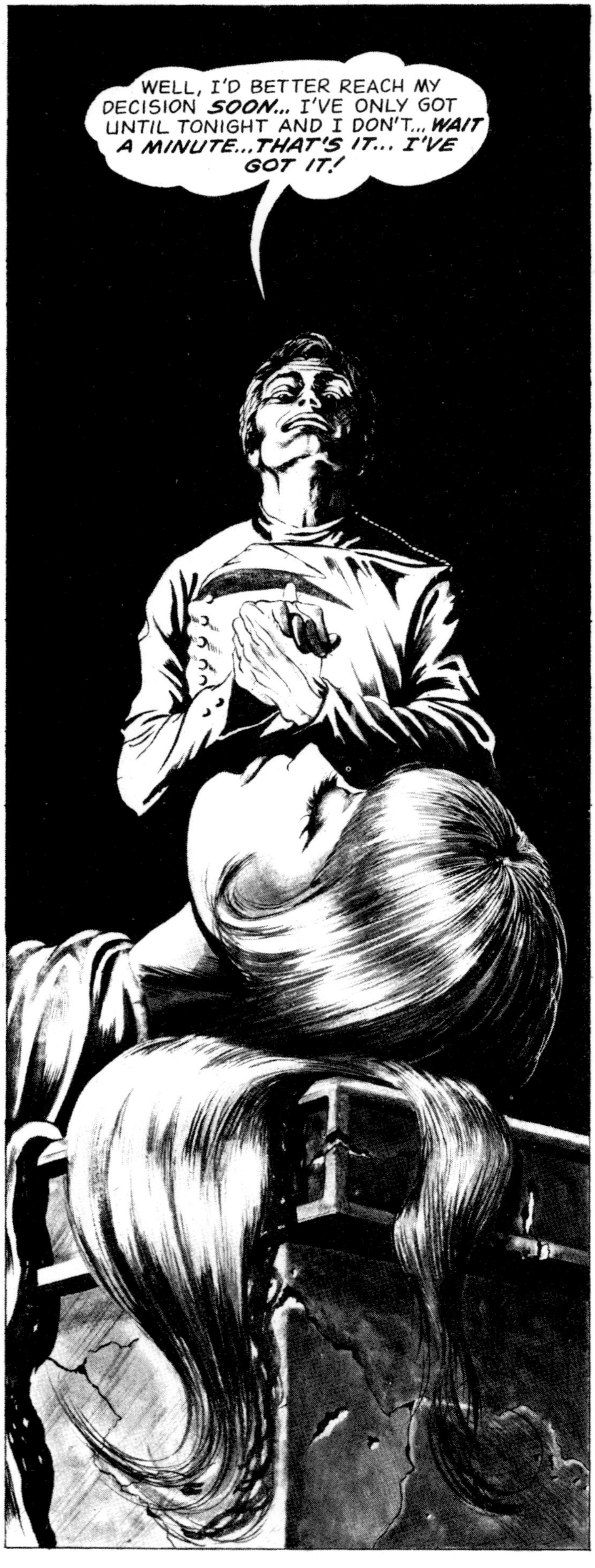
WELL, I'D BETTER REACH MY DECISION SOON... I'VE ONLY GOT UNTIL TONIGHT AND I DON'T... WAIT A MINUTE... THAT'S IT... I'VE GOT IT!

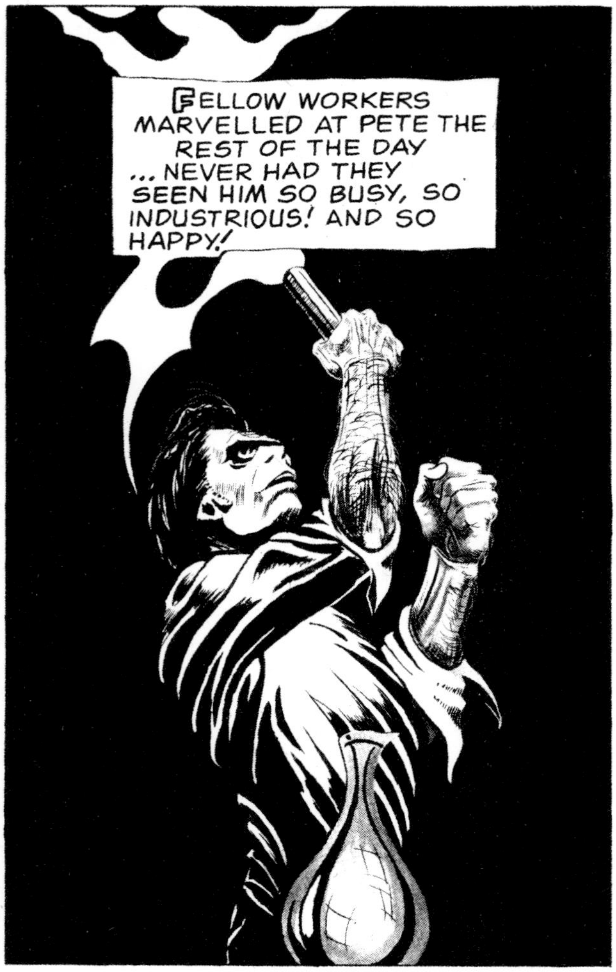
FELLOW WORKERS MARVELLED AT PETE THE REST OF THE DAY ... NEVER HAD THEY SEEN HIM SO BUSY, SO INDUSTRIOUS! AND SO HAPPY!

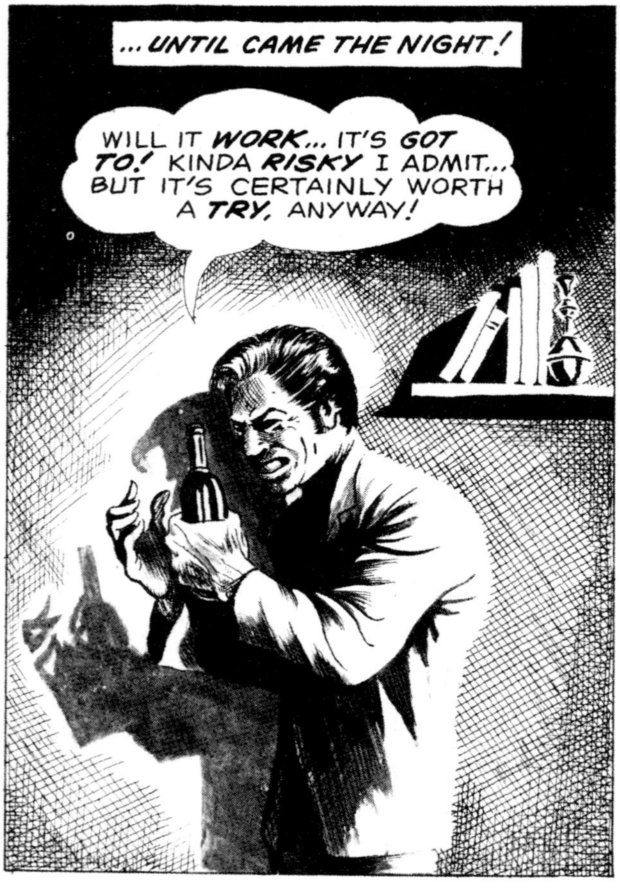
... UNTIL CAME THE NIGHT!
WILL IT WORK... IT'S GOT TO! KINDA RISKY I ADMIT... BUT IT'S CERTAINLY WORTH A TRY, ANYWAY!

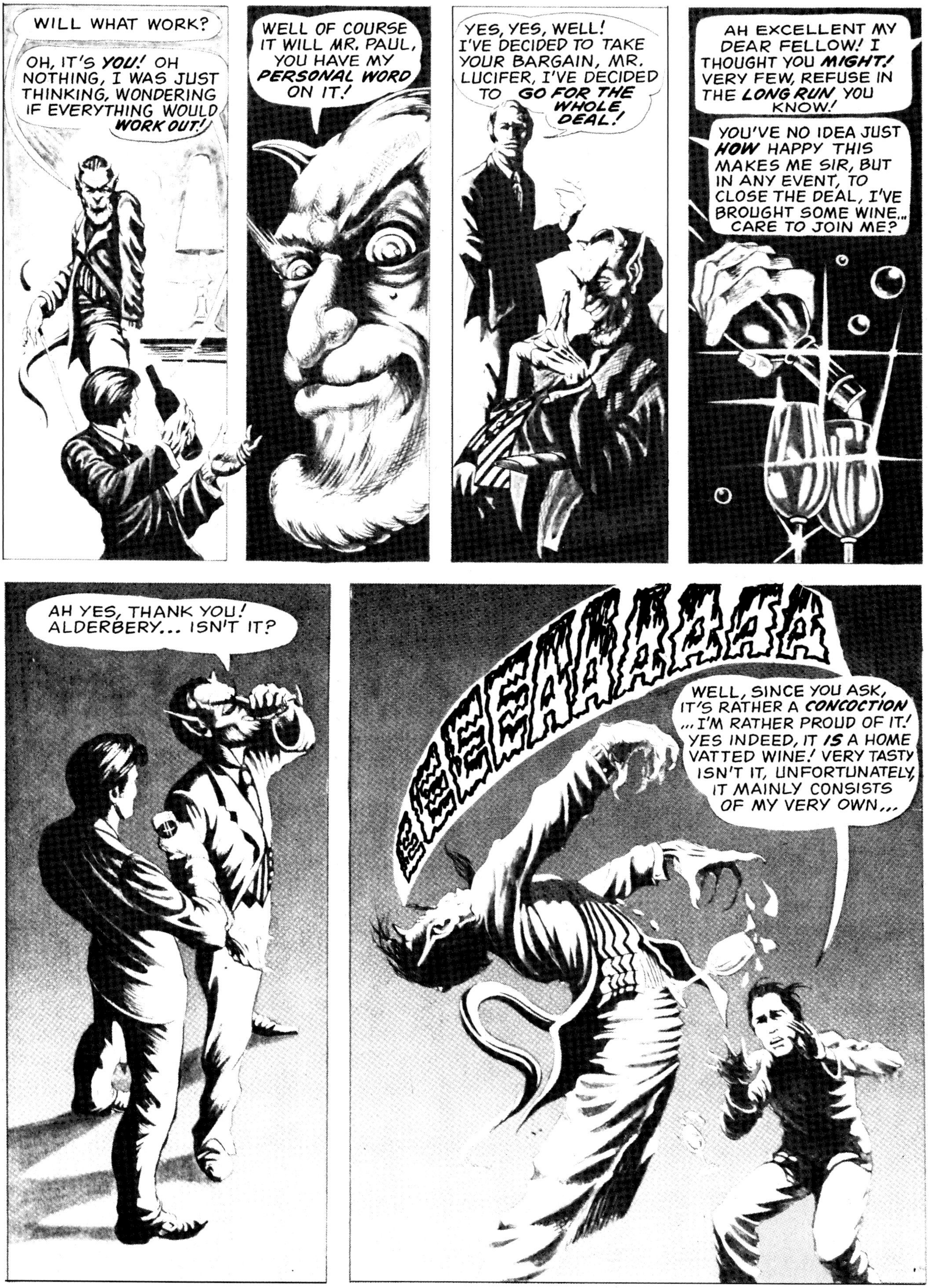

WILL WHAT WORK?
OH, IT'S YOU! OH NOTHING, I WAS JUST THINKING, WONDERING IF EVERYTHING WOULD WORK OUT!
WELL OF COURSE IT WILL MR. PAUL, YOU HAVE MY PERSONAL WORD ON IT!
YES, YES, WELL! I'VE DECIDED TO TAKE YOUR BARGAIN, MR. LUCIFER, I'VE DECIDED TO GO FOR THE WHOLE DEAL!
AH EXCELLENT MY DEAR FELLOW! I THOUGHT YOU MIGHT! VERY FEW, REFUSE IN THE LONG RUN YOU KNOW!
YOU'VE NO IDEA JUST HOW HAPPY THIS MAKES ME SIR, BUT IN ANY EVENT, TO CLOSE THE DEAL, I'VE BROUGHT SOME WINE... CARE TO JOIN ME?"
AH YES, THANK YOU! ALDERBERY... ISN'T IT?
EEEEAAAAAAA
WELL, SINCE YOU ASK, IT'S RATHER A CONCOCTION ... I'M RATHER PROUD OF IT! YES INDEED, IT IS A HOME VATTED WINE! VERY TASTY ISN'T IT, UNFORTUNATELY, IT MAINLY CONSISTS OF MY VERY OWN...

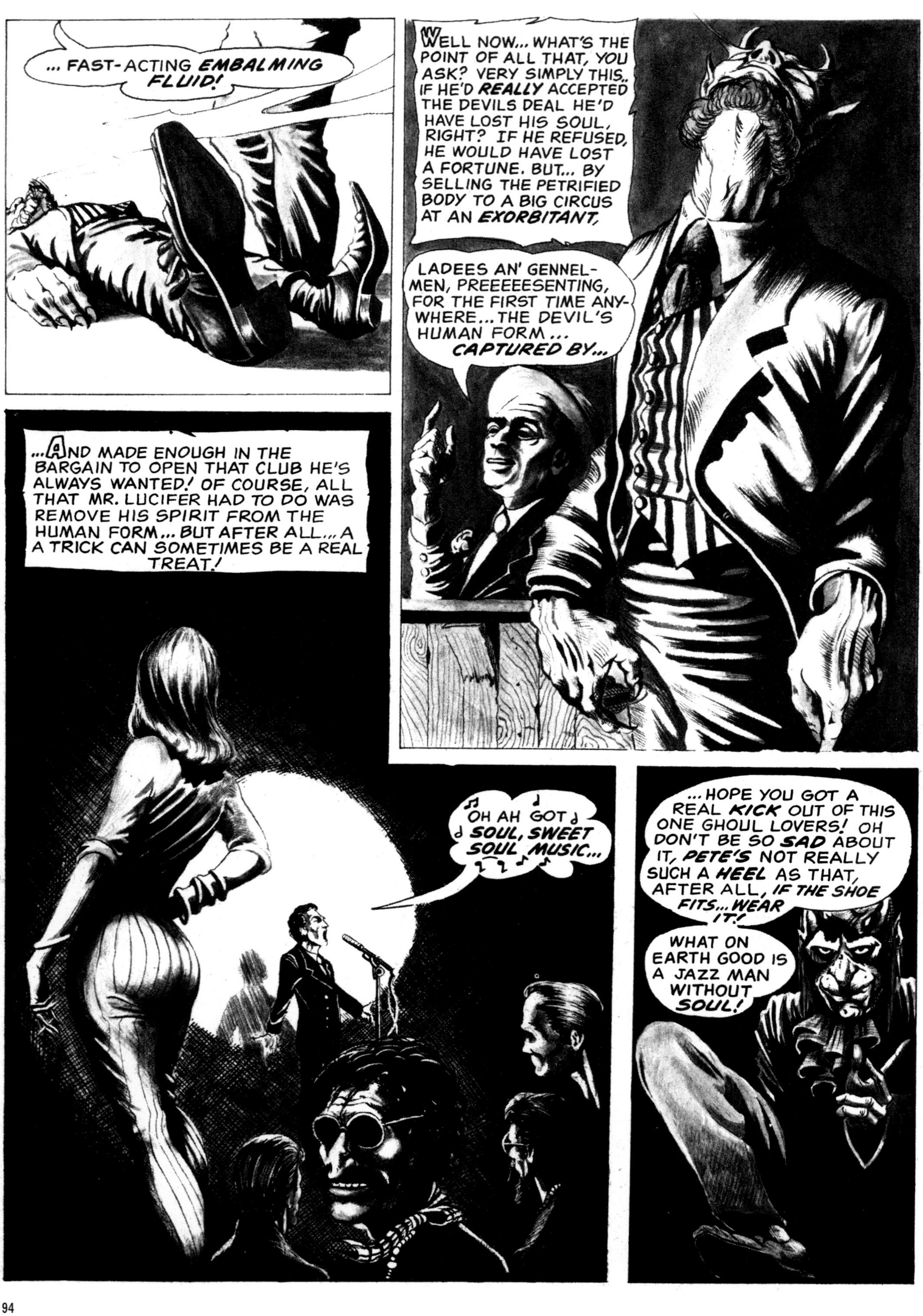
... FAST-ACTING EMBALMING FLUID!
WELL NOW... WHAT'S THE POINT OF ALL THAT, YOU ASK? VERY SIMPLY THIS.. IF HE'D REALLY ACCEPTED THE DEVILS DEAL HE'D HAVE LOST HIS SOUL, RIGHT? IF HE REFUSED, HE WOULD HAVE LOST A FORTUNE. BUT... BY SELLING THE PETRIFIED BODY TO A BIG CIRCUS AT AN EXORBITANT,
LADEES AN' GENNEL-MEN, PREEEEESENTING, FOR THE FIRST TIME ANY-WHERE... THE DEVIL'S HUMAN FORM... CAPTURED BY...
...AND MADE ENOUGH IN THE BARGAIN TO OPEN THAT CLUB HE'S ALWAYS WANTED! OF COURSE, ALL THAT MR. LUCIFER HAD TO DO WAS REMOVE HIS SPIRIT FROM THE HUMAN FORM... BUT AFTER ALL... A A TRICK CAN SOMETIMES BE A REAL TREAT!
OH AH GOT SOUL, SWEET SOUL MUSIC...
...HOPE YOU GOT A REAL KICK OUT OF THIS ONE GHOUL LOVERS! OH DON'T BE SO SAD ABOUT IT, PETE'S NOT REALLY SUCH A HEEL AS THAT, AFTER ALL, IF THE SHOE FITS... WEAR IT!
WHAT ON EARTH GOOD IS A JAZZ MAN WITHOUT SOUL!

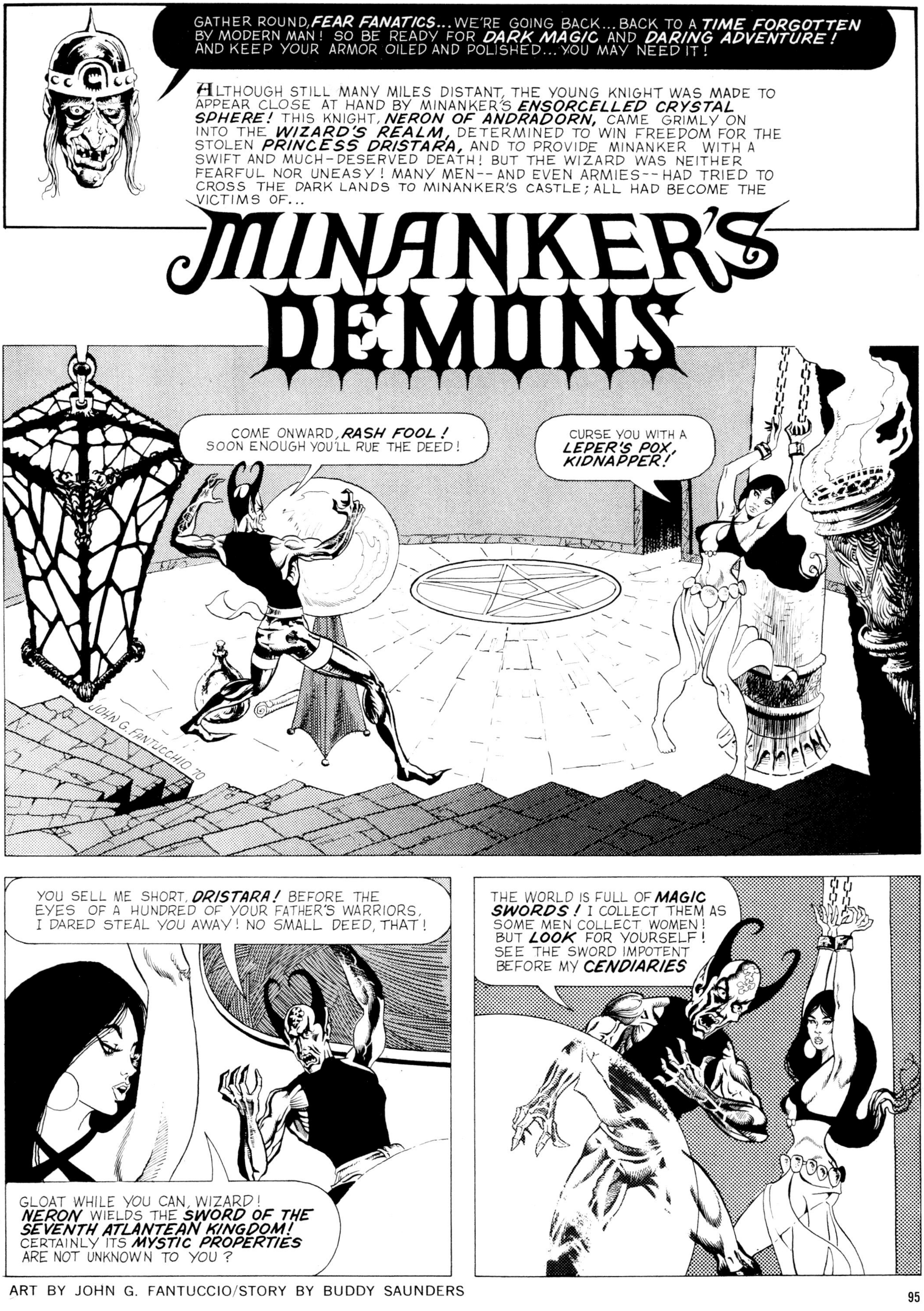
GATHER ROUND, FEAR FANATICS... WE'RE GOING BACK... BACK TO A TIME FORGOTTEN BY MODERN MAN! SO BE READY FOR DARK MAGIC AND DARING ADVENTURE! AND KEEP YOUR ARMOR OILED AND POLISHED... YOU MAY NEED IT!
ALTHOUGH STILL MANY MILES DISTANT, THE YOUNG KNIGHT WAS MADE TO APPEAR CLOSE AT HAND BY MINANKER'S ENSORCELLED CRYSTAL SPHERE! THIS KNIGHT, NERON OF ANDRADORN, CAME GRIMLY ON INTO THE WIZARD'S REALM, DETERMINED TO WIN FREEDOM FOR THE STOLEN PRINCESS DRISTARA, AND TO PROVIDE MINANKER WITH A SWIFT AND MUCH-DESERVED DEATH! BUT THE WIZARD WAS NEITHER FEARFUL NOR UNEASY! MANY MEN-- AND EVEN ARMIES-- HAD TRIED TO CROSS THE DARK LANDS TO MINANKER'S CASTLE; ALL HAD BECOME THE VICTIMS OF...
MINANKER'S DEMONS
COME ONWARD, RASH FOOL! SOON ENOUGH YOU'LL RUE THE DEED!
CURSE YOU WITH A LEPER'S POX, KIDNAPPER!
JOHN G. FANTUCCHIO '70
YOU SELL ME SHORT, DRISTARA! BEFORE THE EYES OF A HUNDRED OF YOUR FATHER'S WARRIORS, I DARED STEAL YOU AWAY! NO SMALL DEED, THAT!
GLOAT WHILE YOU CAN, WIZARD! NERON WIELDS THE SWORD OF THE SEVENTH ATLANTEAN KINGDOM! CERTAINLY ITS MYSTIC PROPERTIES ARE NOT UNKNOWN TO YOU?
THE WORLD IS FULL OF MAGIC SWORDS! I COLLECT THEM AS SOME MEN COLLECT WOMEN! BUT LOOK FOR YOURSELF! SEE THE SWORD IMPOTENT BEFORE MY CENDIARIES

ART BY JOHN G. FANTUCCIO/STORY BY BUDDY SAUNDERS

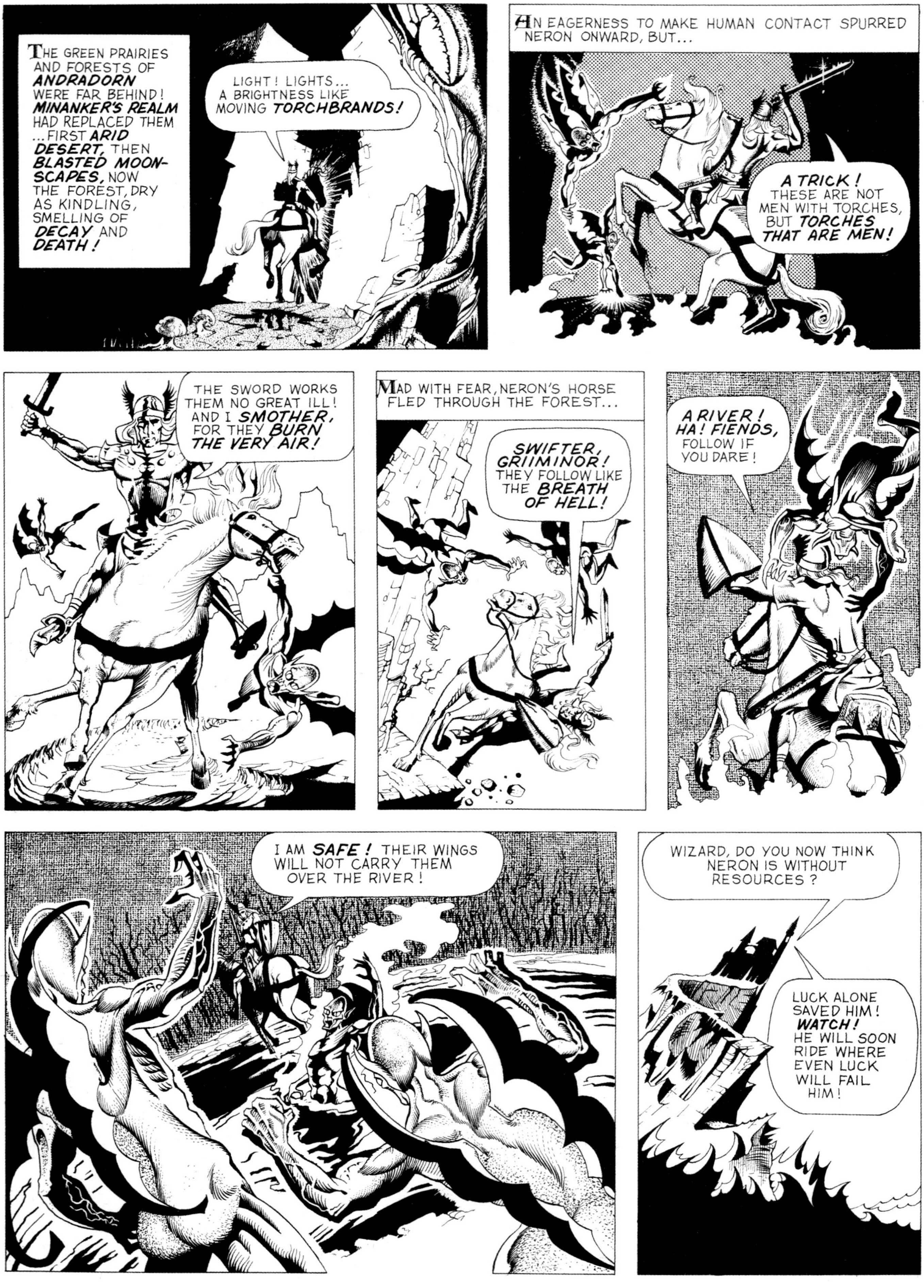
THE GREEN PRAIRIES AND FORESTS OF ANDRADORN WERE FAR BEHIND! MINANKER'S REALM HAD REPLACED THEM ...FIRST ARID DESERT, THEN BLASTED MOON-SCAPES, NOW THE FOREST, DRY AS KINDLING, SMELLING OF DECAY AND DEATH!
LIGHT! LIGHTS... A BRIGHTNESS LIKE MOVING TORCHBRANDS!
AN EAGERNESS TO MAKE HUMAN CONTACT SPURRED NERON ONWARD, BUT...
A TRICK! THESE ARE NOT MEN WITH TORCHES, BUT TORCHES THAT ARE MEN!
THE SWORD WORKS THEM NO GREAT ILL! AND I SMOTHER, FOR THEY BURN THE VERY AIR!
MAD WITH FEAR, NERON'S HORSE FLED THROUGH THE FOREST...
SWIFTER, GRIIMINOR! THEY FOLLOW LIKE THE BREATH OF HELL!
A RIVER! HA! FIENDS, FOLLOW IF YOU DARE!
I AM SAFE! THEIR WINGS WILL NOT CARRY THEM OVER THE RIVER!
WIZARD, DO YOU NOW THINK NERON IS WITHOUT RESOURCES?
LUCK ALONE SAVED HIM! WATCH! HE WILL SOON RIDE WHERE EVEN LUCK WILL FAIL HIM!

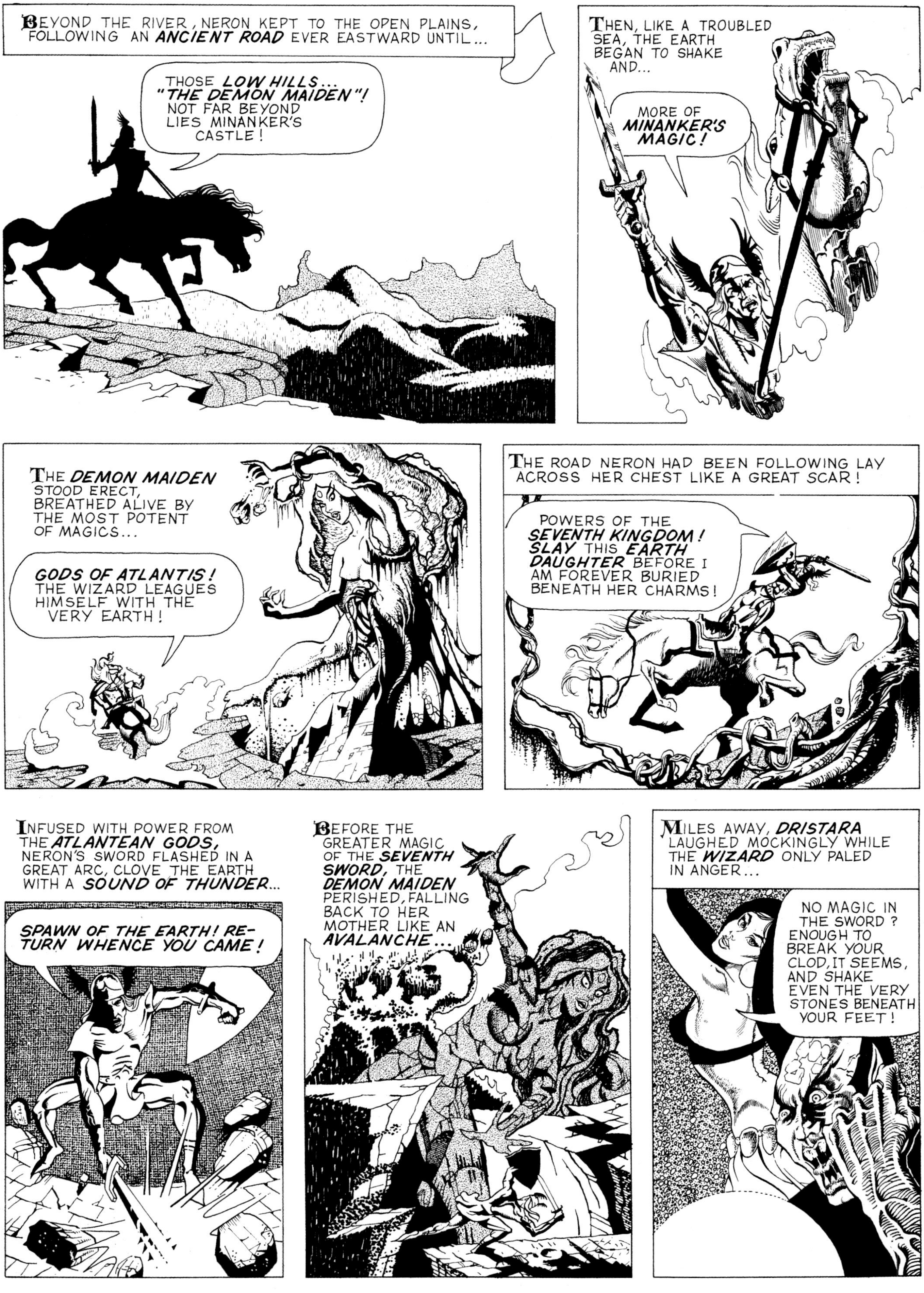

BEYOND THE RIVER, NERON KEPT TO THE OPEN PLAINS, FOLLOWING AN ANCIENT ROAD EVER EASTWARD UNTIL...
THOSE LOW HILLS... "THE DEMON MAIDEN"! NOT FAR BEYOND LIES MINANKER'S CASTLE!
THEN, LIKE A TROUBLED SEA, THE EARTH BEGAN TO SHAKE AND...
MORE OF MINANKER'S MAGIC!
THE DEMON MAIDEN STOOD ERECT, BREATHED ALIVE BY THE MOST POTENT OF MAGICS...
GODS OF ATLANTIS! THE WIZARD LEAGUES HIMSELF WITH THE VERY EARTH!
THE ROAD NERON HAD BEEN FOLLOWING LAY ACROSS HER CHEST LIKE A GREAT SCAR!
POWERS OF THE SEVENTH KINGDOM! SLAY THIS EARTH DAUGHTER BEFORE I AM FOREVER BURIED BENEATH HER CHARMS!
INFUSED WITH POWER FROM THE ATLANTEAN GODS, NERON'S SWORD FLASHED IN A GREAT ARC, CLOVE THE EARTH WITH A SOUND OF THUNDER...
SPAWN OF THE EARTH! RETURN WHENCE YOU CAME!
BEFORE THE GREATER MAGIC OF THE SEVENTH SWORD, THE DEMON MAIDEN PERISHED, FALLING BACK TO HER MOTHER LIKE AN AVALANCHE...
MILES AWAY, DRISTARA LAUGHED MOCKINGLY WHILE THE WIZARD ONLY PALED IN ANGER...
NO MAGIC IN THE SWORD? ENOUGH TO BREAK YOUR CLOD, IT SEEMS, AND SHAKE EVEN THE VERY STONES BENEATH YOUR FEET!

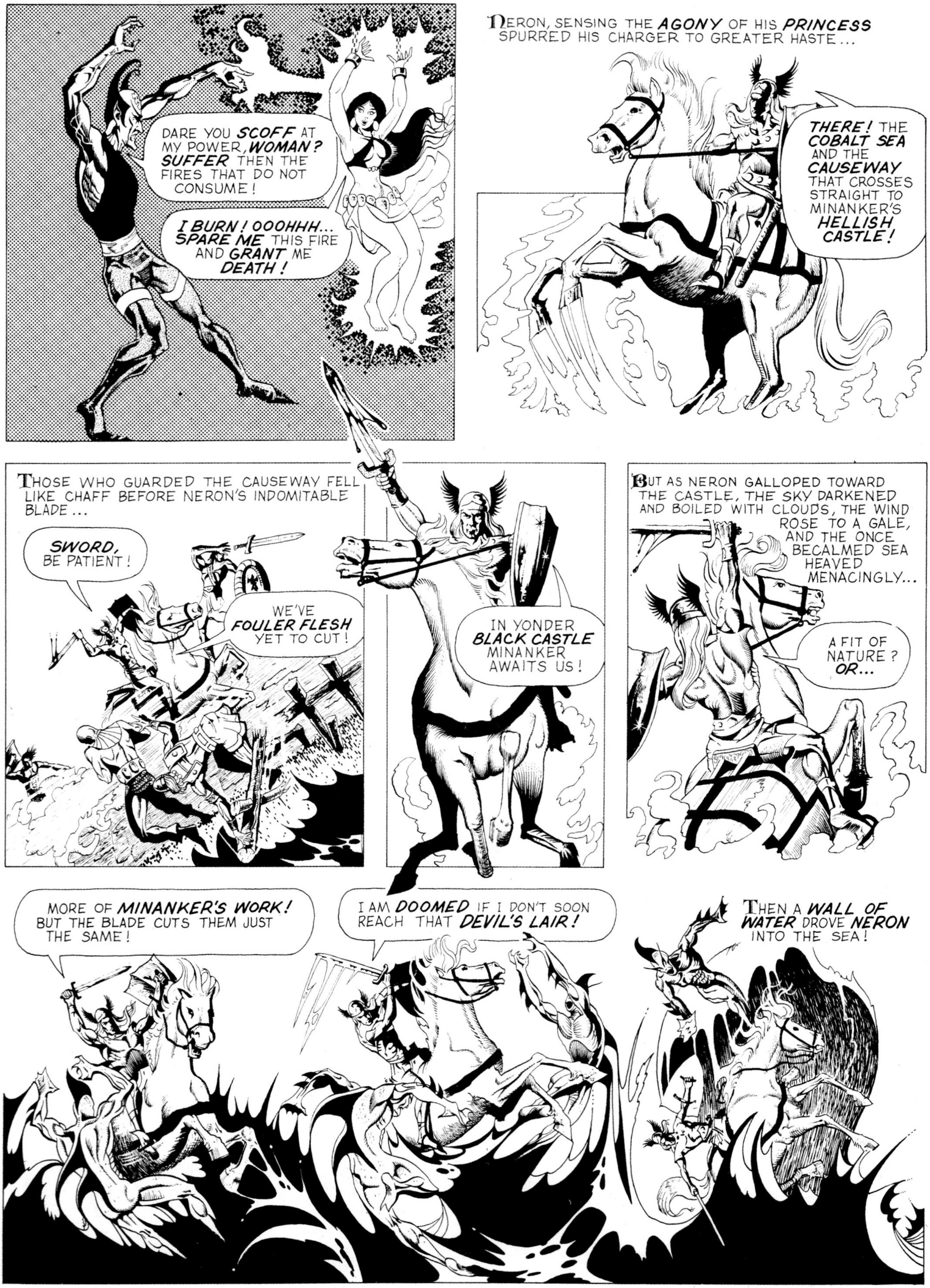

DARE YOU SCOFF AT MY POWER, WOMAN? SUFFER THEN THE FIRES THAT DO NOT CONSUME!
I BURN! OOOHHH... SPARE ME THIS FIRE AND GRANT ME DEATH!
NERON, SENSING THE AGONY OF HIS PRINCESS SPURRED HIS CHARGER TO GREATER HASTE...
THERE! THE COBALT SEA AND THE CAUSEWAY THAT CROSSES STRAIGHT TO MINANKER'S HELLISH CASTLE!
THOSE WHO GUARDED THE CAUSEWAY FELL LIKE CHAFF BEFORE NERON'S INDOMITABLE BLADE...
SWORD, BE PATIENT!
WE'VE FOULER FLESH YET TO CUT!
IN YONDER BLACK CASTLE MINANKER AWAITS US!
BUT AS NERON GALLOPED TOWARD THE CASTLE, THE SKY DARKENED AND BOILED WITH CLOUDS, THE WIND ROSE TO A GALE, AND THE ONCE BECALMED SEA HEAVED MENACINGLY...
A FIT OF NATURE? OR...
MORE OF MINANKER'S WORK! BUT THE BLADE CUTS THEM JUST THE SAME!
I AM DOOMED IF I DON'T SOON REACH THAT DEVIL'S LAIR!
THEN A WALL OF WATER DROVE NERON INTO THE SEA!

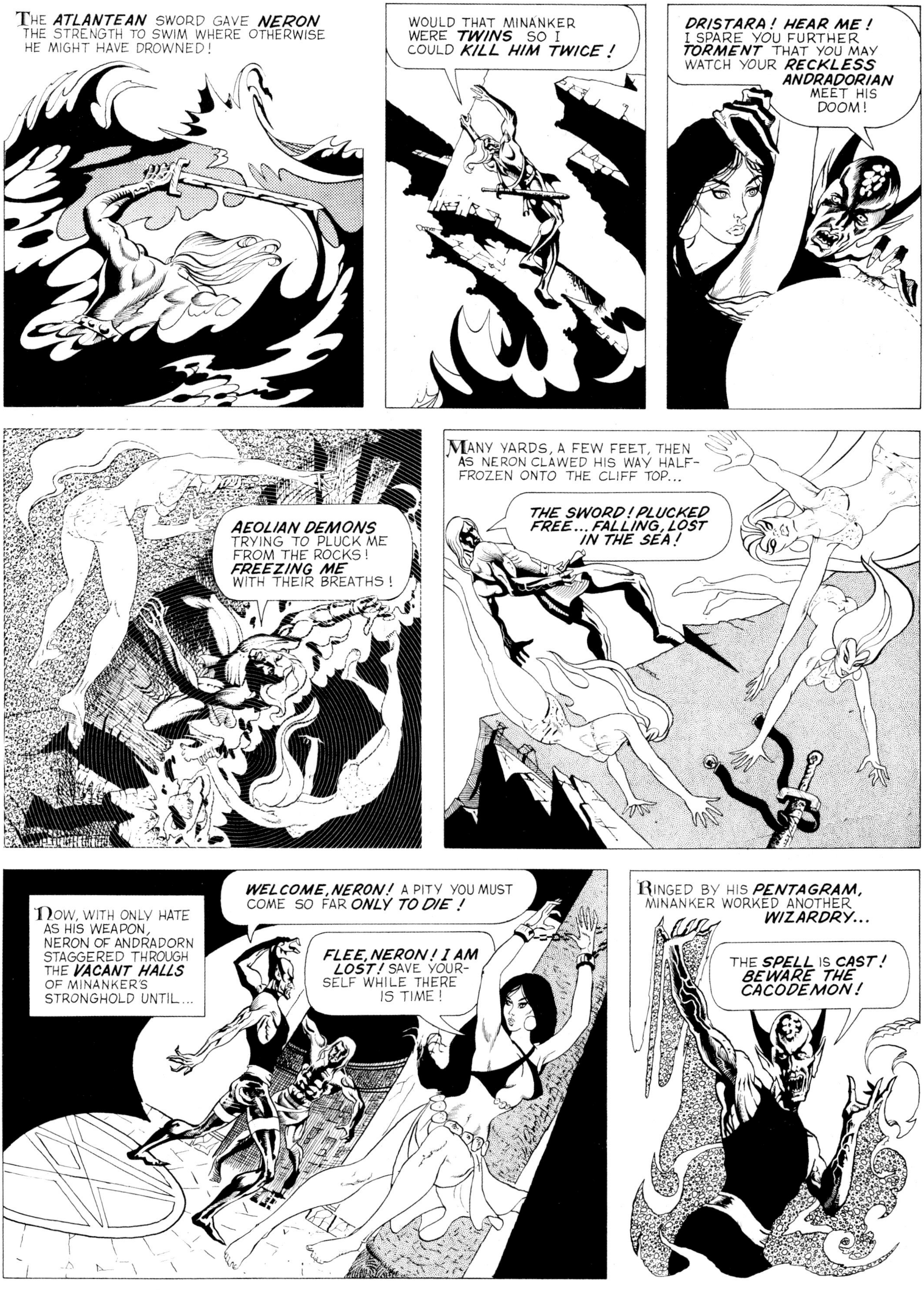
THE ATLANTEAN SWORD GAVE NERON THE STRENGTH TO SWIM WHERE OTHERWISE HE MIGHT HAVE DROWNED!
WOULD THAT MINANKER WERE TWINS SO I COULD KILL HIM TWICE!
DRISTARA! HEAR ME! I SPARE YOU FURTHER TORMENT THAT YOU MAY WATCH YOUR RECKLESS ANDRADORIAN MEET HIS DOOM!
AEOLIAN DEMONS TRYING TO PLUCK ME FROM THE ROCKS! FREEZING ME WITH THEIR BREATHS!
MANY YARDS, A FEW FEET, THEN AS NERON CLAWED HIS WAY HALF-FROZEN ONTO THE CLIFF TOP...
THE SWORD! PLUCKED FREE... FALLING, LOST IN THE SEA!
NOW, WITH ONLY HATE AS HIS WEAPON, NERON OF ANDRADORN STAGGERED THROUGH THE VACANT HALLS OF MINANKER'S STRONGHOLD UNTIL...
WELCOME, NERON! A PITY YOU MUST COME SO FAR ONLY TO DIE!
FLEE, NERON! I AM LOST! SAVE YOURSELF WHILE THERE IS TIME!
RINGED BY HIS PENTAGRAM, MINANKER WORKED ANOTHER WIZARDRY...
THE SPELL IS CAST! BEWARE THE CACODEMON!

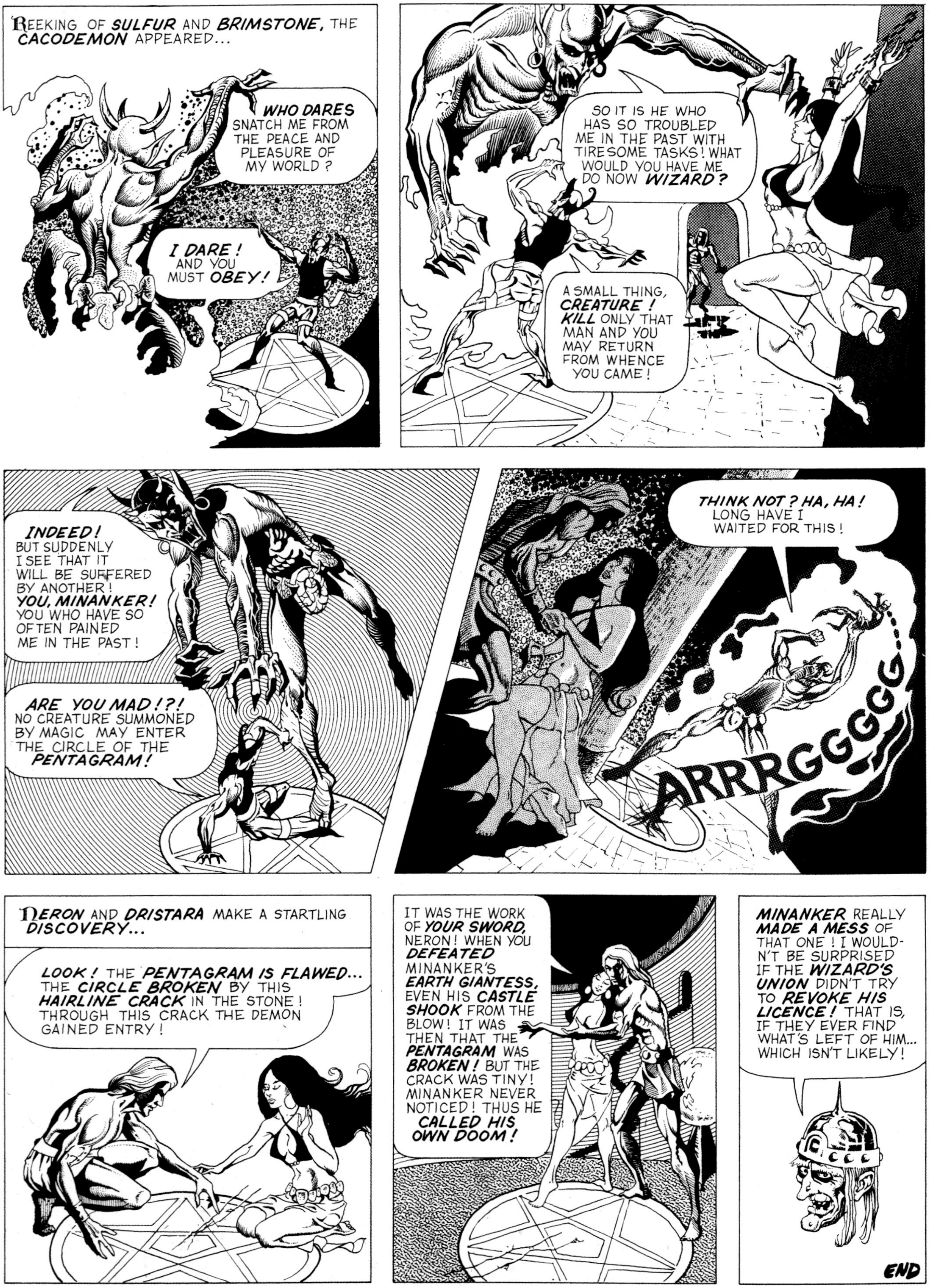
REEKING OF SULFUR AND BRIMSTONE, THE CACODEMON APPEARED...
WHO DARES SNATCH ME FROM THE PEACE AND PLEASURE OF MY WORLD?
I DARE! AND YOU MUST OBEY!
SO IT IS HE WHO HAS SO TROUBLED ME IN THE PAST WITH TIRESOME TASKS! WHAT WOULD YOU HAVE ME DO NOW WIZARD?
A SMALL THING, CREATURE! KILL ONLY THAT MAN AND YOU MAY RETURN FROM WHENCE YOU CAME!
INDEED! BUT SUDDENLY I SEE THAT IT WILL BE SUFFERED BY ANOTHER! YOU, MINANKER! YOU WHO HAVE SO OFTEN PAINED ME IN THE PAST!
ARE YOU MAD!?! NO CREATURE SUMMONED BY MAGIC MAY ENTER THE CIRCLE OF THE PENTAGRAM!
THINK NOT? HA, HA! LONG HAVE I WAITED FOR THIS!
ARRRGGGGG...
NERON AND DRISTARA MAKE A STARTLING DISCOVERY...
LOOK! THE PENTAGRAM IS FLAWED... THE CIRCLE BROKEN BY THIS HAIRLINE CRACK IN THE STONE! THROUGH THIS CRACK THE DEMON GAINED ENTRY!
IT WAS THE WORK OF YOUR SWORD, NERON! WHEN YOU DEFEATED MINANKER'S EARTH GIANTESS, EVEN HIS CASTLE SHOOK FROM THE BLOW! IT WAS THEN THAT THE PENTAGRAM WAS BROKEN! BUT THE CRACK WAS TINY! MINANKER NEVER NOTICED! THUS HE CALLED HIS OWN DOOM!
MINANKER REALLY MADE A MESS OF THAT ONE! I WOULDN'T BE SURPRISED IF THE WIZARD'S UNION DIDN'T TRY TO REVOKE HIS LICENCE! THAT IS, IF THEY EVER FIND WHAT'S LEFT OF HIM... WHICH ISN'T LIKELY!
END

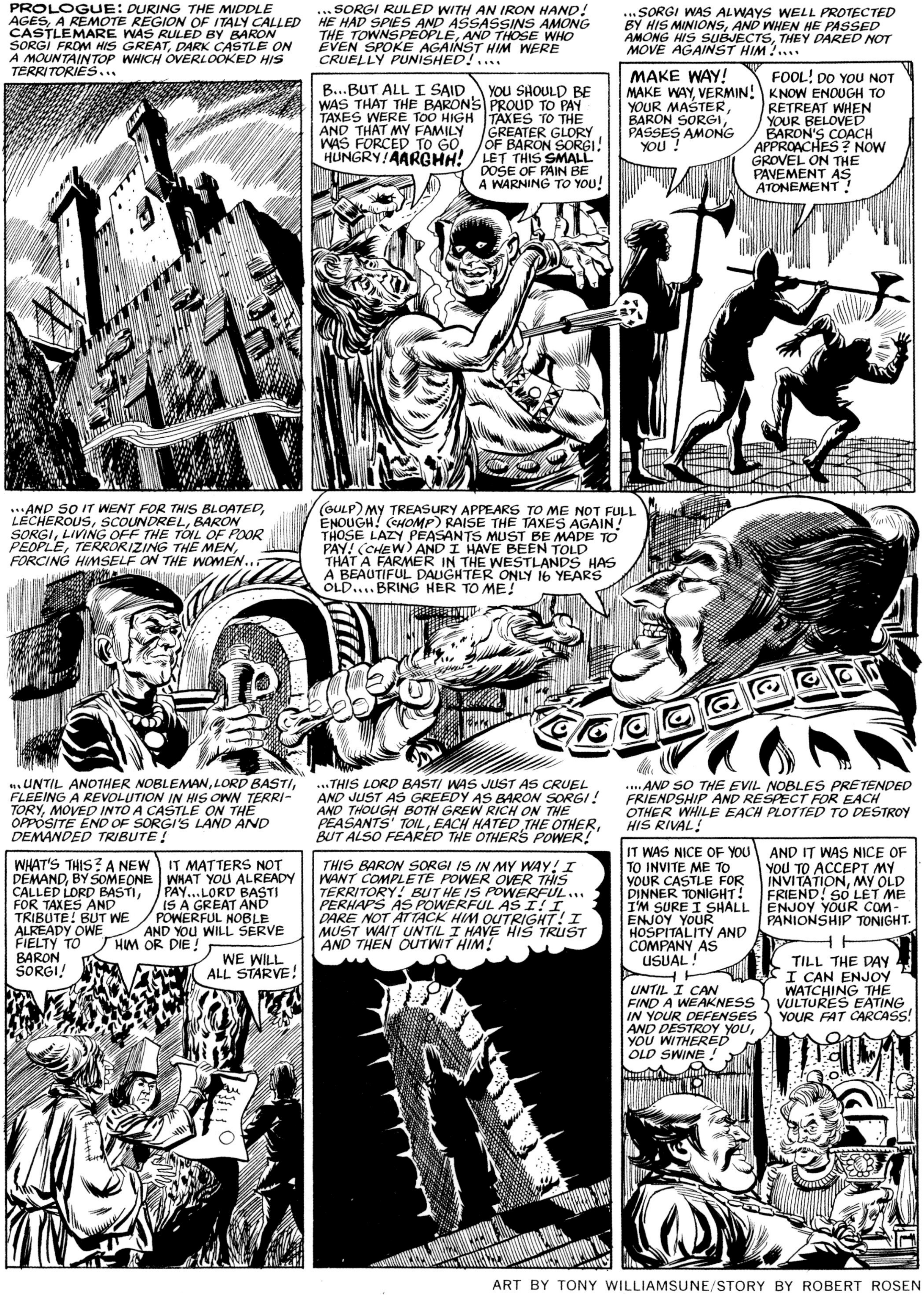
PROLOGUE: DURING THE MIDDLE AGES, A REMOTE REGION OF ITALY CALLED CASTLEMARE WAS RULED BY BARON SORGI FROM HIS GREAT, DARK CASTLE ON A MOUNTAINTOP WHICH OVERLOOKED HIS TERRITORIES...
...SORGI RULED WITH AN IRON HAND! HE HAD SPIES AND ASSASSINS AMONG THE TOWNSPEOPLE, AND THOSE WHO EVEN SPOKE AGAINST HIM WERE CRUELLY PUNISHED!....
B...BUT ALL I SAID WAS THAT THE BARON'S TAXES WERE TOO HIGH AND THAT MY FAMILY WAS FORCED TO GO HUNGRY! AARGHH!
YOU SHOULD BE PROUD TO PAY TAXES TO THE GREATER GLORY OF BARON SORGI! LET THIS SMALL DOSE OF PAIN BE A WARNING TO YOU!
...SORGI WAS ALWAYS WELL PROTECTED BY HIS MINIONS, AND WHEN HE PASSED AMONG HIS SUBJECTS, THEY DARED NOT MOVE AGAINST HIM!....
MAKE WAY! MAKE WAY, VERMIN! YOUR MASTER, BARON SORGI, PASSES AMONG YOU!
FOOL! DO YOU NOT KNOW ENOUGH TO RETREAT WHEN YOUR BELOVED BARON'S COACH APPROACHES? NOW GROVEL ON THE PAVEMENT AS ATONEMENT!
...AND SO IT WENT FOR THIS BLOATED, LECHEROUS, SCOUNDREL, BARON SORGI, LIVING OFF THE TOIL OF POOR PEOPLE, TERRORIZING THE MEN, FORCING HIMSELF ON THE WOMEN...
(GULP) MY TREASURY APPEARS TO ME NOT FULL ENOUGH! (CHOMP) RAISE THE TAXES AGAIN! THOSE LAZY PEASANTS MUST BE MADE TO PAY! (CHEW) AND I HAVE BEEN TOLD THAT A FARMER IN THE WESTLANDS HAS A BEAUTIFUL DAUGHTER ONLY 16 YEARS OLD.... BRING HER TO ME!
...UNTIL ANOTHER NOBLEMAN, LORD BASTI, FLEEING A REVOLUTION IN HIS OWN TERRITORY, MOVED INTO A CASTLE ON THE OPPOSITE END OF SORGI'S LAND AND DEMANDED TRIBUTE!
WHAT'S THIS? A NEW DEMAND, BY SOMEONE CALLED LORD BASTI, FOR TAXES AND TRIBUTE! BUT WE ALREADY OWE FIELTY TO BARON SORGI!
IT MATTERS NOT WHAT YOU ALREADY PAY...LORD BASTI IS A GREAT AND POWERFUL NOBLE AND YOU WILL SERVE HIM OR DIE!
WE WILL ALL STARVE!
...THIS LORD BASTI WAS JUST AS CRUEL AND JUST AS GREEDY AS BARON SORGI! AND THOUGH BOTH GREW RICH ON THE PEASANTS' TOIL, EACH HATED THE OTHER, BUT ALSO FEARED THE OTHER'S POWER!
THIS BARON SORGI IS IN MY WAY! I WANT COMPLETE POWER OVER THIS TERRITORY! BUT HE IS POWERFUL... PERHAPS AS POWERFUL AS I! I DARE NOT ATTACK HIM OUTRIGHT! I MUST WAIT UNTIL I HAVE HIS TRUST AND THEN OUTWIT HIM!
....AND SO THE EVIL NOBLES PRETENDED FRIENDSHIP AND RESPECT FOR EACH OTHER WHILE EACH PLOTTED TO DESTROY HIS RIVAL!
IT WAS NICE OF YOU TO INVITE ME TO YOUR CASTLE FOR DINNER TONIGHT! I'M SURE I SHALL ENJOY YOUR HOSPITALITY AND COMPANY AS USUAL!
AND IT WAS NICE OF YOU TO ACCEPT MY INVITATION, MY OLD FRIEND! SO LET ME ENJOY YOUR COMPANIONSHIP TONIGHT.
UNTIL I CAN FIND A WEAKNESS IN YOUR DEFENSES AND DESTROY YOU, YOU WITHERED OLD SWINE!
TILL THE DAY I CAN ENJOY WATCHING THE VULTURES EATING YOUR FAT CARCASS!

ART BY TONY WILLIAMSUNE/STORY BY ROBERT ROSEN

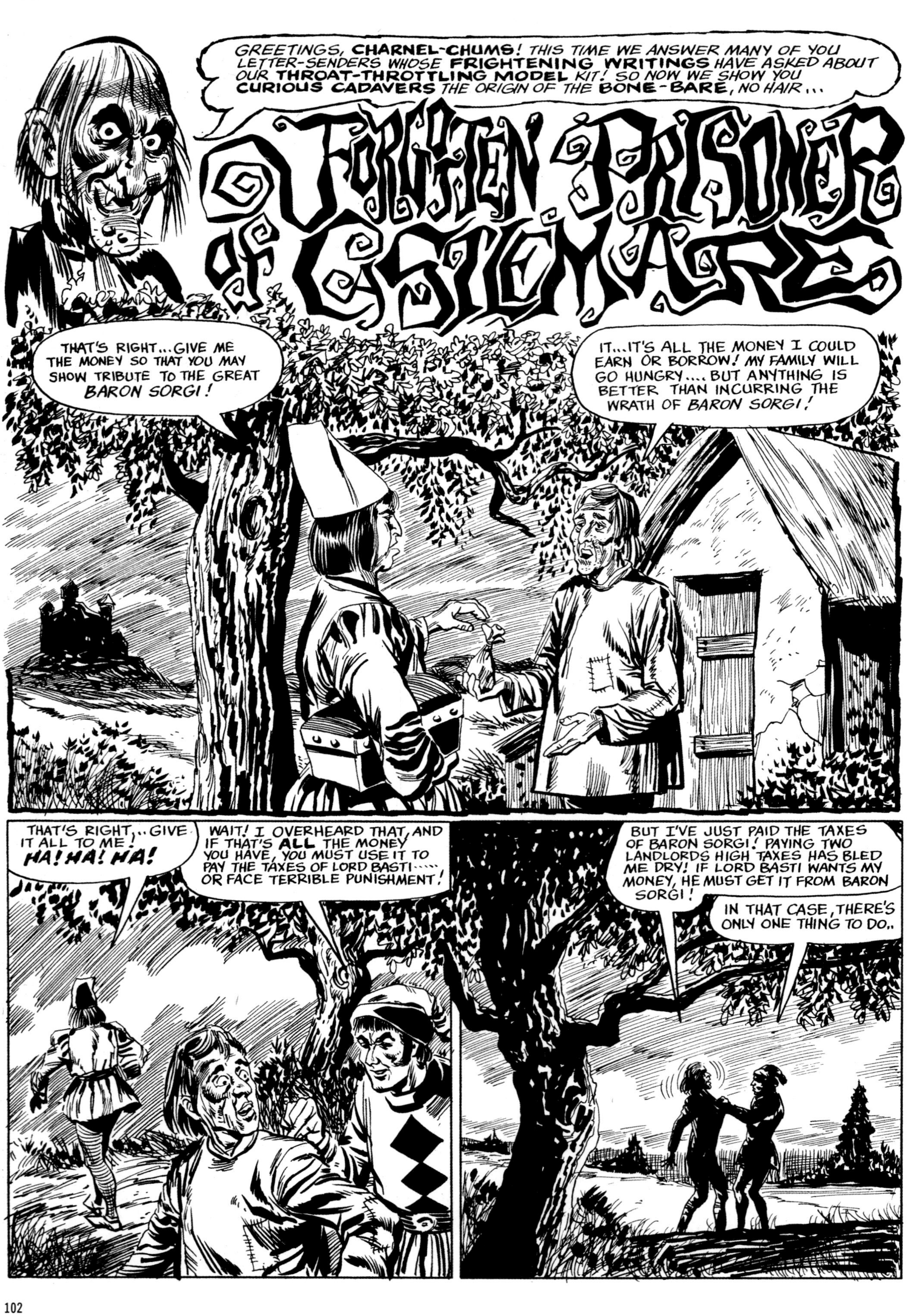
GREETINGS, CHARNEL-CHUMS! THIS TIME WE ANSWER MANY OF YOU LETTER-SENDERS WHOSE FRIGHTENING WRITINGS HAVE ASKED ABOUT OUR THROAT-THROTTLING MODEL KIT! SO NOW WE SHOW YOU CURIOUS CADAVERS THE ORIGIN OF THE BONE-BARE, NO HAIR...
FORGOTTEN PRISONER OF CASTLEMARE
THAT'S RIGHT...GIVE ME THE MONEY SO THAT YOU MAY SHOW TRIBUTE TO THE GREAT BARON SORGI!
IT...IT'S ALL THE MONEY I COULD EARN OR BORROW! MY FAMILY WILL GO HUNGRY.... BUT ANYTHING IS BETTER THAN INCURRING THE WRATH OF BARON SORGI!
THAT'S RIGHT...GIVE IT ALL TO ME! HA! HA! HA!
WAIT! I OVERHEARD THAT, AND IF THAT'S ALL THE MONEY YOU HAVE, YOU MUST USE IT TO PAY THE TAXES OF LORD BASTI..... OR FACE TERRIBLE PUNISHMENT!
BUT I'VE JUST PAID THE TAXES OF BARON SORGI! PAYING TWO LANDLORDS HIGH TAXES HAS BLED ME DRY! IF LORD BASTI WANTS MY MONEY, HE MUST GET IT FROM BARON SORGI!
IN THAT CASE, THERE'S ONLY ONE THING TO DO..

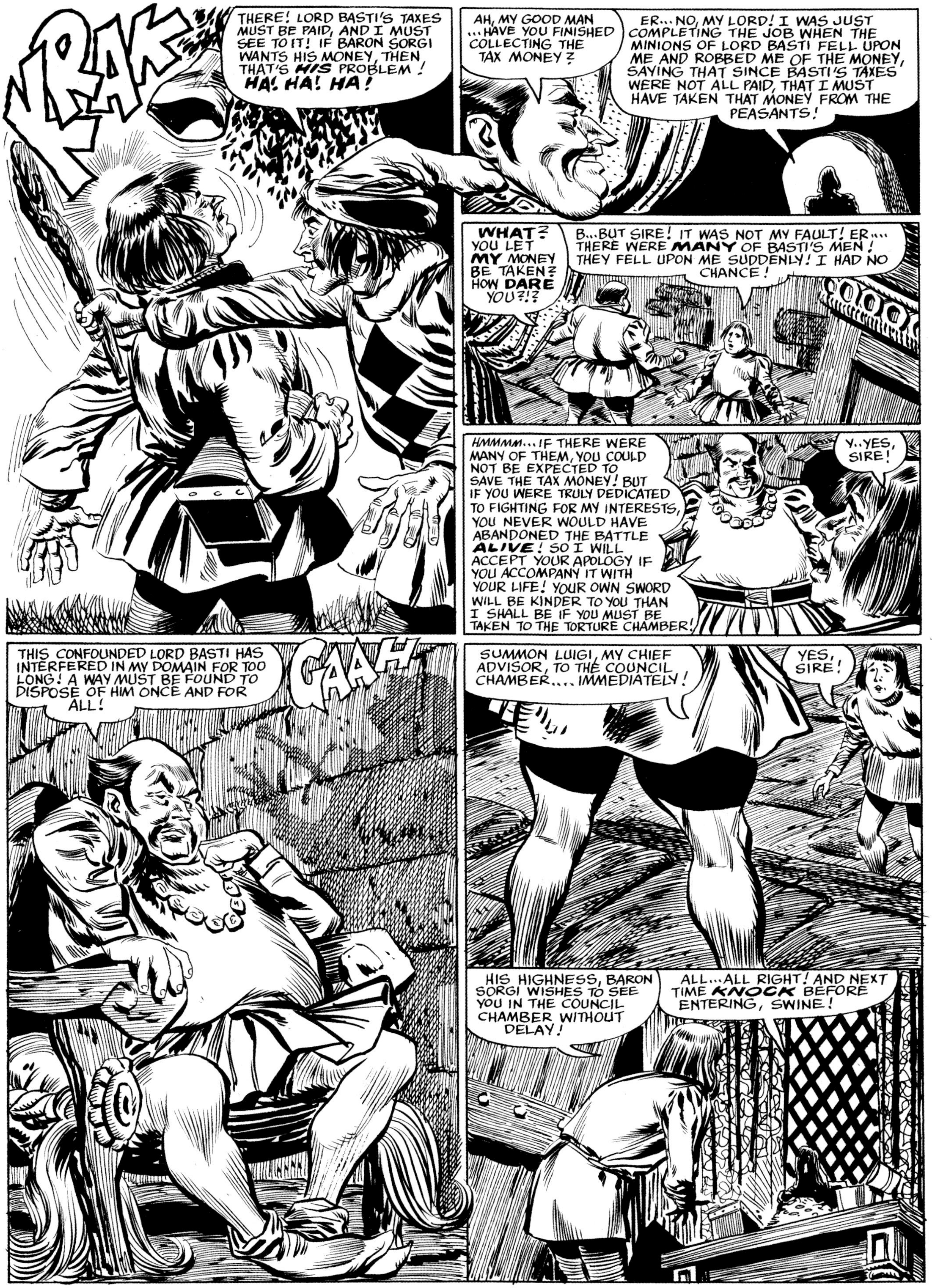
VRAK
THERE! LORD BASTI'S TAXES MUST BE PAID, AND I MUST SEE TO IT! IF BARON SORGI WANTS HIS MONEY, THEN THAT'S HIS PROBLEM! HA! HA! HA!
AH, MY GOOD MAN ...HAVE YOU FINISHED COLLECTING THE TAX MONEY?
ER...NO, MY LORD! I WAS JUST COMPLETING THE JOB WHEN THE MINIONS OF LORD BASTI FELL UPON ME AND ROBBED ME OF THE MONEY, SAYING THAT SINCE BASTI'S TAXES WERE NOT ALL PAID, THAT I MUST HAVE TAKEN THAT MONEY FROM THE PEASANTS!
WHAT? YOU LET MY MONEY BE TAKEN? HOW DARE YOU?!?
B...BUT SIRE! IT WAS NOT MY FAULT! ER.... THERE WERE MANY OF BASTI'S MEN! THEY FELL UPON ME SUDDENLY! I HAD NO CHANCE!
HMMMM...IF THERE WERE MANY OF THEM, YOU COULD NOT BE EXPECTED TO SAVE THE TAX MONEY! BUT IF YOU WERE TRULY DEDICATED TO FIGHTING FOR MY INTERESTS, YOU NEVER WOULD HAVE ABANDONED THE BATTLE ALIVE! SO I WILL ACCEPT YOUR APOLOGY IF YOU ACCOMPANY IT WITH YOUR LIFE! YOUR OWN SWORD WILL BE KINDER TO YOU THAN I SHALL BE IF YOU MUST BE TAKEN TO THE TORTURE CHAMBER!
Y..YES, SIRE!
THIS CONFOUNDED LORD BASTI HAS INTERFERED IN MY DOMAIN FOR TOO LONG! A WAY MUST BE FOUND TO DISPOSE OF HIM ONCE AND FOR ALL!
GAAH
SUMMON LUIGI, MY CHIEF ADVISOR, TO THE COUNCIL CHAMBER.... IMMEDIATELY!
YES, SIRE!
HIS HIGHNESS, BARON SORGI WISHES TO SEE YOU IN THE COUNCIL CHAMBER WITHOUT DELAY!
ALL...ALL RIGHT! AND NEXT TIME KNOCK BEFORE ENTERING, SWINE!

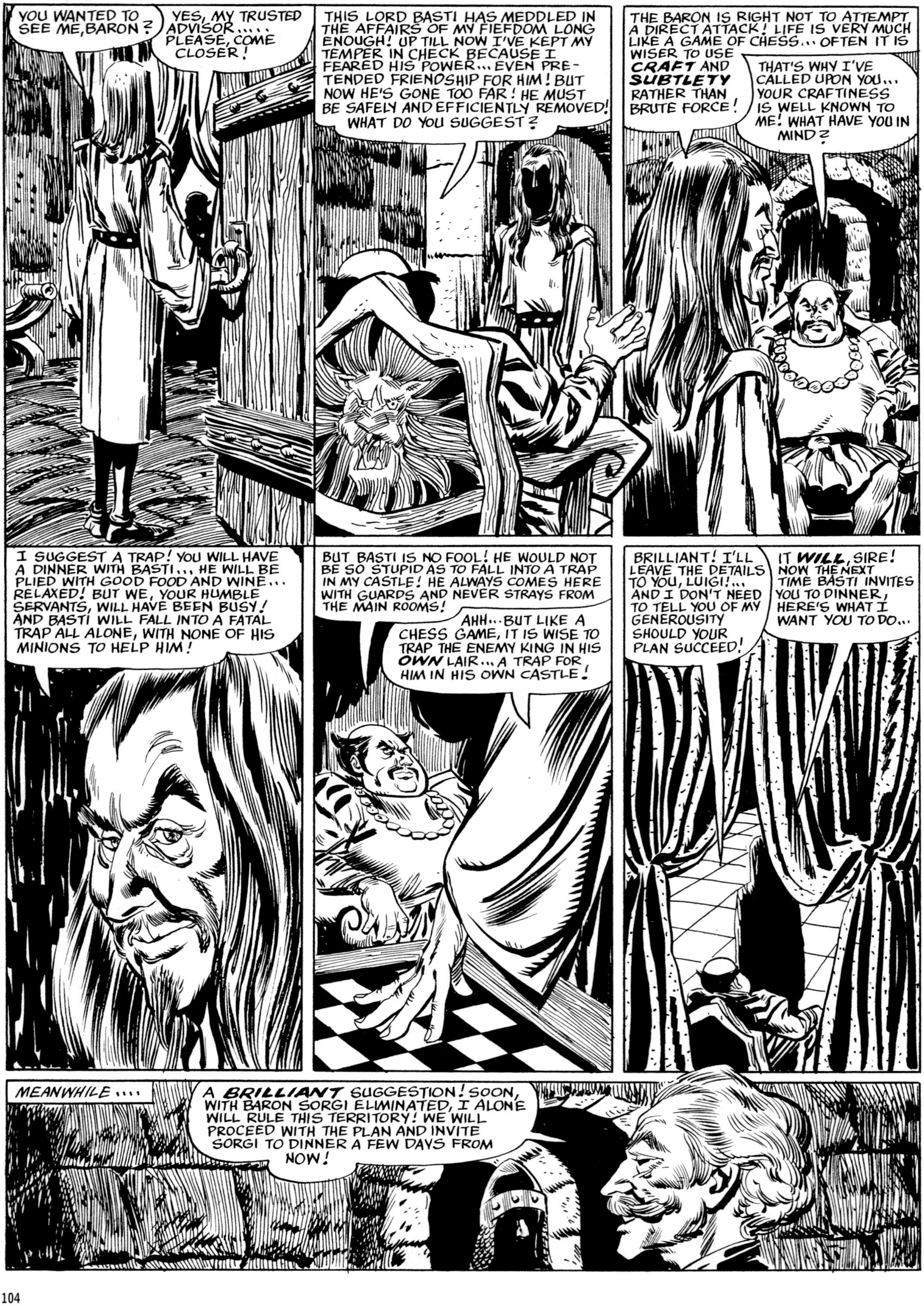
YOU WANTED TO SEE ME, BARON?
YES, MY TRUSTED ADVISOR..... PLEASE, COME CLOSER!
THIS LORD BASTI HAS MEDDLED IN THE AFFAIRS OF MY FIEFDOM LONG ENOUGH! UP TILL NOW I'VE KEPT MY TEMPER IN CHECK BECAUSE I FEARED HIS POWER... EVEN PRETENDED FRIENDSHIP FOR HIM! BUT NOW HE'S GONE TOO FAR! HE MUST BE SAFELY AND EFFICIENTLY REMOVED! WHAT DO YOU SUGGEST?
THE BARON IS RIGHT NOT TO ATTEMPT A DIRECT ATTACK! LIFE IS VERY MUCH LIKE A GAME OF CHESS... OFTEN IT IS WISER TO USE CRAFT AND SUBTLETY RATHER THAN BRUTE FORCE!
THAT'S WHY I'VE CALLED UPON YOU... YOUR CRAFTINESS IS WELL KNOWN TO ME! WHAT HAVE YOU IN MIND?
I SUGGEST A TRAP! YOU WILL HAVE A DINNER WITH BASTI... HE WILL BE PLIED WITH GOOD FOOD AND WINE... RELAXED! BUT WE, YOUR HUMBLE SERVANTS, WILL HAVE BEEN BUSY! AND BASTI WILL FALL INTO A FATAL TRAP ALL ALONE, WITH NONE OF HIS MINIONS TO HELP HIM!
BUT BASTI IS NO FOOL! HE WOULD NOT BE SO STUPID AS TO FALL INTO A TRAP IN MY CASTLE! HE ALWAYS COMES HERE WITH GUARDS AND NEVER STRAYS FROM THE MAIN ROOMS!
AHH... BUT LIKE A CHESS GAME, IT IS WISE TO TRAP THE ENEMY KING IN HIS OWN LAIR... A TRAP FOR HIM IN HIS OWN CASTLE!
BRILLIANT! I'LL LEAVE THE DETAILS TO YOU, LUIGI!... AND I DON'T NEED TO TELL YOU OF MY GENEROUSITY SHOULD YOUR PLAN SUCCEED!
IT WILL, SIRE! NOW THE NEXT TIME BASTI INVITES YOU TO DINNER, HERE'S WHAT I WANT YOU TO DO...
MEANWHILE....
A BRILLIANT SUGGESTION! SOON, WITH BARON SORGI ELIMINATED, I ALONE WILL RULE THIS TERRITORY! WE WILL PROCEED WITH THE PLAN AND INVITE SORGI TO DINNER A FEW DAYS FROM NOW!

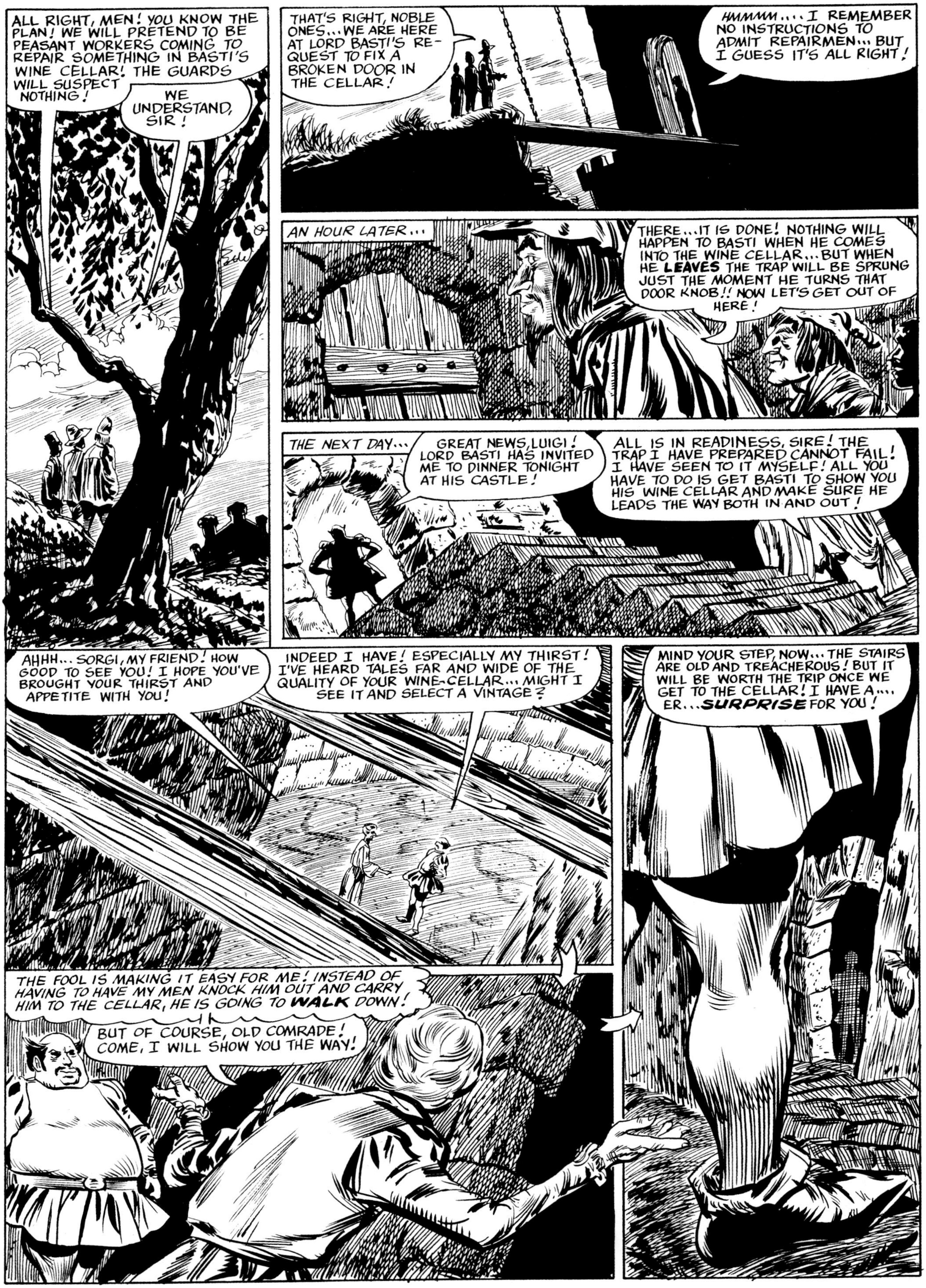
ALL RIGHT, MEN! YOU KNOW THE PLAN! WE WILL PRETEND TO BE PEASANT WORKERS COMING TO REPAIR SOMETHING IN BASTI'S WINE CELLAR! THE GUARDS WILL SUSPECT NOTHING!
WE UNDERSTAND, SIR!
THAT'S RIGHT, NOBLE ONES... WE ARE HERE AT LORD BASTI'S REQUEST TO FIX A BROKEN DOOR IN THE CELLAR!
HMMMM.... I REMEMBER NO INSTRUCTIONS TO ADMIT REPAIRMEN... BUT I GUESS IT'S ALL RIGHT!
AN HOUR LATER...
THERE... IT IS DONE! NOTHING WILL HAPPEN TO BASTI WHEN HE COMES INTO THE WINE CELLAR... BUT WHEN HE LEAVES THE TRAP WILL BE SPRUNG JUST THE MOMENT HE TURNS THAT DOOR KNOB!! NOW LET'S GET OUT OF HERE!
THE NEXT DAY...
GREAT NEWS, LUIGI! LORD BASTI HAS INVITED ME TO DINNER TONIGHT AT HIS CASTLE!
ALL IS IN READINESS, SIRE! THE TRAP I HAVE PREPARED CANNOT FAIL! I HAVE SEEN TO IT MYSELF! ALL YOU HAVE TO DO IS GET BASTI TO SHOW YOU HIS WINE CELLAR AND MAKE SURE HE LEADS THE WAY BOTH IN AND OUT!
AHHH... SORGI, MY FRIEND! HOW GOOD TO SEE YOU! I HOPE YOU'VE BROUGHT YOUR THIRST AND APPETITE WITH YOU!
INDEED I HAVE! ESPECIALLY MY THIRST! I'VE HEARD TALES FAR AND WIDE OF THE QUALITY OF YOUR WINE-CELLAR... MIGHT I SEE IT AND SELECT A VINTAGE?
THE FOOL IS MAKING IT EASY FOR ME! INSTEAD OF HAVING TO HAVE MY MEN KNOCK HIM OUT AND CARRY HIM TO THE CELLAR, HE IS GOING TO WALK DOWN!
BUT OF COURSE, OLD COMRADE! COME, I WILL SHOW YOU THE WAY!
MIND YOUR STEP, NOW... THE STAIRS ARE OLD AND TREACHEROUS! BUT IT WILL BE WORTH THE TRIP ONCE WE GET TO THE CELLAR! I HAVE A.... ER... SURPRISE FOR YOU!

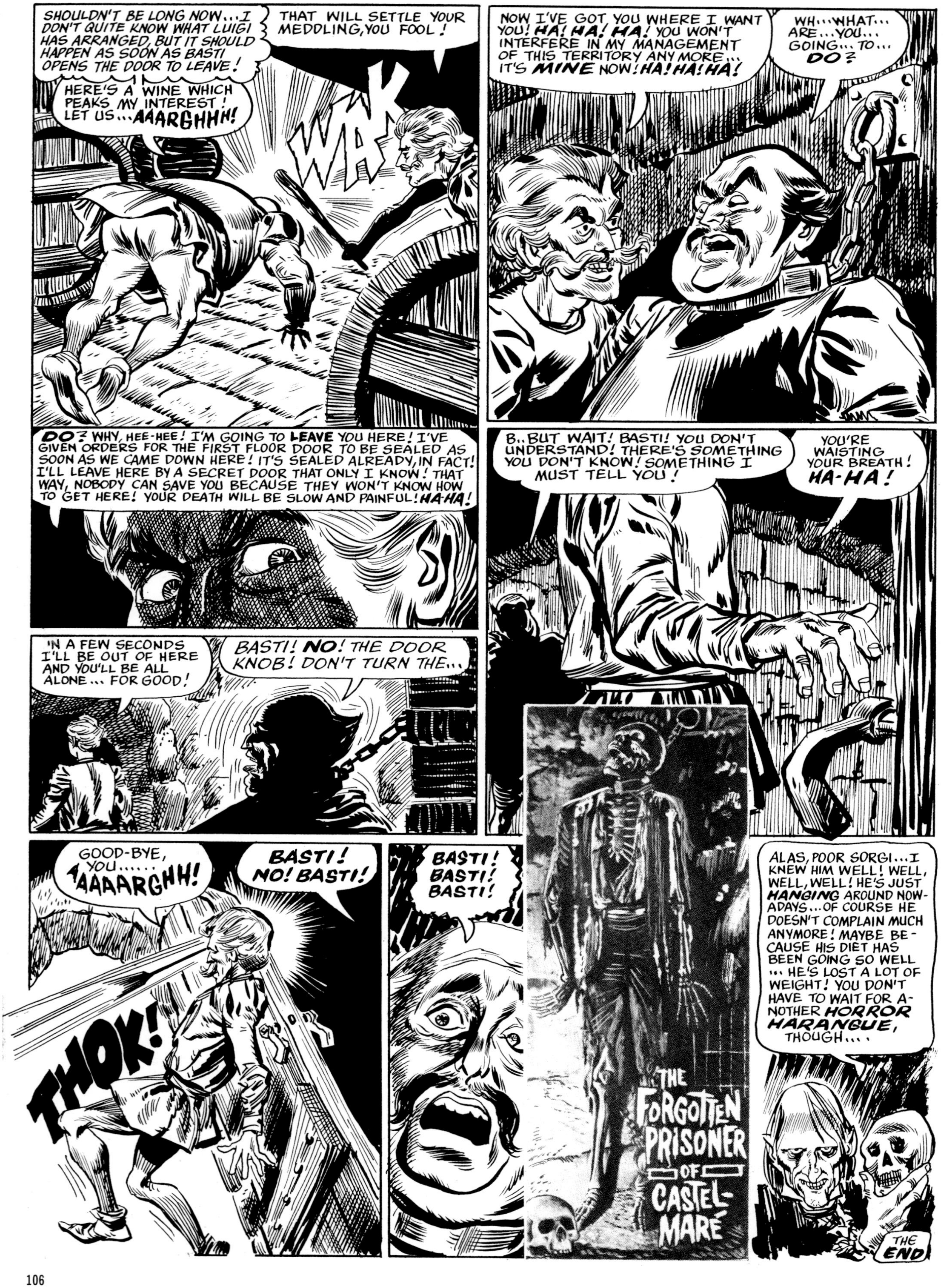

SHOULDN'T BE LONG NOW... I DON'T QUITE KNOW WHAT LUIGI HAS ARRANGED, BUT IT SHOULD HAPPEN AS SOON AS BASTI OPENS THE DOOR TO LEAVE!
HERE'S A WINE WHICH PEAKS MY INTEREST! LET US... AAARGHHH!
THAT WILL SETTLE YOUR MEDDLING, YOU FOOL!
WAK
NOW I'VE GOT YOU WHERE I WANT YOU! HA! HA! HA! YOU WON'T INTERFERE IN MY MANAGEMENT OF THIS TERRITORY ANY MORE... IT'S MINE NOW! HA! HA! HA!
WH... WHAT... ARE... YOU... GOING... TO... DO?
DO? WHY, HEE-HEE! I'M GOING TO LEAVE YOU HERE! I'VE GIVEN ORDERS FOR THE FIRST FLOOR DOOR TO BE SEALED AS SOON AS WE CAME DOWN HERE! IT'S SEALED ALREADY, IN FACT! I'LL LEAVE HERE BY A SECRET DOOR THAT ONLY I KNOW! THAT WAY, NOBODY CAN SAVE YOU BECAUSE THEY WON'T KNOW HOW TO GET HERE! YOUR DEATH WILL BE SLOW AND PAINFUL! HA-HA!
B.. BUT WAIT! BASTI! YOU DON'T UNDERSTAND! THERE'S SOMETHING YOU DON'T KNOW! SOMETHING I MUST TELL YOU!
YOU'RE WAISTING YOUR BREATH! HA-HA!
IN A FEW SECONDS I'LL BE OUT OF HERE AND YOU'LL BE ALL ALONE... FOR GOOD!
BASTI! NO! THE DOOR KNOB! DON'T TURN THE...
GOOD-BYE, YOU...... AAAAARGHH!
BASTI! NO! BASTI!
THOK!
BASTI! BASTI! BASTI!
THE FORGOTTEN PRISONER OF CASTEL-MARÉ
ALAS, POOR SORGI... I KNEW HIM WELL! WELL, WELL, WELL! HE'S JUST HANGING AROUND NOW-ADAYS... OF COURSE HE DOESN'T COMPLAIN MUCH ANYMORE! MAYBE BE-CAUSE HIS DIET HAS BEEN GOING SO WELL ... HE'S LOST A LOT OF WEIGHT! YOU DON'T HAVE TO WAIT FOR A-NOTHER HORROR HARANGUE, THOUGH....
THE END

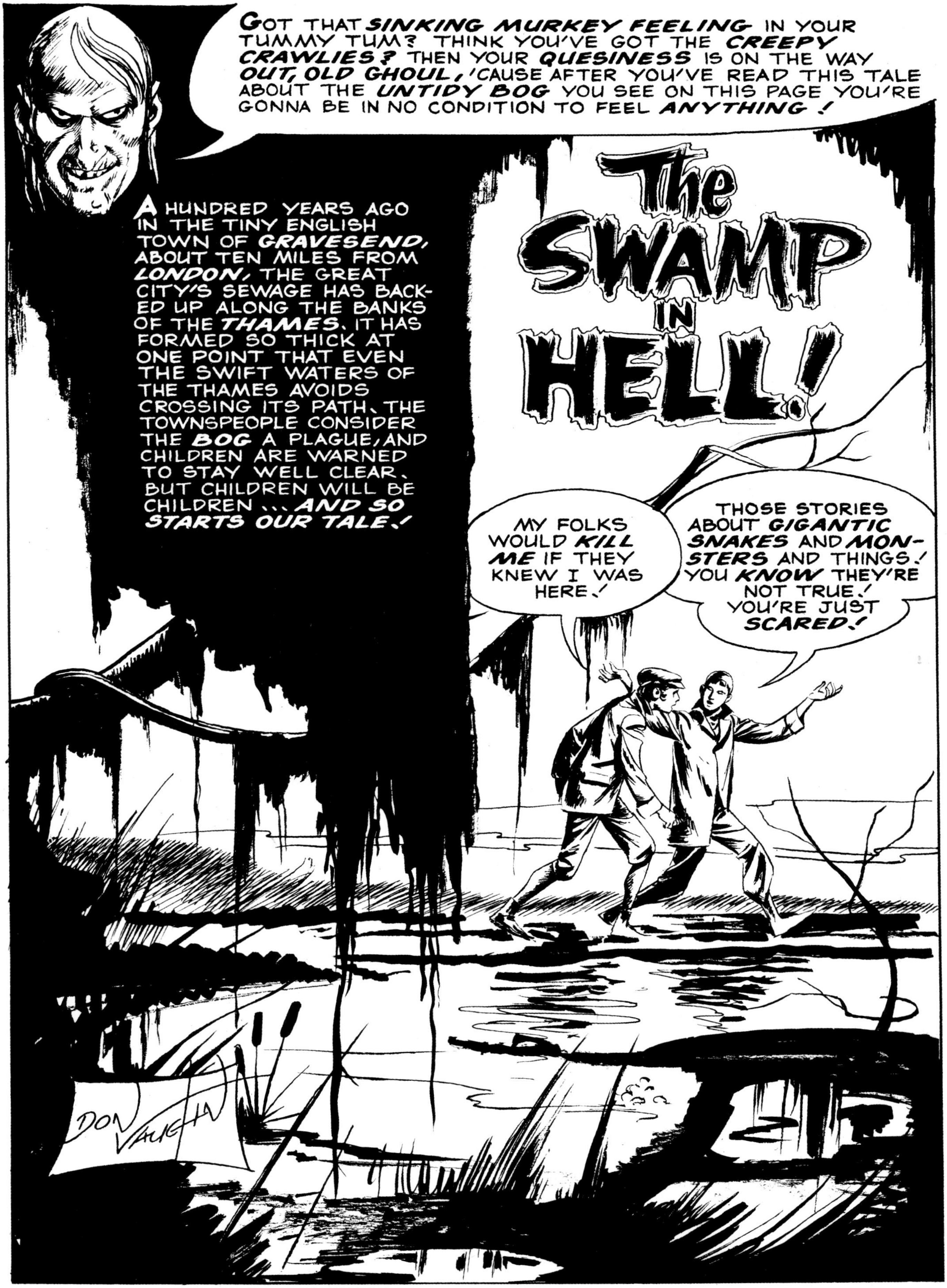
GOT THAT SINKING MURKEY FEELING IN YOUR TUMMY TUM? THINK YOU'VE GOT THE CREEPY CRAWLIES? THEN YOUR QUESINESS IS ON THE WAY OUT, OLD GHOUL, 'CAUSE AFTER YOU'VE READ THIS TALE ABOUT THE UNTIDY BOG YOU SEE ON THIS PAGE YOU'RE GONNA BE IN NO CONDITION TO FEEL ANYTHING!
The SWAMP IN HELL!
A HUNDRED YEARS AGO IN THE TINY ENGLISH TOWN OF GRAVESEND, ABOUT TEN MILES FROM LONDON, THE GREAT CITY'S SEWAGE HAS BACKED UP ALONG THE BANKS OF THE THAMES. IT HAS FORMED SO THICK AT ONE POINT THAT EVEN THE SWIFT WATERS OF THE THAMES AVOIDS CROSSING ITS PATH. THE TOWNSPEOPLE CONSIDER THE BOG A PLAGUE, AND CHILDREN ARE WARNED TO STAY WELL CLEAR. BUT CHILDREN WILL BE CHILDREN ... AND SO STARTS OUR TALE!
MY FOLKS WOULD KILL ME IF THEY KNEW I WAS HERE!
THOSE STORIES ABOUT GIGANTIC SNAKES AND MONSTERS AND THINGS! YOU KNOW THEY'RE NOT TRUE! YOU'RE JUST SCARED!
DON VAUGHN

ART BY DON VAUGHN/STORY BY AL HEWETSON

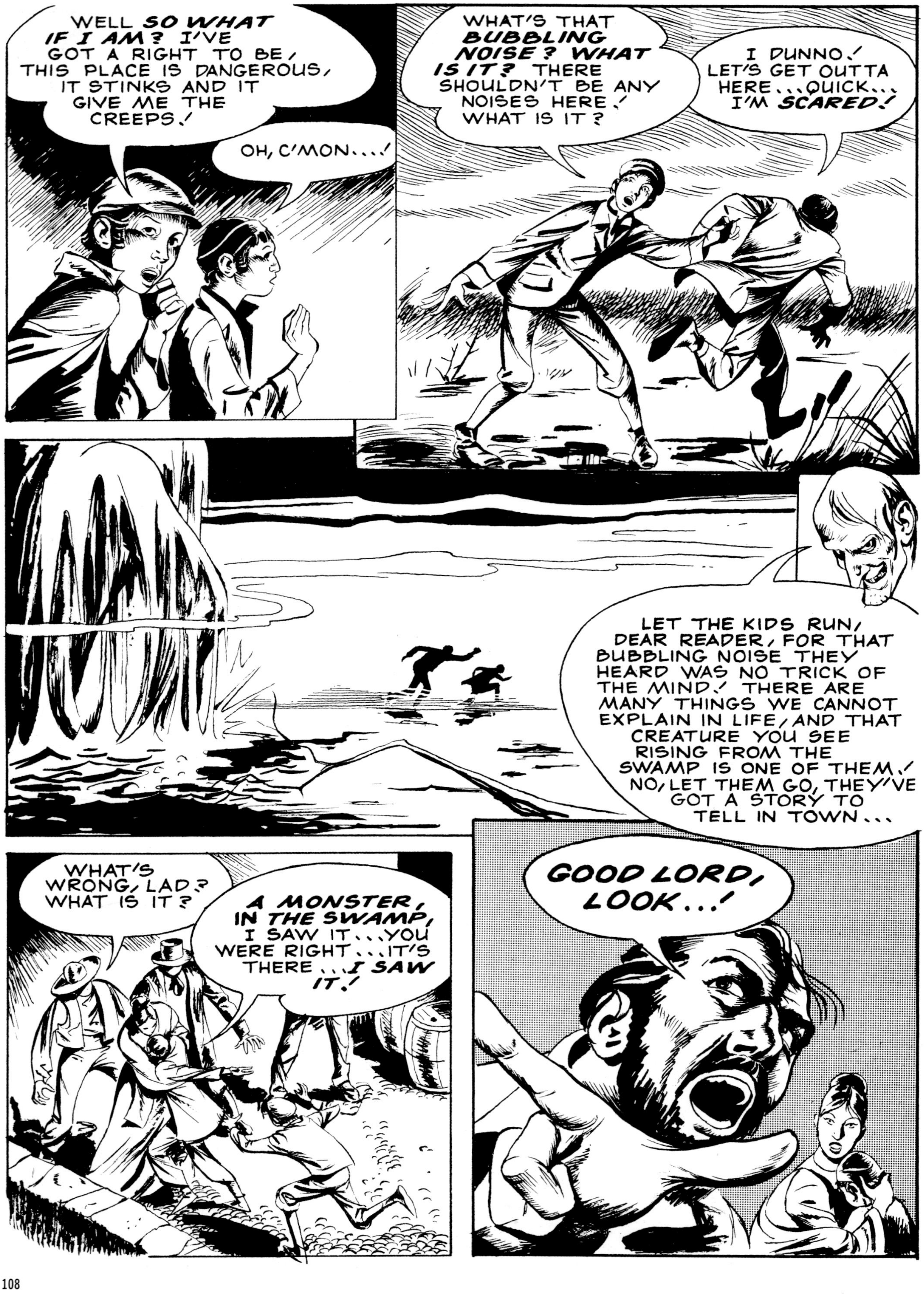
WELL SO WHAT IF I AM? I'VE GOT A RIGHT TO BE, THIS PLACE IS DANGEROUS, IT STINKS AND IT GIVE ME THE CREEPS!
OH, C'MON...!
WHAT'S THAT BUBBLING NOISE? WHAT IS IT? THERE SHOULDN'T BE ANY NOISES HERE! WHAT IS IT?
I DUNNO! LET'S GET OUTTA HERE...QUICK... I'M SCARED!
LET THE KIDS RUN, DEAR READER, FOR THAT BUBBLING NOISE THEY HEARD WAS NO TRICK OF THE MIND! THERE ARE MANY THINGS WE CANNOT EXPLAIN IN LIFE, AND THAT CREATURE YOU SEE RISING FROM THE SWAMP IS ONE OF THEM! NO, LET THEM GO, THEY'VE GOT A STORY TO TELL IN TOWN...
WHAT'S WRONG, LAD? WHAT IS IT?
A MONSTER, IN THE SWAMP, I SAW IT...YOU WERE RIGHT...IT'S THERE...I SAW IT!
GOOD LORD, LOOK...!

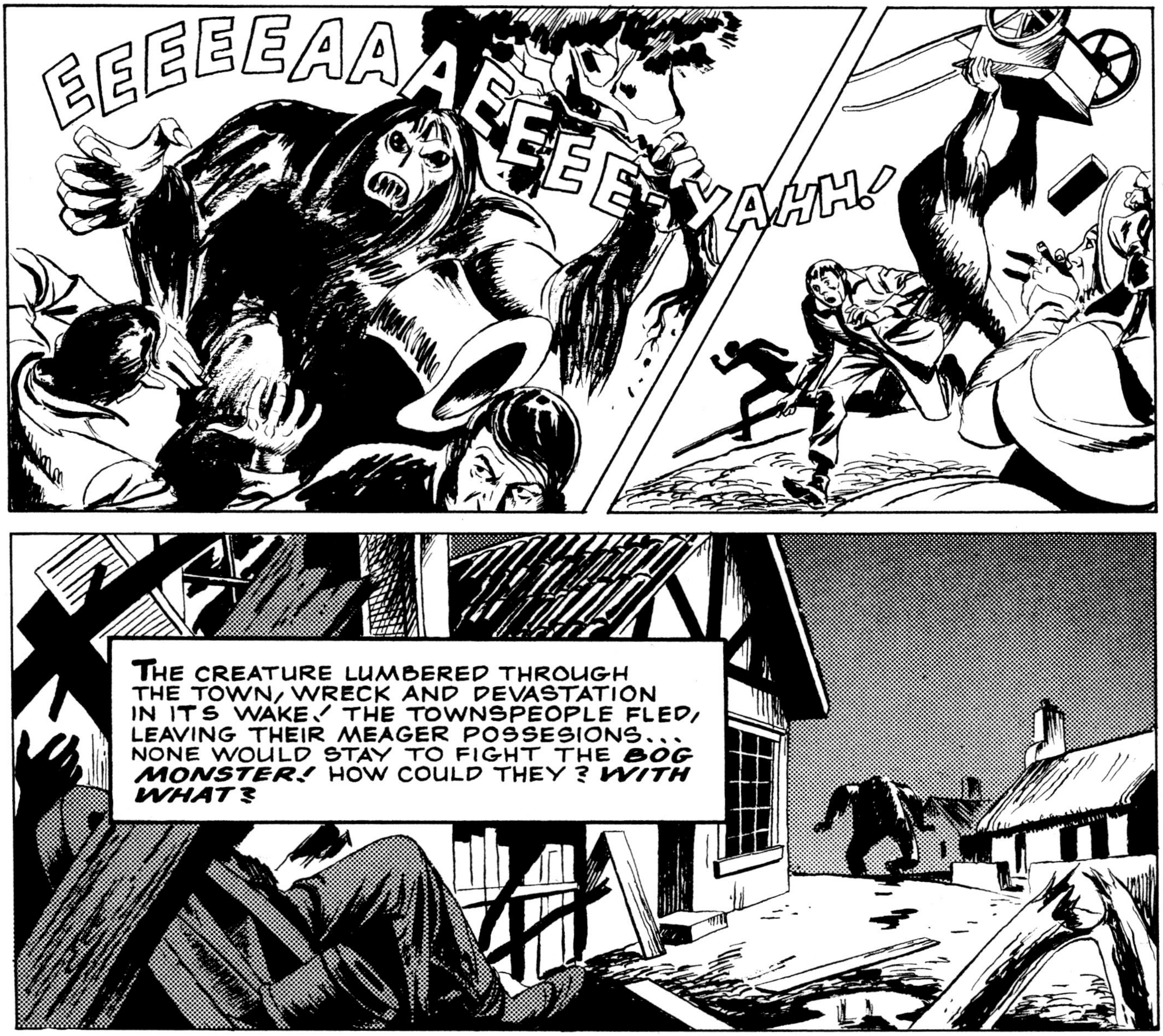
EEEEEAAAEEEEE-YAHH!
THE CREATURE LUMBERED THROUGH THE TOWN, WRECK AND DEVASTATION IN ITS WAKE! THE TOWNSPEOPLE FLED, LEAVING THEIR MEAGER POSSESIONS... NONE WOULD STAY TO FIGHT THE ***BOG MONSTER!*** HOW COULD THEY? ***WITH WHAT?***

BUT THERE WAS ***ONE*** WHO REMAINED...ONE WHO HAD BEEN ***FORGOTTEN!*** ONE WHO COULD NOT RUN FROM ***ANYTHING,*** ONE WHO WAS CRIPPLED, OLD, AND BLIND... ONE WHO DID NOT EVEN ***CARE!***

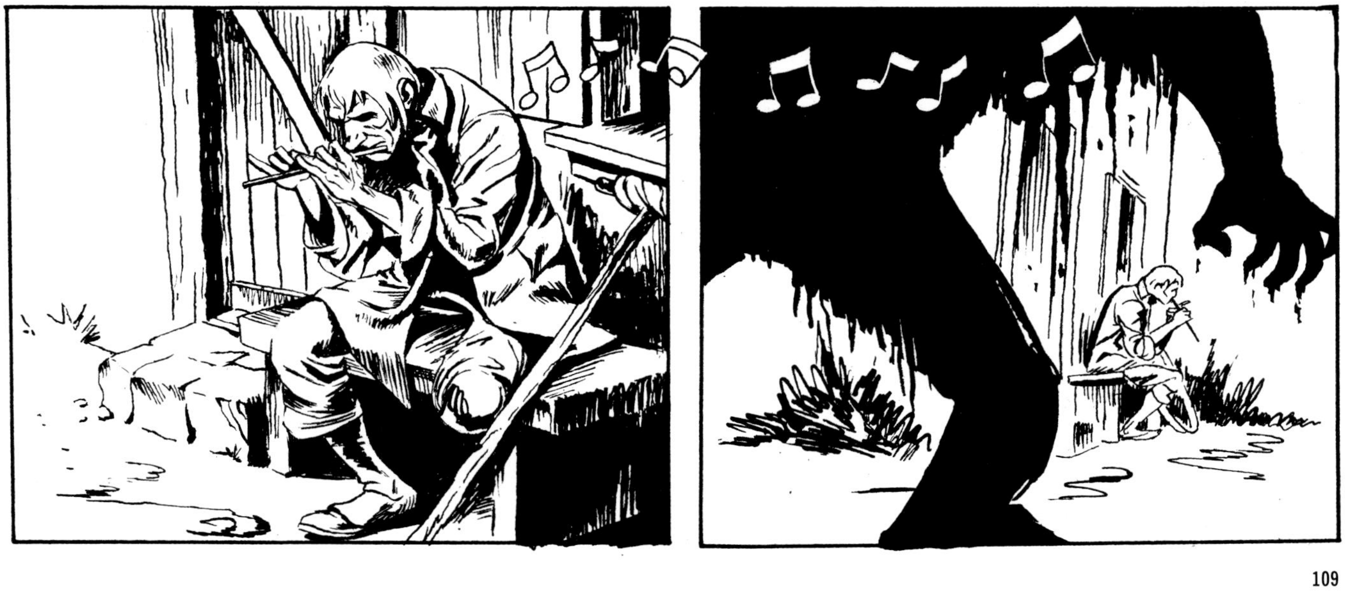

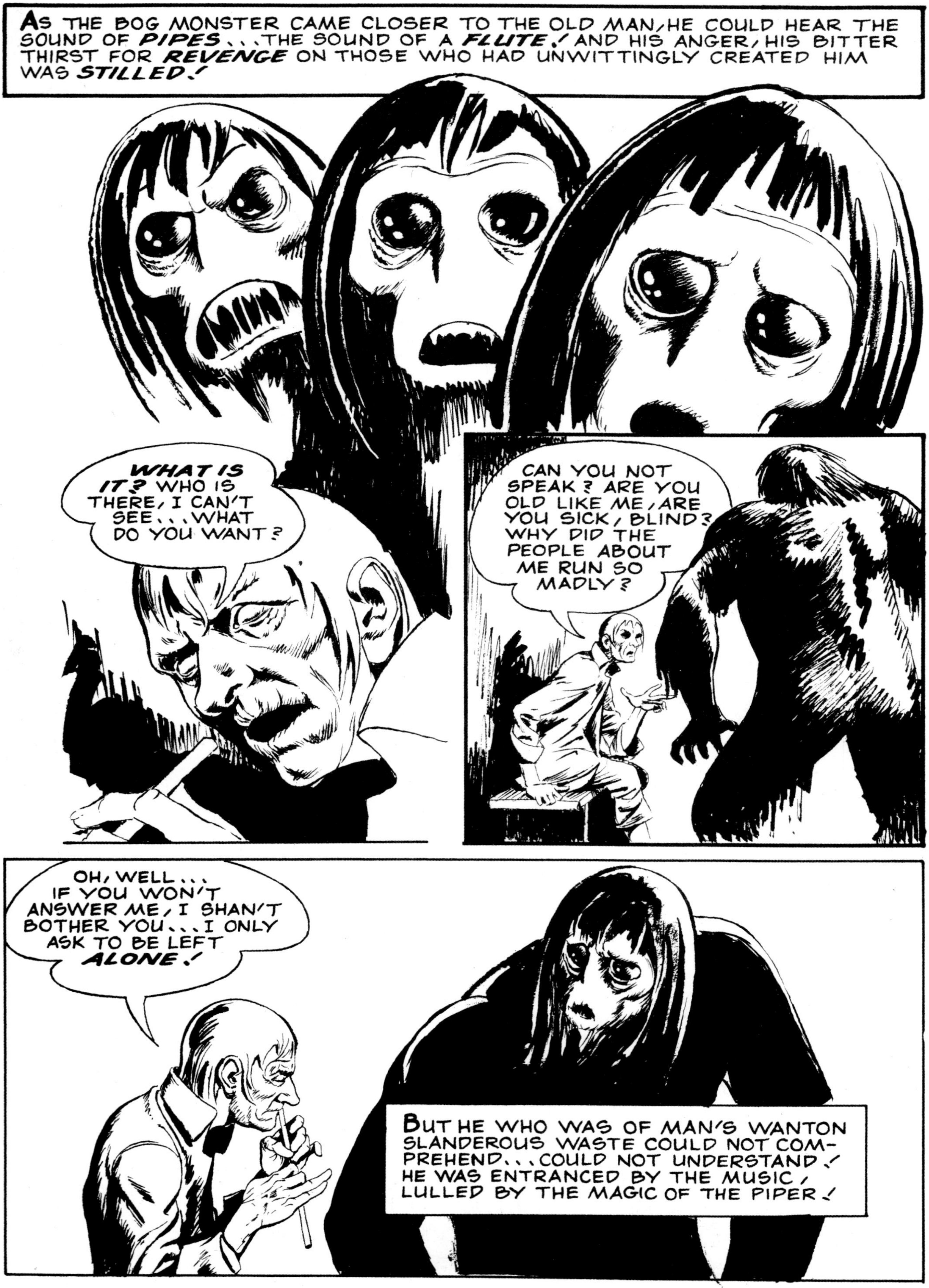

AS THE BOG MONSTER CAME CLOSER TO THE OLD MAN, HE COULD HEAR THE SOUND OF PIPES...THE SOUND OF A FLUTE! AND HIS ANGER, HIS BITTER THIRST FOR REVENGE ON THOSE WHO HAD UNWITTINGLY CREATED HIM WAS STILLED!
WHAT IS IT? WHO IS THERE, I CAN'T SEE...WHAT DO YOU WANT?
CAN YOU NOT SPEAK? ARE YOU OLD LIKE ME, ARE YOU SICK, BLIND? WHY DID THE PEOPLE ABOUT ME RUN SO MADLY?
OH, WELL... IF YOU WON'T ANSWER ME, I SHAN'T BOTHER YOU...I ONLY ASK TO BE LEFT ALONE!
BUT HE WHO WAS OF MAN'S WANTON SLANDEROUS WASTE COULD NOT COMPREHEND...COULD NOT UNDERSTAND! HE WAS ENTRANCED BY THE MUSIC, LULLED BY THE MAGIC OF THE PIPER!

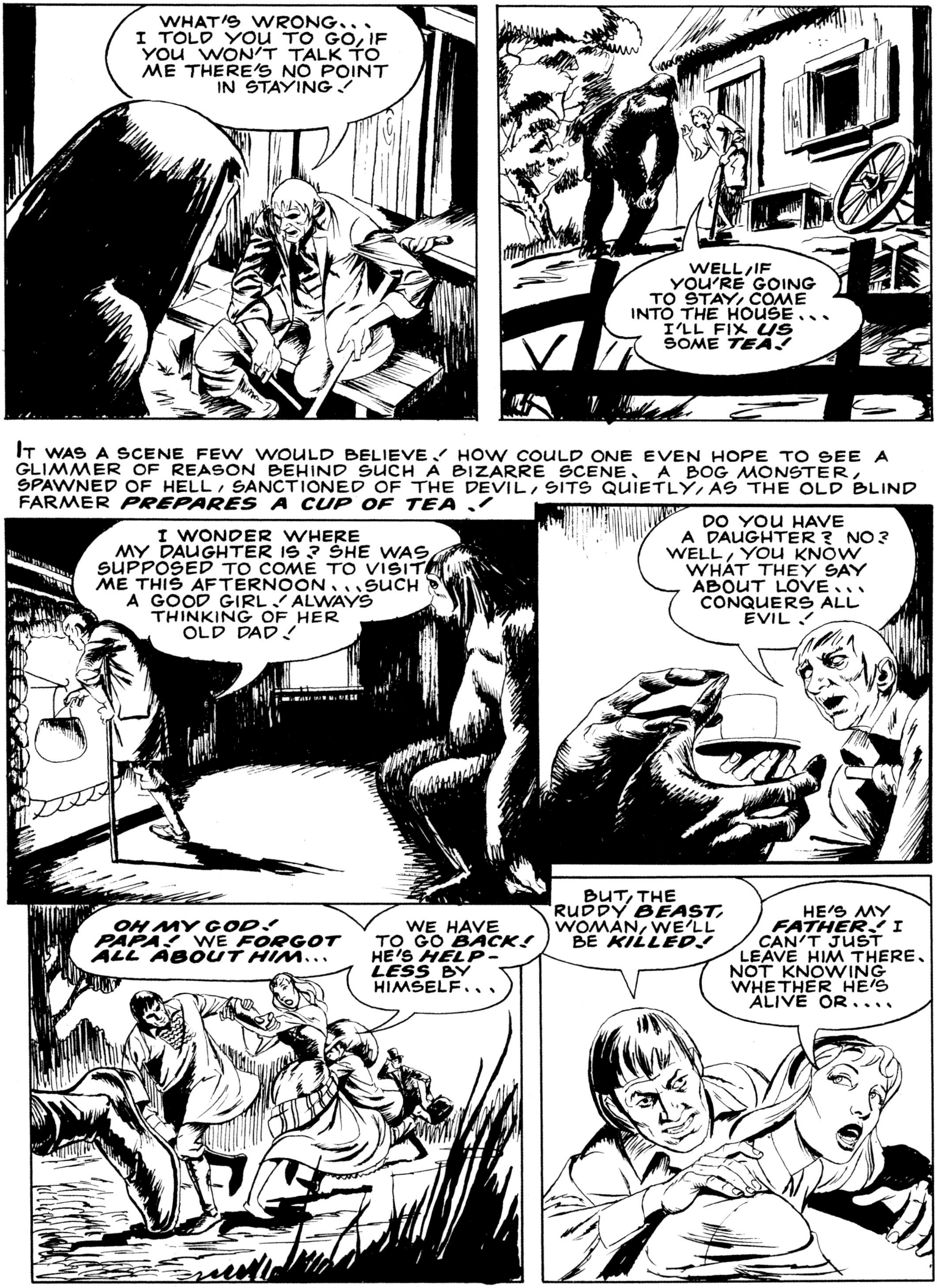
WHAT'S WRONG... I TOLD YOU TO GO, IF YOU WON'T TALK TO ME THERE'S NO POINT IN STAYING!
WELL, IF YOU'RE GOING TO STAY, COME INTO THE HOUSE... I'LL FIX US SOME TEA!
IT WAS A SCENE FEW WOULD BELIEVE! HOW COULD ONE EVEN HOPE TO SEE A GLIMMER OF REASON BEHIND SUCH A BIZARRE SCENE. A BOG MONSTER, SPAWNED OF HELL, SANCTIONED OF THE DEVIL, SITS QUIETLY, AS THE OLD BLIND FARMER PREPARES A CUP OF TEA!
I WONDER WHERE MY DAUGHTER IS? SHE WAS SUPPOSED TO COME TO VISIT ME THIS AFTERNOON...SUCH A GOOD GIRL! ALWAYS THINKING OF HER OLD DAD!
DO YOU HAVE A DAUGHTER? NO? WELL, YOU KNOW WHAT THEY SAY ABOUT LOVE... CONQUERS ALL EVIL!
OH MY GOD! PAPA! WE FORGOT ALL ABOUT HIM...
WE HAVE TO GO BACK! HE'S HELP-LESS BY HIMSELF...
BUT, THE RUDDY BEAST, WOMAN, WE'LL BE KILLED!
HE'S MY FATHER! I CAN'T JUST LEAVE HIM THERE. NOT KNOWING WHETHER HE'S ALIVE OR....

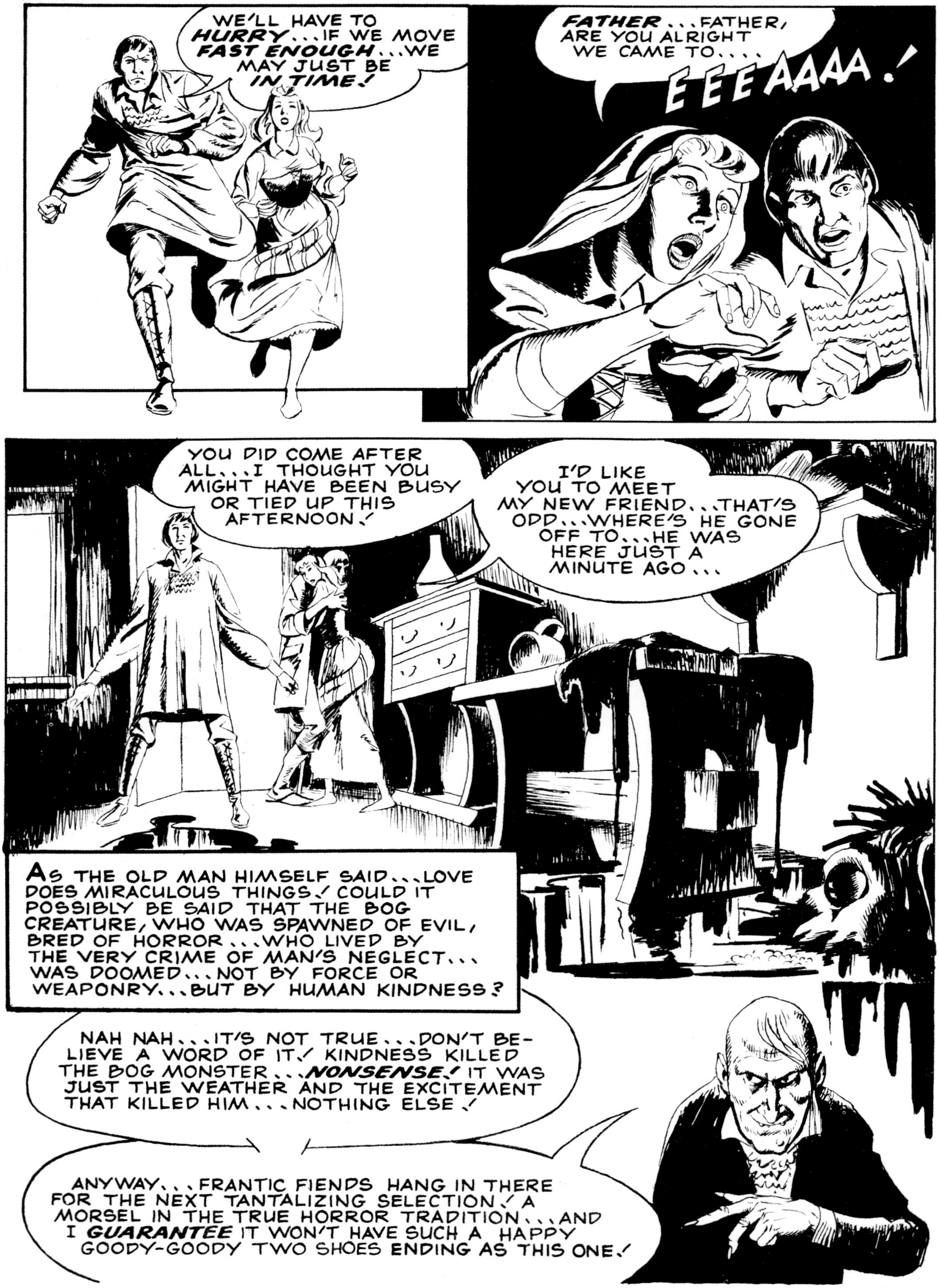
WE'LL HAVE TO HURRY... IF WE MOVE FAST ENOUGH... WE MAY JUST BE IN TIME!
FATHER... FATHER, ARE YOU ALRIGHT WE CAME TO....
EEEAAAA!
YOU DID COME AFTER ALL... I THOUGHT YOU MIGHT HAVE BEEN BUSY OR TIED UP THIS AFTERNOON!
I'D LIKE YOU TO MEET MY NEW FRIEND... THAT'S ODD... WHERE'S HE GONE OFF TO... HE WAS HERE JUST A MINUTE AGO...
AS THE OLD MAN HIMSELF SAID... LOVE DOES MIRACULOUS THINGS! COULD IT POSSIBLY BE SAID THAT THE BOG CREATURE, WHO WAS SPAWNED OF EVIL, BRED OF HORROR... WHO LIVED BY THE VERY CRIME OF MAN'S NEGLECT... WAS DOOMED... NOT BY FORCE OR WEAPONRY... BUT BY HUMAN KINDNESS?
NAH NAH... IT'S NOT TRUE... DON'T BELIEVE A WORD OF IT! KINDNESS KILLED THE BOG MONSTER... NONSENSE! IT WAS JUST THE WEATHER AND THE EXCITEMENT THAT KILLED HIM... NOTHING ELSE!
ANYWAY... FRANTIC FIENDS HANG IN THERE FOR THE NEXT TANTALIZING SELECTION! A MORSEL IN THE TRUE HORROR TRADITION... AND I GUARANTEE IT WON'T HAVE SUCH A HAPPY GOODY-GOODY TWO SHOES ENDING AS THIS ONE!

A COMPLETE COLLECTION OF HORROR & MONSTER MOVIES

WORLD'S ONLY LOW COST ALL-ELECTRIC 8mm MOVIE PROJECTOR with HIGH-PRICE FEATURES!

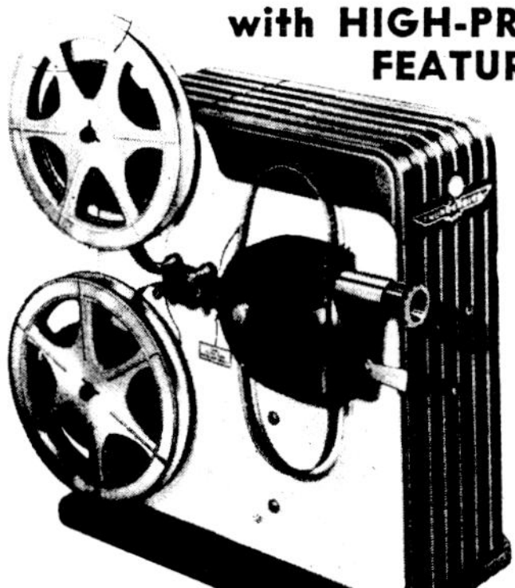

INCLUDES ALL THESE FEATURES—

- SHOWS 200 FEET MONSTER MOVIES!
- COMPLETELY ALL-ELECTRIC OPERATION!
- CONTINUOUS 15-MINUTE SHOWINGS!
- SHARP COLOR OR BLACK & WHITE IMAGES

You'd expect to pay much more for this all-metal, precision-built 8mm MOTION PICTURE PROJECTOR. Now you can show all your 200 foot Monster and Home Movies with professional sharpness. Shows all 8mm film, color and black & white. AND LOOK AT ALL THESE FEATURES: continuous 15 minute showings; blower-cooled; hi-quality coated lens for brightest images, easy, fast film threading; rapid motor film rewind; vertical tilt to aim up or down; 200 ft. takeup reel; manual framer (for correct film adjustment); removable gate for cleaning. A rare ALL-ELECTRIC PROJECTOR at a low, low $29.95, plus $2.00 for safe shipping.

ONLY $29.95

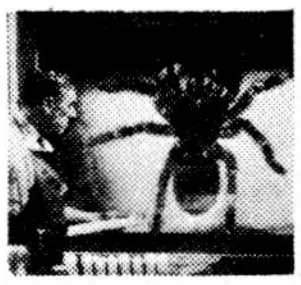

TARANTULA

BE CAREFUL the next time you meet a spider. He may grow bigger than a house if some crazy scientist experimented with him. It happens in TARANTULA. The spider gets bigger and bigger and creeps through the world, hell-bent on destroying it. Does he succeed? You'll find out with the eeriest film ever made, TARANTULA. 8mm, 200 feet, $5.95.

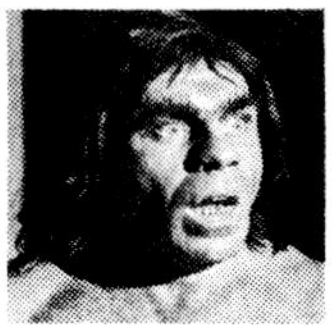

DINOSAURUS!

CAVEMAN & MONSTER BROUGHT BACK TO LIFE!

An American construction engineer accidentally blasts a brontosaurus, a tyrannosaurus rex and a prehistoric cave man up from the depths on an isolated tropical island. During a sudden storm, the creatures are hit by a freak lightning blast and brought back to life. Only $5.95.

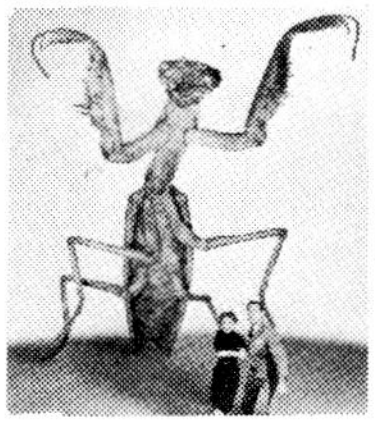

THE DEADLY MANTIS

4,000 TONS OF HORROR!

An incredibly gigantic Mantis swoops from the sky and goes on a raving rampage of earth-shattering destruction and terror. Only $5.95.

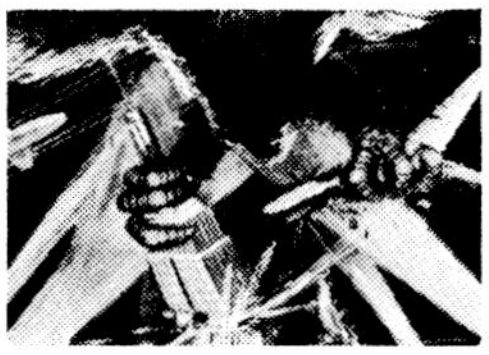

THE GIANT CLAW

From the pre-historic past comes a seemingly unconquerable bird-beast. It attacks, with the destruction of the world as its aim, and is finally destroyed by scientific ingenuity and Air Force weapon-power. Only $5.95.

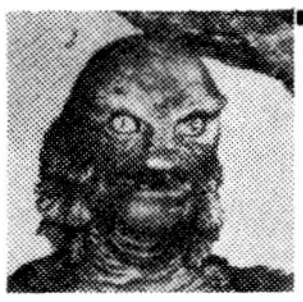

THE CREATURE FROM THE LAGOON

YOU MAY NEVER SWIM AGAIN, after you watch this scary picture. Imagine a living creature from 150 million years ago come out of the water, in Africa. He scares the life out of a party of archaeologists. Full of Black Lagoon scenes, furious spear-gun battles, chases, etc. A creature film every collector cherishes. 8mm, 160 feet, $5.75.

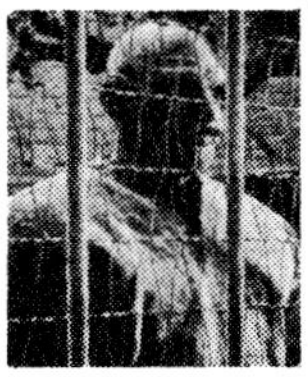

THE CREATURE WALKS AMONG US

The Creature is captured by scientists in an eerie lagoon, and is returned to civilization. He escapes —and leaves a wake of destruction while terrorizing the countryside. Only $5.95.

THE CABINET OF DR. CALIGARI

THE WEIRDEST EERIEST 8mm MOVIE EVER MADE!

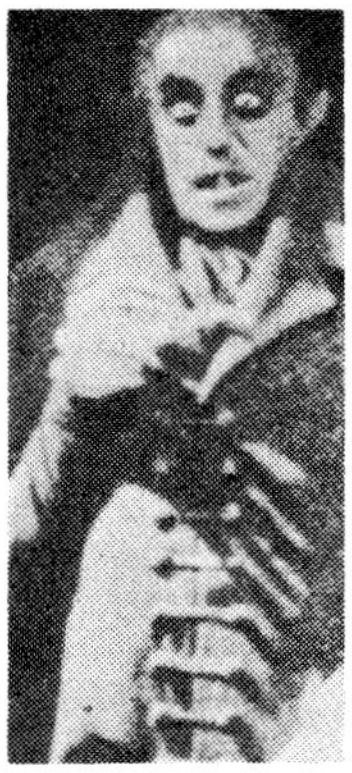

WHEN YOU SHOW this famous film, be prepared for 1 hour and 15 minutes of sheer shocker sensation! Called by many the "father" of all the horror films ever made. DR. CALIGARI will chill you, thrill you . . . . scare you and dare you to walk away. THIS IS THE MASTER MONSTER FILM OF ALL TIME! It featured world-famous Conrad Veidt, Werner Krauss and Lil Dagover. This is the COMPLETE ORIGINAL PRODUCTION. As unforgettable as it is eerie. A true masterpiece, prized by the world's smartest collectors of horror films. COMPLETE 5 BIG REELS, 1,000 FEET, SHOWING TIME A FULL 1¼ HOURS. 8mm. Only $34.95.

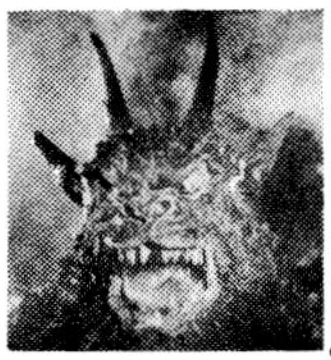

CURSE OF THE DEMON

The Devilworshipping cult of the evil Dr. Kaswell evokes a strange and murderous monster. The gruesome being turns its blood-lust against those who have come to investigate a strange murder. A terrifying tale! Only $5.95.

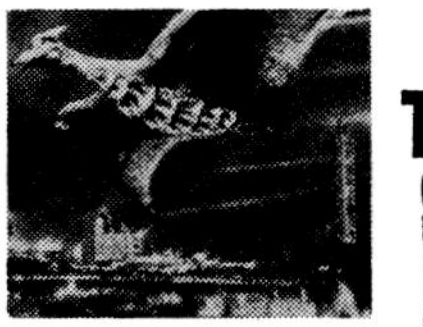

RODAN THE FLYING MONSTER

From pre-historic times, a monster is born again to plague the earth. See the terror of the skies! See the destruction of cities. Watch with horror as this monster flies over the earth terrifying nations. See the forces of man fight and finally conquer the terror that would destroy earth. Only $5.95.

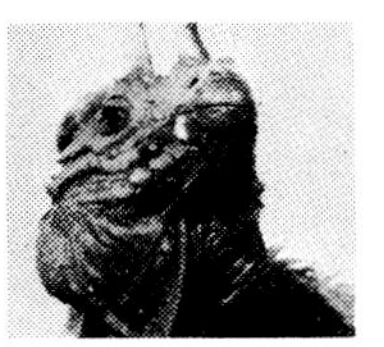

BATTLE OF THE GIANTS

LOOKS LIKE the cavemen had all the fun watching giant dinosaurs fight it out. This film of prehistoric battles between the world's earliest creatures will fascinate you. Was the world really like that? We don't know, but you will have a good time finding out. 160 feet, 8mm, $5.75.

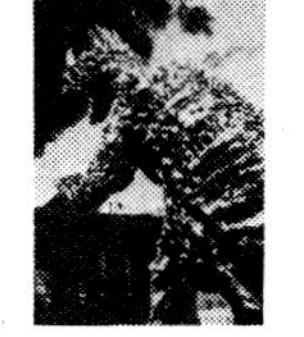

VARAN THE UNBELIEVABLE

Varan came from a World Below—to terrorize, to destroy, to revenge! From the makers of such classics as Godzilla, Rodan & The Mysterians comes the Fantastic VARAN. Only $5.95.

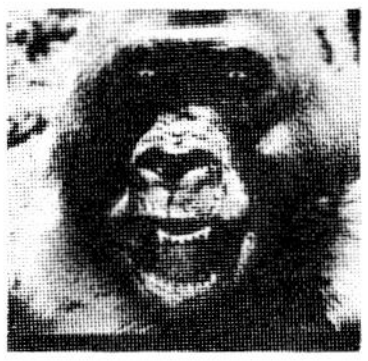

KILLER GORILLA

THE NEXT TIME you wonder how they capture gorillas, and find it hard to believe, here's an idea. Look at the famous film, KILLER GORILLA, and you will see exactly how it is done. Stalked and followed in darkest Africa, the killer Gorilla is finally captured . . . and this film will take you through every thrilling moment. 160 feet, 8mm, $5.75.

Please rush me the following, for which I enclose $.................... plus 25c postage & handling for each film checked below:

- ☐ Tarantula, $5.95
- ☐ Dinosaurus, $5.95
- ☐ The Deadly Mantis, $5.95
- ☐ The Giant Claw, $5.95
- ☐ The Creature From The Lagoon, $5.75
- ☐ The Creature Walks Among Us, $5.95
- ☐ Curse Of The Demon, $5.95
- ☐ Rodan The Flying Monster, $5.95
- ☐ Battle Of The Giants, $5.75
- ☐ Varan The Unbelievable, $5.95
- ☐ The Cabinet Of Dr. Caligari, $34.95
- ☐ Killer Gorilla, $5.75

NAME..

ADDRESS..

CITY..

STATE.............................ZIP CODE NO..........................

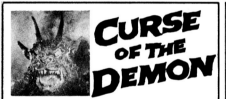

THE CRAWLING HAND

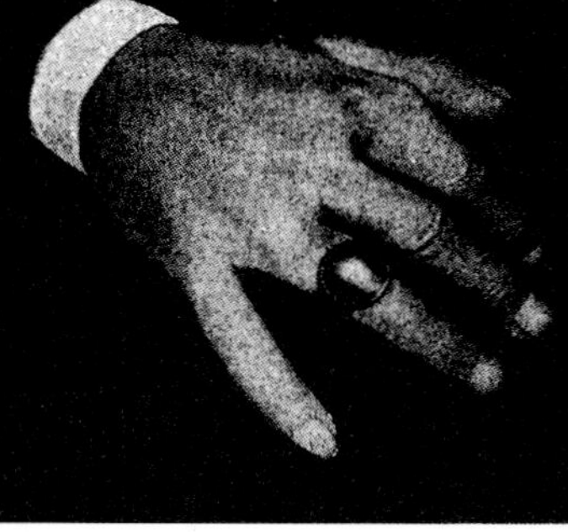

TURN ON the switch and watch! THE HAND comes to life! THE FINGERS flex as the hand starts to walk across the room. The large ring on the third finger sheds a light of erie horror over the room. The silent life-like plastic hand, made of latex rubber with a bandaged wrist, stalks across the room and only YOU know where it came from. Only $4.95 plus 50c for postage and handling.

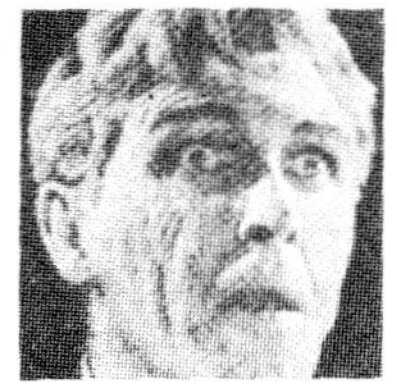

4D MAN

The Corpse-Making 4-Dimensional Man can walk through walls, but needs the life force of others to keep himself from becoming a modern Mummy. Only $5.95.

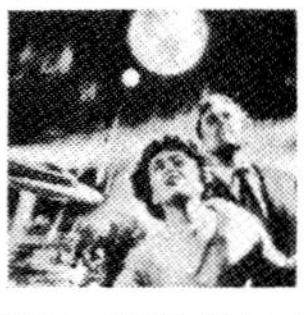

WAR OF THE PLANETS

WHAT HAPPENS when a runaway planet plays hookey from stellar space? Another universe calls in a space scientist to stop exploding missiles, end trouble in the skies. This is a truly wonderful space-and-science film . . . one you won't ever forget. So get it today! 8mm, 160 feet, $5.75.

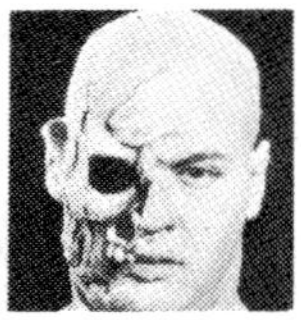

WAR OF THE COLOSSAL BEAST

A monster of the Atomic Age! A towering terror from Hell! The story of a man trapped in the blast of a plutonium bomb—and the terrible events that followed. Only $5.95.

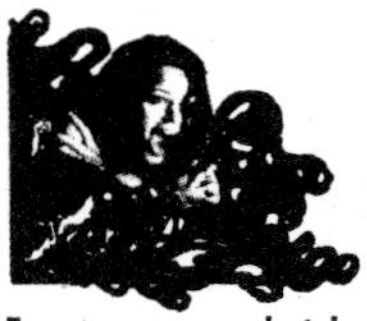

THE BLOB

Teenagers see what looks like a shooting star blaze to earth. At its landing spot they find an old man writhing in pain, his hand covered with a strange substance. They rush him to a doctor, who watched the substance spreading before his eyes. The Blob continues to spread, & terrorize the town. Only $5.95.

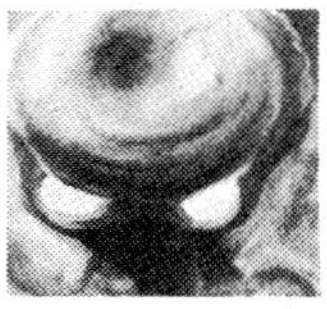

IT CAME FROM OUTER SPACE

WHAT HAPPENS WHEN A SPACE SHIP loaded with stellar monsters goes out of control! They land on earth and battle a brave scientist trying to save the earth. Is he successful? This scary film tells you what really happens. 160 feet, 8mm, $5.75.

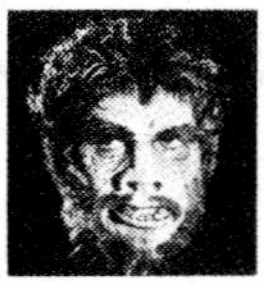

ABBOTT & COSTELLO MEET DR. JEKYLL & MR. HYDE

AMERICA'S MOST MIRTHFUL COMEDIANS meet the world's most monstrous Monsters . . . and that's where the fun begins. Dr. Jekyll gives Costello a drug, turns him into a monster. Everything goes crazy and Scotland Yard goes mad. Monsters can be fun, and this film is the funniest! 8mm, 160 feet, $5.75.

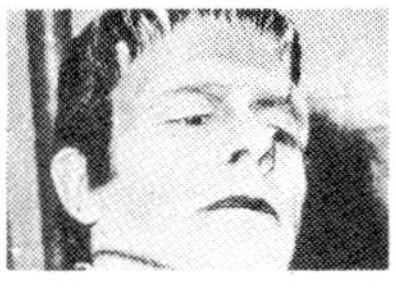

ABBOTT & COSTELLO MEET FRANKENSTEIN

THE WHO'S WHO of the MONSTER WORLD team up in the funniest monster film ever made. Imagine Frankenstein, Dracula, The Wolf Man and The Invisible Man combining their eerie talents to trap Abbott & Costello. They even suggest using Costello's brain for the Monsters. Great fun! 8mm, 100 feet, $5.75.

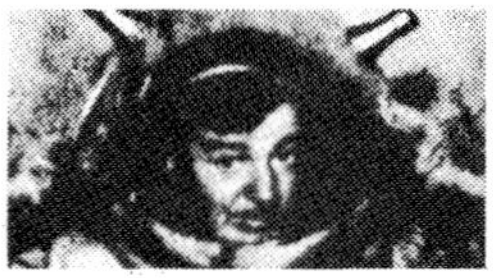

ABBOTT & COSTELLO IN ROCKET & ROLL

THE FUNNIEST COMICS in Hollywood double up for a crazy rocket trip through outer space. Beauties and cuties in Venus tempt them. The runaway rocket ship scares the life out of them. And through it all Abbott & Costello give a hilarious performance that will make you "die" laughing. 8mm, 160 feet, $5.75.

NOW FOR THE FIRST TIME— THE 3 STOOGES IN 3D

Aside from the special color-filter viewers supplied with the film, no special equipment is needed. No special screen . . . no special projector. Just watch the startling action! Sixty feet of film.

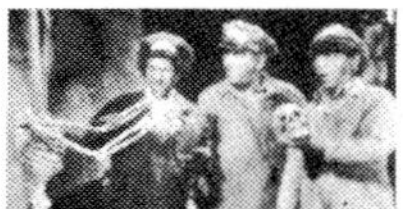

SPOOKS

The Stooges in a hilarious slapstick romp . . . funnier than ever in 3-D. So real they seem to jump right out of the screen. When something is thrown . . . you duck! Only $4.95.

TALES of HORROR

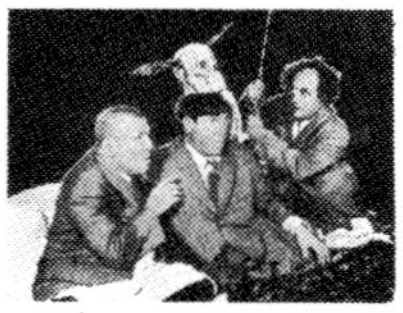

This 3-D Stooge comedy is a wild tale that takes place in an old haunted house. Our 3-Dimensional Stooges are mixed up with all sorts of deadly weapons . . . Only $4.95.

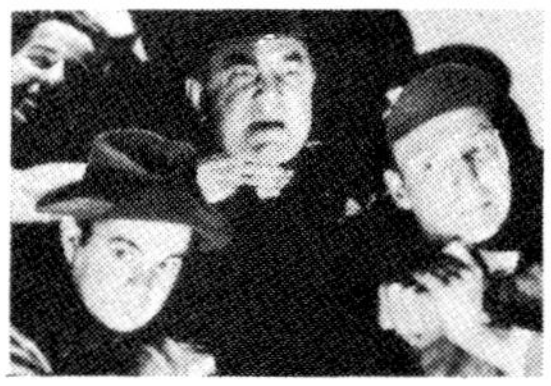

EAST SIDE KIDS MEET BELA LUGOSI

YOU'LL DIE LAUGHING as the East Side Kids match their side-splitting stunts with Bela Lugosi's terror-filled action. Featuring Bela Lugosi and the original East Side Kids. Only $5.95.

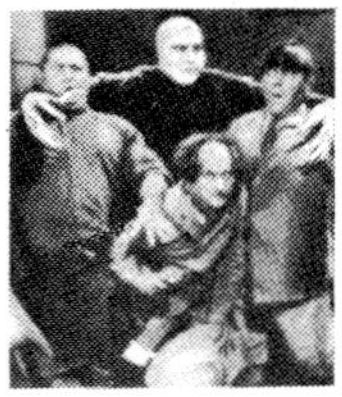

WE WANT OUR MUMMY

Hired as detectives, our 3 friends take a hilarious taxi ride to Egypt. And when they enter the tomb . . . WOW! Only $6.95

Please rush me the following, for which I enclose
$.................... plus 35¢ postage & handling for each film checked

☐ The 4-D Man, $5.95
☐ War Of The Planets, $5.75
☐ War Of The Colossal Beast, $5.95
☐ The Blob, $5.95
☐ It Came From Outer Space, $5.75
☐ A. & C. Meet Dr. Jekyll & Mr. Hyde, $5.75
☐ A. & C. Meet Frankenstein, $5.75
☐ A. & C. in Rocket and Roll, $5.75
☐ East Side Kids Meet Bela Lugosi, $5.95
☐ We Want Our Mummy, $6.95
☐ Spooks in 3-D, $4.95
☐ Tales Of Horror in 3-D, $4.95

NAME..

ADDRESS..

CITY..

STATE....................ZIP CODE NO....................

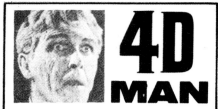

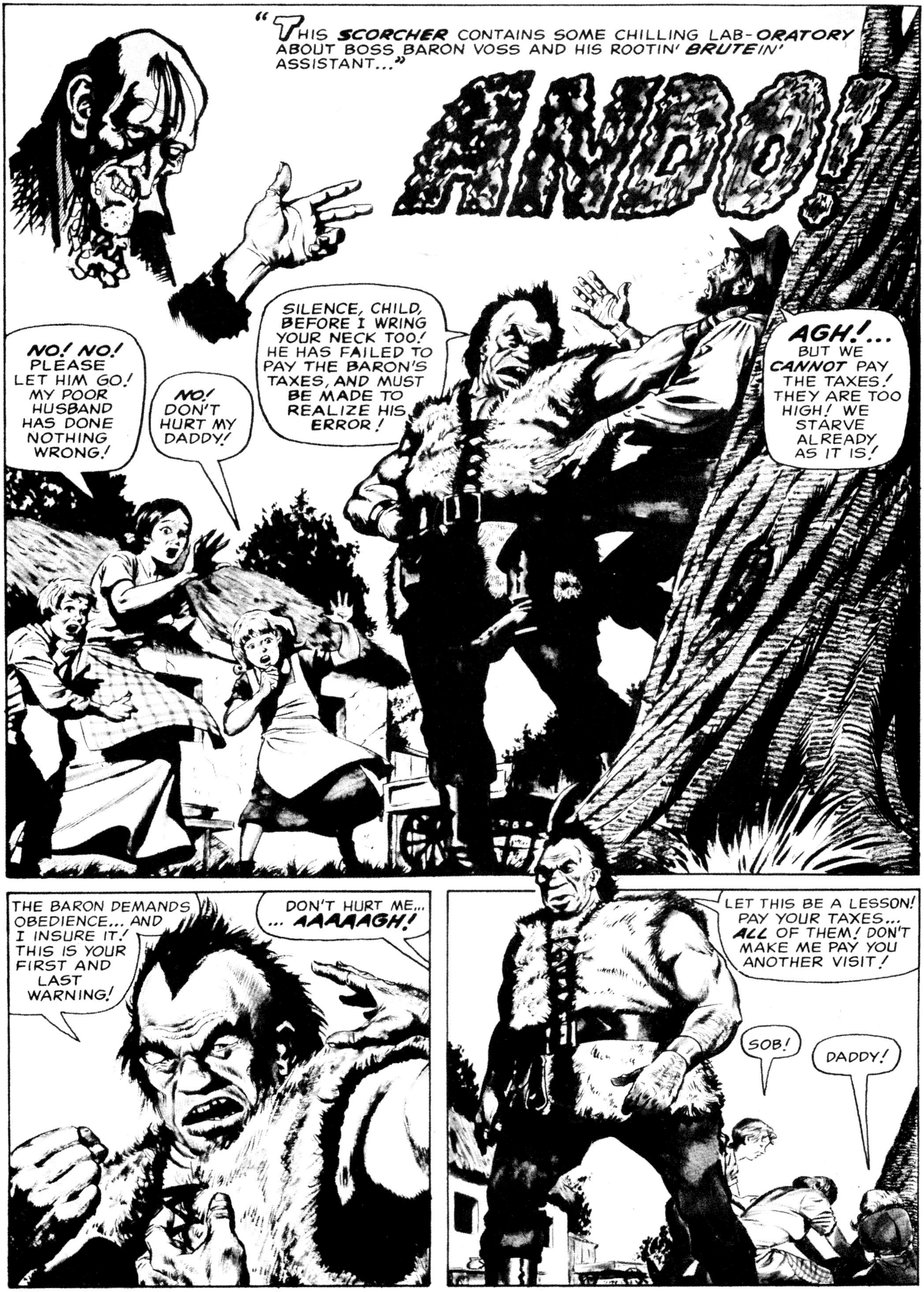
"THIS SCORCHER CONTAINS SOME CHILLING LAB-ORATORY ABOUT BOSS BARON VOSS AND HIS ROOTIN' BRUTEIN' ASSISTANT..."
ANDO!
NO! NO! PLEASE LET HIM GO! MY POOR HUSBAND HAS DONE NOTHING WRONG!
NO! DON'T HURT MY DADDY!
SILENCE, CHILD, BEFORE I WRING YOUR NECK TOO! HE HAS FAILED TO PAY THE BARON'S TAXES, AND MUST BE MADE TO REALIZE HIS ERROR!
AGH!... BUT WE CANNOT PAY THE TAXES! THEY ARE TOO HIGH! WE STARVE ALREADY AS IT IS!
THE BARON DEMANDS OBEDIENCE... AND I INSURE IT! THIS IS YOUR FIRST AND LAST WARNING!
DON'T HURT ME... ...AAAAAGH!
LET THIS BE A LESSON! PAY YOUR TAXES... ALL OF THEM! DON'T MAKE ME PAY YOU ANOTHER VISIT!
SOB!
DADDY!

ART BY SYD SHORES/STORY BY ROBERT ROSEN

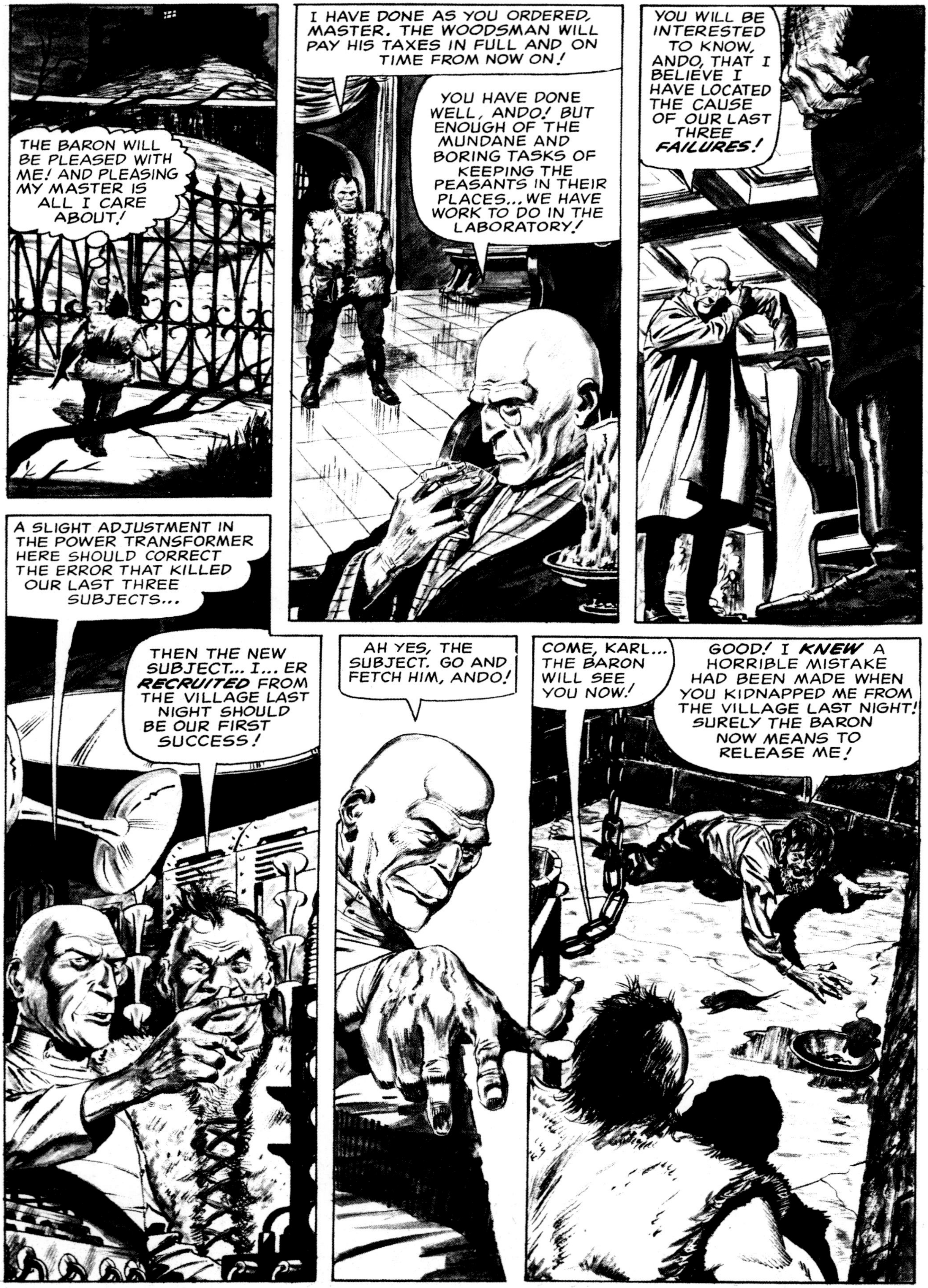
THE BARON WILL BE PLEASED WITH ME! AND PLEASING MY MASTER IS ALL I CARE ABOUT!
I HAVE DONE AS YOU ORDERED, MASTER. THE WOODSMAN WILL PAY HIS TAXES IN FULL AND ON TIME FROM NOW ON!
YOU HAVE DONE WELL, ANDO! BUT ENOUGH OF THE MUNDANE AND BORING TASKS OF KEEPING THE PEASANTS IN THEIR PLACES... WE HAVE WORK TO DO IN THE LABORATORY!
YOU WILL BE INTERESTED TO KNOW, ANDO, THAT I BELIEVE I HAVE LOCATED THE CAUSE OF OUR LAST THREE FAILURES!
A SLIGHT ADJUSTMENT IN THE POWER TRANSFORMER HERE SHOULD CORRECT THE ERROR THAT KILLED OUR LAST THREE SUBJECTS...
THEN THE NEW SUBJECT... I... ER RECRUITED FROM THE VILLAGE LAST NIGHT SHOULD BE OUR FIRST SUCCESS!
AH YES, THE SUBJECT. GO AND FETCH HIM, ANDO!
COME, KARL... THE BARON WILL SEE YOU NOW!
GOOD! I KNEW A HORRIBLE MISTAKE HAD BEEN MADE WHEN YOU KIDNAPPED ME FROM THE VILLAGE LAST NIGHT! SURELY THE BARON NOW MEANS TO RELEASE ME!

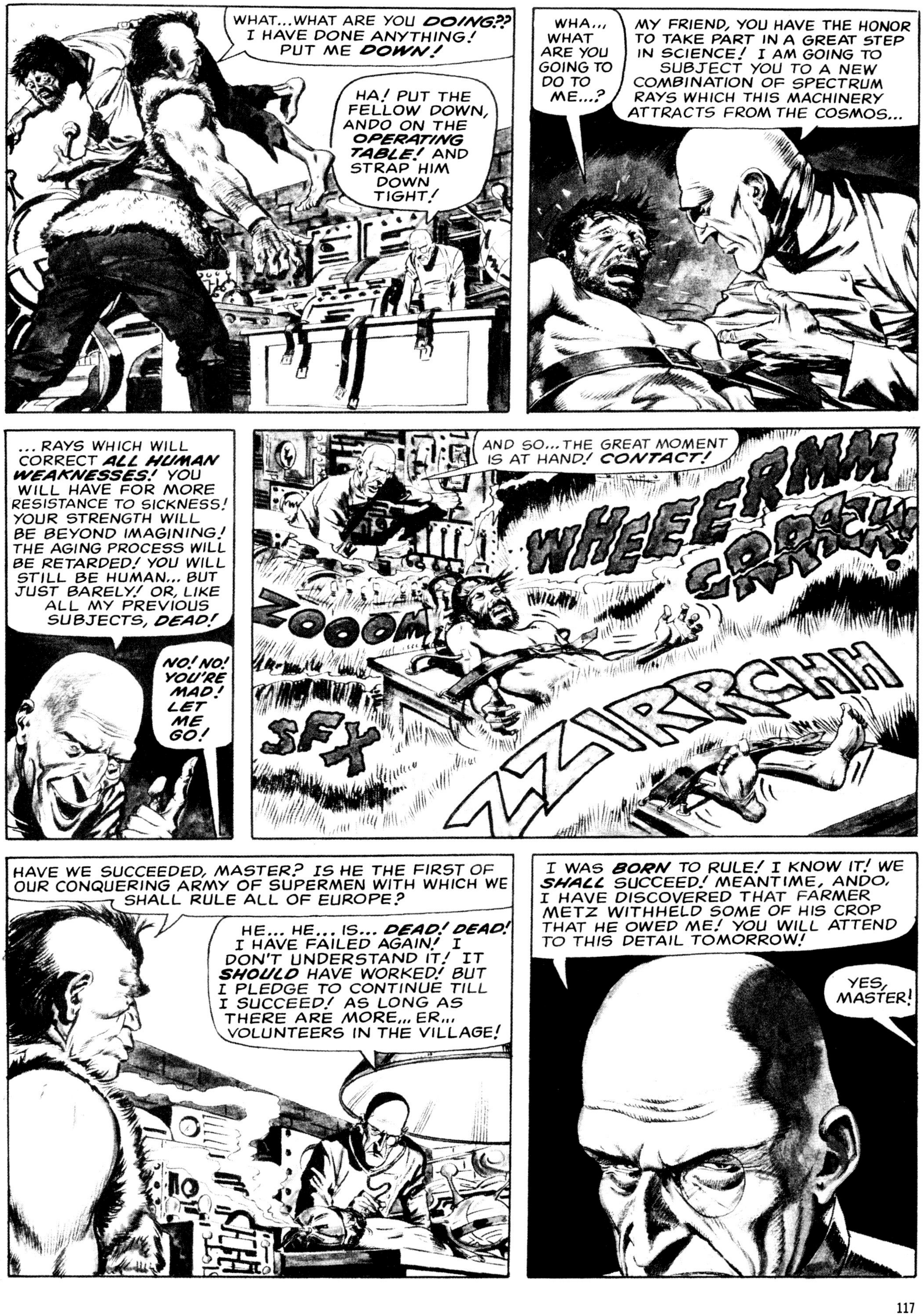
WHAT...WHAT ARE YOU DOING?? I HAVE DONE ANYTHING! PUT ME DOWN!
HA! PUT THE FELLOW DOWN, ANDO ON THE OPERATING TABLE! AND STRAP HIM DOWN TIGHT!
WHA... WHAT ARE YOU GOING TO DO TO ME...?
MY FRIEND, YOU HAVE THE HONOR TO TAKE PART IN A GREAT STEP IN SCIENCE! I AM GOING TO SUBJECT YOU TO A NEW COMBINATION OF SPECTRUM RAYS WHICH THIS MACHINERY ATTRACTS FROM THE COSMOS...
...RAYS WHICH WILL CORRECT ALL HUMAN WEAKNESSES! YOU WILL HAVE FOR MORE RESISTANCE TO SICKNESS! YOUR STRENGTH WILL BE BEYOND IMAGINING! THE AGING PROCESS WILL BE RETARDED! YOU WILL STILL BE HUMAN... BUT JUST BARELY! OR, LIKE ALL MY PREVIOUS SUBJECTS, DEAD!
NO! NO! YOU'RE MAD! LET ME GO!
AND SO...THE GREAT MOMENT IS AT HAND! CONTACT!
WHEEERMM
CRAACK!
ZOOOM
SFX
ZZIRRCHH
HAVE WE SUCCEEDED, MASTER? IS HE THE FIRST OF OUR CONQUERING ARMY OF SUPERMEN WITH WHICH WE SHALL RULE ALL OF EUROPE?
HE... HE... IS... DEAD! DEAD! I HAVE FAILED AGAIN! I DON'T UNDERSTAND IT! IT SHOULD HAVE WORKED! BUT I PLEDGE TO CONTINUE TILL I SUCCEED! AS LONG AS THERE ARE MORE... ER... VOLUNTEERS IN THE VILLAGE!
I WAS BORN TO RULE! I KNOW IT! WE SHALL SUCCEED! MEANTIME, ANDO, I HAVE DISCOVERED THAT FARMER METZ WITHHELD SOME OF HIS CROP THAT HE OWED ME! YOU WILL ATTEND TO THIS DETAIL TOMORROW!
YES, MASTER!

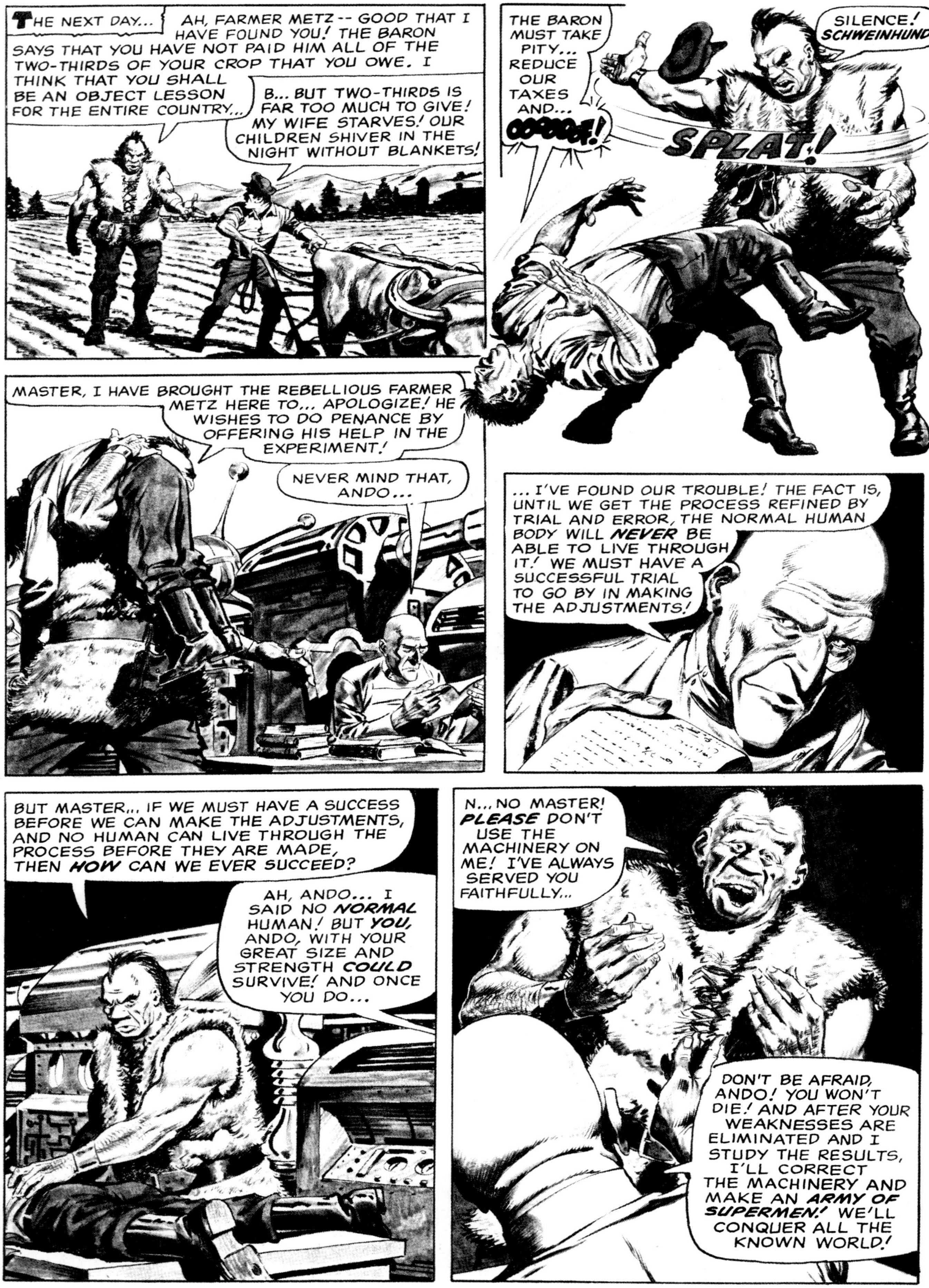
THE NEXT DAY...
AH, FARMER METZ -- GOOD THAT I HAVE FOUND YOU! THE BARON SAYS THAT YOU HAVE NOT PAID HIM ALL OF THE TWO-THIRDS OF YOUR CROP THAT YOU OWE. I THINK THAT YOU SHALL BE AN OBJECT LESSON FOR THE ENTIRE COUNTRY...
B... BUT TWO-THIRDS IS FAR TOO MUCH TO GIVE! MY WIFE STARVES! OUR CHILDREN SHIVER IN THE NIGHT WITHOUT BLANKETS!
THE BARON MUST TAKE PITY... REDUCE OUR TAXES AND...
OOOOOF!
SILENCE! SCHWEINHUND!
SPLAT!
MASTER, I HAVE BROUGHT THE REBELLIOUS FARMER METZ HERE TO... APOLOGIZE! HE WISHES TO DO PENANCE BY OFFERING HIS HELP IN THE EXPERIMENT!
NEVER MIND THAT, ANDO...
... I'VE FOUND OUR TROUBLE! THE FACT IS, UNTIL WE GET THE PROCESS REFINED BY TRIAL AND ERROR, THE NORMAL HUMAN BODY WILL NEVER BE ABLE TO LIVE THROUGH IT! WE MUST HAVE A SUCCESSFUL TRIAL TO GO BY IN MAKING THE ADJUSTMENTS!
BUT MASTER... IF WE MUST HAVE A SUCCESS BEFORE WE CAN MAKE THE ADJUSTMENTS, AND NO HUMAN CAN LIVE THROUGH THE PROCESS BEFORE THEY ARE MADE, THEN HOW CAN WE EVER SUCCEED?
AH, ANDO... I SAID NO NORMAL HUMAN! BUT YOU, ANDO, WITH YOUR GREAT SIZE AND STRENGTH COULD SURVIVE! AND ONCE YOU DO...
N... NO MASTER! PLEASE DON'T USE THE MACHINERY ON ME! I'VE ALWAYS SERVED YOU FAITHFULLY...
DON'T BE AFRAID, ANDO! YOU WON'T DIE! AND AFTER YOUR WEAKNESSES ARE ELIMINATED AND I STUDY THE RESULTS, I'LL CORRECT THE MACHINERY AND MAKE AN ARMY OF SUPERMEN! WE'LL CONQUER ALL THE KNOWN WORLD!

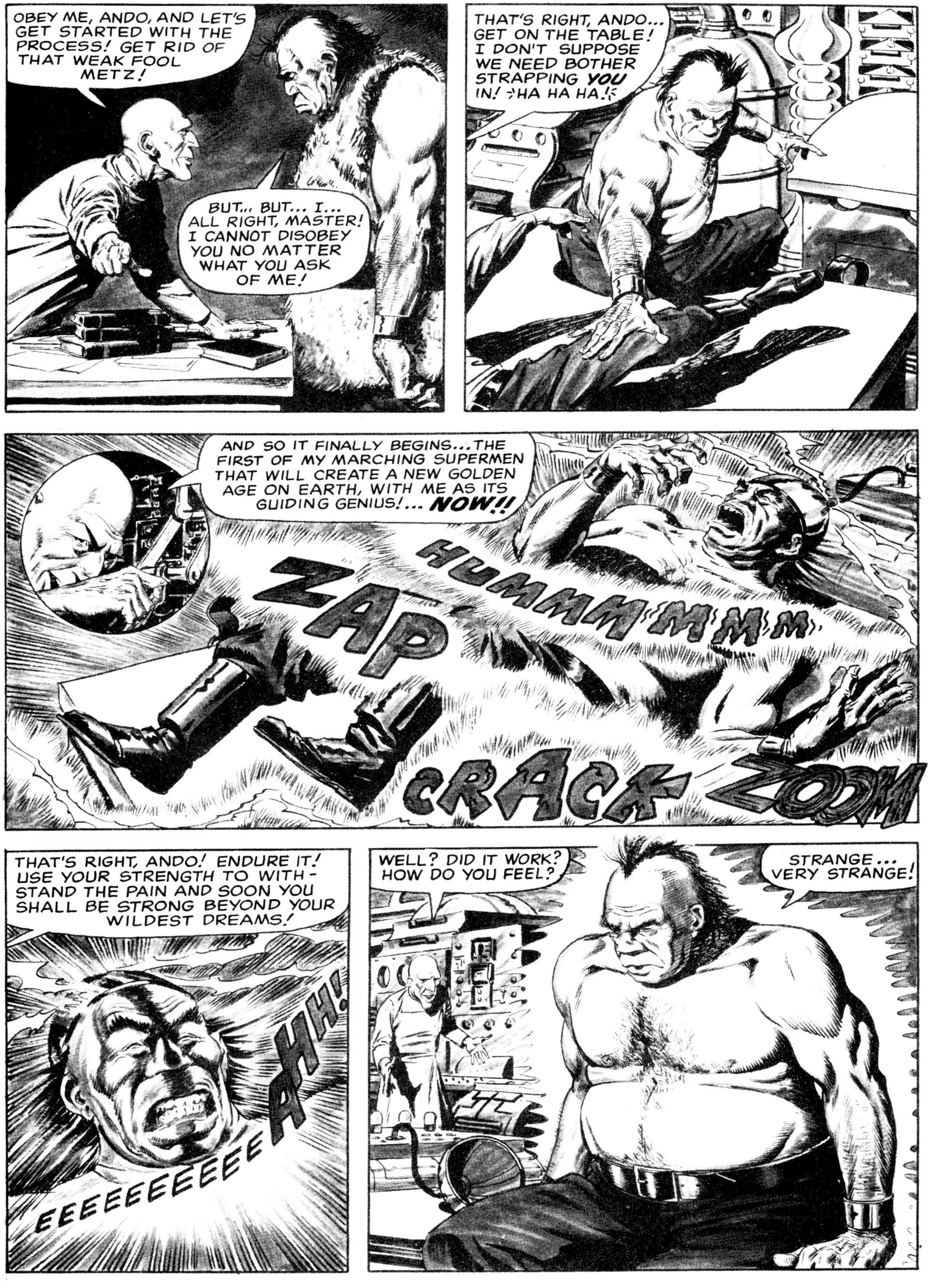
OBEY ME, ANDO, AND LET'S GET STARTED WITH THE PROCESS! GET RID OF THAT WEAK FOOL METZ!
BUT... BUT... I... ALL RIGHT, MASTER! I CANNOT DISOBEY YOU NO MATTER WHAT YOU ASK OF ME!
THAT'S RIGHT, ANDO... GET ON THE TABLE! I DON'T SUPPOSE WE NEED BOTHER STRAPPING YOU IN! HA HA HA!
AND SO IT FINALLY BEGINS... THE FIRST OF MY MARCHING SUPERMEN THAT WILL CREATE A NEW GOLDEN AGE ON EARTH, WITH ME AS ITS GUIDING GENIUS!... NOW!!
HUMMMMMMM
ZAP
CRACK
ZOOM
THAT'S RIGHT, ANDO! ENDURE IT! USE YOUR STRENGTH TO WITHSTAND THE PAIN AND SOON YOU SHALL BE STRONG BEYOND YOUR WILDEST DREAMS!
EEEEEEEEEEEEAHH!
WELL? DID IT WORK? HOW DO YOU FEEL?
STRANGE... VERY STRANGE!

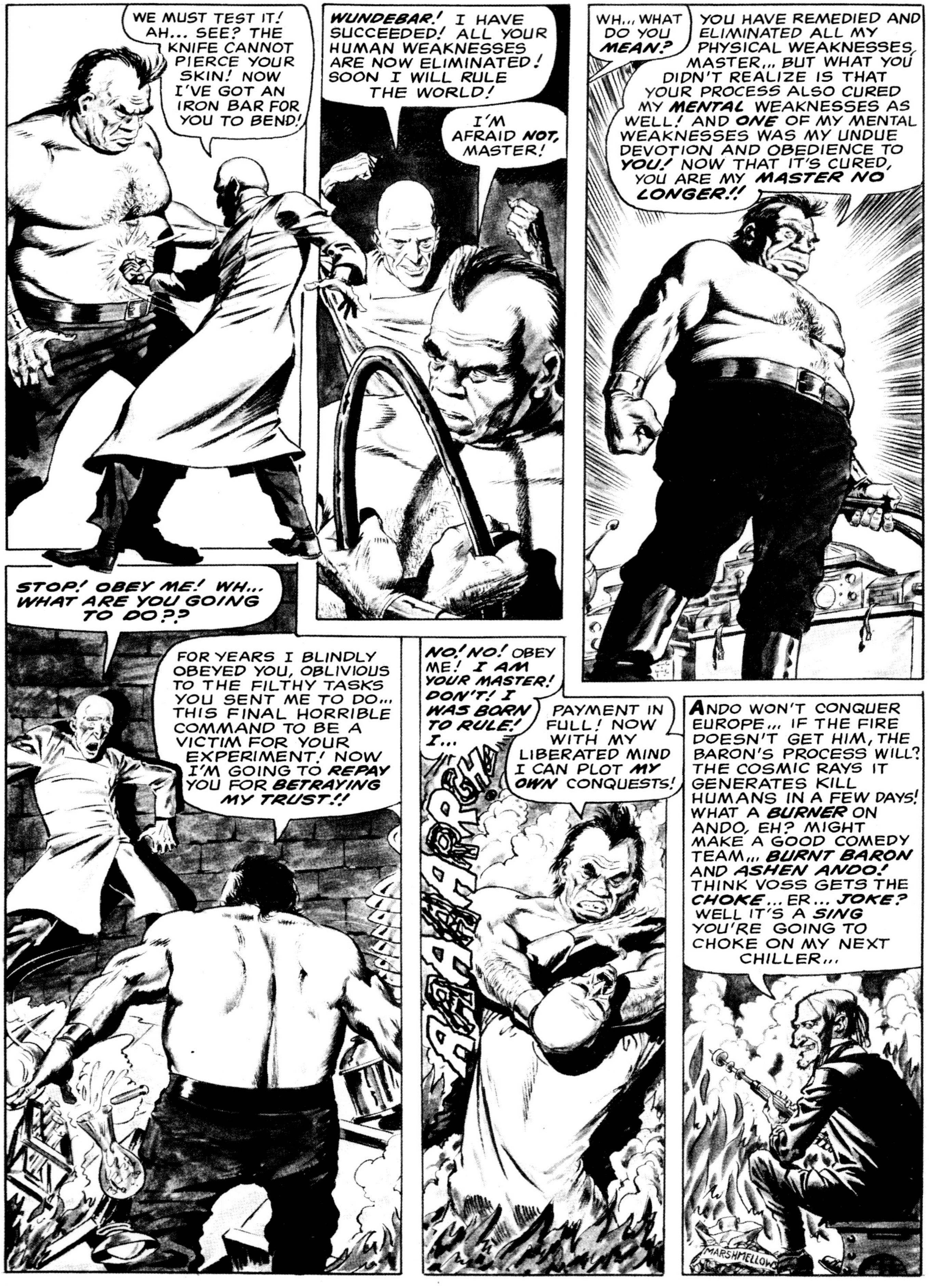
WE MUST TEST IT! AH... SEE? THE KNIFE CANNOT PIERCE YOUR SKIN! NOW I'VE GOT AN IRON BAR FOR YOU TO BEND!
WUNDEBAR! I HAVE SUCCEEDED! ALL YOUR HUMAN WEAKNESSES ARE NOW ELIMINATED! SOON I WILL RULE THE WORLD!
I'M AFRAID NOT, MASTER!
WH... WHAT DO YOU MEAN?
YOU HAVE REMEDIED AND ELIMINATED ALL MY PHYSICAL WEAKNESSES, MASTER... BUT WHAT YOU DIDN'T REALIZE IS THAT YOUR PROCESS ALSO CURED MY MENTAL WEAKNESSES AS WELL! AND ONE OF MY MENTAL WEAKNESSES WAS MY UNDUE DEVOTION AND OBEDIENCE TO YOU! NOW THAT IT'S CURED, YOU ARE MY MASTER NO LONGER!!
STOP! OBEY ME! WH... WHAT ARE YOU GOING TO DO??
FOR YEARS I BLINDLY OBEYED YOU, OBLIVIOUS TO THE FILTHY TASKS YOU SENT ME TO DO... THIS FINAL HORRIBLE COMMAND TO BE A VICTIM FOR YOUR EXPERIMENT! NOW I'M GOING TO REPAY YOU FOR BETRAYING MY TRUST!!
NO! NO! OBEY ME! I AM YOUR MASTER! DON'T! I WAS BORN TO RULE! I...
PAYMENT IN FULL! NOW WITH MY LIBERATED MIND I CAN PLOT MY OWN CONQUESTS!
ANDO WON'T CONQUER EUROPE... IF THE FIRE DOESN'T GET HIM, THE BARON'S PROCESS WILL! THE COSMIC RAYS IT GENERATES KILL HUMANS IN A FEW DAYS! WHAT A BURNER ON ANDO, EH? MIGHT MAKE A GOOD COMEDY TEAM... BURNT BARON AND ASHEN ANDO! THINK VOSS GETS THE CHOKE... ER... JOKE? WELL IT'S A SING YOU'RE GOING TO CHOKE ON MY NEXT CHILLER...
MARSHMELLOWS

FIRST MAGAZINE OF ILLUSTRATED HORROR

CREEPY
#35
SEPT

A WARREN MAGAZINE

PDC

60¢

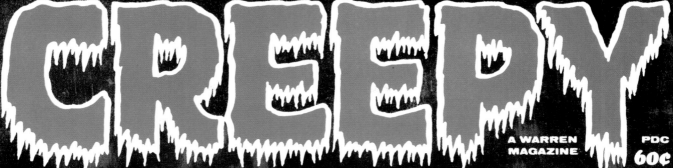

Extra-Special Issue
Featuring 9 great big stories
of illustrated terror
and fantastic suspense!!

Kenneth Smith

AN EDITORIAL TO THE PRESIDENT OF THE UNITED STATES AND ALL THE MEMBERS OF CONGRESS

---ON BEHALF OF OUR READERS, MOST OF WHOM ARE FROM 10 TO 18 YEARS OLD...

WE are a magazine publishing company that is in business to entertain and enlighten our audience. We don't publish politically-oriented magazines (3 of our titles are comics-format), but we do get involved in the serious issues of our times.

BOTH this company and our young readers have felt for some time now that our country is in deep trouble. Our first personal taste of this trouble occurred in 1965 when we came out with BLAZING COMBAT Magazine. Blazing Combat was a comic book that grimly pointed out that war is hell, and inhuman—and not the glamorous, adventurous matter often depicted in the mass media. Editor Archie Goodwin wrote some of the finest anti-war stories ever seen in comics form.

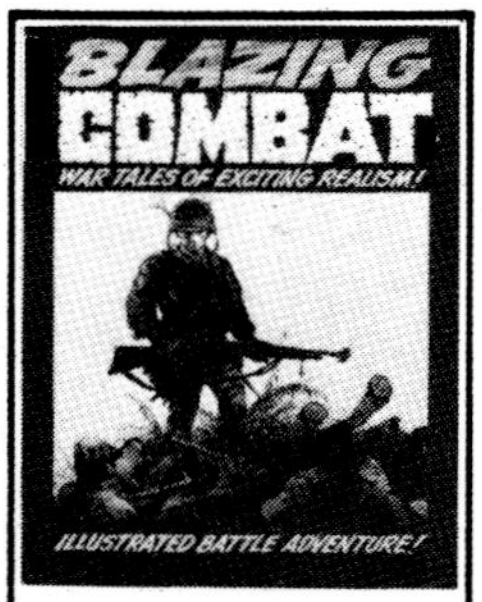
BLAZING
COMBAT
WAR TALES OF EXCITING REALISM!
ILLUSTRATED BATTLE ADVENTURE!
"UNPATRIOTIC?"

It was a publication we were proud of. Yet, Blazing Combat was a failure on the newsstands. It lasted 4 issues.

WE suspect that part of the reason it failed was because some of the people involved in the sales and distribution of our product didn't like the attitude we took on Viet Nam. Back in 1965 it was considered, by most, extremely unpatriotic not to support our country's position. We received complaints along about our second issue. We ignored them, but could not ignore the economic effect of losing thousands of dollars each issue. We ceased publication.

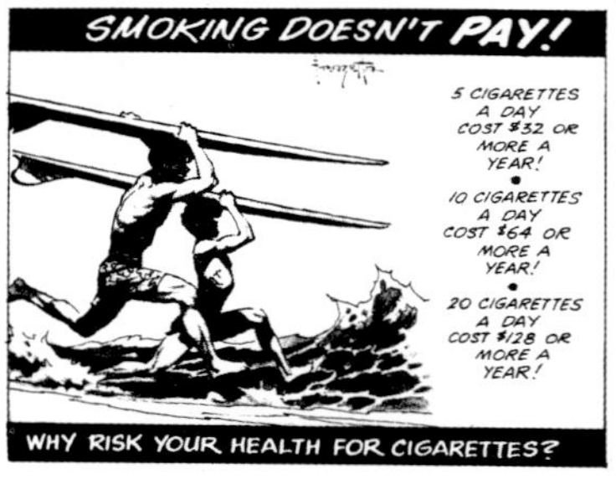
SMOKING DOESN'T PAY!
5 CIGARETTES A DAY COST $32 OR MORE A YEAR!
10 CIGARETTES A DAY COST $64 OR MORE A YEAR!
20 CIGARETTES A DAY COST $128 OR MORE A YEAR!
WHY RISK YOUR HEALTH FOR CIGARETTES?
"MORE IMPORTANT THAN AD REVENUE"

WE were angry—that a magazine we thought deserved to live—had died, possibly because it proclaimed a message that said "War is hell—and the Viet Nam war is not only hell, it's absolute insanity for our country." And so Blazing Combat went quietly out of business.

STILL another involvement for us is the running of our Anti-Cigarette Smoking ad.

CREATED at our own expense, this half-page Comics-Format ad *"EASY WAY TO A TUFF SURFBOARD!"* (written by Archie Goodwin, drawn by Frank Frazetta) has been running in all Warren Magazines for the past 5 summers. It's not the kind of ad you'll see in any other publication in America. It doesn't help sell our magazines, but we run it because we believe the message is important (more important than advertising revenue)—and deserves exposure in our pages.

NOW we must again speak out, concerning that most urgent issue—our involvement in Southeast Asia.

WE realize that only you, Mr. President, can end this war—the longest and costliest war in our history. Failing this, only You—the Members of Congress—can stop the President from continuing a war that is taking the lives and limbs of our youth, soiling our national conscience, and splitting this country down the middle.

MOST of us readers are under 21. We can't vote—yet. But we don't have to be 21 to die in a war that was a mistake to begin with.

That's why we are angry with you adults, Mr. President and Members of Congress. You adults have let this drag on for half of our lives. We've tried to tell you this in our demonstrations. We tried to tell you this at Kent State. Were you listening?

PERHAPS you don't listen because you think we're children. You may even think it strange or odd that words like these appear in a magazine such as this. But we're deadly serious about what we're now saying.

DO something about it NOW.

BEFORE another human life is wasted — give us PEACE, NOW!

James Warren,
President
WARREN PUBLISHING CO.

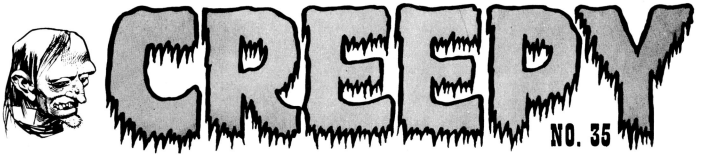

CREEPY

NO. 35

EDITOR and PUBLISHER: JAMES WARREN **ASSOCIATE EDITOR:** ARCHIE GOODWIN
CONTRIBUTING EDITORS: BILL PARENTE, NICOLA CUTI **COVER:** KEN SMITH
ARTISTS THIS ISSUE: PAT BOYETTE, THE BROTHERS CIOCHETTI, ERNIE COLON, MIKE ROYER, SYD SHORES, BILL STILLWELL, TOM SUTTON, ALAN WEISS
WRITERS THIS ISSUE: PAT BOYETTE, T. CASEY BRENNAN, AL HEWETSON, R. MICHAEL ROSEN, BUDDY SAUNDERS, BILL STILLWELL, HOWARD WALDROP, ALAN WEISS

CONTENTS

THIS'LL ONLY TAKE A MINUTE, SNAKE EYES SENDS HIS REGARDS!

GRRRRRRUMMMMMM!

EYE OF FISH AND TOOTH OF MOLE BLACKNESS FROM MY VERY SOUL...

PUT THEM TOGETHER AGAIN!

MAIL

ᵉᵉ Stay away from Science Fiction ᵉᵉ

I've noticed that the more popular comics magazines have started to deal with real social issues. They fight discrimination and the military. They get involved in slum problems.

One of the greatest causes of all is the fight against pollution, and it's one none of the great superheroes have taken on. I think you and that sawed-off runt Cousin Eerie could do a lot to fight that

good fight. Stop littering the landscape with dead bodies. And stop spilling all that blood.

ANN MARIE PETT
New York, N.Y.

Ol' Uncle Creepy has given special consideration to your request since last week, when he found a 3-inch layer of tar & smog residues on his family crypt. Not to mention his family! Hopping into a tub in attempt to wash the grime

& soot from his hide, he was irked to find detergent soap bubbles spilling from a faucet that heretofore poured forth pure, fresh, clean blood. Ol'Uncle Creepy is now IN-CENSED!

The Machinations of Monsterdom are now grinding... so watch for socially pointed stories from our socially pointed heads in future issues of CREEPY, EERIE and VAMPIRELLA.

RENDERING OF POLLUTION PROBLEM AT "W. EISNER'S WHARF"

I was extremely happy to see Reed Crandall's work appear in **CREEPY** after such a long time. The story, "Blue Mum Day," by R. Michael Rosen, was very well done. But why the nude woman in the background of the second panel on page 20? I hope you get some of your artists back on the job, and you seem to be doing so, what with Crandall this issue and Frazetta and Neal Adams in issue #32. Now all you need is Archie Goodwin back. About your other artists, David StClair, Billy Graham and Jack Sparling are your best "regulars," but we older fans wish to see more of Crandall, Adams, Morrow, Colon and Grandenetti like we used to.

The cover on #33 was magnificent, but should never have been bordered. Pat Boyette is good.

The Frazetta-cover and **VAMPIRELLA** posters everyone seems to be mentioning are certainly good ideas. When are you guys going to decide that they're **profitable** ideas?

RANDY PALMER
Arlington, Va.

Archie Goodwin is back, Randy, and he's even writing a 23-page special story for

Vampirella #8, cover by Ken Kelly and interiors by Tom Sutton. Nifty ol' Neal Adams may even appear in that issue, too. As for Jerry Grandenetti, who ever told you he left? Don't tell him he left, or he'll demand a special homecoming party. And if he does, we'll send the bill to you cause you were the one who imagined he went away in the first place.

I usually get my Warren Mags at the corner grocery and when I'm there, I usually take a look at the "cheap" horror mags—just to see if they've gotten any worse. Well, they have. I already knew that they had jumped from 35c to 50c and that most of their material is reprinted stuff. Now, I think they've gotten as bad as they possibly can get. They've actually gone and reprinted a front cover!

I really flipped over your issue #33. It was great. Is Vampirella related to you? Is she your niece? I'm pretty sure I read that somewhere?

JACK AGUGLIARO
Niagra Falls, N.Y.

We are related, yes. But we'd rather not talk about it, if you don't mind.

Lately, I have been observant of a steady downfall in your tales. You seem to be taking the road toward science fiction. Recently I purchased **CREEPY** #33 and **EERIE** #27. First I began reading **CREEPY** and on the very first page of stories was a yarn called "One Too Many," a science fiction story.

Then in **EERIE**, on page 29, what do I see? "The Machine God's Slave." Another science fiction story. And no sooner do I finish that, but you give me another: "Swallowed in Space."

To put it bluntly, This stuff stinks.

If I wanted science fiction, I'd buy a science fiction magazine.

EDWARD POE
Troy, N.Y.

Some of our readers say they like horror stories with a science fiction twist, and SF does give us a chance for a little variety.

Maybe you've just had "one too many."

Perhaps our readers could write in and we could poll response for and against sci-

ence-fiction. Ol' Uncle Creepy isn't saying that this response will particularly mean anything to ye olde editorial staff, but at least it will give us fuel for the long, cold, winter.

The cover of your issue #33 was just great! Pat Boyette and Tom Sutton are very good artists. I've collected horror magazines for years, but the **CREEPYS** I have are the best. I have a few **EERIES**, but they're horrible.

JAY GILBERT
Shively, Ky.

I've been a **CREEPY** fan since issue #1 and a couple of friends and I started the first **CREEPY** Fan Club shortly after that first issue went on sale. We got a letter of recognition from Uncle Creepy and all sorts of weird things.

I'd like to make a plea that you make the covers of your magazines available as pinups. Warren fans could just buy the magazines and tear off the covers. But it gets expensive to have to buy two copies of each one so we have one to read and another for the cover.

Also, any OAF who would destroy an issue of **CREEPY** ought to be drawn and quartered.

It has come to my attention via sayings, rumors and evil premonitions that you obtain your stories by artists submitting their work. I'd appreciate complete information on this subject such as size, media, type of paper, rules, money, minimum age of artists,

---

IS YOUR NEWSSTAND WITH IT?

If you can't find **CREEPY** or **EERIE** or **VAMPIRELLA** on your favorite newsstand, here's something you can do about it. Just fill out this coupon to let us know where that backward newsstand is. We'll see that they get with it.

This store needs (check one) CREEPY ☐ EERIE ☐ VAMPIRELLA ☐:

Store's Name ....

Store's Address ....

City .... State & Zip ....

124

"I have a few EERIES, but they're horrible!"

whether there are Federal rules, etc. I inquire about this because I would rather like to have work in your magazine and I don't mean on the Fan Club page.

KENNETH HUDDLE
Louisville, Ky.

As an age-old fan, I'm sure you've noticed that most of our stories are written by one person and drawn by another. In nearly every case, both are professionals who have decided to make art and writing their life work.

An artist who wants to do a story for this or any other magazine usually submits samples of his work and some background about himself including his training and work experience.

The work must reduce to exactly 10" deep and 7" wide on each page. The best results are often to be had with pen and brush and ink on bristolboard drawing paper. Available in any art store. An artist's samples must be neat & clean, and must evidence that he can draw for mechanical reproduction.

Once he has been accepted, the editor assigns a story to him.

Age isn't important, but experience is. To get that experience, draw as much as possible—for local and school newspapers, yearbooks, class projects. Try to get your work printed as much as you can.

After High School, if your interest is still strong, enroll in a good art school. Your guidance counsellor can help you select one. After that, go to work in an art studio, or for an advertising agency. Every bit of experience is important.

Once you feel you're ready —and it takes a long time— submit printed samples of your work to the editors of our magazines. Send your work to fanzines, and to our own Fan Club pages. It's a step you'd like to skip, but a good way to see how your work looks on a printed page.

In art, as in everything else, work is the important thing. Be prepared to work for a long time without any recognition. Even without much pay. Most importantly, take the advice of teachers. They may not know much about illustrating a horror magazine, but you'll be surprised at the number of things they do know.

Becoming a published illustrator is very much like getting into show business. For every one who makes it, there are hundreds who honestly feel they could do better. They may be right. But proving it isn't easy.

THEY'RE GRINDING...
...ALL THE JUNK FROM THE LOT...
...INTO THAT TRUCK!
ULP!!

From Tom Sutton's "Boxed In" in CREEPY #33, our special slime expose. Kid hid in coffin quickly ka-runched to confetti.

I think you and your magazine are the greatest. I don't know what's the matter with these other freaky wierdos who complain about little things like where animals come from, or which words are spelled wrong. I would like to see any of them do half as well as you do. To come out with so many great new stories every other month.

I have just read your issue #33 and I really liked "Boxed In." I would like to get your back issues, but my family is a little low on money.

ROBERT PHILLIPS
Westfield, N.Y.

Back when I was young, Bob, kids used to trade comic books back and forth among themselves. Since this no ordinary comic, it would be worth several regular books in a trade. But it's a way of picking up back issues when you're short on money. Gives you a great chance to meet new people, too.

It was Monday, a school day. My mother said she was not going to be home, so I had to eat in the restaurant next door. While the food was cooking, I went to look at the magazines and I found an issue of **CREEPY.** By the time the food came, I was finished reading it. I looked at my food, and remembered that last page I had seen in the magazine. Then I was too sick to eat.

BELLA RUDNICK
Chicago, Ill.

We've heard from people who say we take their breath away, but your complaint is a first. Maybe we should sell some of our stuff to WEIGHT-WATCHERS Magazine.

BIG CHANCE

—to meet new people and share their ideas. Rush your raucous responses to:

DEAR UNCLE CREEPY

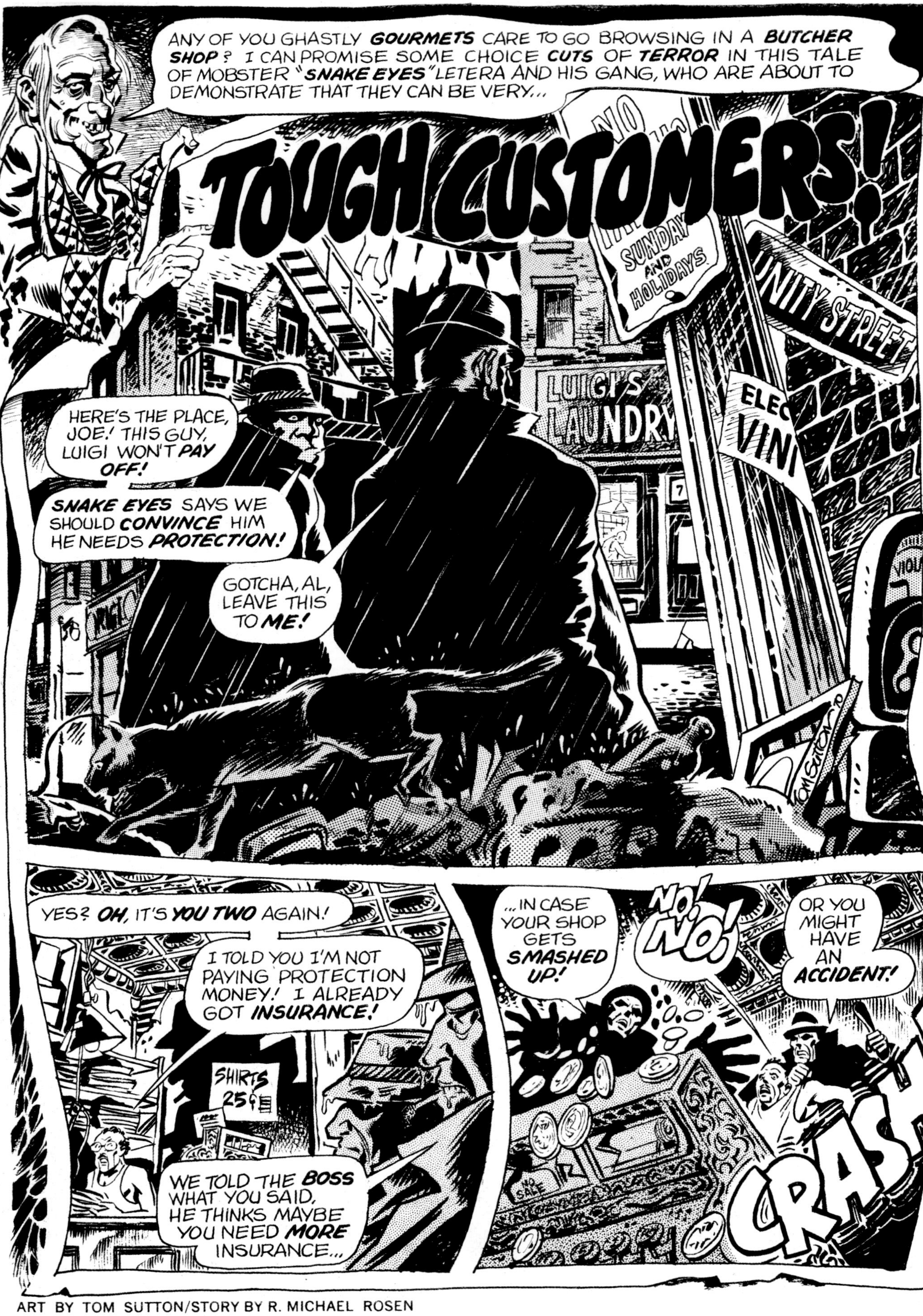
ANY OF YOU GHASTLY GOURMETS CARE TO GO BROWSING IN A BUTCHER SHOP? I CAN PROMISE SOME CHOICE CUTS OF TERROR IN THIS TALE OF MOBSTER "SNAKE EYES" LETERA AND HIS GANG, WHO ARE ABOUT TO DEMONSTRATE THAT THEY CAN BE VERY...
TOUGH CUSTOMERS!
SUNDAY AND HOLIDAYS
UNITY STREET
LUIGI'S LAUNDRY
HERE'S THE PLACE, JOE! THIS GUY, LUIGI WON'T PAY OFF!
SNAKE EYES SAYS WE SHOULD CONVINCE HIM HE NEEDS PROTECTION!
GOTCHA, AL, LEAVE THIS TO ME!
YES? OH, IT'S YOU TWO AGAIN!
I TOLD YOU I'M NOT PAYING PROTECTION MONEY! I ALREADY GOT INSURANCE!
SHIRTS 25¢
WE TOLD THE BOSS WHAT YOU SAID, HE THINKS MAYBE YOU NEED MORE INSURANCE...
...IN CASE YOUR SHOP GETS SMASHED UP!
NO! NO!
OR YOU MIGHT HAVE AN ACCIDENT!
NO SALE
CRASH!

ART BY TOM SUTTON/STORY BY R. MICHAEL ROSEN

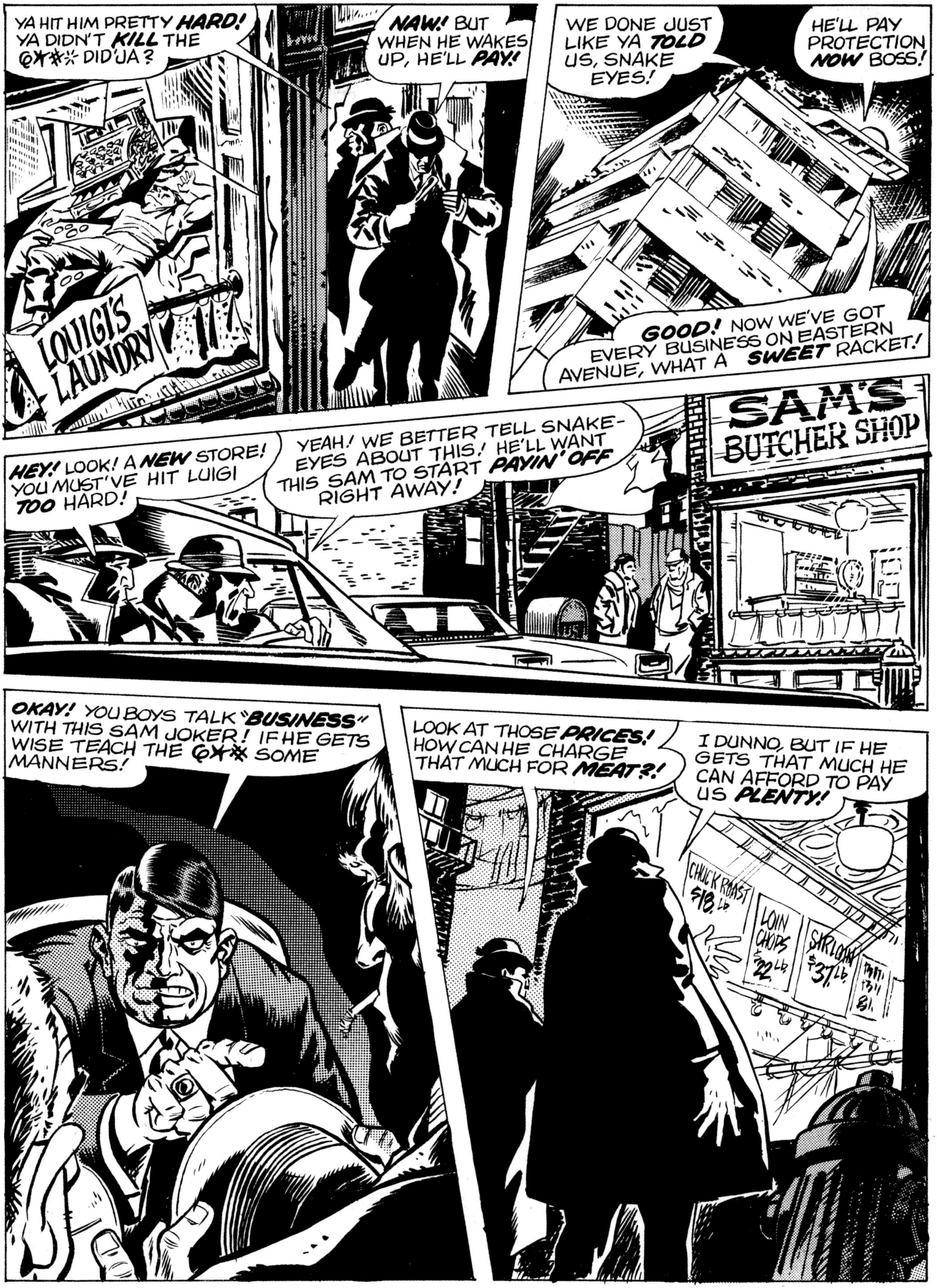
YA HIT HIM PRETTY HARD! YA DIDN'T KILL THE @*#*! DID'JA?
NAW! BUT WHEN HE WAKES UP, HE'LL PAY!
LOUIGI'S LAUNDRY
WE DONE JUST LIKE YA TOLD US, SNAKE EYES!
HE'LL PAY PROTECTION NOW BOSS!
GOOD! NOW WE'VE GOT EVERY BUSINESS ON EASTERN AVENUE, WHAT A SWEET RACKET!
HEY! LOOK! A NEW STORE! YOU MUST'VE HIT LUIGI TOO HARD!
YEAH! WE BETTER TELL SNAKE-EYES ABOUT THIS! HE'LL WANT THIS SAM TO START PAYIN' OFF RIGHT AWAY!
SAM'S BUTCHER SHOP
OKAY! YOU BOYS TALK "BUSINESS" WITH THIS SAM JOKER! IF HE GETS WISE TEACH THE @*# SOME MANNERS!
LOOK AT THOSE PRICES! HOW CAN HE CHARGE THAT MUCH FOR MEAT?!
I DUNNO, BUT IF HE GETS THAT MUCH HE CAN AFFORD TO PAY US PLENTY!
CHUCK ROAST $18. Lb
LOIN CHOPS $22. Lb
SIRLOIN $37. Lb

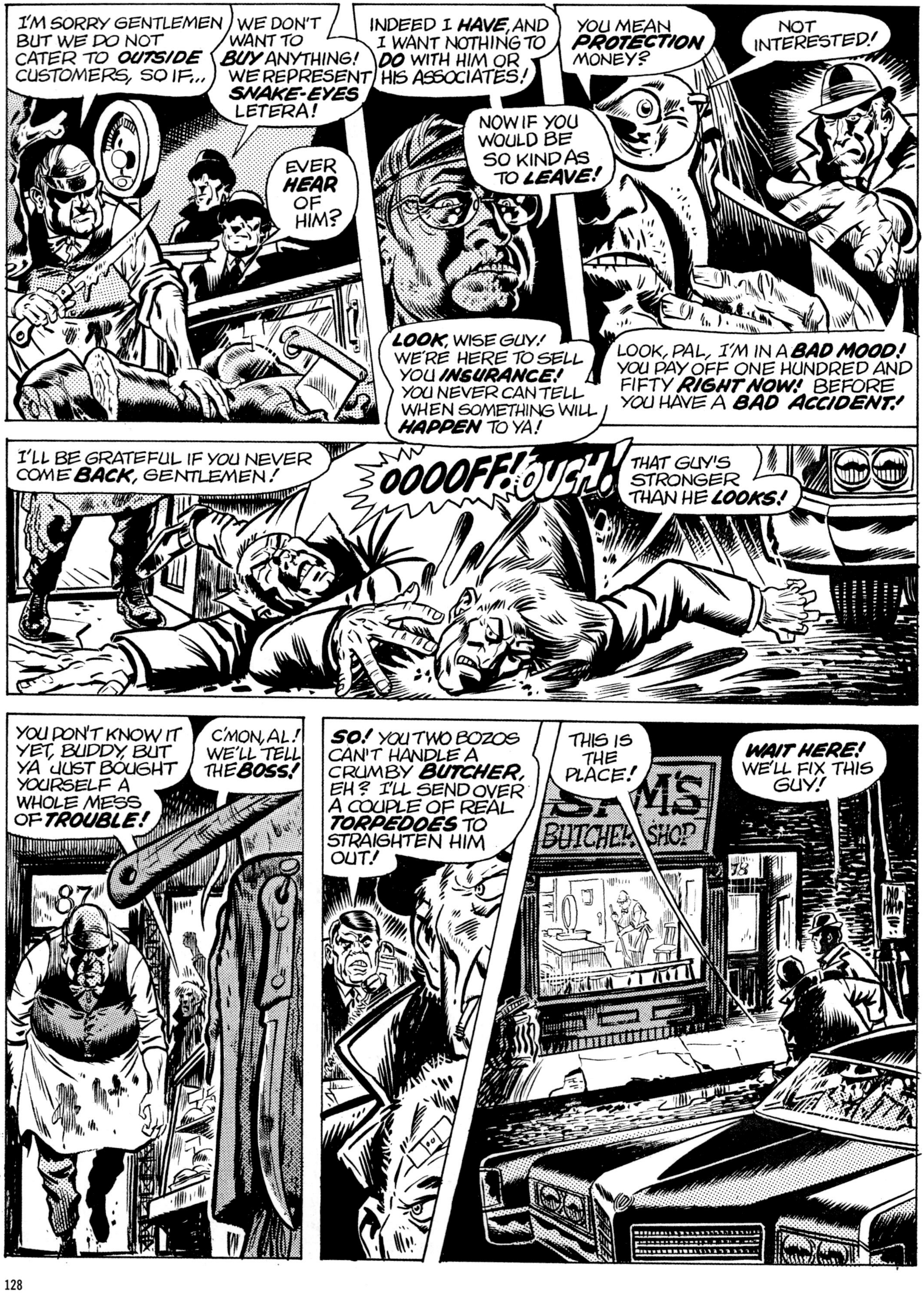
I'M SORRY GENTLEMEN BUT WE DO NOT CATER TO OUTSIDE CUSTOMERS, SO IF...
WE DON'T WANT TO BUY ANYTHING! WE REPRESENT SNAKE-EYES LETERA!
EVER HEAR OF HIM?
INDEED I HAVE, AND I WANT NOTHING TO DO WITH HIM OR HIS ASSOCIATES!
NOW IF YOU WOULD BE SO KIND AS TO LEAVE!
LOOK, WISE GUY! WE'RE HERE TO SELL YOU INSURANCE! YOU NEVER CAN TELL WHEN SOMETHING WILL HAPPEN TO YA!
YOU MEAN PROTECTION MONEY?
NOT INTERESTED!
LOOK, PAL, I'M IN A BAD MOOD! YOU PAY OFF ONE HUNDRED AND FIFTY RIGHT NOW! BEFORE YOU HAVE A BAD ACCIDENT!
I'LL BE GRATEFUL IF YOU NEVER COME BACK, GENTLEMEN!
OOOOFF!
OUCH!
THAT GUY'S STRONGER THAN HE LOOKS!
YOU DON'T KNOW IT YET, BUDDY, BUT YA JUST BOUGHT YOURSELF A WHOLE MESS OF TROUBLE!
C'MON, AL! WE'LL TELL THE BOSS!
87
SO! YOU TWO BOZOS CAN'T HANDLE A CRUMBY BUTCHER, EH? I'LL SEND OVER A COUPLE OF REAL TORPEDOES TO STRAIGHTEN HIM OUT!
THIS IS THE PLACE!
SAM'S
BUTCHER SHOP
78
WAIT HERE! WE'LL FIX THIS GUY!

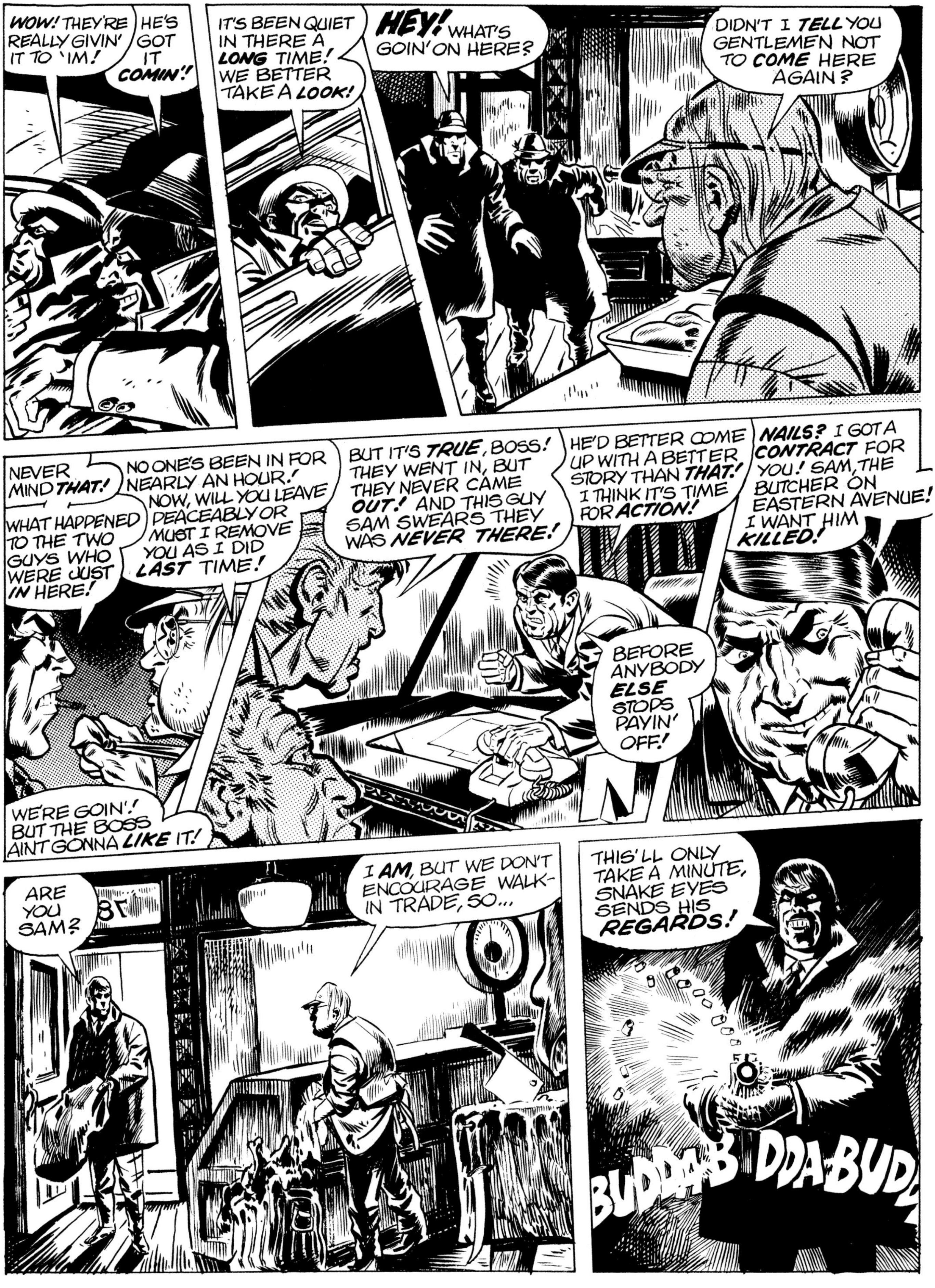
WOW! THEY'RE REALLY GIVIN' IT TO 'IM!
HE'S GOT IT COMIN'!
IT'S BEEN QUIET IN THERE A LONG TIME! WE BETTER TAKE A LOOK!
HEY! WHAT'S GOIN' ON HERE?
DIDN'T I TELL YOU GENTLEMEN NOT TO COME HERE AGAIN?
NEVER MIND THAT!
WHAT HAPPENED TO THE TWO GUYS WHO WERE JUST IN HERE!
NO ONE'S BEEN IN FOR NEARLY AN HOUR! NOW, WILL YOU LEAVE PEACEABLY OR MUST I REMOVE YOU AS I DID LAST TIME!
WE'RE GOIN'! BUT THE BOSS AINT GONNA LIKE IT!
BUT IT'S TRUE, BOSS! THEY WENT IN, BUT THEY NEVER CAME OUT! AND THIS GUY SAM SWEARS THEY WAS NEVER THERE!
HE'D BETTER COME UP WITH A BETTER STORY THAN THAT! I THINK IT'S TIME FOR ACTION!
BEFORE ANYBODY ELSE STOPS PAYIN' OFF!
NAILS? I GOT A CONTRACT FOR YOU! SAM, THE BUTCHER ON EASTERN AVENUE! I WANT HIM KILLED!
ARE YOU SAM?
I AM, BUT WE DON'T ENCOURAGE WALK-IN TRADE, SO...
THIS'LL ONLY TAKE A MINUTE, SNAKE EYES SENDS HIS REGARDS!
BUDDA-B DDA-BUD

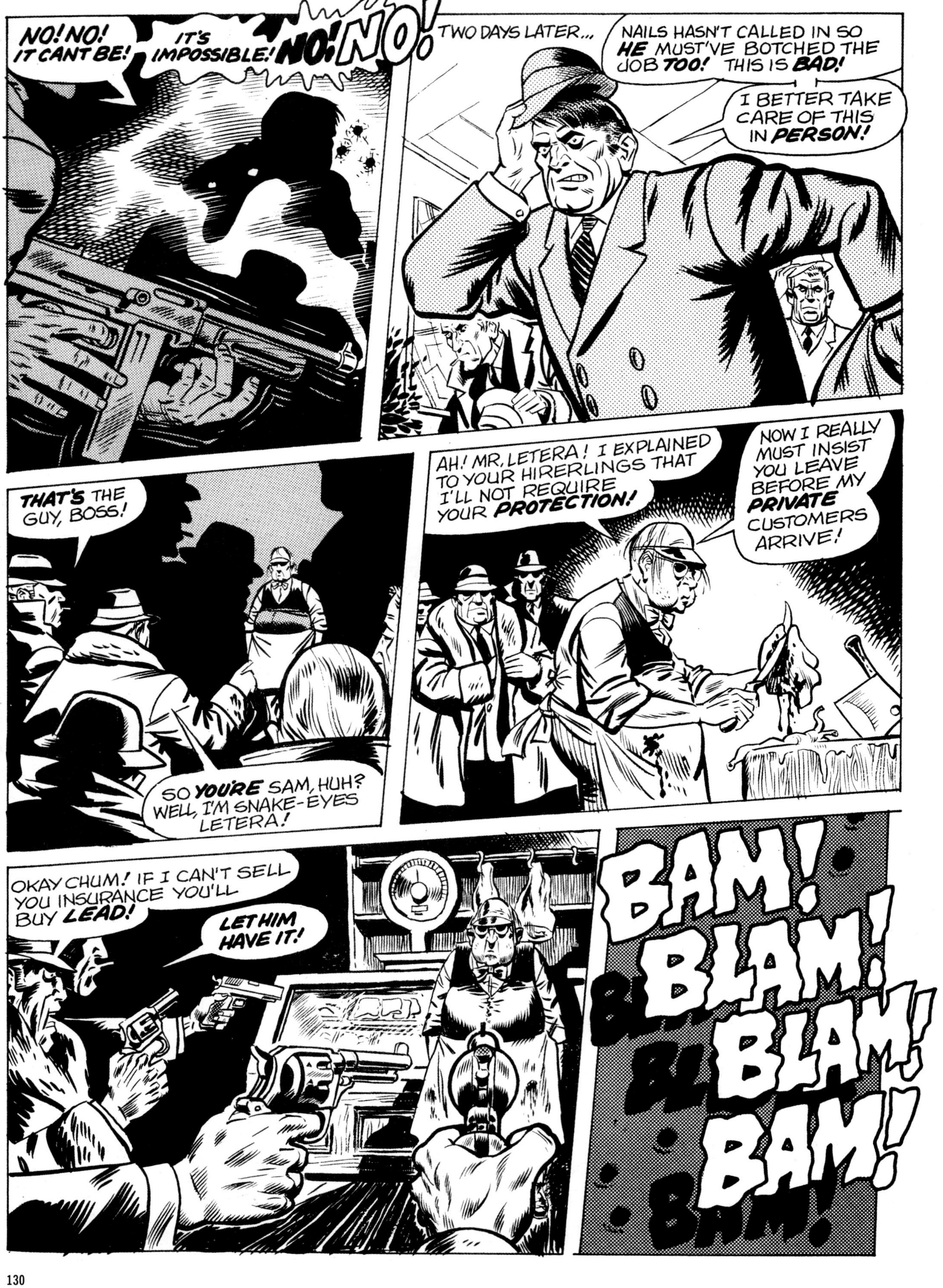
NO! NO! IT CANT BE!
IT'S IMPOSSIBLE! NO! NO!
TWO DAYS LATER...
NAILS HASN'T CALLED IN SO HE MUST'VE BOTCHED THE JOB TOO! THIS IS BAD!
I BETTER TAKE CARE OF THIS IN PERSON!
THAT'S THE GUY, BOSS!
SO YOU'RE SAM, HUH? WELL, I'M SNAKE-EYES LETERA!
AH! MR, LETERA! I EXPLAINED TO YOUR HIRERLINGS THAT I'LL NOT REQUIRE YOUR PROTECTION!
NOW I REALLY MUST INSIST YOU LEAVE BEFORE MY PRIVATE CUSTOMERS ARRIVE!
OKAY CHUM! IF I CAN'T SELL YOU INSURANCE YOU'LL BUY LEAD!
LET HIM HAVE IT!
BAM! BLAM! BLAM! BAM!

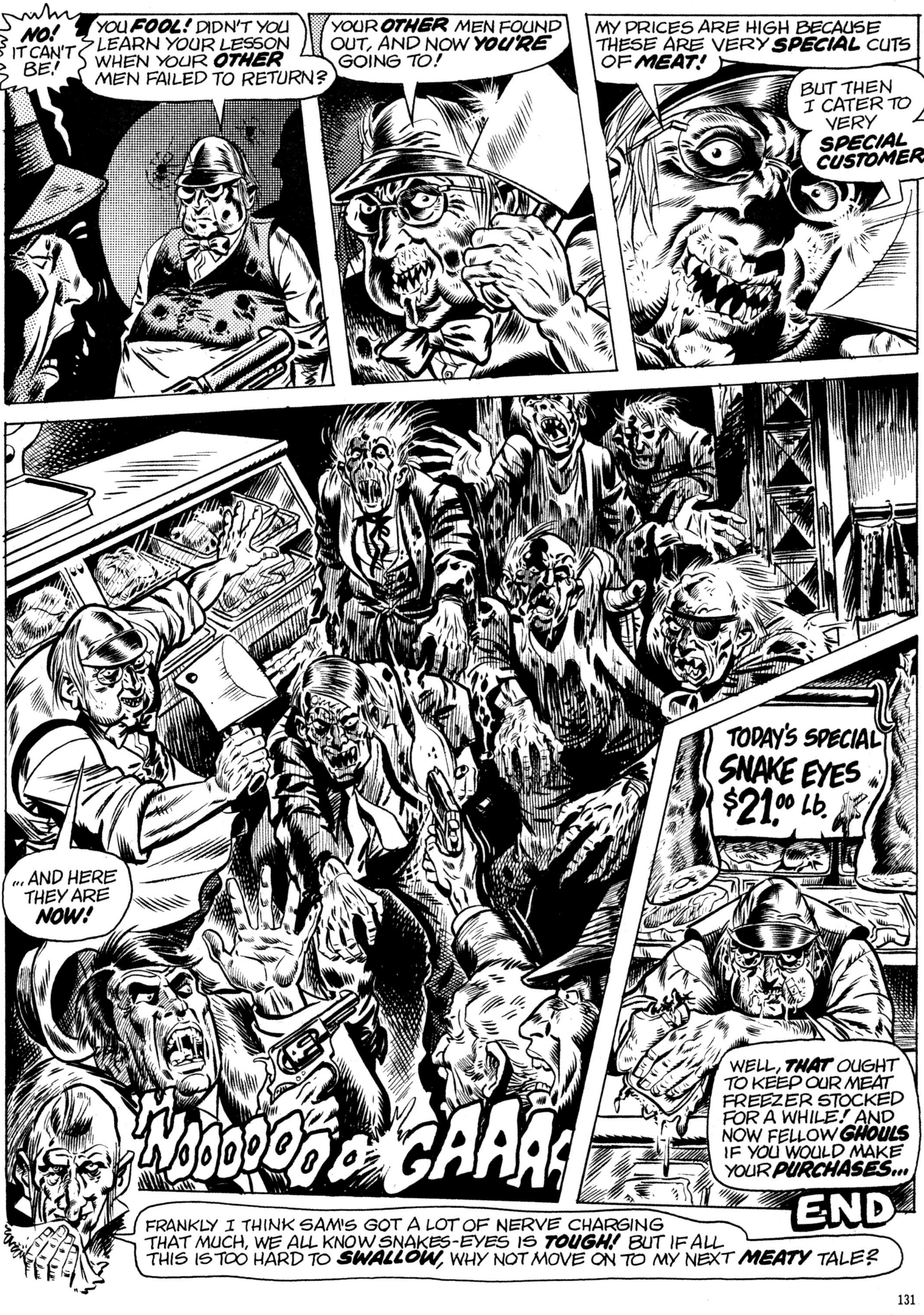
NO! IT CAN'T BE!
YOU FOOL! DIDN'T YOU LEARN YOUR LESSON WHEN YOUR OTHER MEN FAILED TO RETURN?
YOUR OTHER MEN FOUND OUT, AND NOW YOU'RE GOING TO!
MY PRICES ARE HIGH BECAUSE THESE ARE VERY SPECIAL CUTS OF MEAT!
BUT THEN I CATER TO VERY SPECIAL CUSTOMERS!
...AND HERE THEY ARE NOW!
NOOOOOOO
GAAA
TODAY'S SPECIAL
SNAKE EYES
$21.00 Lb.
WELL, THAT OUGHT TO KEEP OUR MEAT FREEZER STOCKED FOR A WHILE! AND NOW FELLOW GHOULS IF YOU WOULD MAKE YOUR PURCHASES...
END
FRANKLY I THINK SAM'S GOT A LOT OF NERVE CHARGING THAT MUCH, WE ALL KNOW SNAKES-EYES IS TOUGH! BUT IF ALL THIS IS TOO HARD TO SWALLOW, WHY NOT MOVE ON TO MY NEXT MEATY TALE?

NEW L.P. RECORD ALBUM!

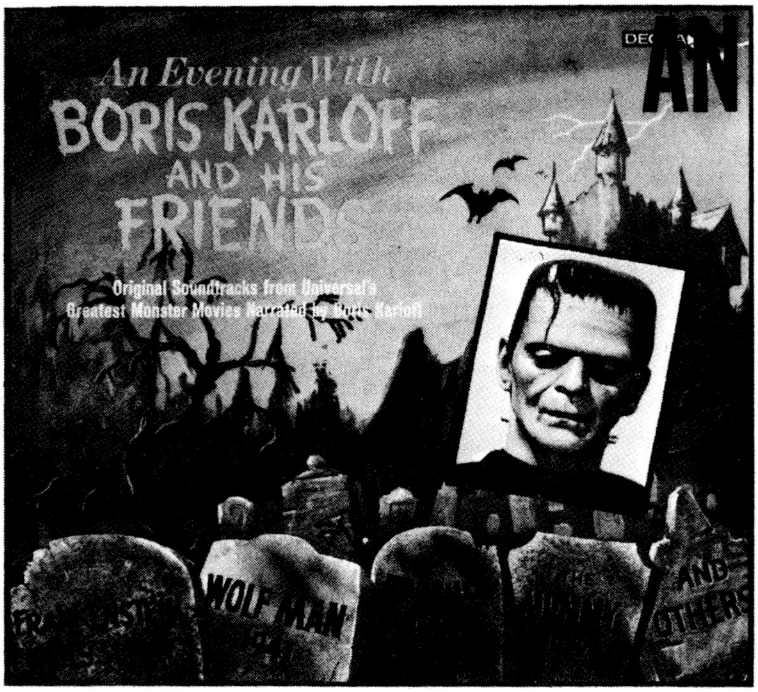
An Evening With
BORIS KARLOFF
AND HIS
FRIENDS
WOLF MAN

AN EVENING WITH BORIS KARLOFF AND HIS FRIENDS

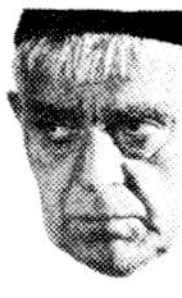

ORIGINAL SOUND TRACK NARRATIVE FROM UNIVERSALS GREATEST MONSTER MOVIES!

NARRATED BY BORIS KARLOFF HIMSELF!

SPOKEN WORDS FROM: FRANKENSTEIN • DRACULA • THE MUMMY • BRIDE OF FRANKENSTEIN • SON OF FRANKENSTEIN • THE WOLF MAN • HOUSE OF FRANKENSTEIN • ALL ABOUT THE MONSTER

BORIS KARLOFF was "born" back in the year 1931, when Colin Clive, as Henry Frankenstein, first spoke on the motion picture screen: "It's moving . . . it's alive . . . it's moving . . . it's alive . . . it's alive! it's alive!!!"; and that triumph of make-up and pantomime, the Frankenstein Monster, built from bodies gathered from the graves, the gallows, the mortuary, rose like a ghoulish, soulless automaton, to stalk the screaming world and invade the nightmares of all mankind.

You will hear that historic moment of creation in this album, as Colin Clive and Dwight Frye live again.

In 1931, Lon Chaney, Sr., the silent Master of Horror, the "Man of a Thousand Faces," was one year dead; ascended to the throne of terror was King Boris, Monster of a Thousand Faces—Frankenstein, Black Cat, Mummy Im-ho-tep, Raven, Fu Manchu, Walking Dead, Haunted Strangler . . . a list long and legendary.

Boris Karloff brings to this recording a rare and singular quality, unmatched in the annals of man or monster. His chilling charm exerts a cobra-like fascination, his mesmeric voice hypnotizing the listener.

This album might be called a chronicle of necrology, a documentary of death, but it is treated in an imaginative rather than a morbid vein. Boris Karloff has approached this project with respect and perspective, as he speaks mainly of those who have passed on into the unknown—Dwight Frye, once Dracula's acolyte of the night, cringing in awe and terror before the wrath of his strange, supernatural master; and we hear again the familiar voice of that master of the macabre, speaking immortal lines from beyond the grave. Boris Karloff re-introduces us to Ernest Thesiger, as the zealous Doctor Pretorius, the skeleton who walked like a man and added a new dimension of diablerie to the experiments of Henry Frankenstein; Lionel Atwill lives again as we hear his cold tones, clipped and harsh, as he attempts to cope with THE SON OF FRANKENSTEIN; venerable Edward Van Sloan is at home once more among ancient mummy cases and barely cold cadavers as he delivers his arresting lines. You'll hear the "*skreeek!*" heard 'round the world when THE BRIDE OF FRANKENSTEIN first beheld her monstrous mate . . . and the late lamented Maria Ouspenskaya, causing shivers as she speaks of the dread curse of lycanthropy and mourns the passing of the man afflicted with werewolfism.

An Evening With BORIS KARLOFF And His FRIENDS is a sincere and moving tribute to the men and women of the netherworld of cinematic science and fantasy terror tales who have made indelible impressions as master menaces and famous monsters. It is an exciting concept, triumphantly realized; and it is a nostalgic listening "must," one you will wish to re-experience frequently . . . whenever the moon is full, the lamp is low, the winter winds are howling, the midnight hour has struck, and you've just read Stoker, Lovecraft or Poe . . . or you just feel in the mood to join in for AN Evening With BORIS KARLOFF And His FRIENDS.

ORDER TODAY! MONEY-BACK GUARANTEE!

RUSH ME AN EVENING WITH BORIS KARLOFF & HIS FRIENDS FOR WHICH I ENCLOSE $3.98 PLUS 25¢ FOR POSTAGE AND HANDLING.

NAME..

ADDRESS..

CITY..........................STATE..........................ZIP CODE..............

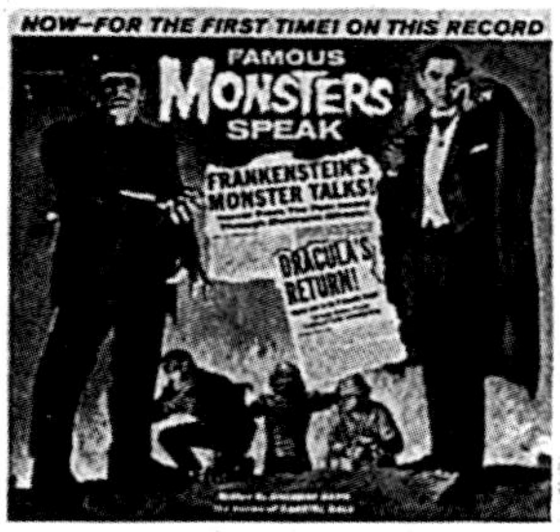
NOW—FOR THE FIRST TIME! ON THIS RECORD
FAMOUS
MONSTERS
SPEAK
FRANKENSTEIN'S MONSTER TALKS!
DRACULA'S RETURN!

FAMOUS MONSTERS SPEAK

50 MINUTES OF SHEER TERROR—BROUGHT TO YOU BY THE EDITORS OF FAMOUS MONSTERS MAGAZINE!

YOU ARE DR. FRANKENSTEIN—for only you can bring his horrible creation back to life . . . through the magic of this real-as-death high fidelity recording! And more! You will also bring Count Dracula back to life! You will hear this human vampire. You will almost feel him as he reaches out for you. This is a collector's item, available in limited edition. Order Today! Only $1.98.

KARLOFF TELLS YOU: "TALES OF MYSTERY & IMAGINATION"

Only as Karloff can tell it . . . "THE LEGEND OF SLEEPY HOLLOW" and "RIP VAN WINKLE". A brand new record by the master story-teller of horror and mystery. In all the frightening powers of his voice with the chilling background of special sound effects, you live the great classic horror tales of the headless horseman. The night lives with terror and you sit in your room and hear the sounds and maybe if you look out your window, you'll catch a fast look at the night rider who roams the countryside. Only $1.98.

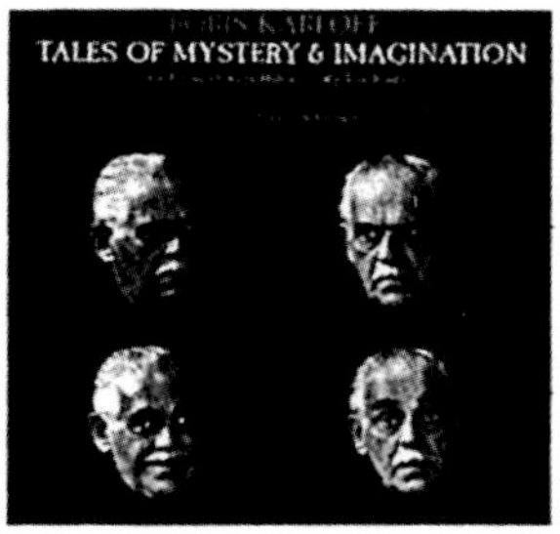
TALES OF MYSTERY & IMAGINATION

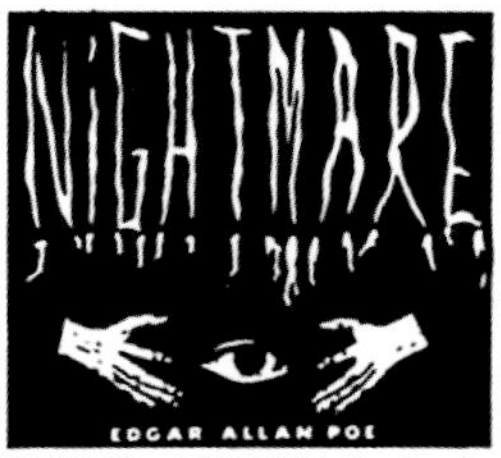
NIGHTMARE
EDGAR ALLAN POE

NIGHTMARE, ANYONE? You've heard of records in a humorous vein—well this one is HORROR IN A JUGULAR VEIN. A frightening narration from the stories of Edgar Allan Poe. THE PIT AND THE PENDULUM is tough on your nerves, but wait until you hear THE TELL-TALE HEART—Poe's most terrorizing stories. Only $1.98.

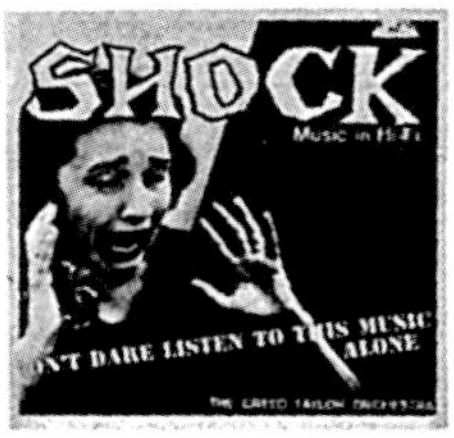
SHOCK
Music in Hi-Fi

Weird music & chilling sound effects created for 12 frightening scenes. HAUNTED HOUSE—groans, rattles & unknown sounds; SPELLBOUND — supernatural theme music; HEARTBEAT, JUNGLE FEVER, THE LONG WALK and others. Long Play Album. Only $3.98.

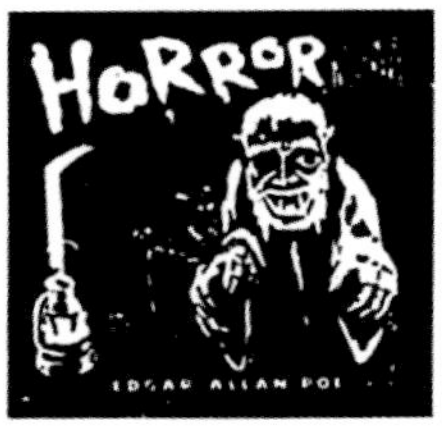
HORROR
EDGAR ALLAN POE

HORROR—THE SON OF NIGHTMARE; a classic tale of terror spoken in eerie tones with the right kind of background music. Actually hearing this story told in your own home is enough to scare you out of your wits. Have your blood curdled by the tale of THE BLACK CAT, by EDGAR ALLAN POE. Only $1.98.

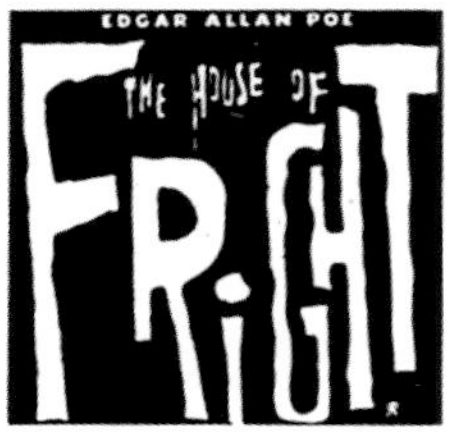
EDGAR ALLAN POE
THE HOUSE OF
FRIGHT

A grim, ghostly, tale of horror that will fill you with lingering FRIGHT, written by the master of thriller-chillers—Edgar Allan Poe. You will remember "THE HOUSE OF USHER" (his most famous tale) with shuddering fear every time you're alone on a deserted street! A sinister narration by Richard Taylor. Only $1.98.

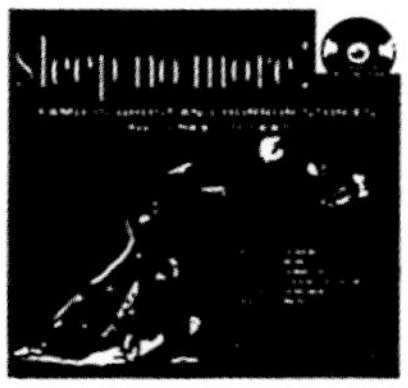
Sleep no more!

FAMOUS GHOST & HORROR STORIES read by Nelson Olmstead, radio's famous sinister voice. Includes THE SIGNAL MAN by Charles Dickens; THE MUMMY'S FOOT, WHAT WAS IT, THE BODY SNATCHER, OCCURRENCE AT OWL CREEK BRIDGE and others. Only $4.98.

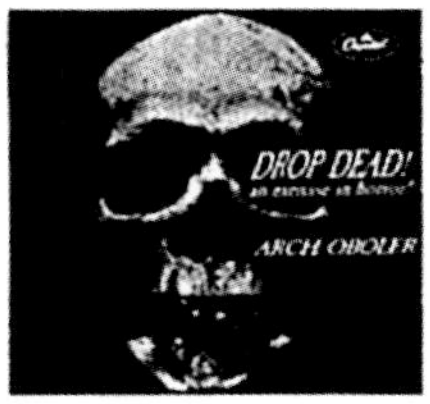
DROP DEAD!
ARCH OBOLER

On any Wednesday night in the late 30's and early 40's, when radio was king, the lights would be on in my house and the radio tuned to a program called "LIGHTS OUT," directed by Arch Oboler, whose talent scared the wits out of America with this blood-chilling series. Here is a sampler of this pioneer of horror that has never been matched. Only $5.98.

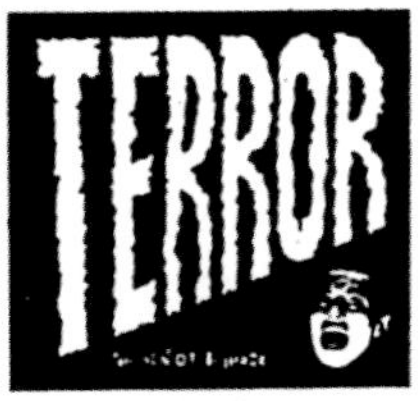
TERROR

CLASSIC TALES OF TERROR to make you shiver in your boots. Be prepared for maniacal action when you listen to these spine-tingling narrations penned by the master of the macabre Edgar Allen Poe. MASQUE OF THE RED DEATH and THE PREMATURE BURIAL, are among these best and most terrifying tales. Only $1.98.

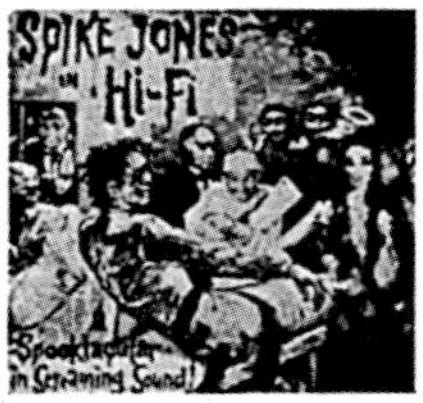
SPIKE JONES
in
Hi-Fi
Spooktacular
in Screaming Sound!

A wild SPIKE JONES album featuring DRACULA, VAMPIRA & THE MAD DOCTOR, in TEENAGE BRAIN SURGEON, MONSTER MOVIE BALL, FRANKENSTEIN'S LAMENT, MY OLD FLAME, plus others specially recorded to drive you mad with ghoulish laughter. Long Play Album. Only $3.98.

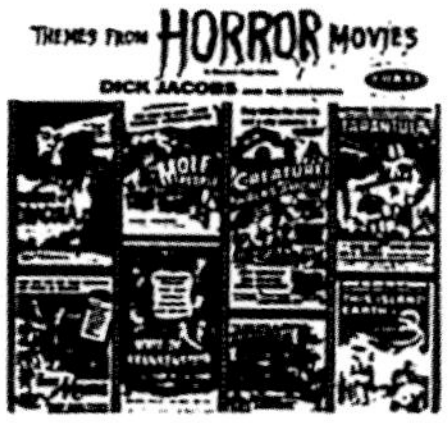
THEMES FROM HORROR MOVIES
DICK JACOBS

Features themes & sound effects from the following motion pictures: House of Frankenstein • Horror of Dracula • Son of Dracula • Creature From the Black Lagoon • Revenge of the Creature • This Island Earth • The Mole People • The Creature Walks Among Us • The Deadly Mantis • It Came From Outer Space • Tarantula • The Incredible Shrinking Man • $3.98.

FEELING CREEPY?

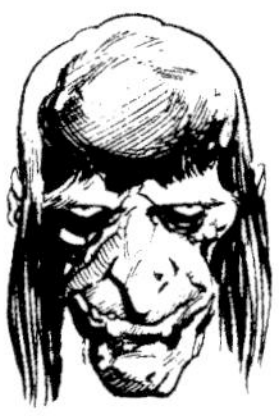

CREEPYUNIVERSE.COM

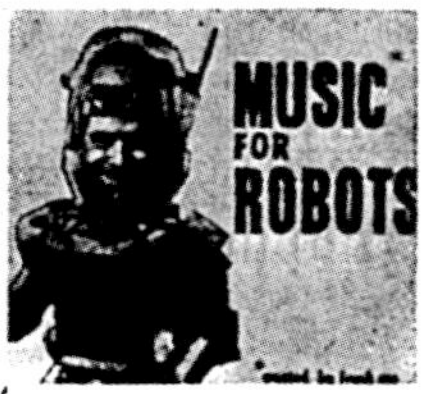
MUSIC
FOR
ROBOTS

Created Just for You — the Most Amazing Half Hour on Record as FORREST J ACKERMAN time-travels to the 21st Century to bring back Music for Robots. FJA talks to YOU for 18 minutes in a thrilling narration about RUR, Tobor, Gort, Robby, Jules Verne, Edgar Allan Poe, the metallic Frankenstein. Hear weird multisonic effects created for the ears of androids! Only $1.98.

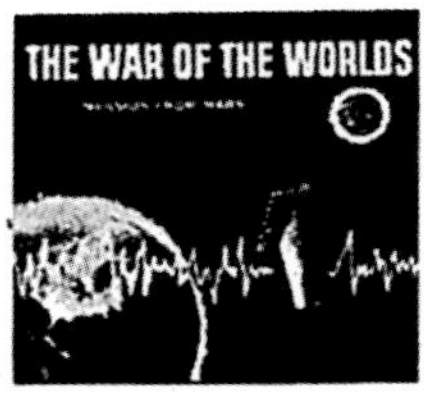
THE WAR OF THE WORLDS

An LP recording of the original Famous Orson Welles broadcast that caused mass hysteria throughout New York and New Jersey. People abandoned their homes—all roads were jammed, and never before had people become so suddenly disturbed as they did on this night. The original broadcast took place on the evening of October 30, 1938. A rare collector's item! Only $5.98.

PLEASE RUSH ME THE FOLLOWING LONG PLAYING ALBUMS:

- ☐ FAMOUS MONSTERS SPEAK; $1.98 plus 25c for postage & handling.
- ☐ TALES OF MYSTERY & IMAGINATION; $1.98 plus 25c for postage & handling.
- ☐ NIGHTMARE; $1.98 plus 25c for postage & handling.
- ☐ SHOCK; $3.98 plus 25c for postage & handling.
- ☐ HORROR; $1.98 plus 25c for postage & handling.
- ☐ THE HOUSE OF FRIGHT; $1.98 plus 25c for postage & handling.
- ☐ BATMAN & ROBIN; $1.79 plus 25c for postage & handling.
- ☐ DROP DEAD; $5.98 plus 25c for postage & handling.
- ☐ TERROR; $1.98 plus 25c for postage & handling.
- ☐ SPIKE JONES IN HI-FI; $3.98 plus 25c for postage & handling.
- ☐ SLEEP NO MORE; $4.98 plus 25c for postage & handling.
- ☐ THEMES FROM HORROR MOVIES; $3.98 plus 25c for postage & handling.
- ☐ MUSIC FOR ROBOTS; $1.98 plus 25c for postage & handling.
- ☐ WAR OF THE WORLDS; $5.98 plus 25c for postage & handling.

NAME..

ADDRESS..

CITY..

STATE.................ZIP CODE NO.....................

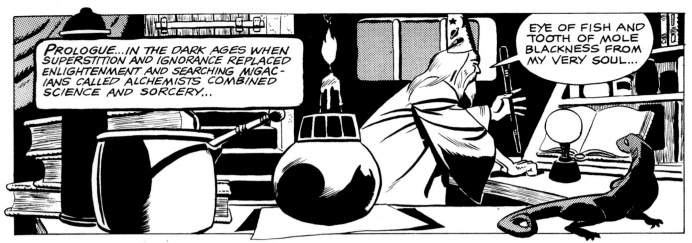

PROLOGUE...IN THE DARK AGES WHEN SUPERSTITION AND IGNORANCE REPLACED ENLIGHTENMENT AND SEARCHING MIGACIANS CALLED ALCHEMISTS COMBINED SCIENCE AND SORCERY...

EYE OF FISH AND TOOTH OF MOLE BLACKNESS FROM MY VERY SOUL...

THESE MEN OFTEN ACHIEVED GREAT THINGS WITHOUT KNOWING THE REAL REASON WHY...

...INSTEAD ATTRIBUTING THE RESULTS TO THEIR MAGIC...

AMAZING! BY STIRRING CREAM IT CAN MAKE IT THICKER AND HARDER!

IT IS OBVIOUSLY MY WAND AND MY SPELL WHICH TRANSFORMED THE CREAM. TRULY I AM A GREAT MAGICIAN!

ALCHEMISTS WERE CONSTANTLY SEEKING THE FABULOUS PHILOSOPHER'S STONE WHICH COULD TURN BASE METALS INTO GOLD!

TOO BAD I HAD TO KILL HIM, BUT THE SECRET OF THE PHILOSOPHER'S STONE MAY BE HIDDEN IN THESE BOOKS. I MUST HAVE IT!

SOME SAY THAT ONE ALCHEMIST DID FIND THE PHILOSOPHER'S STONE!

...BUT SOMETHING MUST HAVE HAPPENED TO HIM AND THE STONE FOR THE SECRET HAS BEEN LOST TO THE AGES!

GOLD! ALL I CAN EVER WANT! I CAN RULE THE WORLD WITH THE PHILOSOPHER'S STONE!

ART BY ROGER BRAND/STORY BY R. MICHAEL ROSEN

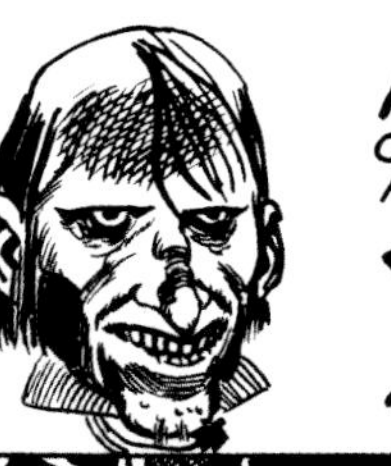

HEY, FORTY NINERS! NOW THAT OUR PULSATING PROLOGUE HAS FILLED YOU IN ON THE PHILOSOPHER'S STONE, JOIN US FOR A DEVILISH DIFFERENT GOLD RUSH THAT WILL LEAD YOU TO THE...

LEGEND IN GOLD

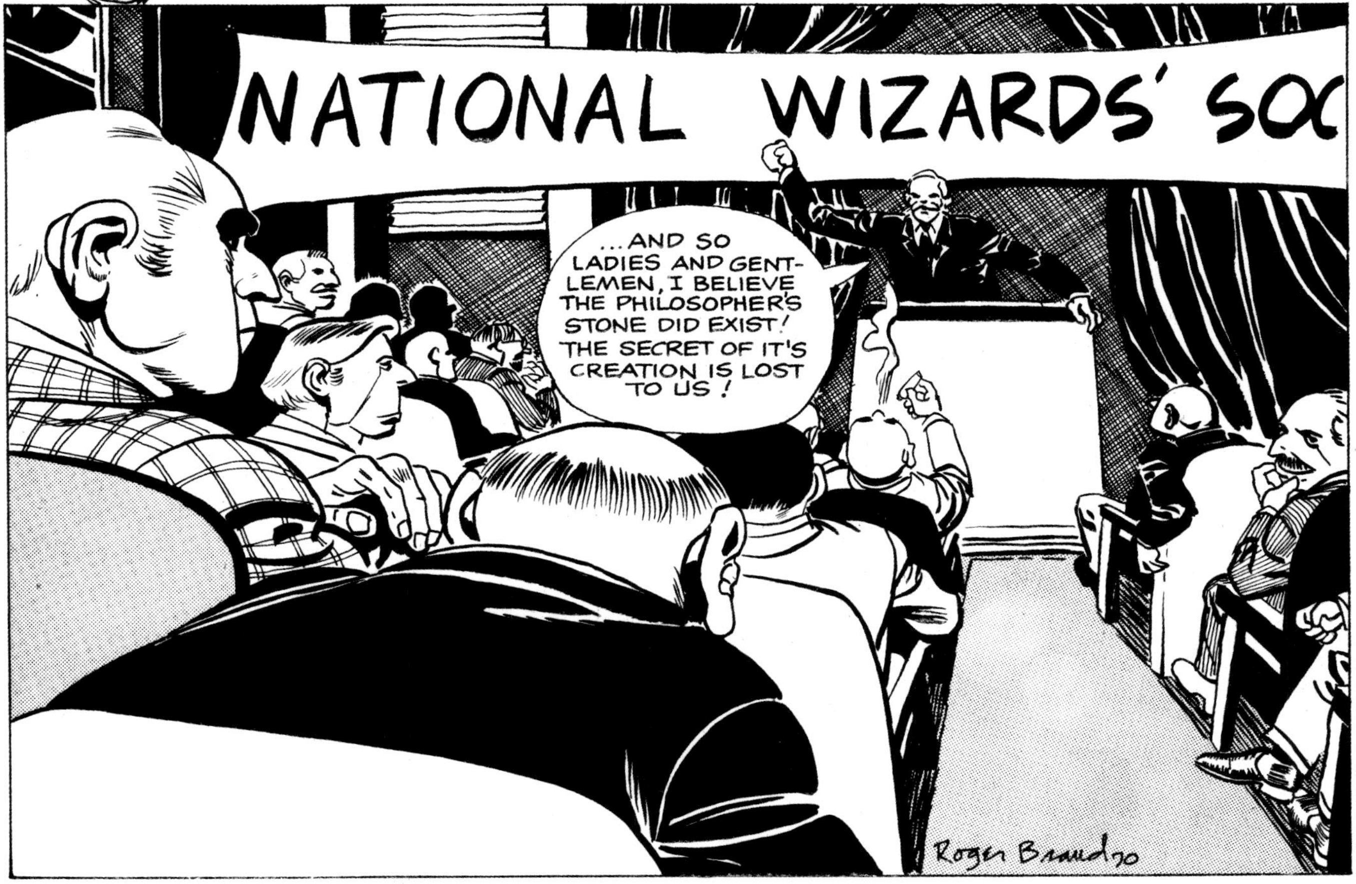
NATIONAL WIZARDS' SOC
...AND SO LADIES AND GENTLEMEN, I BELIEVE THE PHILOSOPHER'S STONE DID EXIST! THE SECRET OF IT'S CREATION IS LOST TO US!
Roger Brand 70

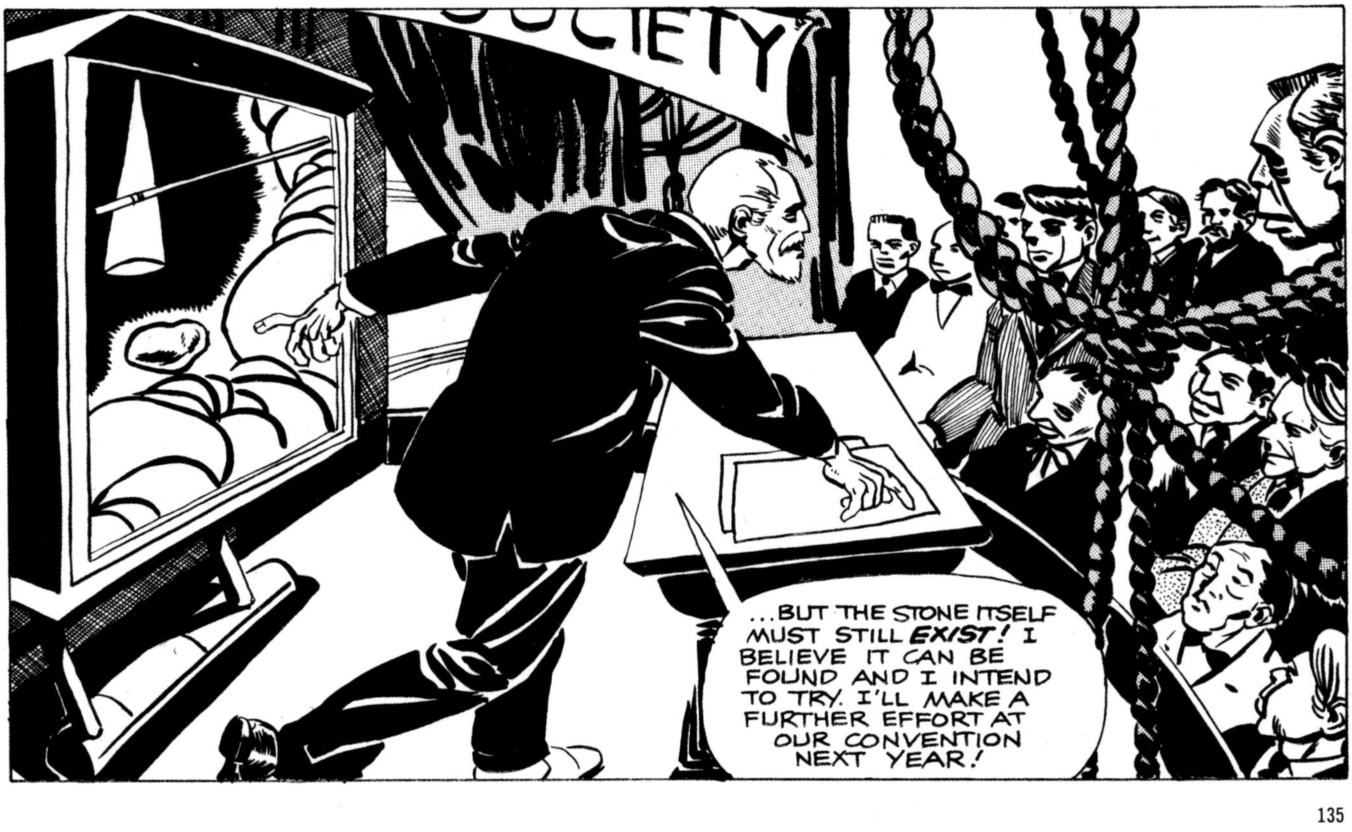
SOCIETY
...BUT THE STONE ITSELF MUST STILL EXIST! I BELIEVE IT CAN BE FOUND AND I INTEND TO TRY. I'LL MAKE A FURTHER EFFORT AT OUR CONVENTION NEXT YEAR!

GREAT SPEECH, DUNN! *HAW, HAW, HAW!* THESE WIZARDS CONVENTIONS ARE THE GREATEST THINGS YET FOR LAUGHS! SAY, WHERE DID YOU *GET* THAT GUFF ABOUT THAT WHATCHA MA-CALL IT STONE?

WELL...ER...THAT IS, I...

EXCUSE ME, MR. DUNN... BUT MAY I SPEAK TO YOU FOR A MOMENT?

NOW...WHAT CAN I DO FOR YOU?

MY NAME IS RICHARD LEWIS... ARE YOU SERIOUS ABOUT SEEKING THE PHILOSOPHER'S STONE?

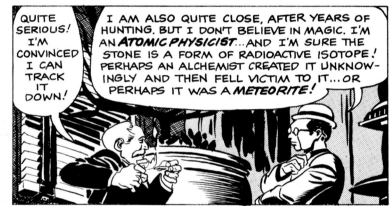

QUITE SERIOUS! I'M CONVINCED I CAN TRACK IT DOWN!

I AM ALSO QUITE CLOSE, AFTER YEARS OF HUNTING. BUT I DON'T BELIEVE IN MAGIC. I'M AN *ATOMIC PHYSICIST*...AND I'M SURE THE STONE IS A FORM OF RADIOACTIVE ISOTOPE! PERHAPS AN ALCHEMIST CREATED IT UNKNOWINGLY AND THEN FELL VICTIM TO IT...OR PERHAPS IT WAS A *METEORITE!*

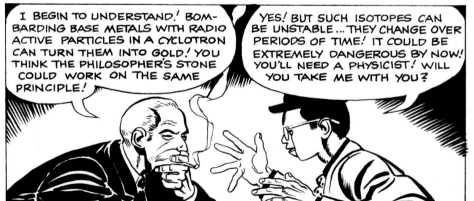

I BEGIN TO UNDERSTAND! BOMBARDING BASE METALS WITH RADIOACTIVE PARTICLES IN A *CYCLOTRON* CAN TURN THEM INTO GOLD! YOU THINK THE PHILOSOPHER'S STONE COULD WORK ON THE SAME PRINCIPLE!

YES! BUT SUCH ISOTOPES CAN BE UNSTABLE...THEY CHANGE OVER PERIODS OF TIME! IT COULD BE EXTREMELY DANGEROUS BY NOW! YOU'LL NEED A PHYSICIST! WILL YOU TAKE ME WITH YOU?

I'D WELCOME SUCH SCIENTIFIC HELP!

I PROPOSE WE GET STARTED AS SOON AS POSSIBLE! I LOST THE TRAIL OF THE STONE IN HAMBURG GERMANY... BUT IT SHOULDN'T BE TOO HARD TO PICK UP!

HERE WE ARE HALFWAY ACROSS THE ATLANTIC, AND I'M JUST BEGINNING TO REALIZE...THE PHILOSOPHER'S STONE WILL MAKE AS MUCH GOLD AS EITHER OF US CAN WANT, SO I LOSE NOTHING BY DIVIDING IT WITH YOU!

A CERTAIN AMOUNT OF WEALTH TO FURTHER MY RESEARCH WOULD NOT BE UNWELCOME, BUT...

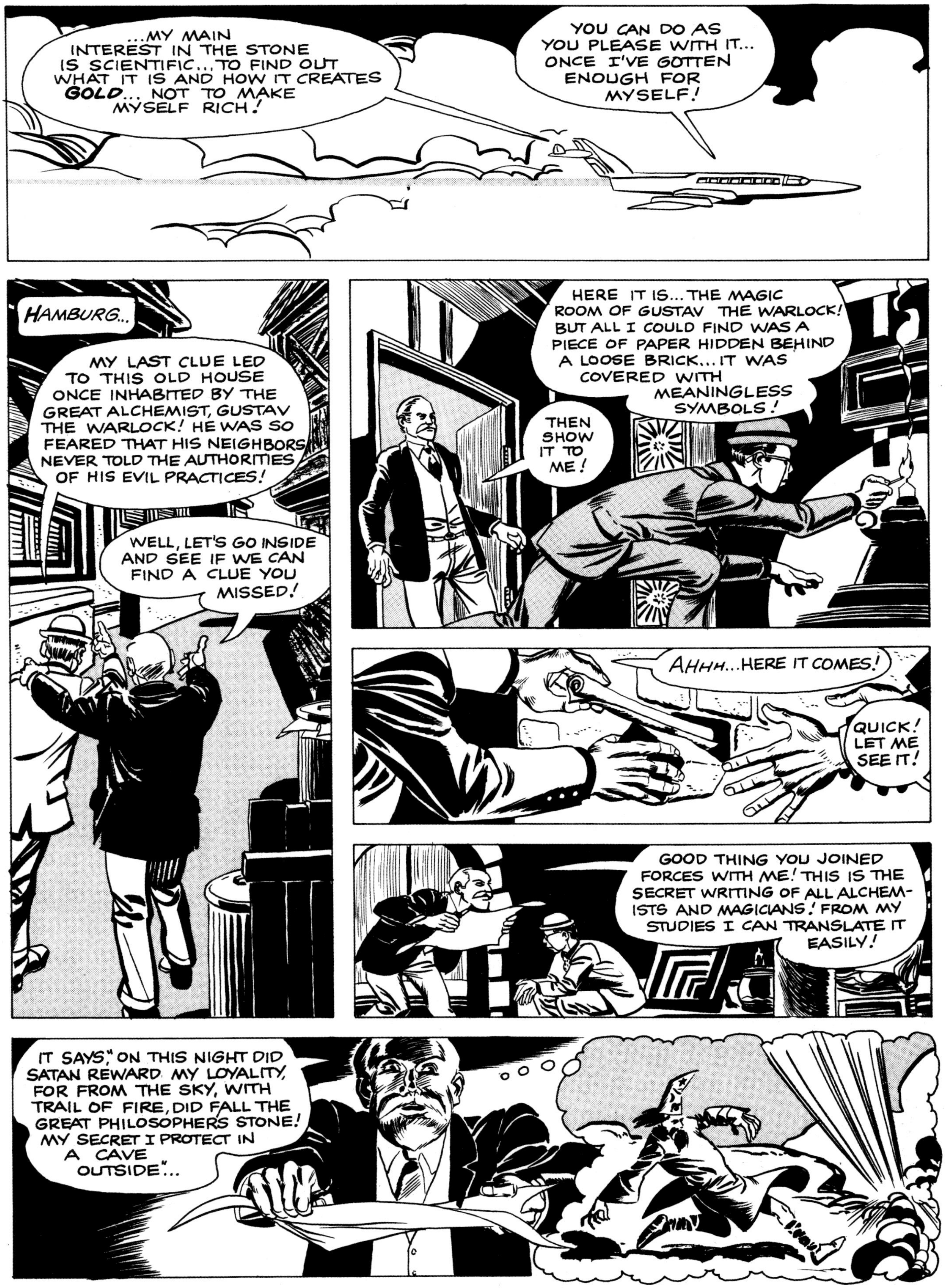
...MY MAIN INTEREST IN THE STONE IS SCIENTIFIC..., TO FIND OUT WHAT IT IS AND HOW IT CREATES GOLD... NOT TO MAKE MYSELF RICH!
YOU CAN DO AS YOU PLEASE WITH IT... ONCE I'VE GOTTEN ENOUGH FOR MYSELF!
HAMBURG...
MY LAST CLUE LED TO THIS OLD HOUSE ONCE INHABITED BY THE GREAT ALCHEMIST, GUSTAV THE WARLOCK! HE WAS SO FEARED THAT HIS NEIGHBORS NEVER TOLD THE AUTHORITIES OF HIS EVIL PRACTICES!
WELL, LET'S GO INSIDE AND SEE IF WE CAN FIND A CLUE YOU MISSED!
HERE IT IS... THE MAGIC ROOM OF GUSTAV THE WARLOCK! BUT ALL I COULD FIND WAS A PIECE OF PAPER HIDDEN BEHIND A LOOSE BRICK... IT WAS COVERED WITH MEANINGLESS SYMBOLS!
THEN SHOW IT TO ME!
AHHH...HERE IT COMES!
QUICK! LET ME SEE IT!
GOOD THING YOU JOINED FORCES WITH ME! THIS IS THE SECRET WRITING OF ALL ALCHEMISTS AND MAGICIANS! FROM MY STUDIES I CAN TRANSLATE IT EASILY!
IT SAYS, "ON THIS NIGHT DID SATAN REWARD MY LOYALITY, FOR FROM THE SKY, WITH TRAIL OF FIRE, DID FALL THE GREAT PHILOSOPHERS STONE! MY SECRET I PROTECT IN A CAVE OUTSIDE"...

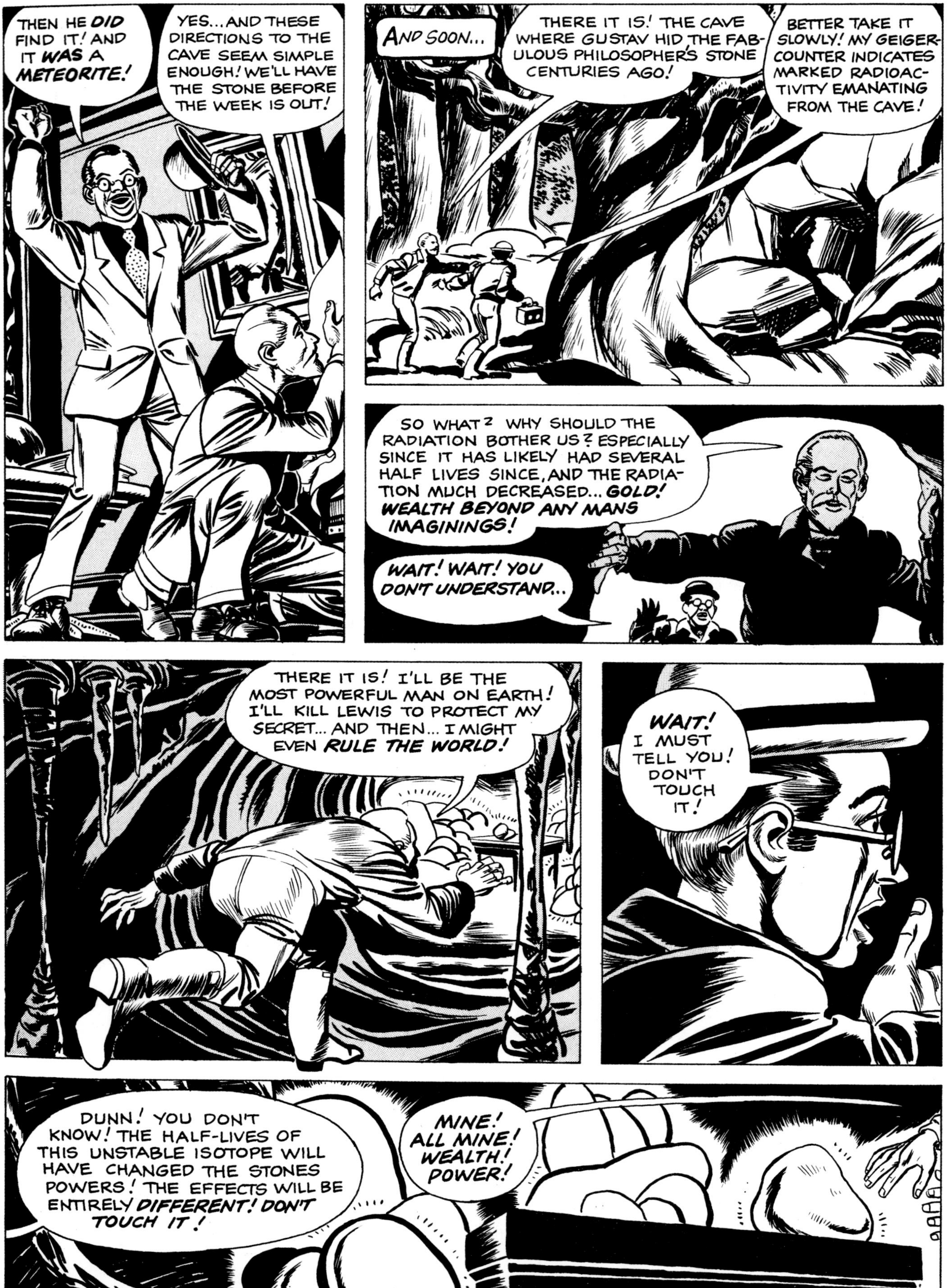
THEN HE DID FIND IT! AND IT WAS A METEORITE!
YES... AND THESE DIRECTIONS TO THE CAVE SEEM SIMPLE ENOUGH! WE'LL HAVE THE STONE BEFORE THE WEEK IS OUT!
AND SOON...
THERE IT IS! THE CAVE WHERE GUSTAV HID THE FABULOUS PHILOSOPHER'S STONE CENTURIES AGO!
BETTER TAKE IT SLOWLY! MY GEIGER-COUNTER INDICATES MARKED RADIOACTIVITY EMANATING FROM THE CAVE!
SO WHAT? WHY SHOULD THE RADIATION BOTHER US? ESPECIALLY SINCE IT HAS LIKELY HAD SEVERAL HALF LIVES SINCE, AND THE RADIATION MUCH DECREASED... GOLD! WEALTH BEYOND ANY MANS IMAGININGS!
WAIT! WAIT! YOU DON'T UNDERSTAND...
THERE IT IS! I'LL BE THE MOST POWERFUL MAN ON EARTH! I'LL KILL LEWIS TO PROTECT MY SECRET... AND THEN... I MIGHT EVEN RULE THE WORLD!
WAIT! I MUST TELL YOU! DON'T TOUCH IT!
DUNN! YOU DON'T KNOW! THE HALF-LIVES OF THIS UNSTABLE ISOTOPE WILL HAVE CHANGED THE STONES POWERS! THE EFFECTS WILL BE ENTIRELY DIFFERENT! DON'T TOUCH IT!
MINE! ALL MINE! WEALTH! POWER!

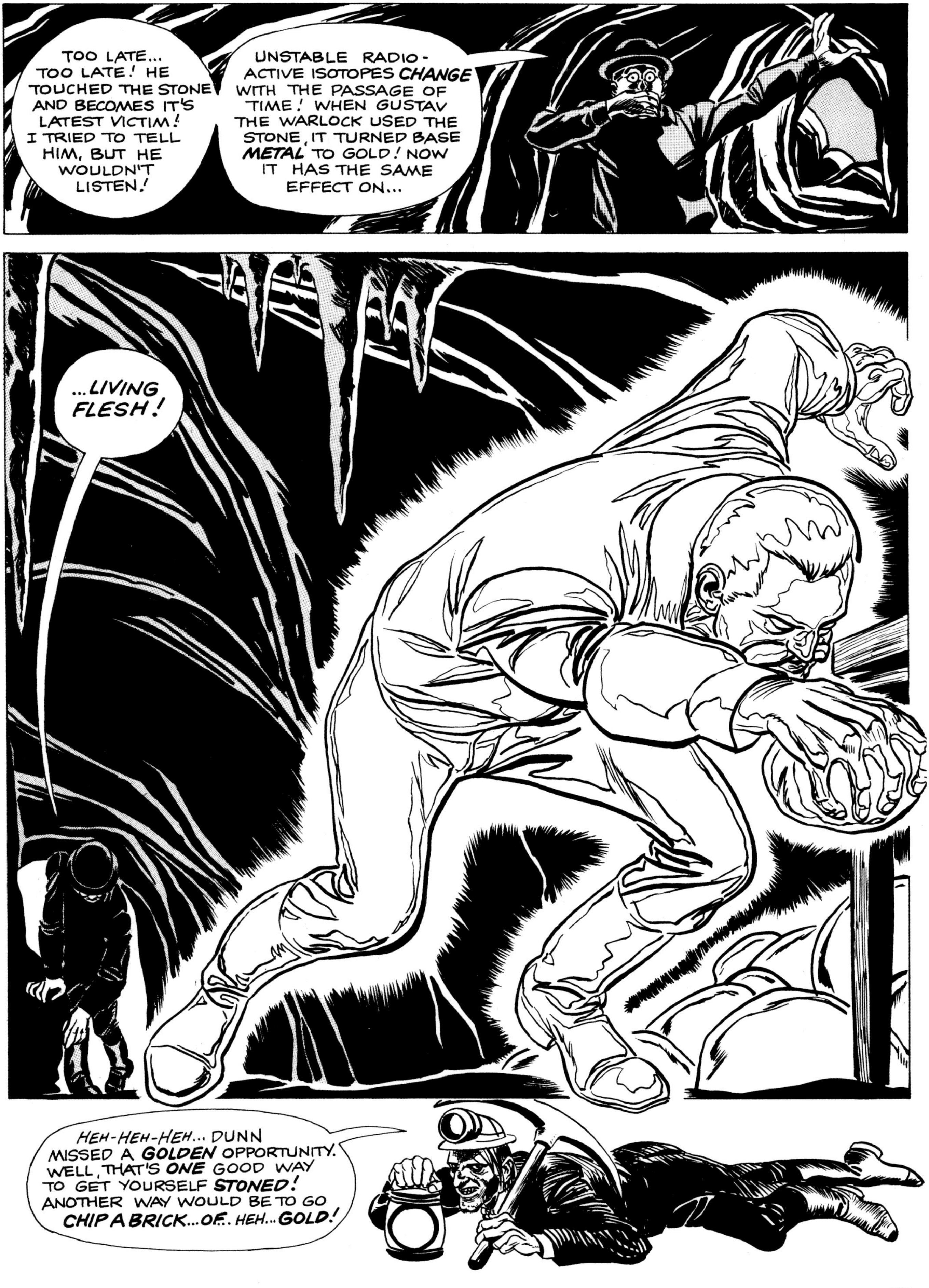
TOO LATE... TOO LATE! HE TOUCHED THE STONE AND BECOMES IT'S LATEST VICTIM! I TRIED TO TELL HIM, BUT HE WOULDN'T LISTEN!
UNSTABLE RADIO-ACTIVE ISOTOPES CHANGE WITH THE PASSAGE OF TIME! WHEN GUSTAV THE WARLOCK USED THE STONE, IT TURNED BASE METAL TO GOLD! NOW IT HAS THE SAME EFFECT ON...
...LIVING FLESH!
HEH-HEH-HEH... DUNN MISSED A GOLDEN OPPORTUNITY. WELL, THAT'S ONE GOOD WAY TO GET YOURSELF STONED! ANOTHER WAY WOULD BE TO GO CHIP A BRICK...OF.. HEH...GOLD!

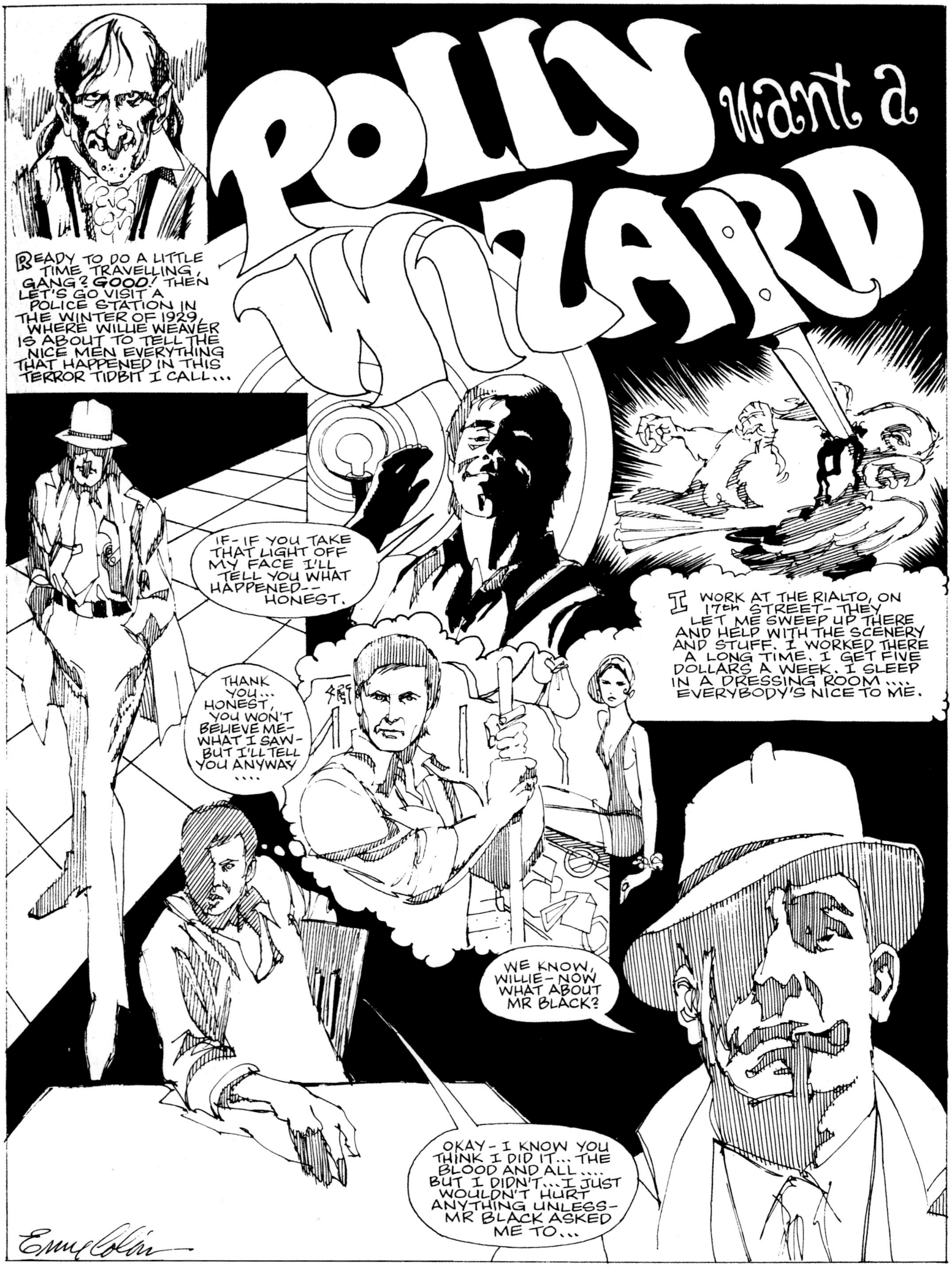
POLLY want a WIZARD
READY TO DO A LITTLE TIME TRAVELLING, GANG? GOOD! THEN LET'S GO VISIT A POLICE STATION IN THE WINTER OF 1929, WHERE WILLIE WEAVER IS ABOUT TO TELL THE NICE MEN EVERYTHING THAT HAPPENED IN THIS TERROR TIDBIT I CALL...
IF- IF YOU TAKE THAT LIGHT OFF MY FACE I'LL TELL YOU WHAT HAPPENED-- HONEST.
I WORK AT THE RIALTO, ON 17th STREET- THEY LET ME SWEEP UP THERE AND HELP WITH THE SCENERY AND STUFF. I WORKED THERE A LONG TIME. I GET FIVE DOLLARS A WEEK. I SLEEP IN A DRESSING ROOM.... EVERYBODY'S NICE TO ME.
THANK YOU... HONEST, YOU WON'T BELIEVE ME- WHAT I SAW- BUT I'LL TELL YOU ANYWAY....
WE KNOW, WILLIE- NOW WHAT ABOUT MR BLACK?
OKAY- I KNOW YOU THINK I DID IT... THE BLOOD AND ALL.... BUT I DIDN'T... I JUST WOULDN'T HURT ANYTHING UNLESS- MR BLACK ASKED ME TO...
Ernie Colón

ART BY ERNIE COLON/STORY BY HOWARD WALDROP

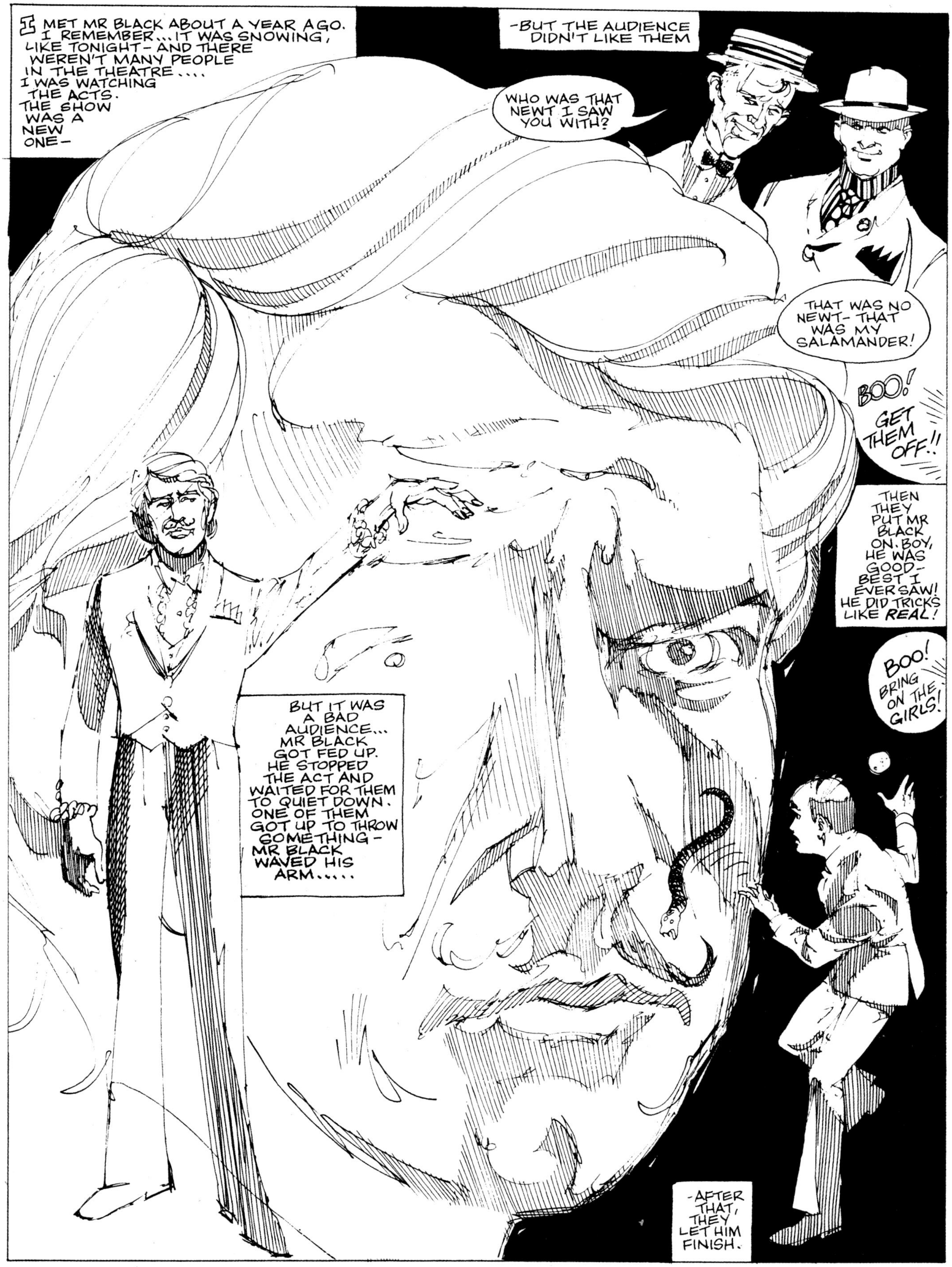
I MET MR BLACK ABOUT A YEAR AGO. I REMEMBER... IT WAS SNOWING, LIKE TONIGHT- AND THERE WEREN'T MANY PEOPLE IN THE THEATRE.... I WAS WATCHING THE ACTS. THE SHOW WAS A NEW ONE-
-BUT THE AUDIENCE DIDN'T LIKE THEM
WHO WAS THAT NEWT I SAW YOU WITH?
THAT WAS NO NEWT- THAT WAS MY SALAMANDER!
BOO! GET THEM OFF!!
THEN THEY PUT MR BLACK ON. BOY, HE WAS GOOD- BEST I EVER SAW! HE DID TRICKS LIKE REAL!
BOO! BRING ON THE GIRLS!
BUT IT WAS A BAD AUDIENCE... MR BLACK GOT FED UP. HE STOPPED THE ACT AND WAITED FOR THEM TO QUIET DOWN. ONE OF THEM GOT UP TO THROW SOMETHING- MR BLACK WAVED HIS ARM.....
-AFTER THAT, THEY LET HIM FINISH.

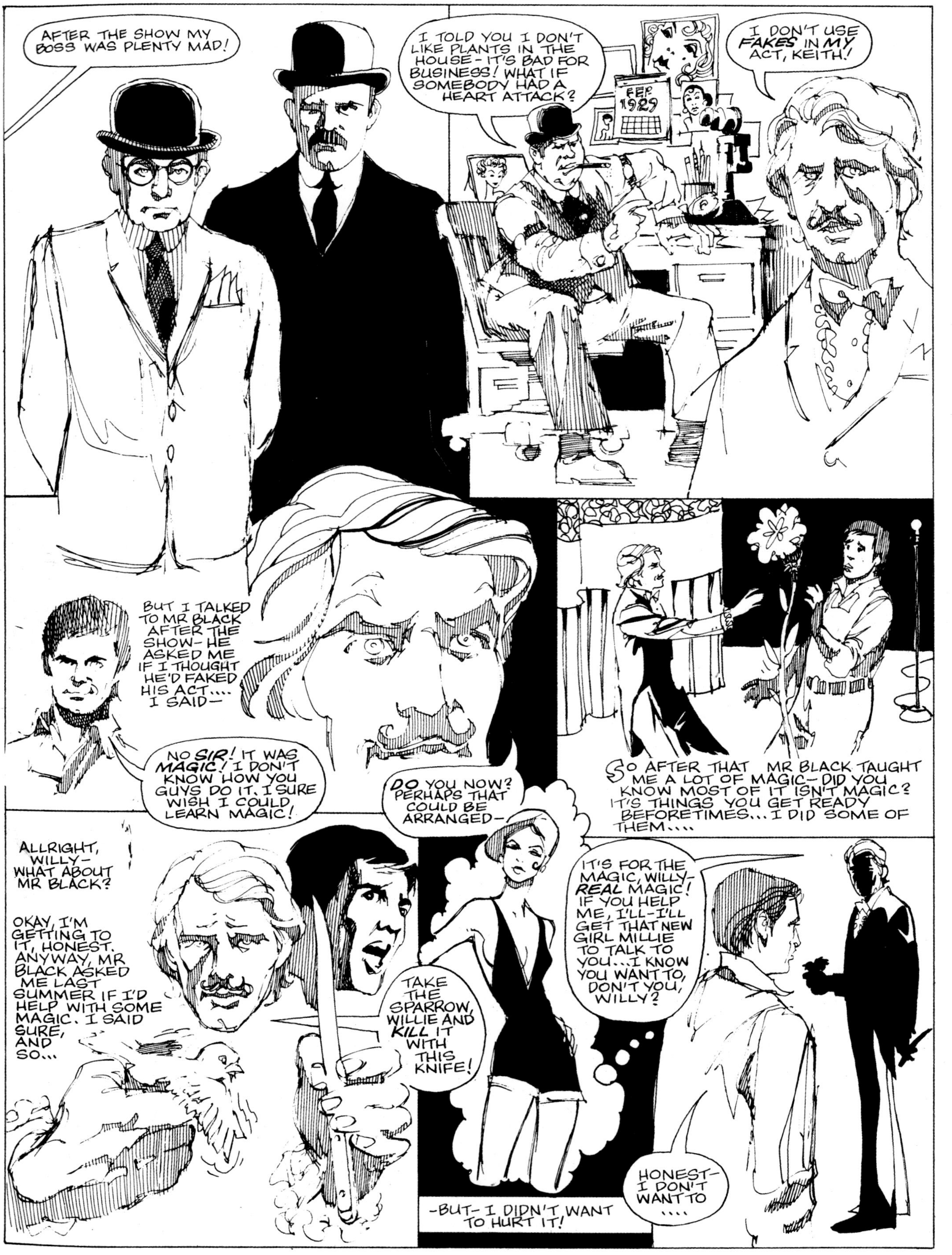
AFTER THE SHOW MY BOSS WAS PLENTY MAD!
I TOLD YOU I DON'T LIKE PLANTS IN THE HOUSE- IT'S BAD FOR BUSINESS! WHAT IF SOMEBODY HAD A HEART ATTACK?
FEB 1929
I DON'T USE FAKES IN MY ACT, KEITH!
BUT I TALKED TO MR BLACK AFTER THE SHOW- HE ASKED ME IF I THOUGHT HE'D FAKED HIS ACT.... I SAID—
NO SIR! IT WAS MAGIC! I DON'T KNOW HOW YOU GUYS DO IT. I SURE WISH I COULD LEARN MAGIC!
DO YOU NOW? PERHAPS THAT COULD BE ARRANGED—
SO AFTER THAT MR BLACK TAUGHT ME A LOT OF MAGIC- DID YOU KNOW MOST OF IT ISN'T MAGIC? IT'S THINGS YOU GET READY BEFORETIMES... I DID SOME OF THEM....
ALLRIGHT, WILLY- WHAT ABOUT MR BLACK?
OKAY, I'M GETTING TO IT, HONEST. ANYWAY, MR BLACK ASKED ME LAST SUMMER IF I'D HELP WITH SOME MAGIC. I SAID SURE, AND SO...
TAKE THE SPARROW, WILLIE AND KILL IT WITH THIS KNIFE!
-BUT- I DIDN'T WANT TO HURT IT!
IT'S FOR THE MAGIC, WILLY- REAL MAGIC! IF YOU HELP ME, I'LL-I'LL GET THAT NEW GIRL MILLIE TO TALK TO YOU...I KNOW YOU WANT TO, DON'T YOU, WILLY?
HONEST- I DON'T WANT TO ....

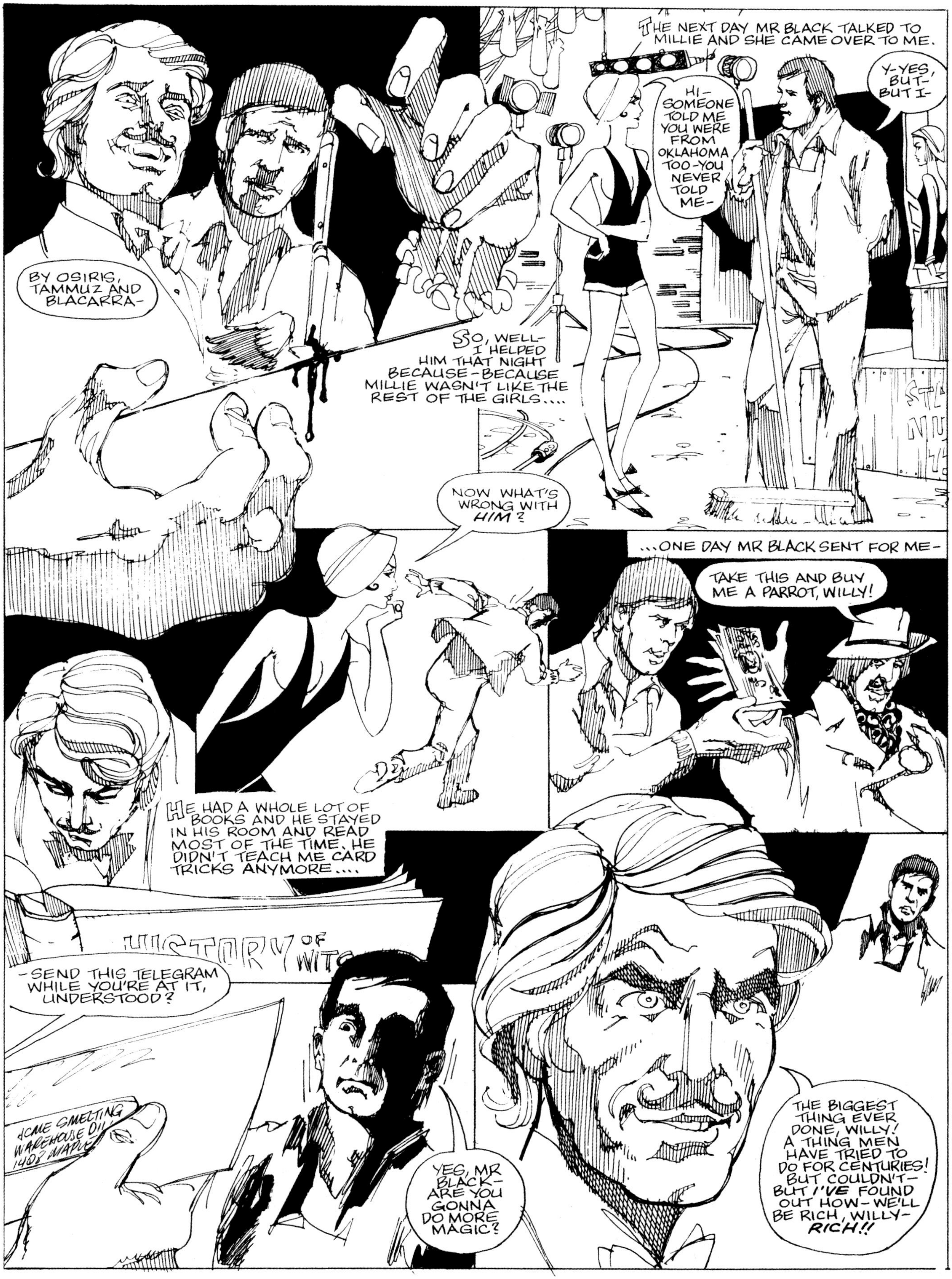
BY OSIRIS, TAMMUZ AND BLACARRA-
SO, WELL- I HELPED HIM THAT NIGHT BECAUSE-BECAUSE MILLIE WASN'T LIKE THE REST OF THE GIRLS....
THE NEXT DAY MR BLACK TALKED TO MILLIE AND SHE CAME OVER TO ME.
HI- SOMEONE TOLD ME YOU WERE FROM OKLAHOMA TOO-YOU NEVER TOLD ME-
Y-YES, BUT-BUT I-
NOW WHAT'S WRONG WITH HIM?
HE HAD A WHOLE LOT OF BOOKS AND HE STAYED IN HIS ROOM AND READ MOST OF THE TIME. HE DIDN'T TEACH ME CARD TRICKS ANYMORE....
...ONE DAY MR BLACK SENT FOR ME-
TAKE THIS AND BUY ME A PARROT, WILLY!
-SEND THIS TELEGRAM WHILE YOU'RE AT IT, UNDERSTOOD?
YES, MR BLACK- ARE YOU GONNA DO MORE MAGIC?
THE BIGGEST THING EVER DONE, WILLY! A THING MEN HAVE TRIED TO DO FOR CENTURIES! BUT COULDN'T- BUT I'VE FOUND OUT HOW-WE'LL BE RICH, WILLY- RICH!!

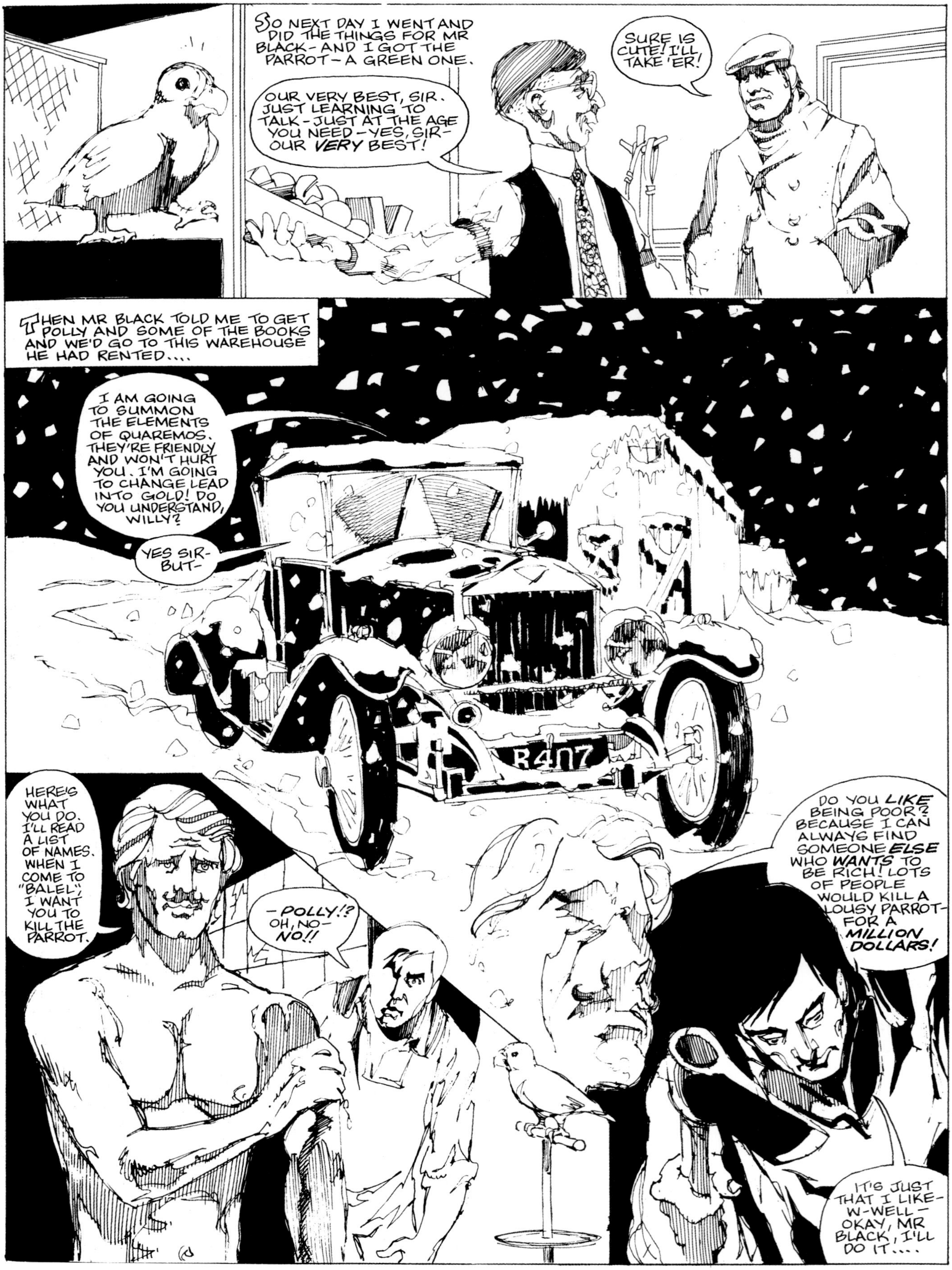
SO NEXT DAY I WENT AND DID THE THINGS FOR MR BLACK - AND I GOT THE PARROT - A GREEN ONE.
OUR VERY BEST, SIR. JUST LEARNING TO TALK - JUST AT THE AGE YOU NEED - YES, SIR - OUR VERY BEST!
SURE IS CUTE! I'LL TAKE 'ER!
THEN MR BLACK TOLD ME TO GET POLLY AND SOME OF THE BOOKS AND WE'D GO TO THIS WAREHOUSE HE HAD RENTED....
I AM GOING TO SUMMON THE ELEMENTS OF QUAREMOS. THEY'RE FRIENDLY AND WON'T HURT YOU. I'M GOING TO CHANGE LEAD INTO GOLD! DO YOU UNDERSTAND, WILLY?
YES SIR - BUT -
R 4117
HERE'S WHAT YOU DO. I'LL READ A LIST OF NAMES. WHEN I COME TO "BALEL", I WANT YOU TO KILL THE PARROT.
- POLLY!? OH, NO - NO!!
DO YOU LIKE BEING POOR? BECAUSE I CAN ALWAYS FIND SOMEONE ELSE WHO WANTS TO BE RICH! LOTS OF PEOPLE WOULD KILL A LOUSY PARROT FOR A MILLION DOLLARS!
IT'S JUST THAT I LIKE - W-WELL - OKAY, MR BLACK, I'LL DO IT....

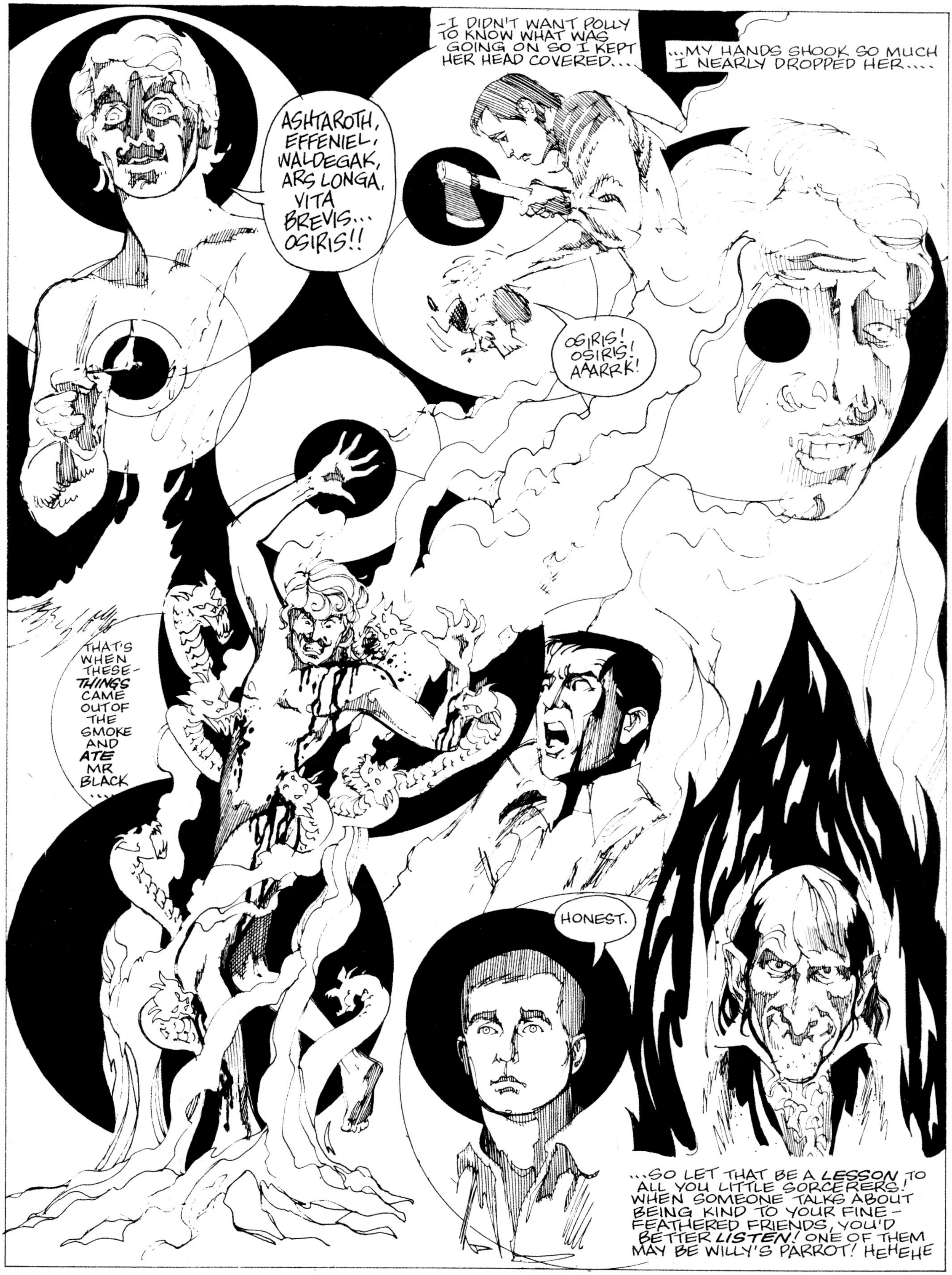
ASHTAROTH, EFFENIEL, WALDEGAK, ARS LONGA, VITA BREVIS... OSIRIS!!
-I DIDN'T WANT POLLY TO KNOW WHAT WAS GOING ON SO I KEPT HER HEAD COVERED...
...MY HANDS SHOOK SO MUCH I NEARLY DROPPED HER....
OSIRIS! OSIRIS! AAARRK!
THAT'S WHEN THESE-THINGS CAME OUT OF THE SMOKE AND ATE MR BLACK....
HONEST.
...SO LET THAT BE A LESSON TO ALL YOU LITTLE SORCERERS! WHEN SOMEONE TALKS ABOUT BEING KIND TO YOUR FINE-FEATHERED FRIENDS, YOU'D BETTER LISTEN! ONE OF THEM MAY BE WILLY'S PARROT! HEHEHE

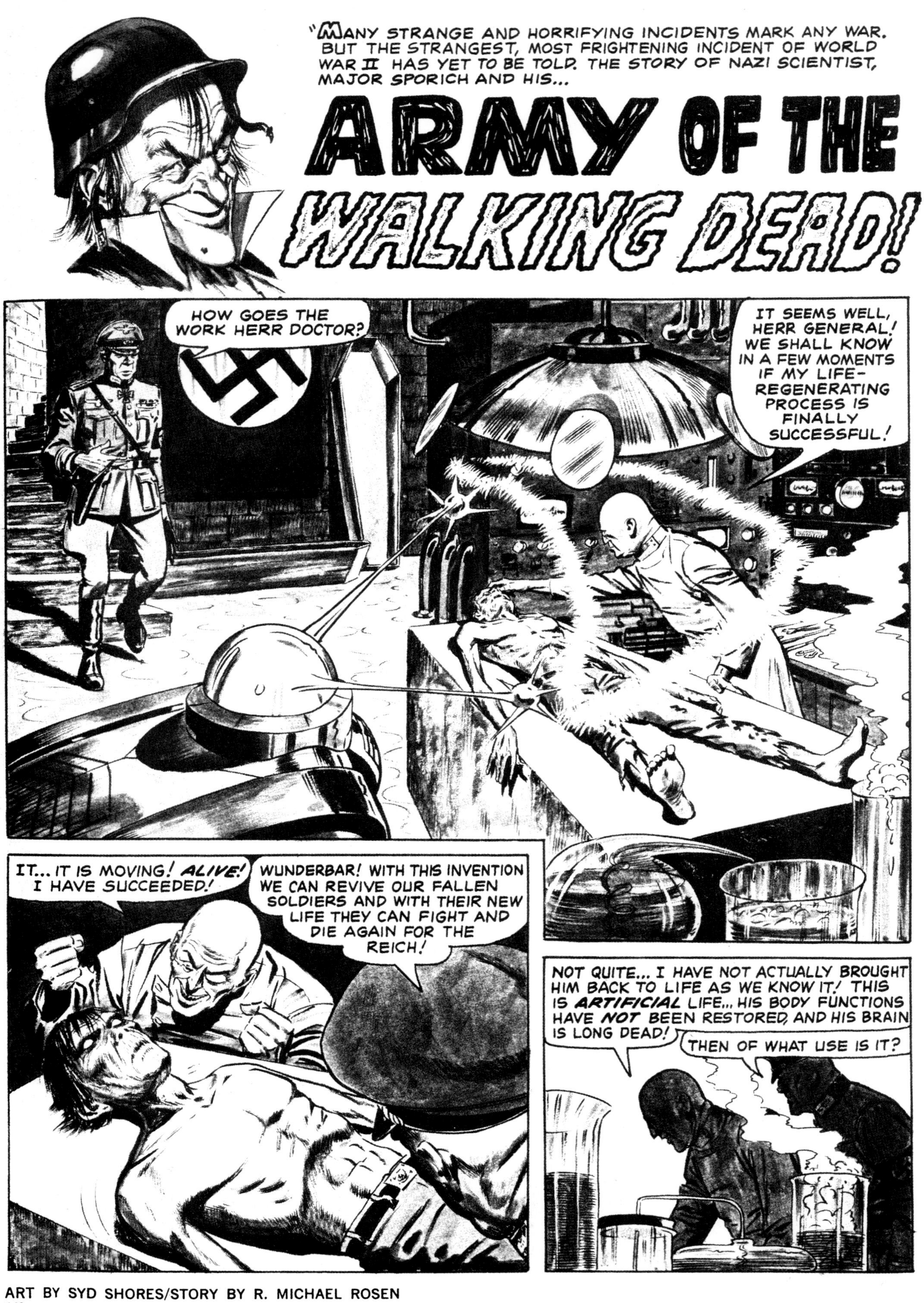
"MANY STRANGE AND HORRIFYING INCIDENTS MARK ANY WAR. BUT THE STRANGEST, MOST FRIGHTENING INCIDENT OF WORLD WAR II HAS YET TO BE TOLD. THE STORY OF NAZI SCIENTIST, MAJOR SPORICH AND HIS...
ARMY OF THE WALKING DEAD!
HOW GOES THE WORK HERR DOCTOR?
IT SEEMS WELL, HERR GENERAL! WE SHALL KNOW IN A FEW MOMENTS IF MY LIFE-REGENERATING PROCESS IS FINALLY SUCCESSFUL!
IT... IT IS MOVING! ALIVE! I HAVE SUCCEEDED!
WUNDERBAR! WITH THIS INVENTION WE CAN REVIVE OUR FALLEN SOLDIERS AND WITH THEIR NEW LIFE THEY CAN FIGHT AND DIE AGAIN FOR THE REICH!
NOT QUITE... I HAVE NOT ACTUALLY BROUGHT HIM BACK TO LIFE AS WE KNOW IT! THIS IS ARTIFICIAL LIFE... HIS BODY FUNCTIONS HAVE NOT BEEN RESTORED, AND HIS BRAIN IS LONG DEAD!
THEN OF WHAT USE IS IT?

ART BY SYD SHORES/STORY BY R. MICHAEL ROSEN

BECAUSE, MY DEAR GENERAL, THESE *ZOMBIES*, AS THE SUPERSTITIOUS CALL SUCH CREATURES, HAVE THE STRENGTH OF TEN MEN! THEY CANNOT BE KILLED SINCE THEY ARE ALREADY DEAD! ONLY THE DESTRUCTION OF THEIR ENTIRE BODIES CAN STOP THEM! AND THEY OBEY ORDERS WITHOUT FEAR!

EXCELLENT! CONFIDENTIALLY, THE WAR IS GOING BADLY! THESE ZOMBIES OF YOURS COULD ASSURE VICTORY IN A MAJOR COUNTER-ATTACK WE PLAN!

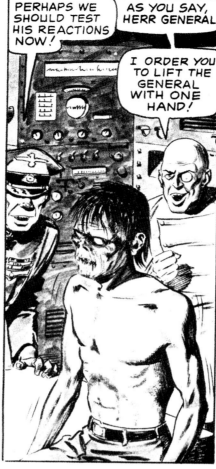

PERHAPS WE SHOULD TEST HIS REACTIONS NOW!

AS YOU SAY, HERR GENERAL.

I ORDER YOU TO LIFT THE GENERAL WITH ONE HAND!

YOU SEE...? HE HAS GREAT STRENTGH, AND OBEYS WITHOUT QUESTION!

ENOUGH! I-I AM CONVINCED... *LET ME DOWN!*

IS HE WITHOUT RESPECT FOR MY IMPORTANCE TO THE REICH... MY GENERAL'S UNIFORM?! A BRUTE LIKE THIS WHO OBEYS *ANY* ORDER COULD EASILY BE TURNED AGAINST US BY THE ENEMY!

HAVE NO FEAR...THESE FINE SOLDIERS CAN RESPOND TO *MY* VOICE ONLY!

THE NEXT DAY... YOUR DEMONSTRATION CONVINCES ME, HERR DOCTOR! YOUR ZOMBIES CAN DO ALL YOU CLAIMED! THEIR COUNTER-ATTACK WILL CRUSH THE ENEMY FRONT... EUROPE SHALL BE *OURS* AGAIN! HOW FAST CAN YOU PRODUCE THEM!

THE PROCESS IS RELATIVELY SIMPLE, MY FUHRER... I NEED ONLY A STEADY SUPPLY OF BODIES OF OUR FALLEN SOLDIERS!

AND SO SPORICH CREATED AN ARMY OF *THE WALKING DEAD*, WHICH WAS SOON TRANSPORTED TO THE FRONT LINES...

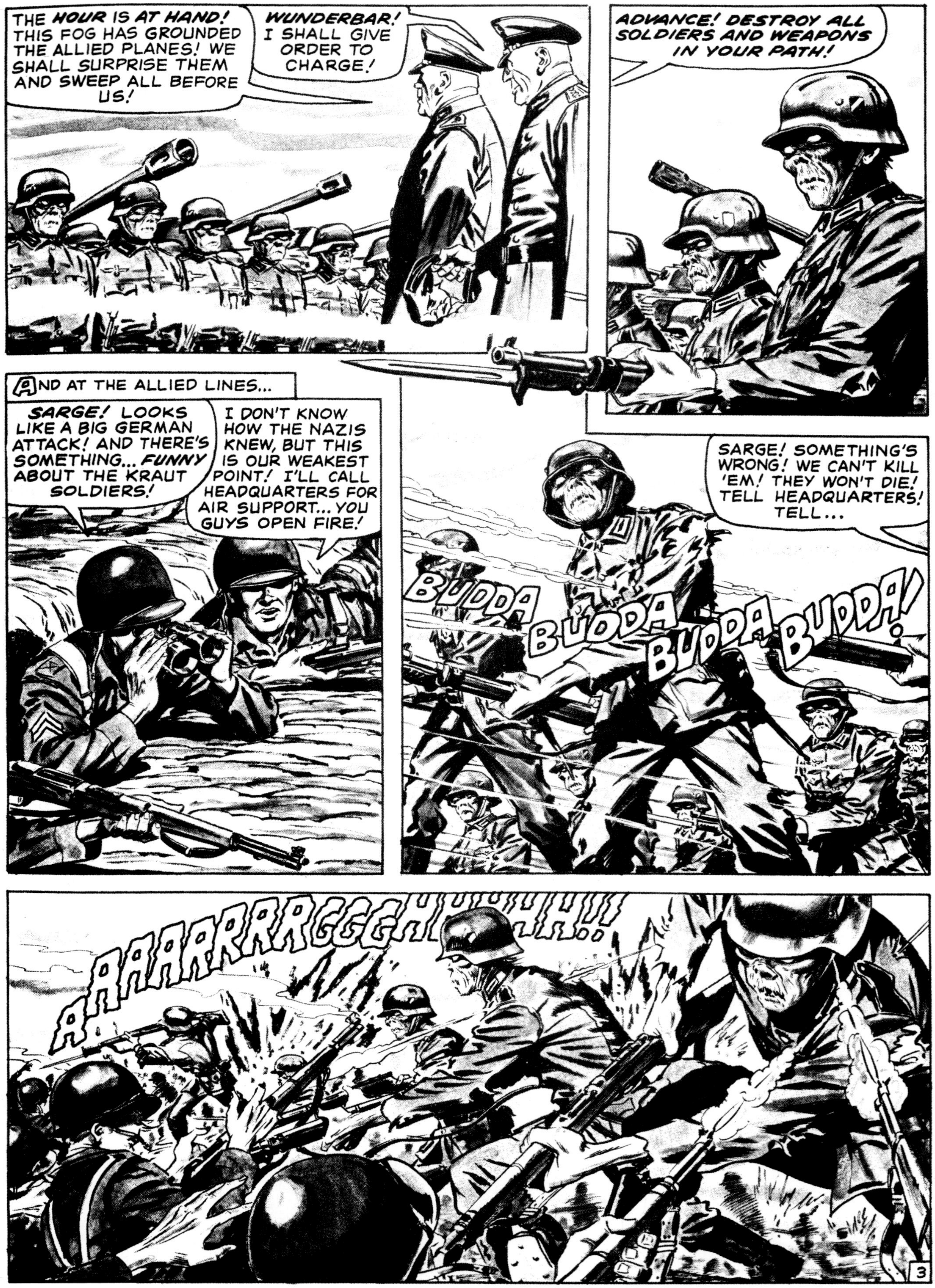
THE HOUR IS AT HAND! THIS FOG HAS GROUNDED THE ALLIED PLANES! WE SHALL SURPRISE THEM AND SWEEP ALL BEFORE US!
WUNDERBAR! I SHALL GIVE ORDER TO CHARGE!
ADVANCE! DESTROY ALL SOLDIERS AND WEAPONS IN YOUR PATH!
AND AT THE ALLIED LINES...
SARGE! LOOKS LIKE A BIG GERMAN ATTACK! AND THERE'S SOMETHING... FUNNY ABOUT THE KRAUT SOLDIERS!
I DON'T KNOW HOW THE NAZIS KNEW, BUT THIS IS OUR WEAKEST POINT! I'LL CALL HEADQUARTERS FOR AIR SUPPORT... YOU GUYS OPEN FIRE!
SARGE! SOMETHING'S WRONG! WE CAN'T KILL 'EM! THEY WON'T DIE! TELL HEADQUARTERS! TELL...
BUDDA BUDDA BUDDA BUDDA!
AAAARRRRGGGGHHHHH!!
3

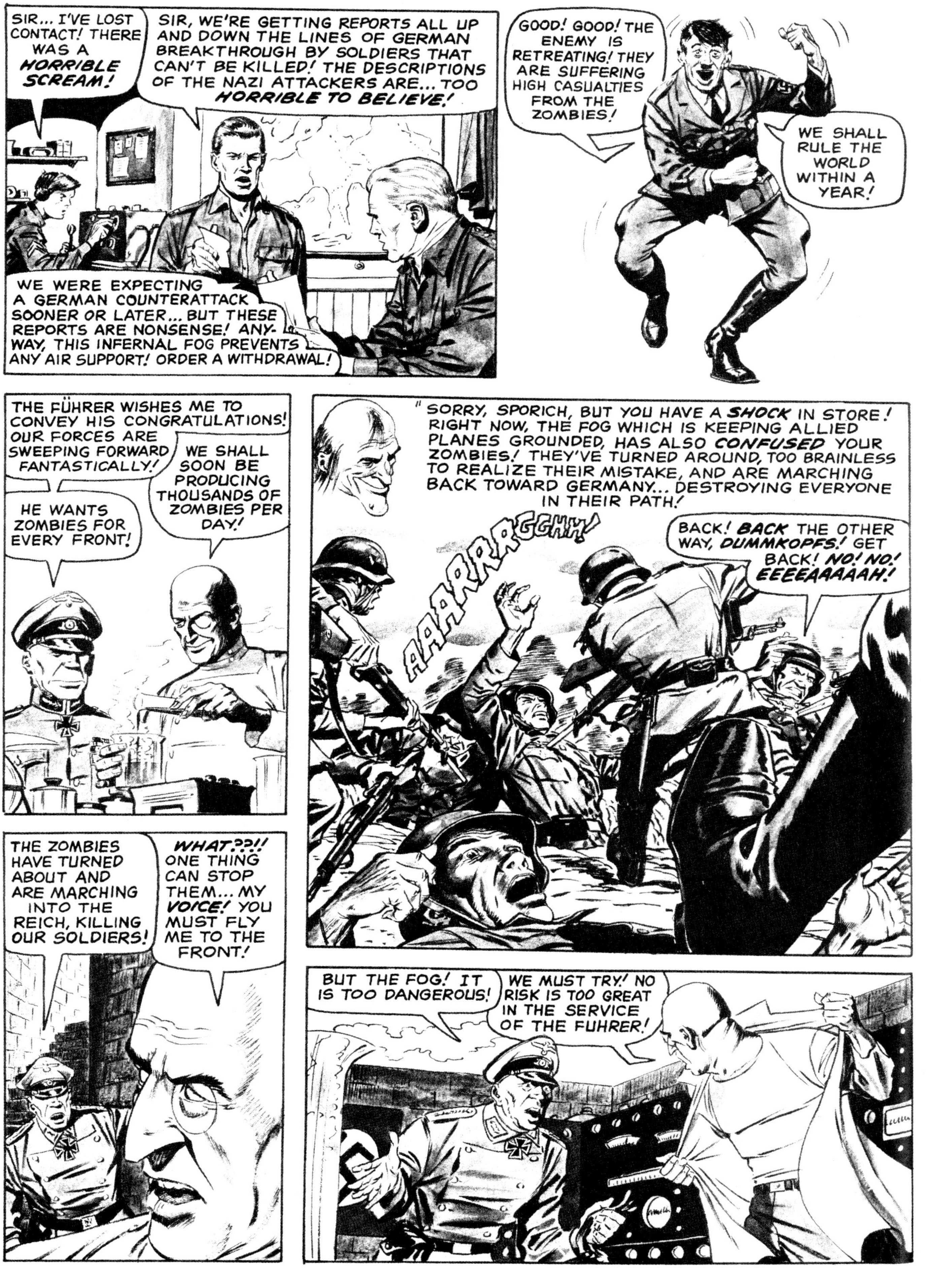
SIR... I'VE LOST CONTACT! THERE WAS A HORRIBLE SCREAM!
SIR, WE'RE GETTING REPORTS ALL UP AND DOWN THE LINES OF GERMAN BREAKTHROUGH BY SOLDIERS THAT CAN'T BE KILLED! THE DESCRIPTIONS OF THE NAZI ATTACKERS ARE... TOO HORRIBLE TO BELIEVE!
WE WERE EXPECTING A GERMAN COUNTERATTACK SOONER OR LATER... BUT THESE REPORTS ARE NONSENSE! ANYWAY, THIS INFERNAL FOG PREVENTS ANY AIR SUPPORT! ORDER A WITHDRAWAL!
GOOD! GOOD! THE ENEMY IS RETREATING! THEY ARE SUFFERING HIGH CASUALTIES FROM THE ZOMBIES!
WE SHALL RULE THE WORLD WITHIN A YEAR!
THE FÜHRER WISHES ME TO CONVEY HIS CONGRATULATIONS! OUR FORCES ARE SWEEPING FORWARD FANTASTICALLY!
HE WANTS ZOMBIES FOR EVERY FRONT!
WE SHALL SOON BE PRODUCING THOUSANDS OF ZOMBIES PER DAY!
"SORRY, SPORICH, BUT YOU HAVE A SHOCK IN STORE! RIGHT NOW, THE FOG WHICH IS KEEPING ALLIED PLANES GROUNDED, HAS ALSO CONFUSED YOUR ZOMBIES! THEY'VE TURNED AROUND, TOO BRAINLESS TO REALIZE THEIR MISTAKE, AND ARE MARCHING BACK TOWARD GERMANY... DESTROYING EVERYONE IN THEIR PATH!
AARRRGGHH!
BACK! BACK THE OTHER WAY, DUMMKOPFS! GET BACK! NO! NO! EEEEAAAAAAH!
AAARRRGH!
THE ZOMBIES HAVE TURNED ABOUT AND ARE MARCHING INTO THE REICH, KILLING OUR SOLDIERS!
WHAT??!! ONE THING CAN STOP THEM... MY VOICE! YOU MUST FLY ME TO THE FRONT!
BUT THE FOG! IT IS TOO DANGEROUS!
WE MUST TRY! NO RISK IS TOO GREAT IN THE SERVICE OF THE FUHRER!

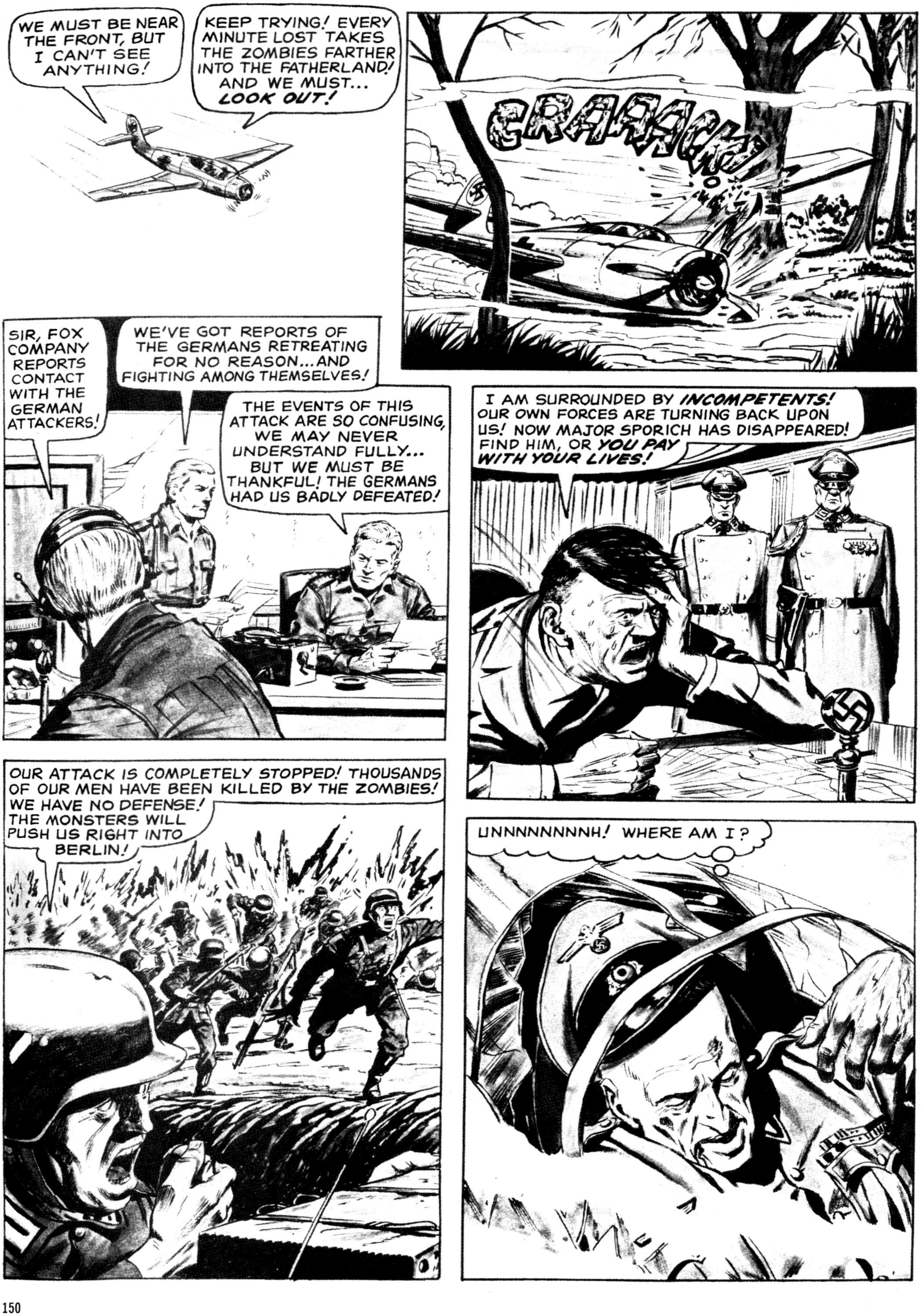
WE MUST BE NEAR THE FRONT, BUT I CAN'T SEE ANYTHING!
KEEP TRYING! EVERY MINUTE LOST TAKES THE ZOMBIES FARTHER INTO THE FATHERLAND! AND WE MUST... LOOK OUT!
CRAAACK!
SIR, FOX COMPANY REPORTS CONTACT WITH THE GERMAN ATTACKERS!
WE'VE GOT REPORTS OF THE GERMANS RETREATING FOR NO REASON... AND FIGHTING AMONG THEMSELVES!
THE EVENTS OF THIS ATTACK ARE SO CONFUSING, WE MAY NEVER UNDERSTAND FULLY... BUT WE MUST BE THANKFUL! THE GERMANS HAD US BADLY DEFEATED!
I AM SURROUNDED BY INCOMPETENTS! OUR OWN FORCES ARE TURNING BACK UPON US! NOW MAJOR SPORICH HAS DISAPPEARED! FIND HIM, OR YOU PAY WITH YOUR LIVES!
OUR ATTACK IS COMPLETELY STOPPED! THOUSANDS OF OUR MEN HAVE BEEN KILLED BY THE ZOMBIES! WE HAVE NO DEFENSE! THE MONSTERS WILL PUSH US RIGHT INTO BERLIN!
UNNNNNNNNH! WHERE AM I?

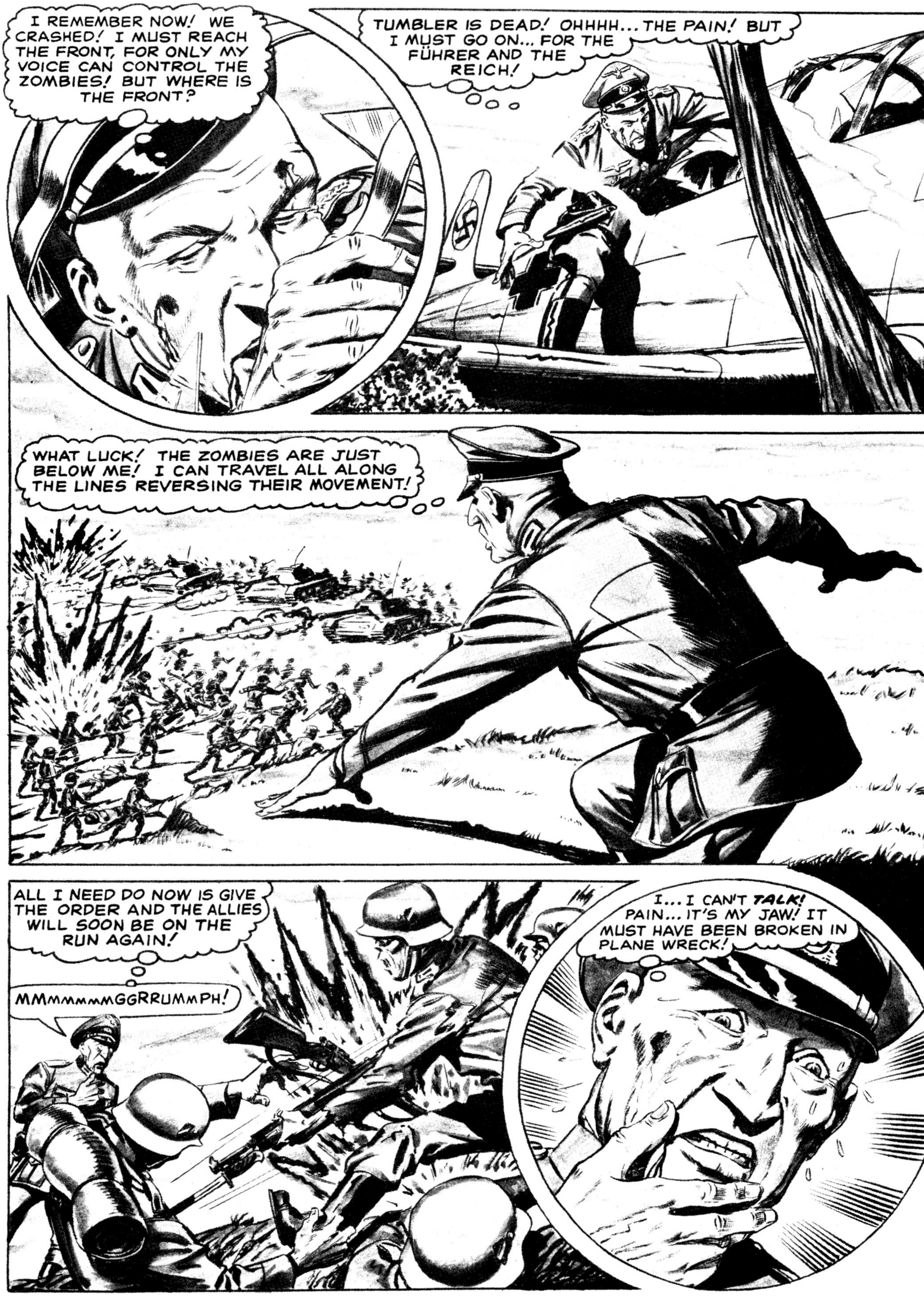
I REMEMBER NOW! WE CRASHED! I MUST REACH THE FRONT, FOR ONLY MY VOICE CAN CONTROL THE ZOMBIES! BUT WHERE IS THE FRONT?
TUMBLER IS DEAD! OHHHH... THE PAIN! BUT I MUST GO ON... FOR THE FÜHRER AND THE REICH!
WHAT LUCK! THE ZOMBIES ARE JUST BELOW ME! I CAN TRAVEL ALL ALONG THE LINES REVERSING THEIR MOVEMENT!
ALL I NEED DO NOW IS GIVE THE ORDER AND THE ALLIES WILL SOON BE ON THE RUN AGAIN!
MMMMMMMGGRRUMMPH!
I... I CAN'T TALK! PAIN... IT'S MY JAW! IT MUST HAVE BEEN BROKEN IN PLANE WRECK!

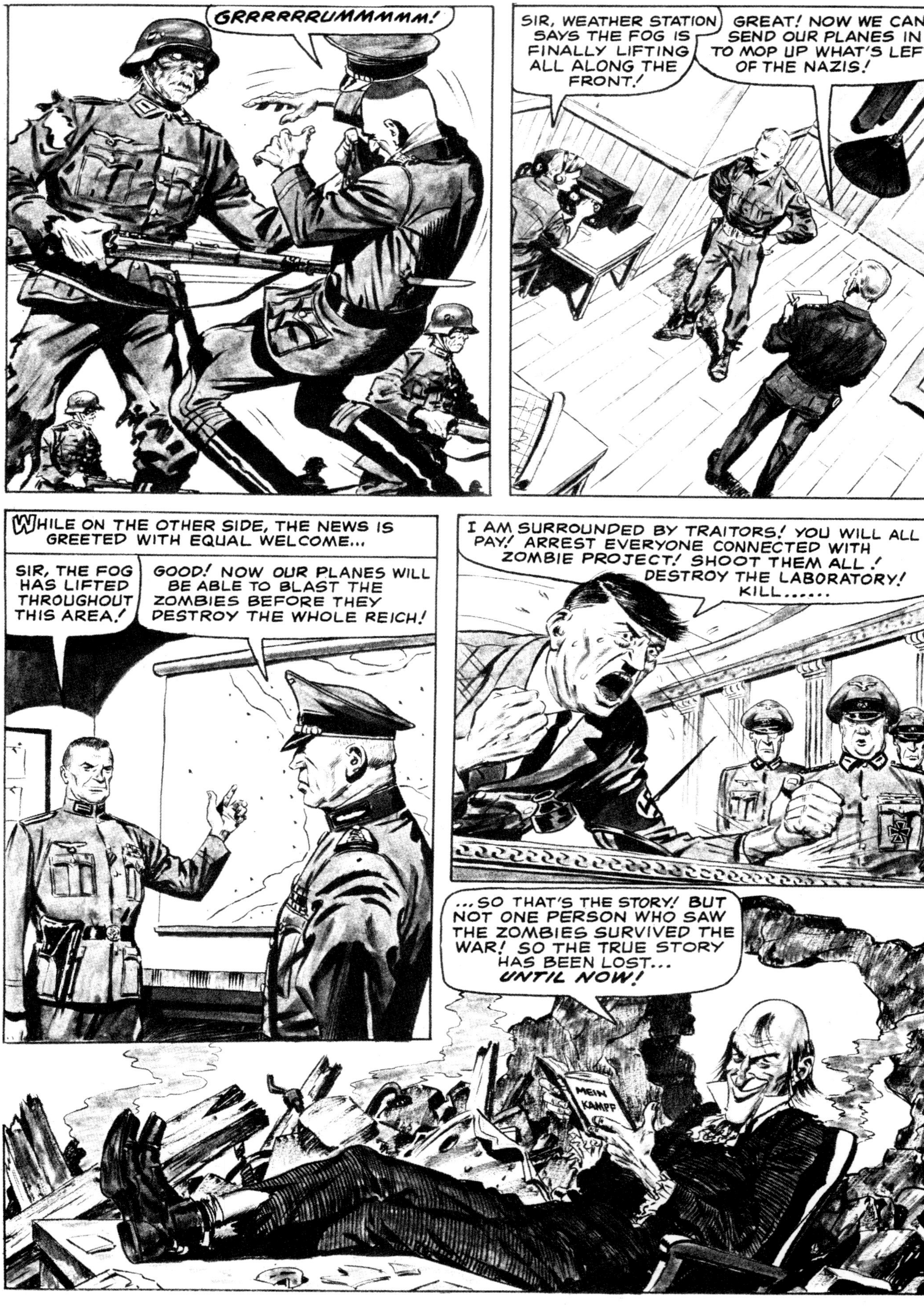
GRRRRRRUMMMMMM!
SIR, WEATHER STATION SAYS THE FOG IS FINALLY LIFTING ALL ALONG THE FRONT!
GREAT! NOW WE CAN SEND OUR PLANES IN TO MOP UP WHAT'S LEFT OF THE NAZIS!
WHILE ON THE OTHER SIDE, THE NEWS IS GREETED WITH EQUAL WELCOME...
SIR, THE FOG HAS LIFTED THROUGHOUT THIS AREA!
GOOD! NOW OUR PLANES WILL BE ABLE TO BLAST THE ZOMBIES BEFORE THEY DESTROY THE WHOLE REICH!
I AM SURROUNDED BY TRAITORS! YOU WILL ALL PAY! ARREST EVERYONE CONNECTED WITH ZOMBIE PROJECT! SHOOT THEM ALL! DESTROY THE LABORATORY! KILL......
...SO THAT'S THE STORY! BUT NOT ONE PERSON WHO SAW THE ZOMBIES SURVIVED THE WAR! SO THE TRUE STORY HAS BEEN LOST... UNTIL NOW!
MEIN KAMPF

THE CREEPY FAN CLUB!

If you're reading this in North America, you'll understand our claim that we've unearthed a real, live alien artist. Our readers in Europe won't exactly agree, because this artist is actually one of them. But around 22 East 42d Street, they call him . . .

KEN BARR: THE ALIEN

Ken is a recent "invader" from the murky shores of farr-off Scotland. He looks like one of us, but there are those in New York who think he talks funny.

Ken doesn't get to the city very often. We keep him caged in a studio in Teaneck, New Jersey. He has an interpreter to help him understand the scripts—his wife, Katherine, a native-born American.

Ken is Scottish, but his background was confused right from the start. He was born on an Irish holiday—St. Patrick's Day—in 1933 in Glasgow.

At the age of ten, he won first prize in the Greenrock (Renfrewshire, Scotland) School competition, in support of the British war effort. His

KEN BARR—SCOTTISH LAD MAKES GOOD

prize-winning sketch was of an incident from the Crimean War.

Ken spent the traditional British six-year apprenticeship as a poster writer in his home town. Between assignments, he snitched the company's paper and paint to make giant poster-size drawings of Tarzan as originally interpreted by Burne Hogarth. He was already sold on the comics. And through him, so were the other apprentices.

At 18, Ken joined the British Army's Royal Signal Corps. But a narrow twist of fate, he just missed being sent off for combat duty in Korea and was assigned to the Middle East instead. A year later, at 19, he became one of the youngest Sergeants in the British Army.

After two years as a coding expert, he was discharged and headed for the bright lights of London and a checkered art career that included a stint with the famous J. Arthur Rank Movie Organization.

Returning to Scotland in the mid-1950's, Ken went to work with D. C. Thompson, one of Britain's largest publishers. He didn't leave Thompson until he married Katherine and fulfilled a life-long dream of emigrating to the United States.

During his years with D. C. Thompson, Kent became a specialist in World War II combat illustration, both in black-and-white line art and in color paintings. He is an expert on fighter aircraft of the period, and is happiest lost in a raging dogfight.

Between assignments at

Thompson's, Ken also found time to do covers and inside art for a British science fiction magazine, NEBULA, which carries stories by well-known authors like Bob Silverberg and Arthur C. Clarke.

In the short time he's been in America, Ken has done a great deal of work for D. C. Comics (no relation to D. C. Thompson, by the way.), and for leading paperback publishers. "I look forward to working on CREEPY, EERIE VAMPIRELLA," he says. "Britain has no equivalent to them." (Who does?)

Ken keeps physically fit. He holds a brown belt in Judo. In any other spare time, he builds out-sized radio-controlled model airplanes.

His highly-detailed art style has been influenced by Hal Foster and Alex Raymond. And by his long-time idol, Burne Hogarth. He also greatly admires jacket illustrators like Frank McCarthy and James Bama.

" I like to do illustrations that are alive and full of action and excitement. I like eye-catching detail, too. I like the reader to really get his money's worth."

Watch him keep his promise in up-coming issues.

FRANK FRAZETTA'S Creation

BRADLEY BURKE, of Memphis, Tenn., was so inspired by ROCKGOD, in issue #32, he wrote a poem about it, and dedicated it to Frank Frazetta, Harlan Ellison and Neal Adams. Oddly enough, he calls it . . .

ROCK GOD
by Bradley Burke

The Rock god stood
  before mankind,
Power he had
  to conquer land.
He was worshipped
  long years ago,
By those he needed
  to help him grow.
He needed sleep
  for eras on,
But then the time
  would not be long.
Up he arose
  out of the ground,
The time had come
  up from a mound.

The diamond grew
  now a new life,
A shape came forth
  ending all strife.
People consumed
  a world in him,
End of humans
  the life to dim.
Rockgod did grow
  the world did shrink
Life would soon go
  left on the brink.
All there was left
  was Rockgod alone,
The world in him
  left not a bone.
What would he do
  no one around,
Search the planets
  absorb more ground.
From one planet
  to find more food,
Travel he must
  changing his mood.
Eons would pass,
  he would live on.
Never an end
  undying mass.

NEAL ADAMS' Rendering

JESSICA CLERK, of New York City, says she stayed up all night to write this story. It could have been something she ate. Or the traffic. But she says it was none of those. She blames it on . . .

THE LITTERED TRASHCAN OF HUMANITY, or THE CONTINUING STORY OF WILLIAM AND DOLORES
by Jessica Clerk

It was a dark and stormy night. William squared his shoulders and gazed through the littered trashcan of humanity. It was cold, and he wondered how he was going to get inside. Suddenly, he saw her.

Lit from behind as she was, her hair formed a dark halo. Her dress was torn. The instant he saw her, he fell in love with her. She was beautiful. Too beautiful for him. His meaningless life would be all the more meaningless without her. He must have her.

"She must needs be mine," he thought. But was he, a bum, good enough for her? Suddenly, a new thought illuminated his mind. "We are all in this gutter, but some of us are looking toward the stars." How beautiful.

"Marry me?" he said as he approached her.

"What is this I'm feeling?" The thought ran insanely around—rather than in—her mind. "Why do I feel so strangely compelled to throw myself at his feet?" Could it be that he was making a go for her succulent flesh? She pondered these thoughts in her small, but perky, brain, while outside a tempest raged.

"Cynthia!" he cried as he rushed toward her.

"The name's Dolores," she said icily.

"What does that matter?" William spoke. "A rose is but a name to smell so sweet." That didn't quite tinkle right in his cybernetic senses. But what of it? He was no effete. Besides, the world nor she would never know. "Dolores, then," he said in an amatory tone. There his thoughts ran dry and his throat grew parched as he waited for her to mumble an appropriate reply. He waited a long time.

"William?" At this point, her thoughts ran dry, too. So, as Electra ran about the walls of Troy, she started running around a nearby table in hopes of giving him an idea. It didn't work.

"Dolores," he began again slowly.

"Yes, William?" she said.

"Call me Winifred," he said as he crushed his fervent lips to hers.

"Oh, Winifred," she murmed. (She wasn't as dumb as she looked.)

"Marry me," he whispered as he kissed her ear.

"Oh, yes, Winifred," she squealed with pure delight. (Meanwhile the storm raged all about them.)

Suddenly, a huge bulk was framed in the doorway. A sound of heavy breathing followed. "It is my stepfather," quivered the young and beautiful girl. "He's drunk. He hates me. He'll kill me. He'll brutalize me . . . the brute," she added as an afterthought.

"Fear not, fair Dolores," cried William. But in his own

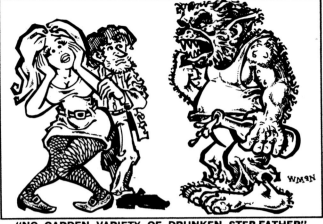

"NO GARDEN VARIETY OF DRUNKEN STEP-FATHER"
Sketch by Winsor McNemo, Cleveland, Ohio

inner mind, he could not believe his words of comfort. He had some odd premonition of danger. For he sensed that this was no ordinary garden-variety mean and drunken stepfather. There was something inordinately evil in his mein. To investigate further, he threw a lighted candle at the man's countenance. In the thin, flickering light, he perceived that this man's face was covered over with hair.

Then, with an alacrity scarcely to be credited, all the facts fell into place:

It was a dark and stormy night. The tempest raged all about them. This guy's face was fantastically covered with hair. Something, or someone, was amiss.

William gathered all the powers at his call, recall and summons. He concentrated all his brain on a single thought: Save Dolores.

On the right lay Dolores, fainting continually—the doctor had warned her about this, but this was clearly no time at all for half-measures. On the left lurked her hairy stepfather, anticipating the lunge. His heavy, panting breath formed an impenetrable cloak about him, which no one in their right mind—and that almost included William—would want to penetrate. North and South were the walls of the alley. Hither & yon were flung the tattered remains of the hairy step-father, thrown a step-farther or two.

"Oh, my dearest, you have shredded him in your teeth!" exclaimed Dolores.

"My darling!" panted William/Winnifred, "I have a confession to make—I am a very long-toothed Vampire, and I haven't had a bite in three days!"

So Dolores bit him.

TED DASEN, of East Lansing, Mich., sent us this little anti-war epic. It's a creepy one called . . .

THE FOOL'S MARCH
by Ted Dasen

The sound is close. The sound is near. TATATATUM . . . TATATATATUM! The sound of the drummer's drum, poetic, beautiful, enchanting. Yet to us it is an insane sound. It is the beat of death. It is surely an insane rhythm. How very true. For that is what each and every one of us patriotic fools march to. A brain-washing, insane rhythm.

It's coming. Slowly. I can sense it. The fog lingers slowly off the morning dew and with each throbbing footstep, I hear and behold the sound of endless gunfire . . . cries of pain . . . booming cannon. Men are tumbling into the earth's crust, fighting their last fight. And yes. Yes, the drum. It's coming. It's getting closer. With each beat, death grows nearer.

Why do we march? Why do we walk to these ungodly hands of death? Who knows? I have **my** reasons. The poor soul next to me has **his** reasons. And, of course, the drummer has his reasons, too.

It is time. Time that we all are to march in our perfectly straight columns for the last time.

Where do we march? We march into battle. We march to our death!

The year? 1776.

Who am I? I am a hero. I am a fool. I am a British soldier.

LISANNE MARDEN, of Pawhuska, Okla., says she doesn't know whether to call this a poem or a story. Whatever it is, she calls it . . .

THE REUNION
by Lisanne Marden

I awoke. Even though in a dazed condition, I realized I was cold. Cold and tired. All I can remember is that the sickness and pain I had felt was now gone. I felt I could move again. I walked down the long dark corridor of death. I felt I was being watched. I turned and saw the glowing eyes of my long-lost love shining upon my face. As we joined in the long-lost greeting, the Children of Darkness howled with joy. For now we would be together. Breeding our own Children of Darkness forever.

PROVE TO US
How talented you are, send your contributions to:

CREEPY FAN CLUB

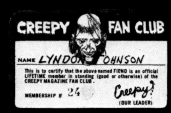

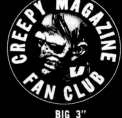

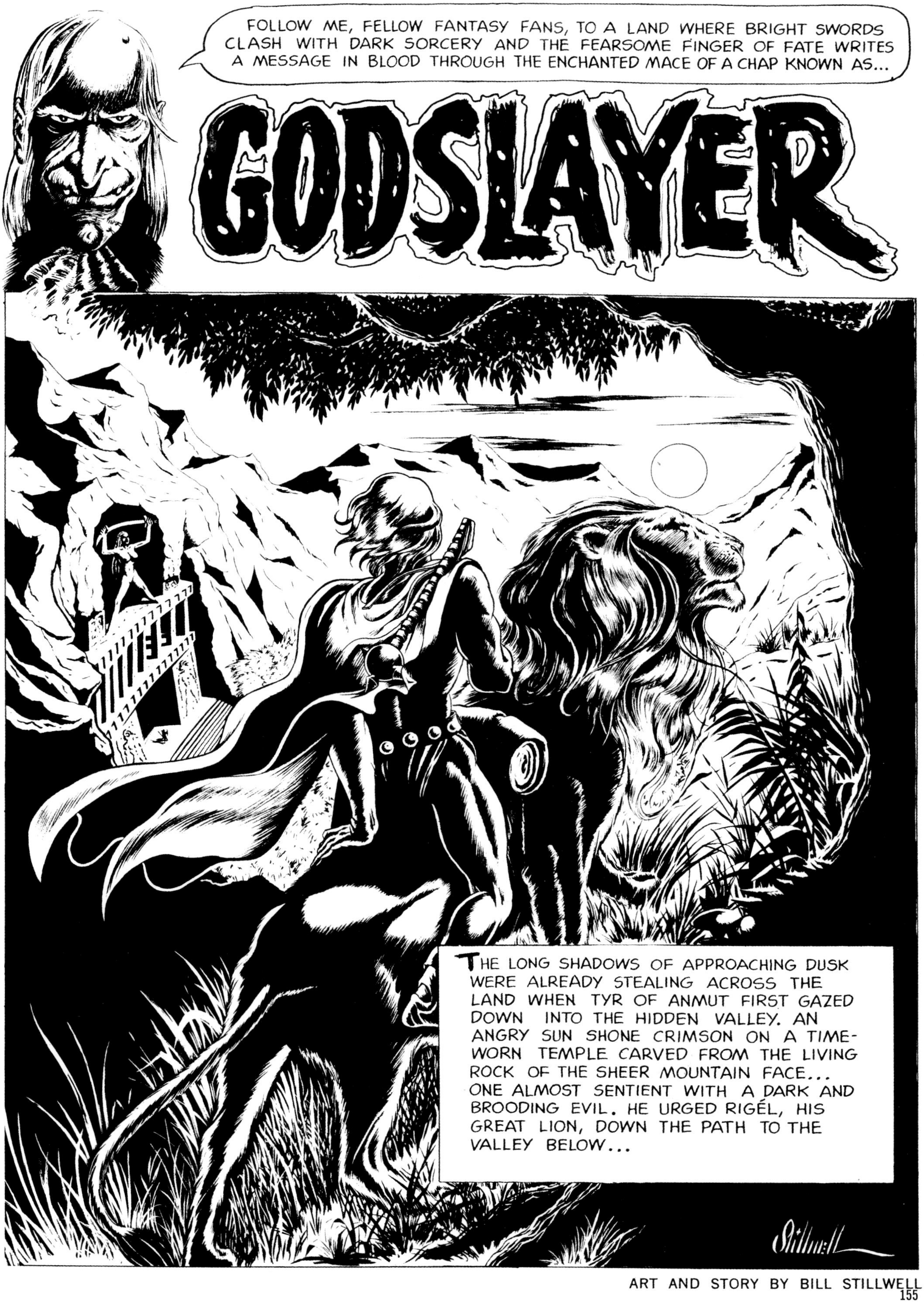
FOLLOW ME, FELLOW FANTASY FANS, TO A LAND WHERE BRIGHT SWORDS CLASH WITH DARK SORCERY AND THE FEARSOME FINGER OF FATE WRITES A MESSAGE IN BLOOD THROUGH THE ENCHANTED MACE OF A CHAP KNOWN AS...
GODSLAYER
THE LONG SHADOWS OF APPROACHING DUSK WERE ALREADY STEALING ACROSS THE LAND WHEN TYR OF ANMUT FIRST GAZED DOWN INTO THE HIDDEN VALLEY. AN ANGRY SUN SHONE CRIMSON ON A TIME-WORN TEMPLE CARVED FROM THE LIVING ROCK OF THE SHEER MOUNTAIN FACE... ONE ALMOST SENTIENT WITH A DARK AND BROODING EVIL. HE URGED RIGÉL, HIS GREAT LION, DOWN THE PATH TO THE VALLEY BELOW...
Stillwell

ART AND STORY BY BILL STILLWELL

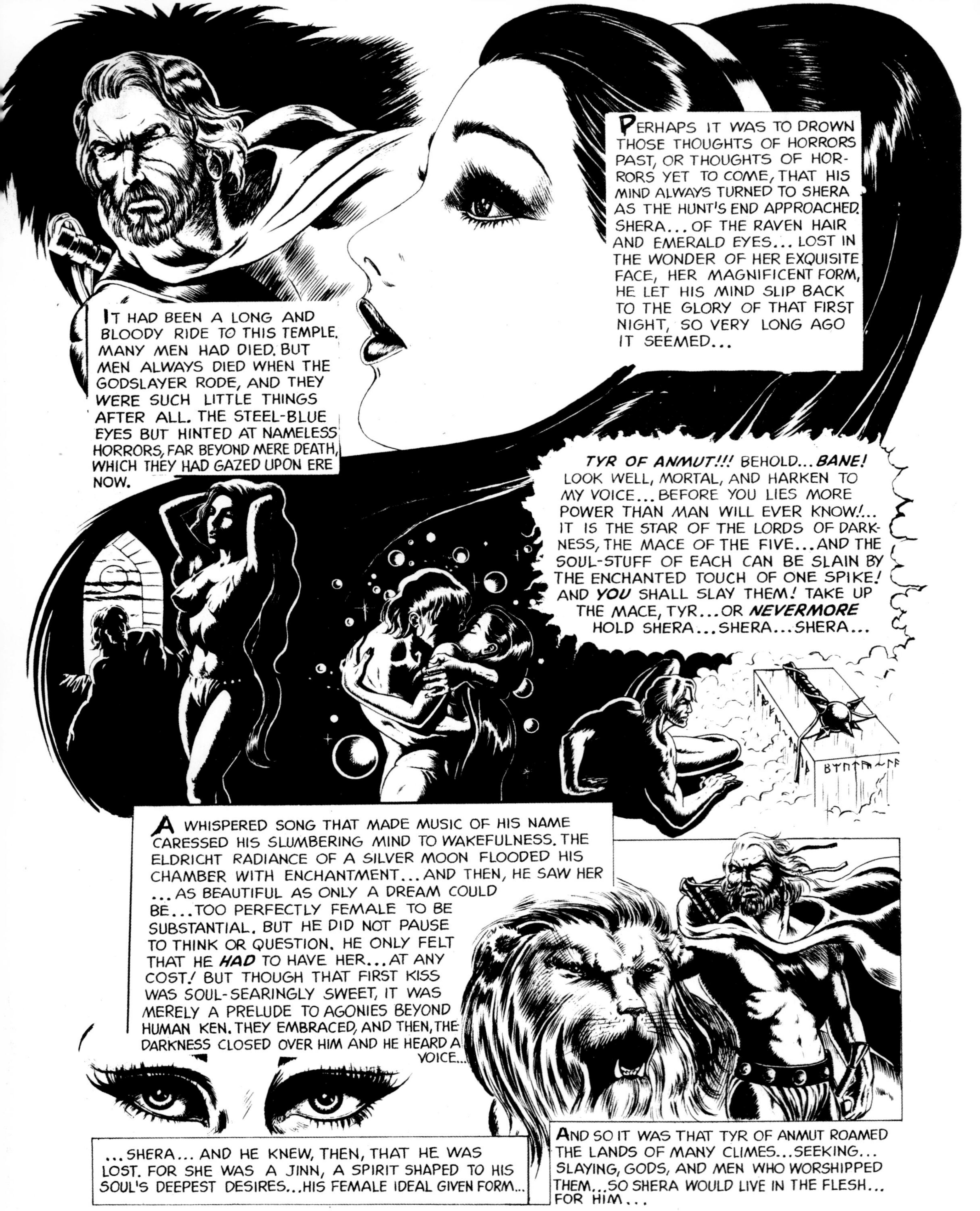
PERHAPS IT WAS TO DROWN THOSE THOUGHTS OF HORRORS PAST, OR THOUGHTS OF HORRORS YET TO COME, THAT HIS MIND ALWAYS TURNED TO SHERA AS THE HUNT'S END APPROACHED. SHERA... OF THE RAVEN HAIR AND EMERALD EYES... LOST IN THE WONDER OF HER EXQUISITE FACE, HER MAGNIFICENT FORM, HE LET HIS MIND SLIP BACK TO THE GLORY OF THAT FIRST NIGHT, SO VERY LONG AGO IT SEEMED...
IT HAD BEEN A LONG AND BLOODY RIDE TO THIS TEMPLE. MANY MEN HAD DIED. BUT MEN ALWAYS DIED WHEN THE GODSLAYER RODE, AND THEY WERE SUCH LITTLE THINGS AFTER ALL. THE STEEL-BLUE EYES BUT HINTED AT NAMELESS HORRORS, FAR BEYOND MERE DEATH, WHICH THEY HAD GAZED UPON ERE NOW.
TYR OF ANMUT!!! BEHOLD... ***BANE!*** LOOK WELL, MORTAL, AND HARKEN TO MY VOICE... BEFORE YOU LIES MORE POWER THAN MAN WILL EVER KNOW!... IT IS THE STAR OF THE LORDS OF DARKNESS, THE MACE OF THE FIVE... AND THE SOUL-STUFF OF EACH CAN BE SLAIN BY THE ENCHANTED TOUCH OF ONE SPIKE! AND ***YOU*** SHALL SLAY THEM! TAKE UP THE MACE, TYR... OR ***NEVERMORE*** HOLD SHERA... SHERA... SHERA...
A WHISPERED SONG THAT MADE MUSIC OF HIS NAME CARESSED HIS SLUMBERING MIND TO WAKEFULNESS. THE ELDRICHT RADIANCE OF A SILVER MOON FLOODED HIS CHAMBER WITH ENCHANTMENT... AND THEN, HE SAW HER ... AS BEAUTIFUL AS ONLY A DREAM COULD BE... TOO PERFECTLY FEMALE TO BE SUBSTANTIAL. BUT HE DID NOT PAUSE TO THINK OR QUESTION. HE ONLY FELT THAT HE ***HAD*** TO HAVE HER... AT ANY COST! BUT THOUGH THAT FIRST KISS WAS SOUL-SEARINGLY SWEET, IT WAS MERELY A PRELUDE TO AGONIES BEYOND HUMAN KEN. THEY EMBRACED, AND THEN, THE DARKNESS CLOSED OVER HIM AND HE HEARD A VOICE...
... SHERA... AND HE KNEW, THEN, THAT HE WAS LOST. FOR SHE WAS A JINN, A SPIRIT SHAPED TO HIS SOUL'S DEEPEST DESIRES... HIS FEMALE IDEAL GIVEN FORM...
AND SO IT WAS THAT TYR OF ANMUT ROAMED THE LANDS OF MANY CLIMES... SEEKING... SLAYING, GODS, AND MEN WHO WORSHIPPED THEM... SO SHERA WOULD LIVE IN THE FLESH... FOR HIM...

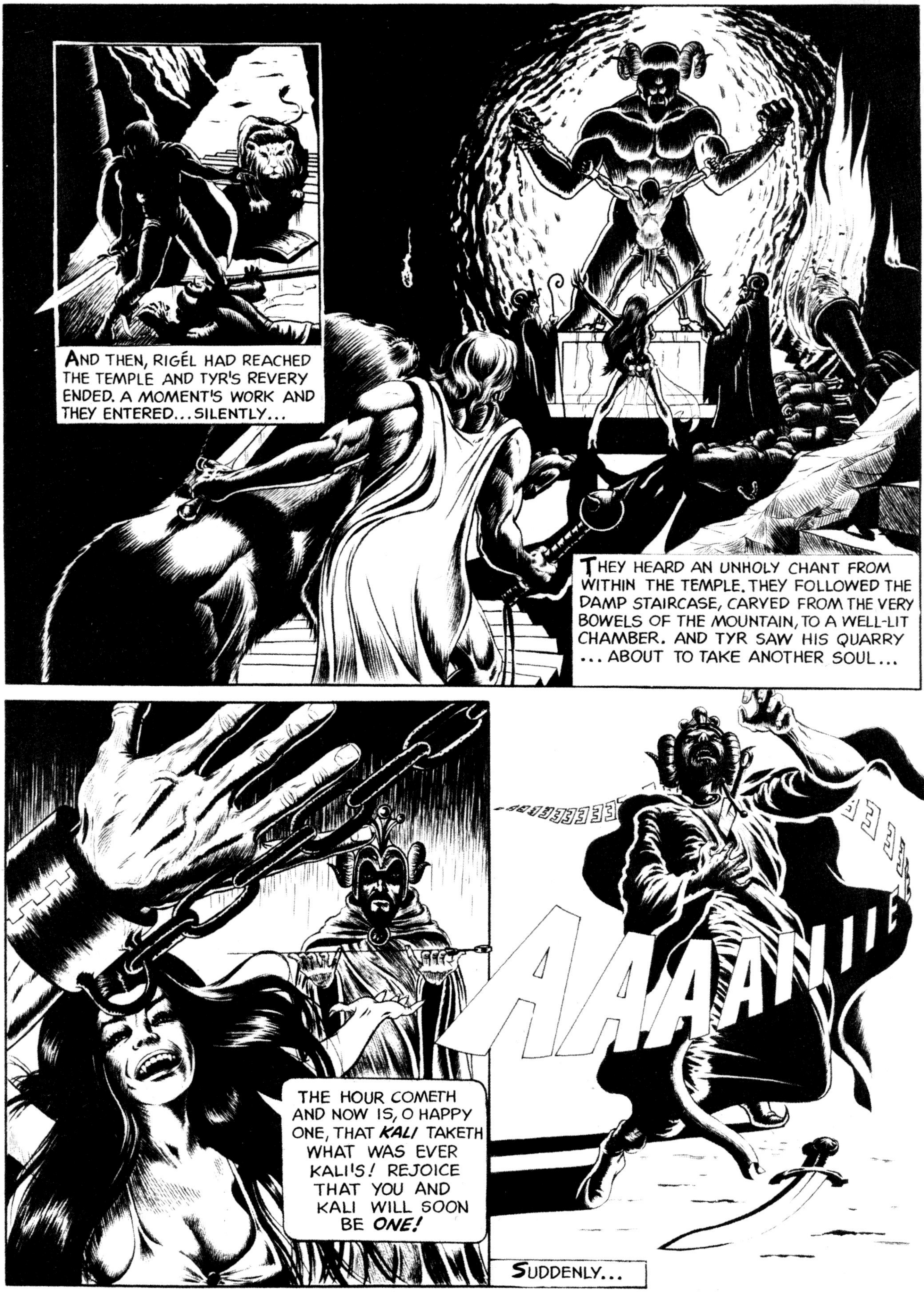
AND THEN, RIGÉL HAD REACHED THE TEMPLE AND TYR'S REVERY ENDED. A MOMENT'S WORK AND THEY ENTERED... SILENTLY...
THEY HEARD AN UNHOLY CHANT FROM WITHIN THE TEMPLE. THEY FOLLOWED THE DAMP STAIRCASE, CARVED FROM THE VERY BOWELS OF THE MOUNTAIN, TO A WELL-LIT CHAMBER. AND TYR SAW HIS QUARRY ... ABOUT TO TAKE ANOTHER SOUL...
THE HOUR COMETH AND NOW IS, O HAPPY ONE, THAT KALI TAKETH WHAT WAS EVER KALI'S! REJOICE THAT YOU AND KALI WILL SOON BE ONE!
SUDDENLY...

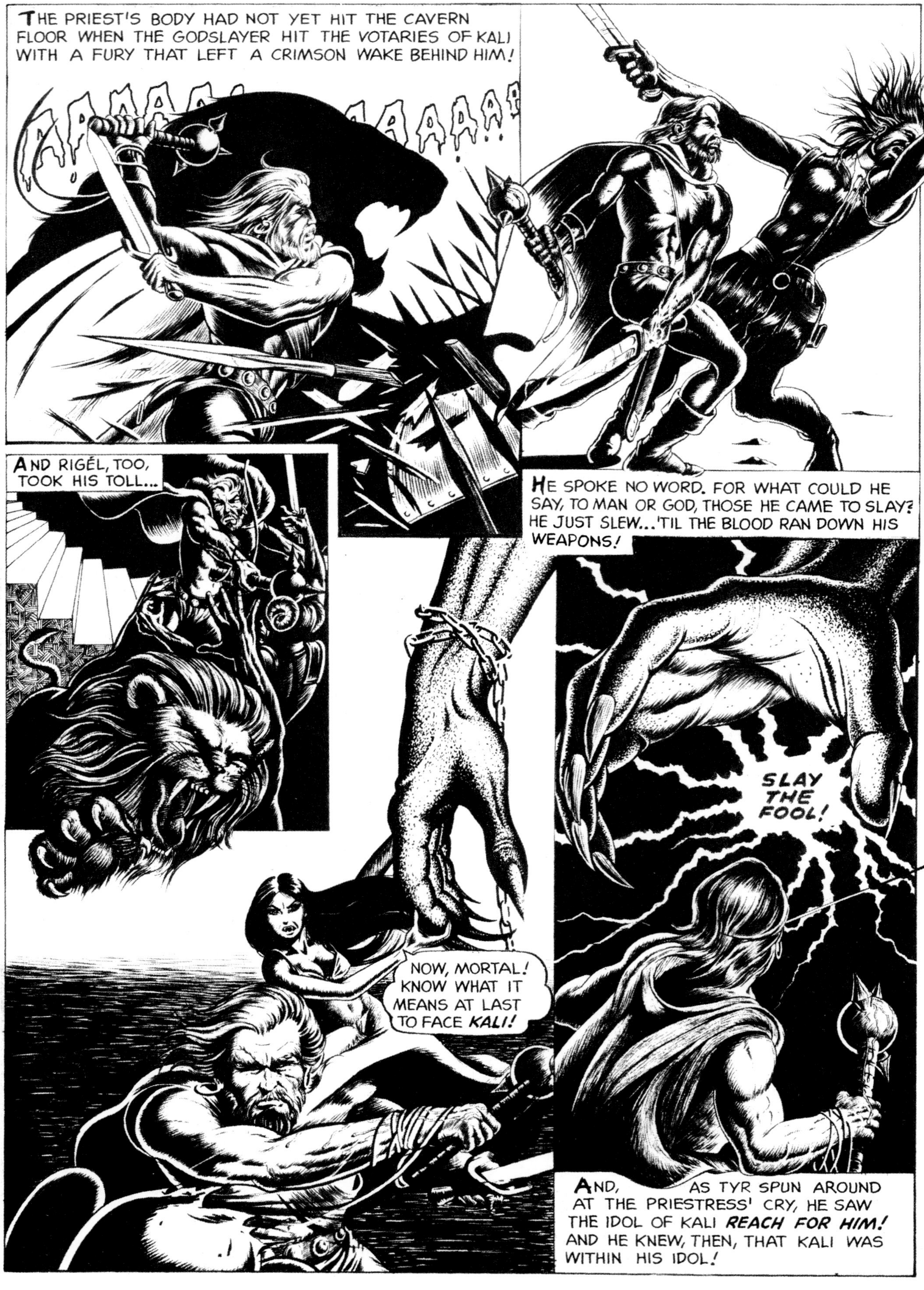
THE PRIEST'S BODY HAD NOT YET HIT THE CAVERN FLOOR WHEN THE GODSLAYER HIT THE VOTARIES OF KALI WITH A FURY THAT LEFT A CRIMSON WAKE BEHIND HIM!
AND RIGÉL, TOO, TOOK HIS TOLL...
HE SPOKE NO WORD. FOR WHAT COULD HE SAY, TO MAN OR GOD, THOSE HE CAME TO SLAY? HE JUST SLEW...'TIL THE BLOOD RAN DOWN HIS WEAPONS!
SLAY THE FOOL!
NOW, MORTAL! KNOW WHAT IT MEANS AT LAST TO FACE KALI!
AND, AS TYR SPUN AROUND AT THE PRIESTRESS' CRY, HE SAW THE IDOL OF KALI REACH FOR HIM! AND HE KNEW, THEN, THAT KALI WAS WITHIN HIS IDOL!

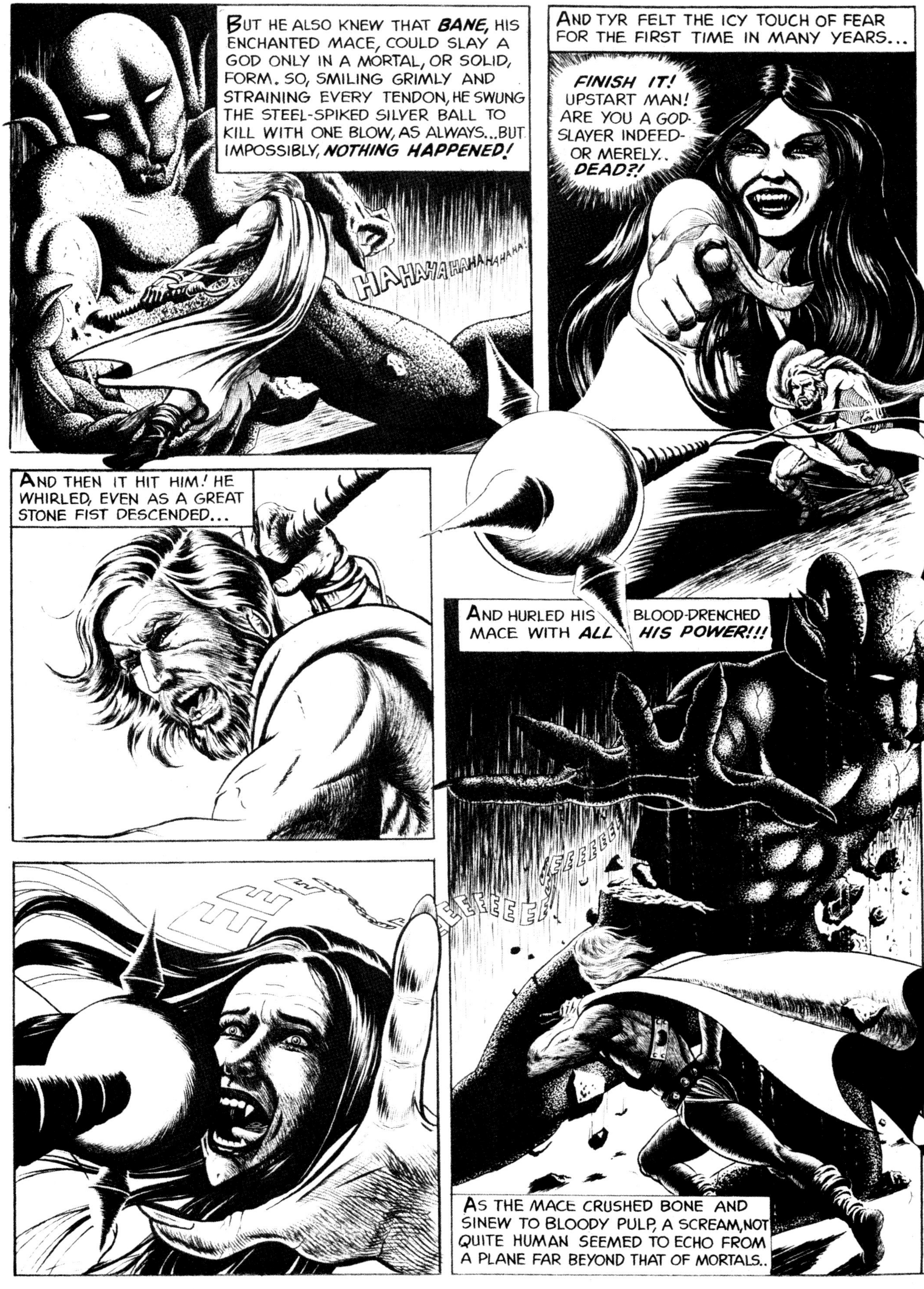
BUT HE ALSO KNEW THAT BANE, HIS ENCHANTED MACE, COULD SLAY A GOD ONLY IN A MORTAL, OR SOLID, FORM. SO, SMILING GRIMLY AND STRAINING EVERY TENDON, HE SWUNG THE STEEL-SPIKED SILVER BALL TO KILL WITH ONE BLOW, AS ALWAYS...BUT IMPOSSIBLY, NOTHING HAPPENED!
HAHAHAHAHAHAHAHAHA!
AND TYR FELT THE ICY TOUCH OF FEAR FOR THE FIRST TIME IN MANY YEARS...
FINISH IT! UPSTART MAN! ARE YOU A GOD-SLAYER INDEED- OR MERELY.. DEAD?!
AND THEN IT HIT HIM! HE WHIRLED, EVEN AS A GREAT STONE FIST DESCENDED...
AND HURLED HIS BLOOD-DRENCHED MACE WITH ALL HIS POWER!!!
EEEEEEEEEEE
AS THE MACE CRUSHED BONE AND SINEW TO BLOODY PULP, A SCREAM, NOT QUITE HUMAN SEEMED TO ECHO FROM A PLANE FAR BEYOND THAT OF MORTALS..

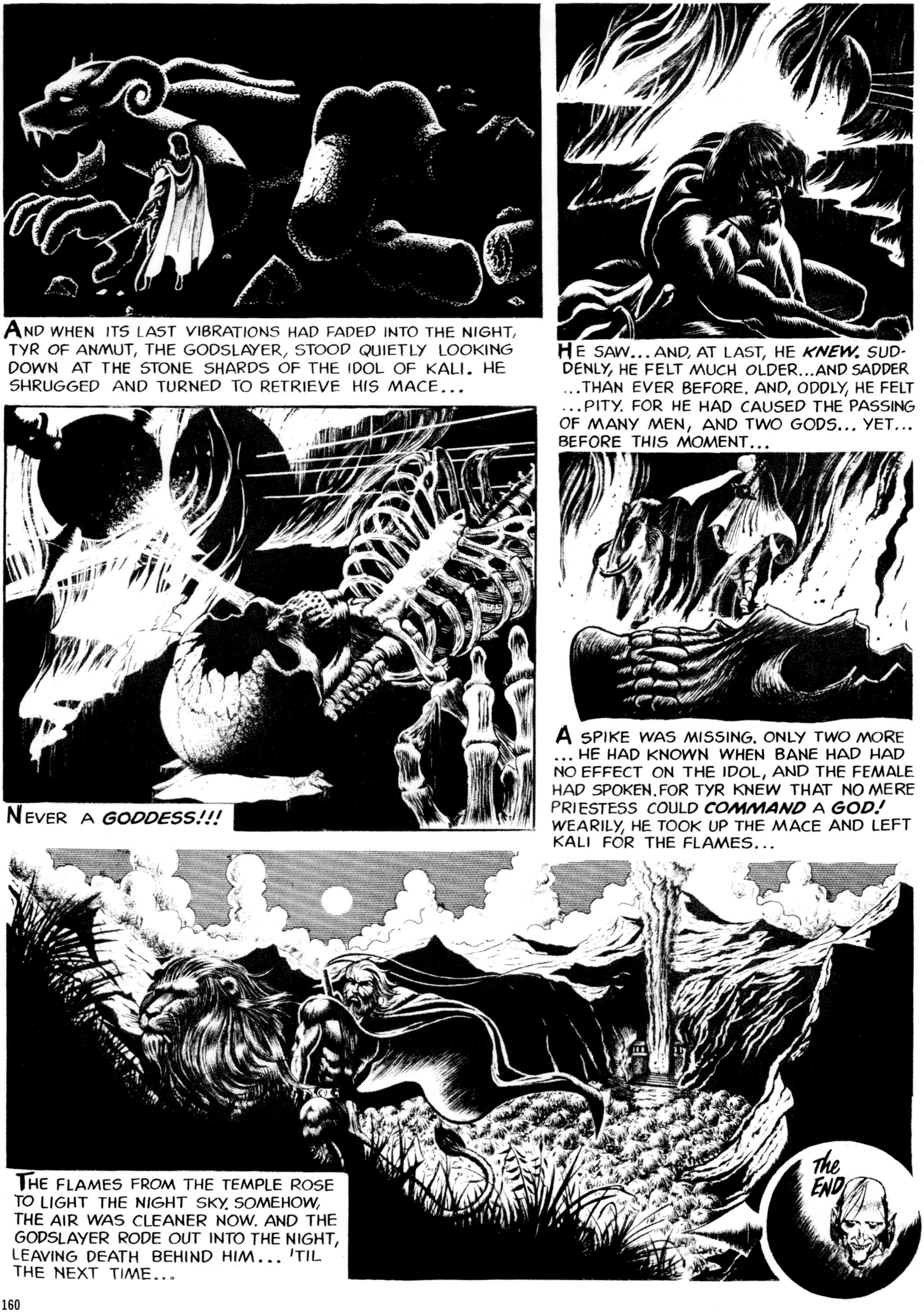
AND WHEN ITS LAST VIBRATIONS HAD FADED INTO THE NIGHT, TYR OF ANMUT, THE GODSLAYER, STOOD QUIETLY LOOKING DOWN AT THE STONE SHARDS OF THE IDOL OF KALI. HE SHRUGGED AND TURNED TO RETRIEVE HIS MACE...
HE SAW... AND, AT LAST, HE *KNEW.* SUDDENLY, HE FELT MUCH OLDER... AND SADDER ...THAN EVER BEFORE. AND, ODDLY, HE FELT ...PITY. FOR HE HAD CAUSED THE PASSING OF MANY MEN, AND TWO GODS... YET... BEFORE THIS MOMENT...
NEVER A ***GODDESS!!!***
A SPIKE WAS MISSING. ONLY TWO MORE ... HE HAD KNOWN WHEN BANE HAD HAD NO EFFECT ON THE IDOL, AND THE FEMALE HAD SPOKEN. FOR TYR KNEW THAT NO MERE PRIESTESS COULD ***COMMAND*** A ***GOD!*** WEARILY, HE TOOK UP THE MACE AND LEFT KALI FOR THE FLAMES...
THE FLAMES FROM THE TEMPLE ROSE TO LIGHT THE NIGHT SKY. SOMEHOW, THE AIR WAS CLEANER NOW. AND THE GODSLAYER RODE OUT INTO THE NIGHT, LEAVING DEATH BEHIND HIM... 'TIL THE NEXT TIME...
The END

SUPER SPECIAL EXCITING PAPERBACK BOOKS!

THE FIEND IN YOU

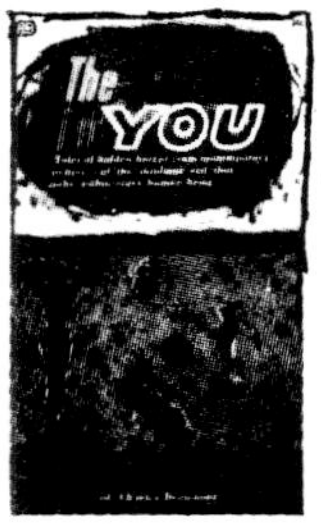
The
YOU

In the long reaches of the night, have you ever cringed in a knot, curdled with terror at something remembered, something, you nearly did, or wanted to do? All roots of abysmal terror and monstrous evil lie in the human mind . . . and this is the fiend in you.

THE INVISIBLE MAN

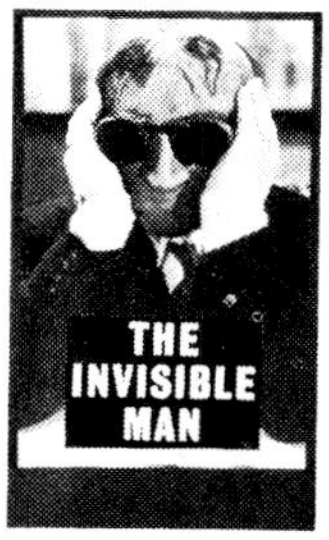
THE
INVISIBLE
MAN

WHO IS THIS Invisible Man who walks into an inn in England and throws fear into the hearts of everyone? Is he a spy, a criminal, a mad scientist, or what? Why is he wrapped in gruesome gauze from head to toe? The answers to these questions, in this horror book by H. G. Wells, make it one of the all-time classics.

THE GHOUL KEEPERS

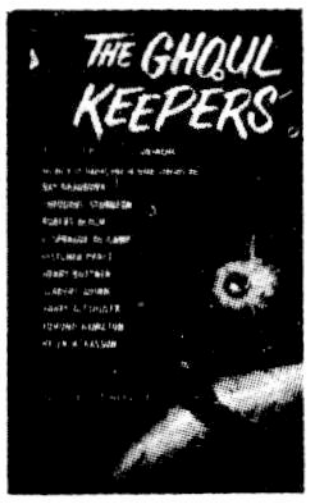
THE GHOUL
KEEPERS

who knows—
how to catch a vampire?
the thing ghosts want most?
how to really saw a woman in half?
what evil lurks in the hearts of men?
The Ghoul Keepsers know and so will you, when you read this collection of nine stories.

VOYAGE TO THE BOTTOM OF THE SEA

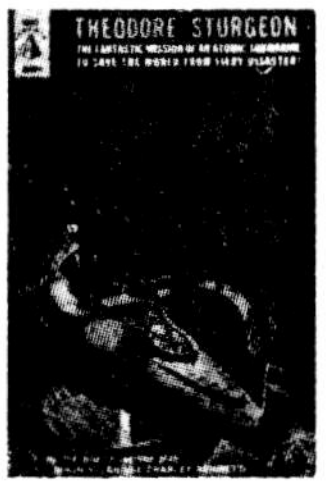
THEODORE STURGEON

The Captain . . . would he meet the test!
The Fanatic . . . why did he hope the world would end!
A mighty epic of undersea adventure, the giant atomic submarine probes the ocean deeps, fights sea monsters and will introduce you to the fabulous world beneath the surface of the sea.

BURN WITCH BURN

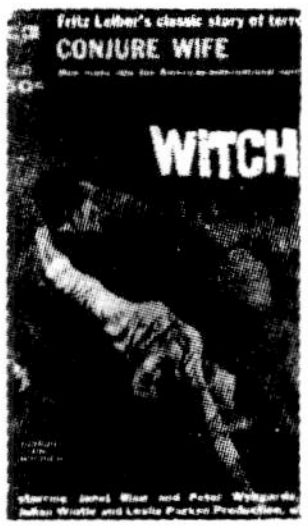
CONJURE WIFE
WITCH

Witchcraft in the 20th Century. Norman Taylor thought it was absurd for his beautiful wife, Tansy to believe in black magic. He made her throw her potions, charms, amulets into the fire. Then his troubles began. Easily the most frightening and the most convincing of all modern horror stories.

PICTURE of DORIAN GRAY

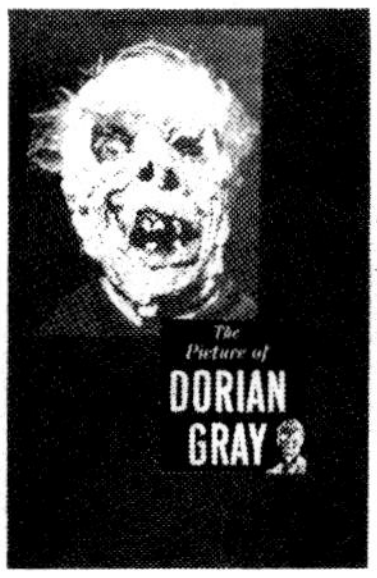
The
Picture of
DORIAN
GRAY

CAN IT HAPPEN? Can a "man of crime" stay young and handsome for years, while a portrait of him grows old and hideous? Oscar Wilde said it could. This supernatural classic combines eternal youth, crime and degeneracy and the moral that criminal acts will show up, even in your oil portrait A wierd, unusual book that will live forever as tops in horror.

GRAVEYARD READER

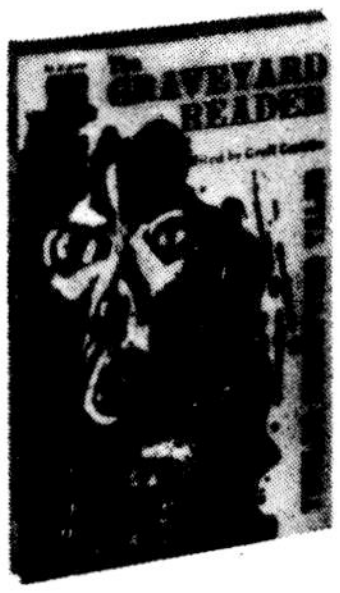
The
GRAVEYARD
READER

Contains 12 of the most frightening short stories ever put together in one book, by H. P. Lovecraft, Henry Kuttner, Charles Beaumont, Ray Bradbury and other greats. Apparitions, ghosts and weird manifestations calculated to paralyze the reader.

THINGS WITH CLAWS

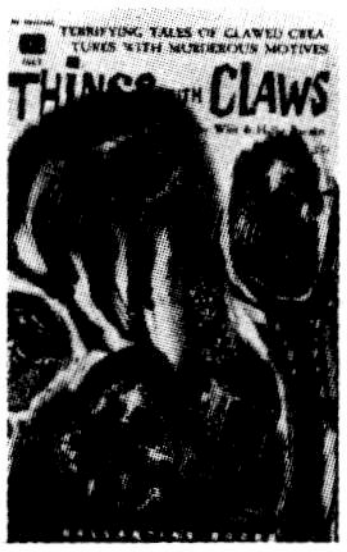
TERRIFYING TALES OF CLAWED CREATURES WITH MURDEROUS MOTIVES
THINGS with CLAWS

Here's one we could not put down until the last page was read! An absolutely fascinating collection of stories having to do with "clawed creatures with murderous motives." Truly terrifying tales of worlds we dream about but wouldn't want to visit—and the creatures that inhabit these dream worlds!

MEN WITHOUT BONES

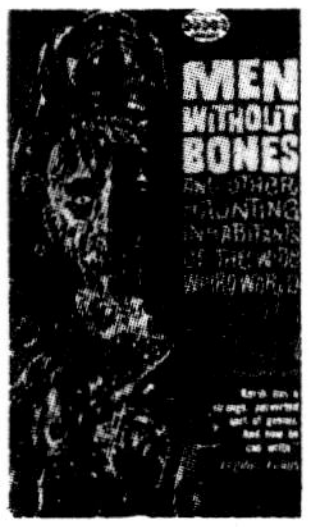
MEN
WITHOUT
BONES

Venture into this alarmingly convincing world of Gerald Kersh. Meet the horse whose stubborness changed history, or the murderer who confessed and confessed and confessed. Learn, too the secret of the Mona Lisa's smile or ponder, if you will, the case of Simple Simon, who lost the only important thing he had.

THE WAR of the WORLDS

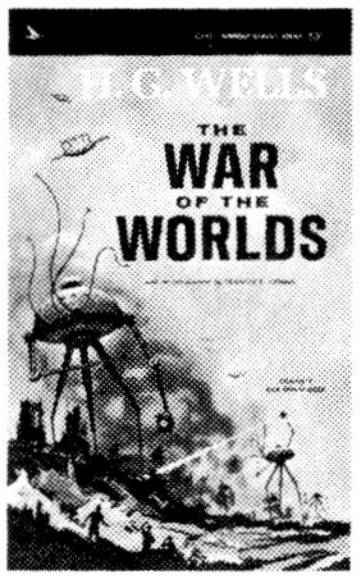
H. G. WELLS
THE
WAR
OF THE
WORLDS

YEARS BEFORE man's conquest of space, H. G. Wells wrote The War of the Worlds. Eerily describes the fight between Earth & Mars. Combines astronomy, space ships and gruesome characters descending on England. A classic horror book.

THE UNEXPECTED

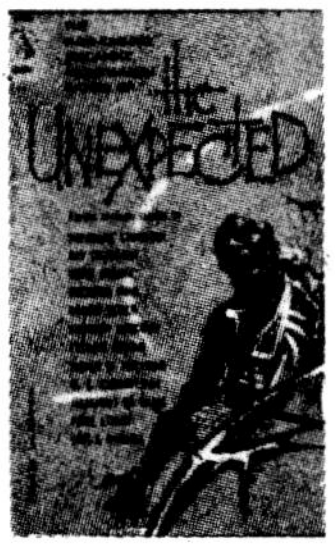
the
UNEXPECTED

Did you ever wonder what hobbies an undertaker has? What it could cost to become the richest man in the world? It's all here in 11 chilling stories. The monsters and hexes, grim demons and gay. Cute fiends at horrible play—some cheerful, some scary . . .

LOVE & HORROR

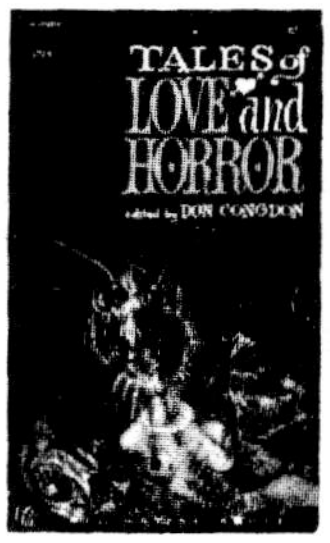
TALES of
LOVE and
HORROR
edited by DON CONGDON

A magnificent collection of horror stories to chill the grisly in heart. Edited by Don Congdon, this paperback is one of the best in the Ballantine CHAMBER OF HORROR SERIES. If you liked SARDONICUS—you'll love this one!

SOME OF YOUR BLOOD

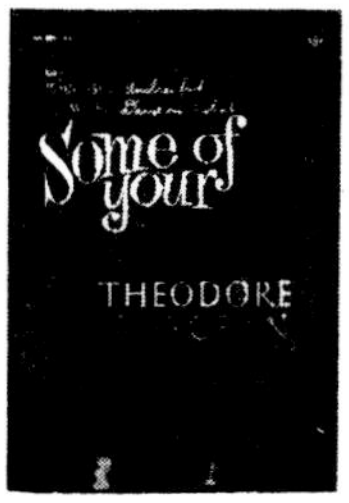
Some of
your
THEODORE

Another great modern horror story by Theodore Sturgeon - one of the most exciting authors of the terrible tale. Here is a short horror novel that reaches a haunting intensity. A brilliant novel of modern times that will play fantastic tricks with your imagination. The best from the master of fantasy!

DR. JEKYLL & MR. HYDE

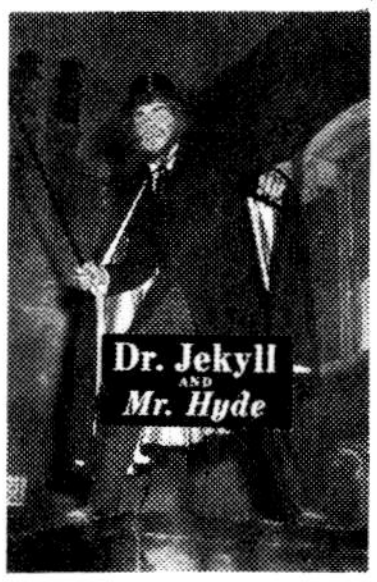
Dr. Jekyll
AND
Mr. Hyde

STEVENSON WROTE this famous book while locked in a room right after a horrible nightmare. It reflects the mysterious, peculiar forces that sometimes make a man into a monster. Fans of horror books will relish the original version by Robert Louis Stevenson. Terror, crime, madness and supernatural things all combined in a very famous classic.

TALES TO BE TOLD IN THE DARK

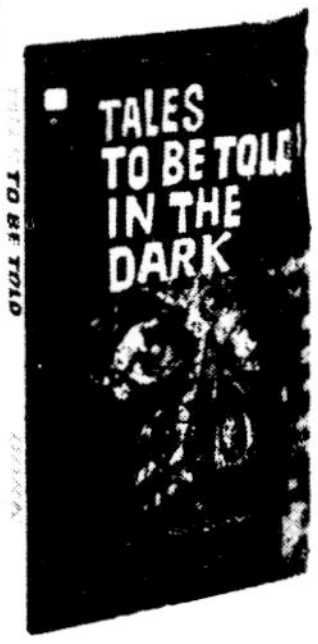
TALES
TO BE TOLD
IN THE
DARK

Do you have a secret desire to chill blood, tingle spines? Here are ten stories by the masters of horror, with hints by the editor on reading them aloud to your own circle. You'll be the life of the wake.

MORE NIGHTMARES

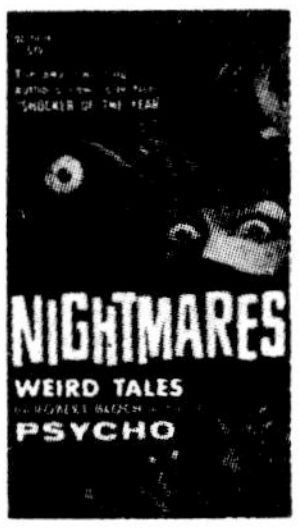
NIGHTMARES
WEIRD TALES
PSYCHO

"FEAR exists. It lurks in the shadows of a lonely night; in the untenanted house and the tenanted tomb; it is at home in all the dark places, including those of the human mind and there are times when we must admit its pressing presence, acknowledge its existence in order to make our own more bearable. It forms the basis of all my work . . .

ANY 2 BOOKS	ANY 3 BOOKS	ANY 4 BOOKS	ANY 5 BOOKS	PLEASE ADD 15¢ PER BOOK FOR POSTAGE & HANDLING
$1.00	$1.50	$2.00	$2.50	

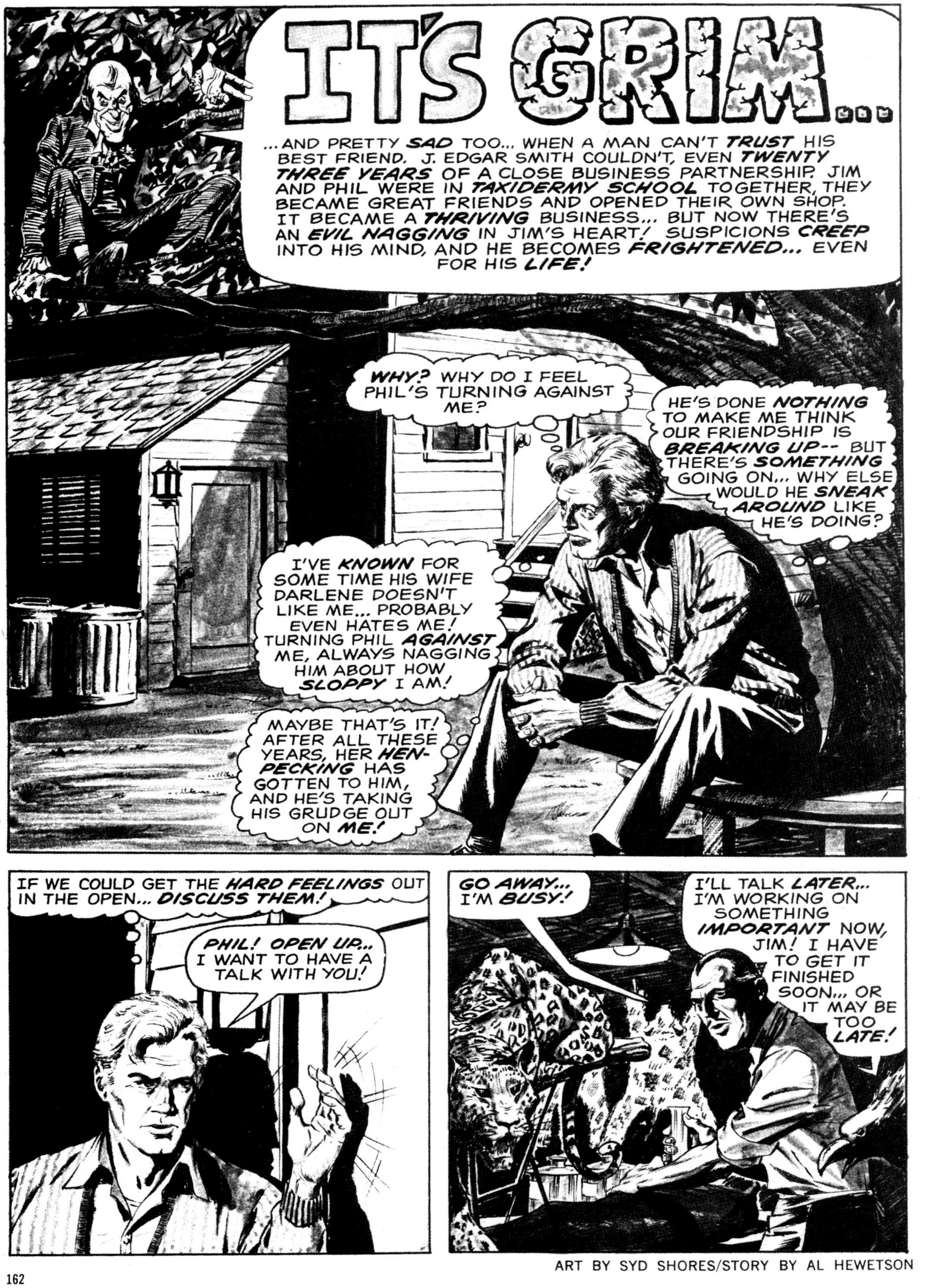
IT'S GRIM...
...AND PRETTY SAD TOO... WHEN A MAN CAN'T TRUST HIS BEST FRIEND. J. EDGAR SMITH COULDN'T, EVEN TWENTY THREE YEARS OF A CLOSE BUSINESS PARTNERSHIP. JIM AND PHIL WERE IN TAXIDERMY SCHOOL TOGETHER, THEY BECAME GREAT FRIENDS AND OPENED THEIR OWN SHOP. IT BECAME A THRIVING BUSINESS... BUT NOW THERE'S AN EVIL NAGGING IN JIM'S HEART! SUSPICIONS CREEP INTO HIS MIND, AND HE BECOMES FRIGHTENED... EVEN FOR HIS LIFE!
WHY? WHY DO I FEEL PHIL'S TURNING AGAINST ME?
HE'S DONE NOTHING TO MAKE ME THINK OUR FRIENDSHIP IS BREAKING UP-- BUT THERE'S SOMETHING GOING ON... WHY ELSE WOULD HE SNEAK AROUND LIKE HE'S DOING?
I'VE KNOWN FOR SOME TIME HIS WIFE DARLENE DOESN'T LIKE ME... PROBABLY EVEN HATES ME! TURNING PHIL AGAINST ME, ALWAYS NAGGING HIM ABOUT HOW SLOPPY I AM!
MAYBE THAT'S IT! AFTER ALL THESE YEARS, HER HEN-PECKING HAS GOTTEN TO HIM, AND HE'S TAKING HIS GRUDGE OUT ON ME!
IF WE COULD GET THE HARD FEELINGS OUT IN THE OPEN... DISCUSS THEM!
PHIL! OPEN UP... I WANT TO HAVE A TALK WITH YOU!
GO AWAY... I'M BUSY!
I'LL TALK LATER... I'M WORKING ON SOMETHING IMPORTANT NOW, JIM! I HAVE TO GET IT FINISHED SOON... OR IT MAY BE TOO LATE!

ART BY SYD SHORES/STORY BY AL HEWETSON

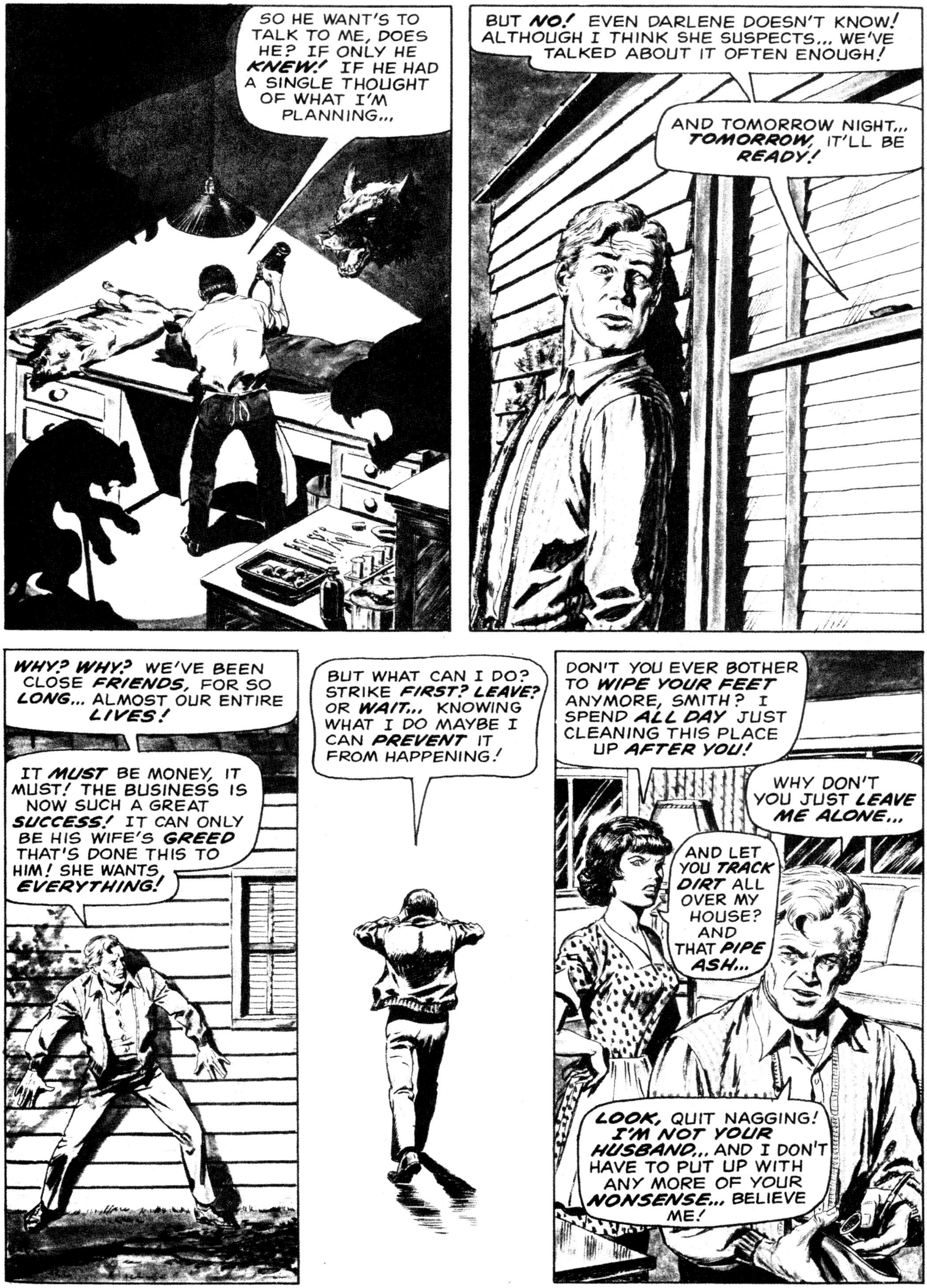
SO HE WANT'S TO TALK TO ME, DOES HE? IF ONLY HE KNEW! IF HE HAD A SINGLE THOUGHT OF WHAT I'M PLANNING...
BUT NO! EVEN DARLENE DOESN'T KNOW! ALTHOUGH I THINK SHE SUSPECTS... WE'VE TALKED ABOUT IT OFTEN ENOUGH!
AND TOMORROW NIGHT... TOMORROW, IT'LL BE READY!
WHY? WHY? WE'VE BEEN CLOSE FRIENDS, FOR SO LONG... ALMOST OUR ENTIRE LIVES!
IT MUST BE MONEY, IT MUST! THE BUSINESS IS NOW SUCH A GREAT SUCCESS! IT CAN ONLY BE HIS WIFE'S GREED THAT'S DONE THIS TO HIM! SHE WANTS EVERYTHING!
BUT WHAT CAN I DO? STRIKE FIRST? LEAVE? OR WAIT... KNOWING WHAT I DO MAYBE I CAN PREVENT IT FROM HAPPENING!
DON'T YOU EVER BOTHER TO WIPE YOUR FEET ANYMORE, SMITH? I SPEND ALL DAY JUST CLEANING THIS PLACE UP AFTER YOU!
WHY DON'T YOU JUST LEAVE ME ALONE...
AND LET YOU TRACK DIRT ALL OVER MY HOUSE? AND THAT PIPE ASH...
LOOK, QUIT NAGGING! I'M NOT YOUR HUSBAND... AND I DON'T HAVE TO PUT UP WITH ANY MORE OF YOUR NONSENSE... BELIEVE ME!

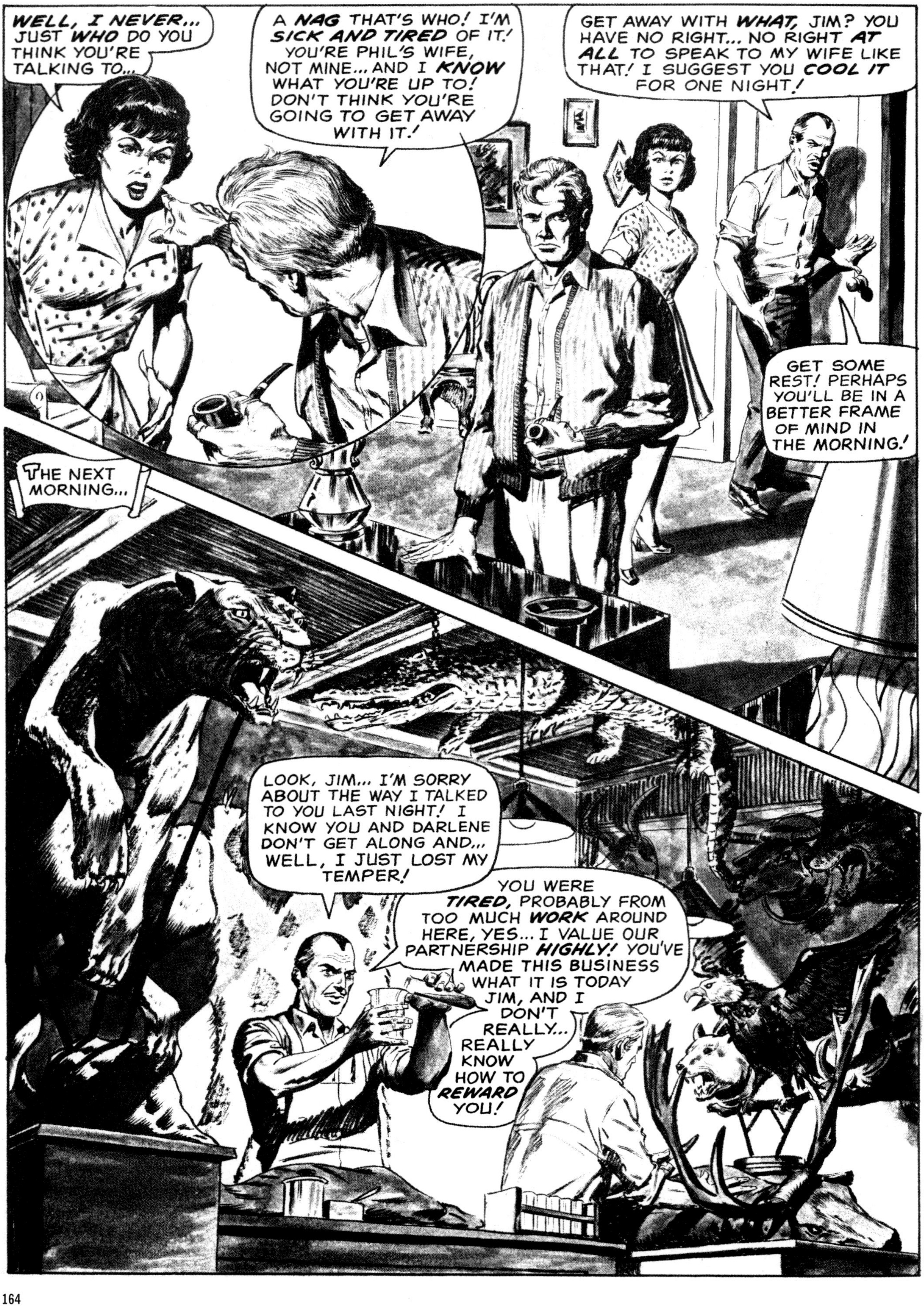
WELL, I NEVER... JUST WHO DO YOU THINK YOU'RE TALKING TO...
A NAG THAT'S WHO! I'M SICK AND TIRED OF IT! YOU'RE PHIL'S WIFE, NOT MINE... AND I KNOW WHAT YOU'RE UP TO! DON'T THINK YOU'RE GOING TO GET AWAY WITH IT!
GET AWAY WITH WHAT, JIM? YOU HAVE NO RIGHT... NO RIGHT AT ALL TO SPEAK TO MY WIFE LIKE THAT! I SUGGEST YOU COOL IT FOR ONE NIGHT!
GET SOME REST! PERHAPS YOU'LL BE IN A BETTER FRAME OF MIND IN THE MORNING!
THE NEXT MORNING...
LOOK, JIM... I'M SORRY ABOUT THE WAY I TALKED TO YOU LAST NIGHT! I KNOW YOU AND DARLENE DON'T GET ALONG AND... WELL, I JUST LOST MY TEMPER!
YOU WERE TIRED, PROBABLY FROM TOO MUCH WORK AROUND HERE, YES... I VALUE OUR PARTNERSHIP HIGHLY! YOU'VE MADE THIS BUSINESS WHAT IT IS TODAY JIM, AND I DON'T REALLY... REALLY KNOW HOW TO REWARD YOU!

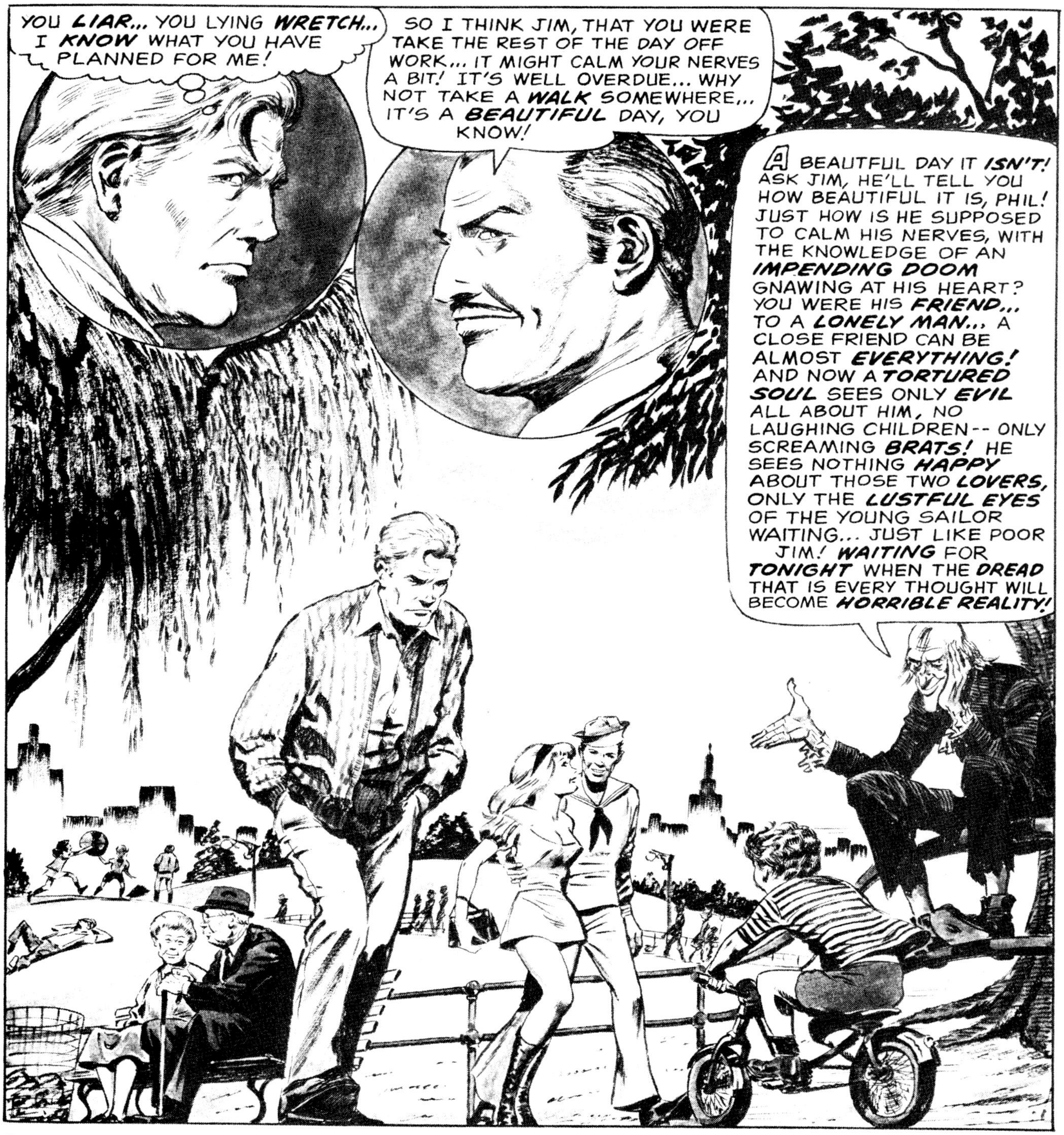
YOU LIAR... YOU LYING WRETCH... I KNOW WHAT YOU HAVE PLANNED FOR ME!
SO I THINK JIM, THAT YOU WERE TAKE THE REST OF THE DAY OFF WORK... IT MIGHT CALM YOUR NERVES A BIT! IT'S WELL OVERDUE... WHY NOT TAKE A WALK SOMEWHERE... IT'S A BEAUTIFUL DAY, YOU KNOW!
A BEAUTIFUL DAY IT ISN'T! ASK JIM, HE'LL TELL YOU HOW BEAUTIFUL IT IS, PHIL! JUST HOW IS HE SUPPOSED TO CALM HIS NERVES, WITH THE KNOWLEDGE OF AN IMPENDING DOOM GNAWING AT HIS HEART? YOU WERE HIS FRIEND... TO A LONELY MAN... A CLOSE FRIEND CAN BE ALMOST EVERYTHING! AND NOW A TORTURED SOUL SEES ONLY EVIL ALL ABOUT HIM, NO LAUGHING CHILDREN-- ONLY SCREAMING BRATS! HE SEES NOTHING HAPPY ABOUT THOSE TWO LOVERS, ONLY THE LUSTFUL EYES OF THE YOUNG SAILOR WAITING... JUST LIKE POOR JIM! WAITING FOR TONIGHT WHEN THE DREAD THAT IS EVERY THOUGHT WILL BECOME HORRIBLE REALITY!

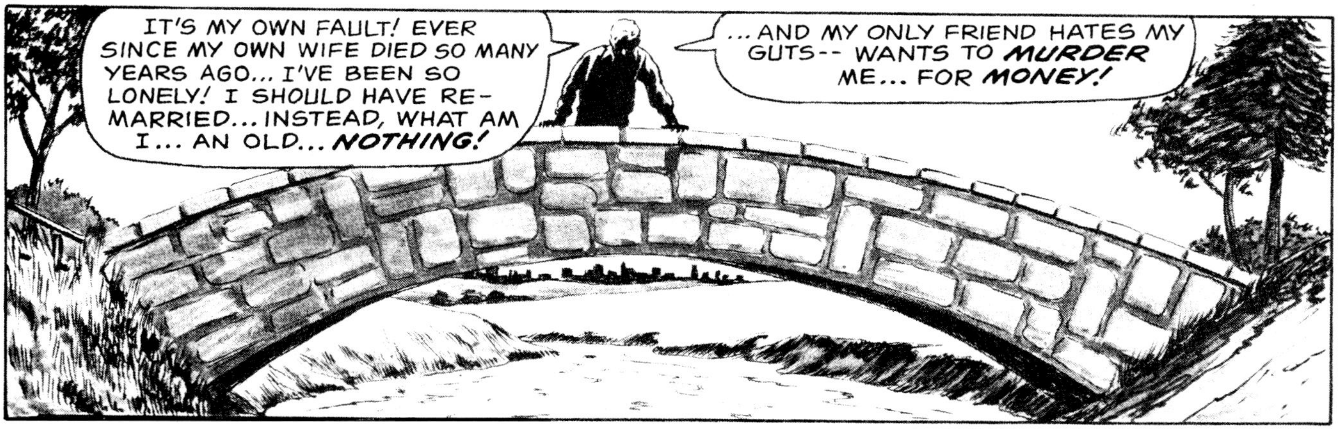
IT'S MY OWN FAULT! EVER SINCE MY OWN WIFE DIED SO MANY YEARS AGO... I'VE BEEN SO LONELY! I SHOULD HAVE RE-MARRIED... INSTEAD, WHAT AM I... AN OLD... NOTHING!
...AND MY ONLY FRIEND HATES MY GUTS-- WANTS TO MURDER ME... FOR MONEY!

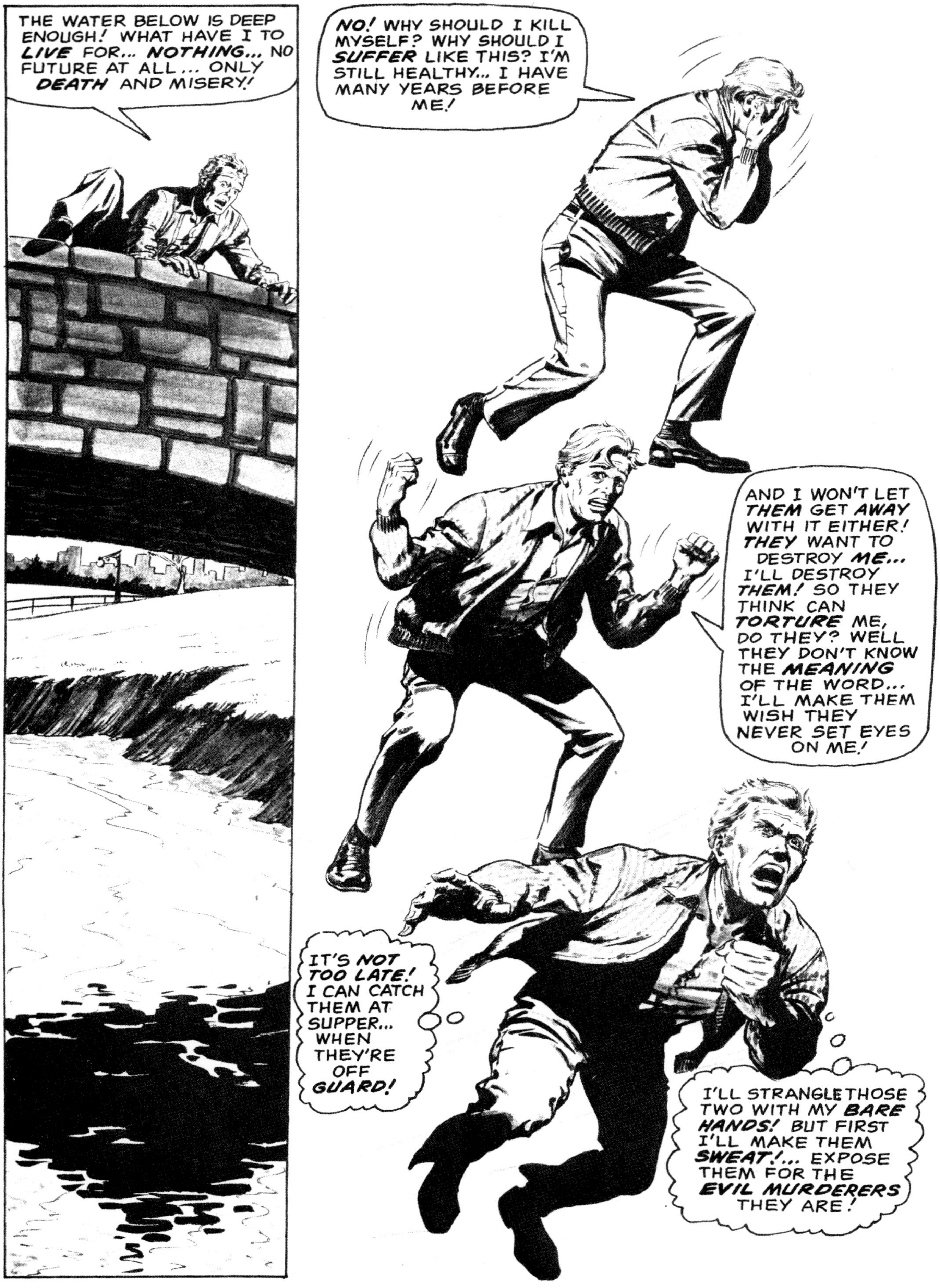
THE WATER BELOW IS DEEP ENOUGH! WHAT HAVE I TO LIVE FOR... NOTHING... NO FUTURE AT ALL... ONLY DEATH AND MISERY!
NO! WHY SHOULD I KILL MYSELF? WHY SHOULD I SUFFER LIKE THIS? I'M STILL HEALTHY... I HAVE MANY YEARS BEFORE ME!
AND I WON'T LET THEM GET AWAY WITH IT EITHER! THEY WANT TO DESTROY ME... I'LL DESTROY THEM! SO THEY THINK CAN TORTURE ME, DO THEY? WELL THEY DON'T KNOW THE MEANING OF THE WORD... I'LL MAKE THEM WISH THEY NEVER SET EYES ON ME!
IT'S NOT TOO LATE! I CAN CATCH THEM AT SUPPER... WHEN THEY'RE OFF GUARD!
I'LL STRANGLE THOSE TWO WITH MY BARE HANDS! BUT FIRST I'LL MAKE THEM SWEAT!... EXPOSE THEM FOR THE EVIL MURDERERS THEY ARE!

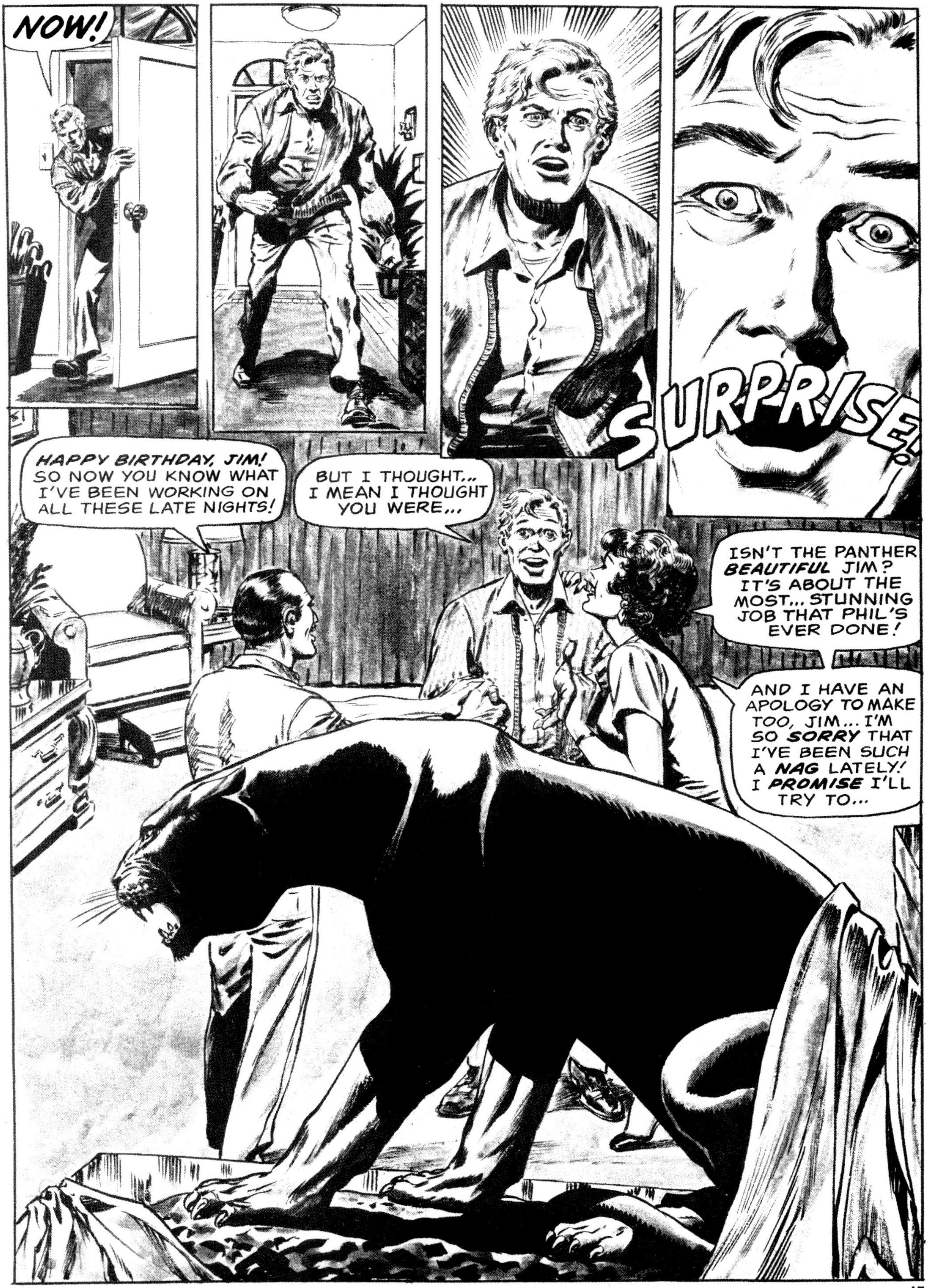
NOW!
SURPRISE!
HAPPY BIRTHDAY, JIM! SO NOW YOU KNOW WHAT I'VE BEEN WORKING ON ALL THESE LATE NIGHTS!
BUT I THOUGHT... I MEAN I THOUGHT YOU WERE...
ISN'T THE PANTHER BEAUTIFUL JIM? IT'S ABOUT THE MOST... STUNNING JOB THAT PHIL'S EVER DONE!
AND I HAVE AN APOLOGY TO MAKE TOO, JIM... I'M SO SORRY THAT I'VE BEEN SUCH A NAG LATELY! I PROMISE I'LL TRY TO...

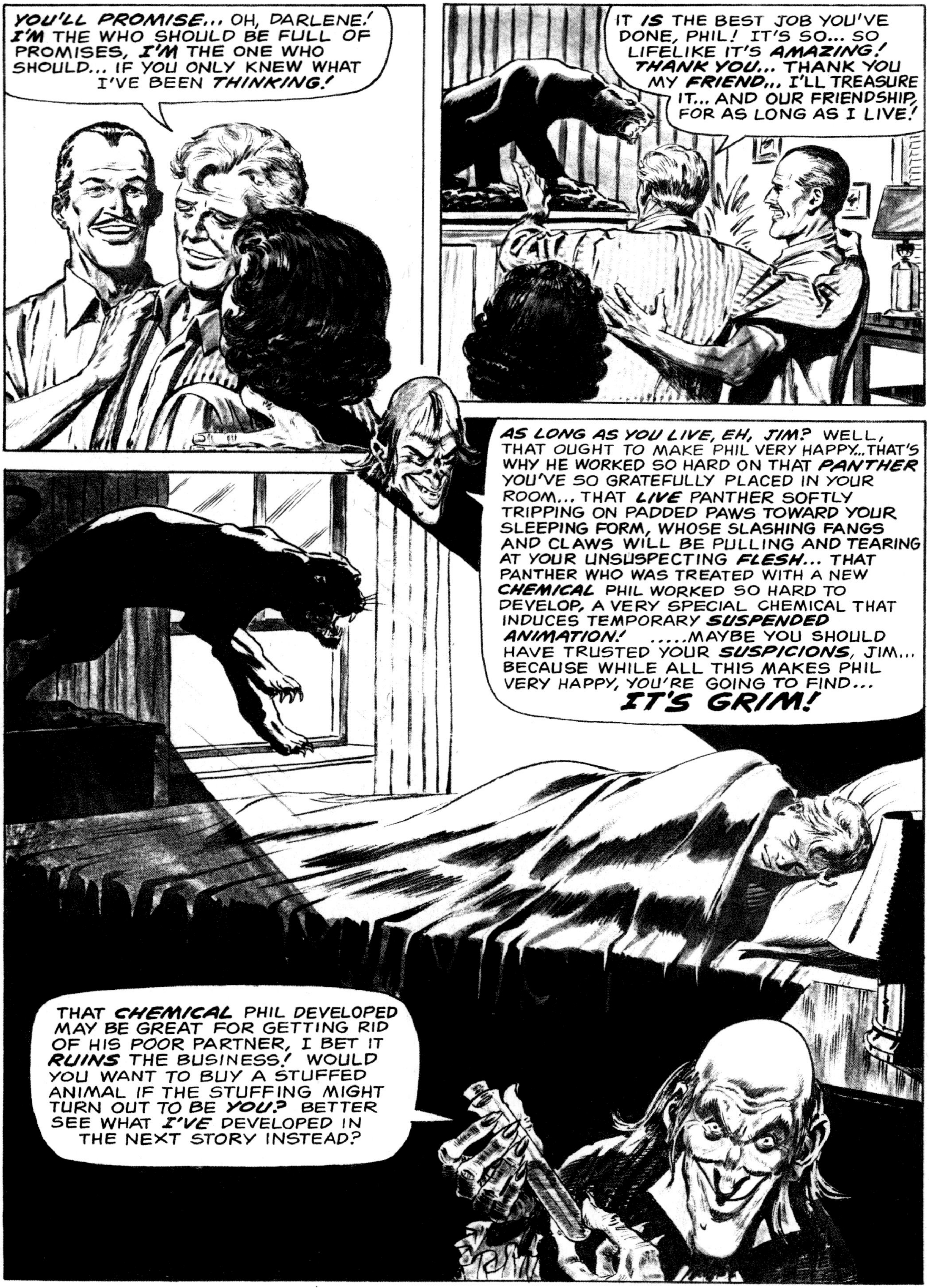
YOU'LL PROMISE... OH, DARLENE! I'M THE WHO SHOULD BE FULL OF PROMISES, I'M THE ONE WHO SHOULD... IF YOU ONLY KNEW WHAT I'VE BEEN THINKING!
IT IS THE BEST JOB YOU'VE DONE, PHIL! IT'S SO... SO LIFELIKE IT'S AMAZING! THANK YOU... THANK YOU MY FRIEND... I'LL TREASURE IT... AND OUR FRIENDSHIP, FOR AS LONG AS I LIVE!
AS LONG AS YOU LIVE, EH, JIM? WELL, THAT OUGHT TO MAKE PHIL VERY HAPPY...THAT'S WHY HE WORKED SO HARD ON THAT PANTHER YOU'VE SO GRATEFULLY PLACED IN YOUR ROOM... THAT LIVE PANTHER SOFTLY TRIPPING ON PADDED PAWS TOWARD YOUR SLEEPING FORM, WHOSE SLASHING FANGS AND CLAWS WILL BE PULLING AND TEARING AT YOUR UNSUSPECTING FLESH... THAT PANTHER WHO WAS TREATED WITH A NEW CHEMICAL PHIL WORKED SO HARD TO DEVELOP, A VERY SPECIAL CHEMICAL THAT INDUCES TEMPORARY SUSPENDED ANIMATION! .....MAYBE YOU SHOULD HAVE TRUSTED YOUR SUSPICIONS, JIM... BECAUSE WHILE ALL THIS MAKES PHIL VERY HAPPY, YOU'RE GOING TO FIND... IT'S GRIM!
THAT CHEMICAL PHIL DEVELOPED MAY BE GREAT FOR GETTING RID OF HIS POOR PARTNER, I BET IT RUINS THE BUSINESS! WOULD YOU WANT TO BUY A STUFFED ANIMAL IF THE STUFFING MIGHT TURN OUT TO BE YOU? BETTER SEE WHAT I'VE DEVELOPED IN THE NEXT STORY INSTEAD?

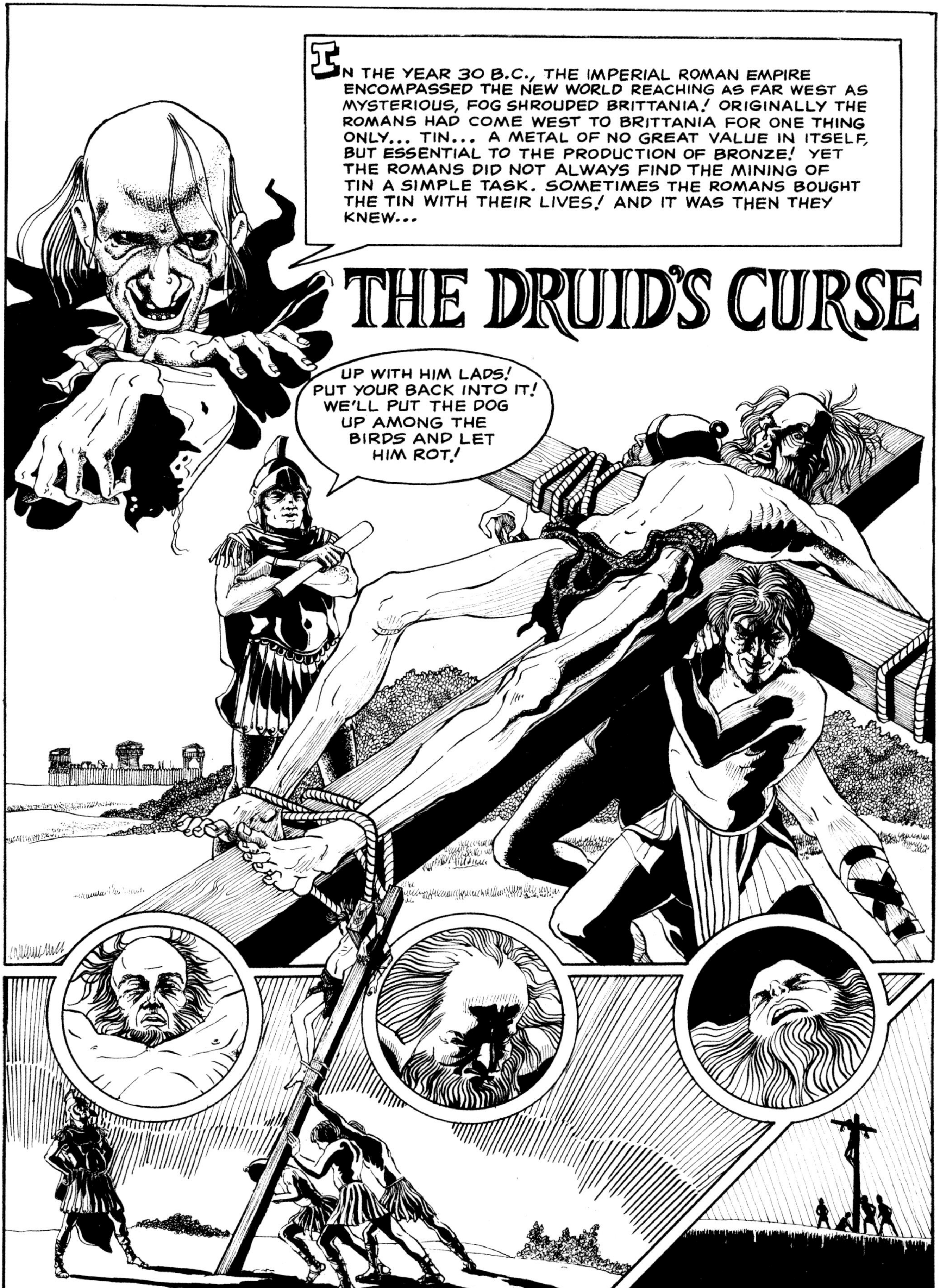
IN THE YEAR 30 B.C., THE IMPERIAL ROMAN EMPIRE ENCOMPASSED THE NEW WORLD REACHING AS FAR WEST AS MYSTERIOUS, FOG SHROUDED BRITTANIA! ORIGINALLY THE ROMANS HAD COME WEST TO BRITTANIA FOR ONE THING ONLY... TIN... A METAL OF NO GREAT VALUE IN ITSELF, BUT ESSENTIAL TO THE PRODUCTION OF BRONZE! YET THE ROMANS DID NOT ALWAYS FIND THE MINING OF TIN A SIMPLE TASK. SOMETIMES THE ROMANS BOUGHT THE TIN WITH THEIR LIVES! AND IT WAS THEN THEY KNEW...
THE DRUID'S CURSE
UP WITH HIM LADS! PUT YOUR BACK INTO IT! WE'LL PUT THE DOG UP AMONG THE BIRDS AND LET HIM ROT!

ART BY THE BROTHERS CIOCHETTI/STORY BY BUDDY SAUNDERS

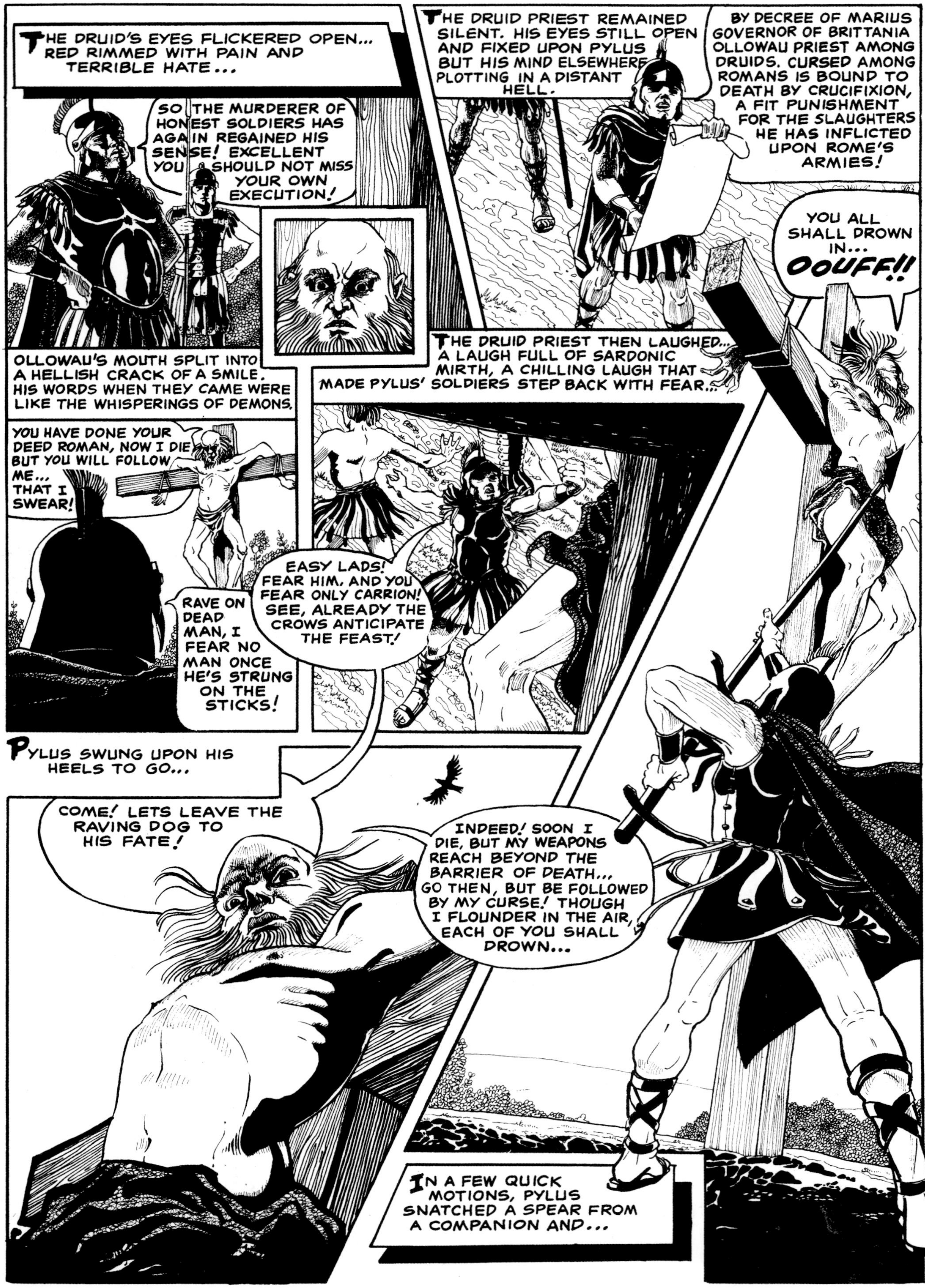
THE DRUID'S EYES FLICKERED OPEN... RED RIMMED WITH PAIN AND TERRIBLE HATE...
SO THE MURDERER OF HONEST SOLDIERS HAS AGAIN REGAINED HIS SENSE! EXCELLENT YOU SHOULD NOT MISS YOUR OWN EXECUTION!
THE DRUID PRIEST REMAINED SILENT. HIS EYES STILL OPEN AND FIXED UPON PYLUS BUT HIS MIND ELSEWHERE PLOTTING IN A DISTANT HELL.
BY DECREE OF MARIUS GOVERNOR OF BRITTANIA OLLOWAU PRIEST AMONG DRUIDS. CURSED AMONG ROMANS IS BOUND TO DEATH BY CRUCIFIXION, A FIT PUNISHMENT FOR THE SLAUGHTERS HE HAS INFLICTED UPON ROME'S ARMIES!
YOU ALL SHALL DROWN IN... OOUFF!!
OLLOWAU'S MOUTH SPLIT INTO A HELLISH CRACK OF A SMILE. HIS WORDS WHEN THEY CAME WERE LIKE THE WHISPERINGS OF DEMONS.
YOU HAVE DONE YOUR DEED ROMAN, NOW I DIE BUT YOU WILL FOLLOW ME... THAT I SWEAR!
RAVE ON DEAD MAN, I FEAR NO MAN ONCE HE'S STRUNG ON THE STICKS!
THE DRUID PRIEST THEN LAUGHED... A LAUGH FULL OF SARDONIC MIRTH, A CHILLING LAUGH THAT MADE PYLUS' SOLDIERS STEP BACK WITH FEAR...
EASY LADS! FEAR HIM, AND YOU FEAR ONLY CARRION! SEE, ALREADY THE CROWS ANTICIPATE THE FEAST!
PYLUS SWUNG UPON HIS HEELS TO GO...
COME! LETS LEAVE THE RAVING DOG TO HIS FATE!
INDEED! SOON I DIE, BUT MY WEAPONS REACH BEYOND THE BARRIER OF DEATH... GO THEN, BUT BE FOLLOWED BY MY CURSE! THOUGH I FLOUNDER IN THE AIR, EACH OF YOU SHALL DROWN...
IN A FEW QUICK MOTIONS, PYLUS SNATCHED A SPEAR FROM A COMPANION AND...

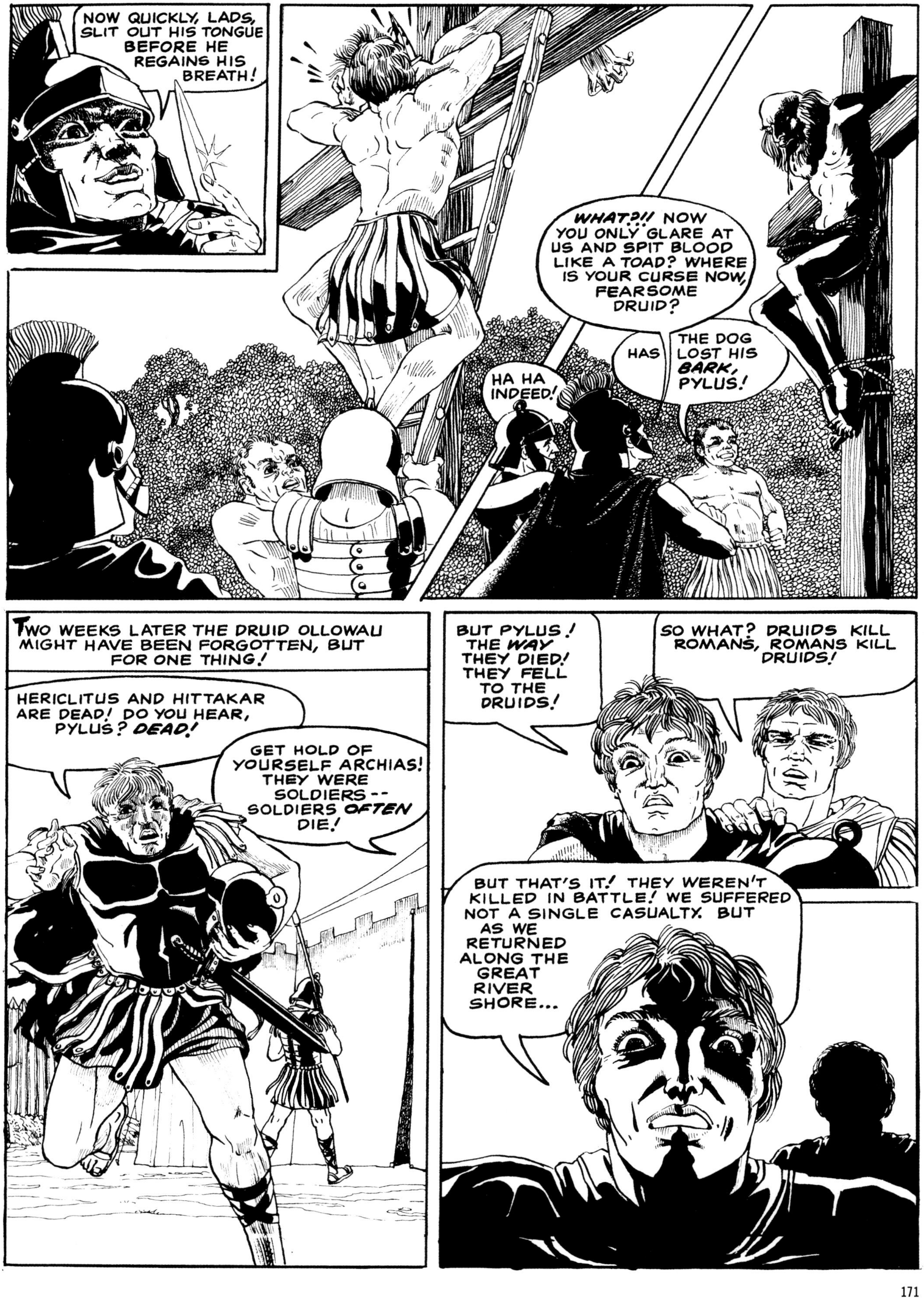
NOW QUICKLY, LADS, SLIT OUT HIS TONGUE BEFORE HE REGAINS HIS BREATH!
WHAT?!! NOW YOU ONLY GLARE AT US AND SPIT BLOOD LIKE A TOAD? WHERE IS YOUR CURSE NOW, FEARSOME DRUID?
HAS
THE DOG LOST HIS BARK, PYLUS!
HA HA INDEED!
TWO WEEKS LATER THE DRUID OLLOWAU MIGHT HAVE BEEN FORGOTTEN, BUT FOR ONE THING!
HERICLITUS AND HITTAKAR ARE DEAD! DO YOU HEAR, PYLUS? DEAD!
GET HOLD OF YOURSELF ARCHIAS! THEY WERE SOLDIERS -- SOLDIERS OFTEN DIE!
BUT PYLUS! THE WAY THEY DIED! THEY FELL TO THE DRUIDS!
SO WHAT? DRUIDS KILL ROMANS, ROMANS KILL DRUIDS!
BUT THAT'S IT! THEY WEREN'T KILLED IN BATTLE! WE SUFFERED NOT A SINGLE CASUALTY. BUT AS WE RETURNED ALONG THE GREAT RIVER SHORE...

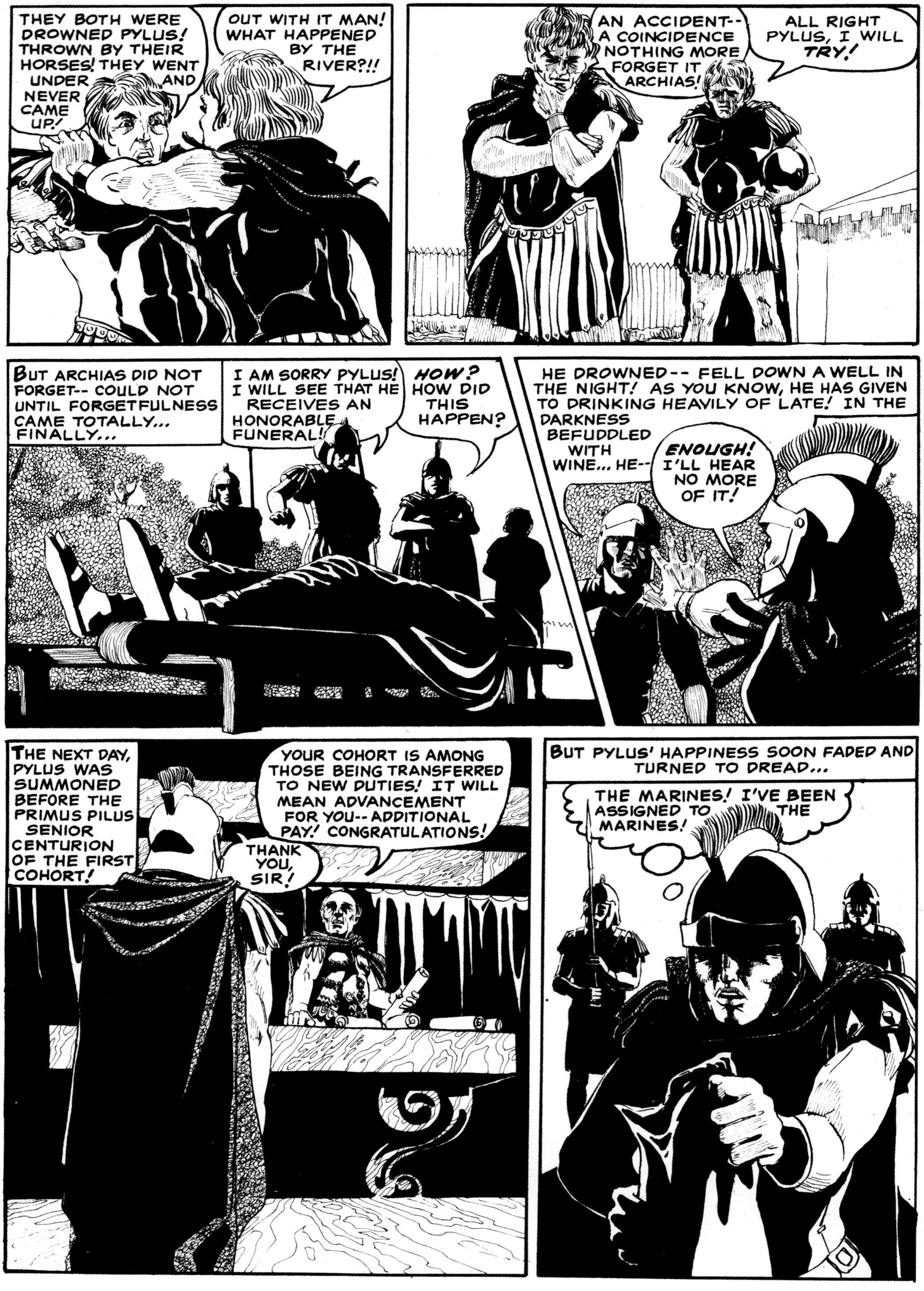
THEY BOTH WERE DROWNED PYLUS! THROWN BY THEIR HORSES! THEY WENT UNDER AND NEVER CAME UP!
OUT WITH IT MAN! WHAT HAPPENED BY THE RIVER?!!
AN ACCIDENT-- A COINCIDENCE NOTHING MORE FORGET IT ARCHIAS!
ALL RIGHT PYLUS, I WILL TRY!
BUT ARCHIAS DID NOT FORGET-- COULD NOT UNTIL FORGETFULNESS CAME TOTALLY... FINALLY...
I AM SORRY PYLUS! I WILL SEE THAT HE RECEIVES AN HONORABLE FUNERAL!
HOW? HOW DID THIS HAPPEN?
HE DROWNED-- FELL DOWN A WELL IN THE NIGHT! AS YOU KNOW, HE HAS GIVEN TO DRINKING HEAVILY OF LATE! IN THE DARKNESS BEFUDDLED WITH WINE... HE--
ENOUGH! I'LL HEAR NO MORE OF IT!
THE NEXT DAY, PYLUS WAS SUMMONED BEFORE THE PRIMUS PILUS SENIOR CENTURION OF THE FIRST COHORT!
YOUR COHORT IS AMONG THOSE BEING TRANSFERRED TO NEW DUTIES! IT WILL MEAN ADVANCEMENT FOR YOU-- ADDITIONAL PAY! CONGRATULATIONS!
THANK YOU, SIR!
BUT PYLUS' HAPPINESS SOON FADED AND TURNED TO DREAD...
THE MARINES! I'VE BEEN ASSIGNED TO THE MARINES!

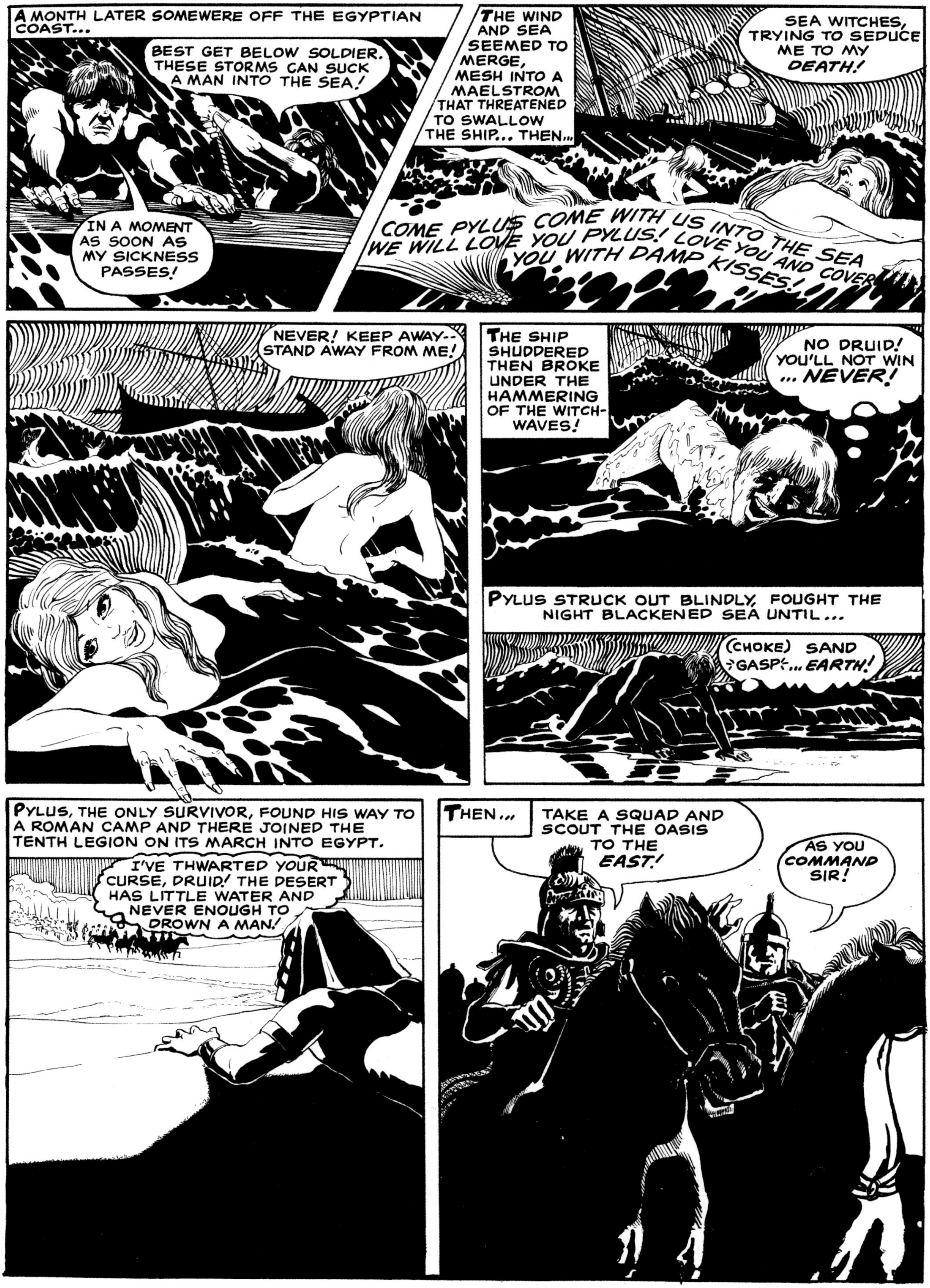
A MONTH LATER SOMEWERE OFF THE EGYPTIAN COAST...
BEST GET BELOW SOLDIER. THESE STORMS CAN SUCK A MAN INTO THE SEA!
IN A MOMENT AS SOON AS MY SICKNESS PASSES!
THE WIND AND SEA SEEMED TO MERGE, MESH INTO A MAELSTROM THAT THREATENED TO SWALLOW THE SHIP... THEN...
SEA WITCHES, TRYING TO SEDUCE ME TO MY DEATH!
COME PYLUS COME WITH US INTO THE SEA WE WILL LOVE YOU PYLUS! LOVE YOU AND COVER YOU WITH DAMP KISSES!
NEVER! KEEP AWAY-- STAND AWAY FROM ME!
THE SHIP SHUDDERED THEN BROKE UNDER THE HAMMERING OF THE WITCH-WAVES!
NO DRUID! YOU'LL NOT WIN ...NEVER!
PYLUS STRUCK OUT BLINDLY, FOUGHT THE NIGHT BLACKENED SEA UNTIL...
(CHOKE) SAND ⁘GASP⁘... EARTH!
PYLUS, THE ONLY SURVIVOR, FOUND HIS WAY TO A ROMAN CAMP AND THERE JOINED THE TENTH LEGION ON ITS MARCH INTO EGYPT.
I'VE THWARTED YOUR CURSE, DRUID! THE DESERT HAS LITTLE WATER AND NEVER ENOUGH TO DROWN A MAN!
THEN...
TAKE A SQUAD AND SCOUT THE OASIS TO THE EAST!
AS YOU COMMAND SIR!

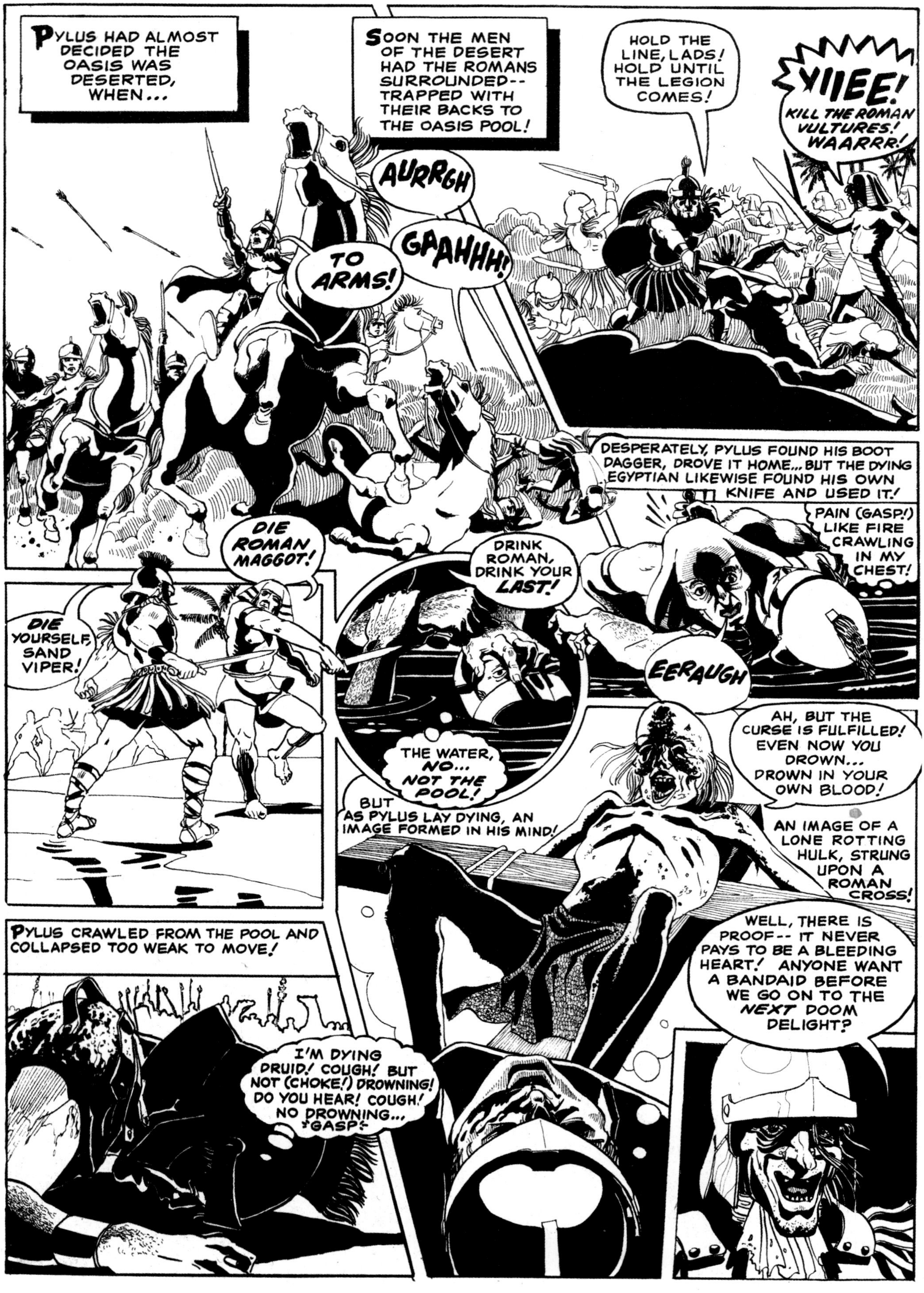
PYLUS HAD ALMOST DECIDED THE OASIS WAS DESERTED, WHEN...
AURRGH
GAAHHH!
TO ARMS!
SOON THE MEN OF THE DESERT HAD THE ROMANS SURROUNDED-- TRAPPED WITH THEIR BACKS TO THE OASIS POOL!
HOLD THE LINE, LADS! HOLD UNTIL THE LEGION COMES!
YIIIEE! KILL THE ROMAN VULTURES! WAARRR!
DIE ROMAN MAGGOT!
DIE YOURSELF, SAND VIPER!
DRINK ROMAN, DRINK YOUR LAST!
THE WATER, NO... NOT THE POOL!
DESPERATELY, PYLUS FOUND HIS BOOT DAGGER, DROVE IT HOME... BUT THE DYING EGYPTIAN LIKEWISE FOUND HIS OWN KNIFE AND USED IT!
PAIN (GASP!) LIKE FIRE CRAWLING IN MY CHEST!
EERAUGH
PYLUS CRAWLED FROM THE POOL AND COLLAPSED TOO WEAK TO MOVE!
I'M DYING DRUID! COUGH! BUT NOT (CHOKE!) DROWNING! DO YOU HEAR! COUGH! NO DROWNING... *GASP*
AH, BUT THE CURSE IS FULFILLED! EVEN NOW YOU DROWN... DROWN IN YOUR OWN BLOOD!
BUT AS PYLUS LAY DYING, AN IMAGE FORMED IN HIS MIND!
AN IMAGE OF A LONE ROTTING HULK, STRUNG UPON A ROMAN CROSS!
WELL, THERE IS PROOF-- IT NEVER PAYS TO BE A BLEEDING HEART! ANYONE WANT A BANDAID BEFORE WE GO ON TO THE NEXT DOOM DELIGHT?

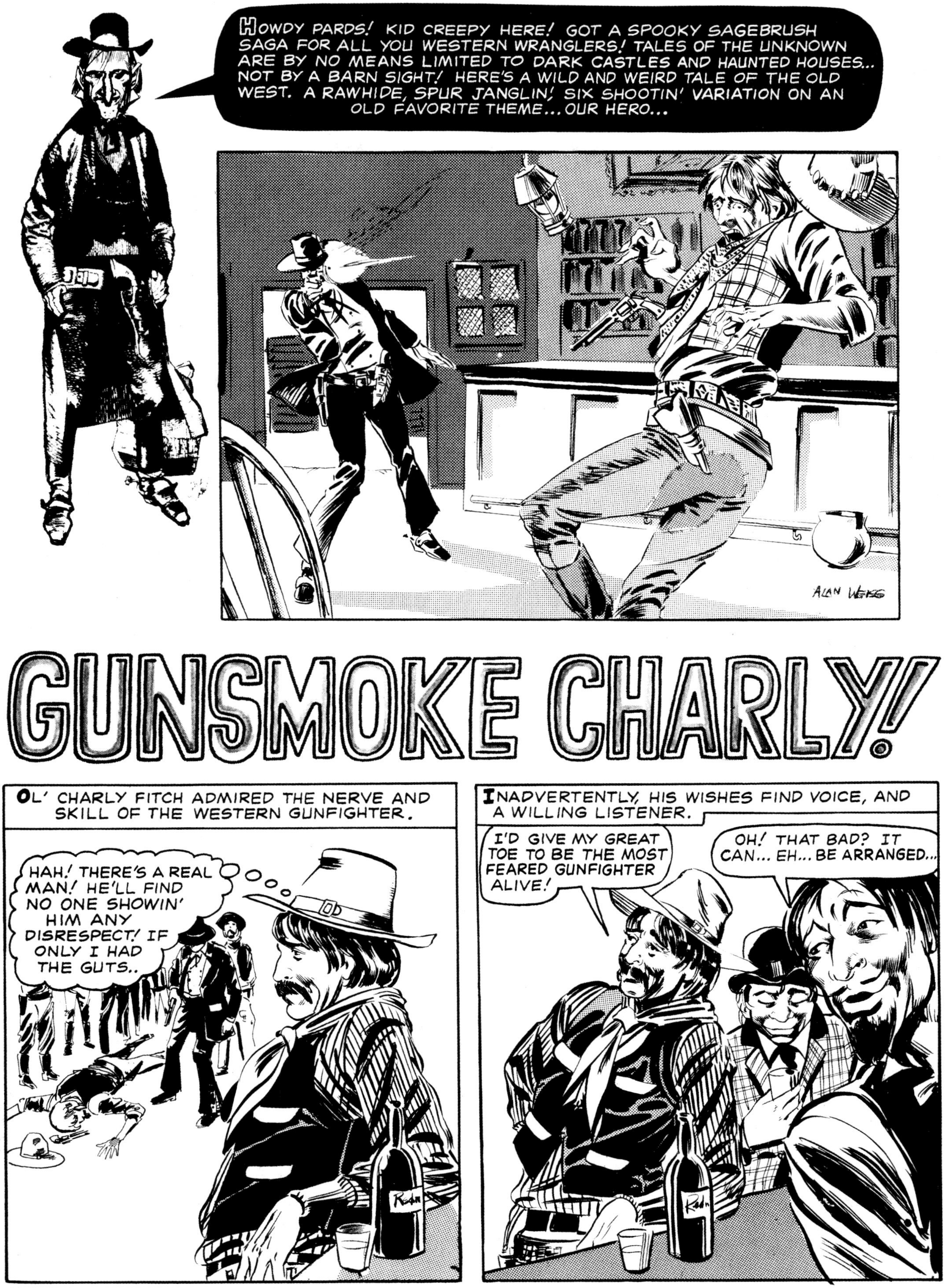
HOWDY PARDS! KID CREEPY HERE! GOT A SPOOKY SAGEBRUSH SAGA FOR ALL YOU WESTERN WRANGLERS! TALES OF THE UNKNOWN ARE BY NO MEANS LIMITED TO DARK CASTLES AND HAUNTED HOUSES... NOT BY A BARN SIGHT! HERE'S A WILD AND WEIRD TALE OF THE OLD WEST. A RAWHIDE, SPUR JANGLIN', SIX SHOOTIN' VARIATION ON AN OLD FAVORITE THEME... OUR HERO...
ALAN WEISS
GUNSMOKE CHARLY!
OL' CHARLY FITCH ADMIRED THE NERVE AND SKILL OF THE WESTERN GUNFIGHTER.
HAH! THERE'S A REAL MAN! HE'LL FIND NO ONE SHOWIN' HIM ANY DISRESPECT! IF ONLY I HAD THE GUTS..
INADVERTENTLY, HIS WISHES FIND VOICE, AND A WILLING LISTENER.
I'D GIVE MY GREAT TOE TO BE THE MOST FEARED GUNFIGHTER ALIVE!
OH! THAT BAD? IT CAN... EH... BE ARRANGED...

ART AND STORY BY ALAN WEISS

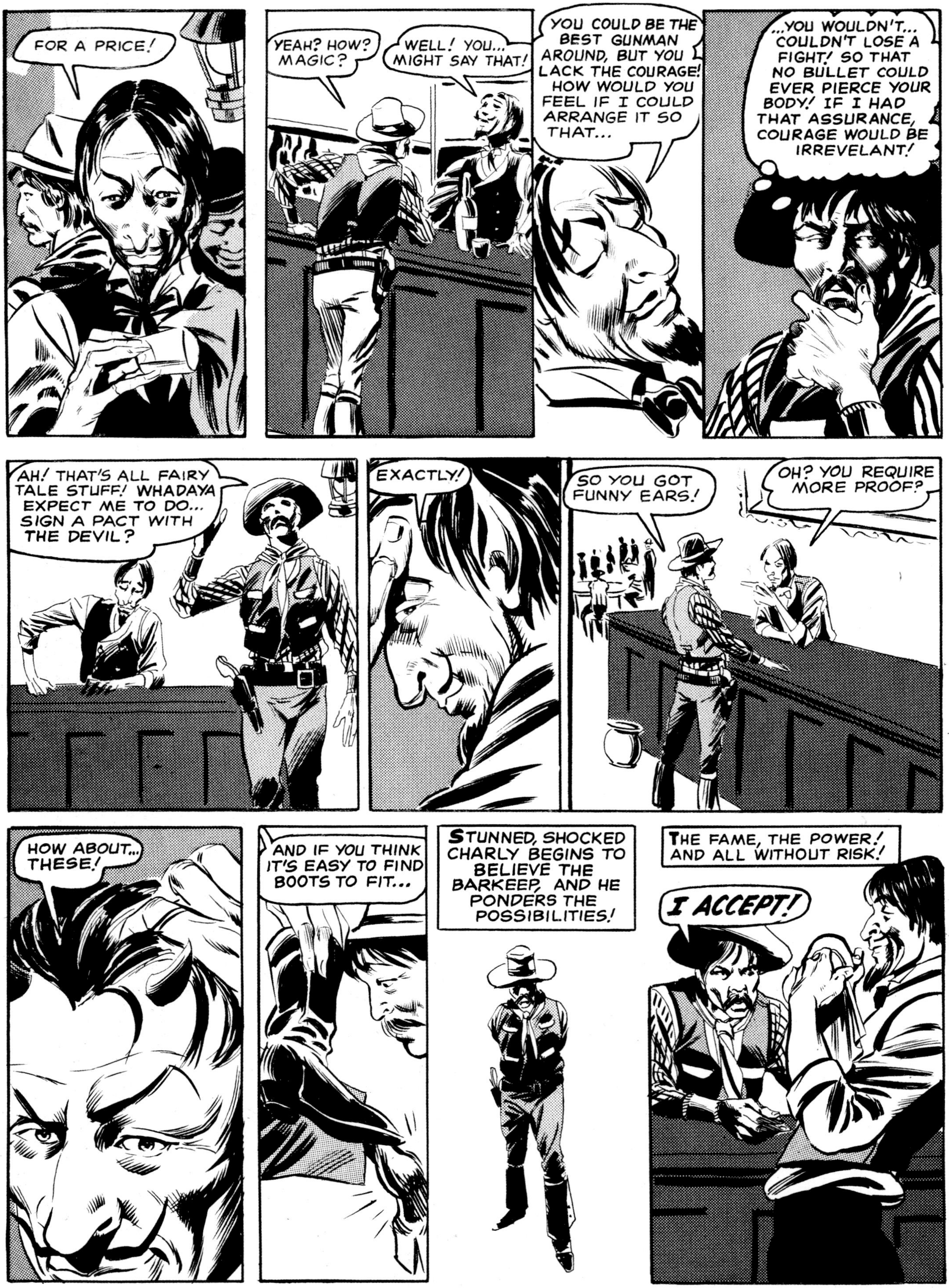
FOR A PRICE!
YEAH? HOW? MAGIC?
WELL! YOU... MIGHT SAY THAT!
YOU COULD BE THE BEST GUNMAN AROUND, BUT YOU LACK THE COURAGE! HOW WOULD YOU FEEL IF I COULD ARRANGE IT SO THAT...
...YOU WOULDN'T... COULDN'T LOSE A FIGHT! SO THAT NO BULLET COULD EVER PIERCE YOUR BODY! IF I HAD THAT ASSURANCE, COURAGE WOULD BE IRRELEVANT!
AH! THAT'S ALL FAIRY TALE STUFF! WHADAYA EXPECT ME TO DO... SIGN A PACT WITH THE DEVIL?
EXACTLY!
SO YOU GOT FUNNY EARS!
OH? YOU REQUIRE MORE PROOF?
HOW ABOUT... THESE!
AND IF YOU THINK IT'S EASY TO FIND BOOTS TO FIT...
STUNNED, SHOCKED CHARLY BEGINS TO BELIEVE THE BARKEEP, AND HE PONDERS THE POSSIBILITIES!
THE FAME, THE POWER! AND ALL WITHOUT RISK!
I ACCEPT!

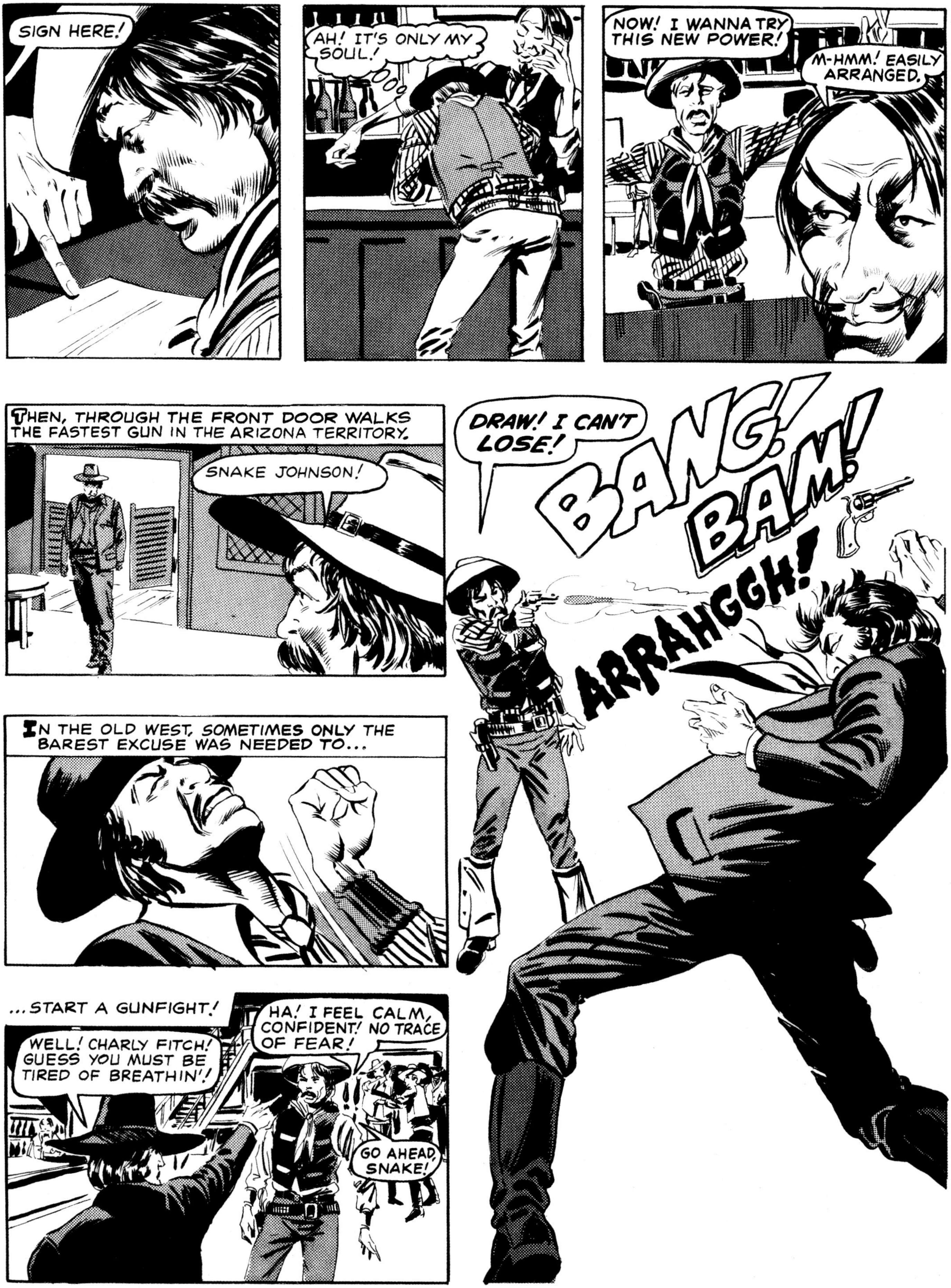
SIGN HERE!
AH! IT'S ONLY MY SOUL!
NOW! I WANNA TRY THIS NEW POWER!
M-HMM! EASILY ARRANGED.
THEN, THROUGH THE FRONT DOOR WALKS THE FASTEST GUN IN THE ARIZONA TERRITORY.
SNAKE JOHNSON!
IN THE OLD WEST, SOMETIMES ONLY THE BAREST EXCUSE WAS NEEDED TO...
...START A GUNFIGHT!
WELL! CHARLY FITCH! GUESS YOU MUST BE TIRED OF BREATHIN'!
HA! I FEEL CALM, CONFIDENT! NO TRACE OF FEAR!
GO AHEAD, SNAKE!
DRAW! I CAN'T LOSE!
BANG!
BAM!
ARRAHGGH!

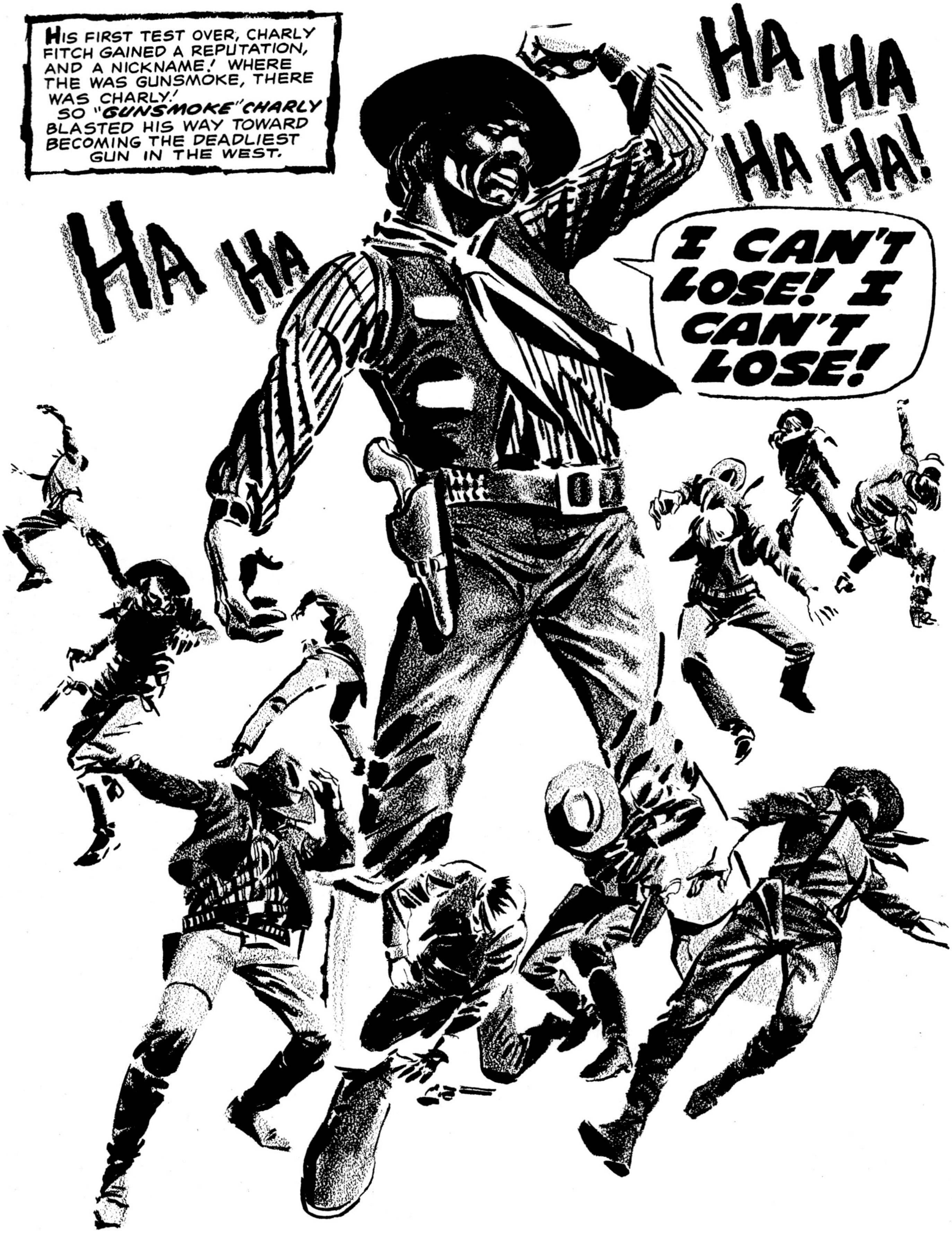
HIS FIRST TEST OVER, CHARLY FITCH GAINED A REPUTATION, AND A NICKNAME! WHERE THE WAS GUNSMOKE, THERE WAS CHARLY! SO "GUNSMOKE" CHARLY BLASTED HIS WAY TOWARD BECOMING THE DEADLIEST GUN IN THE WEST.
HA HA HA HA HA HA!
HA HA
I CAN'T LOSE! I CAN'T LOSE!

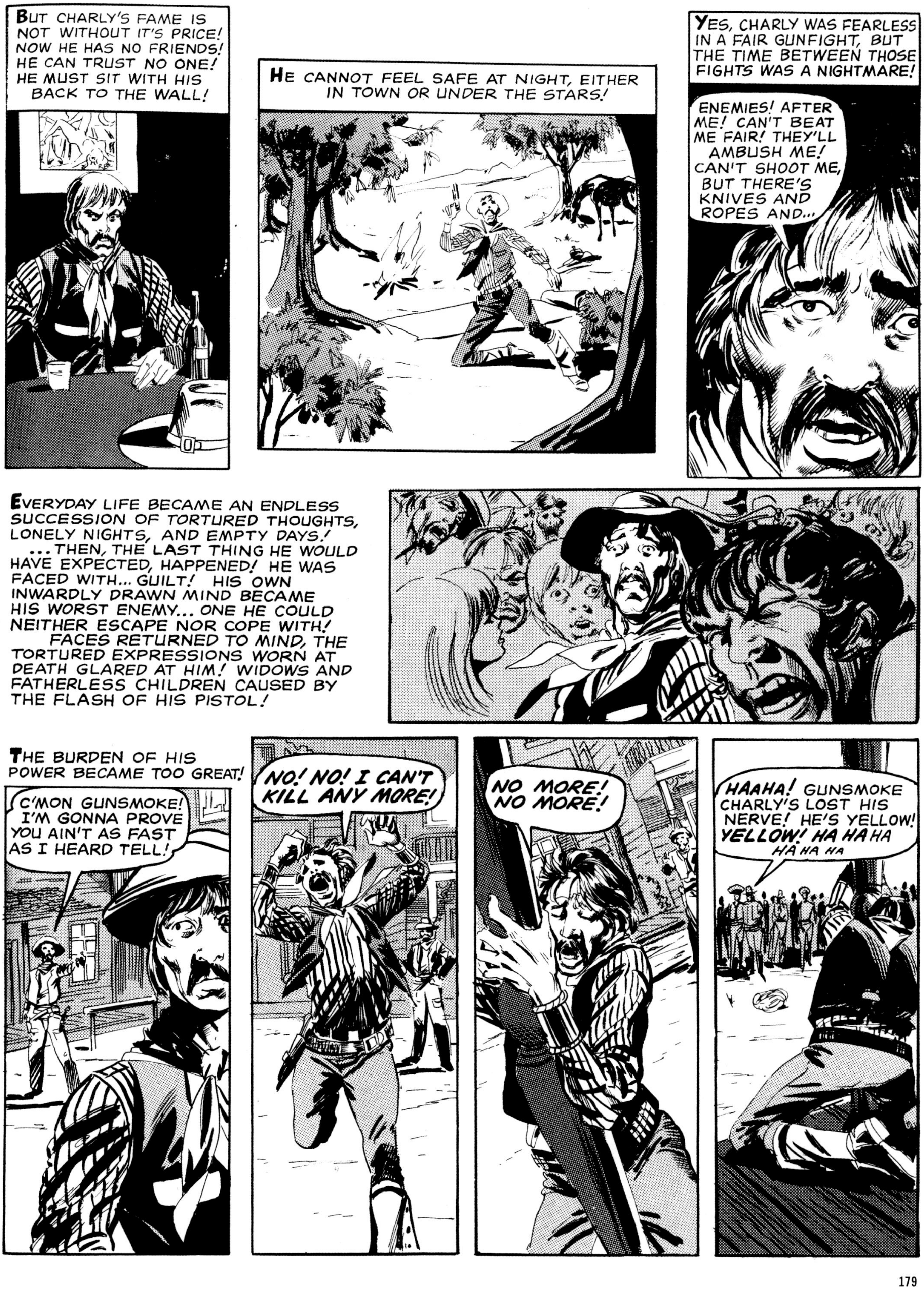
BUT CHARLY'S FAME IS NOT WITHOUT IT'S PRICE! NOW HE HAS NO FRIENDS! HE CAN TRUST NO ONE! HE MUST SIT WITH HIS BACK TO THE WALL!
HE CANNOT FEEL SAFE AT NIGHT, EITHER IN TOWN OR UNDER THE STARS!
YES, CHARLY WAS FEARLESS IN A FAIR GUNFIGHT, BUT THE TIME BETWEEN THOSE FIGHTS WAS A NIGHTMARE!
ENEMIES! AFTER ME! CAN'T BEAT ME FAIR! THEY'LL AMBUSH ME! CAN'T SHOOT ME, BUT THERE'S KNIVES AND ROPES AND...
EVERYDAY LIFE BECAME AN ENDLESS SUCCESSION OF TORTURED THOUGHTS, LONELY NIGHTS, AND EMPTY DAYS! ...THEN, THE LAST THING HE WOULD HAVE EXPECTED, HAPPENED! HE WAS FACED WITH... GUILT! HIS OWN INWARDLY DRAWN MIND BECAME HIS WORST ENEMY... ONE HE COULD NEITHER ESCAPE NOR COPE WITH! FACES RETURNED TO MIND, THE TORTURED EXPRESSIONS WORN AT DEATH GLARED AT HIM! WIDOWS AND FATHERLESS CHILDREN CAUSED BY THE FLASH OF HIS PISTOL!
THE BURDEN OF HIS POWER BECAME TOO GREAT!
C'MON GUNSMOKE! I'M GONNA PROVE YOU AIN'T AS FAST AS I HEARD TELL!
NO! NO! I CAN'T KILL ANY MORE!
NO MORE! NO MORE!
HAHA! GUNSMOKE CHARLY'S LOST HIS NERVE! HE'S YELLOW! YELLOW! HA HA HA HA HA HA

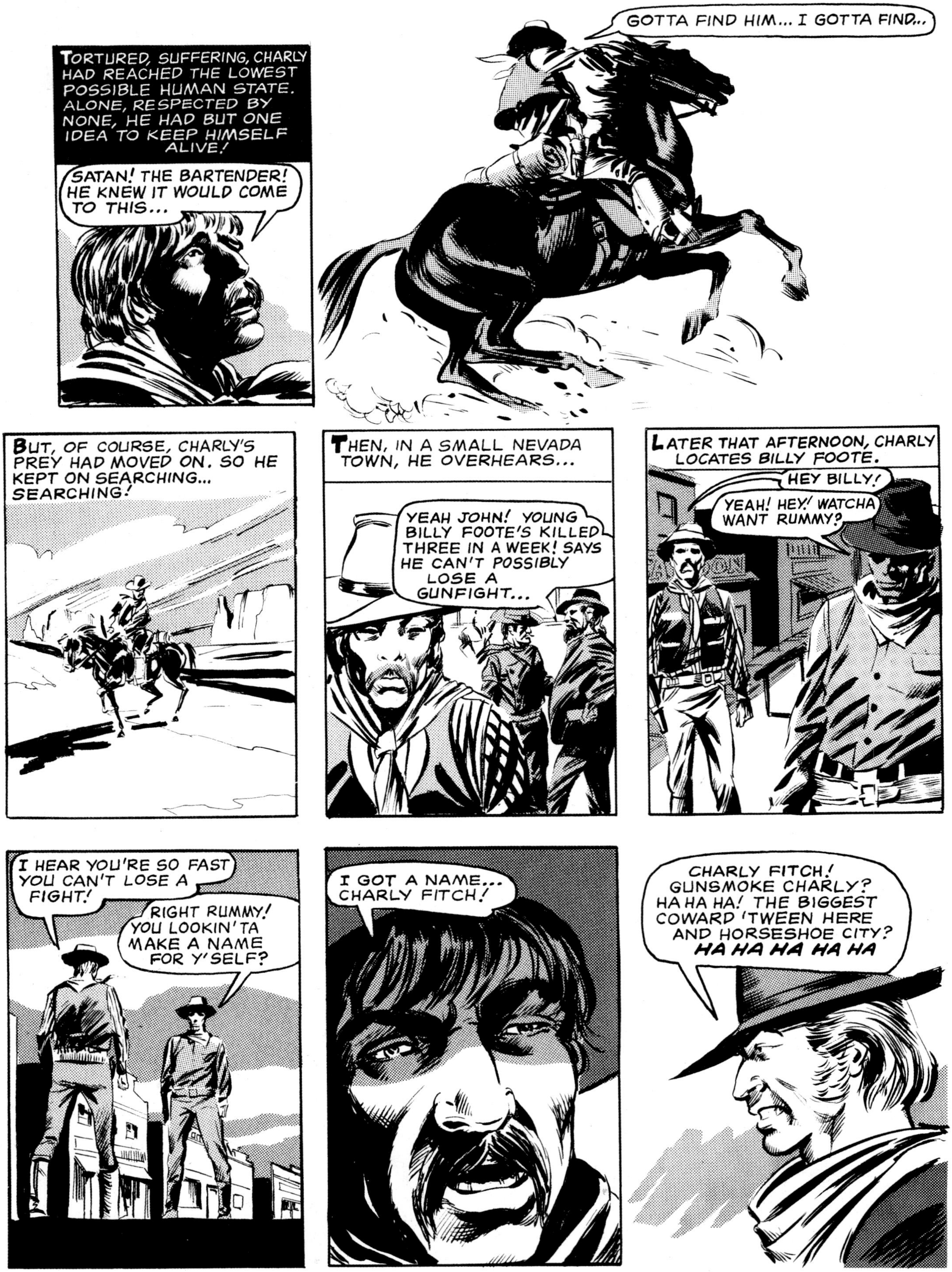
TORTURED, SUFFERING, CHARLY HAD REACHED THE LOWEST POSSIBLE HUMAN STATE. ALONE, RESPECTED BY NONE, HE HAD BUT ONE IDEA TO KEEP HIMSELF ALIVE!
SATAN! THE BARTENDER! HE KNEW IT WOULD COME TO THIS...
GOTTA FIND HIM... I GOTTA FIND...
BUT, OF COURSE, CHARLY'S PREY HAD MOVED ON. SO HE KEPT ON SEARCHING... SEARCHING!
THEN, IN A SMALL NEVADA TOWN, HE OVERHEARS...
YEAH JOHN! YOUNG BILLY FOOTE'S KILLED THREE IN A WEEK! SAYS HE CAN'T POSSIBLY LOSE A GUNFIGHT...
LATER THAT AFTERNOON, CHARLY LOCATES BILLY FOOTE.
HEY BILLY!
YEAH! HEY! WATCHA WANT RUMMY?
I HEAR YOU'RE SO FAST YOU CAN'T LOSE A FIGHT!
RIGHT RUMMY! YOU LOOKIN'TA MAKE A NAME FOR Y'SELF?
I GOT A NAME... CHARLY FITCH!
CHARLY FITCH! GUNSMOKE CHARLY? HA HA HA! THE BIGGEST COWARD 'TWEEN HERE AND HORSESHOE CITY?
HA HA HA HA HA

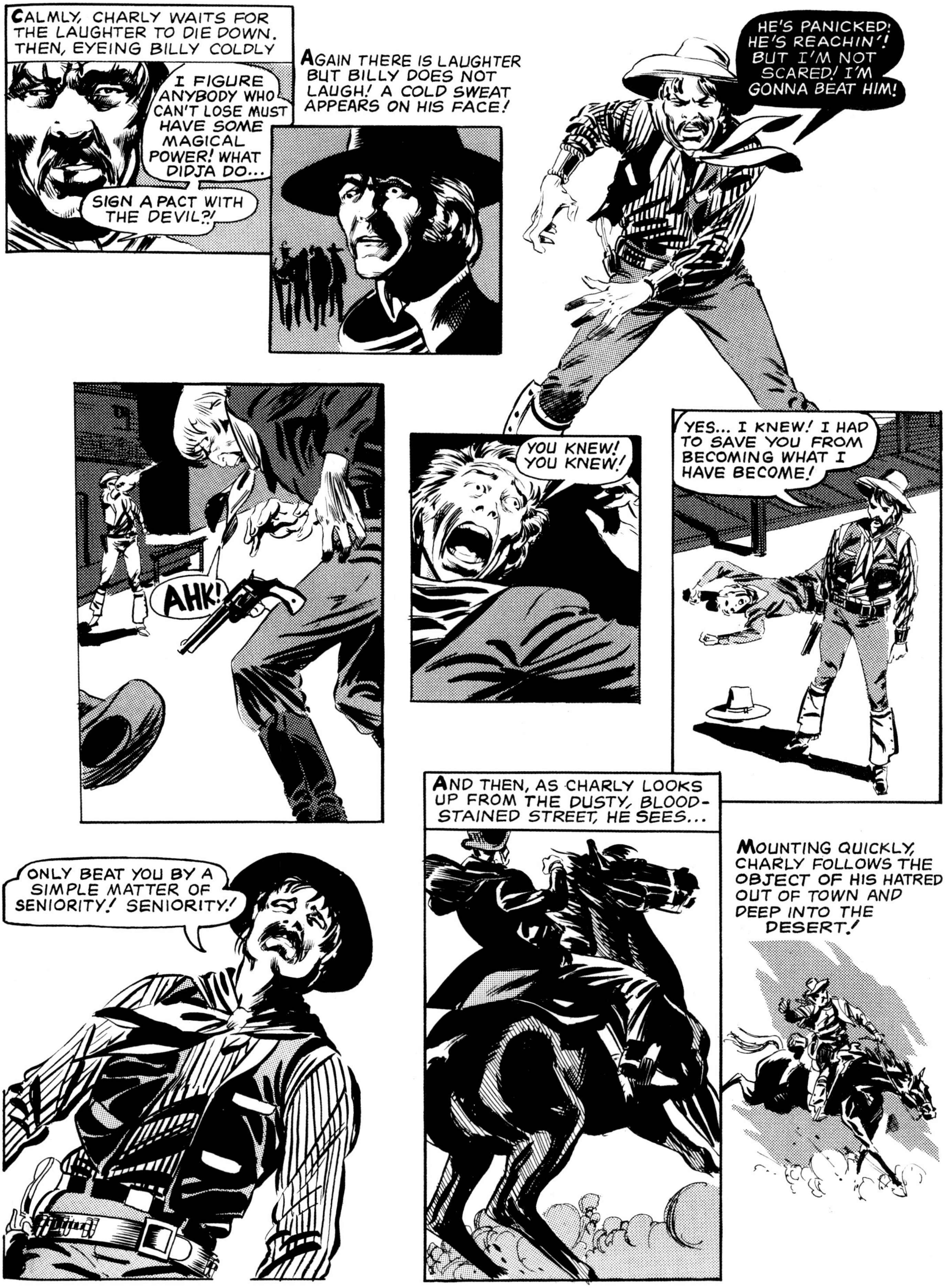
CALMLY, CHARLY WAITS FOR THE LAUGHTER TO DIE DOWN. THEN, EYEING BILLY COLDLY
I FIGURE ANYBODY WHO CAN'T LOSE MUST HAVE SOME MAGICAL POWER! WHAT DIDJA DO...
SIGN A PACT WITH THE DEVIL?!
AGAIN THERE IS LAUGHTER BUT BILLY DOES NOT LAUGH! A COLD SWEAT APPEARS ON HIS FACE!
HE'S PANICKED! HE'S REACHIN'! BUT I'M NOT SCARED! I'M GONNA BEAT HIM!
AHK!
YOU KNEW! YOU KNEW!
YES... I KNEW! I HAD TO SAVE YOU FROM BECOMING WHAT I HAVE BECOME!
ONLY BEAT YOU BY A SIMPLE MATTER OF SENIORITY! SENIORITY!
AND THEN, AS CHARLY LOOKS UP FROM THE DUSTY, BLOOD-STAINED STREET, HE SEES...
MOUNTING QUICKLY, CHARLY FOLLOWS THE OBJECT OF HIS HATRED OUT OF TOWN AND DEEP INTO THE DESERT!

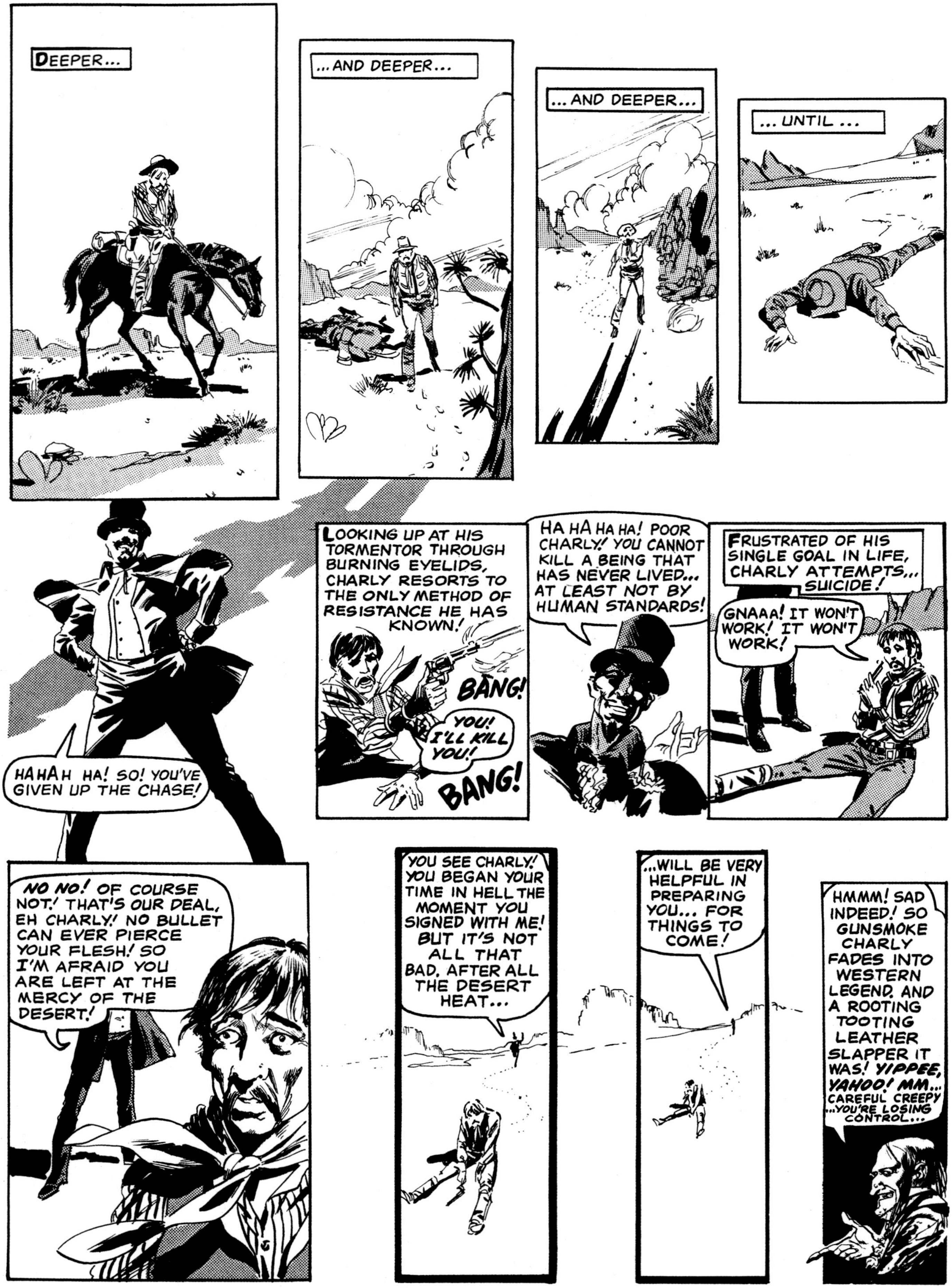
DEEPER...
...AND DEEPER...
...AND DEEPER...
...UNTIL...
HAHAH HA! SO! YOU'VE GIVEN UP THE CHASE!
LOOKING UP AT HIS TORMENTOR THROUGH BURNING EYELIDS, CHARLY RESORTS TO THE ONLY METHOD OF RESISTANCE HE HAS KNOWN!
BANG!
YOU! I'LL KILL YOU!
BANG!
HA HA HA HA! POOR CHARLY! YOU CANNOT KILL A BEING THAT HAS NEVER LIVED... AT LEAST NOT BY HUMAN STANDARDS!
FRUSTRATED OF HIS SINGLE GOAL IN LIFE, CHARLY ATTEMPTS... SUICIDE!
GNAAA! IT WON'T WORK! IT WON'T WORK!
NO NO! OF COURSE NOT! THAT'S OUR DEAL, EH CHARLY! NO BULLET CAN EVER PIERCE YOUR FLESH! SO I'M AFRAID YOU ARE LEFT AT THE MERCY OF THE DESERT!
YOU SEE CHARLY! YOU BEGAN YOUR TIME IN HELL THE MOMENT YOU SIGNED WITH ME! BUT IT'S NOT ALL THAT BAD, AFTER ALL THE DESERT HEAT...
...WILL BE VERY HELPFUL IN PREPARING YOU... FOR THINGS TO COME!
HMMM! SAD INDEED! SO GUNSMOKE CHARLY FADES INTO WESTERN LEGEND AND A ROOTING TOOTING LEATHER SLAPPER IT WAS! YIPPEE, YAHOO! MM... CAREFUL CREEPY ...YOU'RE LOSING CONTROL...

DO YOU HAVE THESE VALUABLE BACK ISSUES OF EERIE IN YOUR MAG COLLECTION?

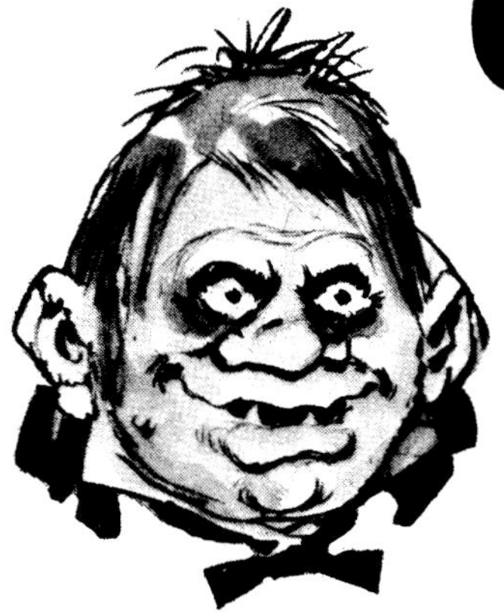

Is your collection of EERIE complete? The small supply of Back Issues of EERIE is disappearing! The few copies still on hand now command large prices in the catalog of the Periodical Collectors League. Buy now, trade later with fellow fans for issues you're missing. You can easily obtain them from our ware (wolf) house below.

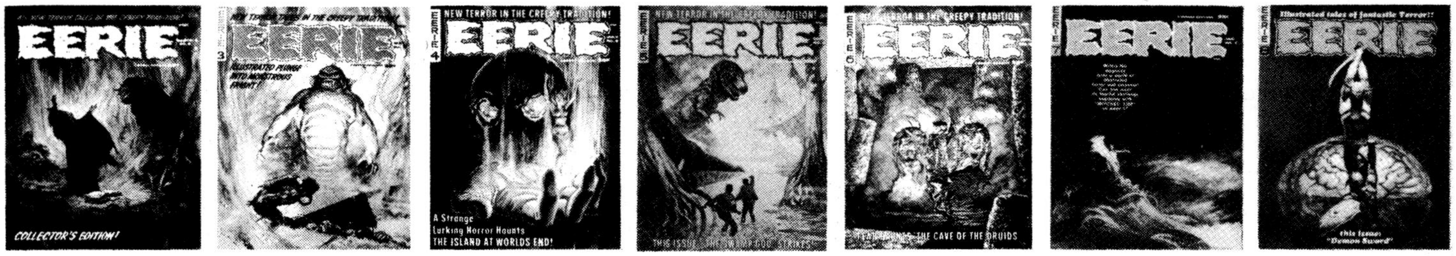

EERIE
COLLECTOR'S EDITION!
NEW TERROR IN THE CREEPY TRADITION!
A Strange Lurking Horror Haunts THE ISLAND AT WORLDS END!
THE CAVE OF THE DRUIDS
this issue: "Demon Sword"

#2 #3 #4 #5 #6 #7 #8

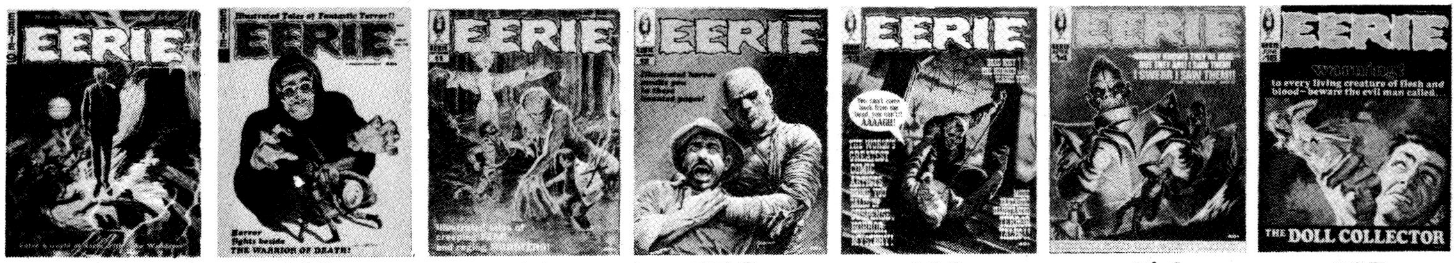

EERIE
Illustrated Tales of Fantastic Terror!!
THE WARRIOR OF DEATH!
THE DOLL COLLECTOR

#9 #10 #11 #12 #13 #14 #15

MAIL COUPON TODAY—WHILE THEY LAST!

All Copies Mailed in a Sturdy Envelope for Protection

- ☐ #2 ($2.50)
- ☐ #3 ($1.00)
- ☐ #4 ($1.00)
- ☐ #5 ($1.00)
- ☐ #6 (75c)
- ☐ #7 (75c)
- ☐ #8 (75c)
- ☐ #9 (75c)
- ☐ #10 (60¢)
- ☐ #11 (60¢)
- ☐ #12 (60¢)
- ☐ #13 (60¢)
- ☐ #14 (60¢)
- ☐ #15 (60¢)

EERIE BACK ISSUE DEPT.

☐ I enclose $__________ for back issues.

☐ I enclose $2.25 for a 6 issue subscription, giving me a full year of future EERIE Magazines!

NAME ______________________________

ADDRESS ______________________________

CITY ______________________________

STATE ______________________ ZIP CODE ____________

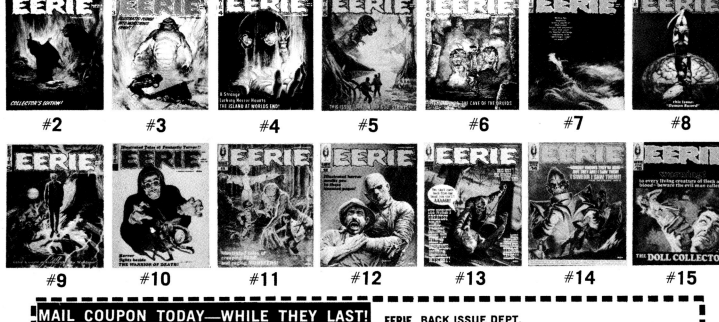

NOW—OWN A REAL
MYSTERY-MAN MASK

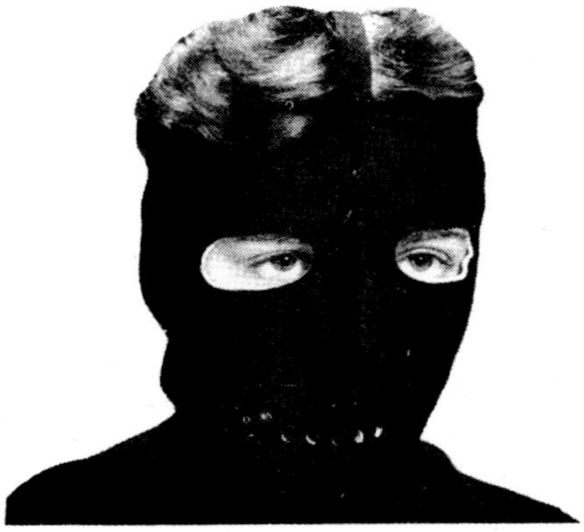

At last, you can have your very own Hollywood MYSTERY-MAN type MASK. The amazing head mask is all genuine wool, double stitched with felt lining for real comfort. For convenience, the mouth flop snaps open or shut. The mask is held in place by elastic head bands, while the special wool collar drapes down over the shoulders. Use your mask to:

1) **Make a movie, with yourself starring as the "Mysterious Avenger!"**
2) **Organize a "Masked Phantom" club with your friends!**
3) **Protect your face against freezing cold weather! Act right now and send for YOUR very own BRAND NEW mask. Only $1.00 each plus 25c for postage and handling.**

3 FAMOUS MONSTER KITS

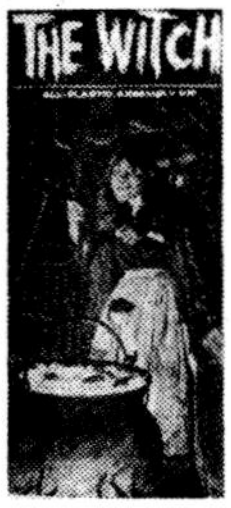
THE WITCH

THE WITCH

WHICH KID isn't awed by the WITCH KIT? Go to work and assemble a Witch's Brew. Everything you need for good, gruesome fun. Once you are boss of this witch, you'll be the envy of all your friends. Only $1.49.

DR. JEKYLL & MR. HYDE

WATCH the transformation take place before your very eyes. Why not? You do it all with the eerie, jeery Monster Kit . . . your hands make Jekyll play Hyde-and-go-seek. Only $1.49.

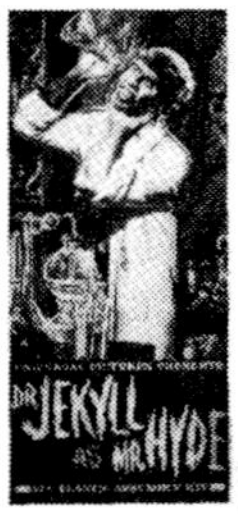
DR JEKYLL AS MR HYDE

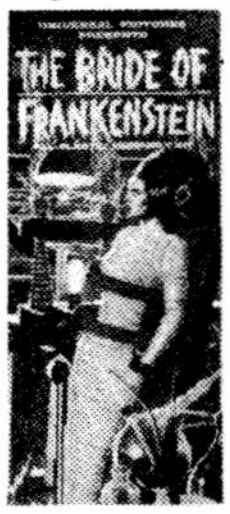
THE BRIDE OF FRANKENSTEIN

THE BRIDE OF FRANKENSTEIN

NOT ALL LADIES are Monsters except the scary new Bride of Frankenstein, all decked out, in this Monster Kit, in her terrible trousseau. Regular cut-up (on the lab table.) Have fun for $1.49.

ADD THESE TO YOUR MONSTER COLLECTION. Have hours of Horror enjoyment, assembling these new kits . . . most gruesome ever made. Specify Kit wanted and mail $1.49, plus 25c for postage & handling.

2 CLASSIC MONSTER KITS!

THE HUNCH BACK OF NOTRE DAME

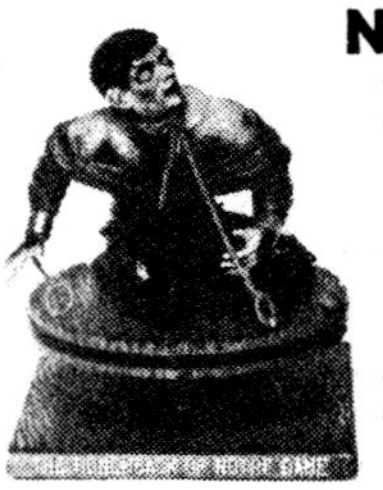

THE HUNCHBACK OF NOTRE DAME. As you start to build this greatest of all Monster characters, you will see not only the physical ugliness, but the beautiful soul that made Lon Chaney's performance a great classic. QUASIMODO, the HORRIBLE, is on the block in the city square. A vicious rope hangs around his neck. His hands are in chains, his throat is parched with thirst. He looks up in ghastly fear at his tormentors. Only 98¢ plus 25¢ for postage and handling.

WOLFMAN

WOLF MAN—In all his gory splendor, arms upraised, ready to clutch his next victim. Complete in every detail, this kit when you assemble it . . . before you run out of the room, is a detailed scale model of "WOLF MAN" surrounded by his favorite playmates. Only 98¢ plus 25¢ for postage & handling.

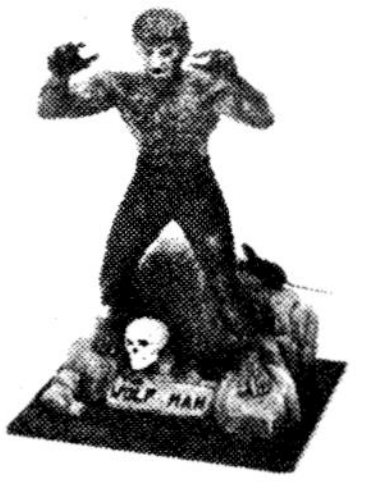
WOLF MAN

WATCH THE
MIRACLE OF BIRTH
BEFORE YOUR VERY EYES

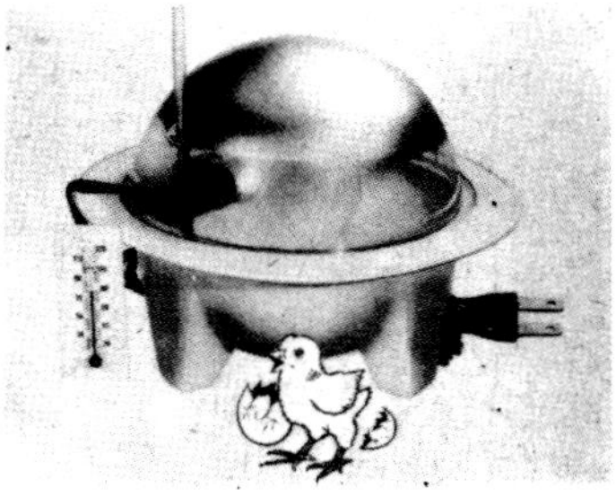

See the entire hatching process . . . from egg to chick . . . through the plastic dome window of this 2 egg incubator. Maintains proper heat and humidity to hatch chicks, ducks, pheasants, quail, etc. Includes bulb, egg holder, thermometer, and instruction book. Stands 6" tall, 7¼" wide. Base converts to a brooder after chick is hatched. Only $2.98 plus 50c postage.

PERPETUAL MOTION
SOLAR ENGINE
NO ELECTRICITY! NO BATTERIES!

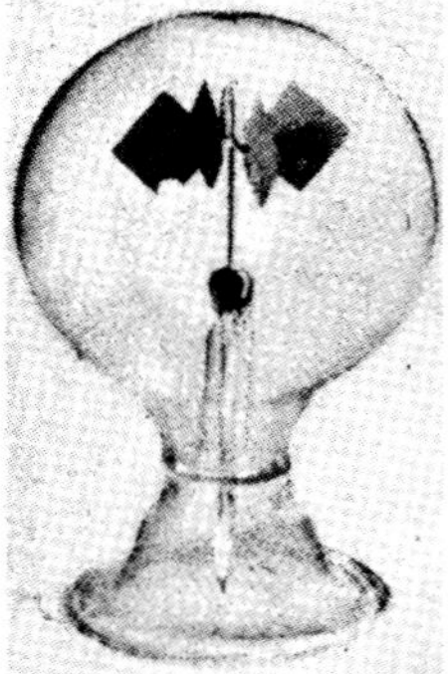

All you need is LIGHT to run this scientific ATOMIC ENERGY ENGINE. The brighter the light—the faster it will spin. Resembles a light bulb (made of quality glass) with a heavy-duty base. Sits anywhere. 6 inches high. No parts to wear out—nothing to get out of order. Any kind of light will cause it to turn—even under water! A truly fascinating and mysterious novelty. Only $1.75 plus 25c postage & handling.

A COMPLETE SET OF 5 DIFFERENT
MONSTER RINGS

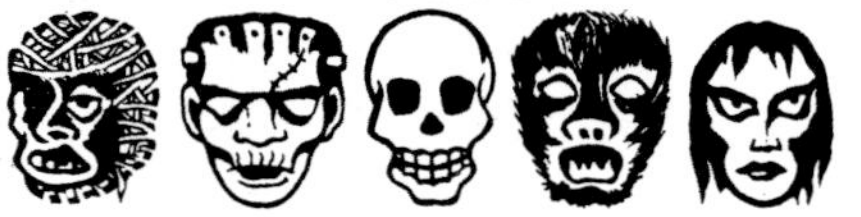

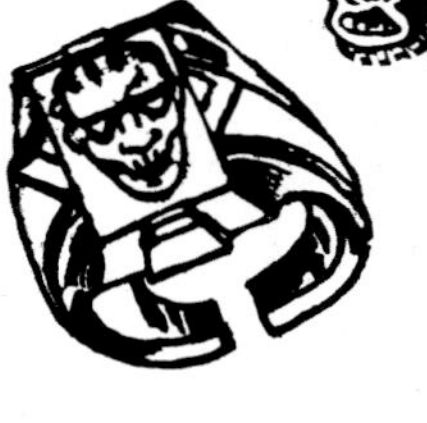

Bright silver-finished MONSTER RINGS with secret flicker designs that jump and change position with each movement of the hand! You get ALL 5 MONSTER RINGS (WEREWOLF, FRANKENSTEIN, VAMPIRE, SKULL & MUMMY) for only 50c plus 25c postage & handling.

USE THIS COUPON TO ORDER NEW MONSTER KITS SHOWN ON PG. 57

☐ Send me THE WITCH for which I enclose $1.79 ($1.49 plus 30c handling & postage). Please rush!

☐ Send me DR. JEKYLL AS MR. HYDE, for which I enclose $1.79 ($1.49 plus 30c handling & postage). Please rush!

☐ Send me THE BRIDE OF FRANKENSTEIN, for which I enclose $1.79 ($1.49 plus 30c handling & postage). Please rush!

NAME ....

ADDRESS ....

CITY .... STATE .... ZIP ....

NO C.O.D.'s PLEASE. Print name & address clearly on all orders.

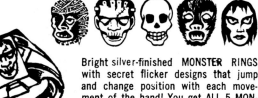

It's dark in this dungeon but I'm not afraid..I'll be safe here while I compile the evidence that will save me from hanging!

My defense has been long in preparation.. but, Judge Head has been most understanding and considerate! He's granted every extension!

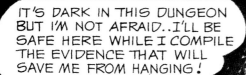

Well now..we're about to learn of a gentle soul and the little failing that led him afoul of the law! However – in a day of judicial awareness, we shall see how he won a verdict with..

JUSTICE!

Members of this honorable court, we know the accused, Winston Fig to be a murderer and a butcher, but we are here today to hang him as a..GHOUL!

To fully understand this 'beast' let us retrace his case! We begin with Winston Fig.. accountant in the import firm of one A.G. Varum..deceased!

Mister Fig! I find it necessary to remind you that you are here to see to my books.. not to ogle my wife!

Sorry... I wasn't aware!

ART AND STORY BY PAT BOYETTE

185

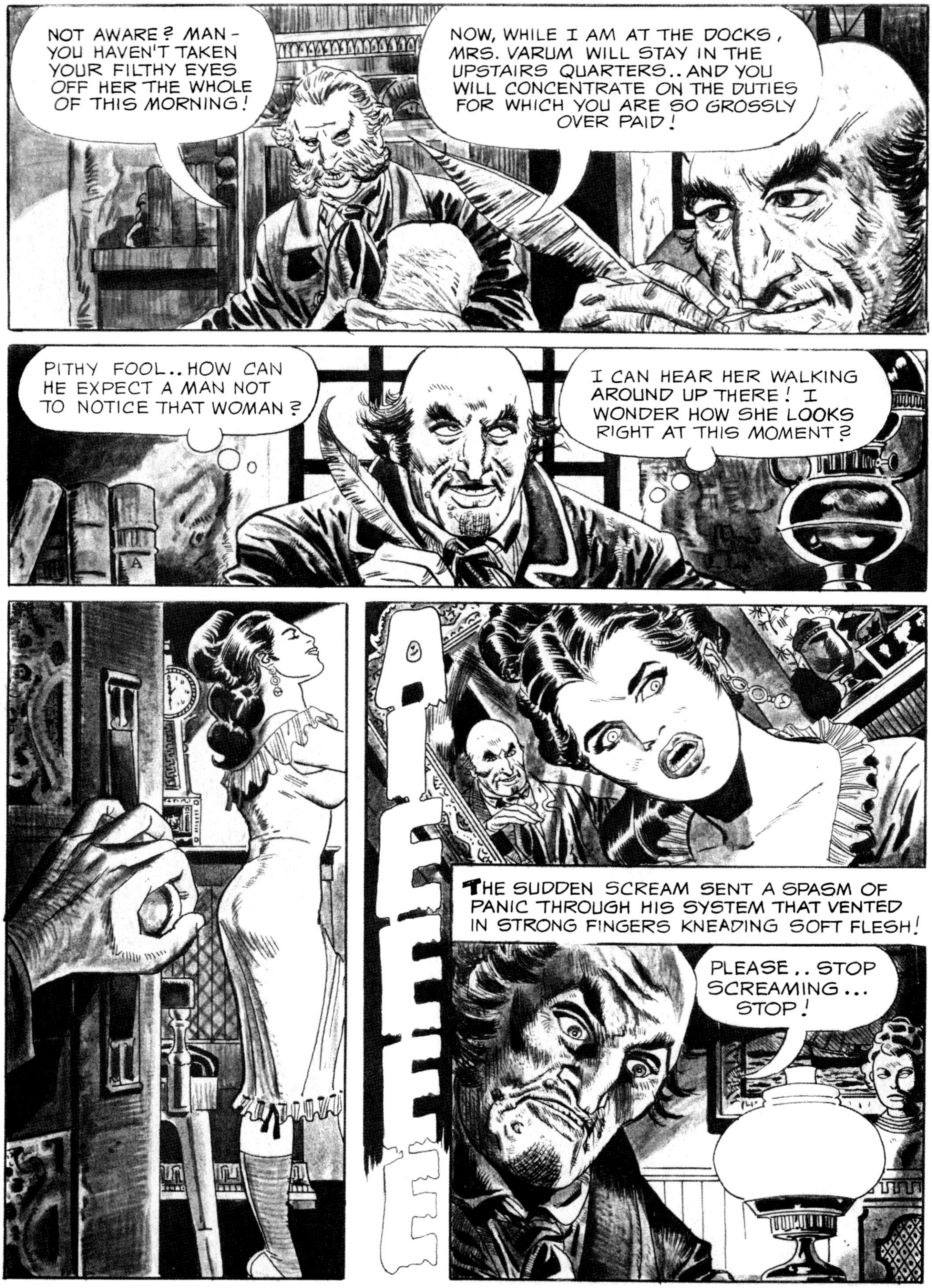
NOT AWARE? MAN - YOU HAVEN'T TAKEN YOUR FILTHY EYES OFF HER THE WHOLE OF THIS MORNING!
NOW, WHILE I AM AT THE DOCKS, MRS. VARUM WILL STAY IN THE UPSTAIRS QUARTERS.. AND YOU WILL CONCENTRATE ON THE DUTIES FOR WHICH YOU ARE SO GROSSLY OVER PAID!
PITHY FOOL.. HOW CAN HE EXPECT A MAN NOT TO NOTICE THAT WOMAN?
I CAN HEAR HER WALKING AROUND UP THERE! I WONDER HOW SHE LOOKS RIGHT AT THIS MOMENT?
THE SUDDEN SCREAM SENT A SPASM OF PANIC THROUGH HIS SYSTEM THAT VENTED IN STRONG FINGERS KNEADING SOFT FLESH!
PLEASE.. STOP SCREAMING... STOP!

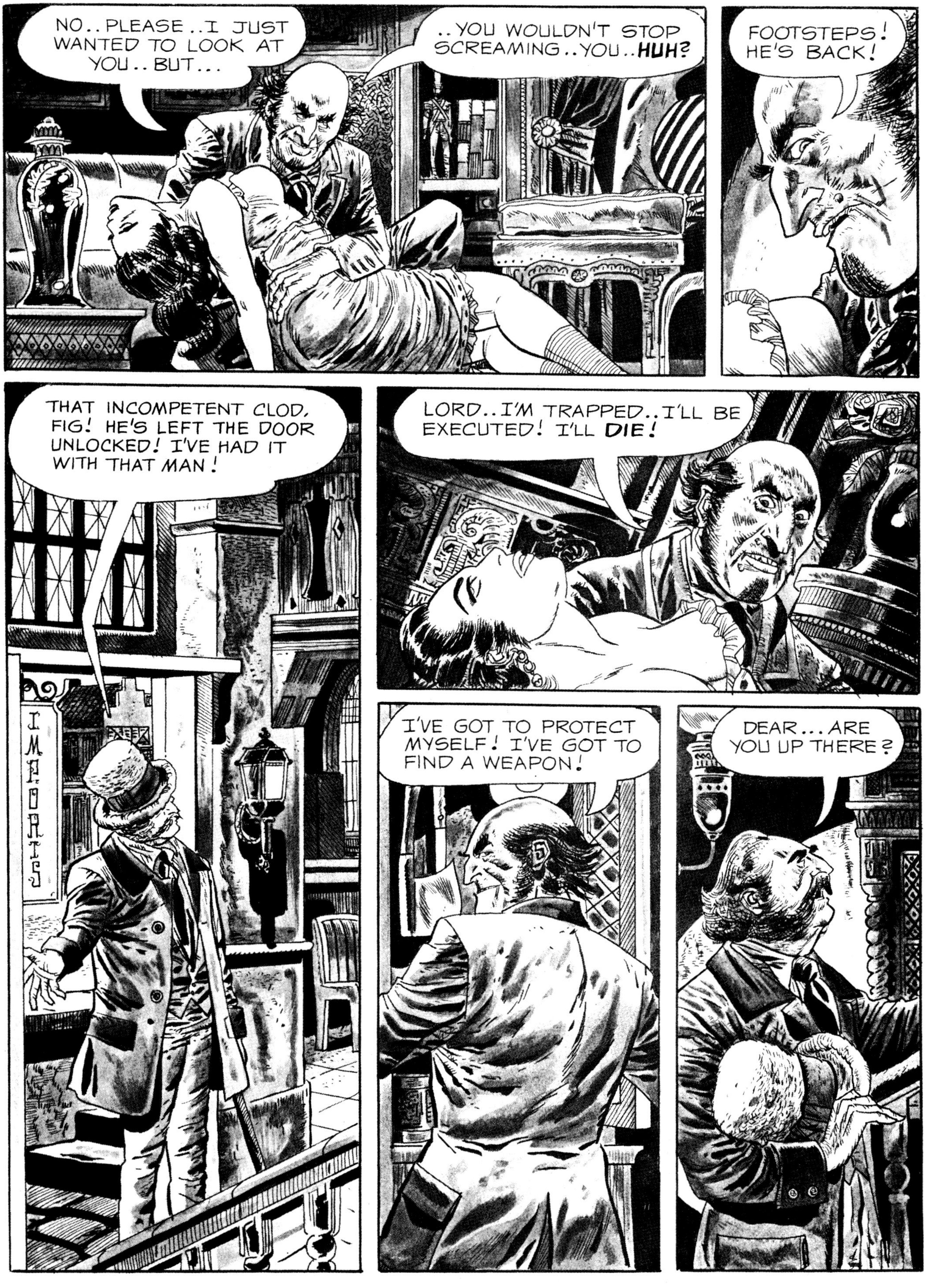
NO..PLEASE..I JUST WANTED TO LOOK AT YOU..BUT...
..YOU WOULDN'T STOP SCREAMING..YOU..HUH?
FOOTSTEPS! HE'S BACK!
THAT INCOMPETENT CLOD, FIG! HE'S LEFT THE DOOR UNLOCKED! I'VE HAD IT WITH THAT MAN!
IMPORTS
LORD..I'M TRAPPED..I'LL BE EXECUTED! I'LL DIE!
I'VE GOT TO PROTECT MYSELF! I'VE GOT TO FIND A WEAPON!
DEAR...ARE YOU UP THERE?

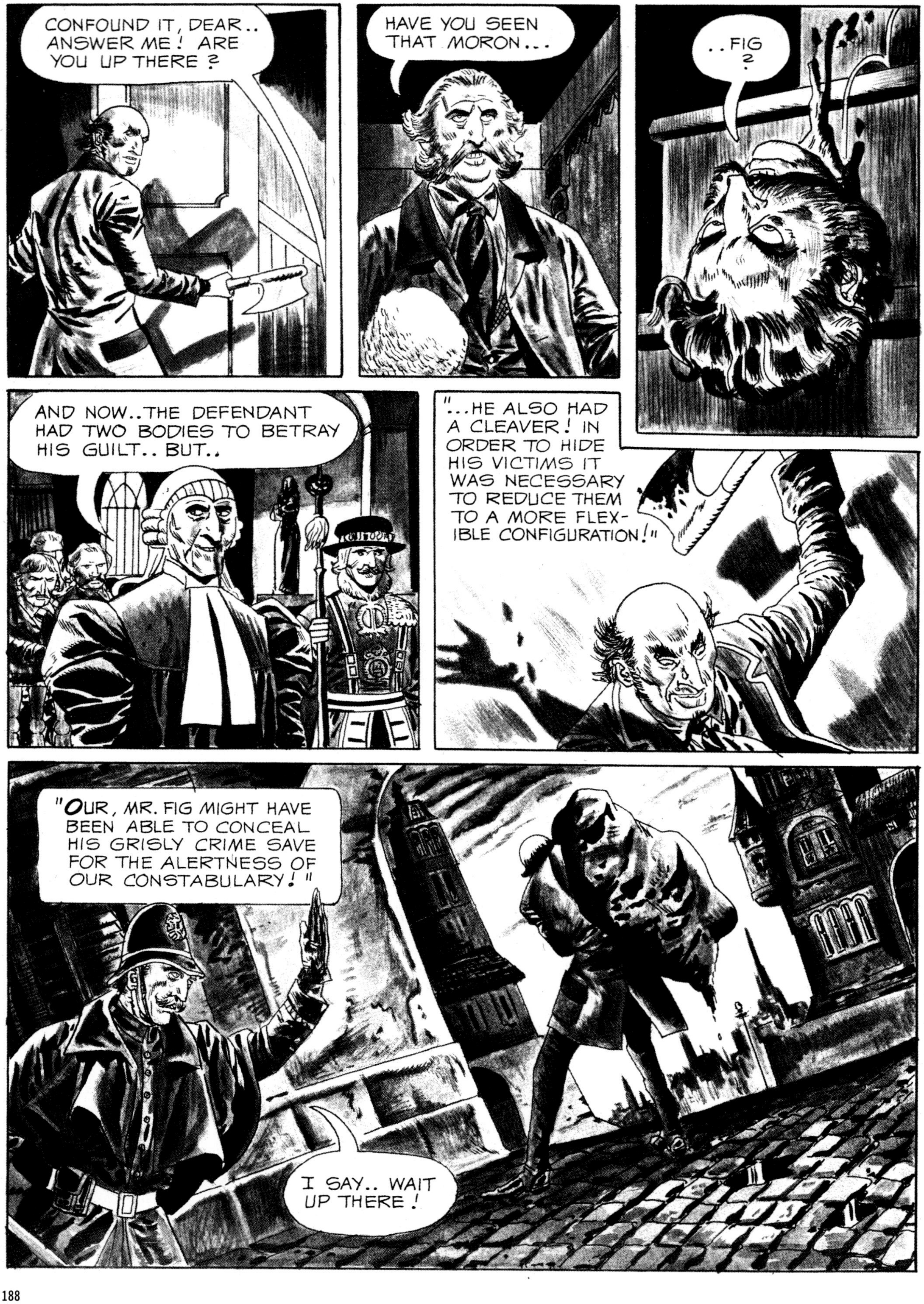
CONFOUND IT, DEAR.. ANSWER ME! ARE YOU UP THERE?
HAVE YOU SEEN THAT MORON...
..FIG?
AND NOW..THE DEFENDANT HAD TWO BODIES TO BETRAY HIS GUILT.. BUT..
"...HE ALSO HAD A CLEAVER! IN ORDER TO HIDE HIS VICTIMS IT WAS NECESSARY TO REDUCE THEM TO A MORE FLEX-IBLE CONFIGURATION!"
"OUR, MR. FIG MIGHT HAVE BEEN ABLE TO CONCEAL HIS GRISLY CRIME SAVE FOR THE ALERTNESS OF OUR CONSTABULARY!"
I SAY.. WAIT UP THERE!

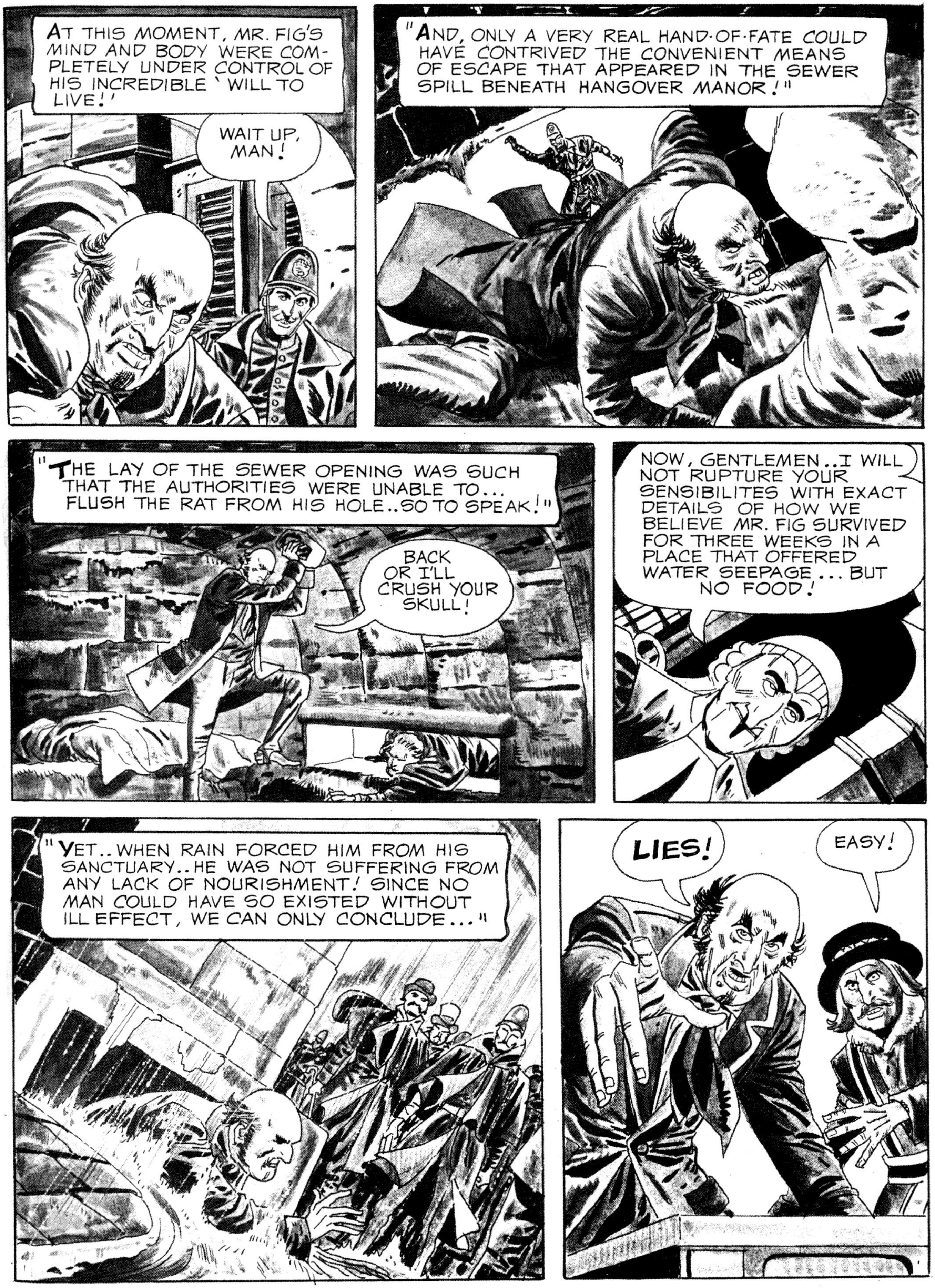
AT THIS MOMENT, MR. FIG'S MIND AND BODY WERE COMPLETELY UNDER CONTROL OF HIS INCREDIBLE 'WILL TO LIVE!'
WAIT UP, MAN!
"AND, ONLY A VERY REAL HAND-OF-FATE COULD HAVE CONTRIVED THE CONVENIENT MEANS OF ESCAPE THAT APPEARED IN THE SEWER SPILL BENEATH HANGOVER MANOR!"
"THE LAY OF THE SEWER OPENING WAS SUCH THAT THE AUTHORITIES WERE UNABLE TO... FLUSH THE RAT FROM HIS HOLE..SO TO SPEAK!"
BACK OR I'LL CRUSH YOUR SKULL!
NOW, GENTLEMEN..I WILL NOT RUPTURE YOUR SENSIBILITES WITH EXACT DETAILS OF HOW WE BELIEVE MR. FIG SURVIVED FOR THREE WEEKS IN A PLACE THAT OFFERED WATER SEEPAGE ... BUT NO FOOD!
"YET..WHEN RAIN FORCED HIM FROM HIS SANCTUARY..HE WAS NOT SUFFERING FROM ANY LACK OF NOURISHMENT! SINCE NO MAN COULD HAVE SO EXISTED WITHOUT ILL EFFECT, WE CAN ONLY CONCLUDE..."
LIES!
EASY!

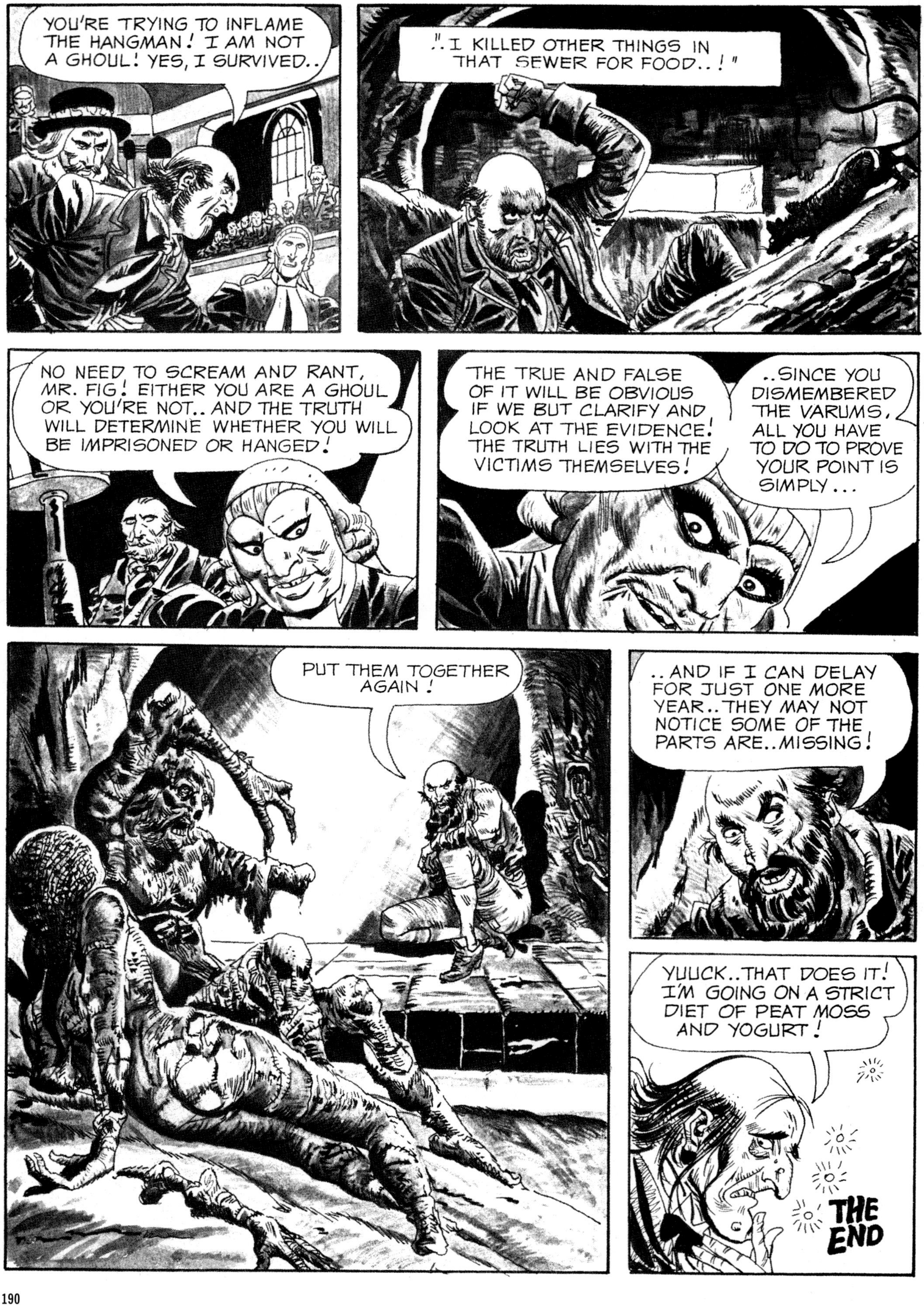
YOU'RE TRYING TO INFLAME THE HANGMAN! I AM NOT A GHOUL! YES, I SURVIVED..
".. I KILLED OTHER THINGS IN THAT SEWER FOR FOOD..!"
NO NEED TO SCREAM AND RANT, MR. FIG! EITHER YOU ARE A GHOUL OR YOU'RE NOT.. AND THE TRUTH WILL DETERMINE WHETHER YOU WILL BE IMPRISONED OR HANGED!
THE TRUE AND FALSE OF IT WILL BE OBVIOUS IF WE BUT CLARIFY AND LOOK AT THE EVIDENCE! THE TRUTH LIES WITH THE VICTIMS THEMSELVES!
..SINCE YOU DISMEMBERED THE VARUMS, ALL YOU HAVE TO DO TO PROVE YOUR POINT IS SIMPLY...
PUT THEM TOGETHER AGAIN!
..AND IF I CAN DELAY FOR JUST ONE MORE YEAR.. THEY MAY NOT NOTICE SOME OF THE PARTS ARE..MISSING!
YUUCK..THAT DOES IT! I'M GOING ON A STRICT DIET OF PEAT MOSS AND YOGURT!
THE END

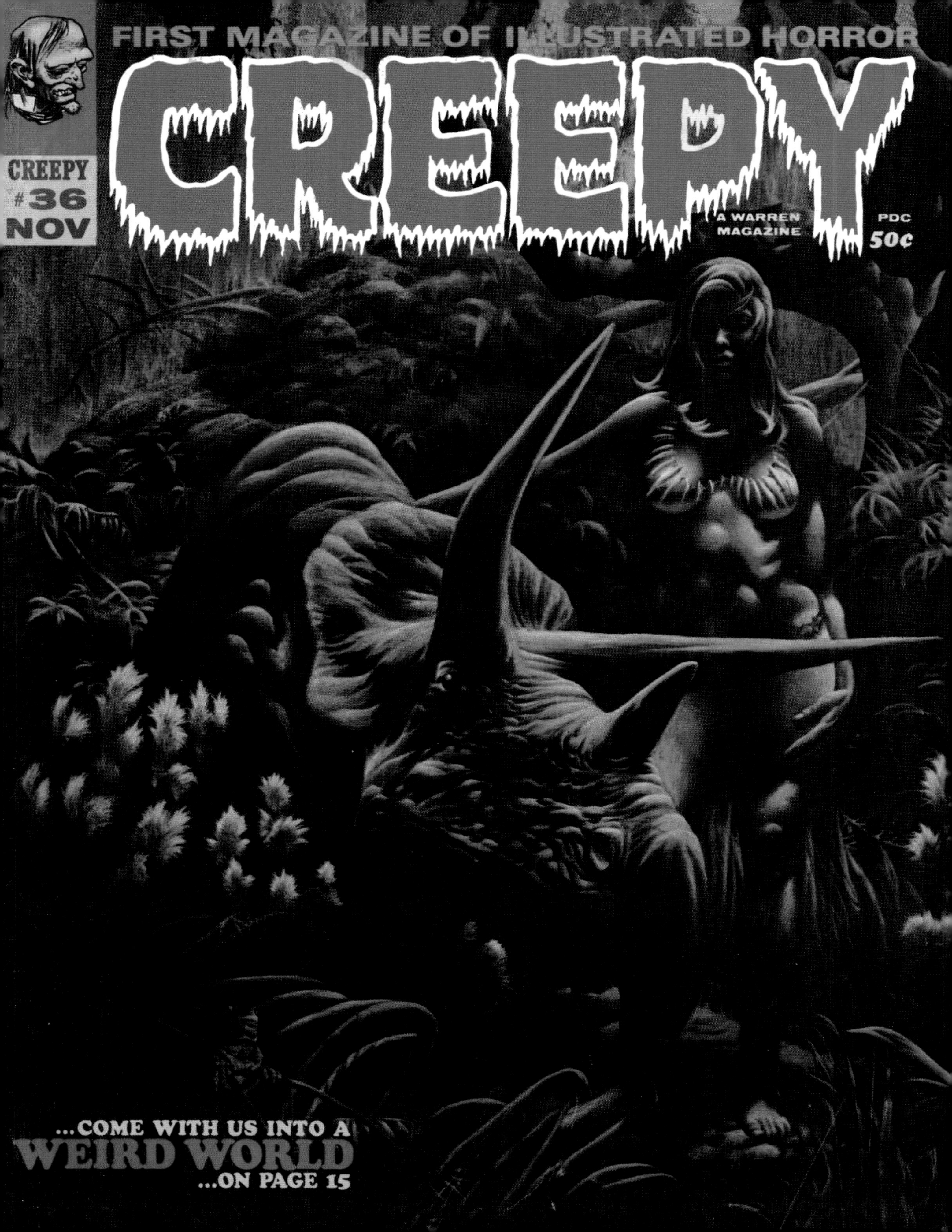
FIRST MAGAZINE OF ILLUSTRATED HORROR
CREEPY
CREEPY
#36
NOV
A WARREN MAGAZINE
PDC
50¢
...COME WITH US INTO A
WEIRD WORLD
...ON PAGE 15

CREEPY'S LOATHSOME LORE
by Tom Sutton '70

I'VE GOT A **BONE** TO PICK WITH MEDDLING **MEDICS** WHO THINK R.I.P. MEANS **REST IN PIECES!** SEE WHAT I MEAN IN...

THE BODY SNATCHERS WHO STOLE A **GIANT!**

1780: AN ENGLISH SIDE SHOW ATTRACTION BECOMES THE OBJECT OF AN EMINENT PHYSICIAN'S **MORBID** FACINATION!

SEE THE **GIANT** CHARLES BYRNE WORLD'S LARGEST MAN!

MARVELOUS SPECIMEN!

I'LL PAY YOU A **FORTUNE** FOR PERMISSION TO **DISSECT** YOUR **BODY** ONCE YOU... AH... NO LONGER HAVE **NEED** OF IT!

YOU WANT ME TO BE A **FREAK** IN **DEATH** AS WELL AS IN LIFE? DR. HUNTER, MY ANSWER IS... **NO!**

THE DOCTOR'S MEN STALKED THEIR MIGHTY PREY FOR THREE LONG YEARS UNTIL BYRNE **DIED** A NEUROTIC ALCHOLIC!

GROG SHOP

BURY ME WHERE THAT... **FIEND** CAN'T GET AT ME!

THE **DEEPEST** PART OF THE THAMES, THAT'S WHERE WE'LL PUT HIM!

THE DOCTOR WILL **NEVER** GET HIM THERE!

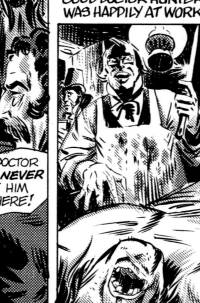

HOWEVER THE GREEDY UNDERTAKER WAS **BRIBED** AND THE GIANT'S COFFIN SWITCHED FOR AN IDENTICAL ONE CONTAINING **ROCKS!** AT THE MOMENT THE GIANT'S FRIENDS THOUGHT THEY CONSIGNED HIM TO THE BOSOM OF THE SEA, THE GOOD DOCTOR HUNTER WAS HAPPILY AT WORK!

THE RESULT OF HIS DEDICATED LABORS WAS EXHIBITED TO AN EXCITED WORLD...

ENTRANCE

LOOK AT **THAT!**

INCREDIBLE!

AN **AMAZING FEAT!**

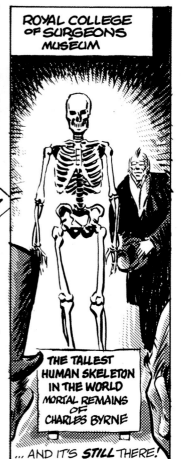

ROYAL COLLEGE OF SURGEONS MUSEUM

THE **TALLEST HUMAN SKELETON IN THE WORLD** MORTAL REMAINS OF **CHARLES BYRNE**

... AND IT'S **STILL** THERE!

ART AND STORY BY TOM SUTTON

CREEPY

NO. 36

EDITOR and PUBLISHER: JAMES WARREN **ASSOCIATE EDITOR:** ARCHIE GOODWIN
CONTRIBUTING EDITORS: BILL PARENTE, NICOLA CUTI **COVER:** KEN SMITH
ARTISTS THIS ISSUE: RICHARD BUCKLER, RICHARD CORBEN, CARLOS GARZON, JERRY GRANDENETTI, JACK SPARLING, TOM SUTTON
WRITERS THIS ISSUE: T. CASEY BRENNAN, RICHARD CORBEN, NICOLA CUTI, JAMES HAGGENMILLER, R. MICHAEL ROSEN, GREG THEAKSTON, BILL WARREN

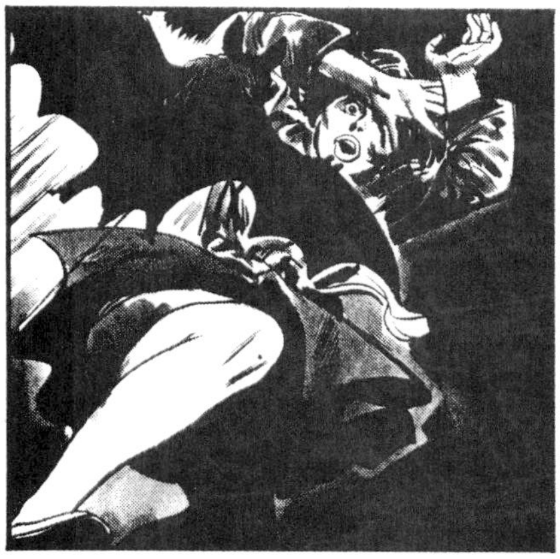

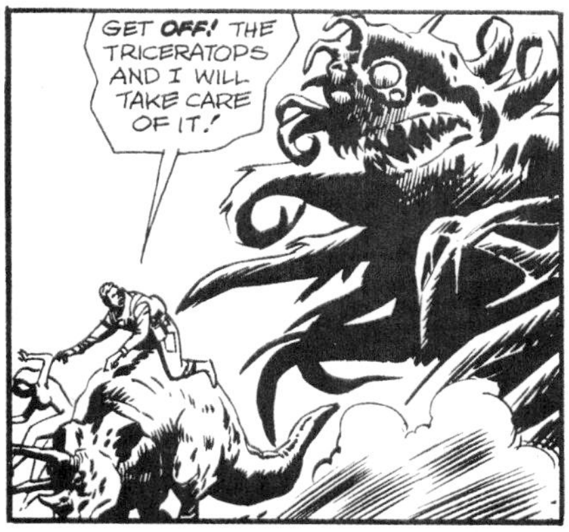
GET OFF! THE TRICERATOPS AND I WILL TAKE CARE OF IT!

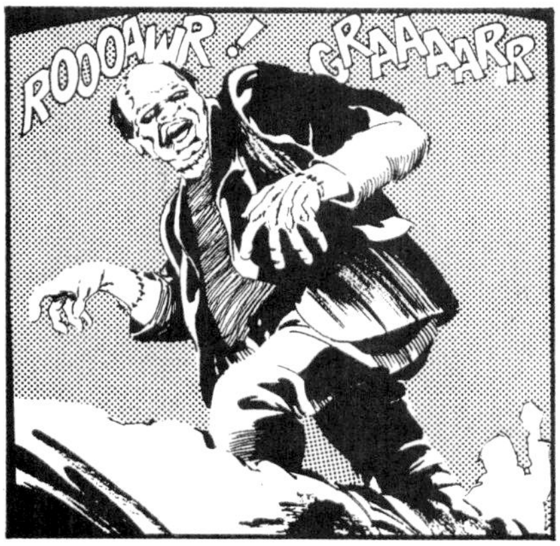
ROOOAWR!
GRAAAARR

CONTENTS

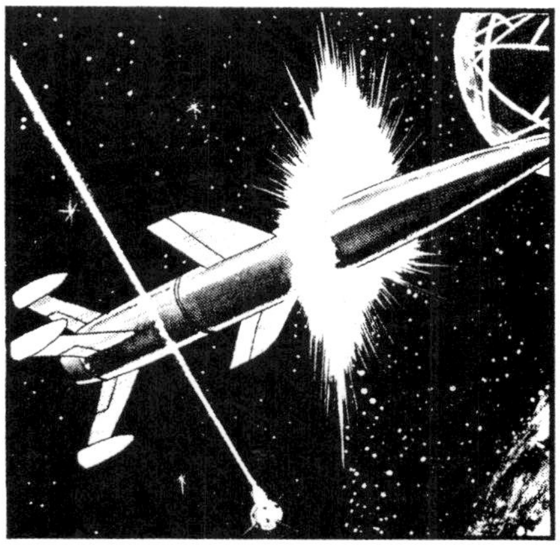

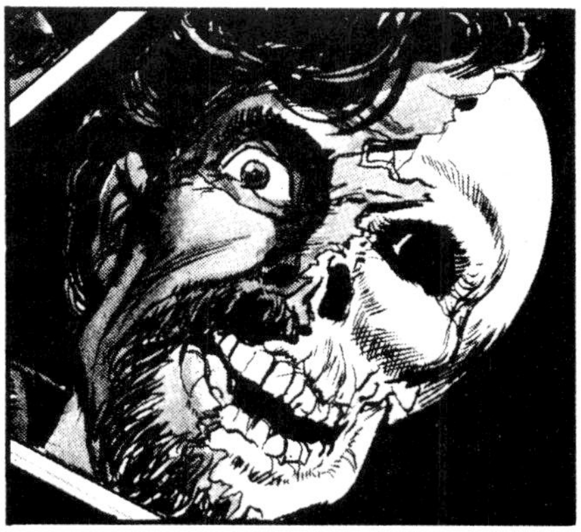

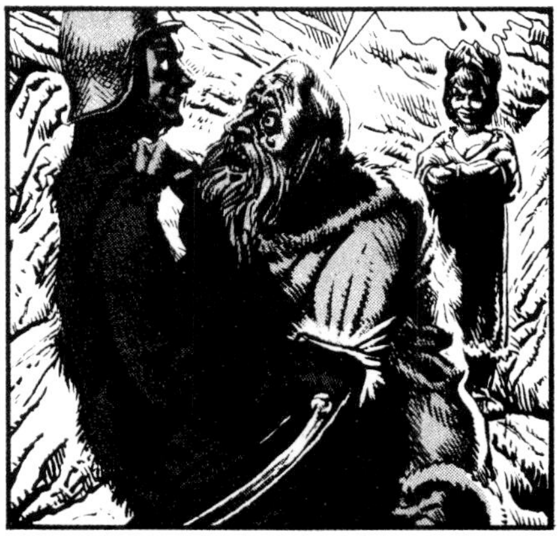

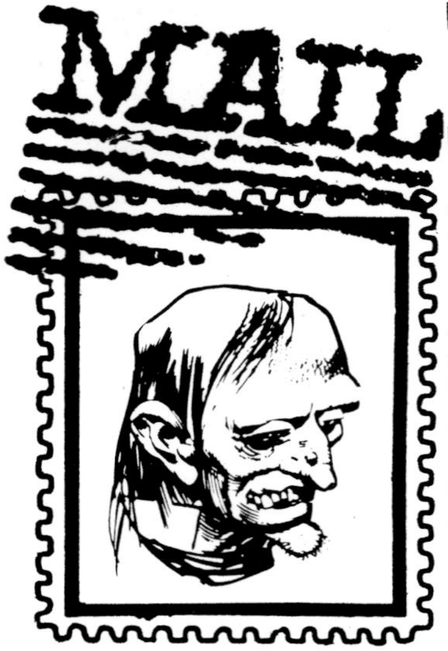
MAIL

"Run a funny story once in awhile!"

Wow! Ken Barr's art and cover for "Lifeboat" in **CREEPY** #34 was extra superb. Man! What a trip! It was really like the resurrection of the now oft-lamented Star Trek!

WINSOR McNEMO
Cleveland, Ohio

Aside from the fact that issue #34 was consistently excellent, artwise; and that "Lifeboat" was probably the best script I've seen for a piece of illustrated fiction in more than two years, I must take issue with author Robert Rosen on some "facts" in the story "X-Tra X." I would suggest that if Mr. Rosen is trying to link lycanthropy with genetic abnormalities, he'd better consult a biology textbook first. The statement "genes . . . are made up of chromosomes," (page 7) is erroneous. Specific genes are located on specific choromsomes.

The only disease I know of which is caused by an extra X chromosome is Kleinfelter's Syndrome, a rare disease in the human male. As yet, direct removal of defective choromosomes is impossible. The only feasible way to correct chromosomal abnormality is the injection of hormones which may in some cases counteract hereditary defects.

Perhaps I'm wrong in expecting an Isaac Asimov script in **CREEPY.** But I think you should stick to innocuous subjects like vampirism, lycanthropy, murder, science fiction, etc., without making any attempt to set a biology curriculum back then thousand years.

THOMAS PREHODA
Schenectady, N.Y.

Hmmm, yes. The doctor was out playing golf the day that script came in. Sorry Tom.

As for your rave for "Lifeboat"—it makes us feel a little edgy and embarrased. Not that ol' Uncle Creep can't take flattery, mind you. You see, the story was attributed to Bill Parente. Actually it was scripted by Nicola Cuti . . . and ol' Unc Creepy was responsible. His foul-up set good magazine publishing back twenty thousand years—if not more!

I am writing this letter in honor of the new member of your faculty, Ken Barr. When I gazed upon the cover of issue #34, I knew that Ken was fast becoming one of the best in your Hall of Fame.

Although Ken is not new to the comic field, I'm sure he will bring up the level of **CREEPY** to what it was back in the good old days. I was even more impressed by the fact that he did the cover story, "Lifeboat." His art was magnificent and Parente's story was more than fabulous. With the addition of Ken Kelly, Dan Adkins, Don Vaughn and Syd Shores, your magazine will never lose its reign as the number one magazine of illustrated horror.

JOHN LIGHTMAN
Toronto, Ontario

Here that, EERIE? He said number one!

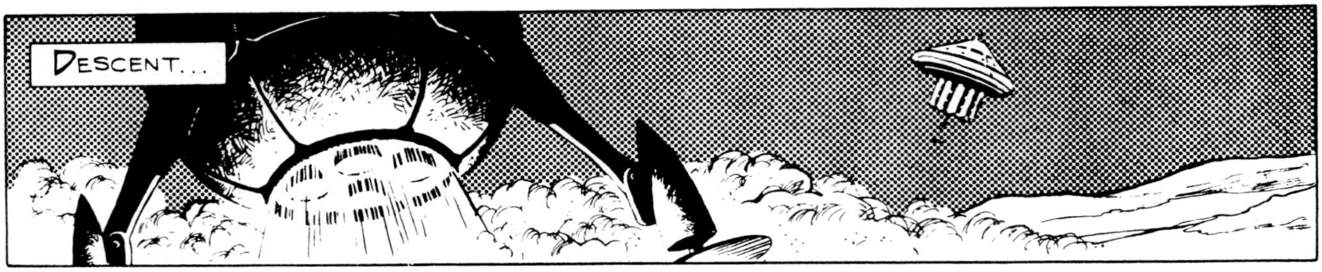
DESCENT...

SCENE BY KEN BARR FROM THE SUPER SCIENCE-FICTION EPIC EFFORT, "LIFEBOAT!"— Correspondents McNemo, Prehoda, and Lightman rave FAN-tabulously in letters above.

A lot of the letters you and your cohorts have been printing lately have been taking swipes at your "competition."

I don't think you really know who your competition is. Have you seen a copy of "Time" lately? Or "Newsweek?" Brother, **that's** your competition!

In case you hadn't noticed, Unc, there's a war on. And the people running it have come up with some pretty groovy ways of getting rid of people. Compared to them, your vampires and ghouls and werewolves are a bunch of rank amateurs.

Your villains kill people one at a time, and for the most part pay for their evil ways in the end. But these guys—the professionals—are coming up with ways of wiping out hundreds at a time. And they get parades in their honor, medals to pin on their chests and the acclaim of a "grateful nation."

Of course, there are some big differences. Your monsters terrorize villages in the mountains of middle Europe. The real monsters are helping to rid the world of the Yellow Peril. The Commie Yellow Peril. And they aren't really like us, as those middle Europeans are. So it's all right. All those years of reading about Ming the Merciless and the bad guys in Buck Rogers' time have made us realize that the world would be much better off without all those yellow people anyway.

I know you're a good American, Unc. You came here by choice from your native Transylvania—or wherever so you must be. But I think it's time you joined the fight against the fighting. It's only a matter of time before your readers realize that they can get more blood and gore in the news magazines than they ever get from you. And don't forget the news magazines come out every week. You only hit the stands every two months.

GENE BARTON
Aurora, Indiana

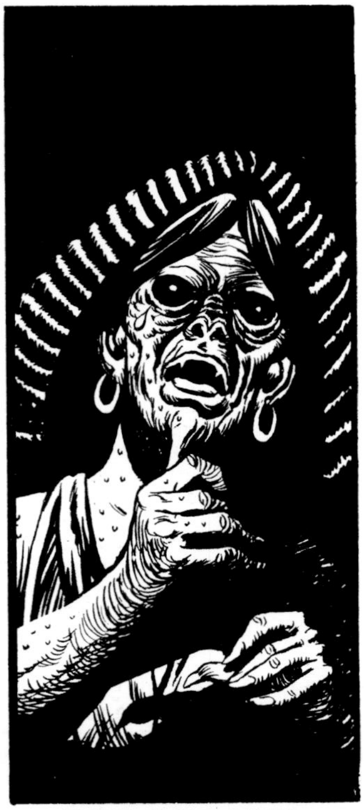

FROM "LIFEBOAT!"
Monster BY KEN BARR

"Readers can get more blood & gore in news magazines!"

I would like to know if you have stopped printing **VAMPIRELLA** Magazine. Except for **CREEPY**, I think it is the best I have ever read, and I have read a lot. I have the first four issues, but would like to get the others if there are any. The store I go to does not get this magazine any more. You're my only hope.

DONALD LUTHER
Riverside, Cal.

Much as I hate to admit it, VAMPIRELLA is still alive and doing very nicely now in her seventh issue. If your store doesn't have it, keep pestering them until they get it. All they have to do is ask for it themselves. If that doesn't work, order a subscription by sending your name and address with your Zip Code and a check to VAMPIRELLA, 22 E. 42d St., New York, N.Y. 10017. A year's subscription is just $3.00; or you can order two years for $5.00. The price is the same for CREEPY, by the way.

You've been making too many mistakes. In issue #34, page 10, 6th panel, you have the same caption as page 11, first panel. The pictures are different, but the words are the same.

But don't worry, your stories are still great and your art is still perfect.

JAY GILBERT
Shively, Ky.

I have been buying your magazine for the past few months, and I am hooked on it again. I first started collecting **CREEPY** with issue #9. But I quit collecting when the art and stories got bad.

But I felt I just had to write to tell you that your magazine has finally come back to the peak of perfection you set with your earlier issues.

A few comments on the Fan Club pages: I'm sick of seeing amateurish pictures of Frankenstein, Dracula, etc. They have to go. In issue #34, three of the pictures turned out muddy-looking. Is that your printer, or just an artist's mistake? The story, "The Search for the Phasimara Plant," put me to sleep after the first two paragraphs.

LOUIS WILSON
Albuquerque, N.M.

The Fan Club page is exactly what the name says it is: A collection of stories and art done by our readers. We don't get many professionals asking to be represented there, and ~~we try to select the best of the~~ material that's mailed to us. This is one time we can honestly say, "Can you do better?" If you think you can, why don't you?

CREEPY
This Issue: DUEL of the MONSTERS!

Frazetta's duel of the Monsters . . . Brought back fan Madeira (letter below).

Of all of your 33 issues, of the 27 issues of **EERIE**, my favorite cover is still the one on **CREEPY** #7. No cover on any magazine anywhere has ever matched it.

Let's see more vampires and werewolves in **CREEPY.** The story in #7, "Duel of the Monsters," was one of the best. This is the kind of stories I want to see again in CREEPY. Let's stop this madness of science fiction.

I've also noticed that lately your heroes are killing off a lot of good monsters. This didn't used to be the case. Your monsters used to wind up on top no matter what. So come on. Wise up.

How about you and Eerie and Vampirella teaming up in one great story together. Sort of a comedy-horror idea. But do it in **her** mag, not yours.

JACK MADEIRA
Toronto, Ontario

Yours truly and Cousin Eerie will appear together in "Where Satan Dwells" in a future ish of CREEPY. Ernie Colon is busy illustrating this episode taken from the true lives of Cousin Eerie and Uncle Creepy which was Chronicled by Ontarian author, Al Hewetsen. Watch for it.

I wonder how many of your readers remember the great Boris Karloff television series, "Thriller." Or the "Twilight Zone" series when it was in its heyday. They don't have anything like either one of those shows any more. Which is one reason I'm thankful for magazines like **CREEPY, EERIE** and **VAMPIRELLA.**

One of the things I enjoyed most about the Karloff show and Rod Serling's great program was that every few weeks or so they'd run a show with a humorous touch. Oh, they managed to hang on to the air of mystery that made them great, but they also managed to get plenty of laughs into the scripts.

And that's something you don't do enough of, Unc.

I don't think you should do it often, but a funny story once in a while would be a very nice addition to your already great magazine. Someone recently wrote to you—or was it to **EERIE?**—telling you that you ought to get Mort Drucker or one of the other **MAD** regulars to do a story for you. The idea isn't as far-fetched as you might think. I say it would be great fun. Does anybody agree with me?

JIM BOWSER
Scranton, Penna.

WHO CARES?

Every letter addressed to DEAR UNCLE CREEPY 22 East 42d Street New York, N.Y. 10017 is carefully read. As many as can be are even printed in the Magazine. . . . And you thought nobody cared!

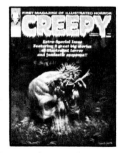

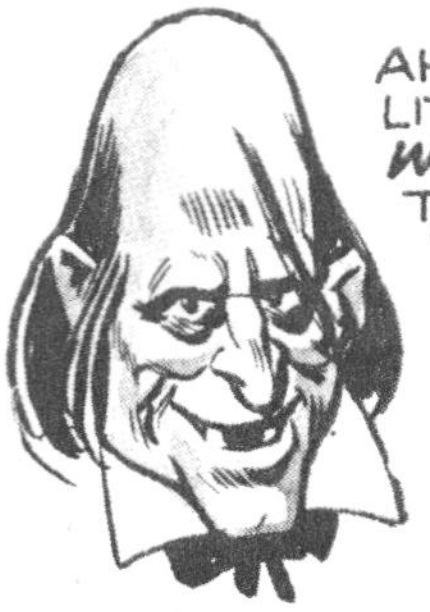

AH! YOU'RE JUST IN TIME LITTLE FRIENDS... WE NEED **WITNESSES** TO A CONTRACT THAT'S ABOUT TO BE SIGNED! THE GENTLEMAN YOU SEE BELOW IS GOING TO MAKE A **DEVILISH DEAL** JUST TO PROVIDE...

ONE WAY TO BREAK THE BOREDOM

THE PLACE: NEW YORK CITY. THE TIME: EARLY EVENING ON A FRIDAY NIGHT. FOR MILLIONAIRE GARY WILLIAMS, IT SHOULD BE THE MOST EXCITING NIGHT OF THE WEEK. GARY IS HANDSOME, RICH, AND USUALLY GETS WHAT HE WANTS. SO WHY IS HE SO ANGRY? LET'S SEE...

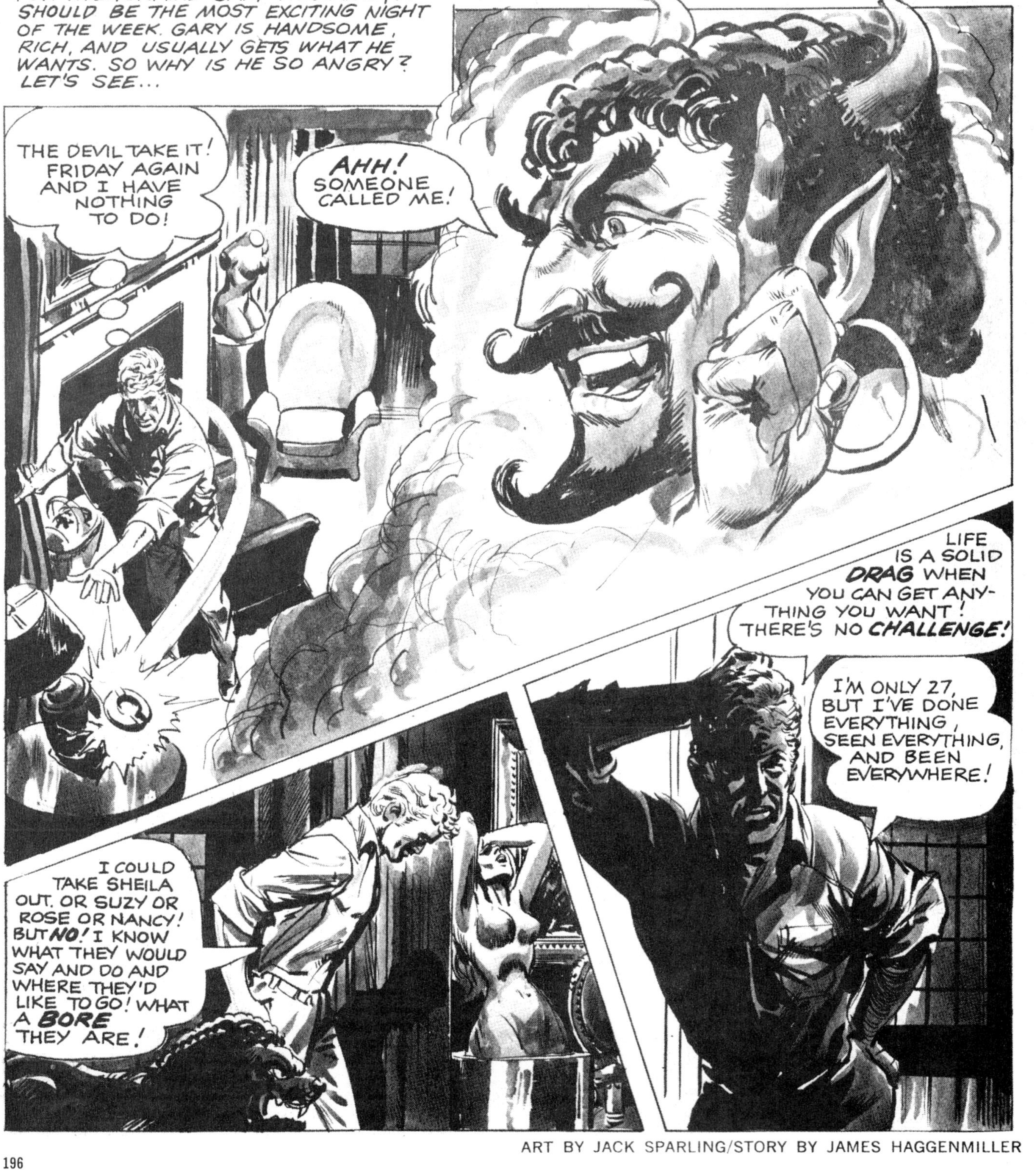

THE DEVIL TAKE IT! FRIDAY AGAIN AND I HAVE NOTHING TO DO!
AHH! SOMEONE CALLED ME!
I COULD TAKE SHEILA OUT. OR SUZY OR ROSE OR NANCY! BUT NO! I KNOW WHAT THEY WOULD SAY AND DO AND WHERE THEY'D LIKE TO GO! WHAT A BORE THEY ARE!
LIFE IS A SOLID DRAG WHEN YOU CAN GET ANYTHING YOU WANT! THERE'S NO CHALLENGE!
I'M ONLY 27, BUT I'VE DONE EVERYTHING, SEEN EVERYTHING, AND BEEN EVERYWHERE!

ART BY JACK SPARLING/STORY BY JAMES HAGGENMILLER

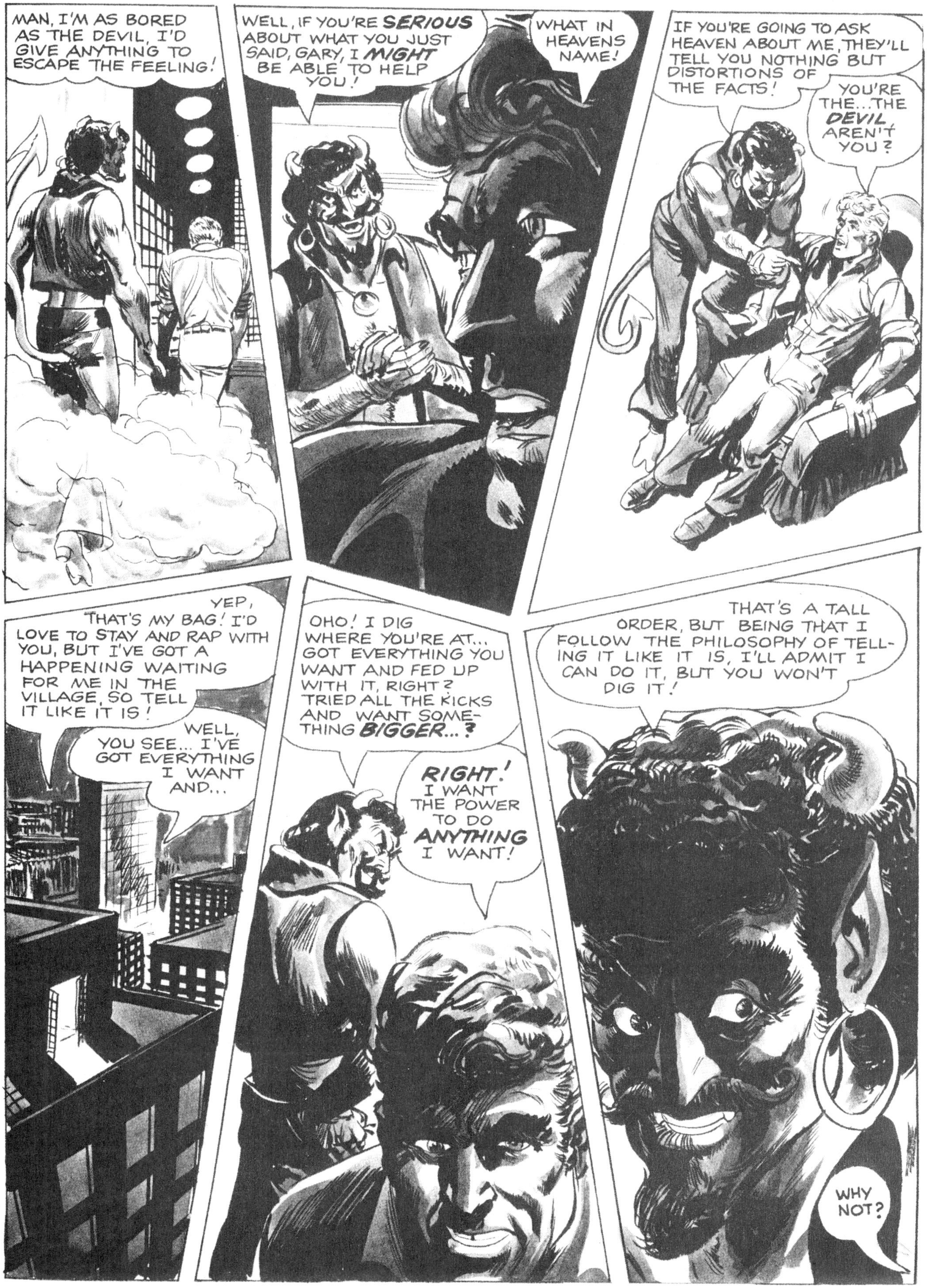
MAN, I'M AS BORED AS THE DEVIL, I'D GIVE ANYTHING TO ESCAPE THE FEELING!
WELL, IF YOU'RE SERIOUS ABOUT WHAT YOU JUST SAID, GARY, I MIGHT BE ABLE TO HELP YOU!
WHAT IN HEAVENS NAME!
IF YOU'RE GOING TO ASK HEAVEN ABOUT ME, THEY'LL TELL YOU NOTHING BUT DISTORTIONS OF THE FACTS!
YOU'RE THE... THE DEVIL, AREN'T YOU?
YEP, THAT'S MY BAG! I'D LOVE TO STAY AND RAP WITH YOU, BUT I'VE GOT A HAPPENING WAITING FOR ME IN THE VILLAGE, SO TELL IT LIKE IT IS!
WELL, YOU SEE... I'VE GOT EVERYTHING I WANT AND...
OHO! I DIG WHERE YOU'RE AT... GOT EVERYTHING YOU WANT AND FED UP WITH IT, RIGHT? TRIED ALL THE KICKS AND WANT SOMETHING BIGGER...?
RIGHT! I WANT THE POWER TO DO ANYTHING I WANT!
THAT'S A TALL ORDER, BUT BEING THAT I FOLLOW THE PHILOSOPHY OF TELLING IT LIKE IT IS, I'LL ADMIT I CAN DO IT, BUT YOU WON'T DIG IT!
WHY NOT?

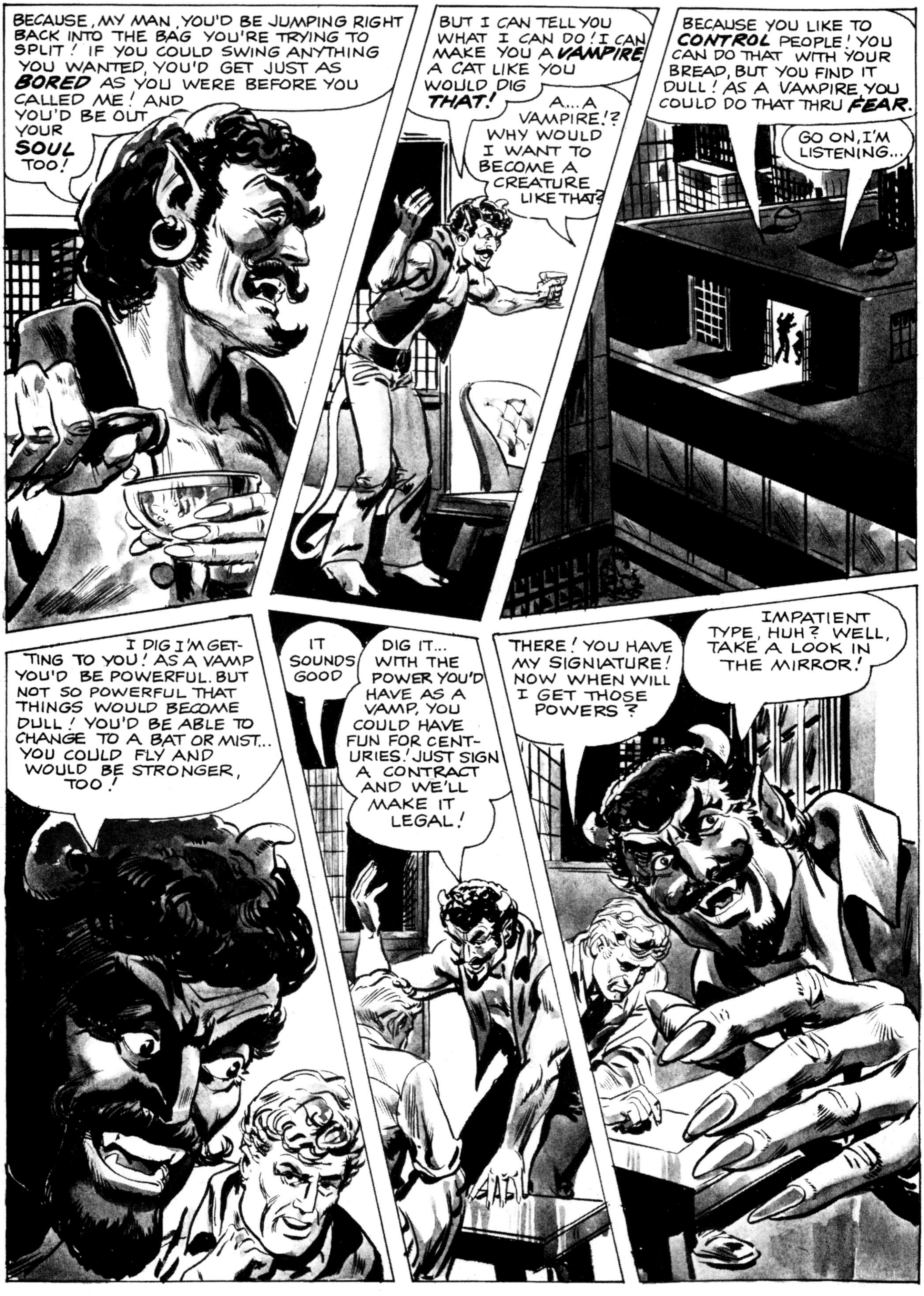
BECAUSE, MY MAN, YOU'D BE JUMPING RIGHT BACK INTO THE BAG YOU'RE TRYING TO SPLIT! IF YOU COULD SWING ANYTHING YOU WANTED, YOU'D GET JUST AS **BORED** AS YOU WERE BEFORE YOU CALLED ME! AND YOU'D BE OUT YOUR **SOUL** TOO!
BUT I CAN TELL YOU WHAT I CAN DO! I CAN MAKE YOU A **VAMPIRE**. A CAT LIKE YOU WOULD DIG **THAT!**
A... A VAMPIRE!? WHY WOULD I WANT TO BECOME A CREATURE LIKE THAT?
BECAUSE YOU LIKE TO **CONTROL** PEOPLE! YOU CAN DO THAT WITH YOUR BREAD, BUT YOU FIND IT DULL! AS A VAMPIRE YOU COULD DO THAT THRU **FEAR**.
GO ON, I'M LISTENING...
I DIG I'M GETTING TO YOU! AS A VAMP YOU'D BE POWERFUL. BUT NOT SO POWERFUL THAT THINGS WOULD BECOME DULL! YOU'D BE ABLE TO CHANGE TO A BAT OR MIST... YOU COULD FLY AND WOULD BE STRONGER, TOO!
IT SOUNDS GOOD
DIG IT... WITH THE POWER YOU'D HAVE AS A VAMP, YOU COULD HAVE FUN FOR CENTURIES! JUST SIGN A CONTRACT AND WE'LL MAKE IT LEGAL!
THERE! YOU HAVE MY SIGNIATURE! NOW WHEN WILL I GET THOSE POWERS?
IMPATIENT TYPE, HUH? WELL, TAKE A LOOK IN THE MIRROR!

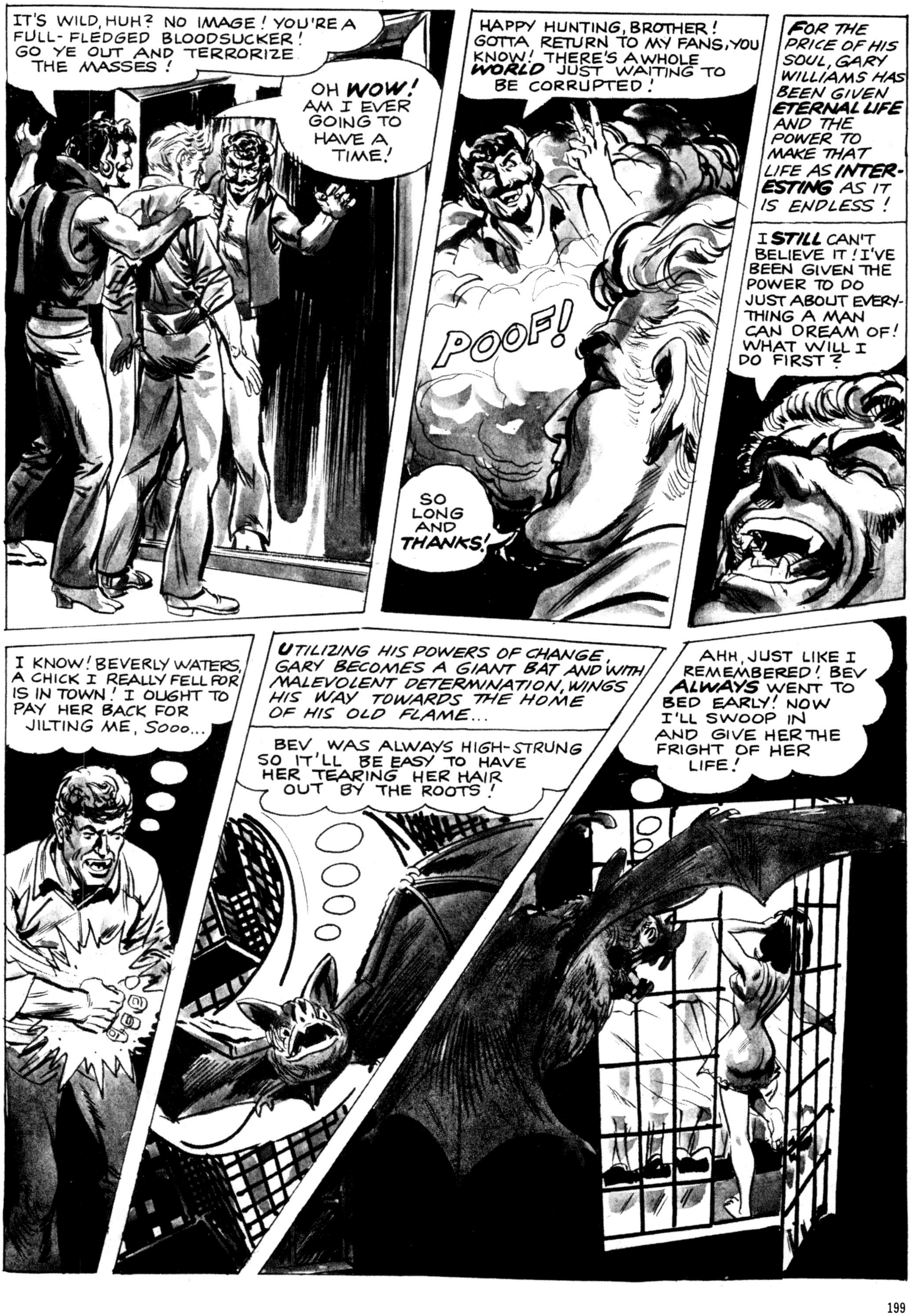
IT'S WILD, HUH? NO IMAGE! YOU'RE A FULL-FLEDGED BLOODSUCKER! GO YE OUT AND TERRORIZE THE MASSES!
OH WOW! AM I EVER GOING TO HAVE A TIME!
HAPPY HUNTING, BROTHER! GOTTA RETURN TO MY FANS, YOU KNOW! THERE'S A WHOLE WORLD JUST WAITING TO BE CORRUPTED!
POOF!
SO LONG AND THANKS!
FOR THE PRICE OF HIS SOUL, GARY WILLIAMS HAS BEEN GIVEN ETERNAL LIFE AND THE POWER TO MAKE THAT LIFE AS INTERESTING AS IT IS ENDLESS!
I STILL CAN'T BELIEVE IT! I'VE BEEN GIVEN THE POWER TO DO JUST ABOUT EVERYTHING A MAN CAN DREAM OF! WHAT WILL I DO FIRST?
I KNOW! BEVERLY WATERS, A CHICK I REALLY FELL FOR IS IN TOWN! I OUGHT TO PAY HER BACK FOR JILTING ME, SOOO...
UTILIZING HIS POWERS OF CHANGE, GARY BECOMES A GIANT BAT AND WITH MALEVOLENT DETERMINATION, WINGS HIS WAY TOWARDS THE HOME OF HIS OLD FLAME...
BEV WAS ALWAYS HIGH-STRUNG SO IT'LL BE EASY TO HAVE HER TEARING HER HAIR OUT BY THE ROOTS!
AHH, JUST LIKE I REMEMBERED! BEV ALWAYS WENT TO BED EARLY! NOW I'LL SWOOP IN AND GIVE HER THE FRIGHT OF HER LIFE!

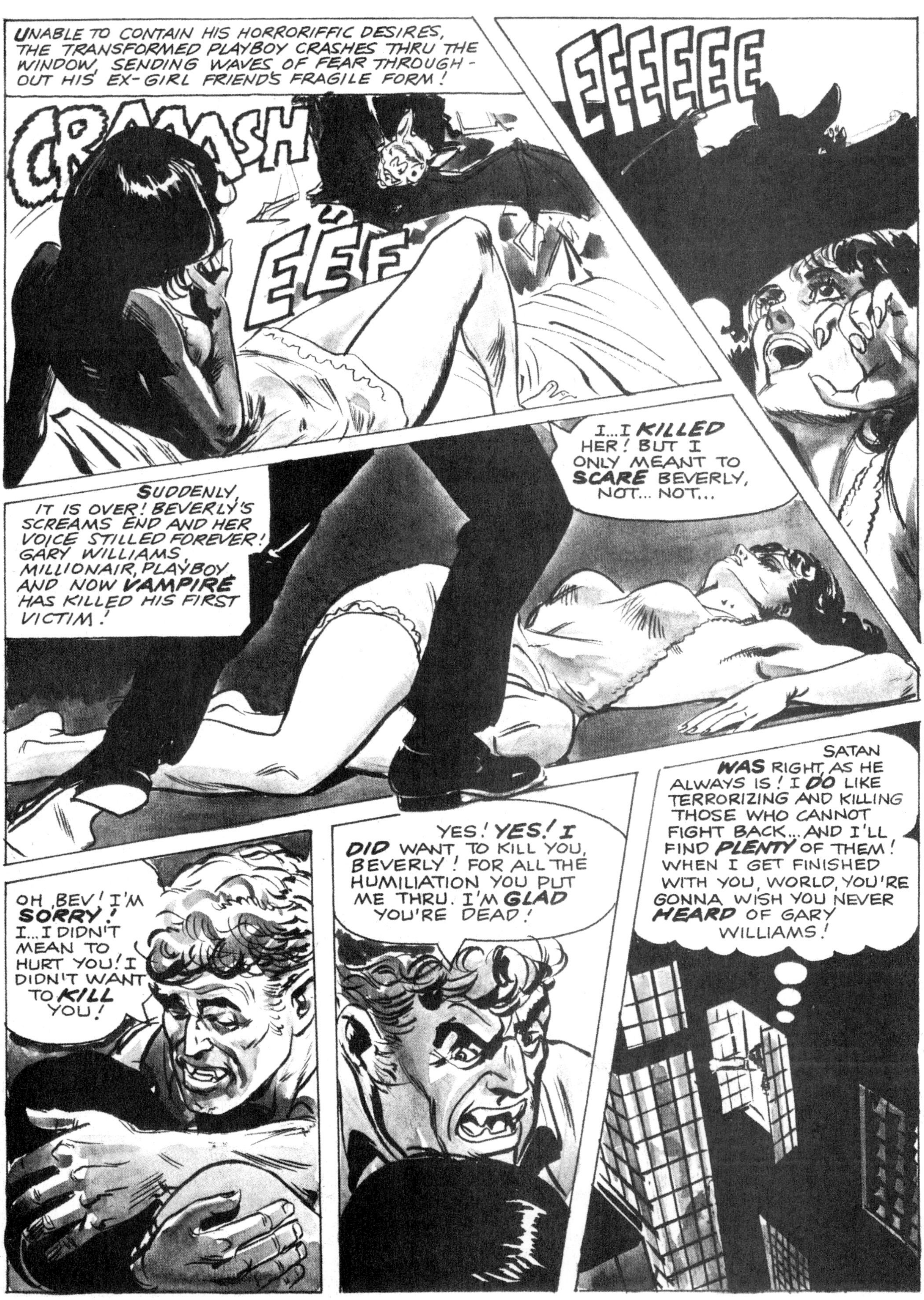
UNABLE TO CONTAIN HIS HORRORIFFIC DESIRES, THE TRANSFORMED PLAYBOY CRASHES THRU THE WINDOW, SENDING WAVES OF FEAR THROUGH-OUT HIS EX-GIRL FRIEND'S FRAGILE FORM!
CRAAASH
EEE
EEEEEE
SUDDENLY, IT IS OVER! BEVERLY'S SCREAMS END AND HER VOICE STILLED FOREVER! GARY WILLIAMS, MILLIONAIR, PLAYBOY AND NOW VAMPIRE HAS KILLED HIS FIRST VICTIM!
I...I KILLED HER! BUT I ONLY MEANT TO SCARE BEVERLY, NOT... NOT...
OH, BEV! I'M SORRY! I...I DIDN'T MEAN TO HURT YOU! I DIDN'T WANT TO KILL YOU!
YES! YES! I DID WANT TO KILL YOU, BEVERLY! FOR ALL THE HUMILIATION YOU PUT ME THRU. I'M GLAD YOU'RE DEAD!
SATAN WAS RIGHT, AS HE ALWAYS IS! I DO LIKE TERRORIZING AND KILLING THOSE WHO CANNOT FIGHT BACK... AND I'LL FIND PLENTY OF THEM! WHEN I GET FINISHED WITH YOU, WORLD, YOU'RE GONNA WISH YOU NEVER HEARD OF GARY WILLIAMS!

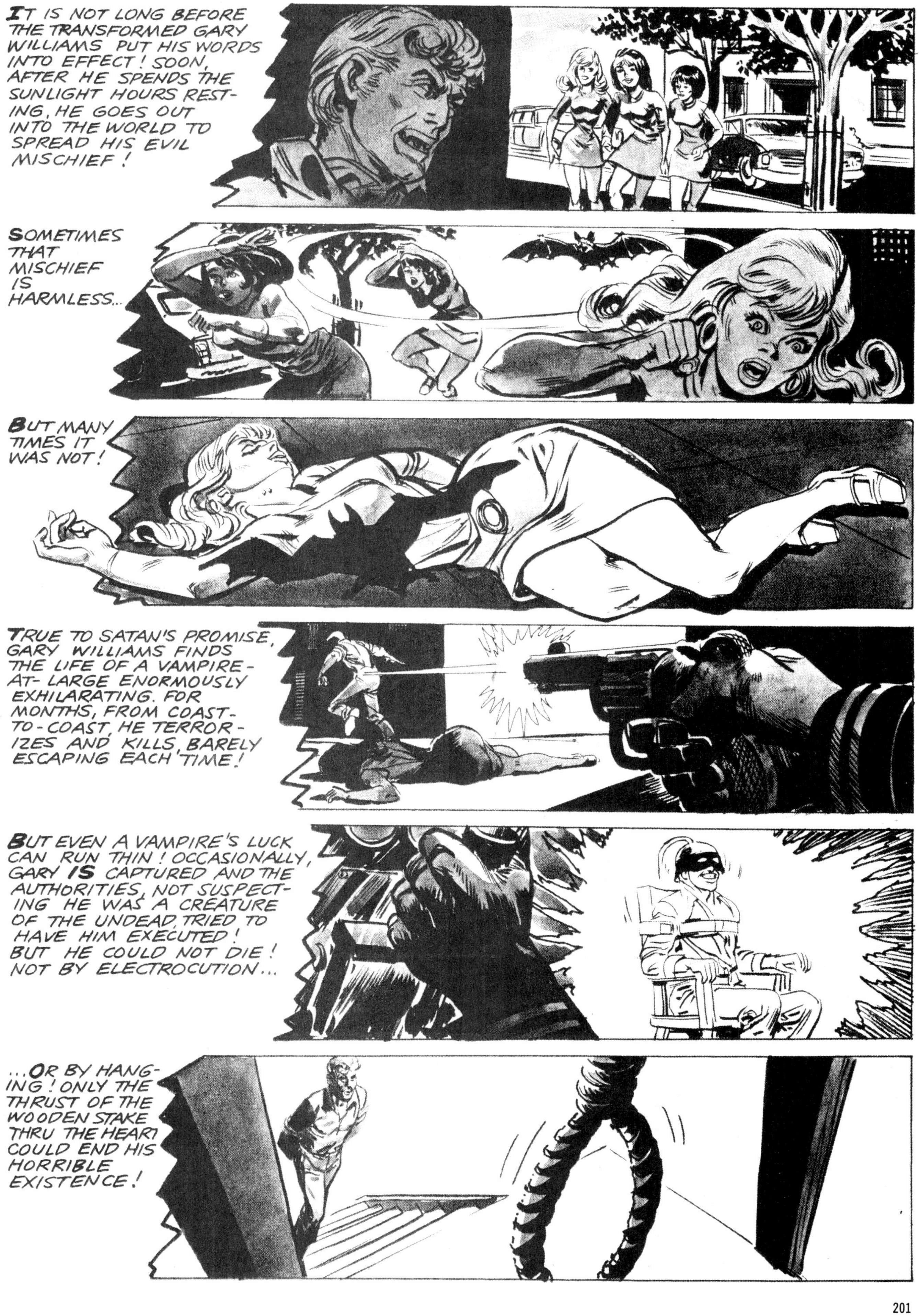
IT IS NOT LONG BEFORE THE TRANSFORMED GARY WILLIAMS PUT HIS WORDS INTO EFFECT! SOON, AFTER HE SPENDS THE SUNLIGHT HOURS RESTING, HE GOES OUT INTO THE WORLD TO SPREAD HIS EVIL MISCHIEF!
SOMETIMES THAT MISCHIEF IS HARMLESS...
BUT MANY TIMES IT WAS NOT!
TRUE TO SATAN'S PROMISE, GARY WILLIAMS FINDS THE LIFE OF A VAMPIRE-AT-LARGE ENORMOUSLY EXHILARATING. FOR MONTHS, FROM COAST-TO-COAST, HE TERRORIZES AND KILLS, BARELY ESCAPING EACH TIME!
BUT EVEN A VAMPIRE'S LUCK CAN RUN THIN! OCCASIONALLY, GARY IS CAPTURED AND THE AUTHORITIES, NOT SUSPECTING HE WAS A CREATURE OF THE UNDEAD, TRIED TO HAVE HIM EXECUTED! BUT HE COULD NOT DIE! NOT BY ELECTROCUTION...
...OR BY HANGING! ONLY THE THRUST OF THE WOODEN STAKE THRU THE HEART COULD END HIS HORRIBLE EXISTENCE!

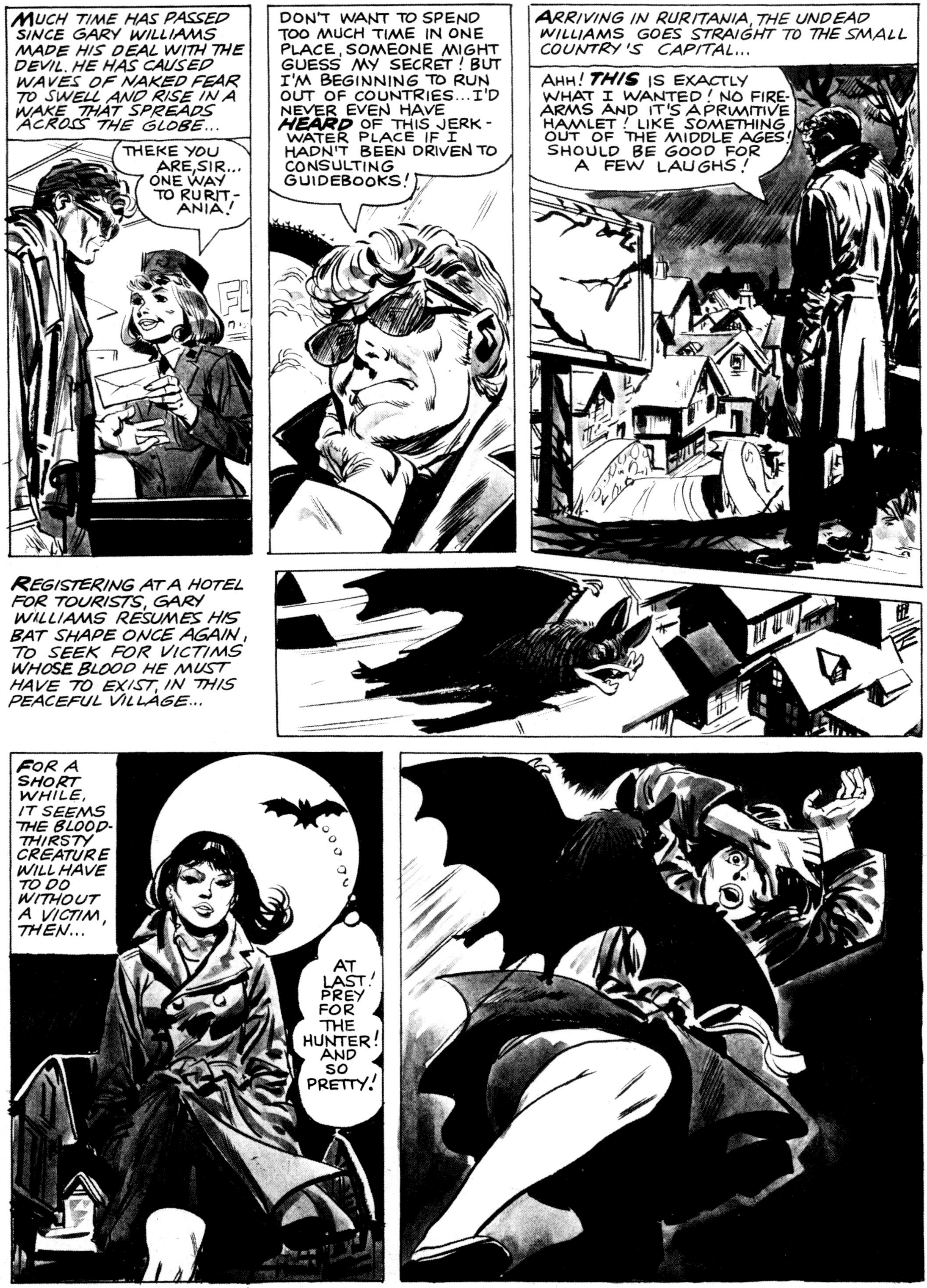
MUCH TIME HAS PASSED SINCE GARY WILLIAMS MADE HIS DEAL WITH THE DEVIL. HE HAS CAUSED WAVES OF NAKED FEAR TO SWELL AND RISE IN A WAKE THAT SPREADS ACROSS THE GLOBE...
THERE YOU ARE, SIR... ONE WAY TO RURITANIA!
DON'T WANT TO SPEND TOO MUCH TIME IN ONE PLACE, SOMEONE MIGHT GUESS MY SECRET! BUT I'M BEGINNING TO RUN OUT OF COUNTRIES... I'D NEVER EVEN HAVE HEARD OF THIS JERK-WATER PLACE IF I HADN'T BEEN DRIVEN TO CONSULTING GUIDEBOOKS!
ARRIVING IN RURITANIA, THE UNDEAD WILLIAMS GOES STRAIGHT TO THE SMALL COUNTRY'S CAPITAL...
AHH! THIS IS EXACTLY WHAT I WANTED! NO FIRE-ARMS AND IT'S A PRIMITIVE HAMLET! LIKE SOMETHING OUT OF THE MIDDLE AGES! SHOULD BE GOOD FOR A FEW LAUGHS!
REGISTERING AT A HOTEL FOR TOURISTS, GARY WILLIAMS RESUMES HIS BAT SHAPE ONCE AGAIN, TO SEEK FOR VICTIMS WHOSE BLOOD HE MUST HAVE TO EXIST, IN THIS PEACEFUL VILLAGE...
FOR A SHORT WHILE, IT SEEMS THE BLOOD-THIRSTY CREATURE WILL HAVE TO DO WITHOUT A VICTIM, THEN...
AT LAST! PREY FOR THE HUNTER! AND SO PRETTY!

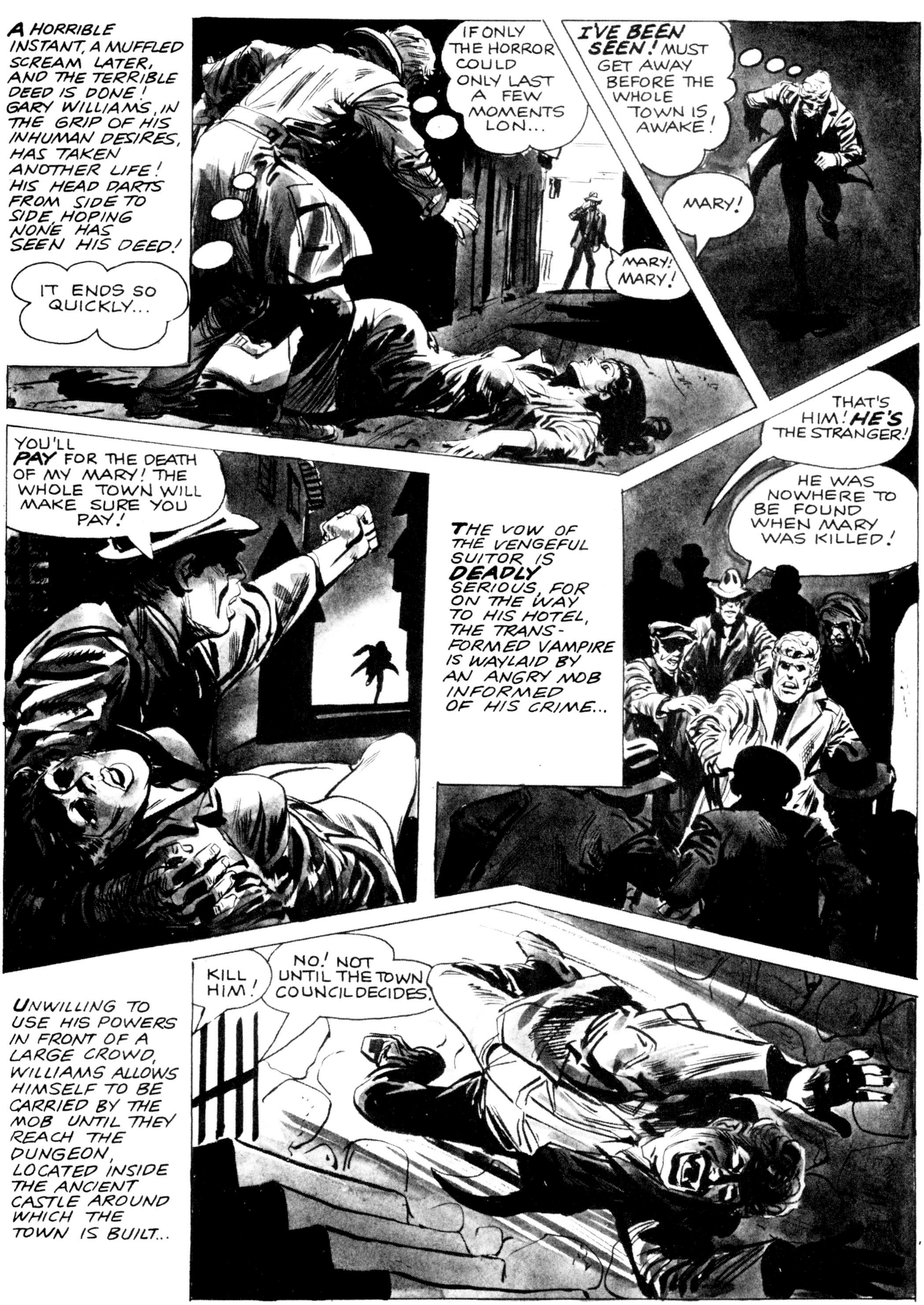
A HORRIBLE INSTANT, A MUFFLED SCREAM LATER, AND THE TERRIBLE DEED IS DONE! GARY WILLIAMS, IN THE GRIP OF HIS INHUMAN DESIRES, HAS TAKEN ANOTHER LIFE! HIS HEAD DARTS FROM SIDE TO SIDE, HOPING NONE HAS SEEN HIS DEED!
IT ENDS SO QUICKLY...
IF ONLY THE HORROR COULD ONLY LAST A FEW MOMENTS LON...
MARY! MARY!
I'VE BEEN SEEN! MUST GET AWAY BEFORE THE WHOLE TOWN IS AWAKE!
MARY!
YOU'LL PAY FOR THE DEATH OF MY MARY! THE WHOLE TOWN WILL MAKE SURE YOU PAY!
THE VOW OF THE VENGEFUL SUITOR IS DEADLY SERIOUS, FOR ON THE WAY TO HIS HOTEL, THE TRANS-FORMED VAMPIRE IS WAYLAID BY AN ANGRY MOB INFORMED OF HIS CRIME...
THAT'S HIM! HE'S THE STRANGER!
HE WAS NOWHERE TO BE FOUND WHEN MARY WAS KILLED!
UNWILLING TO USE HIS POWERS IN FRONT OF A LARGE CROWD, WILLIAMS ALLOWS HIMSELF TO BE CARRIED BY THE MOB UNTIL THEY REACH THE DUNGEON, LOCATED INSIDE THE ANCIENT CASTLE AROUND WHICH THE TOWN IS BUILT...
KILL HIM!
NO! NOT UNTIL THE TOWN COUNCIL DECIDES.

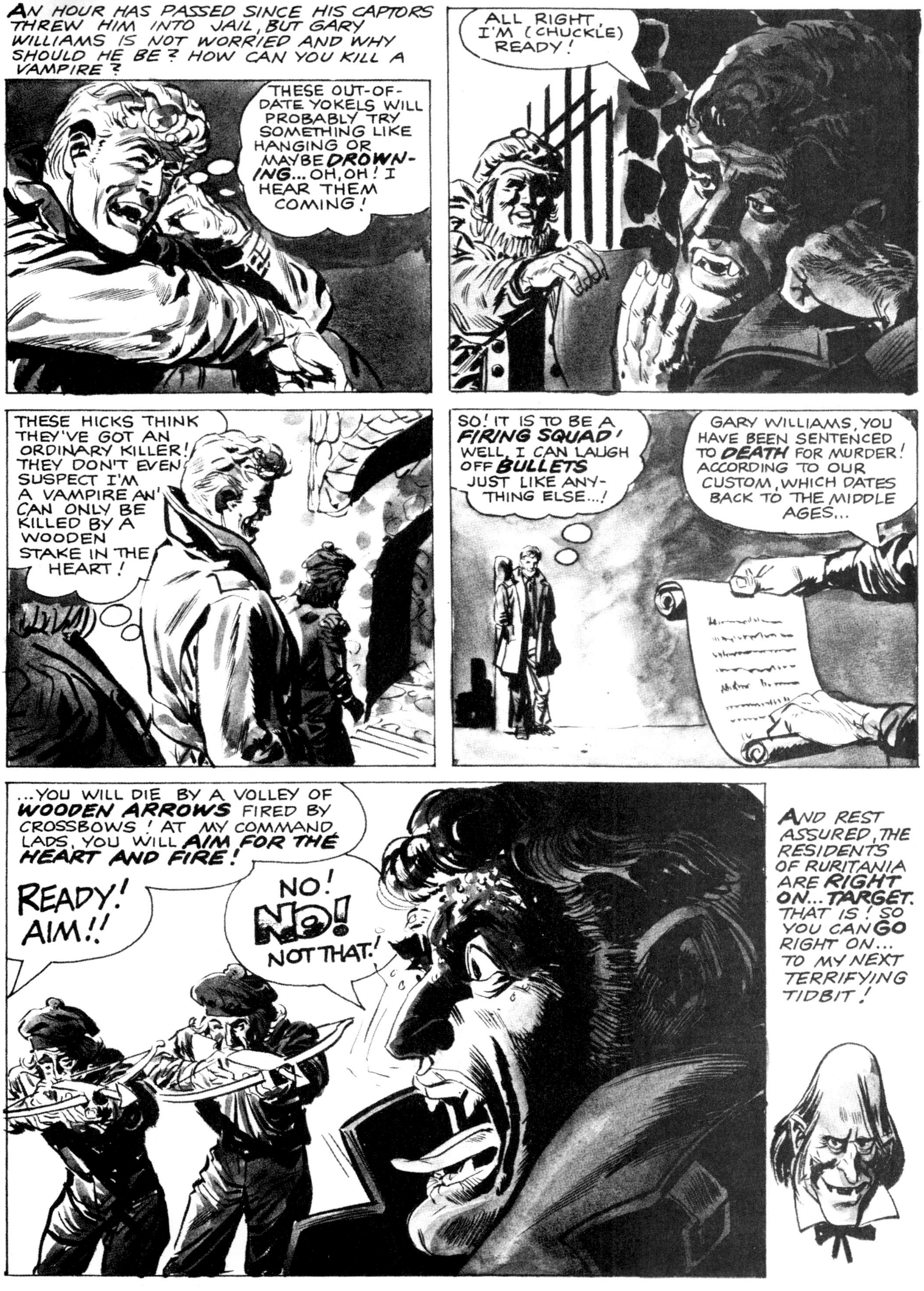
AN HOUR HAS PASSED SINCE HIS CAPTORS THREW HIM INTO JAIL, BUT GARY WILLIAMS IS NOT WORRIED AND WHY SHOULD HE BE? HOW CAN YOU KILL A VAMPIRE?
THESE OUT-OF-DATE YOKELS WILL PROBABLY TRY SOMETHING LIKE HANGING OR MAYBE DROWNING... OH, OH! I HEAR THEM COMING!
ALL RIGHT, I'M (CHUCKLE) READY!
THESE HICKS THINK THEY'VE GOT AN ORDINARY KILLER! THEY DON'T EVEN SUSPECT I'M A VAMPIRE AN' CAN ONLY BE KILLED BY A WOODEN STAKE IN THE HEART!
SO! IT IS TO BE A FIRING SQUAD! WELL, I CAN LAUGH OFF BULLETS JUST LIKE ANYTHING ELSE...!
GARY WILLIAMS, YOU HAVE BEEN SENTENCED TO DEATH FOR MURDER! ACCORDING TO OUR CUSTOM, WHICH DATES BACK TO THE MIDDLE AGES...
...YOU WILL DIE BY A VOLLEY OF WOODEN ARROWS FIRED BY CROSSBOWS! AT MY COMMAND LADS, YOU WILL AIM FOR THE HEART AND FIRE!
READY! AIM!!
NO! NO! NOT THAT!
AND REST ASSURED, THE RESIDENTS OF RURITANIA ARE RIGHT ON... TARGET. THAT IS! SO YOU CAN GO RIGHT ON... TO MY NEXT TERRIFYING TIDBIT!

GREAT 8MM MONSTER MOVIES!

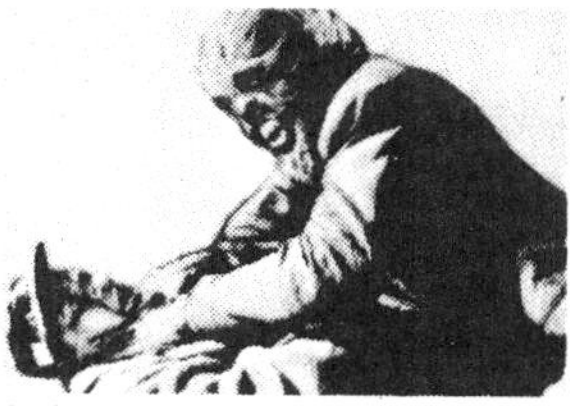

THE WERE-WOLF

A 10,000-year-old legend of bestiality comes to life, tearing the screen to terrified tatters in the body of a bloodthirsty beast. Right before your horror-struck eyes! Only $5.95.

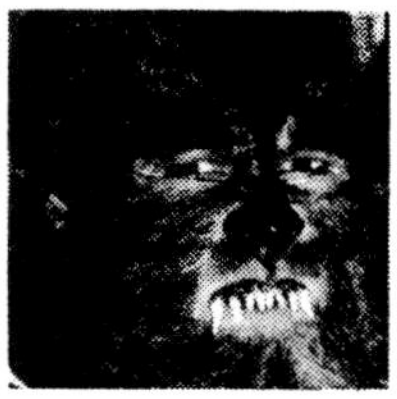

I WAS A TEENAGE WEREWOLF

You asked for it! The companion film to "I was a teenage Frankenstein! Teenage boy turns to horrifying Werewolf who menaces the high school students. Exciting, terrifying film. Only $5.95.

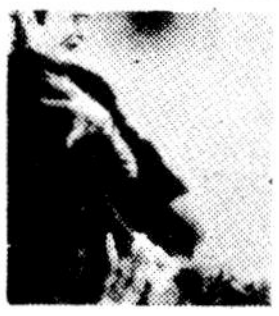

FRANKENSTEIN MEETS THE WOLFMAN

WHO COMES OUT ON TOP . . . Frankenstein or Wolfman? We won't give it away, but here is a 2-Monster Movie that doubles your fun as you watch the world's eeriest adversaries fight it out for the world's Monster Championship. Full of thrills and chills for Monster Movie collectors. 8mm, 160 feet, $5.75.

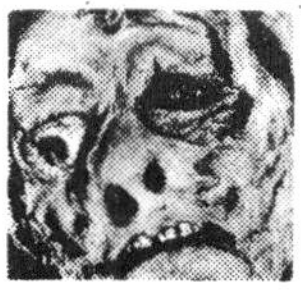

I WAS A TEENAGE FRANKENSTEIN

A MAD DOCTOR sets out to create the most fearsome monster ever born. He winds up with a TEENAGE FRANKENSTEIN combining a boy's body, a monster's mind, a creature's soul. Does the doctor live to regret his fiendish accomplishment? This gruesome movie, a real thriller, gives you the answer. 8mm, 200 feet, $5.95.

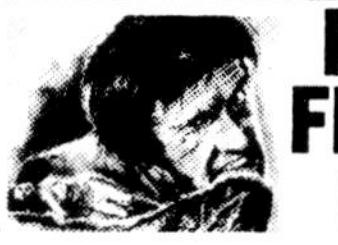

REVENGE OF FRANKENSTEIN

SUPERNATURAL TECHNICOLOR!

FRANKENSTEIN GETS EVEN and his "revenge" makes this the scariest monster movie ever made. The Stalker Walker gives an unforgettable performance. The dark, dank mood of this film is not for the lighthearted. Full of fight and might, it is just right for your Monster Film collection. (Available in both black & white or in supernatural Technicolor.) This 8mm film is a full 200 feet. Black & White, $5.95; Technicolor, $12.95.

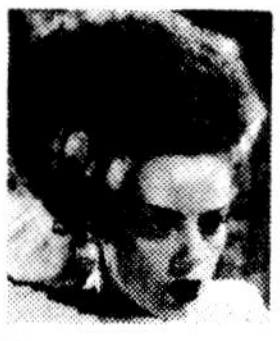

THE BRIDE OF FRANKENSTEIN

FEARFUL FRANKENSTEIN monster Boris Karloff wants to marry Elsa Lanchester. Nothing stops this gruesome two-some . . . not even the fact she is 7 feet tall, is wrapped in gharish gauze . . . and has ragged stitches around her neck. A classic film every collector should own! 8mm, 160 feet, $5.75.

SON OF FRANKENSTEIN

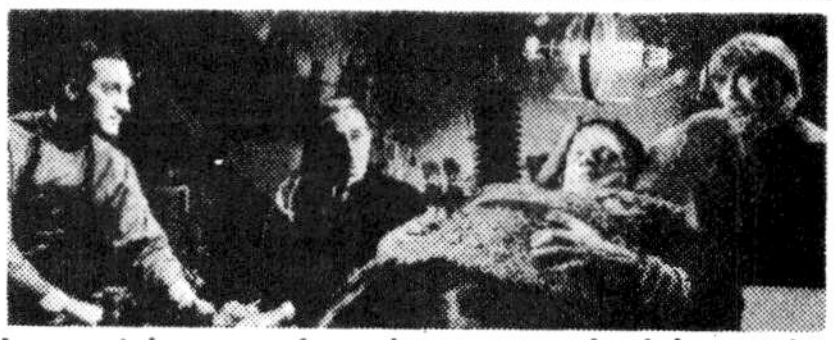

In a nightmare of stark terror and violence the revived Monster threatens death and destruction to a panic-stricken community. Only $5.95.

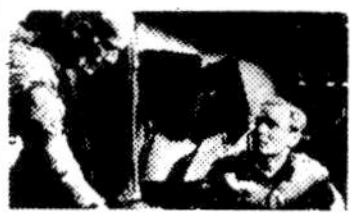

KARLOFF IN THE MUMMY

WOULDN'T YOU KNOW that only Boris Karloff could be so horror-able as the original MUMMY! Back in 1932 he let the Hollywood studio "torture" him for hours, wrapping rotting gauze, spraying chemicals, baking it all with clay. No wonder Karloff was so wonderful as THE MUMMY . . . he felt so horrible he took it out on the film's victims. You'll feel just grand, though, as you watch his eerie performance. 8mm, 160 feet. $5.75.

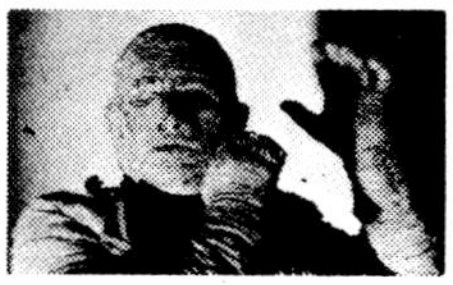

THE MUMMY'S TOMB

DON'T EVER sneak into a Mummy's Tomb. If you do, you may be in for the same revenge as in this movie. A centuries-old mummy starts out to avenge the opening of his crypt in Egypt. How he does his dirty work, and the chills involved, make THE MUMMY'S TOMB a far-from-dreary, excitingly eerie film. 8mm, 200 feet, $5.95.

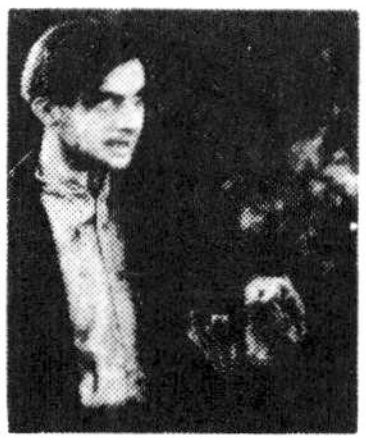

THE VAMPIRE BAT

Most famous and ORIGINAL VAMPIRE film, starring Lionel Atwill, Melvyn Douglas, Fay Wray and Dwight Frye. Full of Vampires, weird characters, mad scientists, etc. A super-shocker. Full 200 feet, 8mm, $4.95.

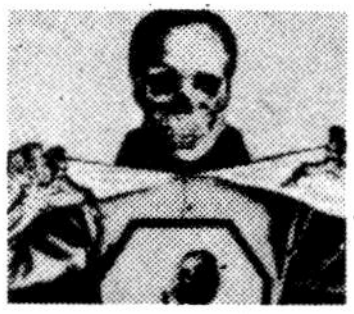

THE UNDEAD

CAN THE GRAVE OPEN UP and give forth its ghostly, ghastly secrets. It sure can, and in THE UNDEAD horror screams from the grave. In the dead of night an evil curse starts a chain of events. You'll sit on the edge of your chair as you walk with THE UNDEAD. 8mm, 200 feet, $5.95.

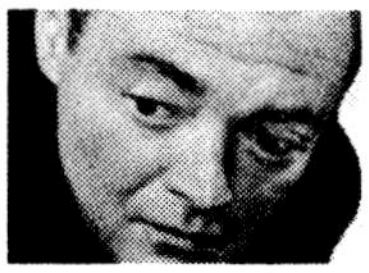

THE BEAST WITH 5 FINGERS

WHAT HAPPENS when stark, staring madness takes over in a famous concert pianist's home? Who is the Beast with 5 Fingers? Peter Lorre stalks through this horror movie at his dramatic best. As scene after terror scene unfolds, you sit on the edge of your chair in absolute suspense. This famous film is now available for the collector. Order today. 8mm, 200 feet, $5.95.

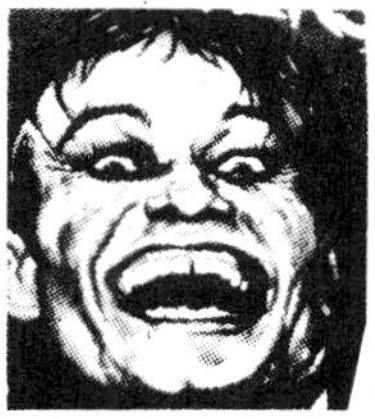

TERROR OF DRACULA

Original 1922 version. Full 400 feet version, full of terror, torment and sensational shock. A must for the horror film collector. Half-hour running time. 8mm, $9.95.

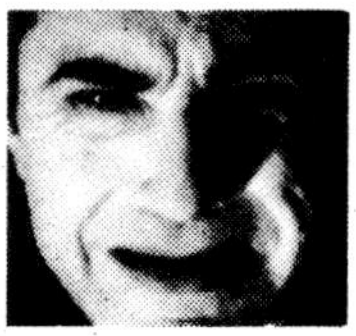

BELA LUGOSI AS DRACULA

DAUNTLESS DRACULA is at it again, slinking through the London fog for his victims. Bela Lugosi gives one of the greatest performances of his career, in this classic film. Fiends, vampires, screams . . . in this famous film. Add this to your collection . . . it is tops. 8mm, 160 feet, $5.75.

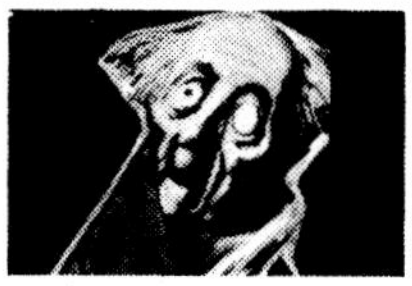

Edgar Allan Poe's TELL TALE HEART

THIS FAMOUS SOUND MOVIE is available, at last, for private collectors. Edgar Allen Poe's creepy, eerie tale of "THE TELLTALE HEART" is a never-to-be-forgotten classic. Here, in 8mm Ultrasonic Sound, you get the original Columbia Pictures film. The incomparable James Mason gives a master narration. You will cherish this film. Order today. 8mm Sound, 200 feet, $11.95 plus 25c for postage

BELA LUGOSI CHILLS YOU THE HUMAN MONSTER

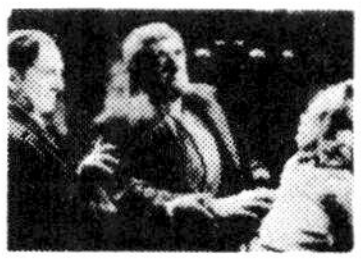

Original Edgar Wallace version, terrifying and chilling. Promises to haunt you again and again; a real shocker for friends you ask to see it. Full 400 feet, 8mm, $10.95.

LON CHANEY AS THE PHANTOM of the OPERA

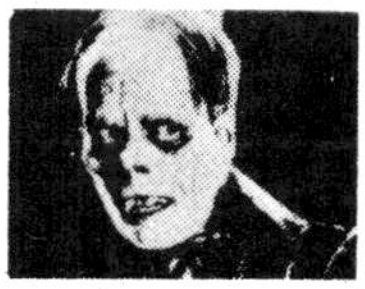

MARY PHILBIN's famous "d u n g e o n unmasking scene." Eerie and unearthly. Famous original movie scene, available for first time in 8mm. Add it to your collection. 100 feet 16MM scene, $5.95. (50 feet, $4.95) Plus 25c postage

- ☐ The Werewolf, $5.95
- ☐ I Was A Teenage Werewolf, $5.95
- ☐ Frankenstein Meets The Wolfman, $5.75
- ☐ I Was A Teenage Frankenstein, $5.95
- ☐ Revenge Of Frankenstein, Black & White, $5.95
- ☐ Revenge Of Frankenstein, Color, $12.95
- ☐ Bride Of Frankenstein, $5.75
- ☐ Son Of Frankenstein, $5.95
- ☐ The Mummy, $5.75
- ☐ The Mummy's Tomb, $5.95
- ☐ The Vampire Bat, $4 95
- ☐ Terror Of Dracula, $9.95
- ☐ The Human Monster, $10.95
- ☐ The Undead, $5.95
- ☐ The Beast With Five Fingers, $5.95
- ☐ Dracula, $5.75
- ☐ Tell-Tale Heart, $11.95
- ☐ Phantom Of The Opera, 100 Ft., 16MM $5.95
- ☐ Phantom Of The Opera, 50 Ft., $4.95

Please rush me the following, for which I enclose $.................... plus 25c postage & handling for each film checked:

NAME..

ADDRESS..

CITY..

STATE....................ZIP CODE NO....................

ALL TIME BEST SELLERS IN PAPERBACKS

SCI-FI! MONSTERS! BEASTS! ADVENTURE!

The FIRST MEN in the MOON

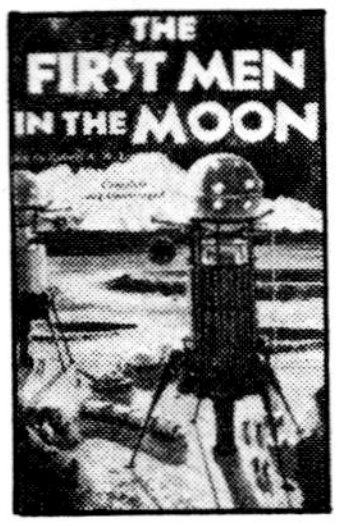
THE FIRST MEN IN THE MOON

A fantastic tale of 2 men on the first flight to the moon! The voyage, landing, and exploration of the Moon in vivid detail. You are there — as they discover an unknown civilization.
No. 2128 .... **68¢**

AROUND the WORLD in 80 DAYS

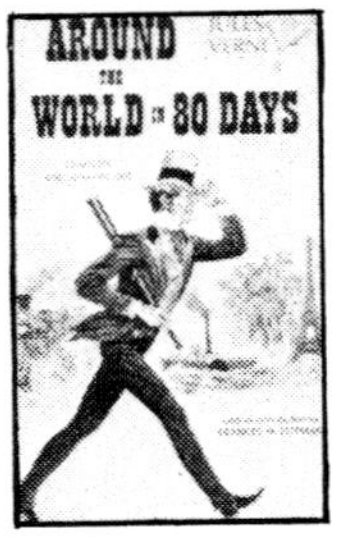
AROUND THE WORLD IN 80 DAYS

The adventures of P. Fogg, Esq. and his French valet, as they travel around the world in a race against time. Full of great suspense, action and drama of world's most famous places.
No. 2127 .... **60¢**

20,000 LEAGUES UNDER THE SEA

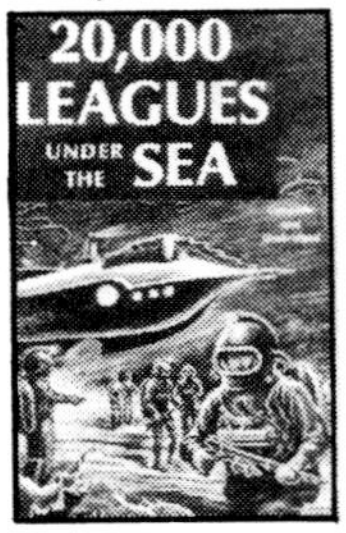
20,000 LEAGUES UNDER THE SEA

Jules Verne creates the fabulous submarine Nautilus, in his predictions of life beneath the sea. Captain Nemo takes you on a strange voyage into the vast watery unknown.
No. 2136 .... **60¢**

A JOURNEY to the CENTER of the EARTH

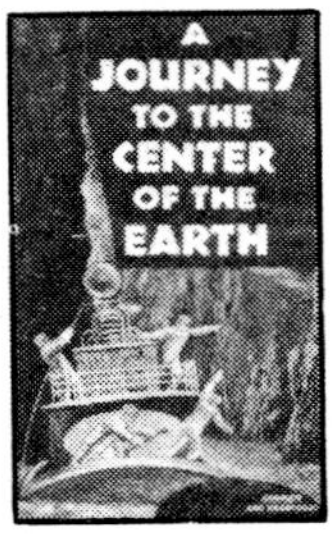
A JOURNEY TO THE CENTER OF THE EARTH

An ancient parchment with a secret message leads to the discovery of the entrance to the center of the world. A bizarre world never before traveled by man.
No. 2132 .... **60¢**

GHOST STORIES

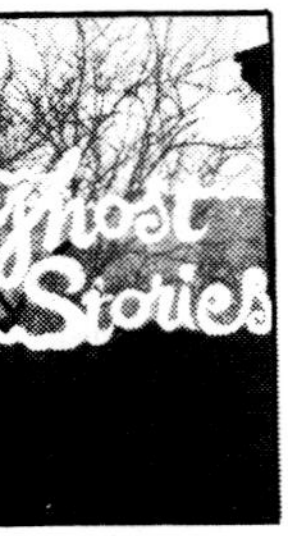
Ghost Stories

Do tales of the supernatural make your spine tingle? Do you believe there really are spooks, or demons or other eerie creatures? There are! Read about them here.
No. 2152 .... **50¢**

MASTER of the WORLD

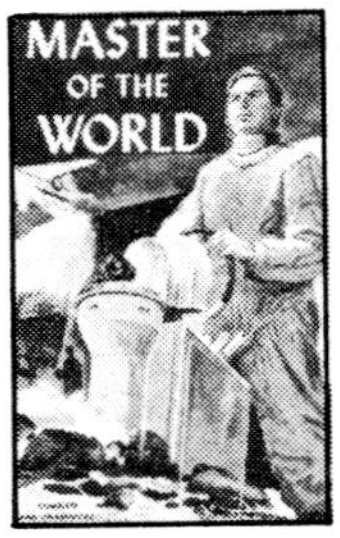
MASTER OF THE WORLD

An unknown inventor gives notice to all the world's governments that his marvelous machines can now control the entire world. Three brave men set out to find and capture him.
No. 2133 .... **60¢**

GREAT GHOST STORIES

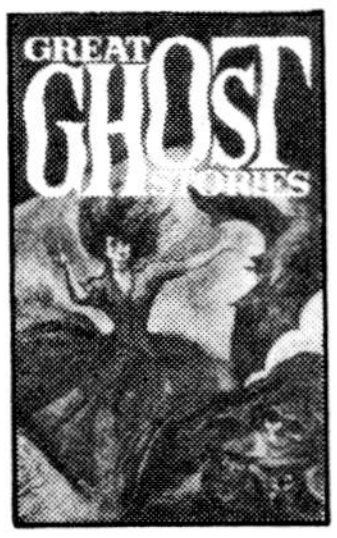
GREAT GHOST STORIES

Thirteen of the most chilling terrifying tales of horror ever written. Each by a writer with great ability to describe the supernatural! Blood tingling!
No. 2193 .... **60¢**

ROUND THE MOON

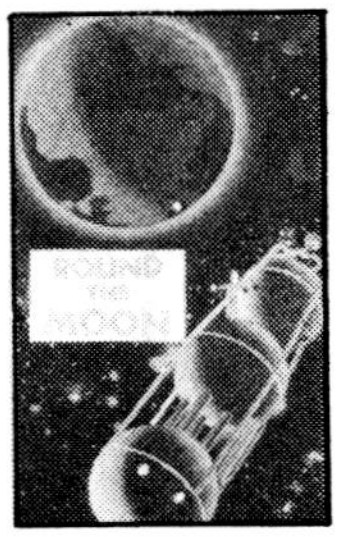
ROUND THE MOON

This history making space journey described in the prophetically scientific style of Jules Verne. He gives us a detailed futuristic view of space travel as never before seen.
No. 2134 .... **60¢**

THE TIME MACHINE

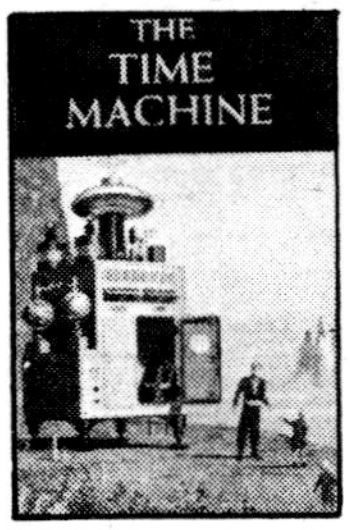
THE TIME MACHINE

How would **you** like to climb into a machine, press a button, and be zoomed into the future, or back into time? It happens in this book!
No. 2135 .... **60¢**

THE UNEXPECTED

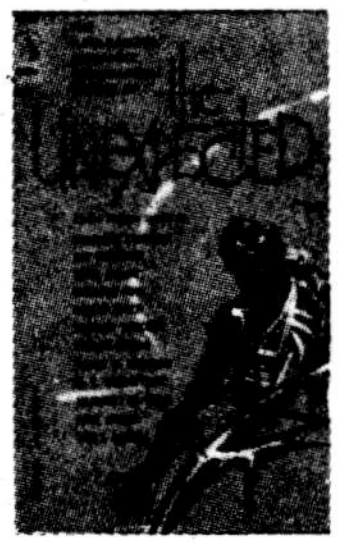

Eleven great stories of the hair-raising, uncanny, nightmarish world of the Unexpected. Twelve of the greatest authors in science-fantasy and the supernatural appear in this classic anthology.
No. 2143 ....60c

THE ISLAND OF DR. MOREAU

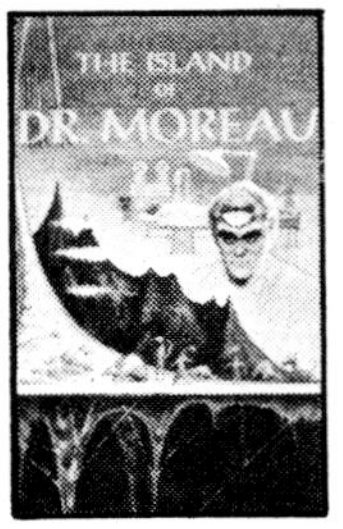
THE ISLAND OF DR. MOREAU

Rescued from the sea and brought to a small out-of-the island, Edward Prendick discovers the terrifying creatures of the island. Real frightening!
No. 2131 .... **60¢**

THE DUNWICH HORROR

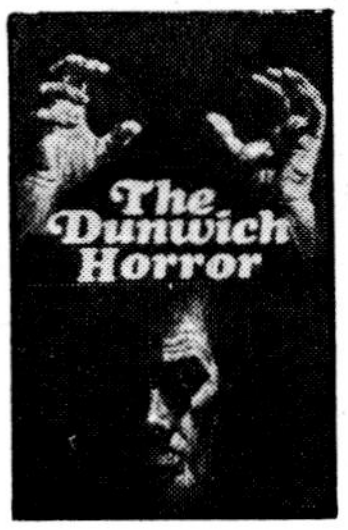
The Dunwich Horror

Read if you dare these frightening world of nightmares, where that scratching in the wall, that suffocation of the heart, that scream torn from the lungs take on forms and shapes!
No. 2159 .... **75¢**

LAND of THE GIANTS #1

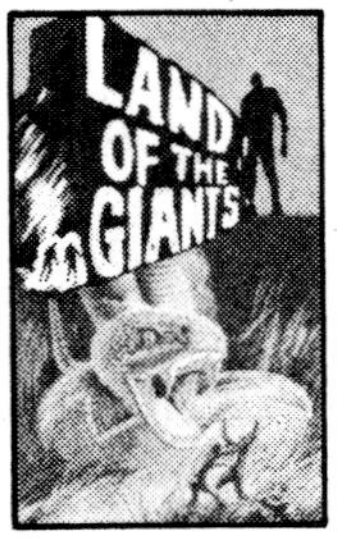
LAND OF THE GIANTS

The grass was six feet high and insects the size of dogs. Men and women were 70-foot giants! Based on the exciting TV Series.
No. 2190 .... **60¢**

LAND of the GIANTS #2 The HOT SPOT

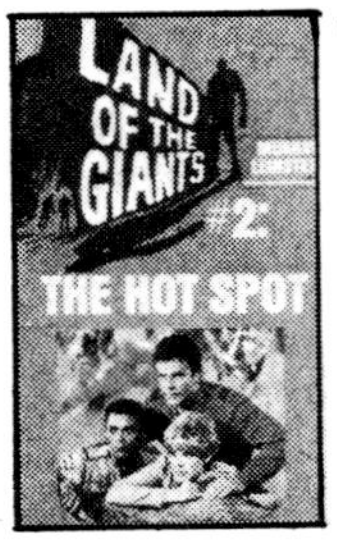
LAND OF THE GIANTS
#2:
THE HOT SPOT

Based on the popular TV series! A tropical paradise turns out to be a terror-racked hell, with mammoth insects and terrifying giant natives.
No. 2191 .... **60¢**

MORE GHOST STORIES

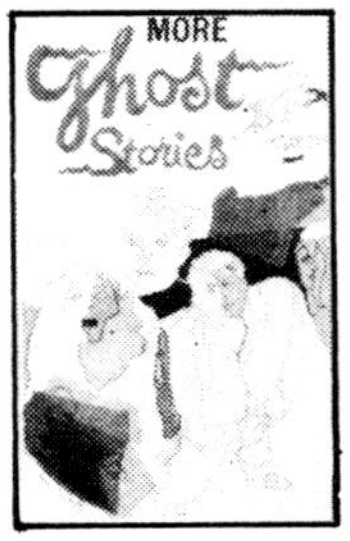
MORE Ghost Stories

Spooks, demons and other creatures of phantasmagorie hover over each eerie page of this new, spine tingling collection. Full of supernatural mystery that will both thrill and scare you!
No. 2186 .... **60¢**

THE FOOD of the GODS

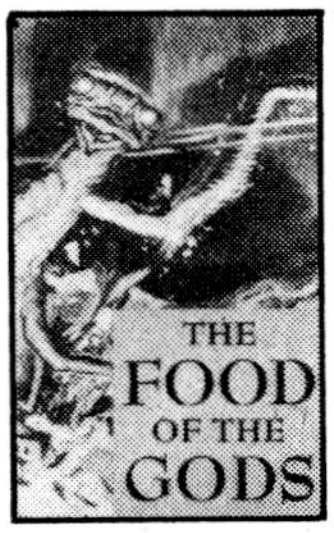
THE FOOD OF THE GODS

Stirs the imagination! What starts off as an experiment soon gets out of hand creating gigantic men, insects and monsters in a world which had no place for them! ! !
No. 2129 .... **60¢**

In THE DAYS OF THE COMET

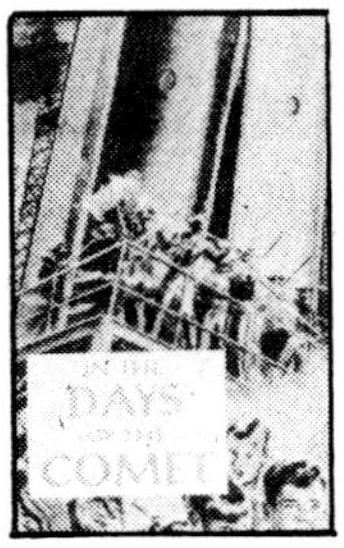
IN THE DAYS OF THE COMET

To awaken . . . changed! Something has happened to human beings all over the world. Makes you wonder and ask yourself, "What if it really happened today!"
No. 2130 .... **60¢**

HAUNTINGS and HORRORS

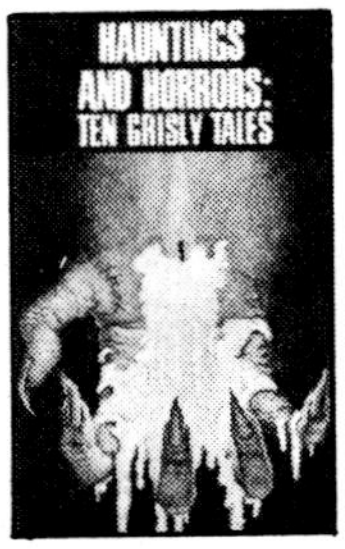
HAUNTINGS AND HORRORS: TEN GRISLY TALES

Ten weird terror-stricken tales. If you like inhuman stories, it's just the thing to turn the blood in your veins to ice water. Only the brave and the strong dare this one!
No. 2185 .... **60¢**

THE COLOUR OUT OF SPACE

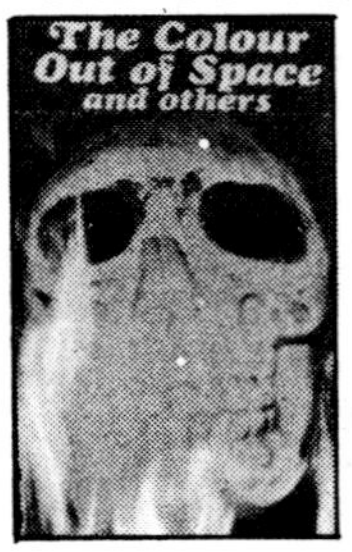
The Colour Out of Space and others

Seven of Lovecraft's masterpieces of horror! Widely acclaimed as surpassing even the great Poe. Full of ancient evils biding their time to break loose again into your world and others.
No. 2182 .... **75¢**

NIGHT of the VAMPIRE

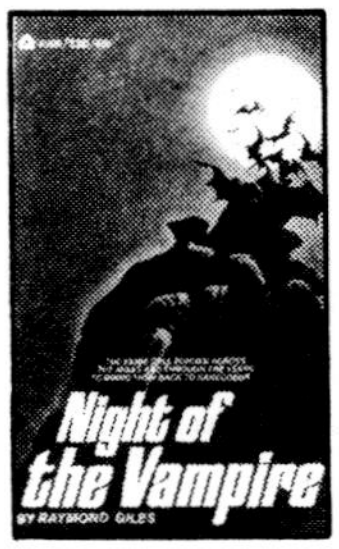
Night of the Vampire
BY RAYMOND GILES

The eerie call echoed across the endless miles and down through the years to bring them back to Sanscoeur! A land where the moon glows green and bats scream in the wind. Scary!
No. 2138 .... **60¢**

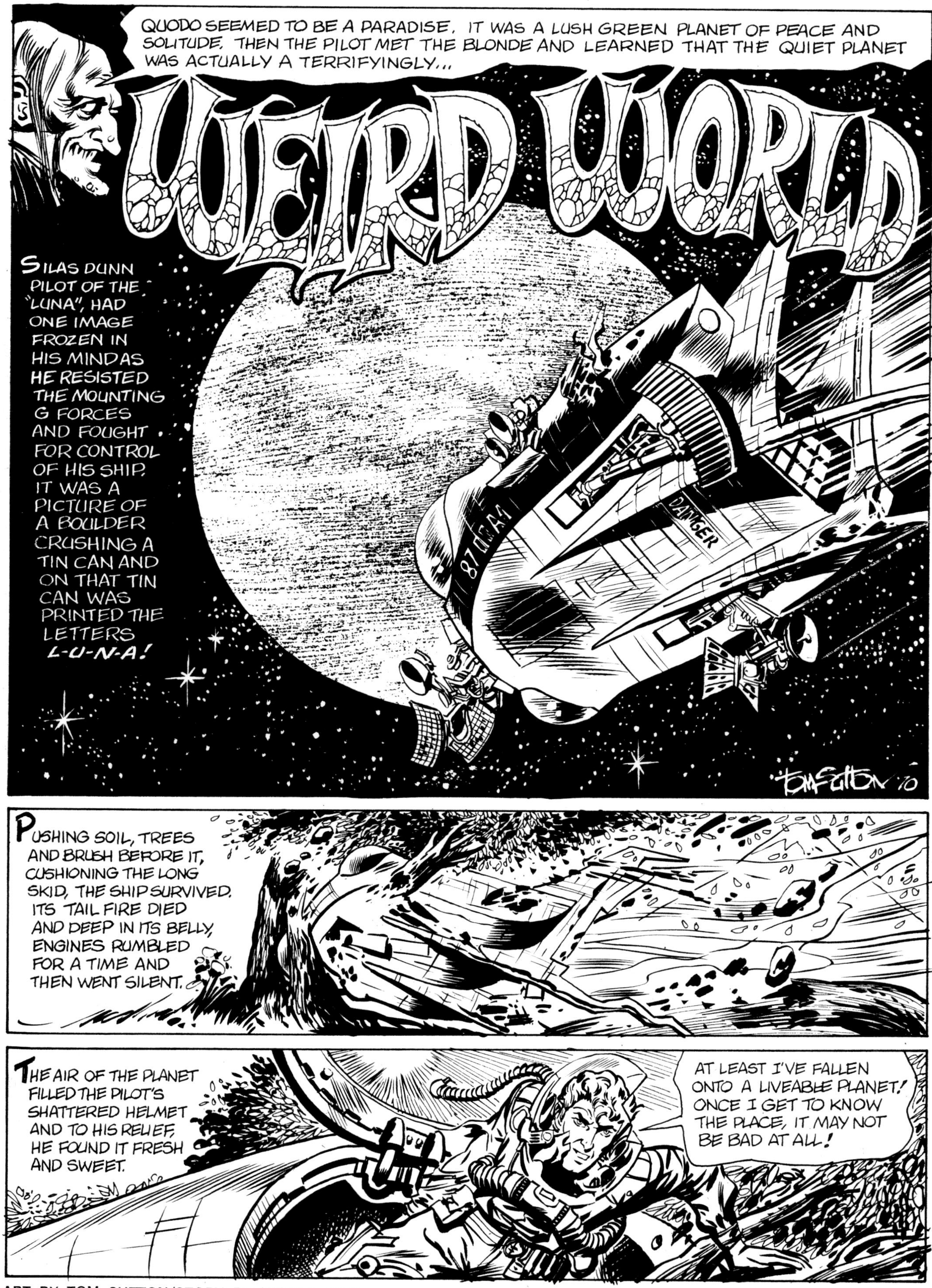
QUODO SEEMED TO BE A PARADISE. IT WAS A LUSH GREEN PLANET OF PEACE AND SOLITUDE. THEN THE PILOT MET THE BLONDE AND LEARNED THAT THE QUIET PLANET WAS ACTUALLY A TERRIFYINGLY...
WEIRD WORLD
SILAS DUNN PILOT OF THE "LUNA", HAD ONE IMAGE FROZEN IN HIS MINDAS HE RESISTED THE MOUNTING G FORCES AND FOUGHT FOR CONTROL OF HIS SHIP. IT WAS A PICTURE OF A BOULDER CRUSHING A TIN CAN AND ON THAT TIN CAN WAS PRINTED THE LETTERS L-U-N-A!
DANGER
TOM SUTTON '70
PUSHING SOIL, TREES AND BRUSH BEFORE IT, CUSHIONING THE LONG SKID, THE SHIP SURVIVED. ITS TAIL FIRE DIED AND DEEP IN ITS BELLY, ENGINES RUMBLED FOR A TIME AND THEN WENT SILENT.
THE AIR OF THE PLANET FILLED THE PILOT'S SHATTERED HELMET AND TO HIS RELIEF, HE FOUND IT FRESH AND SWEET.
AT LEAST I'VE FALLEN ONTO A LIVEABLE PLANET! ONCE I GET TO KNOW THE PLACE, IT MAY NOT BE BAD AT ALL!

ART BY TOM SUTTON/STORY BY NICOLA CUTI

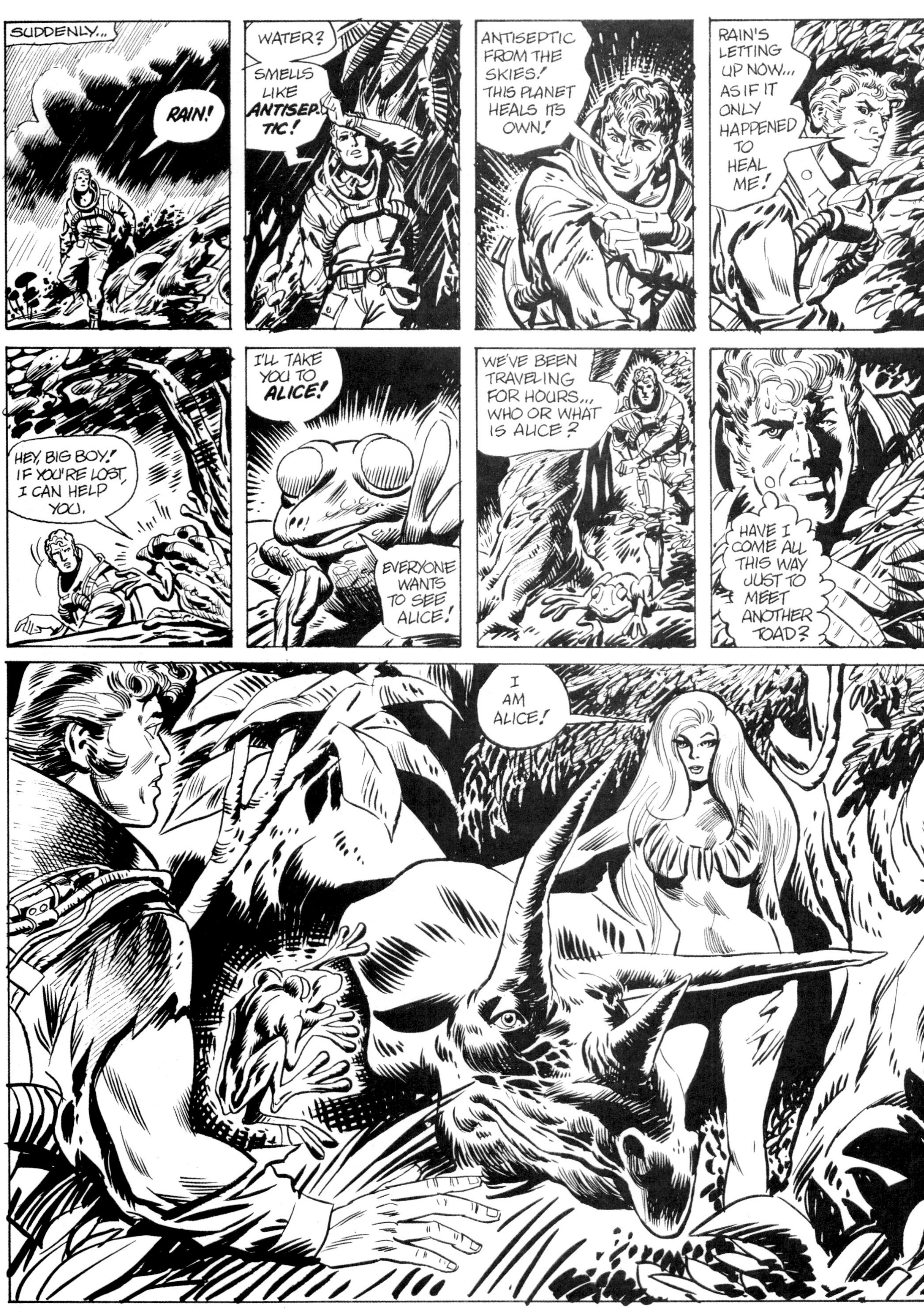
SUDDENLY...
RAIN!
WATER?
SMELLS LIKE ANTISEP-TIC!
ANTISEPTIC FROM THE SKIES! THIS PLANET HEALS ITS OWN!
RAIN'S LETTING UP NOW... AS IF IT ONLY HAPPENED TO HEAL ME!
HEY, BIG BOY! IF YOU'RE LOST, I CAN HELP YOU.
I'LL TAKE YOU TO ALICE!
EVERYONE WANTS TO SEE ALICE!
WE'VE BEEN TRAVELING FOR HOURS... WHO OR WHAT IS ALICE?
HAVE I COME ALL THIS WAY JUST TO MEET ANOTHER TOAD?
I AM ALICE!

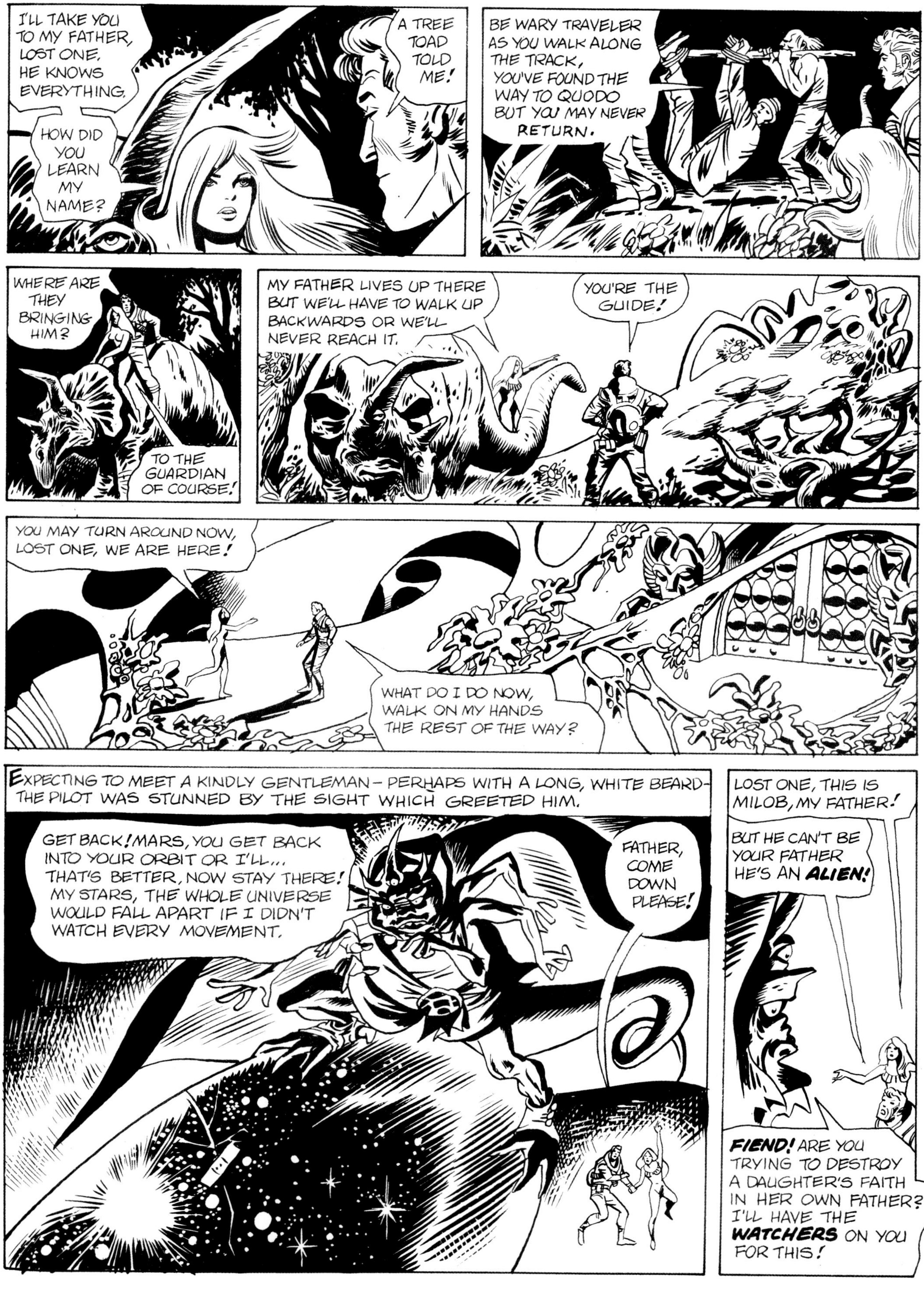
I'LL TAKE YOU TO MY FATHER, LOST ONE. HE KNOWS EVERYTHING.
HOW DID YOU LEARN MY NAME?
A TREE TOAD TOLD ME!
BE WARY TRAVELER AS YOU WALK ALONG THE TRACK, YOU'VE FOUND THE WAY TO QUODO BUT YOU MAY NEVER RETURN.
WHERE ARE THEY BRINGING HIM?
TO THE GUARDIAN OF COURSE!
MY FATHER LIVES UP THERE BUT WE'LL HAVE TO WALK UP BACKWARDS OR WE'LL NEVER REACH IT.
YOU'RE THE GUIDE!
YOU MAY TURN AROUND NOW, LOST ONE, WE ARE HERE!
WHAT DO I DO NOW, WALK ON MY HANDS THE REST OF THE WAY?
EXPECTING TO MEET A KINDLY GENTLEMAN – PERHAPS WITH A LONG, WHITE BEARD – THE PILOT WAS STUNNED BY THE SIGHT WHICH GREETED HIM.
GET BACK! MARS, YOU GET BACK INTO YOUR ORBIT OR I'LL... THAT'S BETTER, NOW STAY THERE! MY STARS, THE WHOLE UNIVERSE WOULD FALL APART IF I DIDN'T WATCH EVERY MOVEMENT.
FATHER, COME DOWN PLEASE!
LOST ONE, THIS IS MILOB, MY FATHER!
BUT HE CAN'T BE YOUR FATHER HE'S AN ALIEN!
FIEND! ARE YOU TRYING TO DESTROY A DAUGHTER'S FAITH IN HER OWN FATHER? I'LL HAVE THE WATCHERS ON YOU FOR THIS!

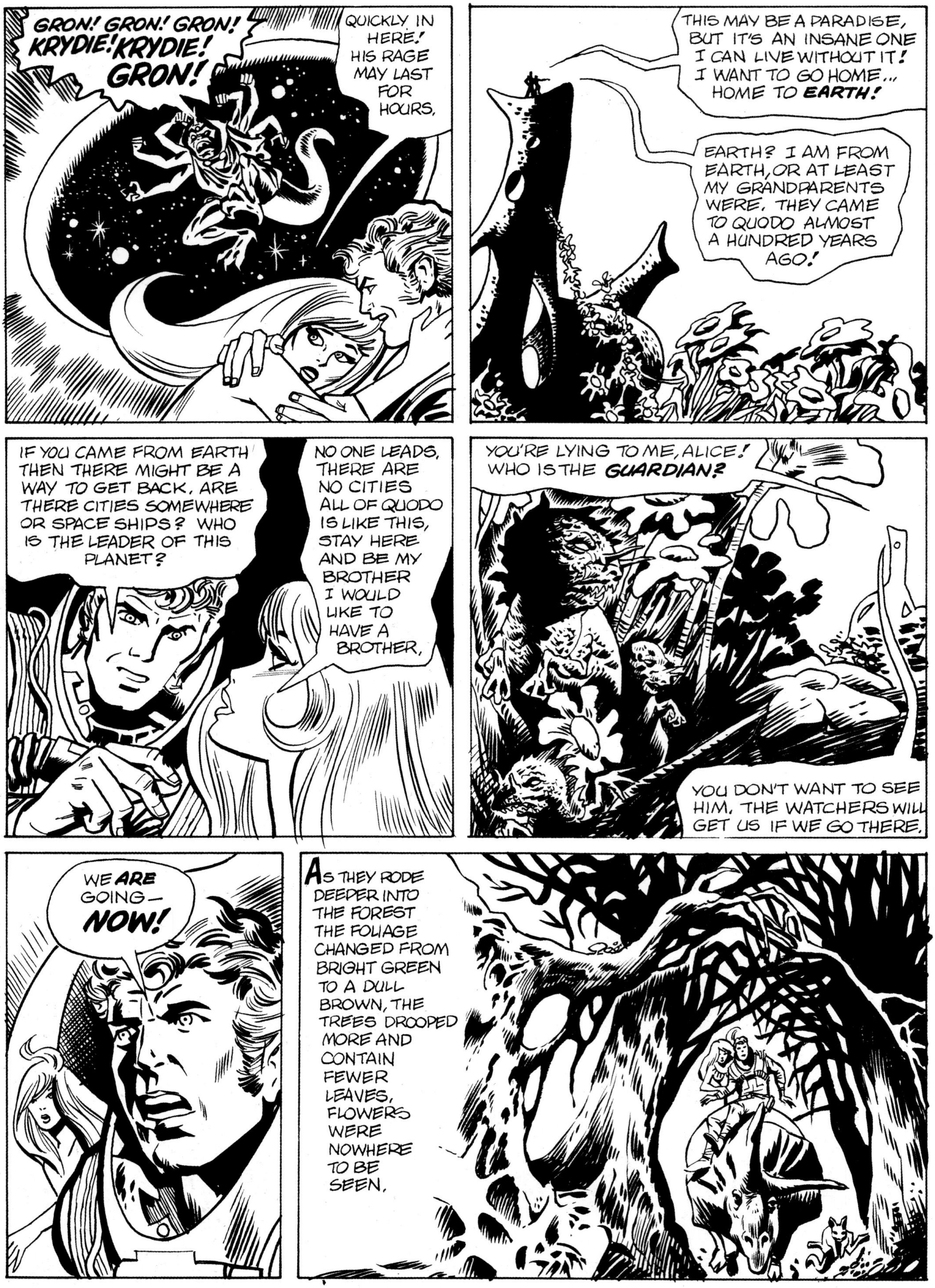
GRON! GRON! GRON! KRYDIE! KRYDIE! GRON!
QUICKLY IN HERE! HIS RAGE MAY LAST FOR HOURS.
THIS MAY BE A PARADISE, BUT IT'S AN INSANE ONE I CAN LIVE WITHOUT IT! I WANT TO GO HOME... HOME TO EARTH!
EARTH? I AM FROM EARTH, OR AT LEAST MY GRANDPARENTS WERE. THEY CAME TO QUODO ALMOST A HUNDRED YEARS AGO!
IF YOU CAME FROM EARTH THEN THERE MIGHT BE A WAY TO GET BACK. ARE THERE CITIES SOMEWHERE OR SPACE SHIPS? WHO IS THE LEADER OF THIS PLANET?
NO ONE LEADS, THERE ARE NO CITIES ALL OF QUODO IS LIKE THIS, STAY HERE AND BE MY BROTHER I WOULD LIKE TO HAVE A BROTHER.
YOU'RE LYING TO ME, ALICE! WHO IS THE GUARDIAN?
YOU DON'T WANT TO SEE HIM. THE WATCHERS WILL GET US IF WE GO THERE.
WE ARE GOING— NOW!
AS THEY RODE DEEPER INTO THE FOREST THE FOLIAGE CHANGED FROM BRIGHT GREEN TO A DULL BROWN, THE TREES DROOPED MORE AND CONTAIN FEWER LEAVES, FLOWERS WERE NOWHERE TO BE SEEN.

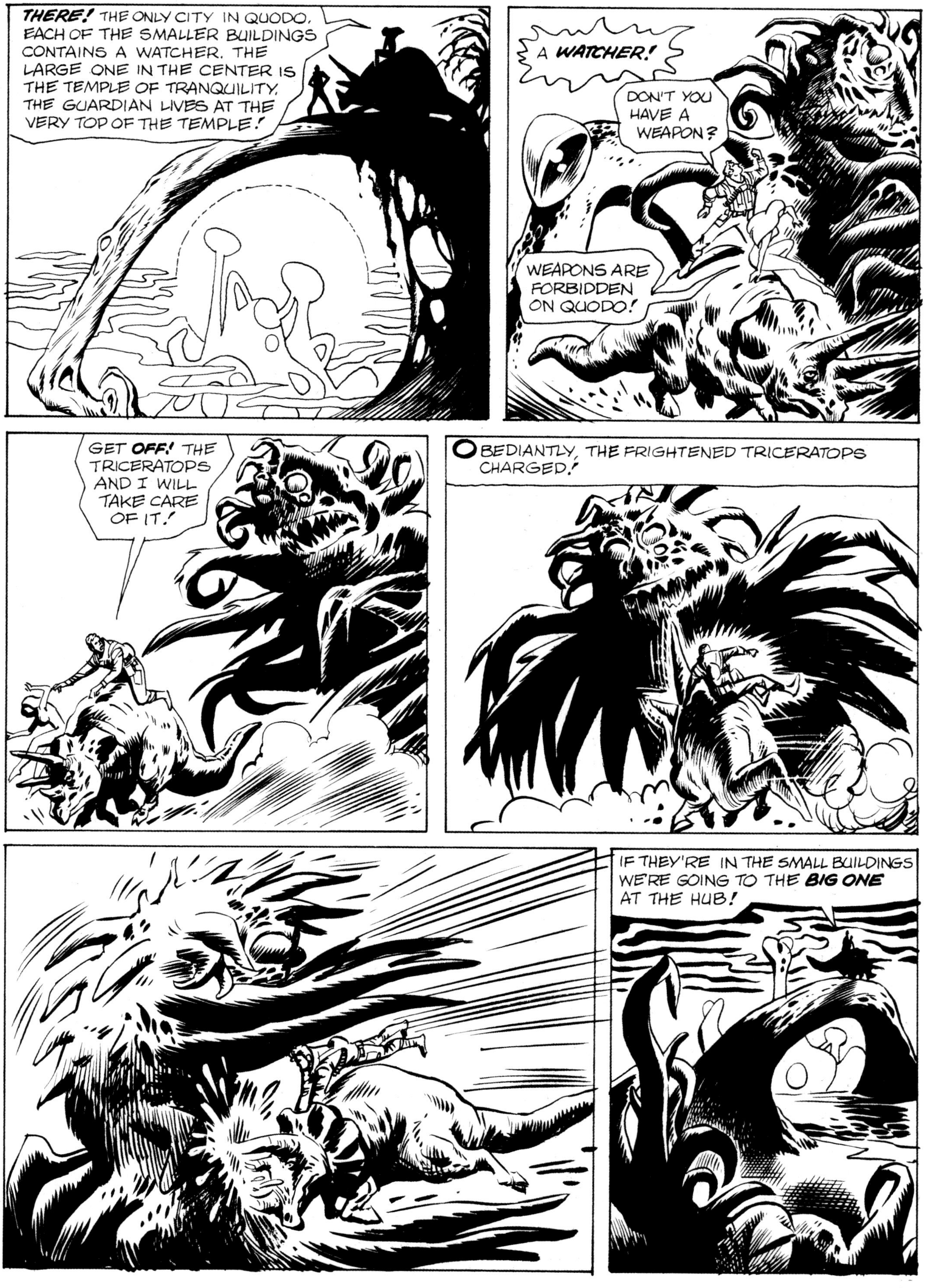
THERE! THE ONLY CITY IN QUODO. EACH OF THE SMALLER BUILDINGS CONTAINS A WATCHER. THE LARGE ONE IN THE CENTER IS THE TEMPLE OF TRANQUILITY. THE GUARDIAN LIVES AT THE VERY TOP OF THE TEMPLE!
A WATCHER!
DON'T YOU HAVE A WEAPON?
WEAPONS ARE FORBIDDEN ON QUODO!
GET OFF! THE TRICERATOPS AND I WILL TAKE CARE OF IT!
OBEDIANTLY, THE FRIGHTENED TRICERATOPS CHARGED!
IF THEY'RE IN THE SMALL BUILDINGS WE'RE GOING TO THE BIG ONE AT THE HUB!

YOU ARE A MIGHTY WARRIOR, LOST ONE, WHAT IS YOUR NAME

MY NAME IS SILAS

THESE ARE THE **VIOLENT ONES** SILAS, THEY HAVE BEEN BROUGHT TO THE TEMPLE OF TRANQUILITY TO BE CURED...

*I*N THE SECOND ROOM, SILAS AND ALICE FIND A THERAPY CHAMBER...

SLEEP, JUDSON, SLEEEP AND DREEEAM, WE ARE YOUR FRIENDS, JUDSON...

HERE IS WHERE THEY ARE CLEANSED

YOU MEAN HERE IS WHERE THEY ARE DRIVEN **MAD!**

NO, MY FRIEND, THE GIRL TELLS THE TRUTH, COME TO MY HIGH CHAMBER AND I'LL EXPLAIN QUODO TO YOU.

THE **GUARDIAN!**

*T*HE MADNESS BELOW SOFTENED TO A MURMUR, THEN VANISHED AS THE DOOR TO THE CHAMBER WAS CLOSED

MY UNFORTUNATE TRAVELER YO HAVE FALLEN INTO A GARDEN THAT IS ALSO AN **INTERPLANETARY INSANE ASYUM!** PEOPLE FROM ALL PLANETS IN THE GALAXY SEND THEIR UNCURABLES HERE WHERE MYSELF AND THE WATCHERS CARE FOR THEM, YOU AND I ARE THE ONLY **SANE** PEOPLE ON QUODO!

YOU'RE GOING TO BE THE ONLY SANE ONE HERE BECAUSE **I'M** LEAVING!

I'M NOT STAYING HERE NO MATTER **HOW** ATTRACTIVE YOU MAKE IT!

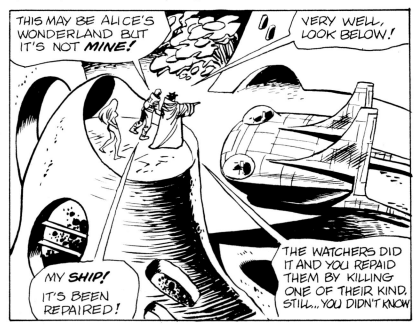

THIS MAY BE ALICE'S WONDERLAND BUT IT'S NOT **MINE!**

MY **SHIP!** IT'S BEEN REPAIRED!

VERY WELL, LOOK BELOW!

THE WATCHERS DID IT AND YOU REPAID THEM BY KILLING ONE OF THEIR KIND, STILL... YOU DIDN'T KNOW

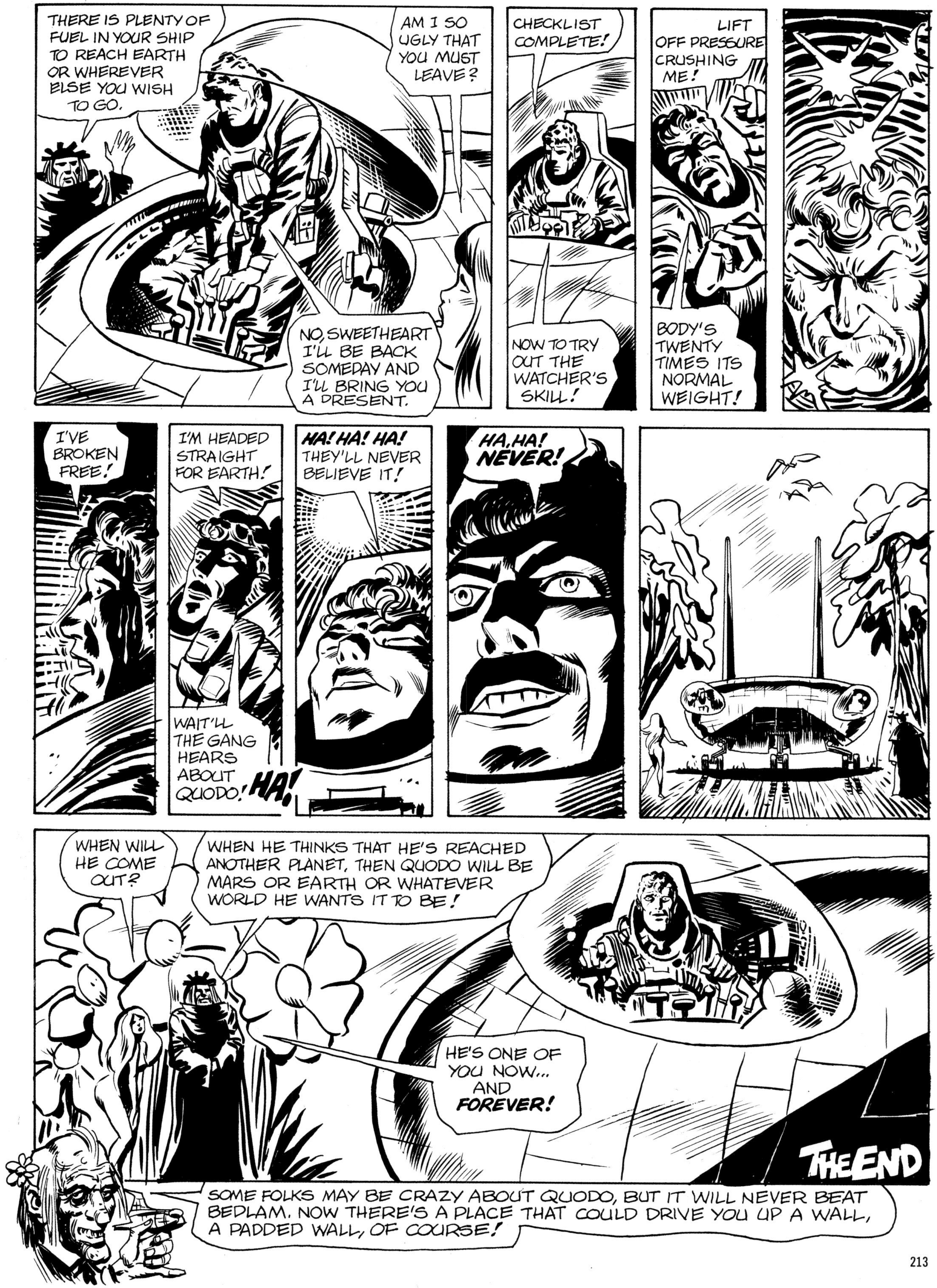
THERE IS PLENTY OF FUEL IN YOUR SHIP TO REACH EARTH OR WHEREVER ELSE YOU WISH TO GO.
AM I SO UGLY THAT YOU MUST LEAVE?
NO, SWEETHEART I'LL BE BACK SOMEDAY AND I'LL BRING YOU A PRESENT.
CHECKLIST COMPLETE!
NOW TO TRY OUT THE WATCHER'S SKILL!
LIFT OFF PRESSURE CRUSHING ME!
BODY'S TWENTY TIMES ITS NORMAL WEIGHT!
I'VE BROKEN FREE!
I'M HEADED STRAIGHT FOR EARTH!
WAIT'LL THE GANG HEARS ABOUT QUODO!
HA!
HA! HA! HA! THEY'LL NEVER BELIEVE IT!
HA, HA! NEVER!
WHEN WILL HE COME OUT?
WHEN HE THINKS THAT HE'S REACHED ANOTHER PLANET, THEN QUODO WILL BE MARS OR EARTH OR WHATEVER WORLD HE WANTS IT TO BE!
HE'S ONE OF YOU NOW... AND FOREVER!
THE END
SOME FOLKS MAY BE CRAZY ABOUT QUODO, BUT IT WILL NEVER BEAT BEDLAM. NOW THERE'S A PLACE THAT COULD DRIVE YOU UP A WALL, A PADDED WALL, OF COURSE!

THE CREEPY FAN CLUB!

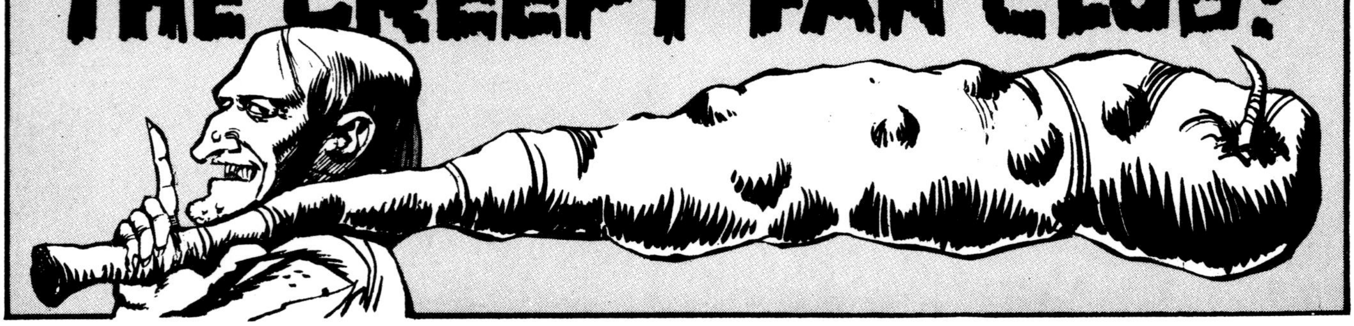

SKETCH BY LARRY DICKISON—ONTARIO, CANADA

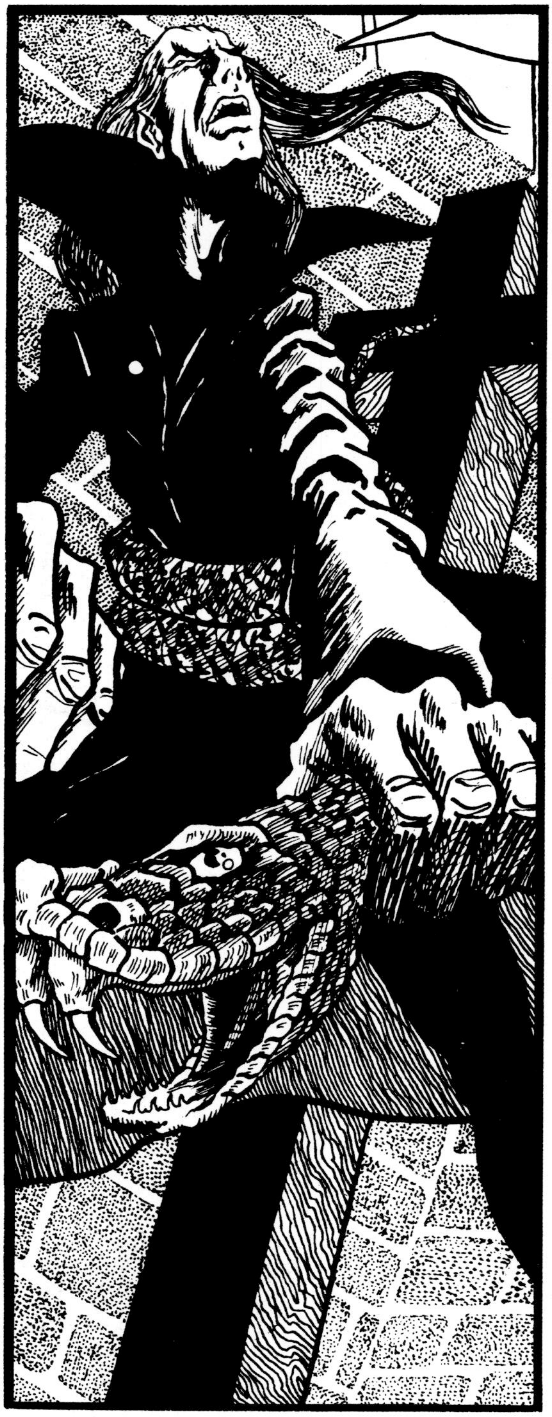

CREEPY POEMS

"Off with their heads!" shouted the Queen. But sometimes, it's the Queen who gets it in the neck. As in this poem by Harry Balmforth of East Sullivan, Maine.

ROYALTY
by Harry Balmforth

The night so black
ever lasting long
The dampness so cold
an everlasting strong
Is love or hate an
everlasting wrong?
Why ask me, why?

Is thought from thought
going to be kind?
Is thought from thought
hoping someone will find?
Is thought from thought
an everlasting bind?
Why ask me, why?

Love for her people
love for you
Love for her people every
trying to get through
Will it be over in the
morning dew?
Why ask me, why?

Never a morning
has anyone seen
Where had the night gone,
where had it been?
The moon's cold light
on the guilotine,
Why ask me, why?

Townspeople listen.
Cake they have et.
The young blood spurts,
for death she has met.
Is it the name that stands
ringing, Marie Antoinette?
Why ask me, why?

A man who calls himself "Count Wolfgang Von Ruebon" wrote this poem. Though he didn't say where he could be found, his letter hinted that his real name might be John Dearden . . .

THE WITCH OF THE CAVE
by John Dearden

Out by yonder archaic willow
There stands
a weatherbeaten cross.
The soil beneath
the ominous memorial
Is throughly scattered
with moss.
Yon marker marks
an ill-dug grave
The site of a witch most dead.
In this grave that I have made,
She was conveniently laid
When a bullet buried
deep in her head!
That witch of the cave is,
thank God,
In her grave.
With a bullet buried
deep in her head.
But when I ponder it
over sometimes,
I wonder if I should
have stabbed
The old crony instead.
When the trigger
was tugged, the
Lead charge was let to fire
And it struck home.
SHAZAM! right between
the eyes!
And for that charitable act,
I'm afraid I must die.
For when I shot yon
evil slattern
All the villagefolk heard
the fateful bang
And for that telltale sound,
I'm afraid at dawn
I must hang.
They call it murder!
I call it charity.
As I watch the breaking dawn,
I know that by next nightfall
I'll be meeting my friend,
The witch of the cave,
Where I know she must
have gone!

Accidents will happen, of course, But there's always someone involved who just can't bring himself to relax and enjoy it. Paul E. King, of Brookfield, Ill., tells of someone like that in his story . . .

TUNNEL OF TERROR
by Paul E. King

"What's happening?"
"We've crashed! Fire!"
"No . . . AIEEEEE! Someone help me. Please!"

A long train had jumped the track into a shallow, muddy ditch. The newspapers and the broadcasters had said the crack flyer was indestructable, yet the tragedy struck. A flaming inferno caused panic as hundreds of frightened passengers fled for their lives. Many were trampled to death, for they stood in the path of others stronger than themselves. There was no room for chivalry here. It was fight or die. Children abandoned all hope for the future. Life, at this moment, was in the cruel hands of fate.

"I've found the door," gasps a middle-aged man, grasping the silver handle in fury.

"Oh, I must escape. I must!" exclaims a teenage girl pressing herself against the exit.

Bounding from the wreckage like torpedoes, they inhale pure air once more. Falling on the sodden ground, some clutch the soil desperately for security. A low rumble stirs the air. Continuing, the sound echoes louder, louder, louder. Then the might marvel explodes like Krakatoa, showering its hapless victims with flying hot metal. Anguished cries fill the air as the horror sinks in. Death swings his accursed sickle in triumph. And eternal sleep comes to all.

In the midst of the wreck, a figure slowly rises. Trembling fingers hold a bleeding forehead as a young man of 27 staggers into the light. He wanders until he finds an old gravel road as his pain grows to almost unbearable proportions. Hours pass. His eyelids begin to flutter as he regains his composure. An icy chill tingles his spine. Gazing into the angry sky, he notices it is raining. A downpour that soaks his very soul.

"My wife. My children. I must get word to them," he mutters. Thankful to be alive, he staggers forward, seeking shelter from the rain. Then he spots a warm cave, and decides to wait there until the deluge is past.

Hurrying into the opening, he slides against the jagged wall, thankful for the security it gives him. Hard draughts of cold air rise up from below him. Turning his head, the wounded man wonders aloud, "Why spend the night in a Godforsaken place like this? Maybe there's another way out down there."

Cautiously, he follows the winding tunnel in search of help and escape. Twice he stumbles on the uneven floor, cutting his hands on the sharp rocks. Blood spilling from his limbs, he presses forward. Then he sees a light. He feels renewed hope.

Running from the narrow confines of the tunnel, he gazes into the vastness of a huge cavern. His head aches violently, and he feels a blast of hot air on his face. Then he sees it. A shrouded figure walking slowly toward him.

"I'm glad you finally arrived. I was a little disturbed when you weren't among the others. But you're here now. And welcome! You'll be most comfortable here, I'm sure. Welcome, my friend, to Hades."

Everybody knows there are monsters everywhere you look. But down in Big Spring, Texas, Rodney E. Hammack was forced to look to the stars to find . . .

DOOMSDAY MONSTERS
by Rodney E. Hammack

The warrior inhabitants of the planet Ferstra IV and their barbaric adversaries of Sestra II had been in continuous battle for more than 12 centuries when the leaders of the two worlds met on a dreary planetoid for an important conference. Both planets realized that their constant conflict had created a severe threat to their whole galaxy. Nuclear attacks had brought about an alarming level of radioactivity in their star system. Both agreed that the time had come to end their war. Or to ban the use of atomic weapons.

The talks lasted for months. Finally, the leaders arrived at a solution. Each would return to his own planet and select a champion to represent his world in a climactic battle. No particulars were discussed about what sort of candidates would be allowable, so each of the leaders schemed to come up with the most ferocious creature his planet could produce.

On a previously agreed-upon date, the two leaders returned to the planetoid. Each with his authorized champion. Both men were confident of success and they watched with eager anticipation as the beasts were unleashed against each other.

The monster from Ferstra IV was a gigantic lizard that towered over the barren plain. The champion of Sestra II was equally awesome. Its evil eyes protruded from its bony skull on two long tentacles. Other tentacles, barbed with deadly-looking claws, snaked out in front of it. The creature moved forward slowly on small root-like structures on its base.

"I see you have brought the gasation lizard," commented the Setrian leader. "But it will be no match for mine."

The two monsters advanced slowly upon each other.

"I've never seen a beast like yours," said the Ferstra commander. "Where did you find it?" The two men's eyes were grimly focused upon the two great beasts on the plain below them.

"Oh, some of my men found it on a small planet near Quastro V," he answered. Suddenly, the face of the Ferstra leader turned deathly pale.

"Don't you know what you've done!?" he shouted. "That beast is pure anti-matter! You have no idea what will happen when it comes in contact with a matter-creature as large as the gasation lizard!"

But before either man could consider the possibilities, the two monsters leapt upon each other with a loud roar that soon blossomed into an awesome sound.

The hellish force of the anti-matter blast surged outward until it had engulfed not just the tiny planetoid, but the entire surrounding star system. Ferstra IV was first to feel the impact. Sestra II was vaporized in minutes.

The shock waves reverberated through the universe for more than 12 centuries.

APOCALYPSE!

Means the end of the world. Something you'll never see if you submit a drawing or story to:

CREEPY FAN CLUB

—because you'll probably keel over from the shock of acceptance!

THIS DOOMSDAY MONSTER

WAS DRAWN BY LARRY DICKISON, OF ONTARIO, CANADA, WHO WILL BE DOING A STORY FOR US IN AN UP-AND-COMING ISSUE OF CREEPY!

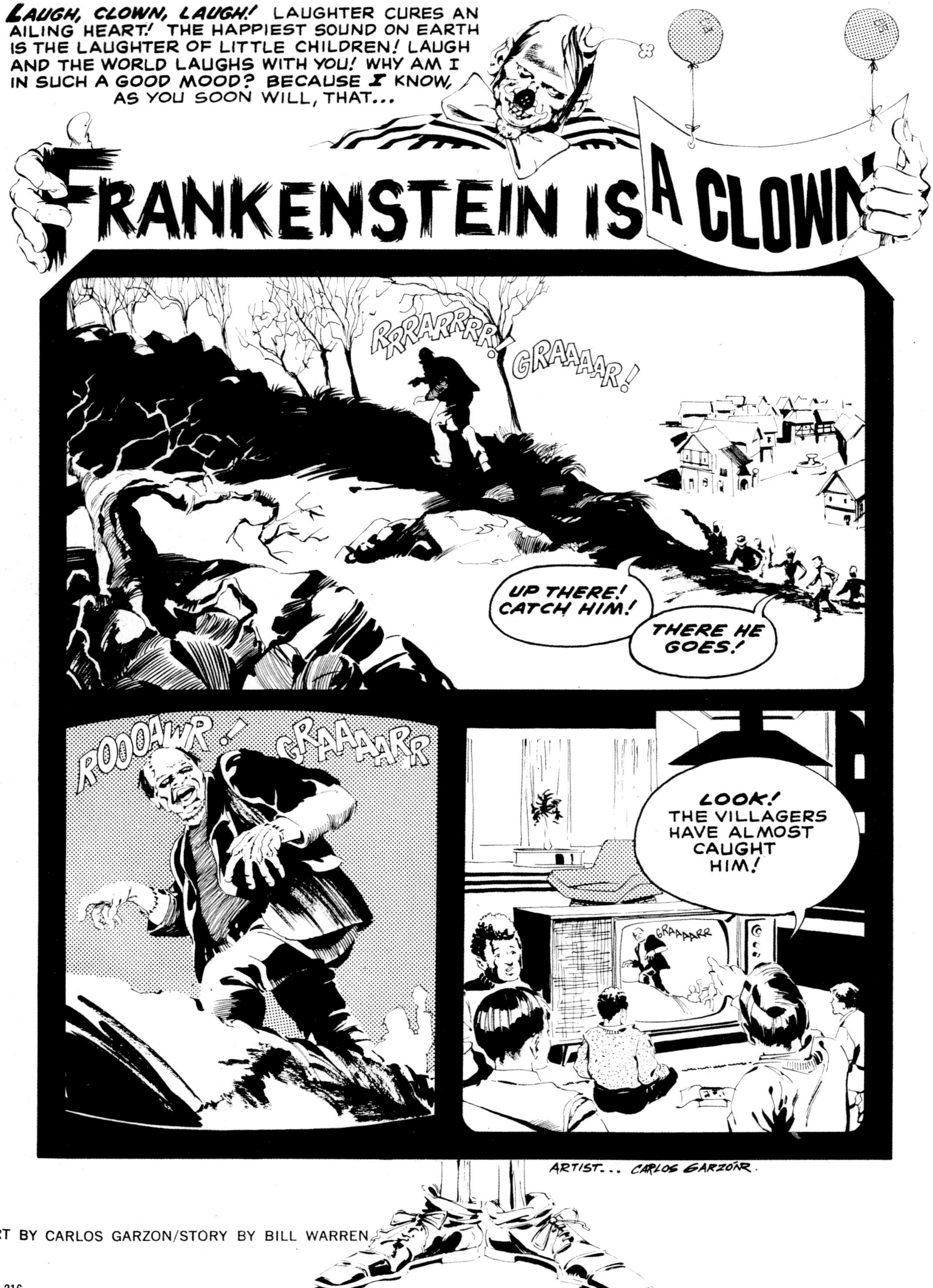
LAUGH, CLOWN, LAUGH! LAUGHTER CURES AN AILING HEART! THE HAPPIEST SOUND ON EARTH IS THE LAUGHTER OF LITTLE CHILDREN! LAUGH AND THE WORLD LAUGHS WITH YOU! WHY AM I IN SUCH A GOOD MOOD? BECAUSE I KNOW, AS YOU SOON WILL, THAT...
FRANKENSTEIN IS A CLOWN
RRRRARRRRR!
GRAAAAAR!
UP THERE! CATCH HIM!
THERE HE GOES!
ROOOAWR!
GRAAAAARR
LOOK! THE VILLAGERS HAVE ALMOST CAUGHT HIM!
GRAAAARR
ARTIST... CARLOS GARZÓN.

ART BY CARLOS GARZON/STORY BY BILL WARREN

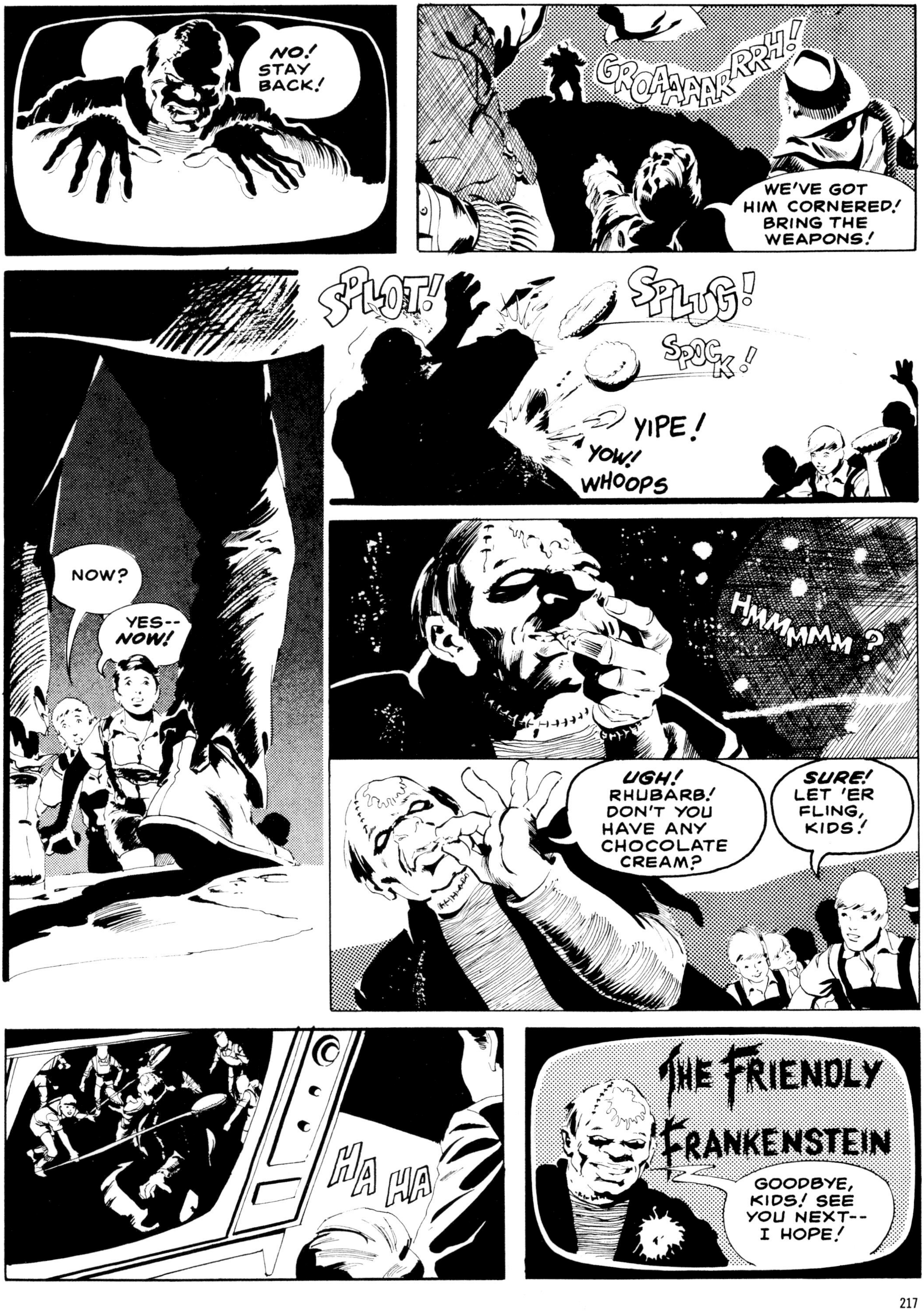
NO! STAY BACK!
GROAAAAARRRH!
WE'VE GOT HIM CORNERED! BRING THE WEAPONS!
SPLOT!
SPLUG!
SPOCK!
YIPE!
YOW! WHOOPS
NOW?
YES-- NOW!
HMMMMM?
UGH! RHUBARB! DON'T YOU HAVE ANY CHOCOLATE CREAM?
SURE! LET 'ER FLING, KIDS!
HA HA
THE FRIENDLY FRANKENSTEIN
GOODBYE, KIDS! SEE YOU NEXT-- I HOPE!

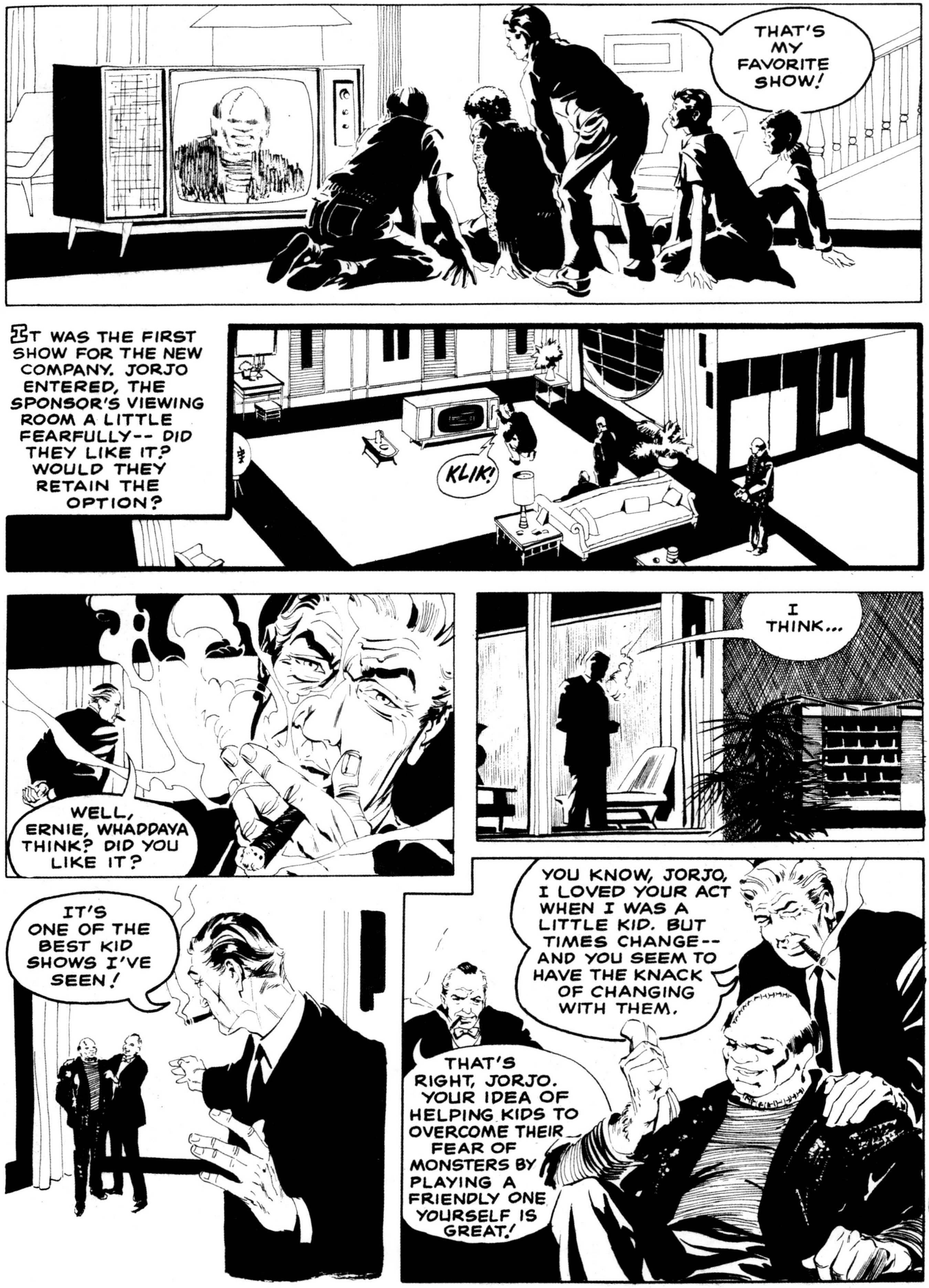
THAT'S MY FAVORITE SHOW!
IT WAS THE FIRST SHOW FOR THE NEW COMPANY. JORJO ENTERED, THE SPONSOR'S VIEWING ROOM A LITTLE FEARFULLY-- DID THEY LIKE IT? WOULD THEY RETAIN THE OPTION?
KLIK!
WELL, ERNIE, WHADDAYA THINK? DID YOU LIKE IT?
I THINK...
IT'S ONE OF THE BEST KID SHOWS I'VE SEEN!
YOU KNOW, JORJO, I LOVED YOUR ACT WHEN I WAS A LITTLE KID. BUT TIMES CHANGE-- AND YOU SEEM TO HAVE THE KNACK OF CHANGING WITH THEM.
THAT'S RIGHT, JORJO. YOUR IDEA OF HELPING KIDS TO OVERCOME THEIR FEAR OF MONSTERS BY PLAYING A FRIENDLY ONE YOURSELF IS GREAT!

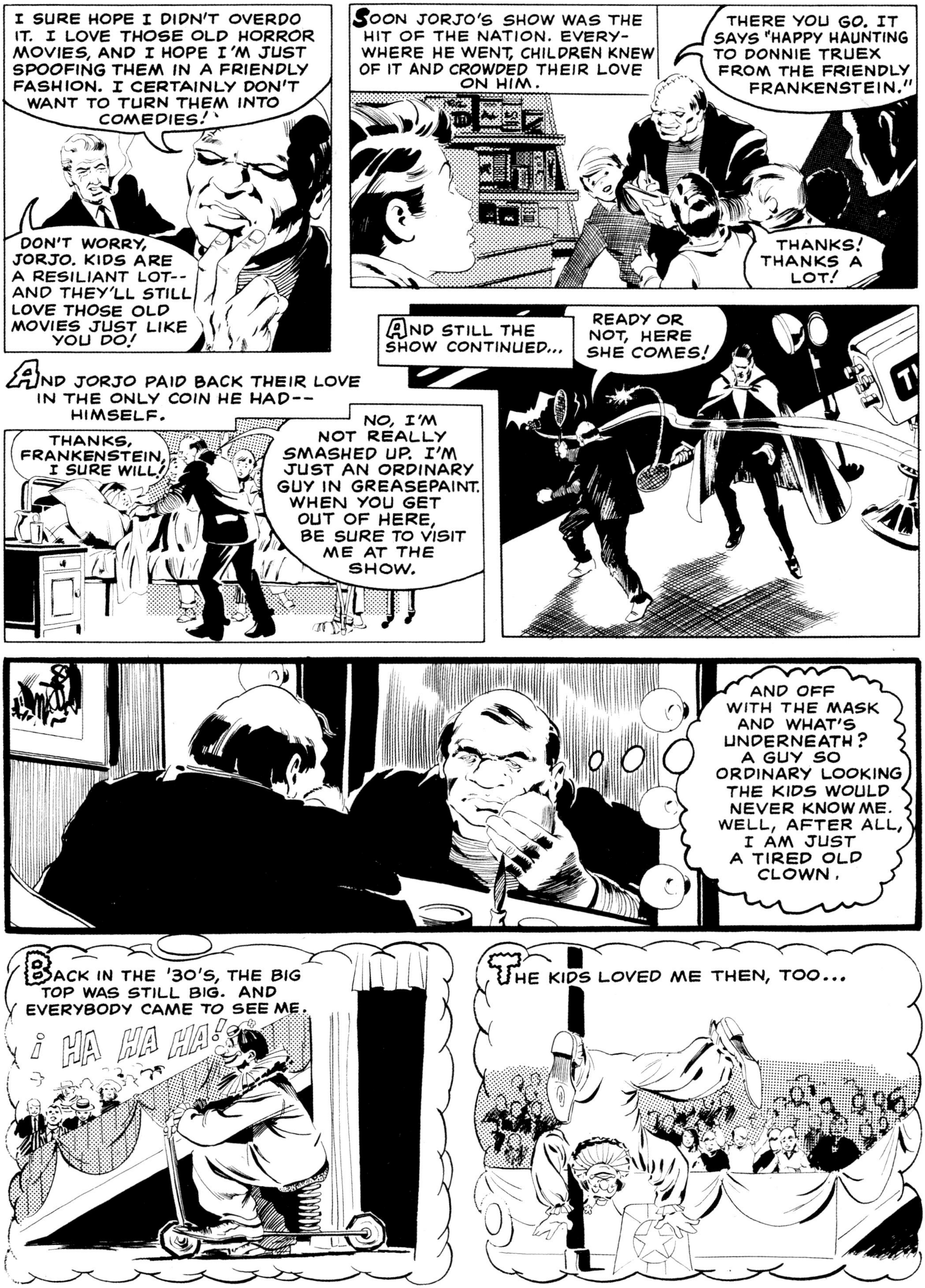
I SURE HOPE I DIDN'T OVERDO IT. I LOVE THOSE OLD HORROR MOVIES, AND I HOPE I'M JUST SPOOFING THEM IN A FRIENDLY FASHION. I CERTAINLY DON'T WANT TO TURN THEM INTO COMEDIES!
DON'T WORRY, JORJO. KIDS ARE A RESILIANT LOT-- AND THEY'LL STILL LOVE THOSE OLD MOVIES JUST LIKE YOU DO!
SOON JORJO'S SHOW WAS THE HIT OF THE NATION. EVERY-WHERE HE WENT, CHILDREN KNEW OF IT AND CROWDED THEIR LOVE ON HIM.
THERE YOU GO. IT SAYS "HAPPY HAUNTING TO DONNIE TRUEX FROM THE FRIENDLY FRANKENSTEIN."
THANKS! THANKS A LOT!
AND JORJO PAID BACK THEIR LOVE IN THE ONLY COIN HE HAD-- HIMSELF.
THANKS, FRANKENSTEIN, I SURE WILL!
NO, I'M NOT REALLY SMASHED UP. I'M JUST AN ORDINARY GUY IN GREASEPAINT. WHEN YOU GET OUT OF HERE, BE SURE TO VISIT ME AT THE SHOW.
AND STILL THE SHOW CONTINUED...
READY OR NOT, HERE SHE COMES!
AND OFF WITH THE MASK AND WHAT'S UNDERNEATH? A GUY SO ORDINARY LOOKING THE KIDS WOULD NEVER KNOW ME. WELL, AFTER ALL, I AM JUST A TIRED OLD CLOWN.
BACK IN THE '30'S, THE BIG TOP WAS STILL BIG. AND EVERYBODY CAME TO SEE ME.
¡HA HA HA!
THE KIDS LOVED ME THEN, TOO...

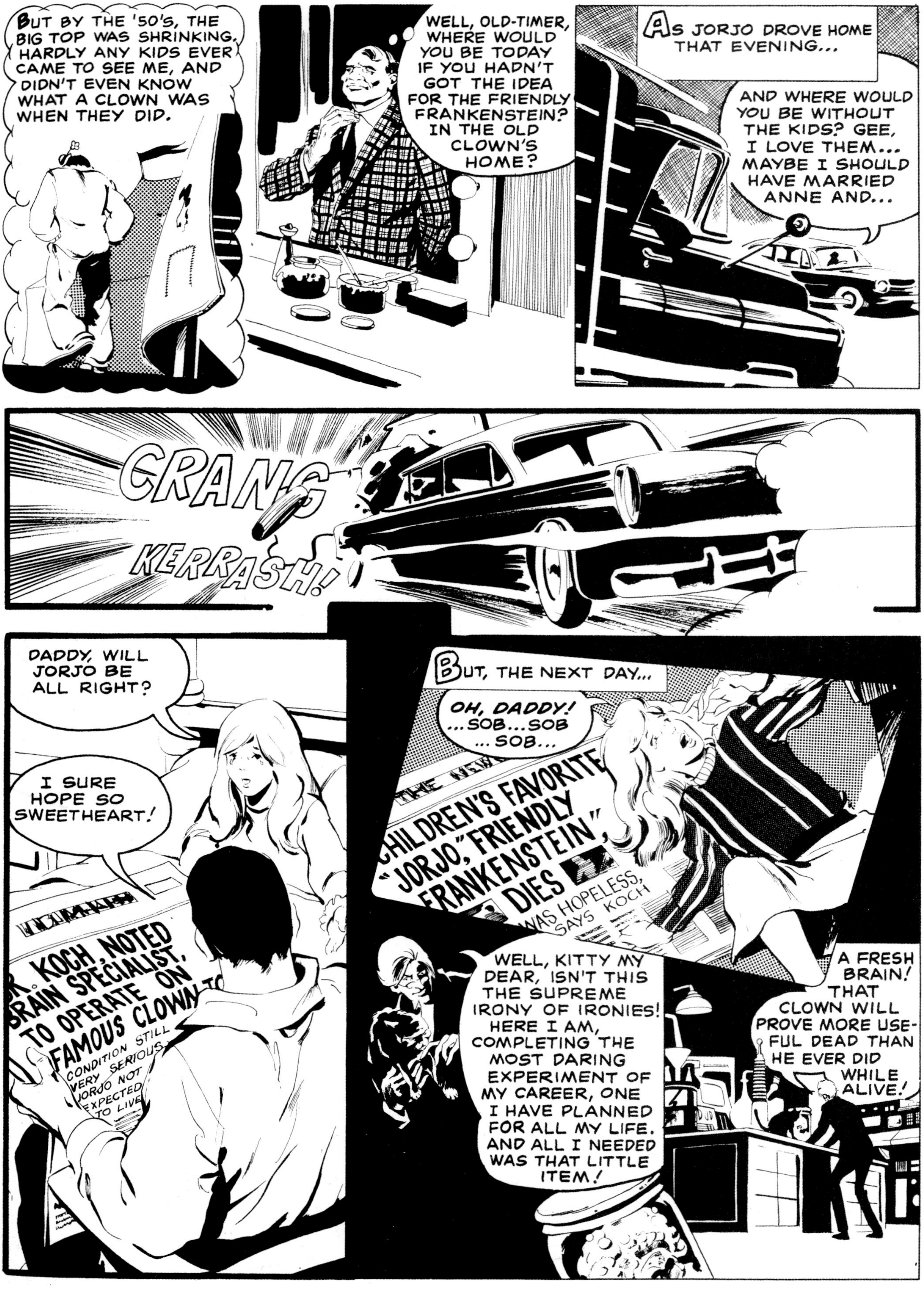
BUT BY THE '50'S, THE BIG TOP WAS SHRINKING. HARDLY ANY KIDS EVER CAME TO SEE ME, AND DIDN'T EVEN KNOW WHAT A CLOWN WAS WHEN THEY DID.
WELL, OLD-TIMER, WHERE WOULD YOU BE TODAY IF YOU HADN'T GOT THE IDEA FOR THE FRIENDLY FRANKENSTEIN? IN THE OLD CLOWN'S HOME?
AS JORJO DROVE HOME THAT EVENING...
AND WHERE WOULD YOU BE WITHOUT THE KIDS? GEE, I LOVE THEM... MAYBE I SHOULD HAVE MARRIED ANNE AND...
CRANG
KERRASH!
DADDY, WILL JORJO BE ALL RIGHT?
I SURE HOPE SO SWEETHEART!
KOCH, NOTED BRAIN SPECIALIST, TO OPERATE ON FAMOUS CLOWN
CONDITION STILL VERY SERIOUS JORJO NOT EXPECTED TO LIVE
BUT, THE NEXT DAY...
OH, DADDY! ...SOB...SOB ...SOB...
CHILDREN'S FAVORITE "JORJO," FRIENDLY FRANKENSTEIN, DIES
WAS HOPELESS, SAYS KOCH
WELL, KITTY MY DEAR, ISN'T THIS THE SUPREME IRONY OF IRONIES! HERE I AM, COMPLETING THE MOST DARING EXPERIMENT OF MY CAREER, ONE I HAVE PLANNED FOR ALL MY LIFE. AND ALL I NEEDED WAS THAT LITTLE ITEM!
A FRESH BRAIN! THAT CLOWN WILL PROVE MORE USEFUL DEAD THAN HE EVER DID WHILE ALIVE!

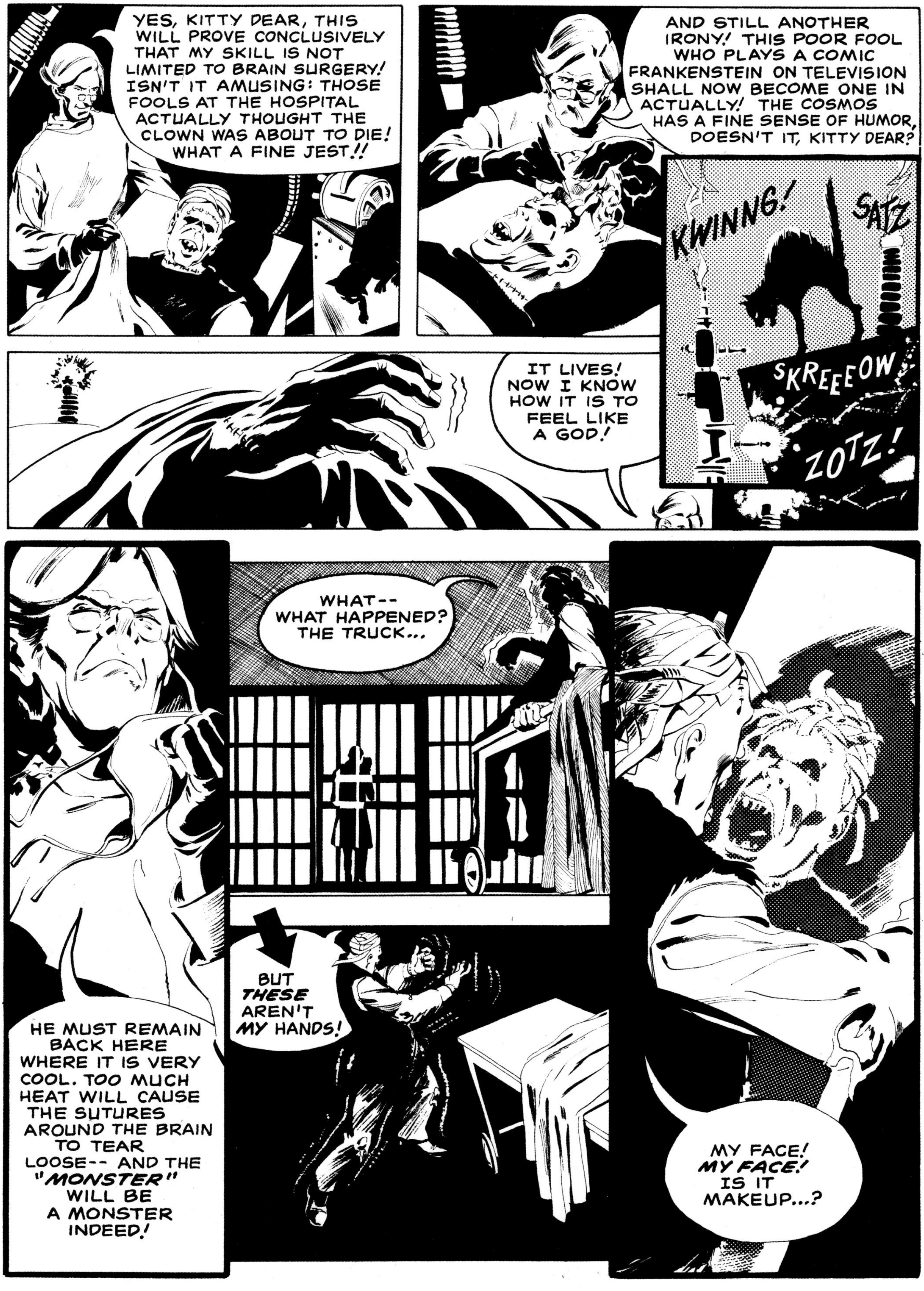
YES, KITTY DEAR, THIS WILL PROVE CONCLUSIVELY THAT MY SKILL IS NOT LIMITED TO BRAIN SURGERY! ISN'T IT AMUSING: THOSE FOOLS AT THE HOSPITAL ACTUALLY THOUGHT THE CLOWN WAS ABOUT TO DIE! WHAT A FINE JEST!!
AND STILL ANOTHER IRONY! THIS POOR FOOL WHO PLAYS A COMIC FRANKENSTEIN ON TELEVISION SHALL NOW BECOME ONE IN ACTUALLY! THE COSMOS HAS A FINE SENSE OF HUMOR, DOESN'T IT, KITTY DEAR?
KWINNG!
SATZ
SKREEEOW
ZOTZ!
IT LIVES! NOW I KNOW HOW IT IS TO FEEL LIKE A GOD!
WHAT-- WHAT HAPPENED? THE TRUCK...
BUT *THESE* AREN'T *MY* HANDS!
HE MUST REMAIN BACK HERE WHERE IT IS VERY COOL. TOO MUCH HEAT WILL CAUSE THE SUTURES AROUND THE BRAIN TO TEAR LOOSE-- AND THE "*MONSTER*" WILL BE A MONSTER INDEED!
MY FACE! *MY FACE!* IS IT MAKEUP...?

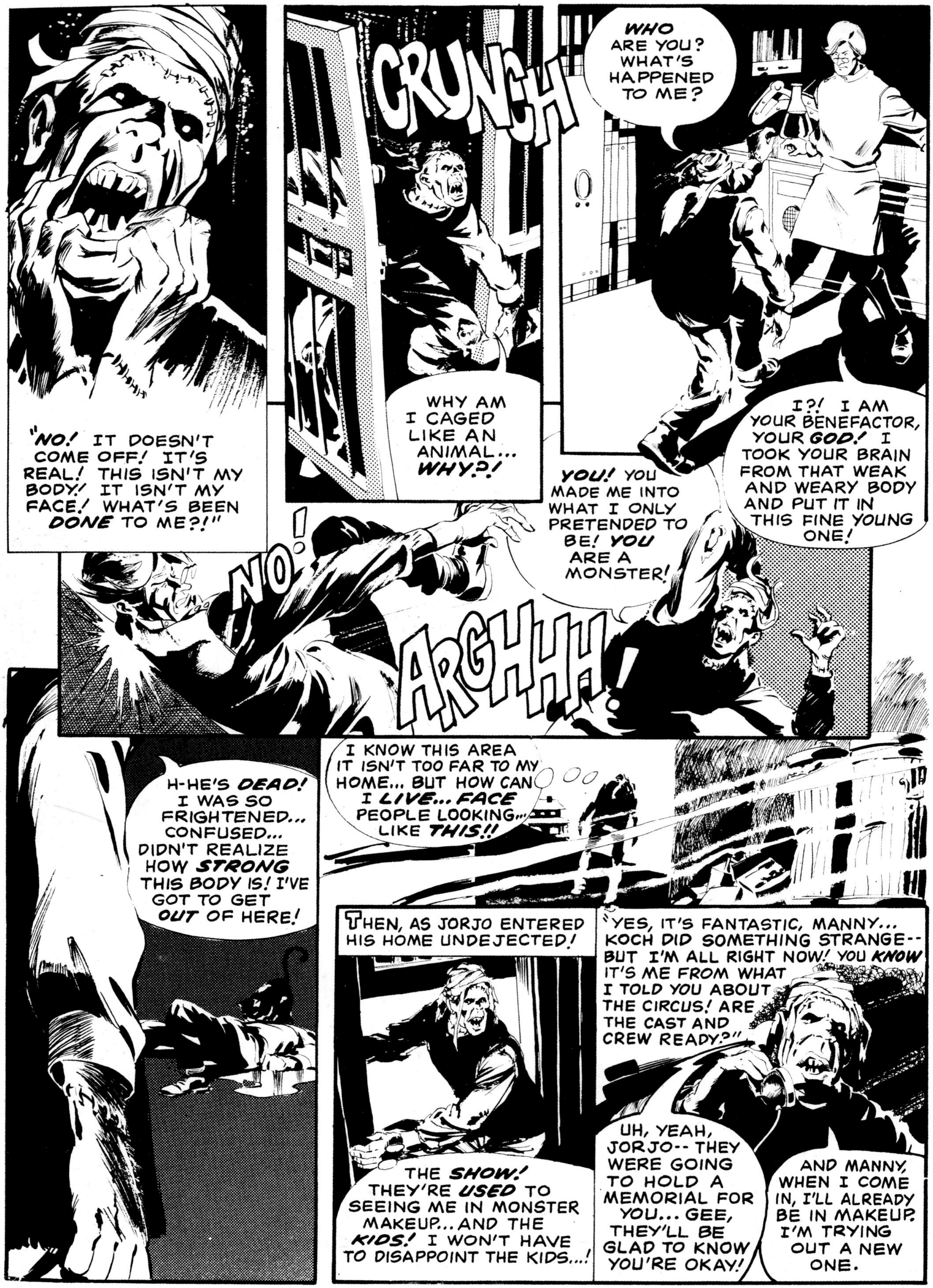
"NO! IT DOESN'T COME OFF! IT'S REAL! THIS ISN'T MY BODY! IT ISN'T MY FACE! WHAT'S BEEN DONE TO ME?!"
CRUNCH
WHY AM I CAGED LIKE AN ANIMAL... WHY?!
WHO ARE YOU? WHAT'S HAPPENED TO ME?
I?! I AM YOUR BENEFACTOR, YOUR GOD! I TOOK YOUR BRAIN FROM THAT WEAK AND WEARY BODY AND PUT IT IN THIS FINE YOUNG ONE!
YOU! YOU MADE ME INTO WHAT I ONLY PRETENDED TO BE! YOU ARE A MONSTER!
NO!
ARGHHH!
H-HE'S DEAD! I WAS SO FRIGHTENED... CONFUSED... DIDN'T REALIZE HOW STRONG THIS BODY IS! I'VE GOT TO GET OUT OF HERE!
I KNOW THIS AREA IT ISN'T TOO FAR TO MY HOME... BUT HOW CAN I LIVE... FACE PEOPLE LOOKING... LIKE THIS!!
THEN, AS JORJO ENTERED HIS HOME UNDEJECTED!
THE SHOW! THEY'RE USED TO SEEING ME IN MONSTER MAKEUP... AND THE KIDS! I WON'T HAVE TO DISAPPOINT THE KIDS...!
"YES, IT'S FANTASTIC, MANNY... KOCH DID SOMETHING STRANGE-- BUT I'M ALL RIGHT NOW! YOU KNOW IT'S ME FROM WHAT I TOLD YOU ABOUT THE CIRCUS! ARE THE CAST AND CREW READY?"
UH, YEAH, JORJO-- THEY WERE GOING TO HOLD A MEMORIAL FOR YOU... GEE, THEY'LL BE GLAD TO KNOW YOU'RE OKAY!
AND MANNY, WHEN I COME IN, I'LL ALREADY BE IN MAKEUP. I'M TRYING OUT A NEW ONE.

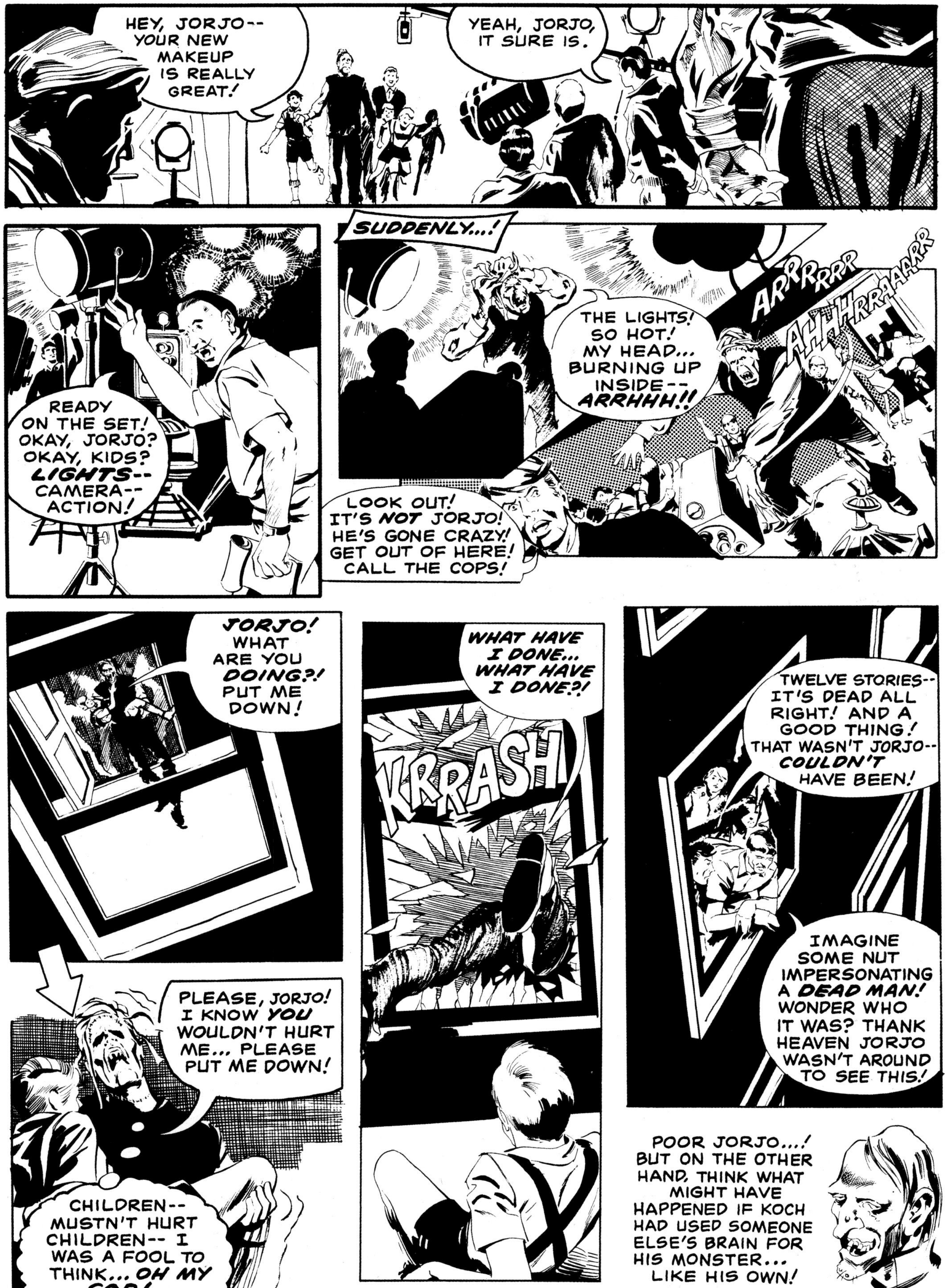
HEY, JORJO-- YOUR NEW MAKEUP IS REALLY GREAT!
YEAH, JORJO, IT SURE IS.
READY ON THE SET! OKAY, JORJO? OKAY, KIDS? LIGHTS-- CAMERA-- ACTION!
SUDDENLY...!
THE LIGHTS! SO HOT! MY HEAD... BURNING UP INSIDE-- ARRHHH!!
ARRRRRR
AHHHRRAAARR
LOOK OUT! IT'S NOT JORJO! HE'S GONE CRAZY! GET OUT OF HERE! CALL THE COPS!
JORJO! WHAT ARE YOU DOING?! PUT ME DOWN!
PLEASE, JORJO! I KNOW YOU WOULDN'T HURT ME... PLEASE PUT ME DOWN!
CHILDREN-- MUSTN'T HURT CHILDREN-- I WAS A FOOL TO THINK... OH MY GOD!
WHAT HAVE I DONE... WHAT HAVE I DONE?!
KRRASH
TWELVE STORIES-- IT'S DEAD ALL RIGHT! AND A GOOD THING! THAT WASN'T JORJO-- COULDN'T HAVE BEEN!
IMAGINE SOME NUT IMPERSONATING A DEAD MAN! WONDER WHO IT WAS? THANK HEAVEN JORJO WASN'T AROUND TO SEE THIS!
POOR JORJO...! BUT ON THE OTHER HAND, THINK WHAT MIGHT HAVE HAPPENED IF KOCH HAD USED SOMEONE ELSE'S BRAIN FOR HIS MONSTER... LIKE HIS OWN!

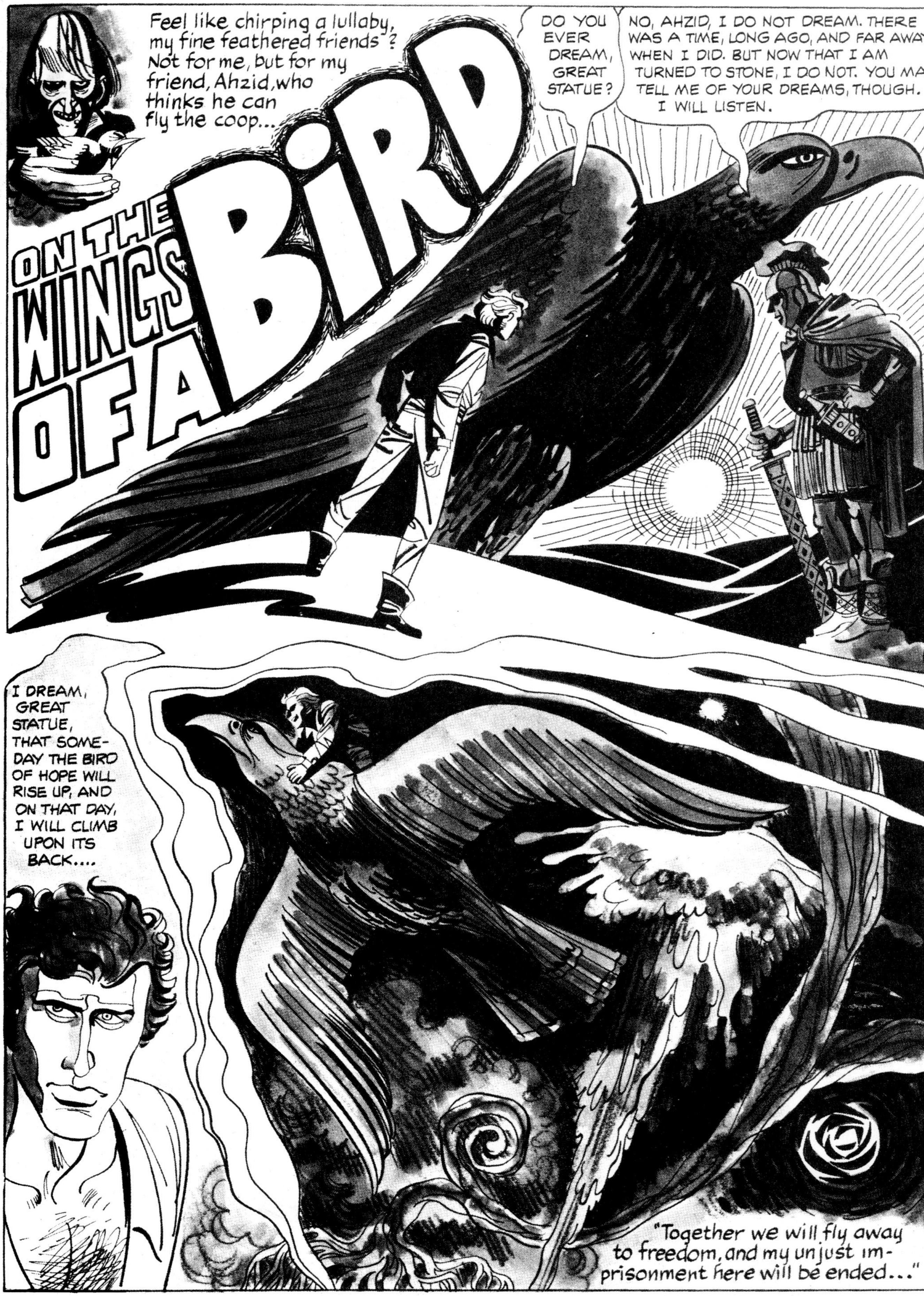
Feel like chirping a lullaby, my fine feathered friends? Not for me, but for my friend, Ahzid, who thinks he can fly the coop...
ON THE WINGS OF A BIRD
DO YOU EVER DREAM, GREAT STATUE?
NO, AHZID, I DO NOT DREAM. THERE WAS A TIME, LONG AGO, AND FAR AWAY WHEN I DID. BUT NOW THAT I AM TURNED TO STONE, I DO NOT. YOU MAY TELL ME OF YOUR DREAMS, THOUGH. I WILL LISTEN.
I DREAM, GREAT STATUE, THAT SOME-DAY THE BIRD OF HOPE WILL RISE UP, AND ON THAT DAY, I WILL CLIMB UPON ITS BACK....
"Together we will fly away to freedom, and my unjust im-prisonment here will be ended..."

ART BY JERRY GRANDENETTI/STORY BY T. CASEY BRENNAN

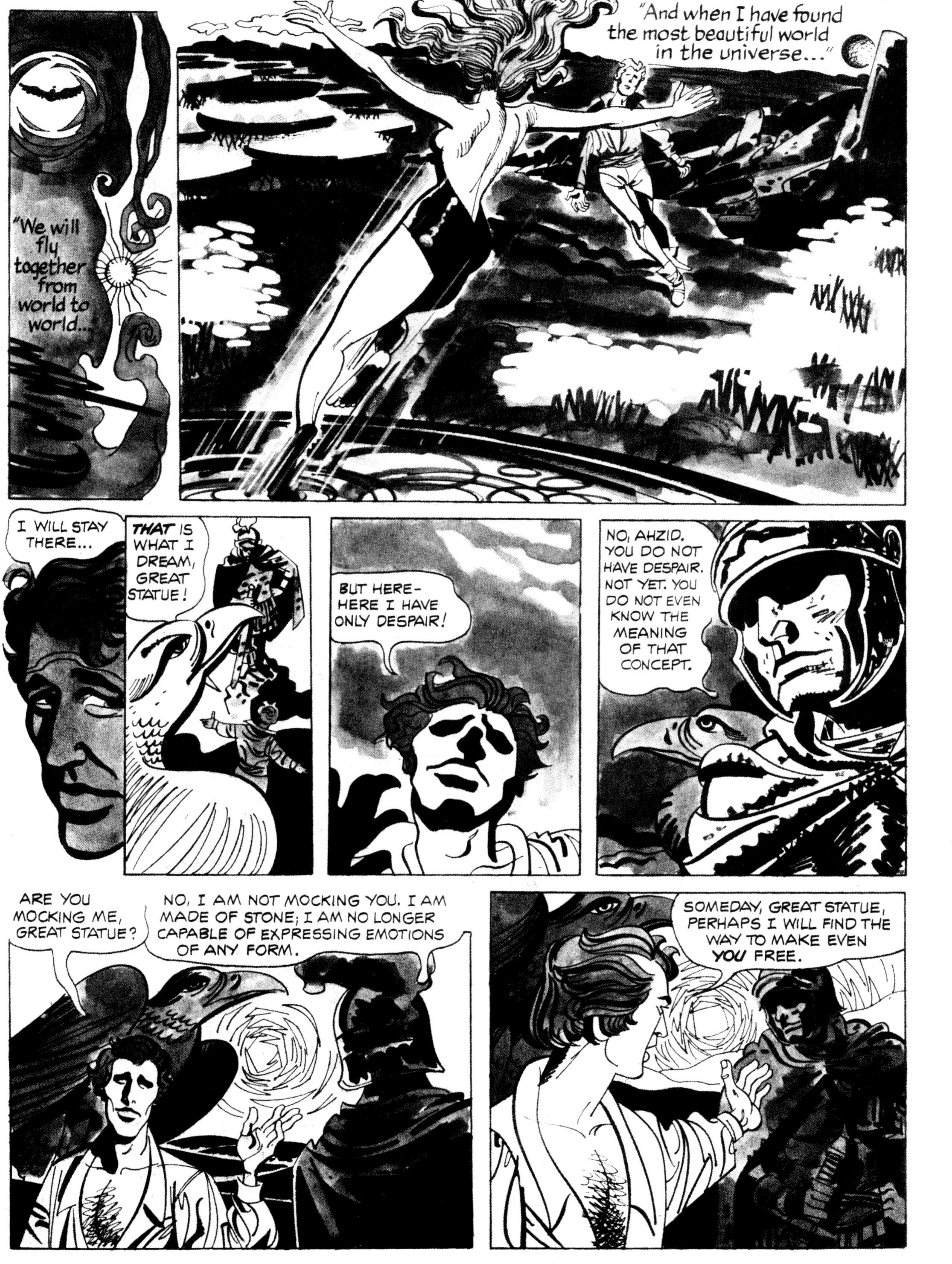
"We will fly together from world to world...
"And when I have found the most beautiful world in the universe..."
I WILL STAY THERE...
THAT IS WHAT I DREAM, GREAT STATUE!
BUT HERE-HERE I HAVE ONLY DESPAIR!
NO, AHZID. YOU DO NOT HAVE DESPAIR. NOT YET. YOU DO NOT EVEN KNOW THE MEANING OF THAT CONCEPT.
ARE YOU MOCKING ME, GREAT STATUE?
NO, I AM NOT MOCKING YOU. I AM MADE OF STONE; I AM NO LONGER CAPABLE OF EXPRESSING EMOTIONS OF ANY FORM.
SOMEDAY, GREAT STATUE, PERHAPS I WILL FIND THE WAY TO MAKE EVEN YOU FREE.

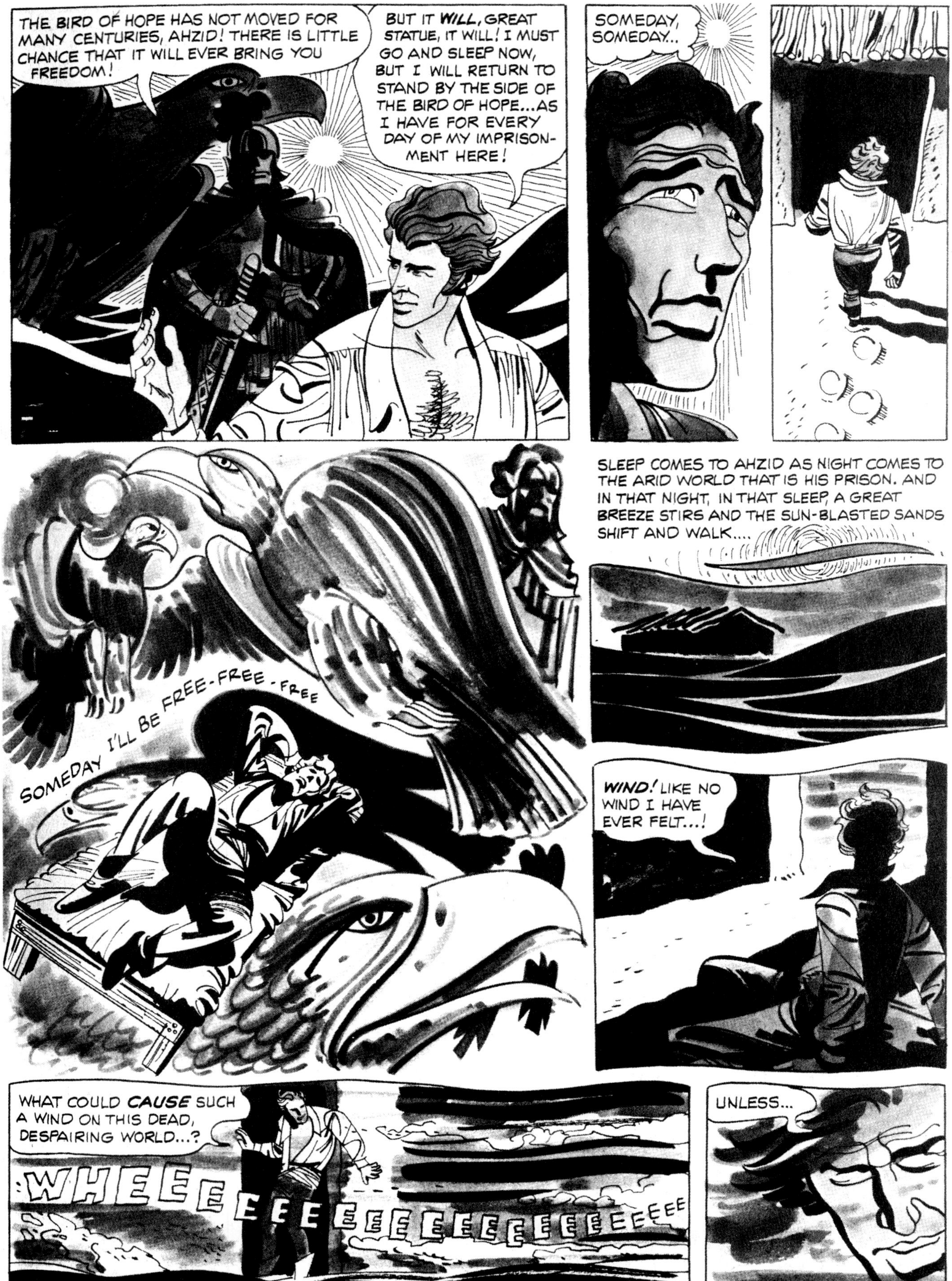

THE BIRD OF HOPE HAS NOT MOVED FOR MANY CENTURIES, AHZID! THERE IS LITTLE CHANCE THAT IT WILL EVER BRING YOU FREEDOM!
BUT IT WILL, GREAT STATUE, IT WILL! I MUST GO AND SLEEP NOW, BUT I WILL RETURN TO STAND BY THE SIDE OF THE BIRD OF HOPE...AS I HAVE FOR EVERY DAY OF MY IMPRISONMENT HERE!
SOMEDAY, SOMEDAY...
SOMEDAY I'LL BE FREE-FREE-FREE
SLEEP COMES TO AHZID AS NIGHT COMES TO THE ARID WORLD THAT IS HIS PRISON. AND IN THAT NIGHT, IN THAT SLEEP, A GREAT BREEZE STIRS AND THE SUN-BLASTED SANDS SHIFT AND WALK....
WIND! LIKE NO WIND I HAVE EVER FELT...!
WHAT COULD CAUSE SUCH A WIND ON THIS DEAD, DESPAIRING WORLD...?
WHEEEEEEEEEEEEEEEEEEEEEEEEEE
UNLESS...

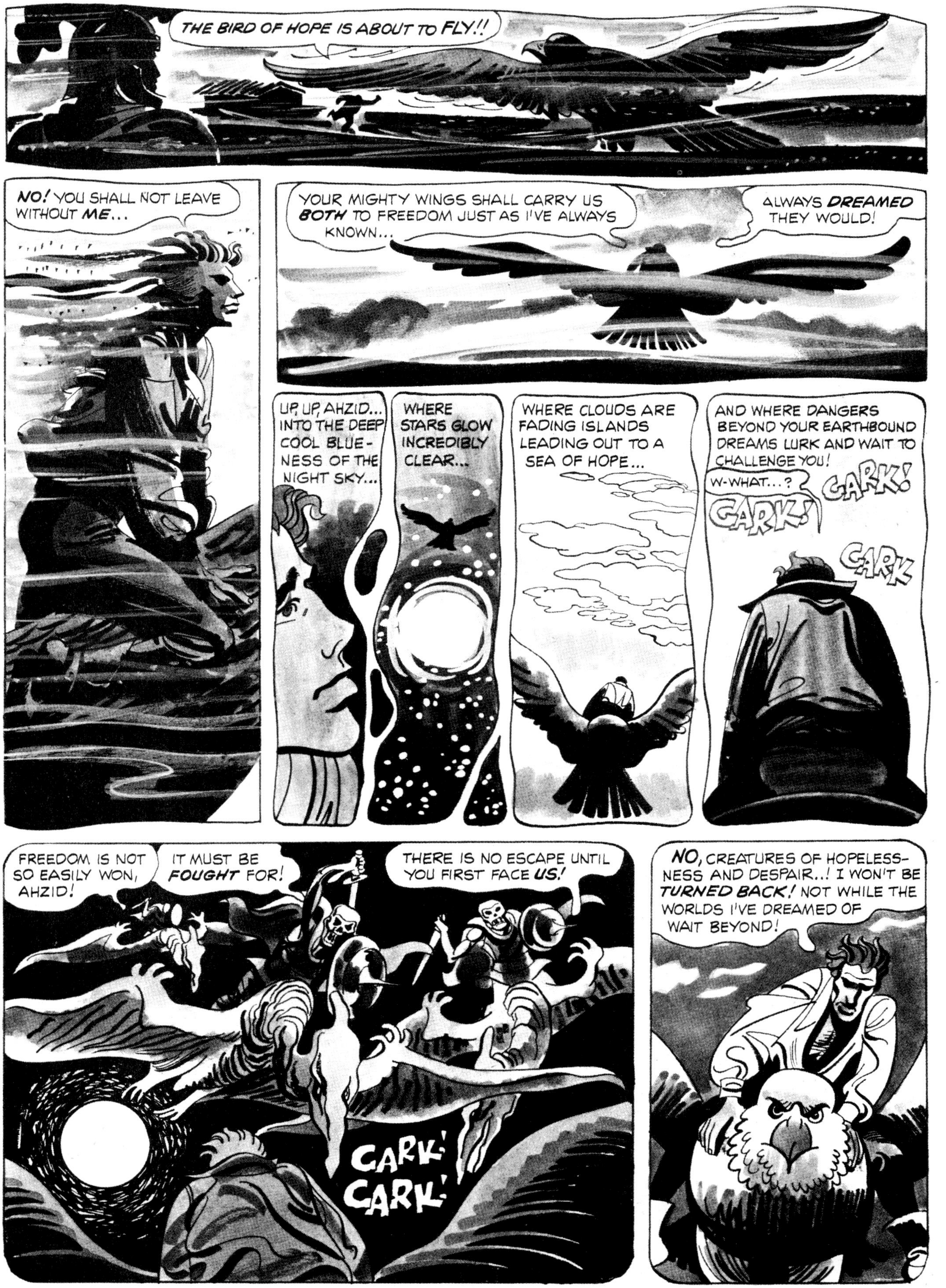
THE BIRD OF HOPE IS ABOUT TO FLY!!
NO! YOU SHALL NOT LEAVE WITHOUT ME...
YOUR MIGHTY WINGS SHALL CARRY US BOTH TO FREEDOM JUST AS I'VE ALWAYS KNOWN...
ALWAYS DREAMED THEY WOULD!
UP, UP, AHZID... INTO THE DEEP COOL BLUE-NESS OF THE NIGHT SKY...
WHERE STARS GLOW INCREDIBLY CLEAR...
WHERE CLOUDS ARE FADING ISLANDS LEADING OUT TO A SEA OF HOPE...
AND WHERE DANGERS BEYOND YOUR EARTHBOUND DREAMS LURK AND WAIT TO CHALLENGE YOU!
W-WHAT...?
CARK!
CARK!
CARK
FREEDOM IS NOT SO EASILY WON, AHZID!
IT MUST BE FOUGHT FOR!
THERE IS NO ESCAPE UNTIL YOU FIRST FACE US!
CARK! CARK!
NO, CREATURES OF HOPELESS-NESS AND DESPAIR...! I WON'T BE TURNED BACK! NOT WHILE THE WORLDS I'VE DREAMED OF WAIT BEYOND!

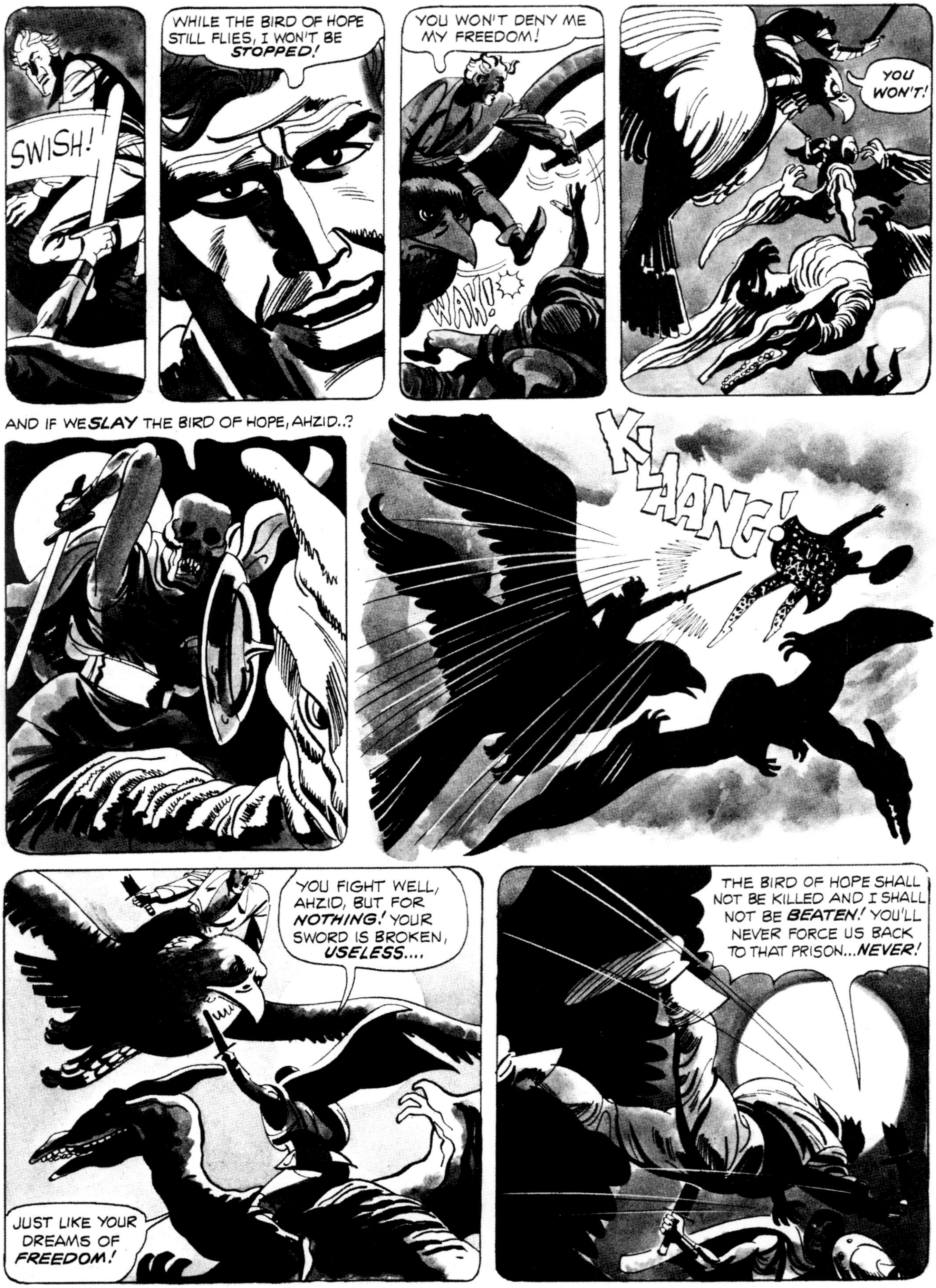
SWISH!
WHILE THE BIRD OF HOPE STILL FLIES, I WON'T BE STOPPED!
YOU WON'T DENY ME MY FREEDOM!
WAK!
YOU WON'T!
AND IF WE SLAY THE BIRD OF HOPE, AHZID..?
KLAANG!
YOU FIGHT WELL, AHZID, BUT FOR NOTHING! YOUR SWORD IS BROKEN, USELESS....
JUST LIKE YOUR DREAMS OF FREEDOM!
THE BIRD OF HOPE SHALL NOT BE KILLED AND I SHALL NOT BE BEATEN! YOU'LL NEVER FORCE US BACK TO THAT PRISON...NEVER!

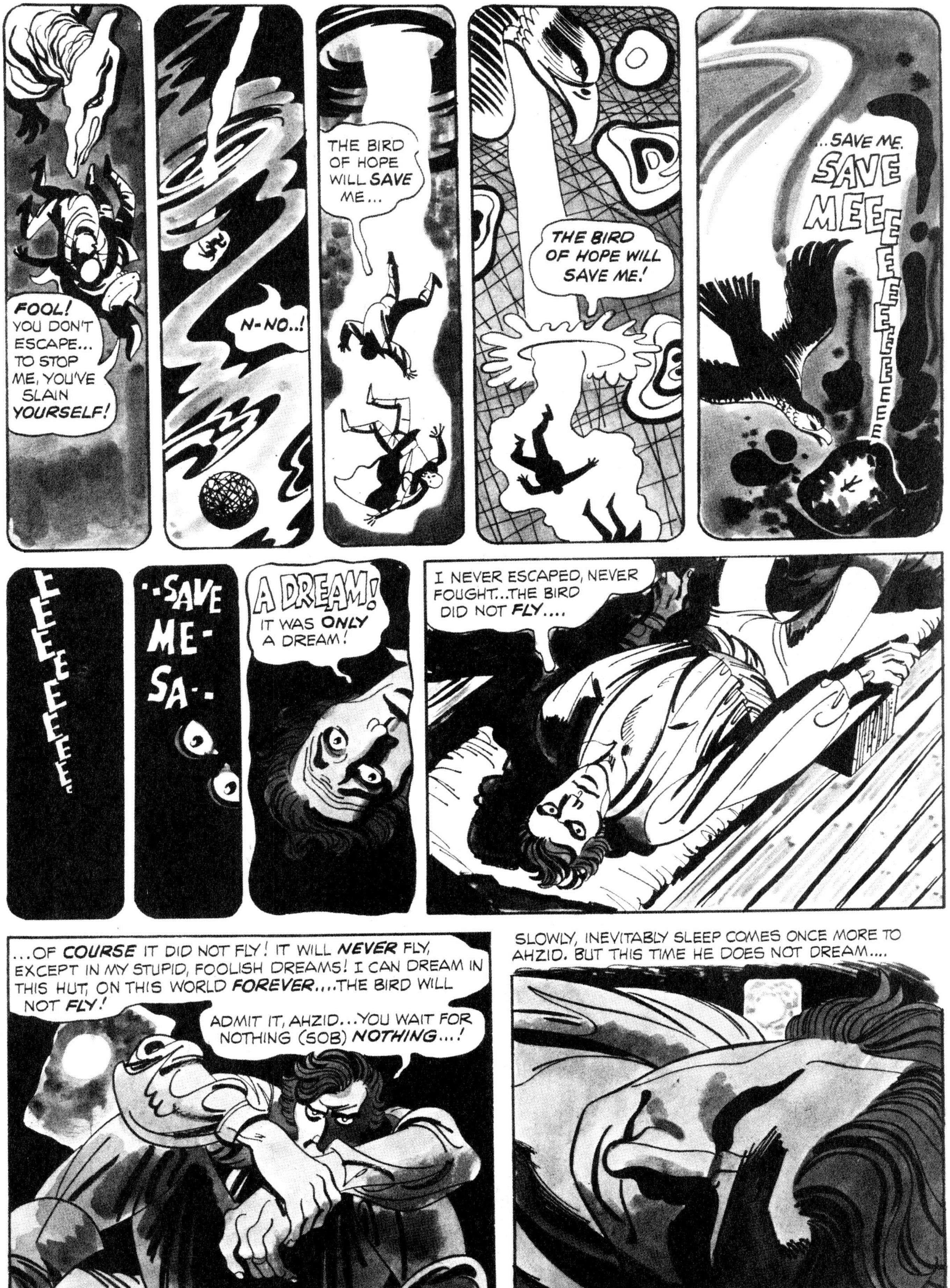
FOOL! YOU DON'T ESCAPE... TO STOP ME, YOU'VE SLAIN YOURSELF!
N-NO..!
THE BIRD OF HOPE WILL SAVE ME...
THE BIRD OF HOPE WILL SAVE ME!
...SAVE ME.
SAVE MEEEEEEEEEEEEE
EEEEEEEE
-- SAVE ME- SA--
A DREAM! IT WAS ONLY A DREAM!
I NEVER ESCAPED, NEVER FOUGHT...THE BIRD DID NOT FLY....
...OF COURSE IT DID NOT FLY! IT WILL NEVER FLY, EXCEPT IN MY STUPID, FOOLISH DREAMS! I CAN DREAM IN THIS HUT, ON THIS WORLD FOREVER....THE BIRD WILL NOT FLY!
ADMIT IT, AHZID...YOU WAIT FOR NOTHING (SOB) NOTHING...!
SLOWLY, INEVITABLY SLEEP COMES ONCE MORE TO AHZID. BUT THIS TIME HE DOES NOT DREAM....

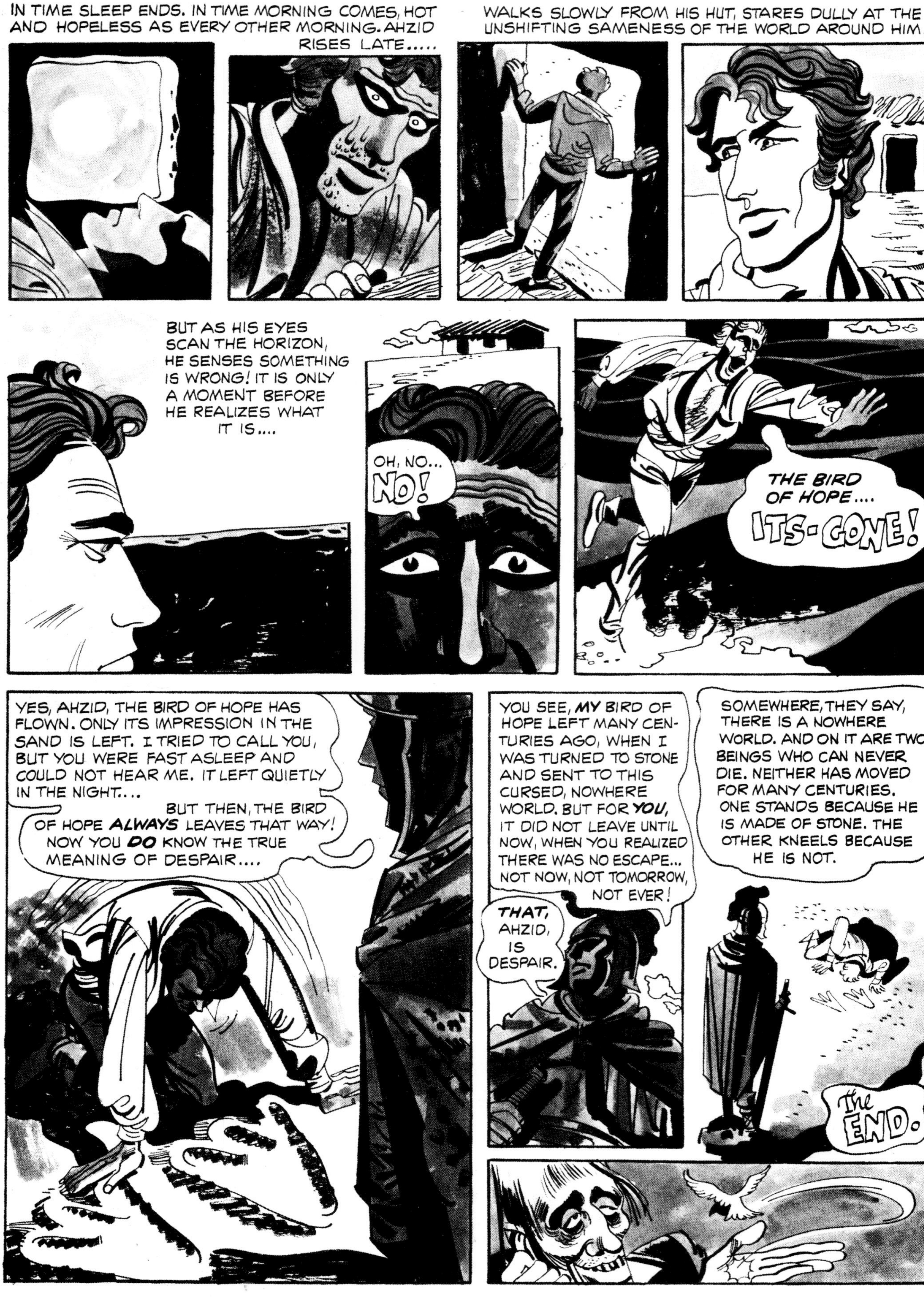
IN TIME SLEEP ENDS. IN TIME MORNING COMES, HOT AND HOPELESS AS EVERY OTHER MORNING. AHZID RISES LATE.....
WALKS SLOWLY FROM HIS HUT, STARES DULLY AT THE UNSHIFTING SAMENESS OF THE WORLD AROUND HIM....
BUT AS HIS EYES SCAN THE HORIZON, HE SENSES SOMETHING IS WRONG! IT IS ONLY A MOMENT BEFORE HE REALIZES WHAT IT IS....
OH, NO... NO!
THE BIRD OF HOPE.... ITS-GONE!
YES, AHZID, THE BIRD OF HOPE HAS FLOWN. ONLY ITS IMPRESSION IN THE SAND IS LEFT. I TRIED TO CALL YOU, BUT YOU WERE FAST ASLEEP AND COULD NOT HEAR ME. IT LEFT QUIETLY IN THE NIGHT....
BUT THEN, THE BIRD OF HOPE ALWAYS LEAVES THAT WAY! NOW YOU DO KNOW THE TRUE MEANING OF DESPAIR....
YOU SEE, MY BIRD OF HOPE LEFT MANY CENTURIES AGO, WHEN I WAS TURNED TO STONE AND SENT TO THIS CURSED, NOWHERE WORLD. BUT FOR YOU, IT DID NOT LEAVE UNTIL NOW, WHEN YOU REALIZED THERE WAS NO ESCAPE... NOT NOW, NOT TOMORROW, NOT EVER!
THAT, AHZID, IS DESPAIR.
SOMEWHERE, THEY SAY, THERE IS A NOWHERE WORLD. AND ON IT ARE TWO BEINGS WHO CAN NEVER DIE. NEITHER HAS MOVED FOR MANY CENTURIES. ONE STANDS BECAUSE HE IS MADE OF STONE. THE OTHER KNEELS BECAUSE HE IS NOT.
The END.

CREEPY PIN-UPS FOR SALE!

GIANT
LIFE SIZE
FRANKENSTEIN
PIN-UP

DRAWN BY Jack Davis

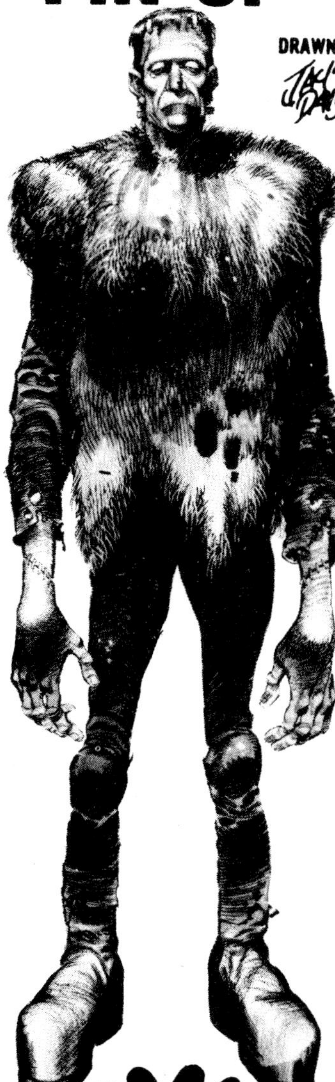

6 FEET TALL!

Never anything like it before! A gigantic, unbelievable drawing of the FRANKENSTEIN MONSTER, over 6 feet tall—by America's greatest cartoonist-artist JACK DAVIS. This is the most striking thing you ever saw! A masterpiece of reproduction that will startle anyone who sees it. The FRANKENSTEIN PIN-UP will supply 100 hours of laughs and thrills: have your picture taken alongside your favorite ghoul; scotch-tape it to the inside of your bedroom or den door; put it between someone's bed sheets, or just pin it on the wall. A million dollars worth of value for a low, low price! Order your's now—supply limited.

A FULL 6 FEET—ONLY $2.00

If you love **GIANT SUPER PIN-UPS**, send for these great goodies! The Frakenstein Poster (left) is a full 6 feet tall, for only $2. All the rest of the posters on this page are 3½ feet by 2½ feet, for only $1 each. All posters printed on heavy paper—perfect for any wall in your house!

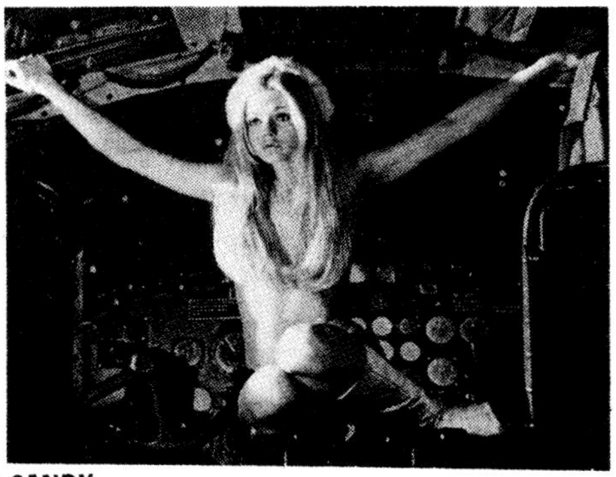

CANDY

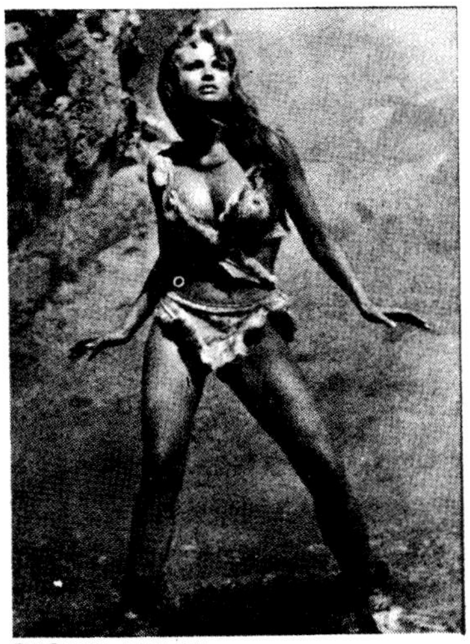

RAQUEL WELCH

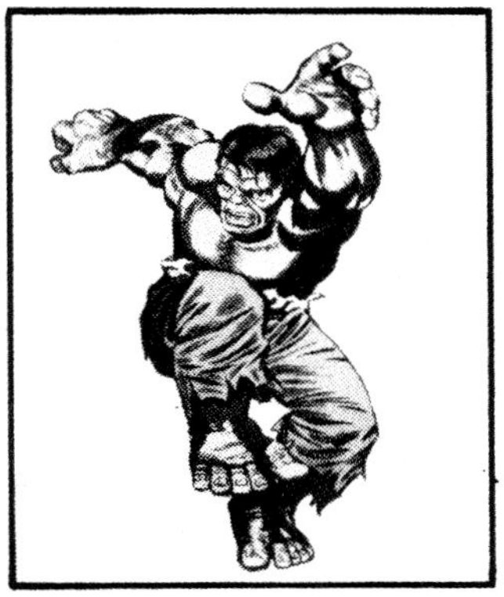

THE HULK

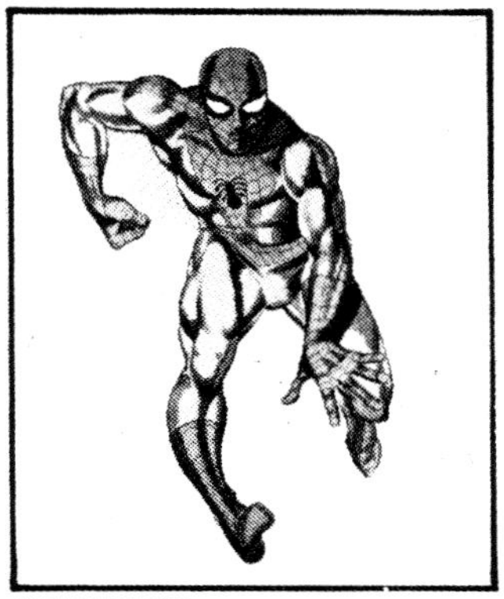

SPIDERMAN

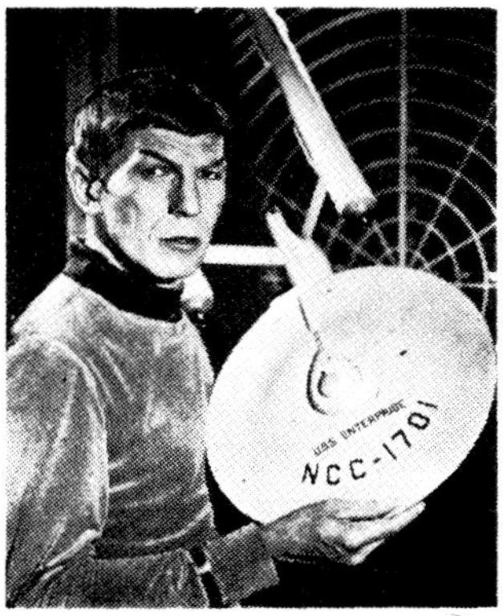
USS ENTERPRISE
NCC-1701

LEONARD NIMOY (STAR TREK)

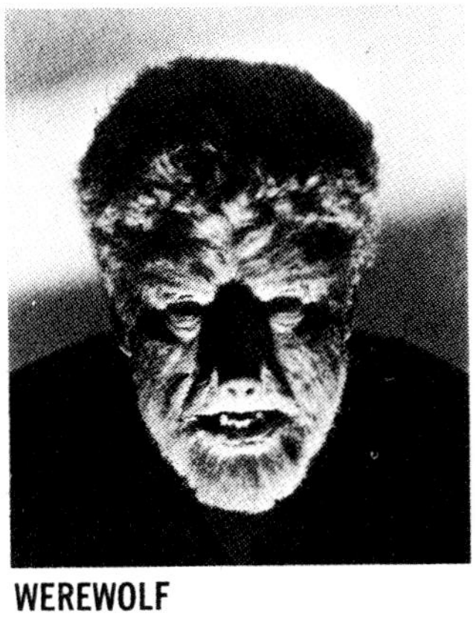

WEREWOLF

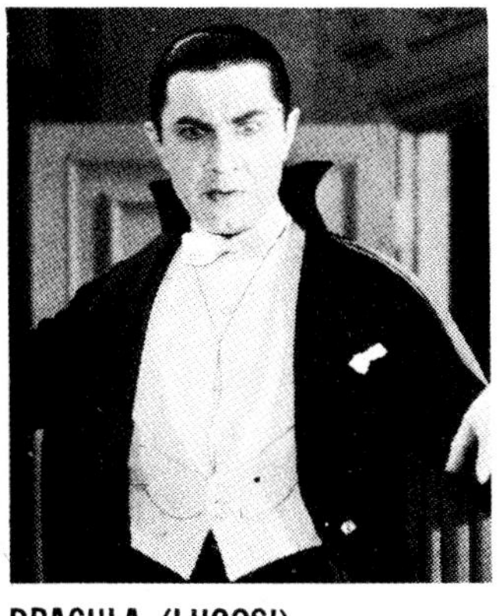

DRACULA (LUGOSI)

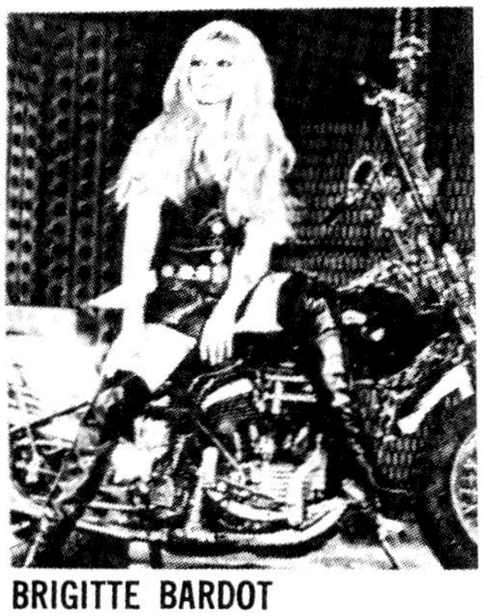

BRIGITTE BARDOT

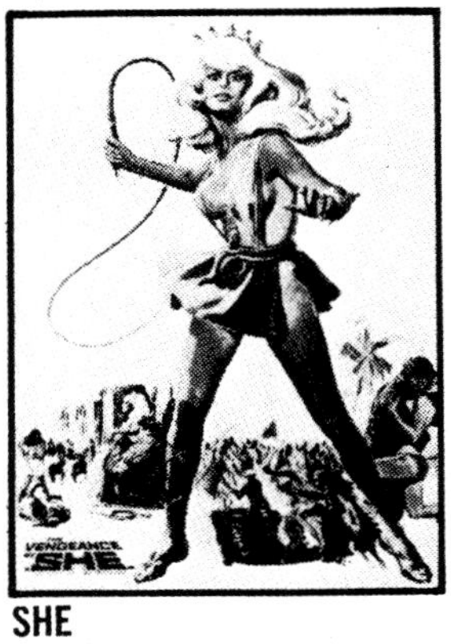

SHE

GIANT SUPER PIN-UPS: Please send me the super-giant pin-up poster indicated below. (The Frankenstein Poster is $2.00 plus 39¢ postage and handling. All other posters are $1.00 plus 39¢ postage and handling for each poster.)

Name..

Address...

City...

State.......................Zip Code...............

Pin-ups...
....
....
....

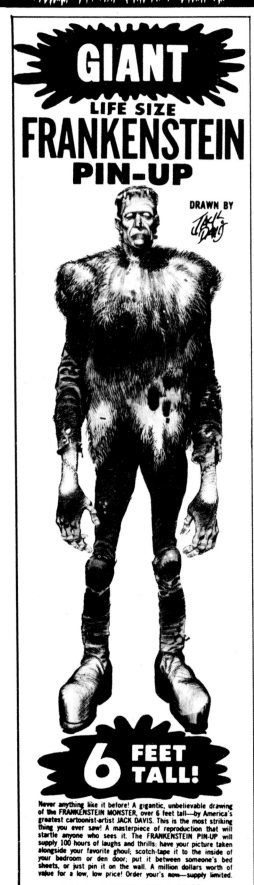

ALL TIME BEST SELLERS IN PAPERBACKS

SCI-FI! MONSTERS! BEASTS! ADVENTURE!

The FIRST MEN in the MOON

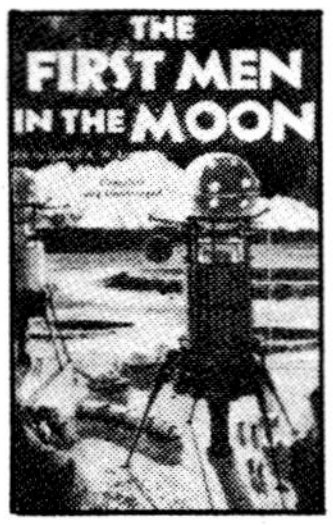
THE FIRST MEN IN THE MOON

A fantastic tale of 2 men on the first flight to the moon! The voyage, landing, and exploration of the Moon in vivid detail. You are there — as they discover an unknown civilization.

No. 2128 .... **68¢**

AROUND the WORLD in 80 DAYS

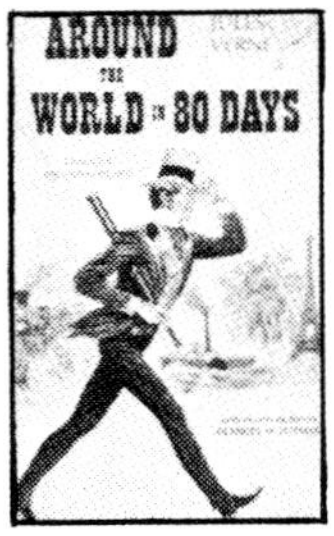
AROUND THE WORLD IN 80 DAYS

The adventures of P. Fogg, Esq. and his French valet, as they travel around the world in a race against time. Full of great suspense, action and drama of world's most famous places.

No. 2127 .... **60¢**

20,000 LEAGUES UNDER THE SEA

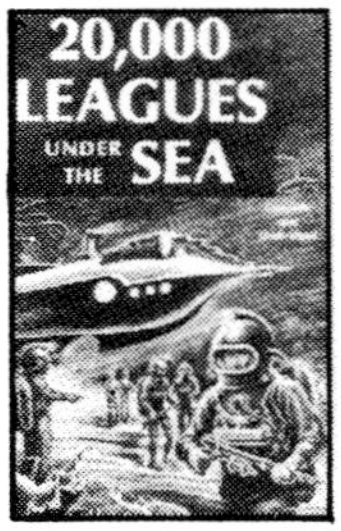
20,000 LEAGUES UNDER THE SEA

Jules Verne creates the fabulous submarine Nautilus, in his predictions of life beneath the sea. Captain Nemo takes you on a strange voyage into the vast watery unknown.

No. 2136 .... **60¢**

A JOURNEY to the CENTER of the EARTH

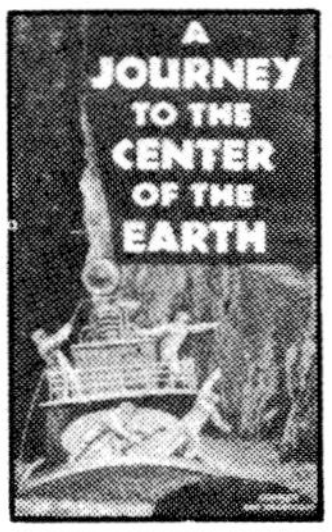
A JOURNEY TO THE CENTER OF THE EARTH

An ancient parchment with a secret message leads to the discovery of the entrance to the center of the world. A bizarre world never before traveled by man.

No. 2132 .... **60¢**

GHOST STORIES

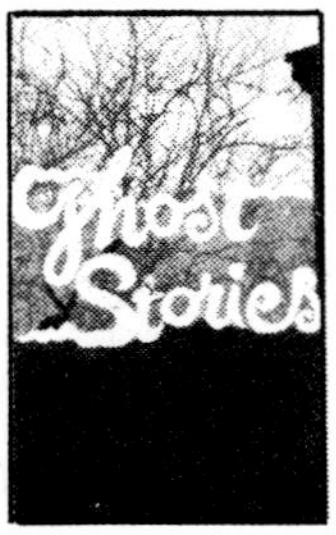
Ghost Stories

Do tales of the supernatural make your spine tingle? Do you believe there really are spooks, or demons or other eerie creatures? There are! Read about them here.

No. 2152 .... **50¢**

MASTER of the WORLD

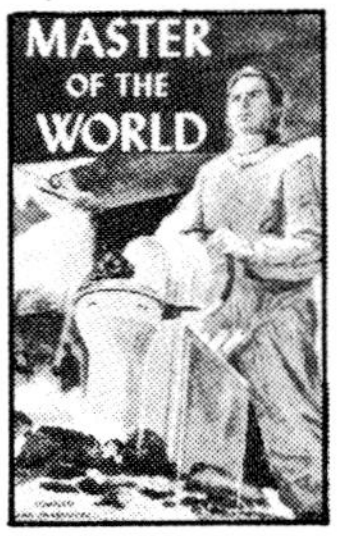
MASTER OF THE WORLD

An unknown inventor gives notice to all the world's governments that his marvelous machines can now control the entire world. Three brave men set out to find and capture him.

No. 2133 .... **60¢**

GREAT GHOST STORIES

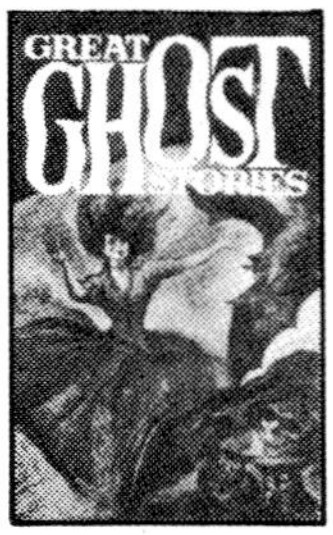
GREAT GHOST STORIES

Thirteen of the most chilling terrifying tales of horror ever written. Each by a writer with great ability to describe the supernatural! Blood tingling!

No. 2193 .... **60¢**

ROUND THE MOON

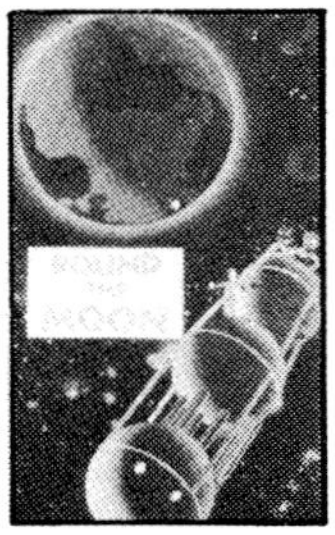

This history making space journey described in the prophetically scientific style of Jules Verne. He gives us a detailed futuristic view of space travel as never before seen.

No. 2134 .... **60¢**

THE TIME MACHINE

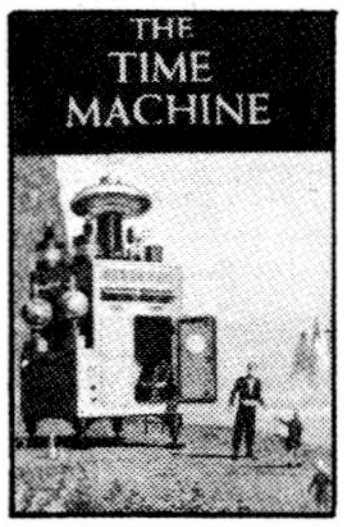
THE TIME MACHINE

How would **you** like to climb into a machine, press a button, and be zoomed into the future, or back into time? It happens in this book!

No. 2135 .... **60¢**

THE UNEXPECTED

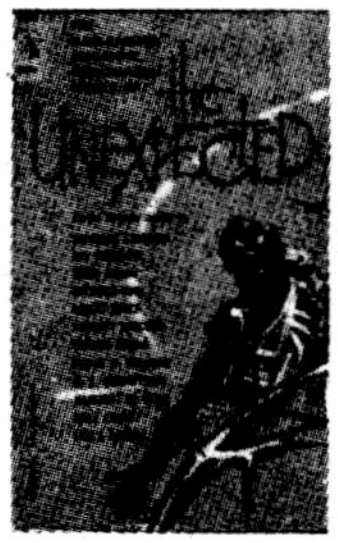

Eleven great stories of the hair-raising, uncanny, nightmarish world of the Unexpected. Twelve of the greatest authors in science-fantasy and the supernatural appear in this classic anthology.

No. 2143 .... **60c**

THE ISLAND OF DR. MOREAU

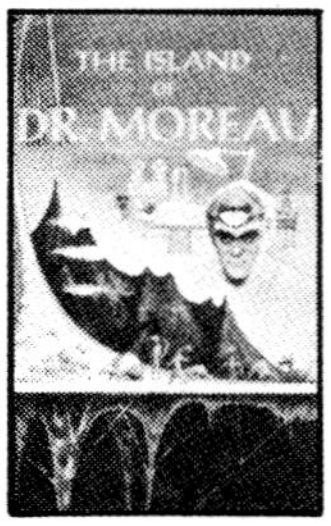
THE ISLAND OF DR. MOREAU

Rescued from the sea and brought to a small out-of-the island, Edward Prendick discovers the terrifying creatures of the island. Real frightening!

No. 2131 .... **60¢**

THE DUNWICH HORROR

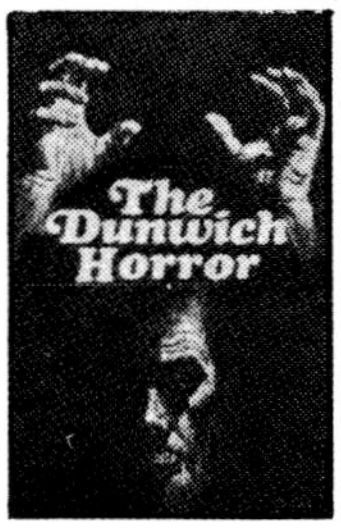
The Dunwich Horror

Read if you dare these frightening world of nightmares, where that scratching in the wall, that suffocation of the heart, that scream torn from the lungs take on forms and shapes!

No. 2159 .... **75¢**

LAND of THE GIANTS #1

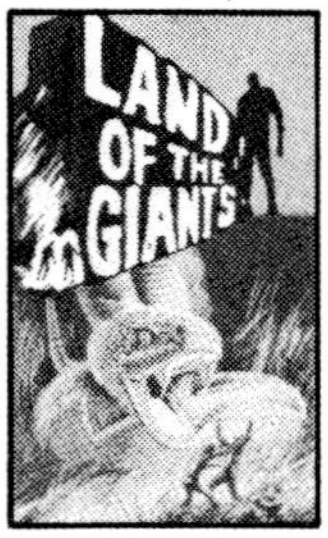
LAND OF THE GIANTS

The grass was six feet high and insects the size of dogs. Men and women were 70-foot giants! Based on the exciting TV Series.

No. 2190 .... **60¢**

LAND of the GIANTS #2 The HOT SPOT

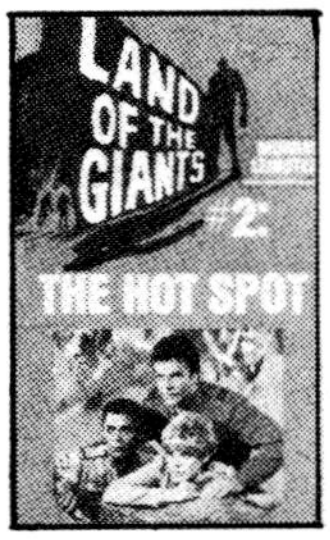
LAND OF THE GIANTS
#2: THE HOT SPOT

Based on the popular TV series! A tropical paradise turns out to be a terror-racked hell, with mammoth insects and terrifying giant natives.

No. 2191 .... **60¢**

MORE GHOST STORIES

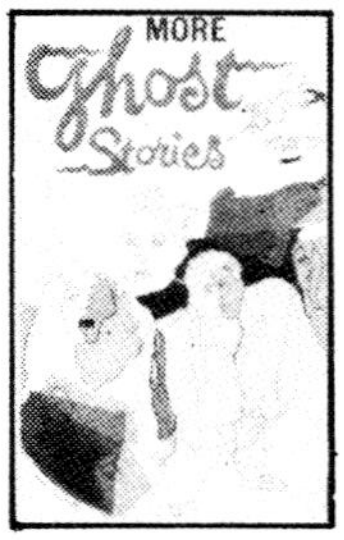
MORE Ghost Stories

Spooks, demons and other creatures of phantasmagorie hover over each eerie page of this new, spine tingling collection. Full of supernatural mystery that will both thrill and scare you!

No. 2186 .... **60¢**

THE FOOD of the GODS

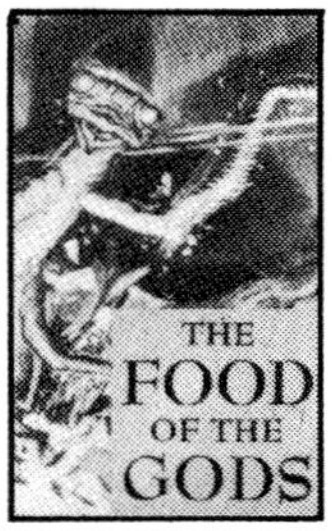
THE FOOD OF THE GODS

Stirs the imagination! What starts off as an experiment soon gets out of hand creating gigantic men, insects and monsters in a world which had no place for them! ! !

No. 2129 .... **60¢**

In THE DAYS OF THE COMET

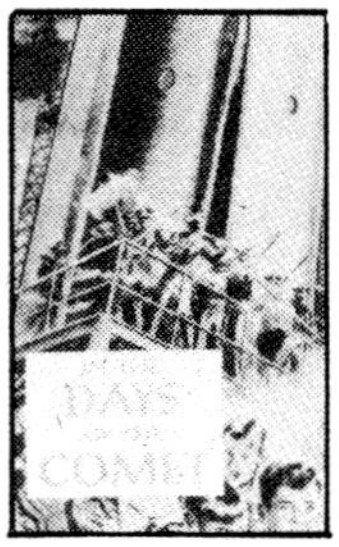

To awaken . . . changed! Something has happened to human beings all over the world. Makes you wonder and ask yourself, "What if it really happened today!"

No. 2130 .... **60¢**

HAUNTINGS and HORRORS

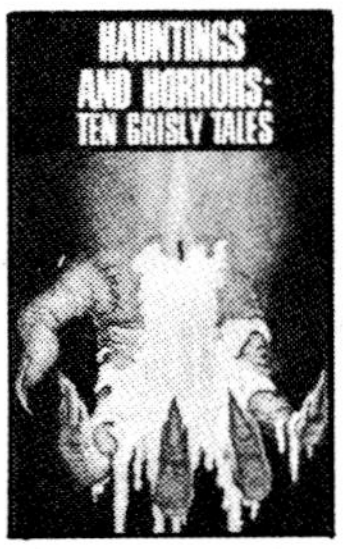
HAUNTINGS AND HORRORS: TEN GRISLY TALES

Ten weird terror-stricken tales. If you like inhuman stories, it's just the thing to turn the blood in your veins to ice water. Only the brave and the strong dare this one!

No. 2185 .... **60¢**

THE COLOUR OUT OF SPACE

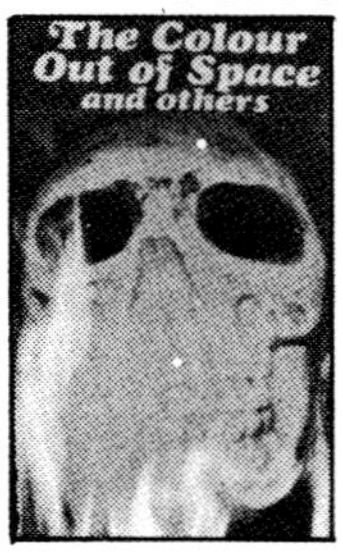
The Colour Out of Space and others

Seven of Lovecraft's masterpieces of horror! Widely acclaimed as surpassing even the great Poe. Full of ancient evils biding their time to break loose again into your world and others.

No. 2182 .... **75¢**

NIGHT of the VAMPIRE

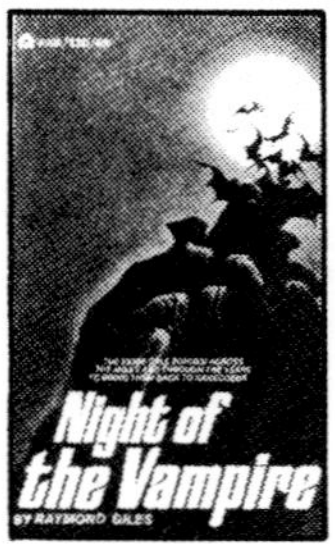
Night of the Vampire

The eerie call echoed across the endless miles and down through the years to bring them back to Sanscoeur! A land where the moon glows green and bats scream in the wind. Scary!

No. 2138 .... **60¢**

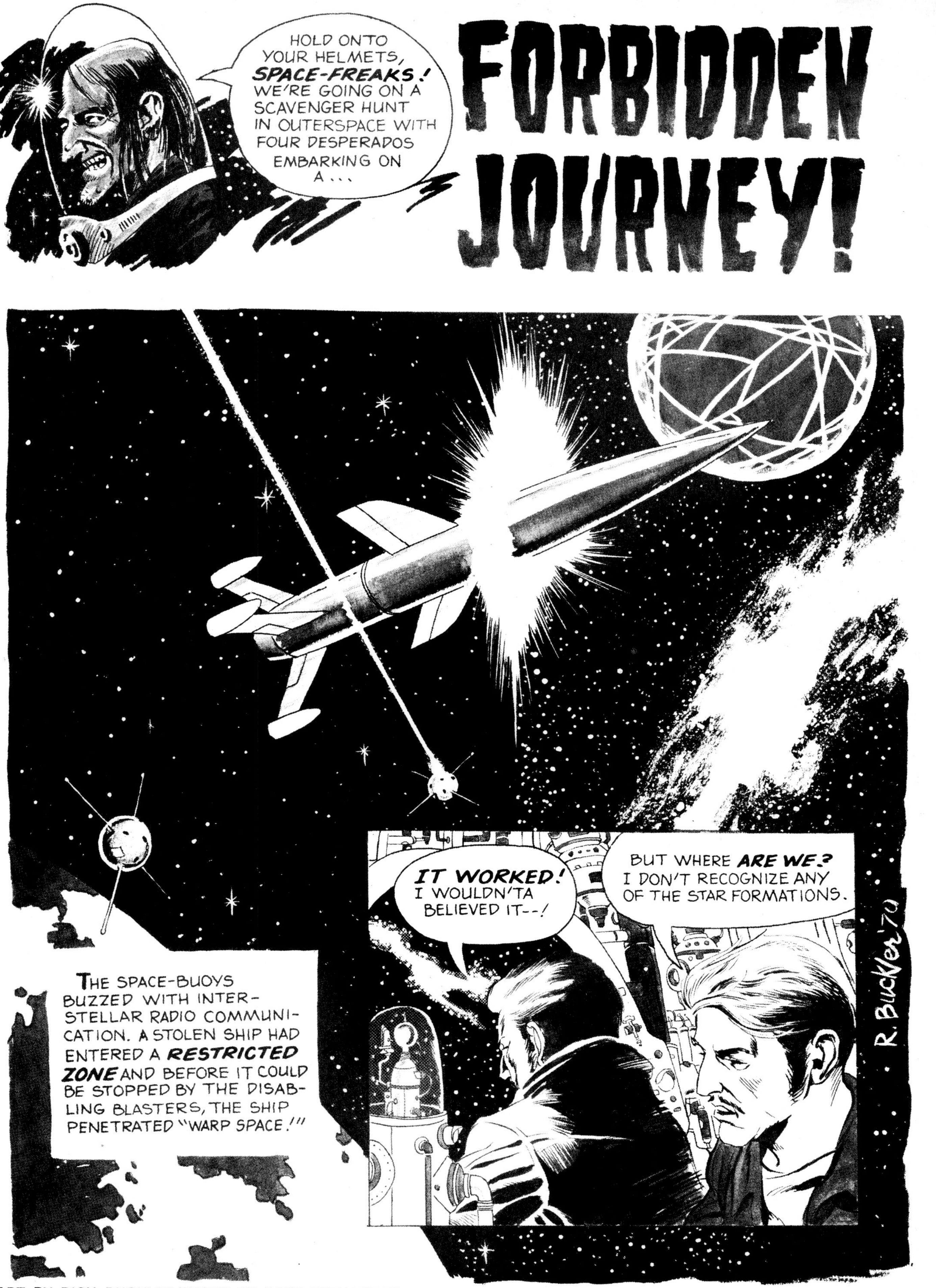
HOLD ONTO YOUR HELMETS, **SPACE-FREAKS!** WE'RE GOING ON A SCAVENGER HUNT IN OUTERSPACE WITH FOUR DESPERADOS EMBARKING ON A...
FORBIDDEN JOURNEY!
THE SPACE-BUOYS BUZZED WITH INTER-STELLAR RADIO COMMUNI-CATION. A STOLEN SHIP HAD ENTERED A **RESTRICTED ZONE** AND BEFORE IT COULD BE STOPPED BY THE DISAB-LING BLASTERS, THE SHIP PENETRATED "WARP SPACE."
IT WORKED! I WOULDN'TA BELIEVED IT--!
BUT WHERE **ARE WE?** I DON'T RECOGNIZE ANY OF THE STAR FORMATIONS.
R. Buckler '70

ART BY RICH BUCKLER/STORY BY GREG THEAKSTON

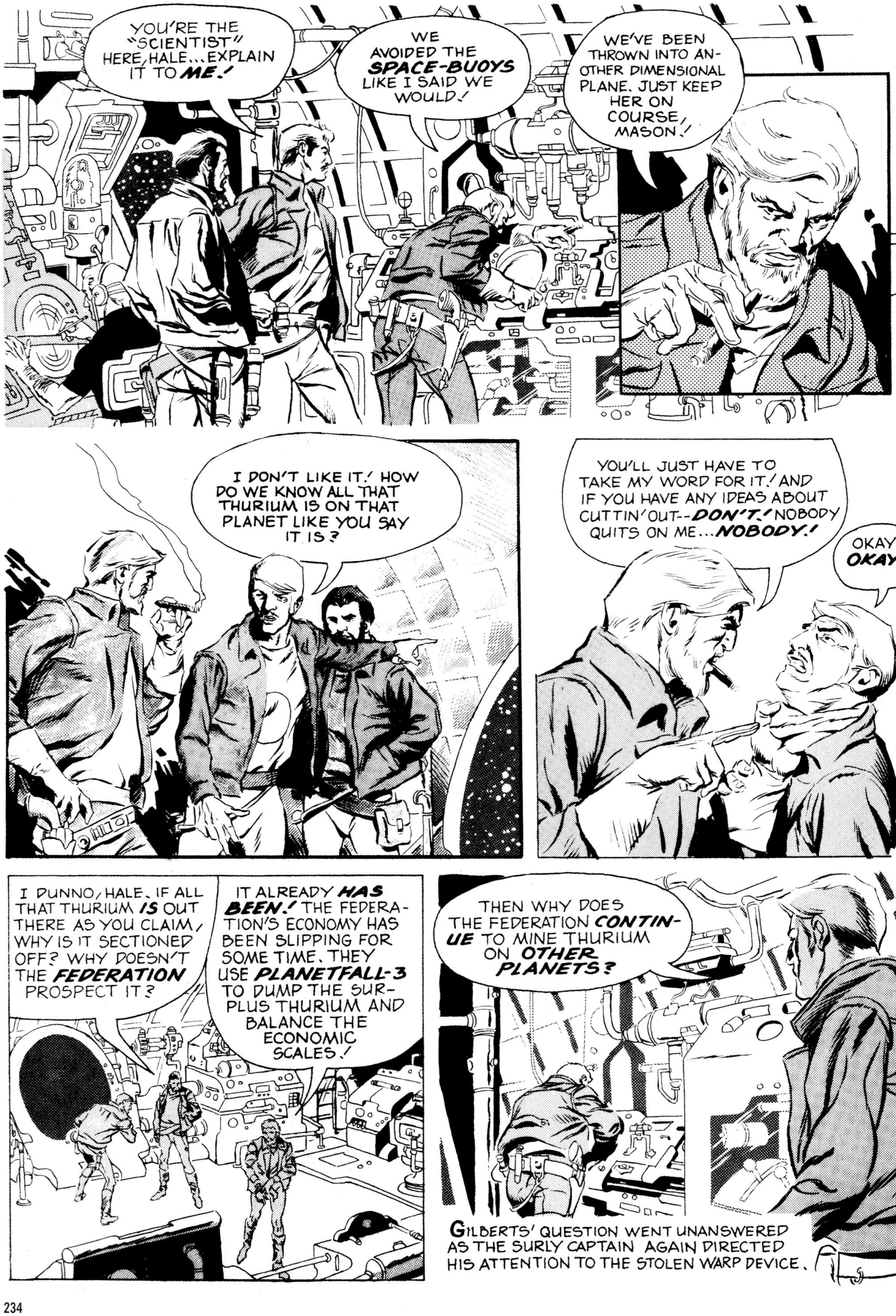
YOU'RE THE "SCIENTIST" HERE, HALE...EXPLAIN IT TO ME.!
WE AVOIDED THE SPACE-BUOYS LIKE I SAID WE WOULD.!
WE'VE BEEN THROWN INTO AN-OTHER DIMENSIONAL PLANE. JUST KEEP HER ON COURSE, MASON.!
I DON'T LIKE IT.! HOW DO WE KNOW ALL THAT THURIUM IS ON THAT PLANET LIKE YOU SAY IT IS?
YOU'LL JUST HAVE TO TAKE MY WORD FOR IT.! AND IF YOU HAVE ANY IDEAS ABOUT CUTTIN'OUT--DON'T.! NOBODY QUITS ON ME...NOBODY.!
OKAY OKAY.!
I DUNNO, HALE. IF ALL THAT THURIUM IS OUT THERE AS YOU CLAIM, WHY IS IT SECTIONED OFF? WHY DOESN'T THE FEDERATION PROSPECT IT?
IT ALREADY HAS BEEN.! THE FEDERA-TION'S ECONOMY HAS BEEN SLIPPING FOR SOME TIME. THEY USE PLANETFALL-3 TO DUMP THE SUR-PLUS THURIUM AND BALANCE THE ECONOMIC SCALES.!
THEN WHY DOES THE FEDERATION CONTIN-UE TO MINE THURIUM ON OTHER PLANETS?
GILBERTS' QUESTION WENT UNANSWERED AS THE SURLY CAPTAIN AGAIN DIRECTED HIS ATTENTION TO THE STOLEN WARP DEVICE.

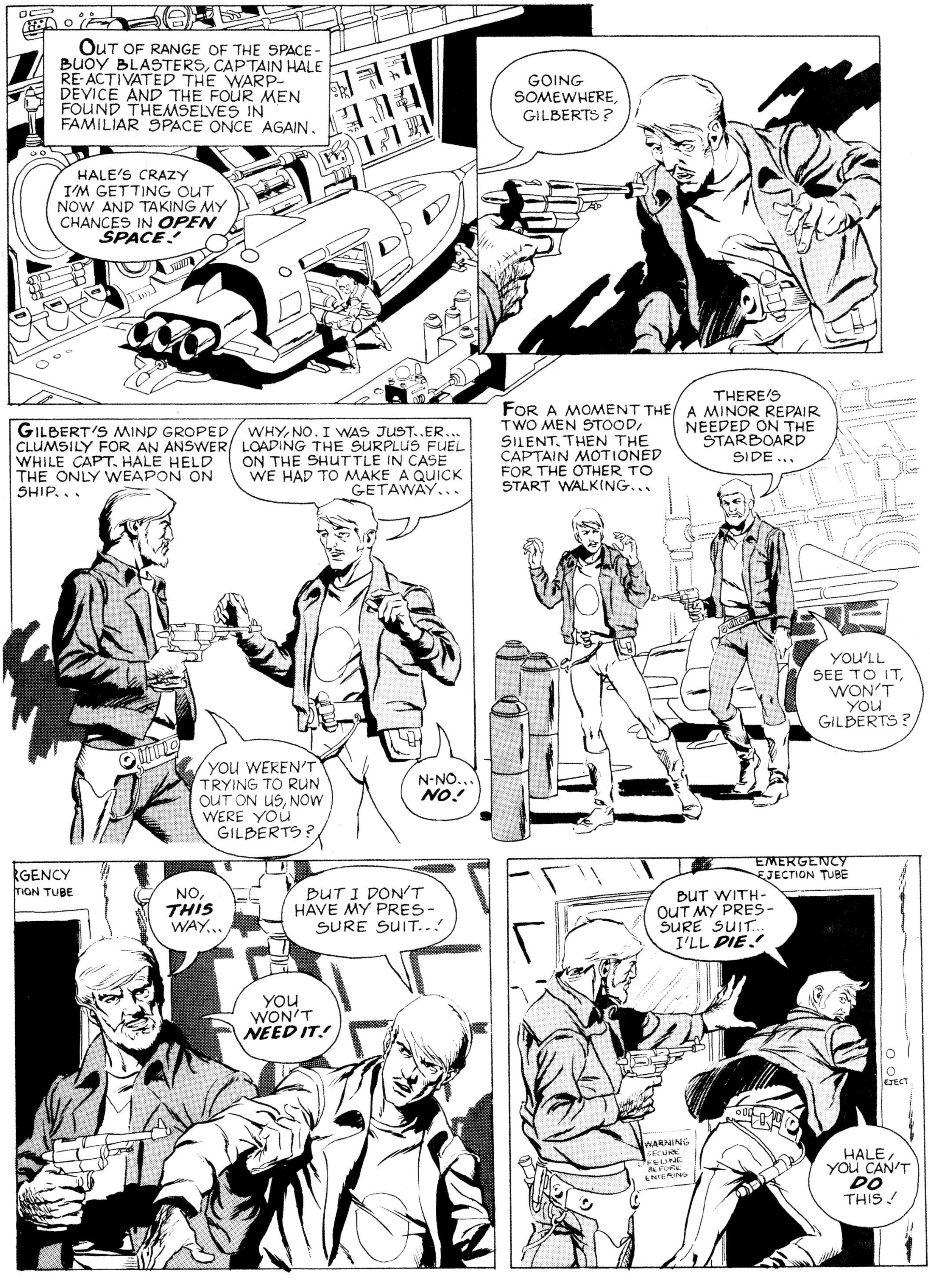
OUT OF RANGE OF THE SPACE-BUOY BLASTERS, CAPTAIN HALE RE-ACTIVATED THE WARP-DEVICE AND THE FOUR MEN FOUND THEMSELVES IN FAMILIAR SPACE ONCE AGAIN.
HALE'S CRAZY I'M GETTING OUT NOW AND TAKING MY CHANCES IN OPEN SPACE!
GOING SOMEWHERE, GILBERTS?
GILBERT'S MIND GROPED CLUMSILY FOR AN ANSWER WHILE CAPT. HALE HELD THE ONLY WEAPON ON SHIP...
WHY, NO. I WAS JUST..ER... LOADING THE SURPLUS FUEL ON THE SHUTTLE IN CASE WE HAD TO MAKE A QUICK GETAWAY...
YOU WEREN'T TRYING TO RUN OUT ON US, NOW WERE YOU GILBERTS?
N-NO... NO!
FOR A MOMENT THE TWO MEN STOOD, SILENT. THEN THE CAPTAIN MOTIONED FOR THE OTHER TO START WALKING...
THERE'S A MINOR REPAIR NEEDED ON THE STARBOARD SIDE...
YOU'LL SEE TO IT, WON'T YOU GILBERTS?
RGENCY
TION TUBE
NO, THIS WAY...
BUT I DON'T HAVE MY PRES-SURE SUIT...!
YOU WON'T NEED IT!
EMERGENCY
EJECTION TUBE
BUT WITH-OUT MY PRES-SURE SUIT... I'LL DIE!
EJECT
WARNING
SECURE LIFELINE BEFORE ENTERING
HALE, YOU CAN'T DO THIS!

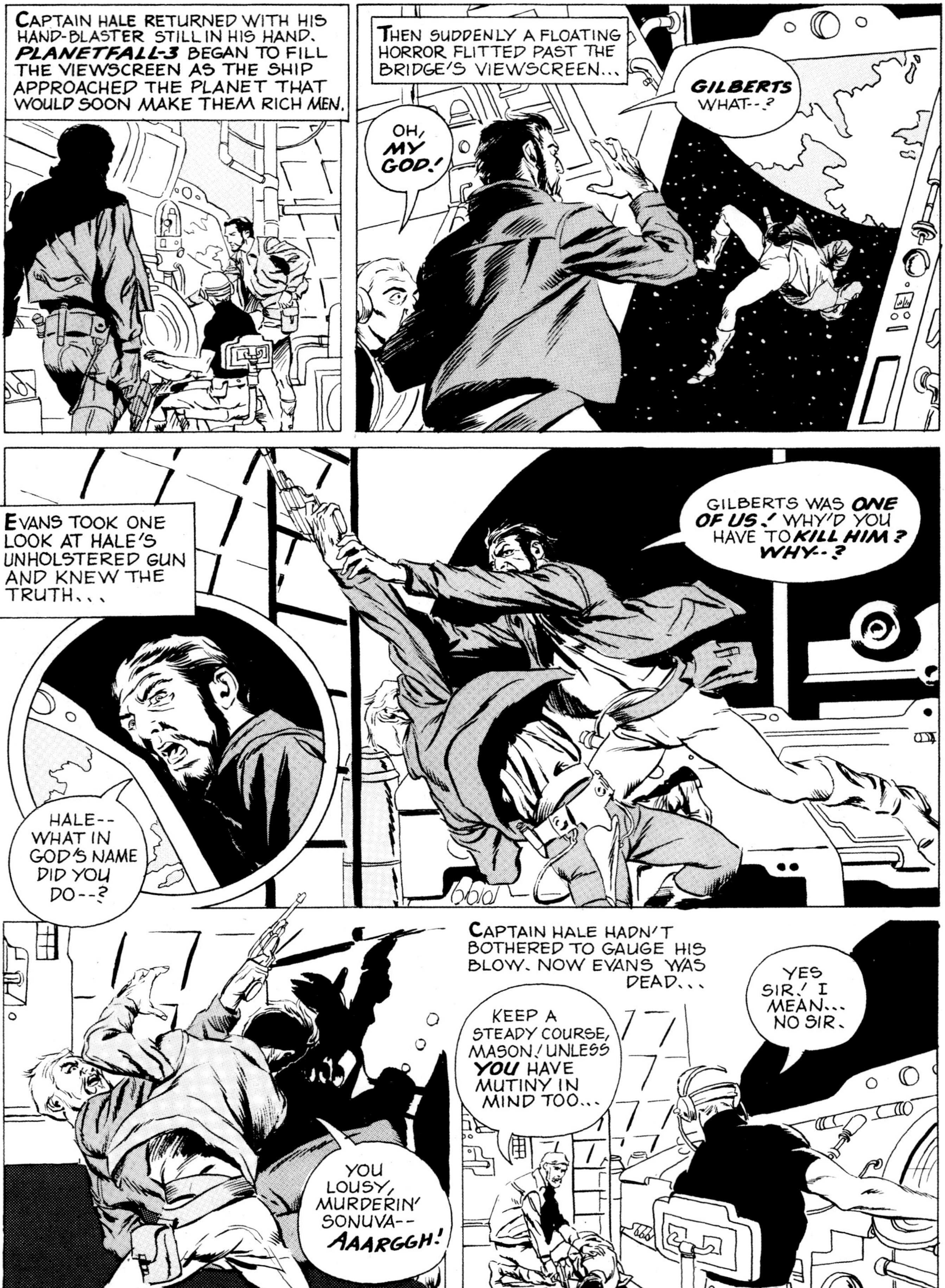

CAPTAIN HALE RETURNED WITH HIS HAND-BLASTER STILL IN HIS HAND. PLANETFALL-3 BEGAN TO FILL THE VIEWSCREEN AS THE SHIP APPROACHED THE PLANET THAT WOULD SOON MAKE THEM RICH MEN.
THEN SUDDENLY A FLOATING HORROR FLITTED PAST THE BRIDGE'S VIEWSCREEN...
GILBERTS WHAT--?
OH, MY GOD!
EVANS TOOK ONE LOOK AT HALE'S UNHOLSTERED GUN AND KNEW THE TRUTH...
HALE--WHAT IN GOD'S NAME DID YOU DO--?
GILBERTS WAS ONE OF US! WHY'D YOU HAVE TO KILL HIM? WHY--?
YOU LOUSY, MURDERIN' SONUVA-- AAARGGH!
CAPTAIN HALE HADN'T BOTHERED TO GAUGE HIS BLOW. NOW EVANS WAS DEAD...
KEEP A STEADY COURSE, MASON! UNLESS YOU HAVE MUTINY IN MIND TOO...
YES SIR! I MEAN... NO SIR.

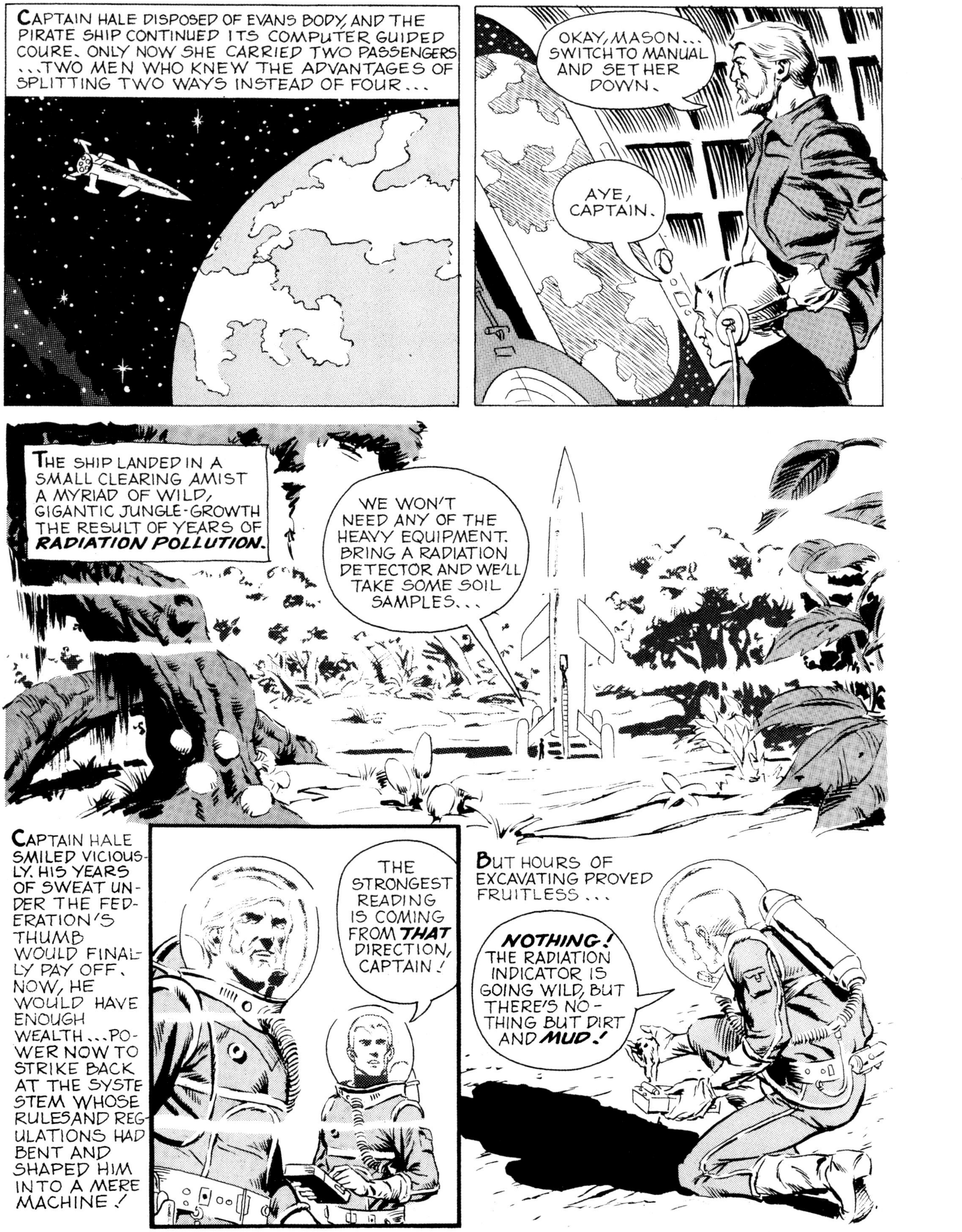
CAPTAIN HALE DISPOSED OF EVANS BODY, AND THE PIRATE SHIP CONTINUED ITS COMPUTER GUIDED COURE. ONLY NOW SHE CARRIED TWO PASSENGERS ...TWO MEN WHO KNEW THE ADVANTAGES OF SPLITTING TWO WAYS INSTEAD OF FOUR...
OKAY, MASON... SWITCH TO MANUAL AND SET HER DOWN.
AYE, CAPTAIN.
THE SHIP LANDED IN A SMALL CLEARING AMIST A MYRIAD OF WILD, GIGANTIC JUNGLE-GROWTH THE RESULT OF YEARS OF RADIATION POLLUTION.
WE WON'T NEED ANY OF THE HEAVY EQUIPMENT. BRING A RADIATION DETECTOR AND WE'LL TAKE SOME SOIL SAMPLES...
CAPTAIN HALE SMILED VICIOUSLY. HIS YEARS OF SWEAT UNDER THE FEDERATION'S THUMB WOULD FINALLY PAY OFF. NOW, HE WOULD HAVE ENOUGH WEALTH...POWER NOW TO STRIKE BACK AT THE SYSTESTEM WHOSE RULES AND REGULATIONS HAD BENT AND SHAPED HIM INTO A MERE MACHINE!
THE STRONGEST READING IS COMING FROM THAT DIRECTION, CAPTAIN!
BUT HOURS OF EXCAVATING PROVED FRUITLESS...
NOTHING! THE RADIATION INDICATOR IS GOING WILD, BUT THERE'S NOTHING BUT DIRT AND MUD!

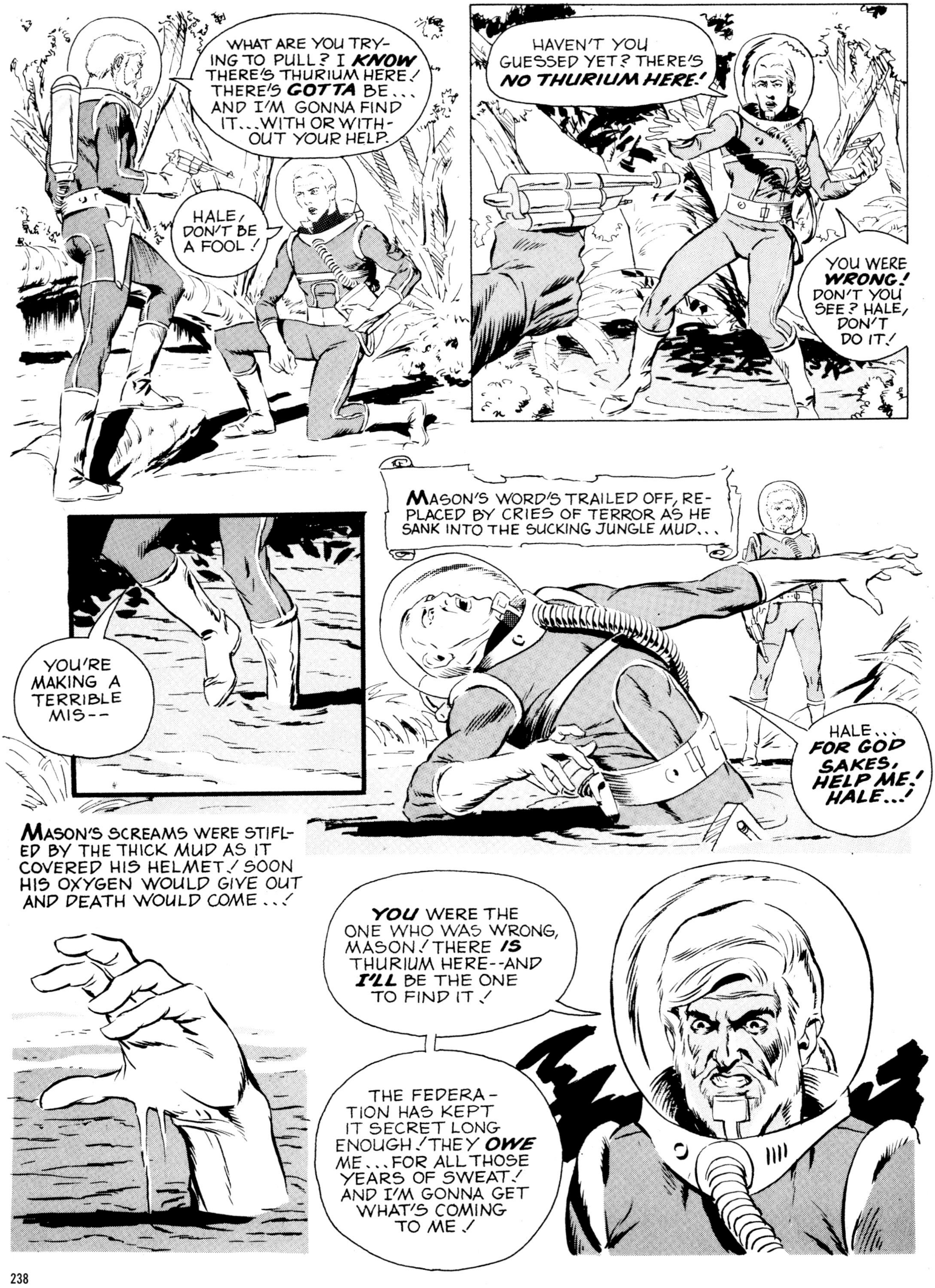
WHAT ARE YOU TRYING TO PULL? I KNOW THERE'S THURIUM HERE! THERE'S GOTTA BE... AND I'M GONNA FIND IT...WITH OR WITHOUT YOUR HELP.
HALE, DON'T BE A FOOL!
HAVEN'T YOU GUESSED YET? THERE'S NO THURIUM HERE!
YOU WERE WRONG! DON'T YOU SEE? HALE, DON'T DO IT!
MASON'S WORD'S TRAILED OFF, REPLACED BY CRIES OF TERROR AS HE SANK INTO THE SUCKING JUNGLE MUD...
YOU'RE MAKING A TERRIBLE MIS--
HALE... FOR GOD SAKES, HELP ME! HALE...!
MASON'S SCREAMS WERE STIFLED BY THE THICK MUD AS IT COVERED HIS HELMET! SOON HIS OXYGEN WOULD GIVE OUT AND DEATH WOULD COME...!
YOU WERE THE ONE WHO WAS WRONG, MASON! THERE IS THURIUM HERE--AND I'LL BE THE ONE TO FIND IT!
THE FEDERATION HAS KEPT IT SECRET LONG ENOUGH! THEY OWE ME...FOR ALL THOSE YEARS OF SWEAT! AND I'M GONNA GET WHAT'S COMING TO ME!

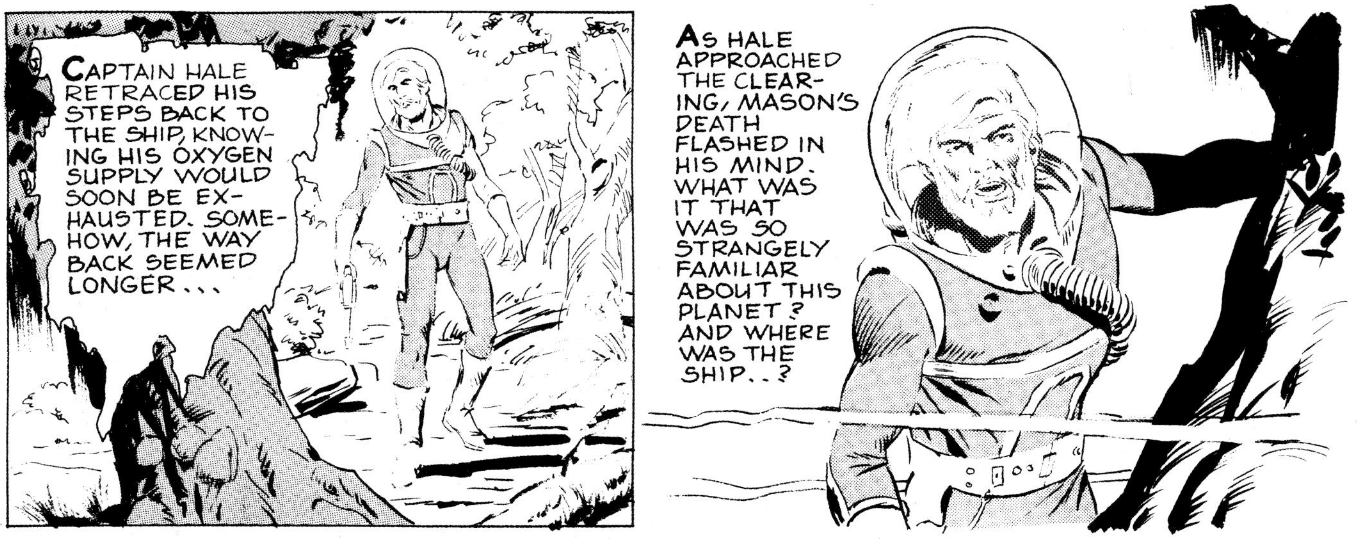
CAPTAIN HALE RETRACED HIS STEPS BACK TO THE SHIP, KNOWING HIS OXYGEN SUPPLY WOULD SOON BE EXHAUSTED. SOMEHOW, THE WAY BACK SEEMED LONGER...
AS HALE APPROACHED THE CLEARING, MASON'S DEATH FLASHED IN HIS MIND. WHAT WAS IT THAT WAS SO STRANGELY FAMILIAR ABOUT THIS PLANET? AND WHERE WAS THE SHIP..?

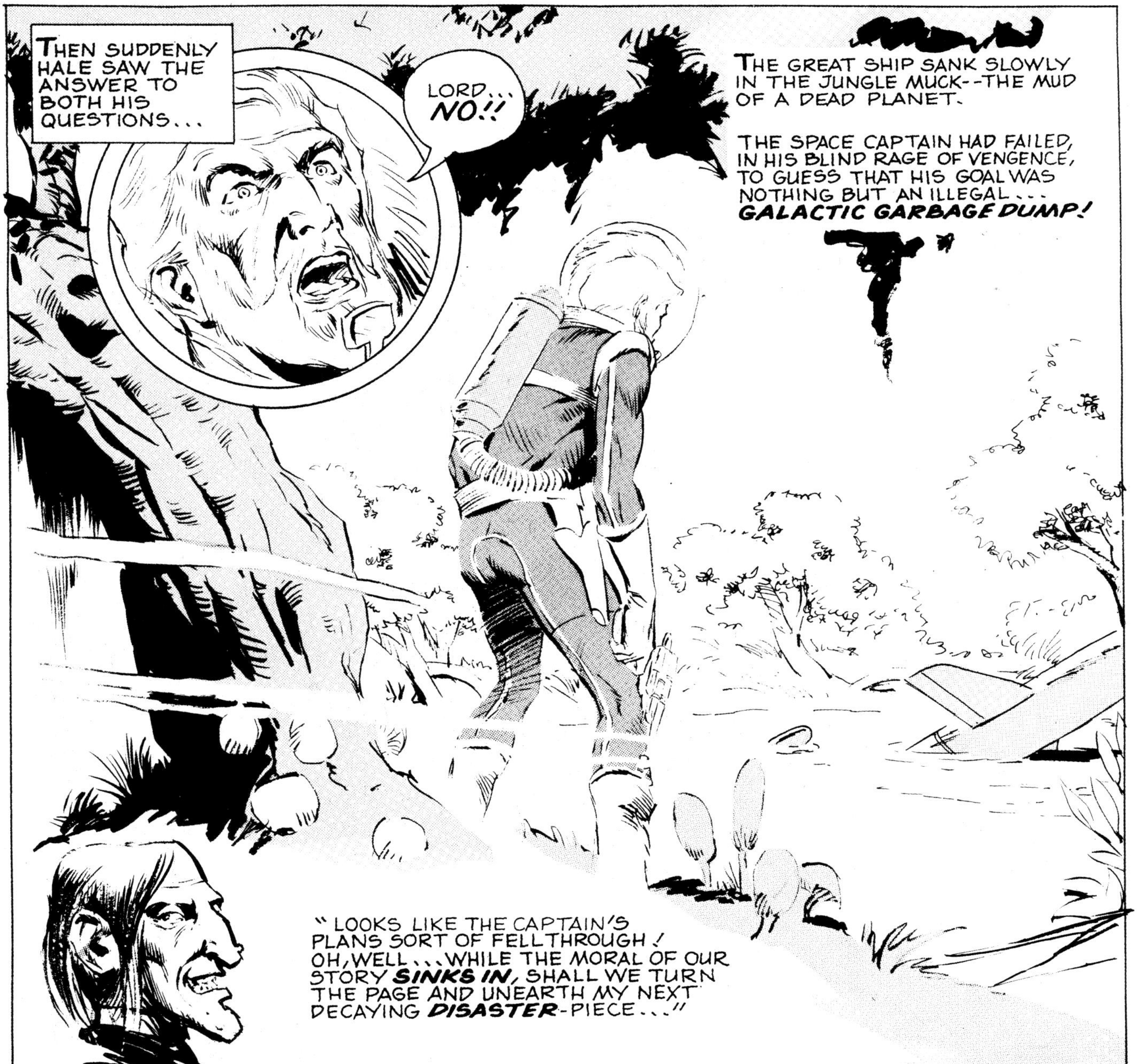
THEN SUDDENLY HALE SAW THE ANSWER TO BOTH HIS QUESTIONS...
LORD... NO!!
THE GREAT SHIP SANK SLOWLY IN THE JUNGLE MUCK--THE MUD OF A DEAD PLANET.
THE SPACE CAPTAIN HAD FAILED, IN HIS BLIND RAGE OF VENGENCE, TO GUESS THAT HIS GOAL WAS NOTHING BUT AN ILLEGAL... GALACTIC GARBAGE DUMP!
"LOOKS LIKE THE CAPTAIN'S PLANS SORT OF FELLTHROUGH! OH, WELL... WHILE THE MORAL OF OUR STORY SINKS IN, SHALL WE TURN THE PAGE AND UNEARTH MY NEXT DECAYING DISASTER-PIECE..."

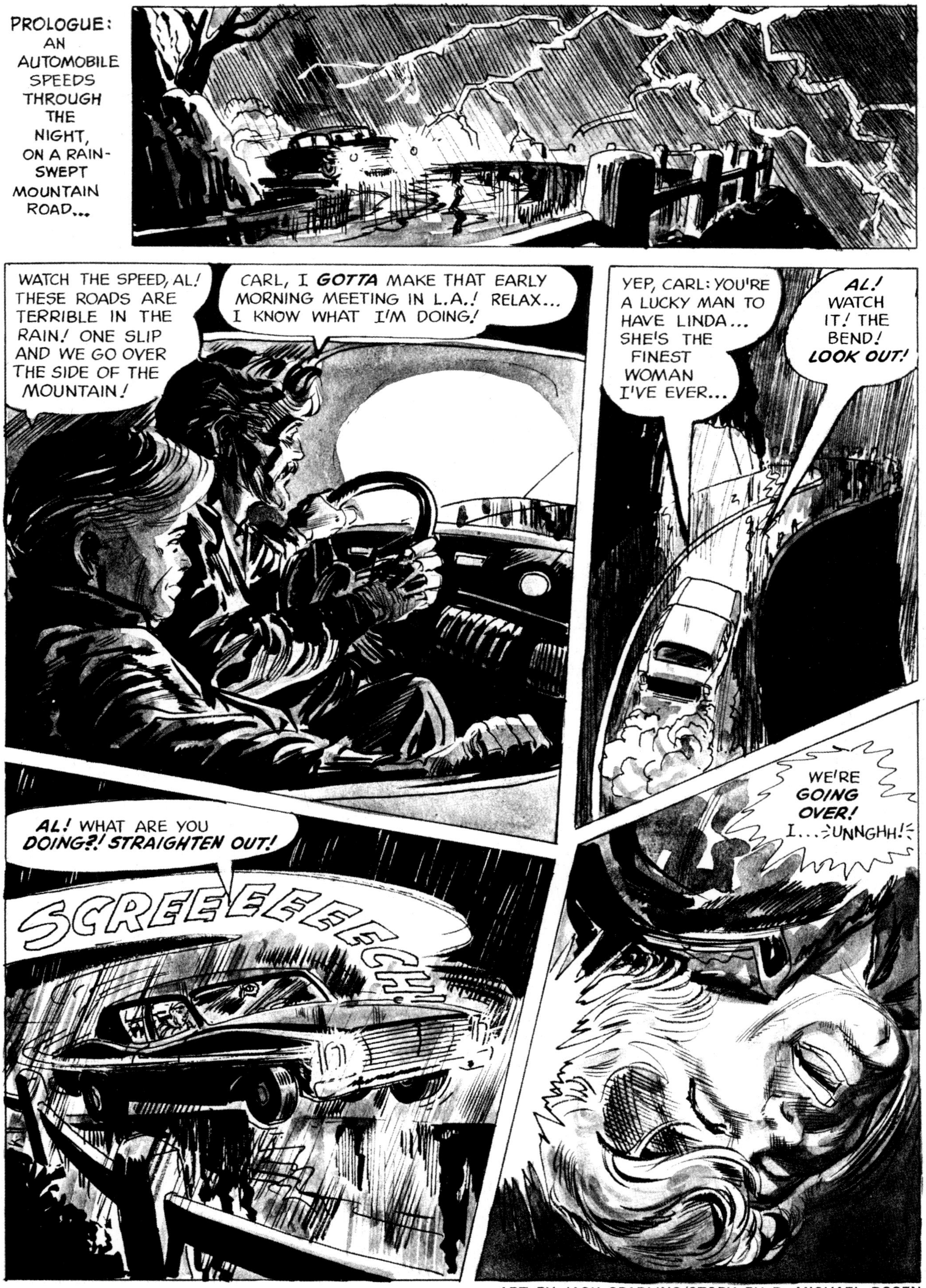

PROLOGUE: AN AUTOMOBILE SPEEDS THROUGH THE NIGHT, ON A RAIN-SWEPT MOUNTAIN ROAD...
WATCH THE SPEED, AL! THESE ROADS ARE TERRIBLE IN THE RAIN! ONE SLIP AND WE GO OVER THE SIDE OF THE MOUNTAIN!
CARL, I GOTTA MAKE THAT EARLY MORNING MEETING IN L.A.! RELAX... I KNOW WHAT I'M DOING!
YEP, CARL: YOU'RE A LUCKY MAN TO HAVE LINDA... SHE'S THE FINEST WOMAN I'VE EVER...
AL! WATCH IT! THE BEND! LOOK OUT!
AL! WHAT ARE YOU DOING?! STRAIGHTEN OUT!
SCREEEEEECH!
WE'RE GOING OVER! I... UNNGHH!

ART BY JACK SPARLING/STORY BY R. MICHAEL ROSEN

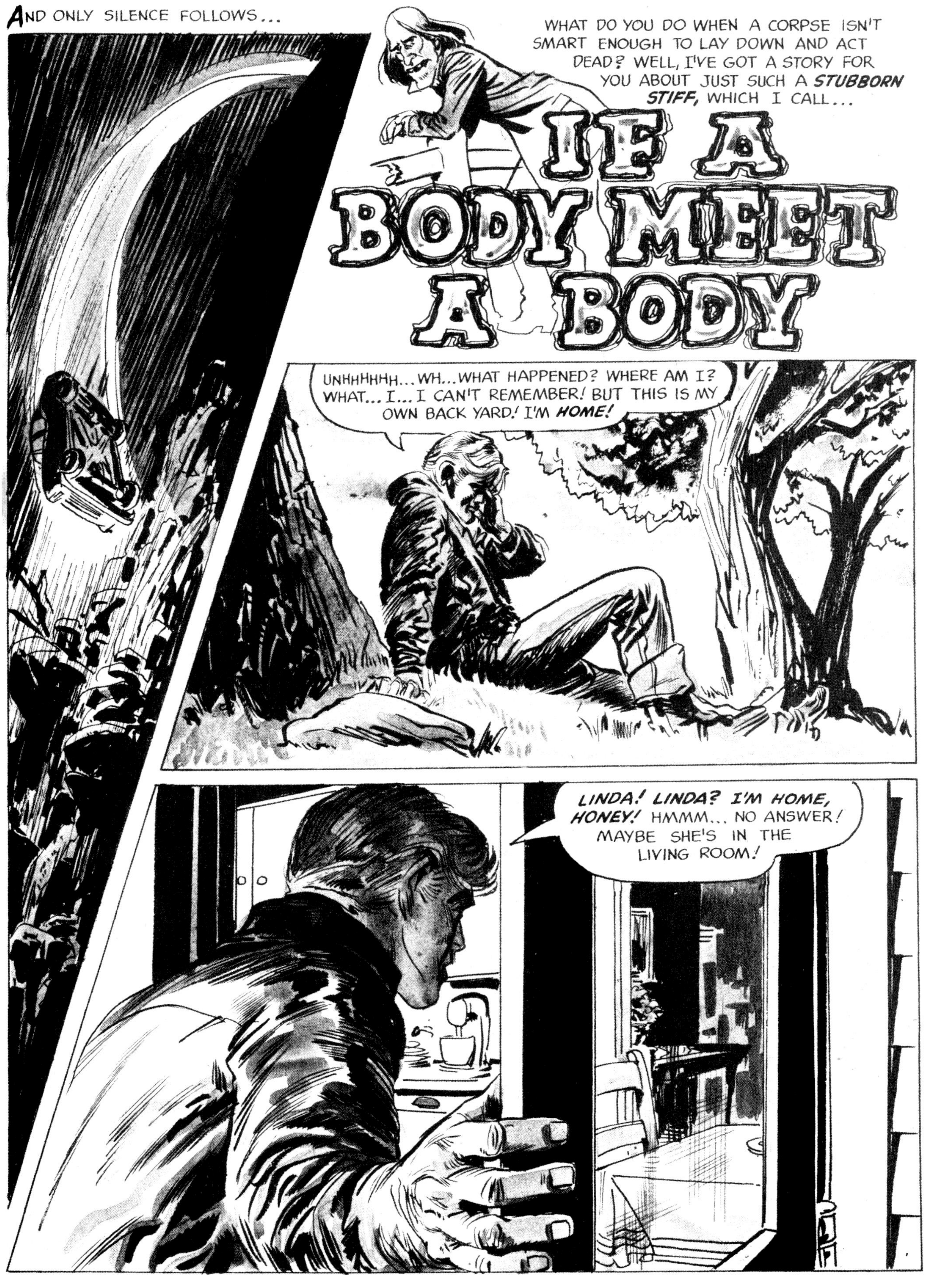
AND ONLY SILENCE FOLLOWS...
WHAT DO YOU DO WHEN A CORPSE ISN'T SMART ENOUGH TO LAY DOWN AND ACT DEAD? WELL, I'VE GOT A STORY FOR YOU ABOUT JUST SUCH A STUBBORN STIFF, WHICH I CALL...
IF A BODY MEET A BODY
UNHHHHHH... WH...WHAT HAPPENED? WHERE AM I? WHAT... I... I CAN'T REMEMBER! BUT THIS IS MY OWN BACK YARD! I'M HOME!
LINDA! LINDA? I'M HOME, HONEY! HMMM... NO ANSWER! MAYBE SHE'S IN THE LIVING ROOM!

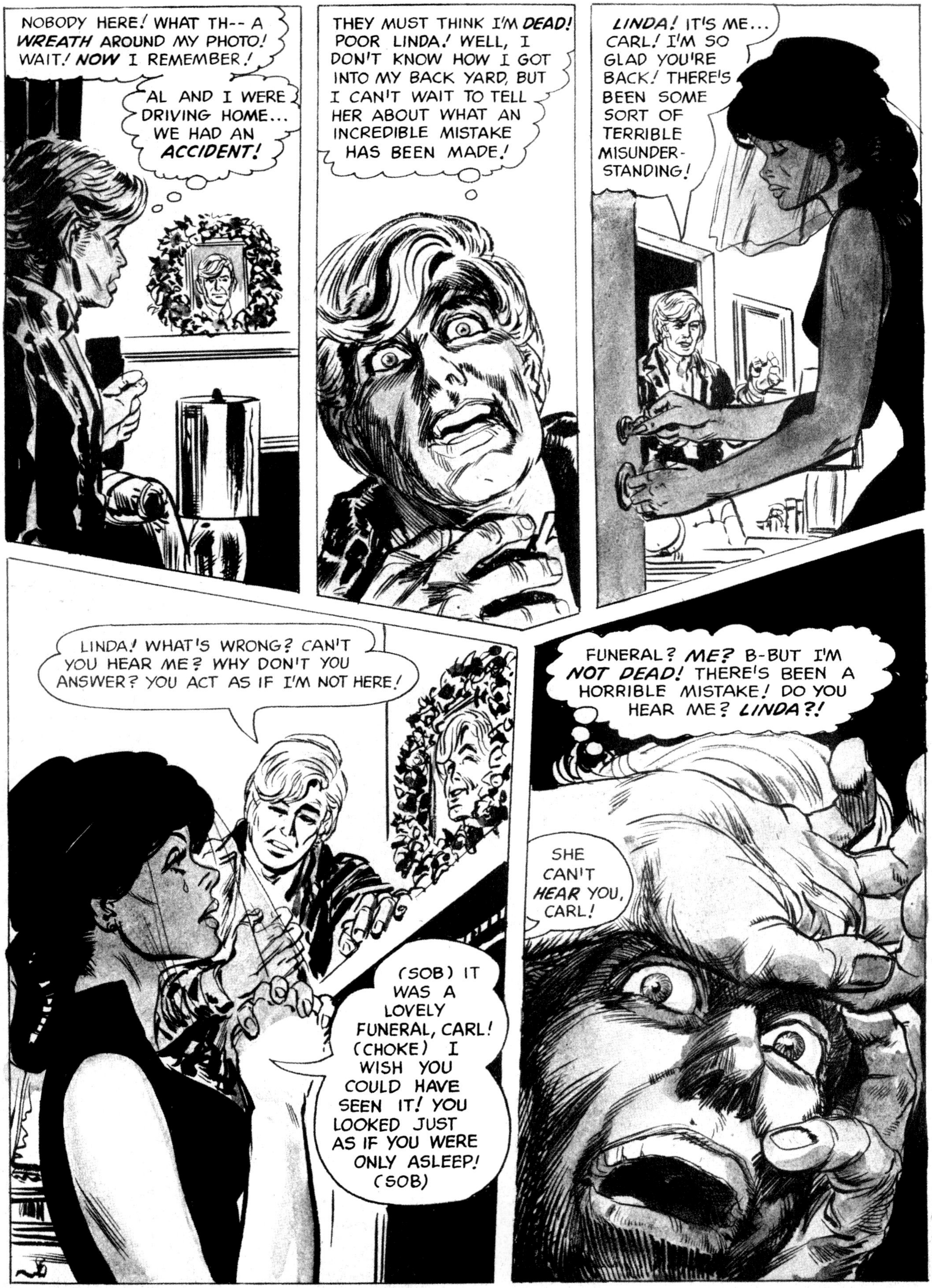
NOBODY HERE! WHAT TH-- A WREATH AROUND MY PHOTO! WAIT! NOW I REMEMBER!
AL AND I WERE DRIVING HOME... WE HAD AN ACCIDENT!
THEY MUST THINK I'M DEAD! POOR LINDA! WELL, I DON'T KNOW HOW I GOT INTO MY BACK YARD, BUT I CAN'T WAIT TO TELL HER ABOUT WHAT AN INCREDIBLE MISTAKE HAS BEEN MADE!
LINDA! IT'S ME... CARL! I'M SO GLAD YOU'RE BACK! THERE'S BEEN SOME SORT OF TERRIBLE MISUNDERSTANDING!
LINDA! WHAT'S WRONG? CAN'T YOU HEAR ME? WHY DON'T YOU ANSWER? YOU ACT AS IF I'M NOT HERE!
(SOB) IT WAS A LOVELY FUNERAL, CARL! (CHOKE) I WISH YOU COULD HAVE SEEN IT! YOU LOOKED JUST AS IF YOU WERE ONLY ASLEEP! (SOB)
FUNERAL? ME? B-BUT I'M NOT DEAD! THERE'S BEEN A HORRIBLE MISTAKE! DO YOU HEAR ME? LINDA?!
SHE CAN'T HEAR YOU, CARL!

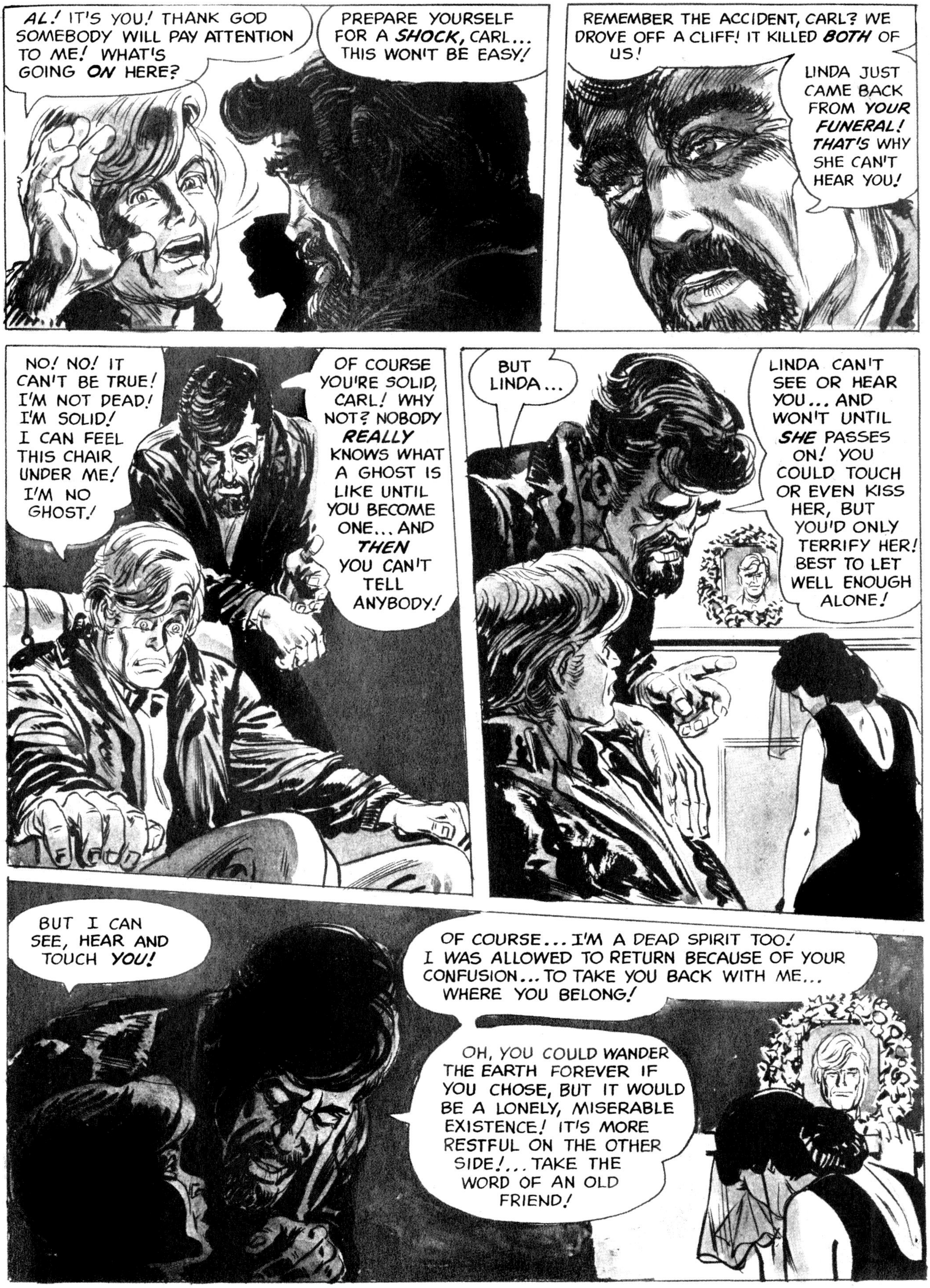
AL! IT'S YOU! THANK GOD SOMEBODY WILL PAY ATTENTION TO ME! WHAT'S GOING ON HERE?
PREPARE YOURSELF FOR A SHOCK, CARL... THIS WON'T BE EASY!
REMEMBER THE ACCIDENT, CARL? WE DROVE OFF A CLIFF! IT KILLED BOTH OF US!
LINDA JUST CAME BACK FROM YOUR FUNERAL! THAT'S WHY SHE CAN'T HEAR YOU!
NO! NO! IT CAN'T BE TRUE! I'M NOT DEAD! I'M SOLID! I CAN FEEL THIS CHAIR UNDER ME! I'M NO GHOST!
OF COURSE YOU'RE SOLID, CARL! WHY NOT? NOBODY REALLY KNOWS WHAT A GHOST IS LIKE UNTIL YOU BECOME ONE... AND THEN YOU CAN'T TELL ANYBODY!
BUT LINDA...
LINDA CAN'T SEE OR HEAR YOU... AND WON'T UNTIL SHE PASSES ON! YOU COULD TOUCH OR EVEN KISS HER, BUT YOU'D ONLY TERRIFY HER! BEST TO LET WELL ENOUGH ALONE!
BUT I CAN SEE, HEAR AND TOUCH YOU!
OF COURSE... I'M A DEAD SPIRIT TOO! I WAS ALLOWED TO RETURN BECAUSE OF YOUR CONFUSION... TO TAKE YOU BACK WITH ME... WHERE YOU BELONG!
OH, YOU COULD WANDER THE EARTH FOREVER IF YOU CHOSE, BUT IT WOULD BE A LONELY, MISERABLE EXISTENCE! IT'S MORE RESTFUL ON THE OTHER SIDE!... TAKE THE WORD OF AN OLD FRIEND!

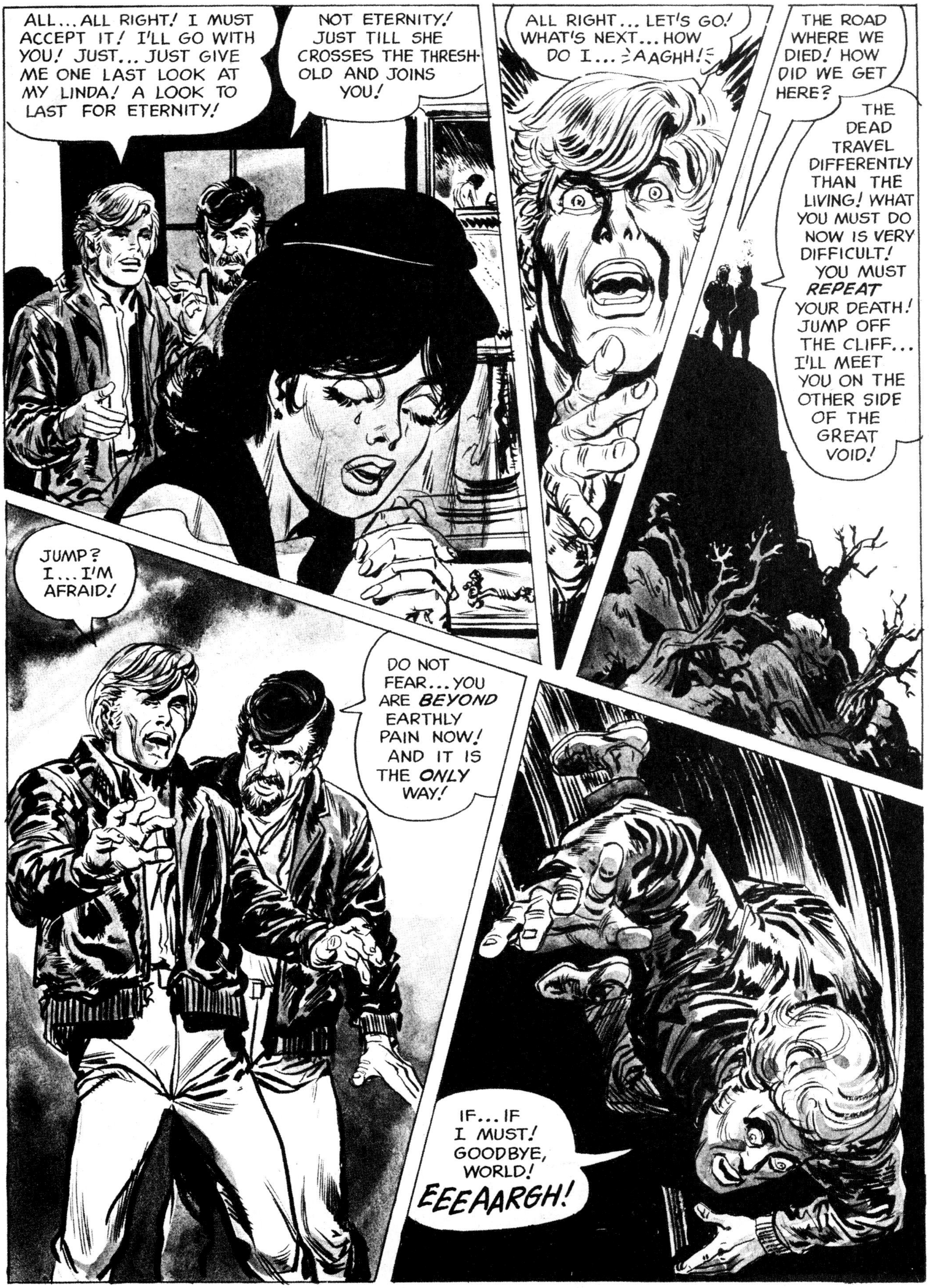
ALL... ALL RIGHT! I MUST ACCEPT IT! I'LL GO WITH YOU! JUST... JUST GIVE ME ONE LAST LOOK AT MY LINDA! A LOOK TO LAST FOR ETERNITY!
NOT ETERNITY! JUST TILL SHE CROSSES THE THRESH-OLD AND JOINS YOU!
ALL RIGHT... LET'S GO! WHAT'S NEXT... HOW DO I... AAGHH!
THE ROAD WHERE WE DIED! HOW DID WE GET HERE?
THE DEAD TRAVEL DIFFERENTLY THAN THE LIVING! WHAT YOU MUST DO NOW IS VERY DIFFICULT! YOU MUST REPEAT YOUR DEATH! JUMP OFF THE CLIFF... I'LL MEET YOU ON THE OTHER SIDE OF THE GREAT VOID!
JUMP? I... I'M AFRAID!
DO NOT FEAR... YOU ARE BEYOND EARTHLY PAIN NOW! AND IT IS THE ONLY WAY!
IF... IF I MUST! GOODBYE, WORLD!
EEEAARGH!

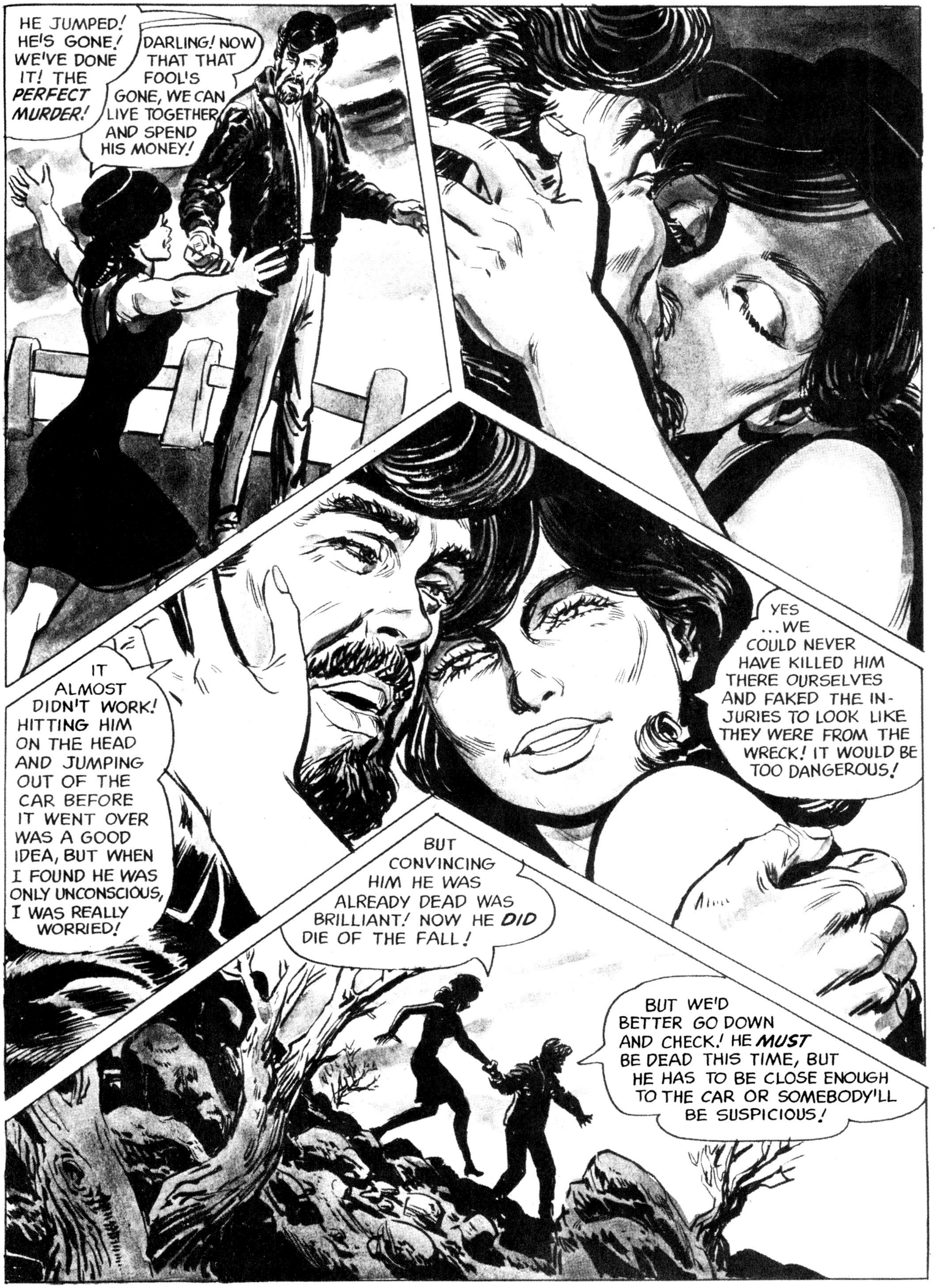
HE JUMPED! HE'S GONE! WE'VE DONE IT! THE PERFECT MURDER!
DARLING! NOW THAT THAT FOOL'S GONE, WE CAN LIVE TOGETHER AND SPEND HIS MONEY!
IT ALMOST DIDN'T WORK! HITTING HIM ON THE HEAD AND JUMPING OUT OF THE CAR BEFORE IT WENT OVER WAS A GOOD IDEA, BUT WHEN I FOUND HE WAS ONLY UNCONSCIOUS, I WAS REALLY WORRIED!
YES ...WE COULD NEVER HAVE KILLED HIM THERE OURSELVES AND FAKED THE IN-JURIES TO LOOK LIKE THEY WERE FROM THE WRECK! IT WOULD BE TOO DANGEROUS!
BUT CONVINCING HIM HE WAS ALREADY DEAD WAS BRILLIANT! NOW HE DID DIE OF THE FALL!
BUT WE'D BETTER GO DOWN AND CHECK! HE MUST BE DEAD THIS TIME, BUT HE HAS TO BE CLOSE ENOUGH TO THE CAR OR SOMEBODY'LL BE SUSPICIOUS!

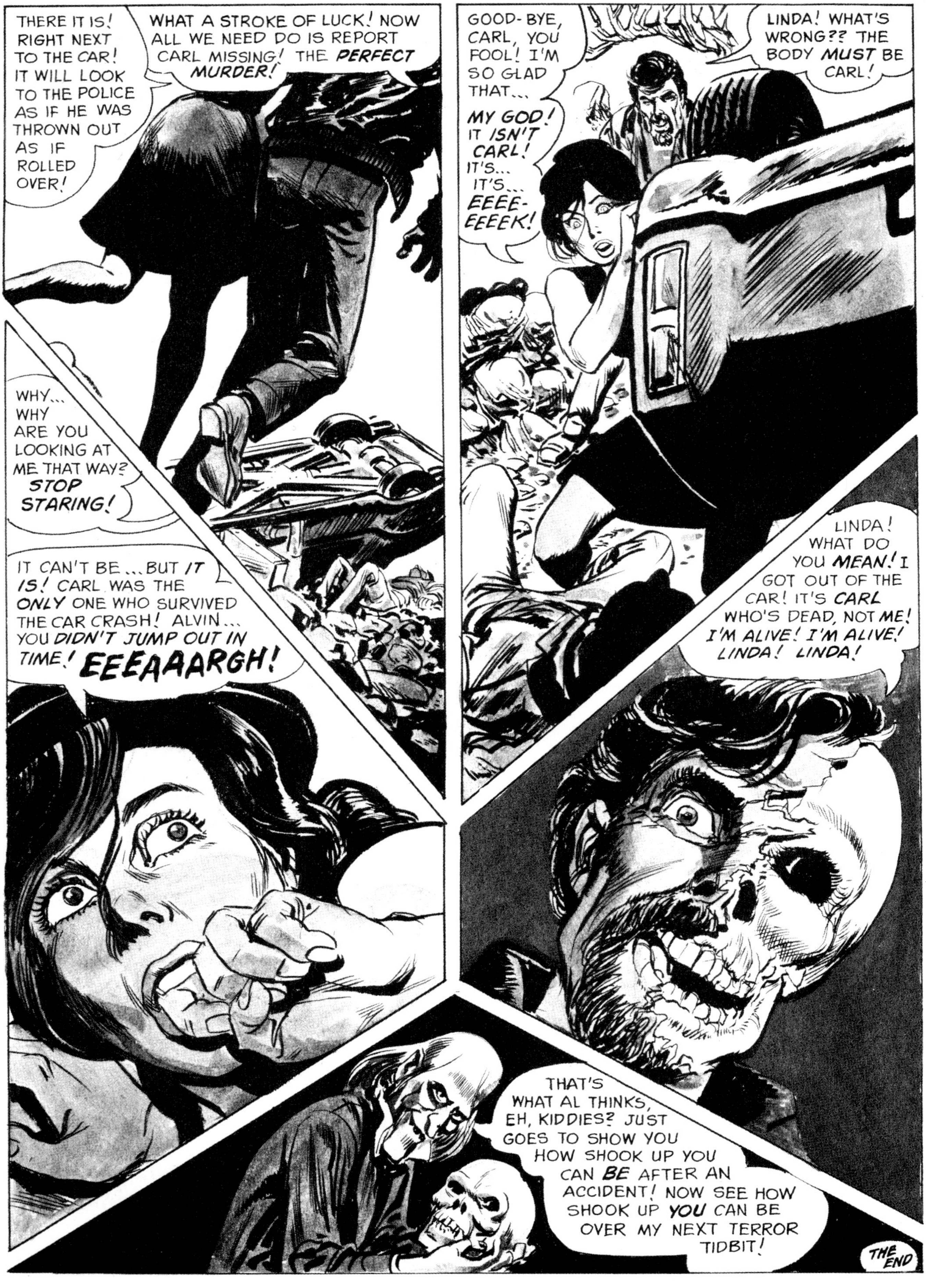
THERE IT IS! RIGHT NEXT TO THE CAR! IT WILL LOOK TO THE POLICE AS IF HE WAS THROWN OUT AS IF ROLLED OVER!
WHAT A STROKE OF LUCK! NOW ALL WE NEED DO IS REPORT CARL MISSING! THE PERFECT MURDER!
GOOD-BYE, CARL, YOU FOOL! I'M SO GLAD THAT...
LINDA! WHAT'S WRONG?? THE BODY MUST BE CARL!
MY GOD! IT ISN'T CARL! IT'S... IT'S... EEEE-EEEEK!
WHY... WHY ARE YOU LOOKING AT ME THAT WAY? STOP STARING!
IT CAN'T BE ... BUT IT IS! CARL WAS THE ONLY ONE WHO SURVIVED THE CAR CRASH! ALVIN... YOU DIDN'T JUMP OUT IN TIME! EEEAAARGH!
LINDA! WHAT DO YOU MEAN! I GOT OUT OF THE CAR! IT'S CARL WHO'S DEAD, NOT ME! I'M ALIVE! I'M ALIVE! LINDA! LINDA!
THAT'S WHAT AL THINKS, EH, KIDDIES? JUST GOES TO SHOW YOU HOW SHOOK UP YOU CAN BE AFTER AN ACCIDENT! NOW SEE HOW SHOOK UP YOU CAN BE OVER MY NEXT TERROR TIDBIT!
THE END

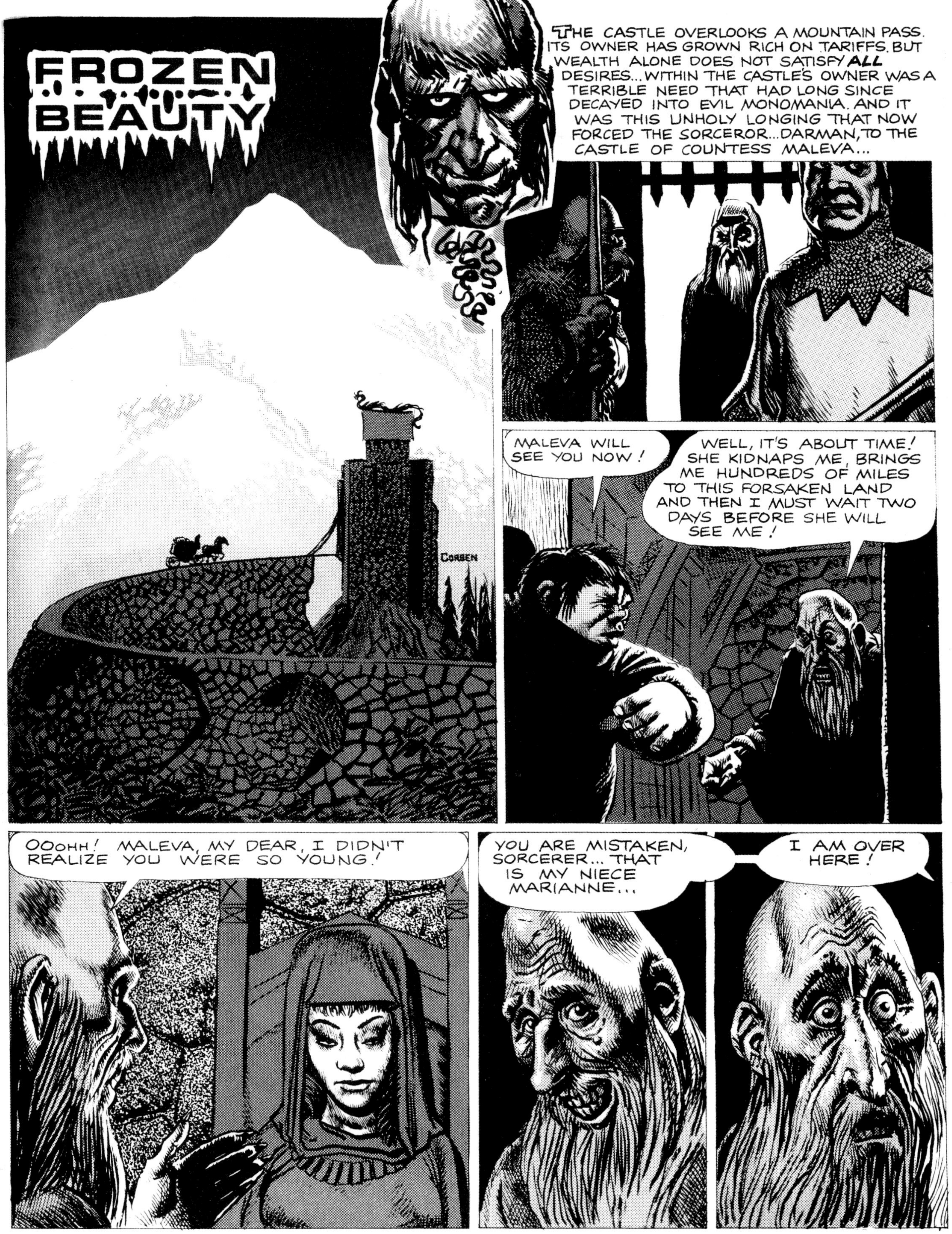
FROZEN BEAUTY
THE CASTLE OVERLOOKS A MOUNTAIN PASS. ITS OWNER HAS GROWN RICH ON TARIFFS. BUT WEALTH ALONE DOES NOT SATISFY ALL DESIRES... WITHIN THE CASTLE'S OWNER WAS A TERRIBLE NEED THAT HAD LONG SINCE DECAYED INTO EVIL MONOMANIA. AND IT WAS THIS UNHOLY LONGING THAT NOW FORCED THE SORCEROR... DARMAN, TO THE CASTLE OF COUNTESS MALEVA...
CORBEN
MALEVA WILL SEE YOU NOW!
WELL, IT'S ABOUT TIME! SHE KIDNAPS ME, BRINGS ME HUNDREDS OF MILES TO THIS FORSAKEN LAND AND THEN I MUST WAIT TWO DAYS BEFORE SHE WILL SEE ME!
OOOHH! MALEVA, MY DEAR, I DIDN'T REALIZE YOU WERE SO YOUNG!
YOU ARE MISTAKEN, SORCERER... THAT IS MY NIECE MARIANNE...
I AM OVER HERE!

ART AND STORY BY RICHARD CORBEN

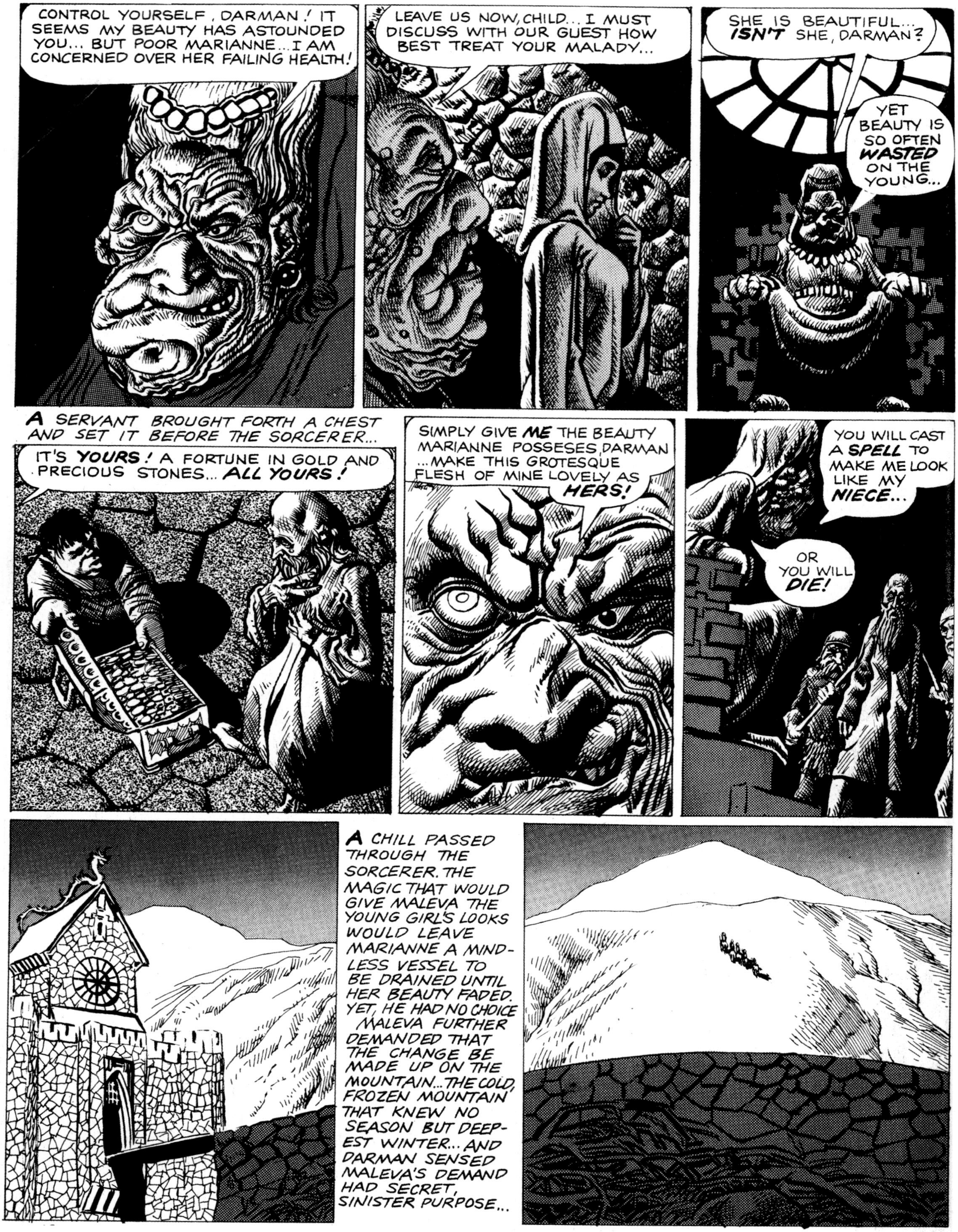
CONTROL YOURSELF, DARMAN! IT SEEMS MY BEAUTY HAS ASTOUNDED YOU... BUT POOR MARIANNE... I AM CONCERNED OVER HER FAILING HEALTH!
LEAVE US NOW, CHILD... I MUST DISCUSS WITH OUR GUEST HOW BEST TREAT YOUR MALADY...
SHE IS BEAUTIFUL... ISN'T SHE, DARMAN?
YET BEAUTY IS SO OFTEN WASTED ON THE YOUNG...
A SERVANT BROUGHT FORTH A CHEST AND SET IT BEFORE THE SORCERER...
IT'S YOURS! A FORTUNE IN GOLD AND PRECIOUS STONES... ALL YOURS!
SIMPLY GIVE ME THE BEAUTY MARIANNE POSSESES, DARMAN ...MAKE THIS GROTESQUE FLESH OF MINE LOVELY AS HERS!
YOU WILL CAST A SPELL TO MAKE ME LOOK LIKE MY NIECE...
OR YOU WILL DIE!
A CHILL PASSED THROUGH THE SORCERER. THE MAGIC THAT WOULD GIVE MALEVA THE YOUNG GIRL'S LOOKS WOULD LEAVE MARIANNE A MIND-LESS VESSEL TO BE DRAINED UNTIL HER BEAUTY FADED. YET, HE HAD NO CHOICE. MALEVA FURTHER DEMANDED THAT THE CHANGE BE MADE UP ON THE MOUNTAIN... THE COLD, FROZEN MOUNTAIN THAT KNEW NO SEASON BUT DEEP-EST WINTER... AND DARMAN SENSED MALEVA'S DEMAND HAD SECRET, SINISTER PURPOSE...

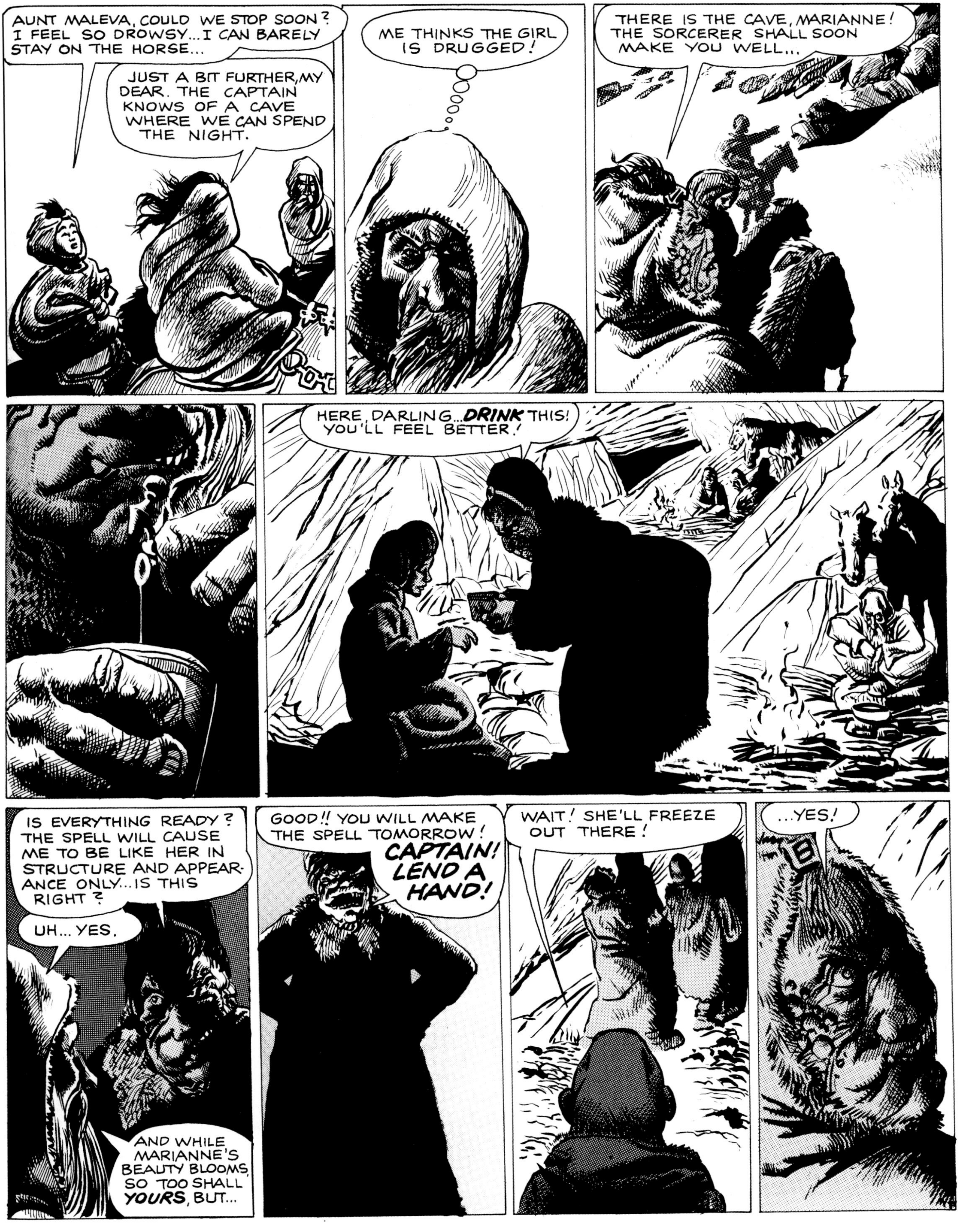

AUNT MALEVA, COULD WE STOP SOON? I FEEL SO DROWSY... I CAN BARELY STAY ON THE HORSE...
JUST A BIT FURTHER, MY DEAR. THE CAPTAIN KNOWS OF A CAVE WHERE WE CAN SPEND THE NIGHT.
ME THINKS THE GIRL IS DRUGGED!
THERE IS THE CAVE, MARIANNE! THE SORCERER SHALL SOON MAKE YOU WELL...
HERE, DARLING... DRINK THIS! YOU'LL FEEL BETTER!
IS EVERYTHING READY? THE SPELL WILL CAUSE ME TO BE LIKE HER IN STRUCTURE AND APPEARANCE ONLY... IS THIS RIGHT?
UH... YES.
AND WHILE MARIANNE'S BEAUTY BLOOMS, SO TOO SHALL YOURS, BUT...
GOOD!! YOU WILL MAKE THE SPELL TOMORROW!
CAPTAIN! LEND A HAND!
WAIT! SHE'LL FREEZE OUT THERE!
...YES!

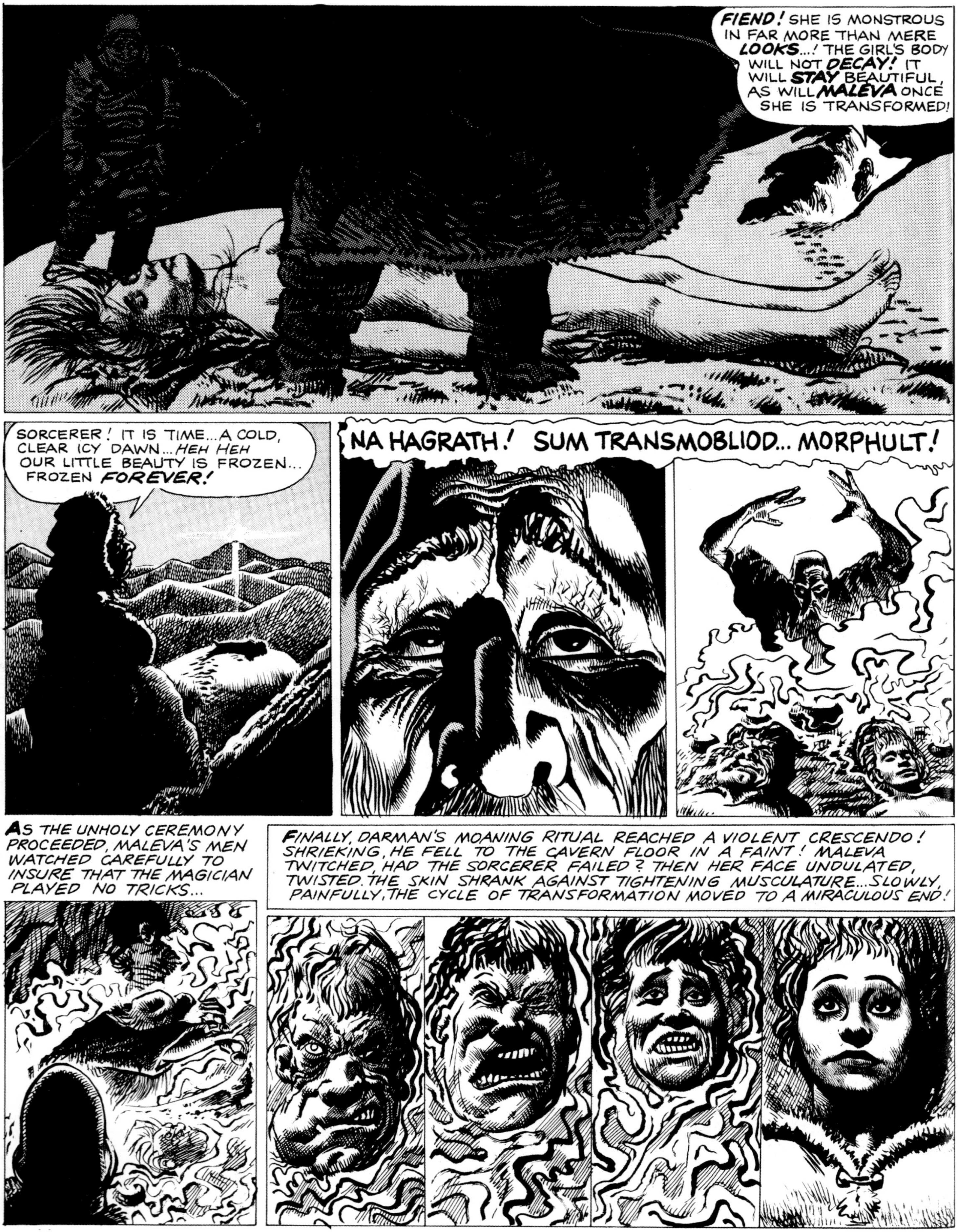
FIEND! SHE IS MONSTROUS IN FAR MORE THAN MERE LOOKS...! THE GIRL'S BODY WILL NOT DECAY! IT WILL STAY BEAUTIFUL, AS WILL MALEVA ONCE SHE IS TRANSFORMED!
SORCERER! IT IS TIME... A COLD, CLEAR ICY DAWN... HEH HEH OUR LITTLE BEAUTY IS FROZEN... FROZEN FOREVER!
NA HAGRATH! SUM TRANSMOBLIOD... MORPHULT!
AS THE UNHOLY CEREMONY PROCEEDED, MALEVA'S MEN WATCHED CAREFULLY TO INSURE THAT THE MAGICIAN PLAYED NO TRICKS...
FINALLY, DARMAN'S MOANING RITUAL REACHED A VIOLENT CRESCENDO! SHRIEKING, HE FELL TO THE CAVERN FLOOR IN A FAINT! MALEVA TWITCHED, HAD THE SORCERER FAILED? THEN HER FACE UNDULATED, TWISTED. THE SKIN SHRANK AGAINST TIGHTENING MUSCULATURE... SLOWLY, PAINFULLY, THE CYCLE OF TRANSFORMATION MOVED TO A MIRACULOUS END!

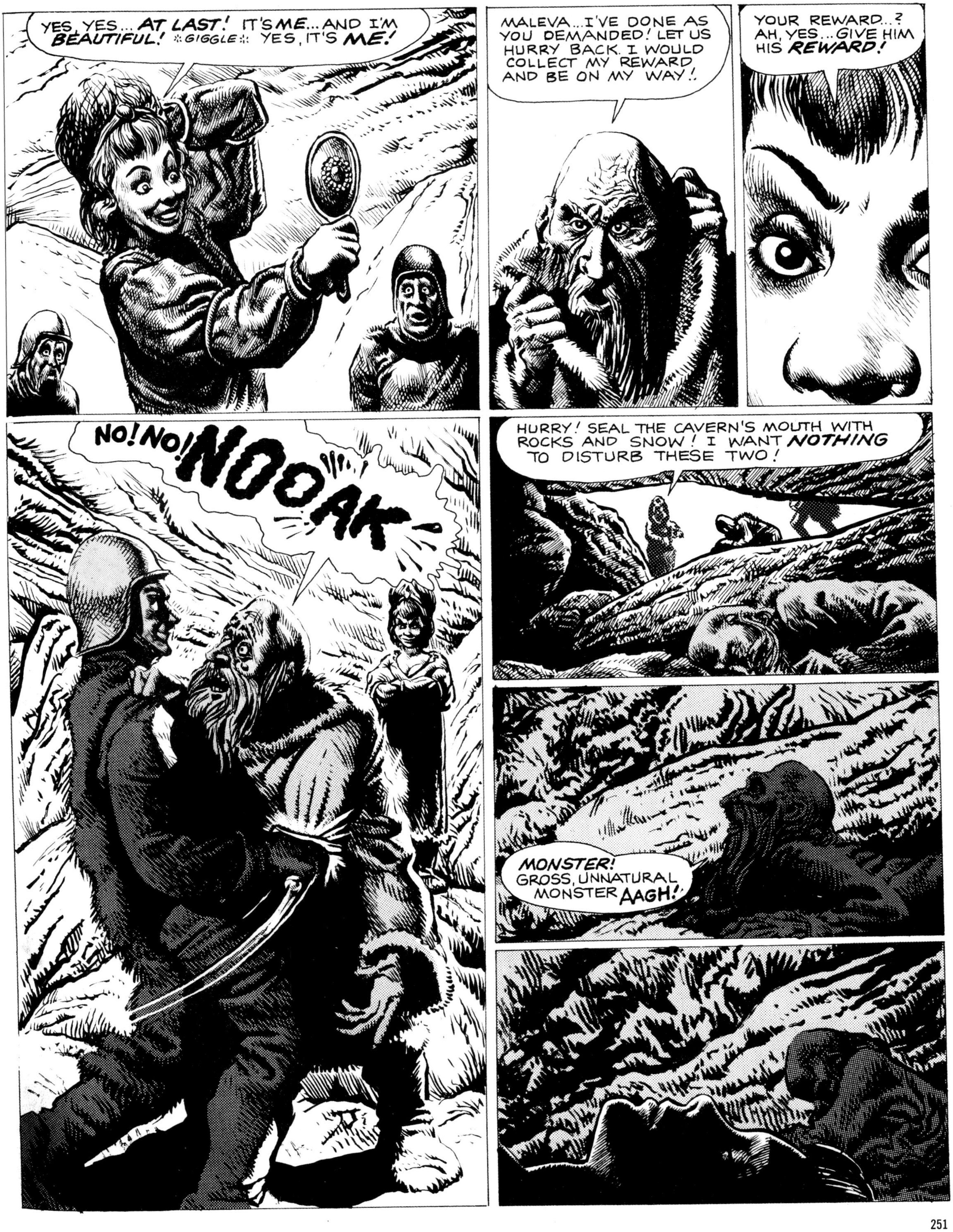
YES, YES... AT LAST! IT'S ME... AND I'M BEAUTIFUL! *GIGGLE* YES, IT'S ME!
MALEVA... I'VE DONE AS YOU DEMANDED! LET US HURRY BACK. I WOULD COLLECT MY REWARD AND BE ON MY WAY!
YOUR REWARD..? AH, YES... GIVE HIM HIS REWARD!
NO! NO! NOOAK
HURRY! SEAL THE CAVERN'S MOUTH WITH ROCKS AND SNOW! I WANT NOTHING TO DISTURB THESE TWO!
MONSTER! GROSS, UNNATURAL MONSTER AAGH!

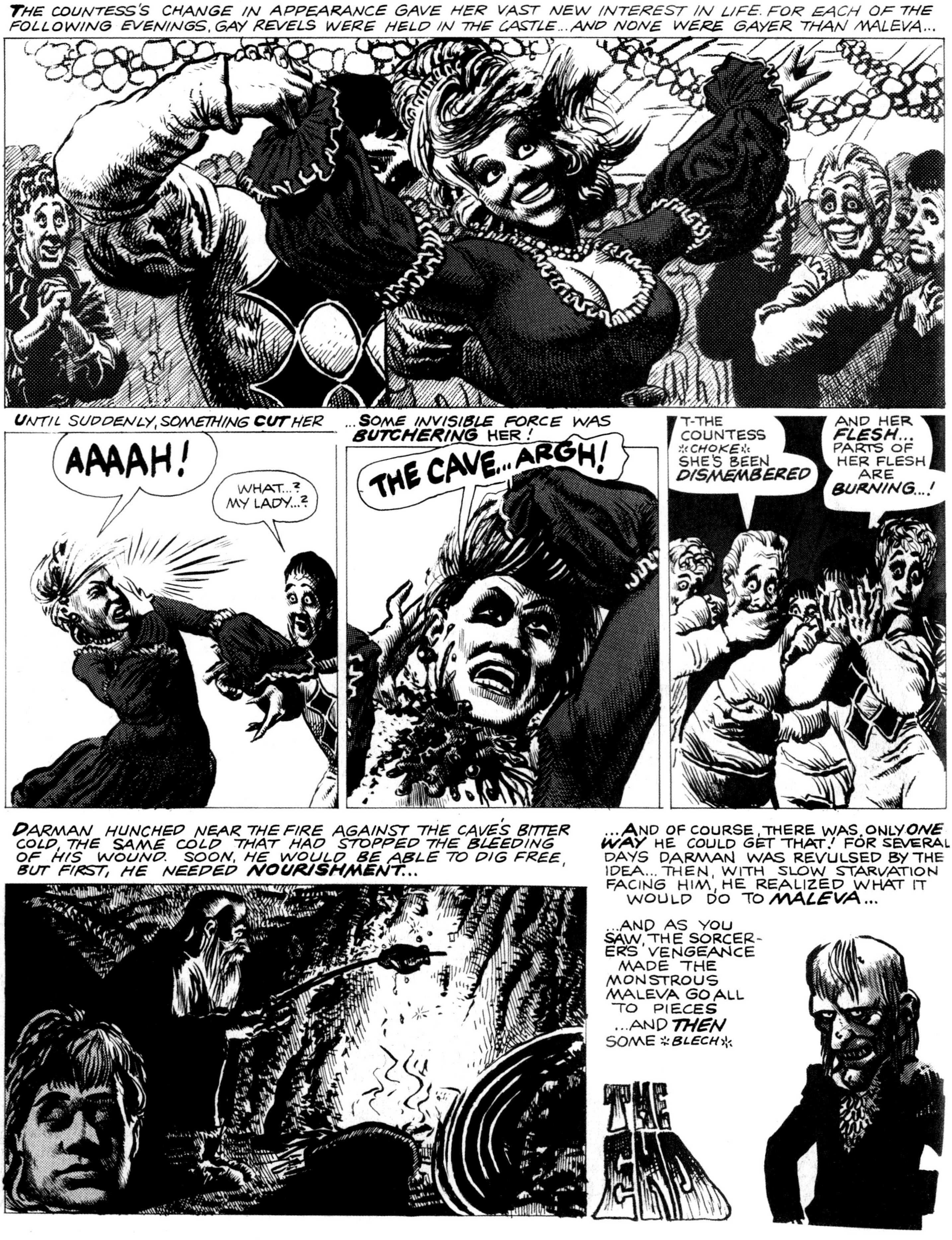
THE COUNTESS'S CHANGE IN APPEARANCE GAVE HER VAST NEW INTEREST IN LIFE. FOR EACH OF THE FOLLOWING EVENINGS, GAY REVELS WERE HELD IN THE CASTLE... AND NONE WERE GAYER THAN MALEVA...
UNTIL SUDDENLY, SOMETHING CUT HER
AAAAH!
WHAT...? MY LADY...?
...SOME INVISIBLE FORCE WAS BUTCHERING HER!
THE CAVE... ARGH!
T-THE COUNTESS *CHOKE* SHE'S BEEN DISMEMBERED
AND HER FLESH... PARTS OF HER FLESH ARE BURNING...!
DARMAN HUNCHED NEAR THE FIRE AGAINST THE CAVE'S BITTER COLD, THE SAME COLD THAT HAD STOPPED THE BLEEDING OF HIS WOUND. SOON, HE WOULD BE ABLE TO DIG FREE, BUT FIRST, HE NEEDED NOURISHMENT...
...AND OF COURSE, THERE WAS ONLY ONE WAY HE COULD GET THAT! FOR SEVERAL DAYS DARMAN WAS REVULSED BY THE IDEA... THEN, WITH SLOW STARVATION FACING HIM, HE REALIZED WHAT IT WOULD DO TO MALEVA...
...AND AS YOU SAW, THE SORCERER'S VENGEANCE MADE THE MONSTROUS MALEVA GO ALL TO PIECES ...AND THEN SOME *BLECH*
THE END

VOLUME ONE · COLLECTING CREEPY 1-5

WEIRD AND HAUNTING TALES OF FRIGHT!
DARK HORSE ARCHIVES

Volume 1   ISBN 978-1-59307-973-4

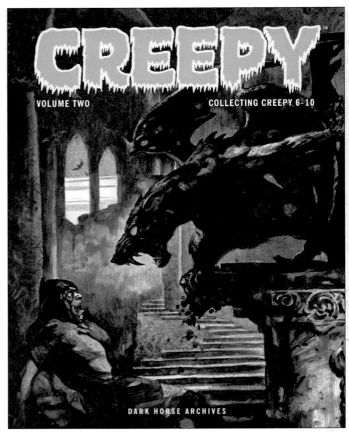

VOLUME TWO · COLLECTING CREEPY 6-10

DARK HORSE ARCHIVES

Volume 2   ISBN 978-1-59582-168-3

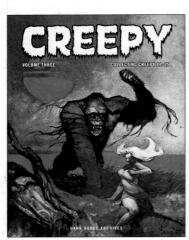

VOLUME THREE · COLLECTING CREEPY 11-15

DARK HORSE ARCHIVES

Volume 3   ISBN 978-1-59582-259-8

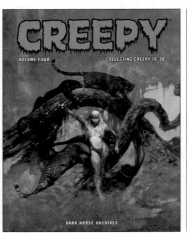

VOLUME FOUR · COLLECTING CREEPY 16-20

DARK HORSE ARCHIVES

Volume 4   ISBN 978-1-59582-308-3

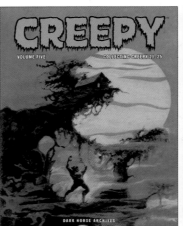

VOLUME FIVE · COLLECTING CREEPY 21-25

DARK HORSE ARCHIVES

Volume 5   ISBN 978-1-59582-353-3

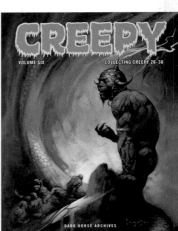

VOLUME SIX · COLLECTING CREEPY 26-30

DARK HORSE ARCHIVES

Volume 6   ISBN 978-1-59582-354-0

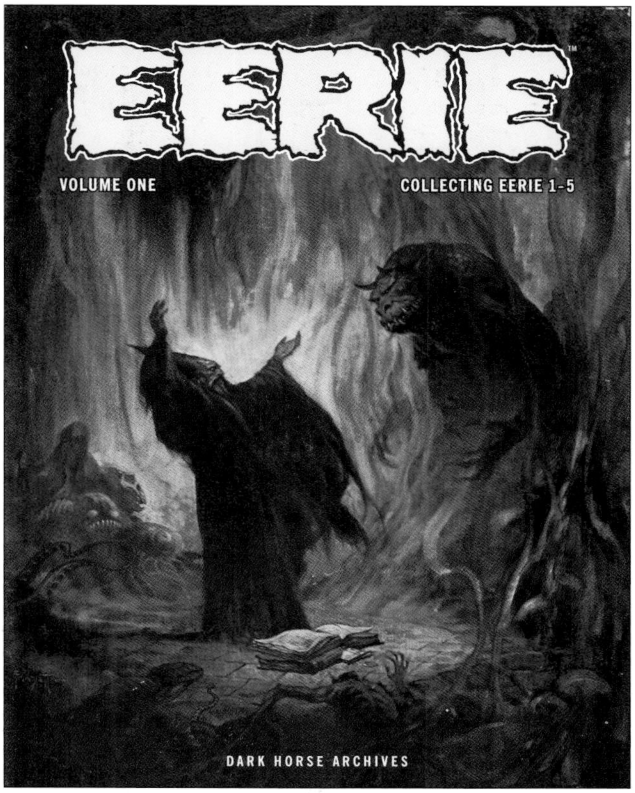
EERIE
VOLUME ONE
COLLECTING EERIE 1-5
DARK HORSE ARCHIVES
Volume 1 ISBN 978-1-59582-245-1

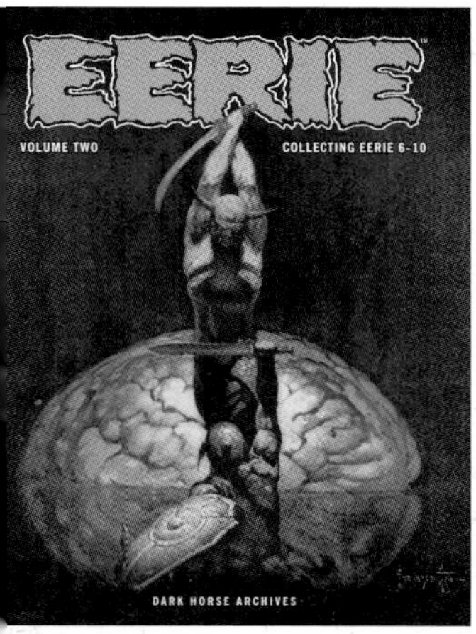
EERIE
VOLUME TWO
COLLECTING EERIE 6-10
DARK HORSE ARCHIVES
lume 2 ISBN 978-1-59582-315-1

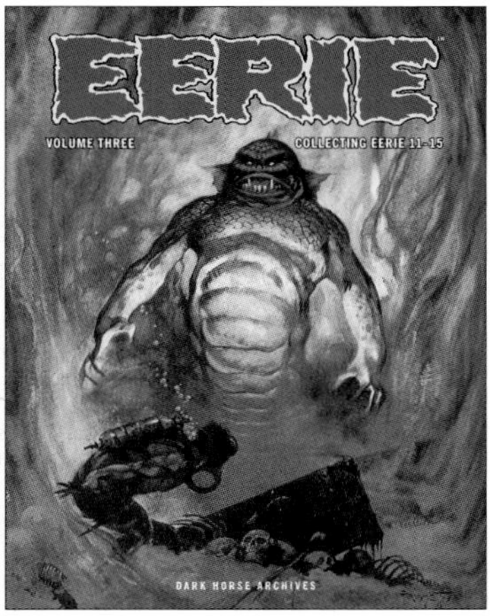
EERIE
VOLUME THREE
COLLECTING EERIE 11-15
DARK HORSE ARCHIVES
Volume 3 ISBN 978-1-59582-369-4

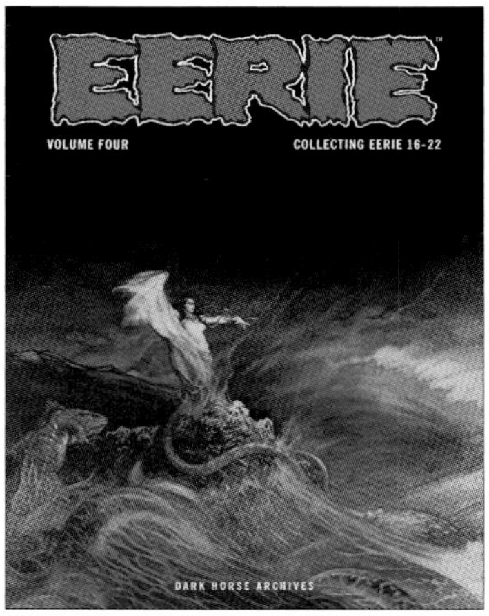
EERIE
VOLUME FOUR
COLLECTING EERIE 16-22
DARK HORSE ARCHIVES
Volume 4 ISBN 978-1-59582-429-5

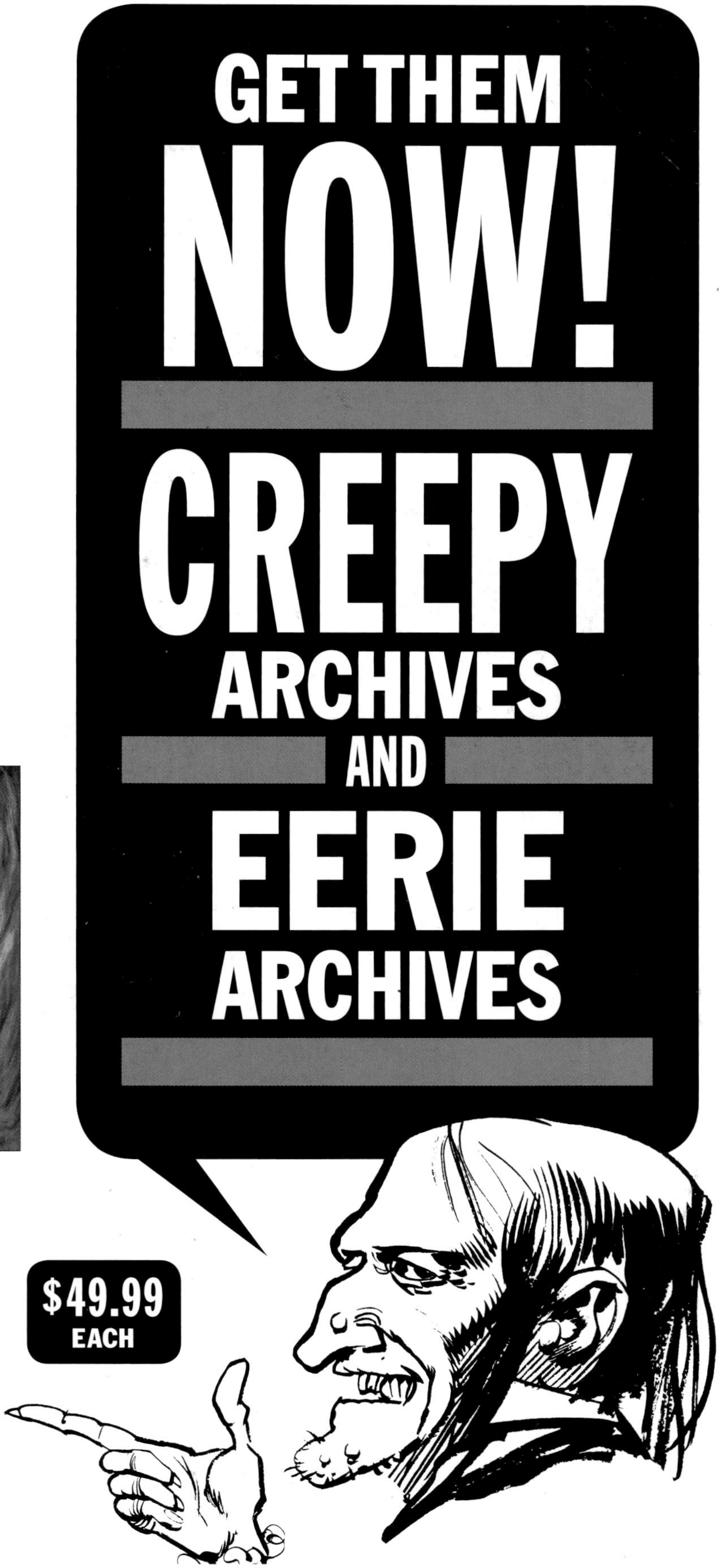
GET THEM
NOW!
CREEPY
ARCHIVES
AND
EERIE
ARCHIVES
$49.99
EACH

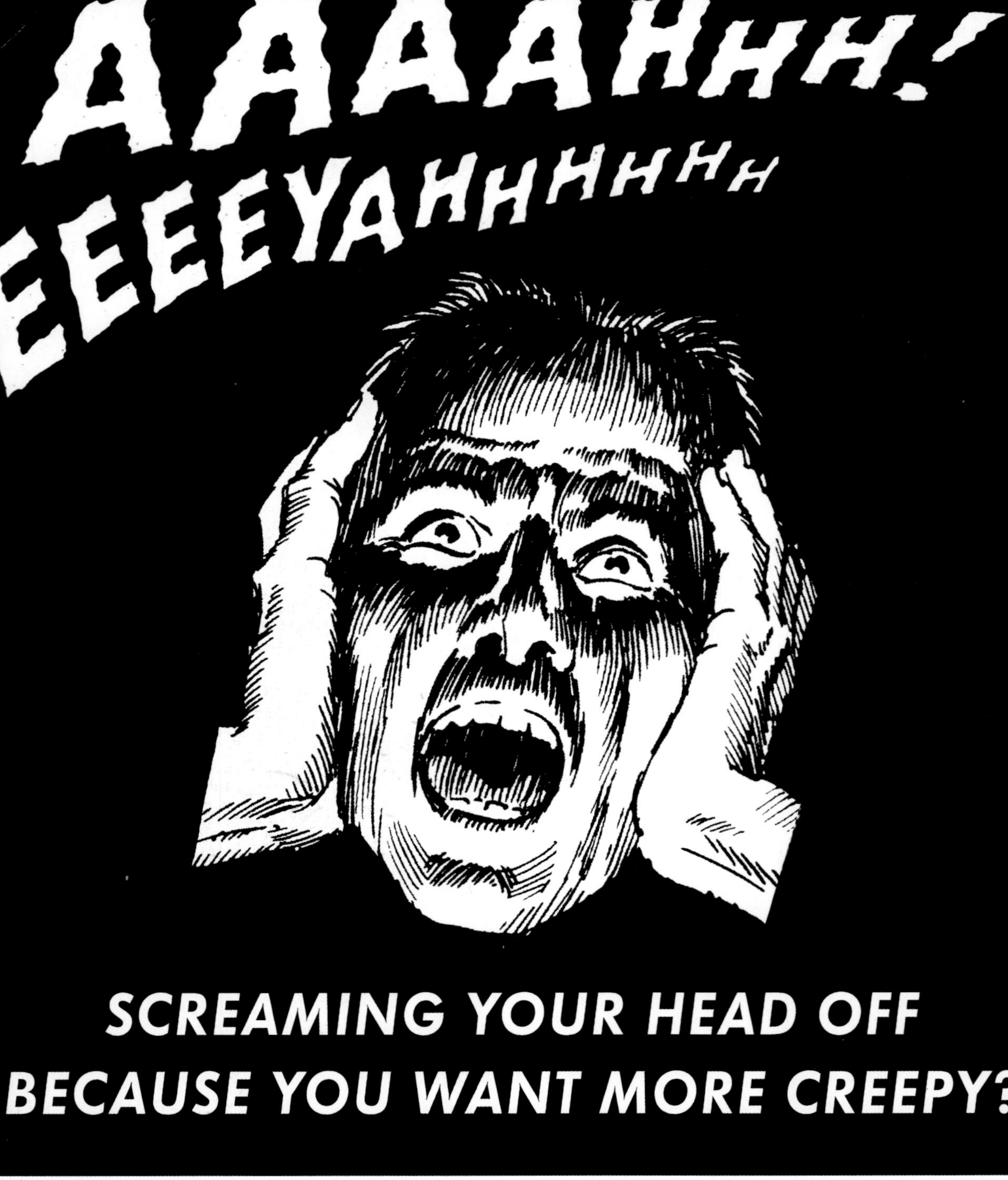
AAAAHHH!
EEEEYAHHHHHHH

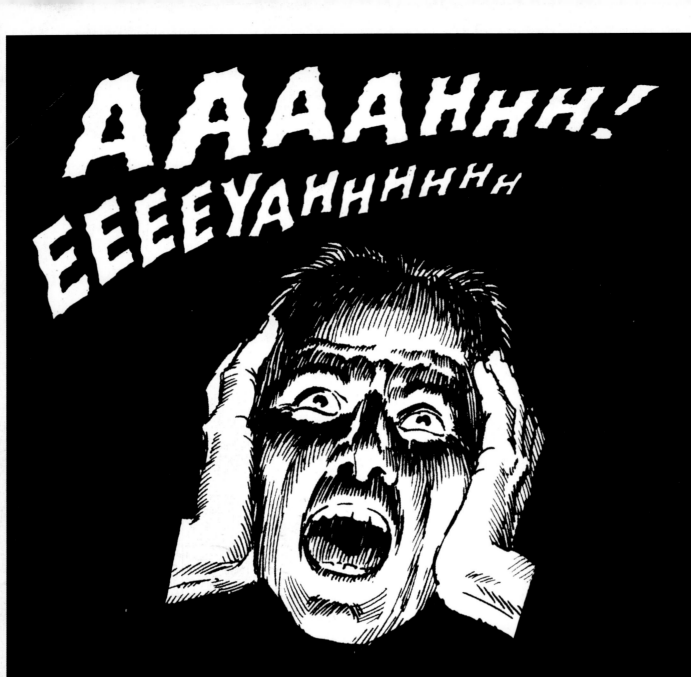